The Mathematics of Finite Networks

Since the early eighteenth century, the theory of networks and graphs has matured into an indispensable tool for describing countless real-world phenomena. However, the study of large-scale features of a network often requires unrealistic limits, such as taking the network size to infinity or assuming a continuum. These asymptotic and analytic approaches can significantly diverge from real or simulated networks when applied at the finite scales of real-world applications. This book offers an approach to overcoming these limitations by introducing operator graph theory, an exact, non-asymptotic set of tools combining graph theory with operator calculus. The book is intended for mathematicians, physicists, and other scientists interested in discrete finite systems and their graph-theoretical description, and in delineating the abstract algebraic structures that characterise such systems. All the necessary background on graph theory and operator calculus is included for readers to understand the potential applications of operator graph theory.

MICHAEL RUDOLPH is a mathematical physicist of the French National Centre for Scientific Research at the Denis Poisson Institute. His research includes graph theory and classical number theory, and is directed towards understanding physical reality from an inherently finite discrete perspective, both mathematically and philosophically.

The Mathematics of Finite Networks

An Introduction to Operator Graph Theory

MICHAEL RUDOLPH

CNRS / Institute Denis Poisson, University of Tours

CAMBRIDGE
UNIVERSITY PRESS

CAMBRIDGE
UNIVERSITY PRESS

University Printing House, Cambridge CB2 8BS, United Kingdom

One Liberty Plaza, 20th Floor, New York, NY 10006, USA

477 Williamstown Road, Port Melbourne, VIC 3207, Australia

314–321, 3rd Floor, Plot 3, Splendor Forum, Jasola District Centre, New Delhi – 110025, India

103 Penang Road, #05–06/07, Visioncrest Commercial, Singapore 238467

Cambridge University Press is part of the University of Cambridge.

It furthers the University's mission by disseminating knowledge in the pursuit of education, learning, and research at the highest international levels of excellence.

www.cambridge.org
Information on this title: www.cambridge.org/9781107134430
DOI: 10.1017/9781316466919

First published 2022

A catalogue record for this publication is available from the British Library.

Library of Congress Cataloging-in-Publication Data
Names: Rudolph, Michael, 1969– author.
Title: The mathematics of finite networks : an introduction to operator graph theory / Michael Rudolph.
Description: Cambridge ; New York, NY : Cambridge University Press, 2022. | Includes bibliographical references and index.
Identifiers: LCCN 2021058077 (print) | LCCN 2021058078 (ebook) | ISBN 9781107134430 (hardback) | ISBN 9781316466919 (epub)
Subjects: LCSH: Graph theory. | Operator theory. | System analysis. | BISAC: COMPUTERS / General
Classification: LCC QA166 .R83 2022 (print) | LCC QA166 (ebook) | DDC 511/.5–dc23/eng/20220126
LC record available at https://lccn.loc.gov/2021058077
LC ebook record available at https://lccn.loc.gov/2021058078

ISBN 978-1-107-13443-0 Hardback

For Uesat

— in memoriam —

Contents

Preface

Imagine for a moment that you stroll through a beautiful city like London with its dizzying array of inspiring detail. An overwhelming number of small streets, unpredictably intersecting with one another, wind around busy alleyways which themselves appear to stretch endlessly into all directions. Finding your way in this arguably chaotic mesh of interconnected paths and roadways by foot or by car without resorting to a memorised representation or detailed map of its layout would require the often time-consuming search through a vast number of possibilities until, eventually, the desired destination is reached. Taking a bird's-eye perspective, however, this confusing maze of small streets and mews seems to magically disappear and reveal, with concentric rings of expressways framing a star of boulevards which emanate from the metropole's centre, a different, much simpler pattern. Although such a coarser structural view certainly helps to confine your search, it does so at the expense of abstracting from finer details, – the small, narrow streets which are not only an integral part of the cultural and historical lifeblood of a city like London but reside at the very heart of its flair. Naturally, you might then wonder whether it is possible to hold on to these pertinent details alongside the more crude structural peculiarities which emerge at larger scales and hold, not unlike a skeleton, those details together.

When thinking of city maps, we instinctively envision a network of links along which an ever-changing flow of traffic is carried. Such an idealised description, however, is not limited to the maps we are all familiar with. From the interactions between atoms and subatomic particles to the gravitational forces which act between the billions of galaxies stretching across the known universe, from the transmission of electrical signals in our brains to the complexity of social interactions between people, most if not all of the phenomena we encounter, consciously or not, all around us find a natural representation in the form of networks. Indeed, it can be indubitably argued that the abstract notion of interacting objects resides at the very heart of our conceptual understanding of nature as it touches upon the very fabric of physical reality with its finite and discrete makeup. It is for that reason that we now find the mathematical study of interconnected objects, the theory of networks and graphs, branching deeply through all fields of science and its innumerable applications.

Since its formal inception in the early eighteenth century, graph theory has constructed a solid foundation on which its conceptual and mathematical roots now comfortably rest. In doing so, it has amassed a plethora of useful tools which allow for a thorough qualification and quantification of the sheer uncountable number of networks we find all around us. Unfortunately, such a realisation of graph-theoretical concepts does not come without its limitations. All too often, it is the very nature of a studied system which also can, and does, throw stones in the way of its graph-theoretical formalisation or viable qualifying generalisations. Worse even, many real-world systems defiantly refuse an analytical treatment with the toolkit of graph theory and can only be studied numerically, thus, they are inadvertently yet inescapably tied to the efficiency of our computational hardware, or the lack thereof.

To bypass these limitations, and to capture the essential structural properties of real-world networks, the construction of simplified mathematical models is required. However, as in the example of London's map, many of the current mathematical approaches provide only a bird's-eye view, at the expense of the finer details, in order to reveal the large-scale features of the network that may exist, or to allow certain simplifications to become effective. Indeed, these approaches regularly consider unrealistic limits, such as taking the network size to infinity or abstracting from a network's defining discrete makeup by assuming a continuum. While such 'asymptotic' and 'analytic' approaches can certainly provide simple representations of the dominant structural features and, thus, often succeed at describing network structure in the aggregate, however, the equations at their core can diverge from real or simulated networks quite significantly, especially when applied to the finite scales occurring in the real world. What if the algorithms behind network models – and, for good models, behind real-world data as well – could be cast in mathematical terms that would allow for direct manipulations and, in some cases, exact solutions without the necessity of imposing limits? What if such algorithms could be cast into a form which would allow one to consider specific graph ensembles all at once, without the need to computationally construct and assess concrete individual realisation?

In this book, we aim to introduce, or at least propose, exactly such an approach to graph theory. The mathematical language used for formalising this discrete and finite algebraic framework lends itself to operator calculus, and we have termed this framework *operator graph theory*. Irrespective of being tackled from a computational or more mathematical perspective, the investigation of large yet finite networks and their defining structural peculiarities still remains largely out of reach. Algorithmic approaches often become lost in a vast set of possibilities, as computational methods cannot cope with the combinatorial complexities inherent to many graph-theoretical problems; while asymptotic approaches are often unable to capture the very structure they are obliged to exclude, especially where real-world data are concerned. With this in mind, it is our great hope that operator graph theory may provide a viable language capable of casting such descriptions, by providing an exact, non-asymptotic set of tools which can be applied to, and provides links between, real-world data and their graph-theoretical representations.

This book is intended primarily for physicists, mathematicians, biologists and computer scientists, among others, who are interested in discrete, finite real-world systems that can be described in graph-theoretical terms, as well as in delineating the abstract algebraic structures characterising such systems. Including all the necessary background material on graph theory and operator calculus, and requiring no specific prerequisites other than linear algebra and calculus at the undergraduate level, this book is essentially self-contained and suitable for advanced undergraduates, postgraduates and researchers from a variety of backgrounds. However, it is important to stress that this book has to be understood as nothing more than a mere proposition which attempts the natural, yet arguably novel, fusion of graph theory and operator calculus. With many details in need of being fleshed out by the unforgiving demands of mathematical rigour still at large, I nevertheless hope to provide sufficient inspiration and motivation for an exciting explorative journey across uncharted waters. Let us take this journey together and see where it will lead us, because, after all, this is what science is all about.

I humbly admit that this book has been some years in the making, during a time of great professional and personal hardship. For that reason, I must first and foremost thank my ever-patient editor Lauren Cowles and her editorial assistant Amy He for their unwavering support and understanding nature. The same applies to my fellow colleagues at the Institute Denis Poisson in Tours and Orleans, who gave me in the 'Year of Crazy' a new comfortable home and awoke a memory of still-existing places in which only the sky is the limit, a cherished memory I thought had long been lost. When thinking about the tranquility of a new home, it is impossible not to see Madame Gigi and Daniel 'Rambo72' who not only helped me to build, from nothing, a secluded Asgardian paradise deep in the intoxicating beauty of Sarthe, France, but gave me through their kindness, friendship and unconditional support the strength to master the uncompromising waves of fate crashing down on me. Writing these lines would also have been impossible without my ever-growing family of cats who finally can, like their 'Old Man', enjoy a simple life in nature and the freedom we are born with. Accompanied by the words of the great Charles Dickens, 'what a greater gift than the love of a cat', my beyond-infinite thanks go to Uesat and Black Mountain, Schmusie and Flusie, as well as the many cats I could not save from the abyss of human savagery. Last but not least, my profound and eternal thanks to Morgan and the two 'Hepburns', Audrey and Katherine, and Mark and Andrew, for their selfless support in the dark times I endured, as well as to Claude for keeping alive the fire of passion which burns in each true explorer of the mysteries of nature. To all of you I owe my life, and the candle of hope which, once again, is shining brightly deep inside me. Finally, thanks go to Lyle E. Muller for his help in preparing the original proposal for this book, as well as to J.A.G. Willow, C.O. Cain, S. Hower and L.S. Dee for their invaluable guidance, without which the conclusion of this work would have been impossible.

1
Introduction

When on sunny days in the early years of the eighteenth century people hastened through the narrow streets of Königsberg, now Kaliningrad in Russia, it was not for catching a breeze of fresh air, but for being the lucky first to unlock the mystery of its now famous bridges. Not a valuable golden treasure was to be unearthed, but the solution to the simple problem of finding a path over the seven bridges that connect both banks of the river Pregel with the two islands around which that beautiful Prussian town was built. The goal, however, was not to find just any path, but one along which each bridge was crossed only once. A futile endeavour indeed, and it is unknown how many of Königsberg's inhabitants and intrigued travellers from afar succumbed to this formidable challenge before in 1736 the brilliant mind of a young genius named Leonard Euler provided the definite answer. *Such a path does not exist!* [42].

What was Euler's deep insight which allowed him to solve the problem of Königsberg's bridges without setting foot on any of them, the insight which had eluded all mathematical treasure hunters, professional and recreational alike, before him? In short, seven bridges connect the four main geographical areas of Königsberg, but only one or two of these areas can serve as start and finish of the sought-after path through the city. This means that at least two areas must be traversed and, in order to do so, must be connected by an even number of bridges across the river Pregel. However, as a quick look at the map of Königsberg reveals (Fig. 1.1a), each of its four areas was accessible only through an odd number of bridges, thus rendering the existence of a valid path an impossibility.

Although it still took many decades after Euler's simple yet brilliant resolution of the now famous *Königsberg bridge problem* before a coherent and rigorous mathematical framework was established, it undoubtedly marks both historically and conceptually the beginning of what is now known as network or *graph theory*. Indeed, his contribution in this regard cannot be overstated.

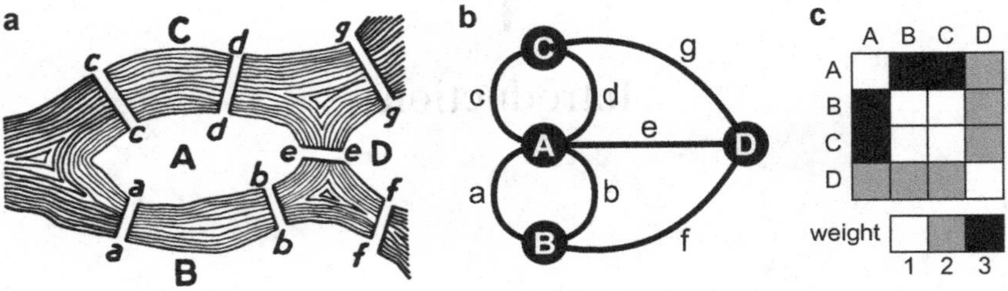

Figure 1.1 The bridges of Königsberg and their graph-theoretical representation. **a:** Seven bridges (*a* through *f*) connect both sides of the river Pregel (*B* and *C*) with the large islands Kneiphof and Lomse (*A* and *D*). Is it possible to reach all four parts of the city by crossing each bridge once and only once? **b:** Euler's ingenious solution rests on the abstraction of the problem, replacing *A*, *B*, *C* and *D* by nodes, and the bridges by links, or edges, interconnecting these nodes. As all nodes are connected by an odd number of edges, the problem's solution is in the negative [42]. **c:** Visualisation of the weighted adjacency relations defining the network at the heart of the Königsberg bridge problem in the form of a matrix. Rows and columns represent the departure and arrival areas, respectively, the weights indicate the number of bridges connecting each of these areas with one another. Panels **a** and **b** are modified from Kraitchik [68, Chapter 8.4].

By stripping colourful yet less relevant details off the given original problem, Euler single-handedly introduced an abstract notion which not just allowed him to uncover its defining essence, but in fact touches upon the very fabric of physical reality. *Each real-world system is finite and discrete*, comprised of discernible parts which share links to, interact with or assert an action on other parts of the system. Be it the plethora of elementary particles interacting with one another through the exchange of virtual bosons, the complex dendritic and axonal trees which carry electrical signals through a network of synaptically interlinked neurons in our brains, or the arrangement of galaxies into large filaments through the action of the gravitational force, all natural phenomena we discovered so far can be abstractly described by and modelled as networks of interconnected objects. These objects are called *nodes* or *vertices*, their connections *edges*, and graph theory, in its most general sense, is the mathematical framework for the study of networks formed by nodes and edges.

Truth be told, it would be an almost futile endeavour to present just a glimpse of the large body of graph-theoretical literature which emerged in the past three centuries since Euler's time. For that reason, we must, and only humbly can, refer the interested reader to the historically first textbook written by Kőnig [65], the still-unmatched definite textbook on the subject by Harary [59] and perhaps the most comprehensive presentation of modern applications of graph theory by Newman [86], and by doing so challenge, somewhat self-servingly, each reader to construct from these initial literature nodes his or her very own 'network of exploration' of the formidable world of graph-theoretical literature. From this it will become immediately clear that not even a genius such as Euler could have envisioned the undoubtedly overwhelming success of graph theory, its underpinning conceptual beauty and far-reaching applications in the study, modelling and characterisation of real-world systems. Unfortunately, however, even the greatest success story hides a tiny stain, some form of caveat hinting at a possible limitation or complication, and it is such a stain on the Michelangelonian masterpiece of graph theory which this book intends to identify and eventually target.

As we already asserted above, due to the very makeup of physical reality, most, if not all, real-world phenomena can be described in terms of networks of interconnected objects. Graph theory, as the mathematical framework formalising such a description, has over the past century not just provided us with a vast yet ever-growing number of concrete examples of networks – ranging in size from a few nodes, such as in the case of the Königsberg bridges, to hundreds of million of nodes in the case of the World Wide Web – but also amassed a plethora of tools and methods for analysing and understanding these networks. Most of these tools and applied methods, however, are of a quantitative nature and, thus, inherently rely on numerical evaluations by hand or, more contemporarily, the use of computers. Although big advances in computational hardware over the past few decades have made it possible to characterise and delineate finer structural details of increasingly larger networks, the question of principal limitations of computational approaches looms like the sword of destiny over the head of every researcher who dares to venture into the seemingly endless realms of graph theory. How far can we go, or – more importantly – how far will we be ever able to go?

To illustrate the more fundamental nature of this question, let us return to the seven bridges of Königsberg and ignore for a moment Euler's definite, and simple, solution of the associated problem in the negative. How many paths through the city are possible? More precisely, how many *Eulerian walks* – that is, paths which traverse each bridge at most once, do exist – and how many of these walks define *Eulerian paths* by crossing each bridge exactly once? It will not take long to draw a tree of all possibilities, a small fraction of which is shown in Fig. 1.2, and count a total of 90 Eulerian walks starting from either bank of the river Pregel (node B or C, Fig. 1.1), 6 of which leave three bridges uncrossed, 12 of which leave two bridges uncrossed, and 72 of which end with one bridge remaining untraversed. None of these 90 walks – nor, for that matter, any of the possible walks emanating from the other parts of the city – is,

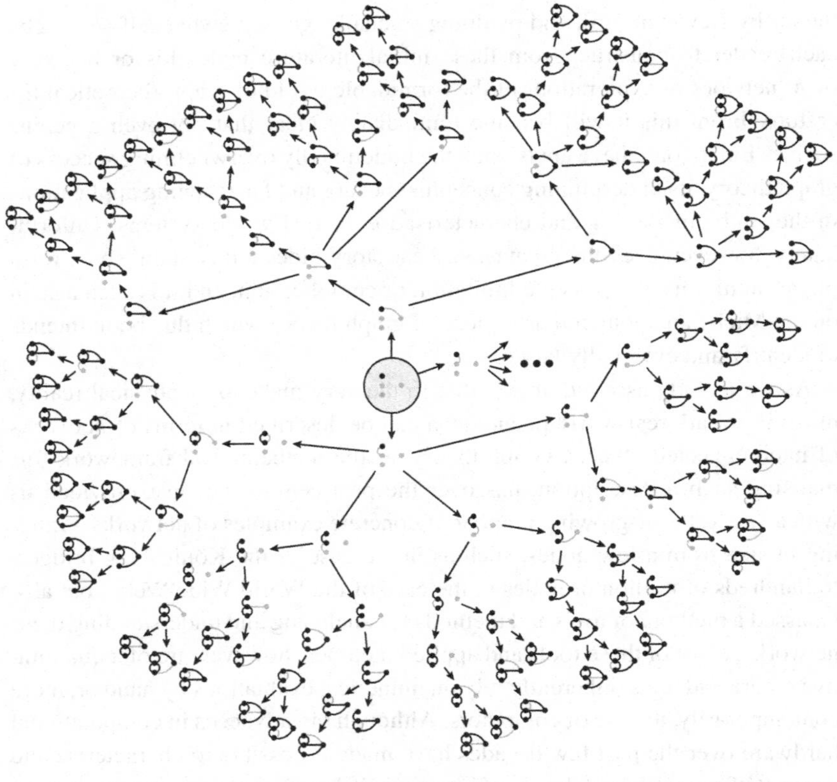

Figure 1.2 Solving the problem of Königsberg's seven bridges through an exhaustive search. Each branch in this tree constructs a possible Eulerian walk, with bridges being crossed marked in grey and bridges already traversed in black. Shown are only Eulerian walks starting from one bank of the river Pregel, omitting all walks which begin by crossing the second bridge to the south. Each branch of this tree of possibilities leaves at least one bridge uncrossed; thus, none of the constructed walks constitutes a sought-after Eulerian path.

thus, an Eulerian path. Without having ever set foot in Königsberg, we just solved the problem of its bridges by brute force on a piece of paper. But today, one can find some 100 bridges and overpasses in Kaliningrad. How long would it take now to draw a tree of all possible walks through the city?

In short, about 10^{150} times as long, give or take some orders of magnitude! A formidable exercise which undoubtedly lies beyond the capacity of even the most modern computers, let alone a wholeheartedly motivated researcher with paper and pencil. The longer and more nuanced answer to this question necessitates the introduction of the notion of *computational complexity*, a measure which, in the most general sense, quantifies the scaling behaviour of computational algorithms with respect to the magnitude of their input variables, in our case the number of bridges and overpasses. To distinguish further the time it takes to run a given algorithm from the storage space it requires, both defining aspects quantifying the efficiency of a computational algorithm in relation to the stringent constraints imposed by the utilised computational hardware, one typically differentiates *time complexity* and *space complexity*, respectively.

Let us first take a look at the time complexity of our little exercise. Drawing a single walk through the city which traverses each bridge – that is, each edge in the associated graph – at most once certainly scales linearly with the total number of bridges E. In mathematical terms, one expresses such a scaling behaviour with the notion $\mathcal{O}(E)$. However, our exercise requires us to draw all Eulerian walks and identify potential Eulerian paths, a rather brute-force approach which is called *exhaustive search*. In order to do so, we must start at every possible point and traverse all the possible paths from that point onwards (Fig. 1.2), a task with a staggering time complexity of not less than $\mathcal{O}(E!)$. Luckily for us, the original problem absolves us from having to cope with such an unmanageable complexity, as it requires us only to decide wether an Eulerian path exists or not. Indeed, following Euler's inspiring solution, we only need to calculate the number of edges connected to each node and test wether any of these numbers is even, a task which can certainly be performed in $\mathcal{O}(E)$ and leaves us off the hook, this time. Unfortunately, however, many of the quantitative graph-theoretical methods and measures do not allow for such an elegant approach, and they typically scale polynomially with the size of the graph, that is, with a time complexity of $\mathcal{O}(E^k)$ for some $k \gg 1$. Undeniably, such a scaling is certainly better than the factorial scaling we encountered above in a brute-force construction. But even with the development of computational hardware in the foreseeable future or the conception of novel, highly efficient computational algorithms, such a polynomial time complexity is still hard to cope with and likely renders the exact quantification of larger networks difficult or even impossible for many decades to come.

The situation regarding space complexity does not look much less gloomy when dealing with graph-theoretical formulations of real-world phenomena. Although efficient representations for a small subset of special graphs exist, generally one is left with a matrix representation of a graph's adjacency relations (see Fig. 1.1c), an approach with a space complexity of $\mathcal{O}(N^2)$ in the number of nodes N. Certainly, neither the seven bridges of Königsberg during Euler's time nor the more numerous bridges in current-day Kaliningrad pose a representational problem here. But what about the graph describing the World Wide Web with its hundreds of millions of nodes [1, 34]? Even if we assign only a Boolean number in the form of a computational bit to indicate the presence, or absence, of an edge between any given pair of nodes, it would require a staggering 1000 terabytes to store the complete adjacency matrix of a graph describing only 100 million linked websites. Luckily for us, in this specific case, a linear list of source and target nodes would suffice, as each node of this graph is, at average, connected to only seven or eight other nodes (e.g., see [26, 54] but also [77]). But even such a sparse representation would still require about one gigabyte of memory alone for storing the graph's defining structure, without any computational analysis having yet been performed on it. When considering still larger or less sparsely connected graphs, such as the network of neurons in the human brain with thousands of connections embedding each of its 100 billion nodes [11, 23], we quickly run out of options as the memory requirements for their representation alone will breach the storage capacity made available in modern computers, perhaps even the computational devices of the next few generations.

The question, then, is, where does this leave us? Of course, a computational analysis is just one of several available options when facing a graph-theoretical formulation of a natural phenomenon. Indeed, the very limitation of a purely numerical approach has led to the development of a whole host of new and exciting methods and continues to stimulate novel ideas and techniques beyond the mere optimisation of computational algorithms. Arguably, one of the conceptually most important and fruitful of these ideas is the distinction of real-world networks into classes of simplified, heavily idealised graph models. Examples of such idealised models include perhaps the most-widely known Erdős–Rényi model [22, 38] which generally serves as the prototype when referring to random graphs, the small-world graph of Watts and Strogatz [109] inspired by Stanley Milgram's infamous 'six degrees of separation' [78] and the scale-free graph of Barabási and Albert [12] which captures the property of self-similarity found in complex systems, to mention but a few. Most of these models are conceived by abstracting from many of the finer structural peculiarities we observe in real-world networks, details which are, as we argued above, increasingly harder to delineate through computational approaches in cases where larger or densely connected networks are concerned. With these graph models typically requiring less than a handful of parameters for their construction and characterisation, the simplified nature of the models then not only allows for the application of numerical optimisation techniques which significantly reduce their computational complexity, but eventually opens the door for a more rigorous mathematical exploration by allowing for an algebraic formalisation of their algorithmic construction.

In this book, we will propose and motivate exactly such a rigorous mathematical approach. By embarking on this adventurous journey, however, we will seek to avoid at least one of the major caveats accompanying many of the idealised graph-theoretical models proposed as descriptions of real-world phenomena since the time of Euler. To briefly illustrate this caveat, let us consider perhaps the simplest of these abstract models, that of the Erdős–Rényi random graph. For each point in its two-dimensional parameter space, which is spanned by the number of nodes and the number of edges, or, alternatively but with subtle conceptual differences, the connection probability between pairs of nodes, a whole ensemble of possible realisations exists, each of which describes a distinct connectivity pattern between all possible pairs of nodes. Although the algebraic formalisation of this model allows, at least in principle, access to this ensemble, most of the defining characteristics of the Erdős–Rényi model can still only be assessed numerically, ideally so over a large number of realisations for each parameter set in order to ensure statistical significance of the obtained results.

Naturally, just as in the case of graph-theoretical descriptions of real-world phenomena, such a computational approach is subject to the stringent limitations mentioned earlier, especially when models of larger graphs are considered. Due to its mathematically well-rooted conception, however, the Erdős–Rényi random graph model also invites a more rigorous analytical examination. Some of its characteristics, such as the number and distribution of edges connected to each node, are indeed governed by exact formulae which, due to the random makeup of the Erdős–Rényi model, are probabilistic in nature and deliver the expectation value for those characteristics across the entire parameter space and, thus, the whole ensemble of possible realisations. With other properties – such as the shortest distance between any pair of nodes, measured in number of edges which must at least be traversed to reach a target node, or the clustering, quantified by the abundance of triangular cycles – we are unfortunately not so lucky. Indeed, many if not most of the properties allow for an analytical take only in some parts of the model's parameter space, that is, under certain and often stringent conditions imposed on the graph's makeup.

It was the meticulous work of Paul Erdős and Alfréd Rényi in the early second half of the last century which eventually established what is now called *random graph theory*, the mathematical study of properties of the probability space of random graphs, a field which stretches today with applications far beyond the random graph model named after its original architects (for a comprehensive introduction, see [22]). The conceptual core of this theory defines a set of conditions which allow for a mathematically rigorous quantification of a random graph's properties. But – and herein lies the problem or caveat hinted at above – these very conditions are rooted in asymptotic considerations, specifically and most importantly the heavy-weighting assumption which demands that the network size should become infinitely large. Although for the math-savvy reader such a demand might certainly appear as nothing unusual, as something being widely employed in mathematics and its many applications – a trick if you will, to establish some form of analytical framework for describing a physical phenomenon or, as in the case of random graphs, for formalising a theoretical model – we must stop here and evaluate its potentially pernicious repercussions and pitfalls.

The important question to ask before issuing any demands on our approach is, do we find in nature any system which we know for certain is infinite in one or more of its properties or, alternatively, is genuinely continuous in an analytical or, if you like, Cantorian sense? Or is it that our models, describing these systems, assume such an idealising makeup for reasons of simplicity, or the sheer lack of a more suitable approach in tune with our study of nature and, thus, epistemology? We could go as far as posing the heretical question of whether the fabric of physical reality itself is algebraic, that is finite and discrete, or analytic, that is infinite and continuous, in nature? Although on first sight such questions might appear far removed from an graph-theoretical inquiry of our world – indeed, as being of little or no relevance today as our analytical formulation of real-world phenomena has undeniably demonstrated tremendous success – their gravity continues to penetrate philosophical discussions and, arguably, lies at the very bedrock of modern science and its mathematical foundation (a comprehensive review of arguments from both sides can be found in Hagar [56]).

To illustrate this point, arguably naively so, in the context of this book, let us take a look at a physical phenomenon which many of us encounter on a daily basis, namely preparing, and eventually enjoying, a nice cup of coffee. Hot water is poured on finely grained coffee and finds its way – 'percolates' – through the porous brown powder to finally yield the tasty, longed-for beverage. This mundane process is just one example of a whole class of phenomena in condensed matter physics which finds a natural representation in terms of random graph theory. However, due to its analytical foundation, the obtained results are, at best, valid only in the case that the number of nodes in the associated graph-theoretical models approaches infinity – that is, we deal with an impossible-to-imagine amount of coffee in front of us – or if the connection probability between nodes is small enough that the connectivity pattern of the model graph resembles that of a tree, a structure that is devoid of cycles or loops and resembles, to stick with our illustrative example, anything but the coffee we are all familiar with. Indeed, the reality of making coffee certainly looks much different from the model we use to describe it, as we do not have at our disposal an (almost) infinite quantity of coffee powder for quenching our desire, nor do we find a resemblance between a sparsely connected tree and the gaps separating the coffee grains through which the water finds its way into our cups!

Despite the fact that theoretical models, by their very conceptual definition, can provide only a simplified, more abstract view of natural phenomena, the above highlighted differences are certainly, or at least arguably, not even close to being a viable reflection of the real-world system in question. Thus, reiterating the above questions, we must ask whether random graph theory, indeed graph theory in general, with its analytical core is the right mathematical approach to describe the discrete and finite phenomena, such as percolation, which we find all around us. After all, every system we can discern in nature, in lack of a proof to the opposite, is both finite and discrete. An answer to this question becomes even more pressing when considering systems which, by their very definition, are bound in size, such as the game of chess, or display boundaries which crucially shape the system's defining behavioural characteristics, such as the aromatic powder in a coffee machine. In such cases we have no choice but to strictly adhere to a finite description, as each simplifying asymptotic assumption will necessarily push us outside the defining premise of the studied phenomenon and eventually deliver a model which no longer observes the phenomenon being considered.

Is it possible to conceive of a mathematical framework which is capable of more precisely capturing finite and discrete graph-theoretical models, thus allowing for a more viable and, arguably, more accurate and thus valid description of real-world phenomena? In this book, we will answer this question affirmatively and motivate a rigorous algebraic approach for the construction, analysis and characterisation of finite graphs. This approach, which we will term *operator graph theory*, comes at the price of abandoning the original definition of a network, or graph, which resides at the very core of classical graph theory in favour of a more dynamic, operational viewpoint. A graph will no longer be a mere static collection of nodes and edges, but instead a construct which can evolve and change due to the actions of operators. We will argue that by studying the algebraic properties typically associated with such operators, this approach opens up a new dimension of qualitative and quantitative insights into the very properties which define a given finite graph, insights which find a viable mathematical representation without resorting to the dangerous tool bag of asymptotic approximations and throttling limitations. In order to further stress, on epistemological grounds and in full awareness of its heretical nature, this very rejection of a continuous, thus analytic, description of real-world phenomena in favour of a finite, thus algebraic, approach, we will restrict, unless otherwise motivated, to the ring of rational numbers $\mathbb{Q}$ instead of the ring of real numbers $\mathbb{R}$ throughout the presentation.

However, before we embark on this adventurous journey, it is of upmost importance to note that the approach presented in this book must and can only be viewed as a coarse introduction, primarily focusing on the mere motivation of a new angle from which to view graph theory and its utilisation as a descriptive tool in the understanding of real-world phenomena. For that reason, the book is divided into two main parts. In the first part, we will lay the necessary theoretical foundation for operator graph theory. To that end, Chapter 2 will provide a necessarily incomplete introduction into classical graph theory by focusing on the presentation of concepts, terminology and mathematical notions needed for the comprehension of the material in the remainder of this book. A similar approach holds for Chapter 3, in which we will take a brief look at the essential fundamentals of the vast field of discrete operator calculus. By fusing the notion of a classical graph with concepts of operator theory introduced in these two chapters, we will then be ready to define the central contribution that this book is aiming for, namely that of an operator graph. In Chapter 4, concluding the first part, not only will this fusion be motivated, but the core conceptual notions of operator graph theory, along with definitions and a presentation of its mathematical framework, will be justified and, hopefully, accessibly illustrated.

The second part of this book focuses on exemplifying the proposed operator graph-theoretical framework by presenting its applications to a few relatable systems and well-known conceptual models of real-world phenomena. Specifically, we will formalise the rigorous algebraic generation of the most-widely used finite random graph models in Chapter 5, and then use this formalisation in Chapter 6 to obtain exact algebraic expressions for a variety of properties characterising these graphs, without resorting to asymptotic approximations. Closing with Chapter 7, we will finish our journey with a brief stroll through the playful realms of game theory by demonstrating the potential usefulness of our operator graph-theoretical framework in the construction and analysis of the game of chess.

We ardently hope that with the chosen examples and applications, the interested reader will be inspired to partake in the furthering of the yet-to-be-fleshed-out theoretical foundations of the operator graph-theoretical framework and be thoroughly motivated not just to consider the latter as a potentially powerful ally in the graph-theoretical description and analysis of real-world phenomena, but to actively utilise this exciting novel approach in the conquest of understanding nature.

PART I

OPERATOR GRAPH THEORY

2
Classical Graph Theory: The Mathematical Description of Networks

What do the bridges of Königsberg, synaptically connected neurons in our brains, or the galaxies illuminating the dark voids of our universe have in common? All of these real-world phenomena can be described as collections of discrete discernible objects which are interlinked to form weblike structures called networks. This chapter will introduce the mathematical representation of such networks and familiarise us with the basic concepts, ideas and terminology of a vast and ever-growing research field whose roots date back to the work of Leonard Euler. Naturally, such an introduction must remain short and will aim primarily at building an intuition for the basic elements necessary to arrive at an algebraic formalisation of networks and their structural characteristics. By taking a closer look at a number of concrete network models, specifically the random graph models which prominently feature as descriptive vessels for many natural phenomena, and briefly exploring some deep-rooted conceptual limitations of these models at the end of this chapter, we hope not only to motivate the need for a rigorous mathematical framework for the study of networks at finite scales, but also to accentuate the potential advantages of a more dynamic vantage point from which to view networks and their defining characteristics in later chapters of this book.

2.1 Graphs and Networks

Let us begin our journey by formalising the core object with which graph theory is concerned. On its most basic conceptual level, a *network*, or *graph* in the mathematical literature, is comprised of a collection of discrete objects, interchangeably called *vertices* or *nodes*, and a collection of *edges*, also called *links* or *bonds*, which describe relations between these objects. Remaining with the example of Königsberg as the iconic city whose now historical mystery inspired the mathematical field of network studies, or *graph theory*, we find that each of the city's four river banks and islands constitutes a node, while the seven bridges connecting these areas establish relations between these nodes and, thus, can be viewed as comprising a set of edges. The collection of areas and bridges then forms the *graph of Königsberg's bridges*, as illustrated in Fig. 1.1. This brilliant insight of Leonard Euler, by abstracting from colourful yet less relevant details, not only allowed for a new way to look at and eventually solve the historical problem associated with Königsberg's seven bridges itself, but indeed established a new powerful framework which matured since Euler's time into an indispensable tool for studying the governing structural and functional characteristics of a sheer unlimited range of real-world phenomena and physical systems. In order to fully realise and harness the power of this framework beyond a mere descriptive vessel, however, we certainly require a mathematically more rigorous representation of a network and its conceptual makeup. To that end, we formulate

Definition 2.1 (finite graph) A *finite network* or *graph* $\mathcal{G}$ is an ordered tuple $\mathcal{G} = (\mathcal{N}, \mathcal{E})$ of a set $\mathcal{N} \neq \emptyset$ of nodes i with cardinality $|\mathcal{N}| \in \mathbb{N}$: $|\mathcal{N}| < \infty$, and a set $\mathcal{E}$ of edges with cardinality $|\mathcal{E}| \in \mathbb{N}_0$ comprised of ordered pairs $(i, j) \in \mathcal{N} \times \mathcal{N}$, each denoting an adjacency relation, or link, between a source node i and a target node j.

Although this now most commonly cited definition constitutes the very foundation of classical graph theory, it must be cautioned that the defined notion also remains rather limited in its scope and suffices only as a portrayal of the principal algebraic building blocks which describe the structural makeup of a given finite graph. Indeed, as each student of real-world graphs will quickly realise, an algebraically more precise description and subsequent exploration of a network's characteristics necessitates a more suitable mathematical representation of the set of nodes and their existing relations. This often includes, or even requires, a quantification of the strength, or *weight*, of the relations established between the nodes beyond the mere existence, or absence, of adjacency relations themselves. Such a representation can be achieved by assigning to each pair of nodes (i, j) with $i, j \in \mathcal{N}$ a number $w_{ij} \in \mathbb{Q}$, such that

$$w_{ij}\colon \mathcal{N} \times \mathcal{N} \to \mathbb{Q} \text{ with } \begin{cases} w_{ij} \neq 0 & \text{iff } (i, j) \in \mathcal{E}, \\ w_{ij} = 0 & \text{otherwise.} \end{cases} \tag{2.1}$$

Referring to a node i by its order in the set $\mathcal{N}$, this mapping is typically represented as $|\mathcal{N}| \times |\mathcal{N}|$ matrix and called the *weight matrix* $\boldsymbol{w}$ of the graph $\mathcal{G}$. Throughout this book – and, arguably, somewhat in defiance of the vast majority of introductory textbooks of graph theory – we will accommodate this more general stance and consider each of a finite graph's edges as being weighted. As we will see below, the various types of networks utilised in the applied graph-theoretical literature then appear as special cases defined by imposing constraints on the weight matrix.

Before utilising Definition 2.1 and the weight matrix (2.1) to furnish a classical graph-theoretical framework, however, let us briefly illustrate the algebraic representation of a graph in the case of Königsberg's bridges. The city's four areas (Kneiphof, Haberberg or Vorstadt, Löbenicht or Altstadt, and Lomse) comprise all nodes of this graph and find a suitable representation in form of the set $\mathcal{N} = \{1, 2, 3, 4\}$ by assigning a number to each area consecutively. With this enumeration, the seven bridges connecting between the city's areas can then be listed as pairs $(1, 2)$ and $(2, 1)$ for the Grüne Brücke and Köttelbrücke, $(1, 3)$ and $(3, 1)$ for the Krämerbrücke and Schmiedebrücke, $(1, 4)$ and $(4, 1)$ for the Honigbrücke, $(2, 4)$ and $(4, 2)$ for the Hohebrücke, and $(3, 4)$ and $(4, 3)$ for the Holzbrücke, and comprise the elements of $\mathcal{E}$. In order to account for the two bridges connecting Kneiphof and Haberberg, the adjacency relations $(1, 2)$ and $(2, 1)$ are both assigned a weight of two. The same applies to the adjacency relation between nodes 1 (Kneiphof) and 3 (Löbenicht), thus leaving us with the weight matrix

$$\boldsymbol{w} = \begin{pmatrix} 0 & 2 & 2 & 1 \\ 2 & 0 & 0 & 1 \\ 2 & 0 & 0 & 1 \\ 1 & 1 & 1 & 0 \end{pmatrix} \tag{2.2}$$

as not only an algebraic description of the graph associated with Königsberg's bridges (Fig. 2.1a), but also a suitable mathematical representation which will ease the further analysis of this historically important graph.

2.1.1 Types of Graphs

The set of edges $\mathcal{E}$ together with the weight w_{ij} associated with each element (i, j) of $\mathcal{E}$ provides a complete mathematical description of the adjacency relations between the nodes of a given graph $\mathcal{G}$. Depending on the specific properties of the set $\mathcal{E}$ and weight matrix $\boldsymbol{w}$, various types of graphs can then be distinguished, some of which are illustrated in Fig. 2.1 and listed in Table 2.1. Definition 2.1 describes what is generally called a *directed graph*, or *digraph* for short, as each $(i, j) \in \mathcal{E}$ is an ordered pair of nodes describing a *directed edge* whose presence in $\mathcal{E}$ neither requires the existence of the associated reciprocal adjacency relations (j, i) nor imposes conditions on the weight of an eventually existing reciprocal adjacency relation $(j, i) \in \mathcal{E}$.

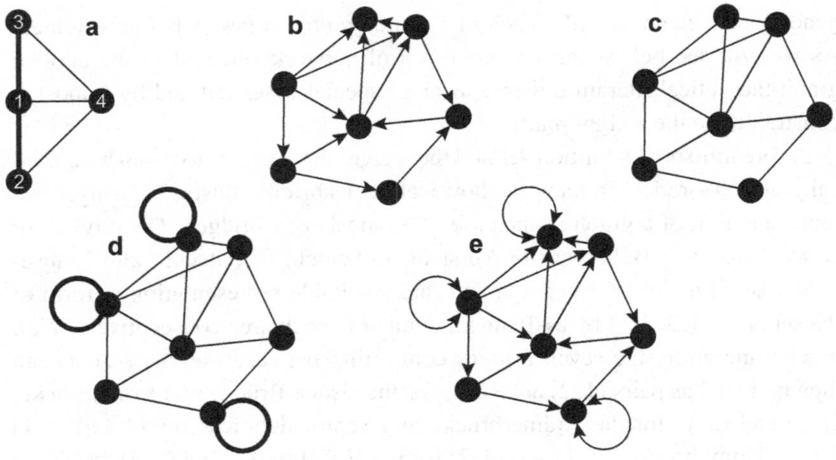

Figure 2.1 Examples of various types of graphs. **a:** The seven bridges of Königsberg form an undirected multigraph, with the weight of the graph's edges representing the number of bridges connecting each of the city's four areas (thin solid: 1 bridge, thick solid: 2 bridges). **b:** A relational digraph in which pairs of nodes are connected by directed edges. **c:** The same graph with undirected edges, forming a simple graph. **d:** A self-looped undirected multigraph. Although all edges between pairs of distinct nodes are unweighted, a self-loop is considered as either two directed links each carrying a weight of 1 or, as shown here, as one undirected edge of weight 2. **e:** A self-looped directed multigraph in which each self-loop is represented by two directed edges (indicated by double-arrows) each carrying a weight of 1. Graphs **a**, **c** and **d** are examples of undirected graphs, while **b** and **e** are digraphs. Due to the presence of weighted edges and self-loops, graphs displayed in **a**, **d** and **e** require a weight matrix (2.3) for their correct representation, while in the cases displayed in **b** and **c**, an adjacency matrix (2.4) suffices.

In terms of the weight matrix, we can thus define a graph as being directed if $\exists (i, j) \in \mathcal{E}$ with $i, j \in \mathcal{N}$: $w_{ij} \neq 0 \wedge w_{ji} = 0$. On the other hand, the Königsberg's bridge graph is a classical example of an *undirected graph*, as here for each $(i, j) \in \mathcal{E}$ also $(j, i) \in \mathcal{E}$ such that $w_{ij} = w_{ji}$ for all $i, j \in \mathcal{N}$ and each unordered pair (i, j): $w_{ij} \neq 0$ defines an *undirected edge* (Fig. 2.1a). On closer inspection, we furthermore notice that in this particular graph none of its nodes serves both as source and target of an edge. A graph for which $\nexists i \in \mathcal{N}$: $(i, i) \in \mathcal{E}$ is called a *not self-looped graph*, and a *self-looped graph* if and only if there exists at least one *self-loop*, that is, an edge which connects a node with itself such that $w_{ii} \neq 0$ for at least one $i \in \mathcal{N}$.

Following historically established terminology, the assignment of a weight $w_{ij} \in \mathbb{Q}$ to each adjacency relation $(i, j) \in \mathcal{E}$ of a directed graph with $w_{ij} \neq 1$

Table 2.1 *Major graph types and their weight matrix representation.*

directed	$\exists i, j \in \mathcal{N}\colon w_{ij} \neq 0 \wedge w_{ji} = 0$	undirected	$\forall i, j \in \mathcal{N}\colon w_{ij} = w_{ji}$
self-looped	$\exists i \in \mathcal{N}\colon w_{ii} \neq 0$	not self-looped	$\forall i \in \mathcal{N}\colon w_{ii} = 0$
weighted	$\exists (i, j) \in \mathcal{E}\colon w_{ij} \neq 1$	unweighted	$\forall i, j \in \mathcal{N}\colon w_{ij} \in \mathbb{B}$

multidigraph	$\forall i, j \in \mathcal{N}\colon w_{ij} \in \mathbb{N}_0 \wedge \exists i, j \in \mathcal{N} : w_{ij} \neq w_{ji} \wedge \exists (i, j) \in \mathcal{E} : w_{ij} > 1$
multigraph	$\forall i, j \in \mathcal{N}\colon w_{ij} \in \mathbb{N}_0 \wedge w_{ij} = w_{ji} \wedge \exists (i, j) \in \mathcal{E} : w_{ij} > 1$
relational digraph	$\forall i, j \in \mathcal{N}\colon w_{ij} \in \mathbb{B} \wedge \forall i \in \mathcal{N} : w_{ii} = 0$
simple graph	$\forall i, j \in \mathcal{N}\colon w_{ij} \in \mathbb{B} \wedge w_{ij} = w_{ji} \wedge \forall i \in \mathcal{N} : w_{ii} = 0$

for at least one $(i, j) \in \mathcal{E}$ defines a *weighted digraph*. A first special case of a weighted digraph is obtained if we set $w_{ij} = w_{ji}$ for each $(i, j) \in \mathcal{E}$. In this case, the graph is undirected and simply called a *weighted graph*. By further restricting each non-zero element of the weight matrix to the set of natural numbers $\mathbb{N}$, we have

$$w_{ij}\colon \mathcal{N} \times \mathcal{N} \to \mathbb{N}_0 \text{ with } \begin{cases} w_{ij} \in \mathbb{N} & \text{iff } (i, j) \in \mathcal{E}, \\ w_{ij} = 0 & \text{otherwise,} \end{cases} \tag{2.3}$$

and the corresponding graph is called a *directed multigraph*, or *multidigraph*, if $\exists (i, j) \in \mathcal{E} : w_{ij} > 1$, and an *undirected multigraph* or simply *multigraph* if, in addition, its weight matrix is symmetric. In a multigraph or multidigraph, each adjacency relation $(i, j) \in \mathcal{E}$ with weight $w_{ij} > 1$ can be viewed as representing either w_{ij} edges of weight 1 linking nodes i and j, or a single *multiedge* of weight w_{ij}. Recalling the weight matrix (2.2), the graph of Königsberg's bridges provides a classical example of such a multigraph (Fig. 2.1a). A final special type of weighted digraph we will entertain here is realised if each element of the weight matrix of a not self-looped digraph maps a pair of nodes into the Boolean set $\mathbb{B} := \{0, 1\}$. The weight matrix is then commonly referred to as *adjacency matrix* $\boldsymbol{a}$ with elements

$$a_{ij}\colon \mathcal{N} \times \mathcal{N} \to \mathbb{B} \text{ with } a_{ij} = \begin{cases} 1 & \text{iff } (i, j) \in \mathcal{E} \text{ and } i \neq j, \\ 0 & \text{otherwise,} \end{cases} \tag{2.4}$$

and defines a *relational digraph* (Fig. 2.1b) or, in the undirected case with symmetric adjacency matrix $a_{ij} = a_{ji}$, a *simple graph* (Fig. 2.1c).

It is this type of simple – that is, undirected, not self-looped and single-edged – graph which most prominently features in the contemporary applied graph-theoretical literature. Indeed, and somewhat unfortunately, the overwhelming majority of notions and measures introduced into graph theory since Euler's time is attuned to utilising the adjacency matrix (2.4), a simplification which, arguably, only rarely is justified when dealing with graph-theoretical descriptions of real-world phenomena. For that reason, the presentation in the remainder of this book will focus, whenever possible, on the most general, i.e. weighted, directed and self-looped, type of graph formalised in Definition 2.1 together with equation (2.1), and highlight, whenever necessary, results and subtleties for the specific types of graphs introduced above as special cases.

One of these subtleties concerns the incorporation of nodes with self-loops in a graph. In order to explore the complication associated with the presence of self-loops, let us first consider the case of an unweighted undirected graph. Here, for each ordered pair $(i, j) \in \mathcal{E}$ of distinct nodes, (j, i) must also be an element of $\mathcal{E}$. If the source and target node of an edge are identical and each edge carries a weight of 1, we obtain for the associated adjacency relations

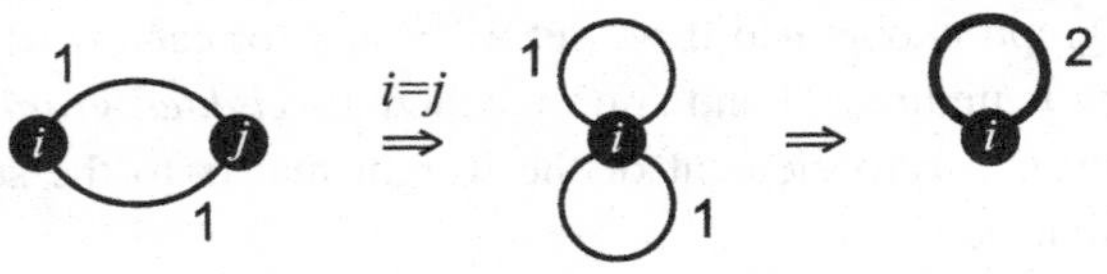

which suggests that each pair (i, i) must be counted twice in $\mathcal{E}$. Although it is possible to account for this doubling in the mathematical definition of graph-theoretical quantities by treating self-loops separately from undirected edges between distinct nodes, it is often more convenient to represent a self-loop as one edge and assign to it a weight of two, as illustrated above and exemplified in Fig. 2.1d. However, such an approach carries the subtle disadvantage that unweighted undirected graphs with self-loops can no longer be represented by employing an adjacency matrix (2.4), as in this case $a_{ii} = 2 \notin \mathbb{B}$ if $(i, i) \in \mathcal{E}$, and thus limits the commonly used notion of an adjacency matrix to an unweighted undirected graph without self-loops; that is, simple graphs. In the presence of self-loops, such graphs are multigraphs and therefore require a weight matrix with $w_{ii} = 2 \; \forall \, (i, i) \in \mathcal{E}$ for their representation.

Naturally, this convention can be generalised to incorporate undirected multigraphs with self-loops and arbitrary edge weights, in which case $w_{ii} = 2\mathbb{N}_0$ for all $i \in \mathcal{N}$, as well as undirected graphs with edges taking weights in $\mathbb{Q}$. Moreover, and most importantly, the above approach with its associated conditions imposed on the diagonal elements of the weight matrices (2.1) and (2.3) also applies to directed graphs if we consider that, by definition, each self-looped node serves as both source and target of an adjacency relation and, thus, each self-loop necessarily corresponds to an undirected edge (Fig. 2.1e). Indeed, in a directed graph, an undirected adjacency relation of weight w between two distinct nodes i and j can be generated by either adding a reciprocal directed edge to $\mathcal{E}$ (symmetrisation) or discarding the direction of the given edge which, again, necessitates the addition of a reciprocal directed edge to $\mathcal{E}$ (doubling). In both cases, a self-loop is conceptually consistent with the presence of two directed edges each carrying a weight of w, or one undirected edge of weight $2w$, as illustrated in

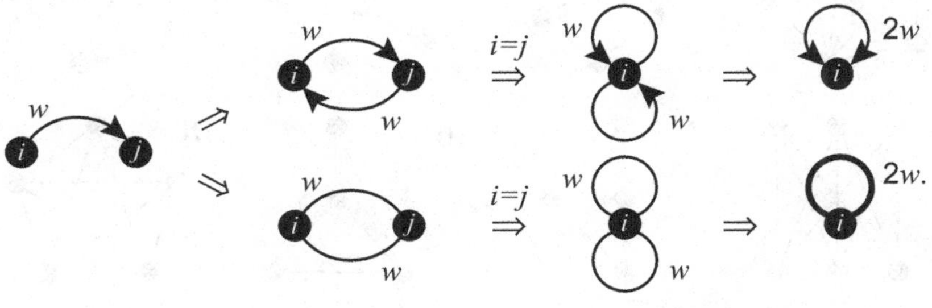

It is important to stress that, unfortunately, in many applications of graph theory this subtle conceptual difference between self-loops and edges between distinct nodes is largely ignored in order to remain with an adjacency matrix as a representational vessel. This is typically addressed by discarding self-loops from graph models – that is, by modifying the very structural makeup of a given graph – altogether. The convention introduced above and adhered to throughout this book avoids such a heavy-handed approach, but does so at the expense of surrendering the commonly used notion of an adjacency matrix a_{ij} to the consideration of relational digraphs and simple graphs only, that is, unweighted directed and undirected graphs without self-loops.

2.1.2 Classes of Graphs

In addition to the various types of graphs introduced above and distinguished by general properties of the set of edges $\mathcal{E}$ and the weights assigned to each of its elements, we can also identify a number of graph classes, some of which are illustrated in Fig. 2.2 and listed in Table 2.2, by considering more specific structural characteristics shared between graphs. An important first example of such a graph class is given by the *complete graph*, commonly defined as a fully connected simple graph in which each node establishes edges to all other nodes such that $a_{ij} = 1$ for all $i, j \in \mathcal{N}: i \neq j$ (Fig. 2.2a). This notion of a complete graph can certainly be generalised to incorporate relational digraphs, in which case each pair of distinct nodes is connected by two edges, one in each direction, to form a *complete digraph*. Moreover, as the definition of a complete graph requires only the presence of edges between each pair of distinct nodes in $\mathcal{N}$, this class can be further expanded to include not self-looped weighted graphs. In what follows, we will therefore refer to a complete digraph as a generally weighted graph for which $w_{ij} \neq 0$ for all $i, j \in \mathcal{N}: i \neq j$, and a complete graph if, in addition, $\forall i, j \in \mathcal{N}: i \neq j$ we have $w_{ij} = w_{ji}$. We recognise,

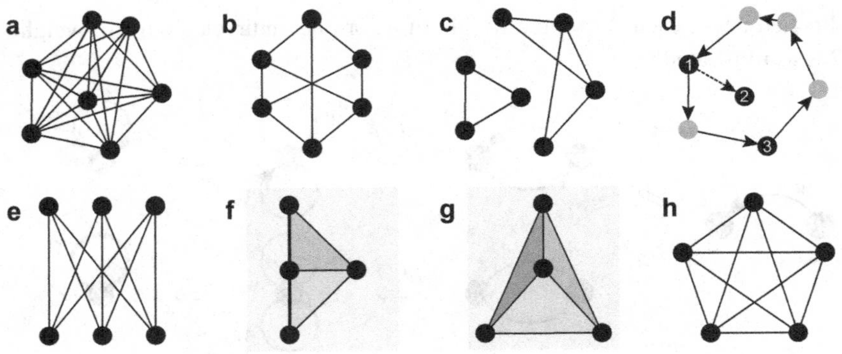

Figure 2.2 Representative examples of various classes of graphs. Illustrated are a complete graph (**a**), a 3-regular graph (**b**), a disconnected graph (**c**), a weakly connected digraph (**d**), a bipartite graph (also known as a utility graph) (**e**), the planar graph of Königsberg's bridges (**f**), a complete planar (**g**) and a complete non-planar graph (**h**). With the exception of the weakly connected digraph and the weighted Königsberg bridge graph, the displayed examples are all simple graphs. In the case of the weakly connected digraph (**d**), nodes 1 and 3 are strongly connected (black solid), while nodes 1 and 2 establish only a weak connection (black dashed). The grey areas in (**f**) and (**g**) mark the different faces of the illustrated planar graphs.

however, that such a generalisation runs into conflict somewhat with the type of directed graphs introduced in the previous section, a situation which will be salvaged in Section 2.2.3 with the introduction of the type of weight-directed graph. An illustrative example of a complete digraph is given by a small collaboration network of scientists in which each individual member will contribute, depending on expertise and relevance, to further the other members' research. As a representative example, for a complete graph we find the network of gravitational interactions between galaxies, as each galaxy exerts an attractive force on all others while the strength of this force and, thus, the weight of each edge in the associated graph will vary between different pairs as a function of the galaxies' spatial distance.

Inherently related to the notion of a complete graph is that of a *graph complement*, also called a *graph edge-complement* or *graph inverse* [53]. Given a relational digraph $\mathcal{G} = (\mathcal{N}, \mathcal{E})$, the complement of $\mathcal{G}$ is typically defined as a relational digraph $\bar{\mathcal{G}} = (\bar{\mathcal{N}}, \bar{\mathcal{E}})$ with the same set of nodes $\bar{\mathcal{N}} = \mathcal{N}$ and a set of edges $\bar{\mathcal{E}}$ such that for all $i, j \in \mathcal{N}: i \neq j$ we have $(i, j) \in \bar{\mathcal{E}}$ if and only if $(i, j) \notin \mathcal{E}$. If a_{ij} denotes the adjacency matrix of $\mathcal{G}$, the adjacency matrix of its complement is thus given by $\bar{a}_{ij} = 1 - a_{ij}$ for all $i, j \in \mathcal{N}: i \neq j$ and $\bar{a}_{ii} = 0$. With this, the sum of $\mathcal{G}$ and its complement $\bar{\mathcal{G}}$ then yields a complete digraph formed by the set of nodes $\mathcal{N}$. Here, the *graph sum* of two relational digraphs

$\mathcal{G}_1 = (\mathcal{N}, \mathcal{E}_1)$ and $\mathcal{G}_2 = (\mathcal{N}, \mathcal{E}_2)$ sharing the same set of nodes $\mathcal{N}$ and edge sets $\mathcal{E}_1, \mathcal{E}_2 : \mathcal{E}_1 \cap \mathcal{E}_2 = \emptyset$ is defined as the relational digraph $\mathcal{G}_1 \triangledown \mathcal{G}_2 := (\mathcal{N}, \mathcal{E}_1 \cup \mathcal{E}_2)$. In case two given graphs share at least one common edge or at least one of the graphs is weighted, their graph sum will necessarily yield a weighted graph. This generalisation allows naturally extending the notion of a graph complement to include not self-looped weighted graphs, such that in the remainder of this book we will refer to a graph complement $\bar{\mathcal{G}}$ of a not self-looped graph or digraph $\mathcal{G}$ if their sum $\mathcal{G} \triangledown \bar{\mathcal{G}}$ respectively forms a complete graph or digraph.

Another important graph class is comprised of simple graphs in which each node establishes the same number of edges to other nodes in the graph, and is called a *regular graph* or *k-regular graph* (Fig. 2.2b). Mathematically, the requirement defining a k-regular graph can be expressed as

$$\forall i \in \mathcal{N}\colon \sum_{j \in \mathcal{N}} a_{ij} = k = const,$$

where the sum runs over all nodes in the graph. As in the case of a complete graph, this notion also can be generalised to cover relational digraphs, in which case each node is required to have the same number of outgoing and incoming directed edges, that is,

$$\forall i \in \mathcal{N}\colon \sum_{j \in \mathcal{N}} a_{ij} = \sum_{j \in \mathcal{N}} a_{ji} = k = const\,.$$

Such a graph is then called a *k-regular digraph*. Finally, if the edges of a not self-looped directed graph are weighted, we can formulate

$$\forall i \in \mathcal{N}\colon \sum_{j \in \mathcal{N}} w_{ij} = \sum_{j \in \mathcal{N}} w_{ji} = w = const$$

as a necessary condition defining a *w-regular digraph* and, in the case of symmetric w_{ij}, a *w-regular graph*, although these generalising notions are not yet employed in the wider graph-theoretical literature. We note that each complete graph or digraph with node set $\mathcal{N}$ and unweighted edges is also a k-regular graph or digraph with $k = |N| - 1$, while it is generally not true that a complete weighted graph is also a w-regular graph.

A third major class of graphs concerns the existence of connections between possible pairs of nodes. A simple graph in which each node can be reached from at least one other node by following existing edges is called a *connected graph*. Conversely, in a *disconnected graph*, there exists at least one pair of nodes which cannot be linked through edges forming the graph. The presence of an *isolated node* – that is, a node without associated adjacency relations – is a trivial example of a disconnected graph; while the disconnected graph depicted in Fig. 2.2c is comprised of two independent smaller graphs.

Table 2.2 *Important graph classes and their weight matrix representation.*

Class	Type[a] *d*	*ud*	*w*	*uw*	Representation
complete	•	•	•	•	$\forall i, j \in \mathcal{N}, i \neq j : w_{ij} \neq 0$
k-regular	•	•		•	$\forall i, j \in \mathcal{N} : w_{ij} \in \mathbb{B} \wedge \forall i \in \mathcal{N} : \sum_{j\in\mathcal{N}} w_{ij} = \sum_{j\in\mathcal{N}} w_{ji} = k$
w-regular	•	•	•		$\forall i \in \mathcal{N} : \sum_{j\in\mathcal{N}} w_{ij} = \sum_{j\in\mathcal{N}} w_{ji} = w$
connected		•	•	•	$\forall i, j \in \mathcal{N}, i \neq j\ \exists j_l \in \mathcal{N}, l \in [1, k], j_1 = i, j_{k+1} = j : w_{j_l j_{l+1}} \neq 0$
bipartite	•	•	•	•	$\exists \mathcal{N}' \subset \mathcal{N}, \mathcal{N}' \neq \emptyset$ such that $\forall i, j \in \mathcal{N}' : w_{ij} = 0 \wedge \forall i, j \in \mathcal{N} \setminus \mathcal{N}' : w_{ij} = 0$ and $\exists i \in \mathcal{N}', j \in \mathcal{N} \setminus \mathcal{N}' : w_{ij} \neq 0 \vee w_{ji} \neq 0$
biclique	•	•	•	•	$\exists \mathcal{N}' \subset \mathcal{N}, \mathcal{N}' \neq \emptyset$ such that $\forall i, j \in \mathcal{N}' : w_{ij} = 0 \wedge \forall i, j \in \mathcal{N} \setminus \mathcal{N}' : w_{ij} = 0$ and $\forall i \in \mathcal{N}', j \in \mathcal{N} \setminus \mathcal{N}' : w_{ij} \neq 0 \wedge w_{ji} \neq 0$

[a] Graph types (see Table 2.1) to which the given representation applies. Here *d*, *ud*, *w* and *uw* denote directed, undirected, weighted and unweighted graphs respectively.

Naturally, the notion of a connected graph can again be expanded to include undirected weighted graphs, with the graph of Königsberg's bridges being an illustrative example of a connected multigraph. In the case of relational or, more generally, weighted directed graphs, however, the situation is slightly more involved and requires the notion of strongly and weakly connected nodes. In the example illustrated in Fig. 2.2d, both nodes 2 and 3 can be reached from node 1 by following a path of directed edges, but the converse is true only for node 3. We refer to nodes 1 and 3 as being *strongly connected*, while nodes 1 and 2 are not. However, node 1 can be reached from node 2 if the directed edge connecting both nodes is complemented by a directed edge pointing in the opposite direction, or is simply replaced by an undirected edge, thus rendering nodes 1 and 2 *weakly connected.* If each pair of nodes in a directed graph is strongly connected, the graph is called a *strongly connected digraph*; while in a *weakly connected digraph*, there exists at least one pair of only weakly connected nodes. As each strongly connected node pair is also weakly connected, all strongly connected digraphs are necessarily and sufficiently weakly connected digraphs, while the opposite is not true.

With complete, regular and connected graphs, we certainly have not yet exhausted the long list of classes which distinguish possible connectivity patterns in graphs. Indeed, by considering patterns of connections between subsets of nodes, many more graph classes can be defined which, in some cases, find important applications as models in the description of real-world phenomena. As an illustrative example, let us focus here on one of these more specific classes. If in a given simple graph $\mathcal{G} = (\mathcal{N}, \mathcal{E})$, two distinct subsets

$\mathcal{N}_1$ and $\mathcal{N}_2$ of nodes can be identified such that adjacency relations exist only between nodes which reside in different subsets, that is, if $\mathcal{N} = \mathcal{N}_1 \cup \mathcal{N}_1$ and for all $(i, j) \in \mathcal{E}$: $(i \in \mathcal{N}_1 \wedge j \in \mathcal{N}_2) \vee (i \in \mathcal{N}_2 \wedge j \in \mathcal{N}_1)$, the graph is called a *bipartite graph*, and a *complete bipartite graph*, or simply *biclique*, in the case all nodes in $\mathcal{N}_1$ are connected to all nodes in set $\mathcal{N}_2$ (Fig. 2.2e). This notion applies to both weighted and unweighted as well as directed and undirected not self-looped graphs. Due to their conceptional simplicity, bipartite graphs find widespread use not only as models of interactions between groups of objects whose members share common characteristics [10], but also in the modelling of feedforward networks such as artificial neural networks [46, 75] and a variety of biological neural networks along with their functional properties [93].

The final and, historically, arguably most intriguing class of graphs to be introduced in this abridged presentation of classical graph theory is comprised of networks which allow for a planar embedding. Such an embedding is defined as a visual representation of a given graph on a two-dimensional surface such that edges intersect only at the nodes to which they connect. A simple graph which allows for such a representation is then called a *planar graph*, and it is called a *non-planar graph* if no such planar embedding exists. The graph of Königsberg's bridges (Fig 2.2f) and the complete simple graph with four nodes depicted in Fig 2.2g are planar, while the bipartite graph shown in Fig 2.2e and complete simple graph with five nodes in Fig 2.2h are examples of non-planar graphs. Indeed, the latter two graphs are instrumental in deciding whether a given simple graph allows for a planar embedding or not, a remarkable insight formalised in Kuratowski's theorem [72]. Unfortunately, a just presentation of this historically significant result along with its many proofs [64, 104] is beyond the scope of this brief introduction, and we must refer the interested reader to the excellent textbook by Nishizeki and Chiba [89].

Instead, let us take a closer look at another important contribution which not only resides at the very heart of the theory of planar graphs but unearthed one of the most beautiful equations in the theory of finite graphs altogether, *Euler's formula*. Owing to its definition, a planar graph $\mathcal{G} = (\mathcal{N}, \mathcal{E})$ necessarily divides the plane into distinct regions or *faces*, each encircled by a subset of edges forming a *cycle*. Let us denote with $\mathcal{F}$ the set of these faces, including the unbounded region outside the graph, such that the cardinality $|\mathcal{F}|$ yields the number of faces. Euler's formula then states that the number of nodes, given by $|\mathcal{N}|$, the number of edges, given by $|\mathcal{E}|$, and the number of faces $|\mathcal{F}|$ are subject to the strict identity

$$|\mathcal{N}| - |\mathcal{E}| + |\mathcal{F}| = 2 \tag{2.5}$$

for any finite connected planar graph $\mathcal{G}$. In the graph of Königsberg's bridges (Fig. 2.2f), for example, we find $|\mathcal{N}| = 4$, $|\mathcal{E}| = 5$ and $|\mathcal{F}| = 3$. For the complete graph with $|\mathcal{N}| = 4$ depicted in Fig. 2.2g, we have $|\mathcal{E}| = 6$ and $|\mathcal{F}| = 4$. Thus both examples of planar graphs satisfy (2.5).

Due to the historical significance of Euler's formula, and its importance for many real-world applications, we will present here a simple proof demonstrating its validity. To that end, let us first introduce the notion of a *tree graph* as a simple planar graph which has only one face, and show by induction on the number of nodes that (2.5) holds for this type of graph. If a tree graph contains only one node and no edge, Euler's formula clearly applies. We now assume that (2.5) is true for all tree graphs with $|\mathcal{N}| \geq 1$ nodes. Following its definition, each such graph must have $|\mathcal{N}| - 1$ edges. Let $\mathcal{T}' = (\mathcal{N}', \mathcal{E}')$ be a tree graph with $|\mathcal{N}'| = |\mathcal{N}| + 1$ nodes and $|\mathcal{E}'|$ edges. Starting at any of its nodes, we then follow an arbitrary path comprised of edges between connected nodes but without revisiting nodes. As a tree graph has only one face, and thus no cycle, such a path will not return to the initially chosen node but instead must necessarily terminate at a node which is connected by only one edge. By removing the path's final node along with its sole edge, we then construct a new tree $\mathcal{T}'' = (\mathcal{N}'', \mathcal{E}'')$ with $|\mathcal{N}''| = |\mathcal{N}'| - 1 = |\mathcal{N}|$ nodes and $|\mathcal{E}''| = |\mathcal{E}'| - 1$ edges. By the induction hypothesis, as $\mathcal{T}''$ is a tree graph with $|\mathcal{N}|$ nodes, we must have $|\mathcal{E}''| = |\mathcal{N}| - 1$, from which $|\mathcal{E}'| = |\mathcal{N}|$ for $\mathcal{T}'$ and the validity of Euler's formula for trees with $|\mathcal{N}| + 1$ nodes, thus for all tree graphs, follows.

For arbitrary planar graphs, the proof of Euler's formula (2.5) follows a similar approach using induction on the number of edges. A connected planar graph with $|\mathcal{N}| \geq 1$ nodes must have at least $|\mathcal{N}| - 1$ edges. If the graph has exactly $|\mathcal{N}| - 1$ edges, it is a tree graph and, as shown above, Euler's formula certainly applies. Assuming that (2.5) is true for graphs with $|\mathcal{N}| \geq 1$ nodes and $|\mathcal{E}| \geq |\mathcal{N}| - 1$ edges, we have $\mathcal{F} \geq 1$. Let $\mathcal{G}' = (\mathcal{N}', \mathcal{E}')$ be a connected simple graph with $|\mathcal{N}'| = |\mathcal{N}|$ nodes and $|\mathcal{E}'| = |\mathcal{E}| + 1$ edges. Then $\mathcal{F} > 1$, and $\mathcal{G}$ must have at least one cycle. By choosing any of these cycles and removing one of the chosen cycle's edges, we then construct a new graph $\mathcal{G}'' = (\mathcal{N}'', \mathcal{E}'')$ with $|\mathcal{N}''| = |\mathcal{N}'| = |\mathcal{N}|$ nodes, $|\mathcal{E}''| = |\mathcal{E}'| - 1 = |\mathcal{E}|$ edges and two merged faces, i.e. $|\mathcal{F}''| = |\mathcal{F}'| - 1$. By the induction hypothesis, as $\mathcal{G}''$ is a connected planar graph with $|\mathcal{N}|$ nodes and $|\mathcal{E}|$ edges, we have $|\mathcal{N}''| - |\mathcal{E}''| + |\mathcal{F}''| = 2$, from which $|\mathcal{N}'| - (|\mathcal{E}'| - 1) + (|\mathcal{F}'| - 1) = |\mathcal{N}'| - |\mathcal{E}'| + |\mathcal{F}'| = 2$ for $\mathcal{G}'$ and eventually the validity of (2.5) for all finite connected planar graphs follows.

The theory of planar graphs undoubtedly forms the root of one of the historically most influential branches of graph theory, from which a whole host of important real-world applications was spawned. Certainly high among these applications ranks the *four-colour theorem*, which states that four colours

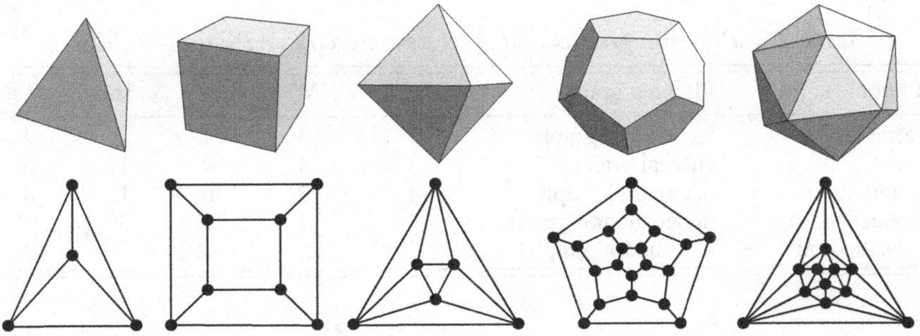

Figure 2.3 The Platonic solids (tetrahedron, cube, octahedron, dodecahedron and icosahedron) and their associated planar graphs (tetrahedral graph, cubical graph, octahedral graph, dodecahedral graph and icosahedral graph). Using Euler's formula, it can easily be shown that only five Platonic solids are possible.

suffice to draw the faces of a planar graph in such a way that no adjacent faces have the same colour [7, 8, 9], and which provides the mathematical foundation for the accessible visual representation of contiguous regions on the many maps we encounter in our everyday lives. Unfortunately, our necessarily brief introduction to classical graph theory does not permit a worthy presentation of this or other important results of planar graph theory. However, we will entertain the intrigued reader with a beautiful yet simple graph-theoretical proof of another historically significant mathematical theorem which states that there can be only five *Platonic solids*: the tetrahedron, cube, octahedron, dodecahedron and icosahedron (Fig. 2.3, top). Platonic solids are defined as convex polyhedra whose faces are comprised of congruent convex regular polygons. These iconic geometrical objects not only were the subject of extensive studies in antiquity, but they played an important role in a variety of fields throughout history. It was Euclid in his *Elements* who first showed rigorously that only five such solids are possible [41].

Here we will present a simple proof utilising Euler's formula (2.5). To that end, we first represent each solid as a planar graph $\mathcal{G} = (\mathcal{N}, \mathcal{E})$, called a *Platonic graph*, by associating a node with each corner of the solid, and a graph edge with each of the solid's edges (Fig. 2.3). By construction, the faces of the Platonic graphs correspond to the faces of the Platonic solid, with each face of a given solid being encircled by the same number of edges $N_e^{\mathcal{F}}$, and each node establishing the same number of adjacency relations $N_e^{\mathcal{N}}$. As furthermore, each edge of our Platonic graphs belongs to exactly two distinct faces, we have $N_e^{\mathcal{F}}|\mathcal{F}| = 2|\mathcal{E}|$, and as each edge links two distinct nodes, we find $N_e^{\mathcal{N}}|\mathcal{N}| = 2|\mathcal{E}|$. Employing Euler's formula and some simple algebraic

Table 2.3 *Platonic graphs and their associated five Platonic solids.*

Platonic solid	Platonic graph	$N_e^{\mathcal{N}}$	$N_e^{\mathcal{F}}$	$\lvert\mathcal{N}\rvert$	$\lvert\mathcal{E}\rvert$	$\lvert\mathcal{F}\rvert$
tetrahedron	tetrahedral graph	3	3	4	6	4
cube	cubical graph	3	4	8	12	6
octahedron	octahedral graph	4	3	6	12	8
dodecahedron	dodecahedral graph	3	5	20	30	12
icosahedron	icosahedral graph	5	3	12	30	20

manipulations, which we leave as an exercise for the reader, we are then left with the diophantine equation

$$\frac{1}{N_e^{\mathcal{N}}} + \frac{1}{N_e^{\mathcal{F}}} = \frac{1}{|\mathcal{E}|} + \frac{1}{2}$$

as a necessary condition governing the existence of Platonic graphs. By noting that $N_e^{\mathcal{N}} \geq 3$ and $N_e^{\mathcal{F}} \geq 3$, and that Platonic graphs must have at least one edge such that $|\mathcal{E}| \geq 1$, we find that this equation can only have the five integer solutions for $N_e^{\mathcal{N}}$, $N_e^{\mathcal{F}}$ and $|\mathcal{E}|$ listed in Table 2.3, thus demonstrating that only five Platonic graphs, hence only five Platonic solids, are possible.

With this brief excursion into the realms of our antique forefathers, we will conclude our brief introduction to the basic notions and conceptual foundation at the heart of the theory of graphs and networks. These preliminaries should suffice as a framework for the material presented in the remainder of this book. In the next section, we will return to general weighted digraphs and introduce, on more rigorous grounds, some of the concepts and concrete quantities which are commonly employed throughout the applied graph-theoretical literature to characterise and measure graphs.

2.2 Graph Measures

Although the classical notion of a graph introduced in Definition 2.1 along with the small selection of types and classes exemplified in the last section already allow for a coarse distinction of a graph's structural makeup, the delineation and quantification of finer structural characteristics certainly require a more detailed assessment. Indeed, since Euler's time, a plethora of such quantities has emerged, and hundreds of measures are now being commonly employed throughout the contemporary literature in the comparative analysis of graphs and real-world networks. A thorough presentation of this ever-growing host of graph-theoretical measures, however, lies beyond the scope of this book, and we must refer the interested reader to the recent textbook of Newman [86] or the excellent review by Boccaletti and colleagues [20] for a more comprehensive and detailed overview. Instead, we will focus here on only the most basic and prominent measures of relevance for presentation in later chapters, and we will categorise these measures into general measures, degree-based, weight-based and distance-based measures, as well as measures associated with network motifs and graph spectra. With this necessarily abridged presentation, we nevertheless hope to motivate the serious student to further explore this vast and fluent branch of graph theory and its countless real-world applications.

2.2.1 General Measures

In Section 2.1, we already encountered some of the graph-theoretical notions associated with a general characterisation of a given network, its size, type and class. To formalise these notions and set the foundation for a mathematically more rigorous framework, let us begin by introducing a number of measures with values in the Boolean set $\mathbb{B}$ which allow us to distinguish whether a given graph $\mathcal{G} = (\mathcal{N}, \mathcal{E})$ *is directed*,

$$\lambda_d \in \mathbb{B} : \lambda_d := \begin{cases} 1 & \text{iff } \exists\, i, j \in \mathcal{N}, (i, j) \in \mathcal{E} : w_{ij} \neq 0 \wedge w_{ji} = 0, \\ 0 & \text{otherwise,} \end{cases} \tag{2.6}$$

is weighted,

$$\lambda_w \in \mathbb{B} : \lambda_w := \begin{cases} 1 & \text{iff } \exists\, i, j \in \mathcal{N}, (i, j) \in \mathcal{E} : w_{ij} \neq 1, \\ 0 & \text{otherwise,} \end{cases} \tag{2.7}$$

or *is self-looped*

$$\lambda_l \in \mathbb{B} : \lambda_l := \begin{cases} 1 & \text{iff } \exists\, i \in \mathcal{N}, (i, i) \in \mathcal{E} : w_{ii} \neq 0, \\ 0 & \text{otherwise.} \end{cases} \tag{2.8}$$

A simple graph, for example, is then a graph for which $\lambda_d = 0$, $\lambda_w = 0$ and $\lambda_l = 0$, the undirected multigraph of Königsberg's bridges (Fig. 2.1a) is a network with $\lambda_d = 0$, $\lambda_w = 1$ and $\lambda_l = 0$, and the directed graph illustrated in Fig. 2.1e is one with $\lambda_d = 1$, $\lambda_w = 1$ and $\lambda_l = 1$. These Boolean measures thus present a more formal means with which to identify the graph types listed in Table 2.1.

Returning to Definition 2.1, we will henceforth refer to the cardinality of the set of nodes $\mathcal{N}$ as the *number of nodes*

$$N_n \in \mathbb{N} : N_n := |\mathcal{N}| \tag{2.9}$$

and utilise N_n as a general measure of the size or *order* of a graph $\mathcal{G}$. Similarly, the cardinality $|\mathcal{E}|$ of the set of edges $\mathcal{E}$ provides a count of the total number of existing adjacency relations between nodes, a measure we will term *total adjacency count*

$$N_a \in \mathbb{N}_0 : N_a := |\mathcal{E}|. \tag{2.10}$$

However, it is important to stress here that this notion applies only to graphs without self-loops, as each self-loop $(i, i) \in \mathcal{E}$, according to the convention argued for in Section 2.1.1, will contribute a total of two directed edges. In order to generalise the total adjacency count to also encompass self-looped graphs, we first define the subset

$$\mathcal{L} \subset \mathcal{N} : \forall\, i \in \mathcal{L} \Rightarrow w_{ii} \neq 0 \text{ and } \forall\, i \in \mathcal{N}, i \notin \mathcal{L} \Rightarrow w_{ii} = 0 \tag{2.11}$$

of nodes with self-loops. The cardinality of $\mathcal{L}$ is called the *number of self-loops* of a graph and corresponds to the number of non-zero diagonal elements in its weight matrix representation, that is,

$$N_l \in \mathbb{N}_0 : N_l := |\mathcal{L}| = N_n - \sum_{i \in \mathcal{N}} \delta[w_{ii}], \tag{2.12}$$

where we introduced

$$\delta[q] : \mathbb{Q} \to \mathbb{B}\ ,\ \delta[q] := \begin{cases} 1 & \text{iff } q = 0, \\ 0 & \text{iff } q \neq 0 \end{cases} \tag{2.13}$$

as a generalisation of the Kronecker delta function. With this, the *total adjacency* of a graph is defined as

$$A \in \mathbb{N}_0 : A := N_n^2 + N_l - \sum_{i,j \in \mathcal{N}} \delta[w_{ij}], \tag{2.14}$$

where the sum in the last term runs over all possible ordered pairs of nodes, including cases in which both nodes are identical.

As each non-zero element of the weight matrix in a directed graph contributes one edge, with self-loops contributing two, the total adjacency A defined in (2.14) also counts a digraph's edges. Similarly, in undirected graphs, each edge between two nodes is represented by two non-zero elements in its weight matrix, with each self-loop counting as one edge of weight 2 (see Section 2.1.1). This allows us to formalise

$$N_e \in \mathbb{N}_0 : N_e := \frac{1}{2}(1 + \lambda_d)\, A = \begin{cases} A & \text{if } \mathcal{G} \text{ is directed,} \\ A/2 & \text{if } \mathcal{G} \text{ is undirected} \end{cases} \tag{2.15}$$

as the *number of edges* of a graph $\mathcal{G}$. In a complete graph of order N_n, the number of edges takes on its maximum value $N_e^{\max}$ possible for any not self-looped graph of the same order. With the notions introduced above, however, we also easily find a generalisation which covers self-looped graphs, yielding

$$N_e^{\max} \in \mathbb{N}_0 : N_e^{\max} := \frac{1}{2}(1 + \lambda_d)\left(N_n^2 + (2\lambda_l - 1)\,N_n\right). \tag{2.16}$$

By considering the fraction of actually present edges N_e, we can then quantify how densely populated with edges a given graph is and define a measure of relative graph connectivity, or *connectedness*

$$\rho \in \mathbb{Q}\,,\, \rho \in [0,1] : \rho := \frac{N_e}{N_e^{\max}}. \tag{2.17}$$

Utilising ρ, a graph $\mathcal{G}$ is commonly referred to as being *sparse* if $N_e \ll N_n^2$, i.e. $\rho \ll 1$, and as being *dense* if $N_e = \mathcal{O}(N_n^2)$, i.e. $\rho \sim 1$. It is important to note here that both qualifiers experience large variations across different research fields and, thus, should be employed with care.

Although the presence of a single directed edge $(i, j) \in \mathcal{E}$ with $w_{ij} \neq 0$ and $w_{ji} = 0$ already suffices to render the type of a given weighted graph $\mathcal{G}$ directed (see Table 2.1), one can conceive of a viable measure which, similar to ρ, counts the fraction of directed edges among all adjacency relations and thus quantifies the extent to which a given graph is directed, or asymmetric, by taking a closer look at the individual elements of $\mathcal{E}$ or the weight matrix w_{ij} of $\mathcal{G}$. In order to arrive at such a measure, let us define

$$N_{se} \in \mathbb{N}_0 : N_{se} := \frac{1}{2}\left(N_l + \sum_{i,j \in \mathcal{N}} (1 - \delta[w_{ij} w_{ji}])\right) \tag{2.18}$$

as the *number of symmetrical edges* counting the number of ordered pairs $(i, j) \in \mathcal{E}$ for which also $(j, i) \in \mathcal{E}$, and with

$$N_{ae} \in \mathbb{N}_0 : N_{ae} := \sum_{i,j \in \mathcal{N}} \delta[w_{ij}]\,(1 - \delta[w_{ji}]) \tag{2.19}$$

the *number of asymmetrical edges* counting all adjacency relations $(i, j) \in \mathcal{E}$ for which $(j, i) \notin \mathcal{E}$. Noting that the Kronecker delta introduced in (2.13) satisfies $\forall p, q \in \mathbb{Q} : \delta[p] + \delta[q] = \delta[pq] + \delta[p]\delta[q]$, it can easily be shown that

$$2N_{se} + N_{ae} = A. \tag{2.20}$$

For graphs with non-zero total adjacency, the scalar

$$\alpha \in \mathbb{Q}\,,\, \alpha \in [0,1] : \alpha := \frac{N_{ae}}{A - N_{se}} \tag{2.21}$$

then delivers the ratio between the number of asymmetrical and symmetrical edges and is called the *asymmetry index* of a graph (see [88, 101, 107], but also [48]). In a fully asymmetric graph in which no adjacency relation is bidirectional, we have $N_{se} = 0$ and, with (2.15), find $N_{ae} = N_e = A$ such that $\alpha = 1$. In contrast, for undirected graphs such as the network of Königsberg's bridges, the number of symmetrical edges is $N_{se} = N_e = A/2$, which then, with $N_{ae} = 0$, yields $\alpha = 0$. It is necessary, however, to stress here that the notion of a graph's asymmetry relies solely on the existence of reciprocal adjacency relations, irrespective of their weight. Indeed, a weighted graph can already be viewed as being asymmetric if $\exists\,(i, j) \in \mathcal{E}$ for which $w_{ij} \neq w_{ji}$, a viewpoint which naturally invites not only to explore the generalisation of the notion of a directed graph as defined in (2.6), but also to consider edge weights in the definitions of N_{se}, N_{ae} and α. Such a generalisation will be presented later in conjunction with the introduction of weight-based measures in Section 2.2.3.

Let us conclude our presentation of general graph measures with an interesting exercise regarding the relation between the asymmetry index and the connectedness of a directed graph and its corresponding undirected representation [95]. The construction of the undirected counterpart of a digraph is called graph *symmetrisation*, and it is often utilised in the applied graph-theoretical literature for the purpose of comparative analysis or the easing of a graph's computational representation. A symmetrisation is achieved by simply replacing each directed edge with an undirected edge of equal weight. Naturally, such a symmetrisation must render the connectedness ρ of a graph intrinsically dependent on its asymmetry α, as one edge will be added for each asymmetrical edge in the original digraph, thus resulting in a more pronounced increase of ρ the larger α. To formalise this dependence, we will respectively denote with A^d and A^{ud} the total adjacency, and with ρ^d and ρ^{ud} the connectedness of a given digraph and its symmetrised counterpart. Each undirected edge in a digraph contributes two adjacency relations, thus $A^d = N_{ae} + 2N_{se}$ in accordance with (2.20), and each symmetrised directed edge contributes one additional adjacency relation to the eventually undirected graph, thus, $A^{ud} = 2(N_{ae}+N_{se})$. Noting that $\alpha(A^d - N_{se}) = N_{ae}$ according to (2.21), we then find $2A^d = A^{ud}(2 - \alpha)$ which, together with (2.17), eventually yields

$$\rho^d/\rho^{ud} = 1 - \alpha/2 \tag{2.22}$$

as the sought-after relation between the connectedness of a digraph with asymmetry index α and the connectedness of its symmetrised counterpart.

2.2.2 Degree-Based Measures

The general measures introduced so far already allow for a quantification of more specific structural characteristics of a given graph beyond its mere type.

Other insights into the structural makeup of a network can be obtained by taking a closer look at the connectivity patterns of individual nodes themselves. To that end, let us first introduce the notion of *node connectivity*, or *node degree*. In order to arrive at a viable measure which covers both undirected and directed graphs, however, we must distinguish the *node in-degree*,

$$a_i^{in} : \mathcal{N} \to \mathbb{N}_0 \, , \, a_i^{in} := N_n - \sum_{j \in \mathcal{N}} \delta[w_{ji}] + (1 - \delta[w_{ii}]), \tag{2.23}$$

counting the number of incoming edges of each node, and the *node out-degree*,

$$a_i^{out} : \mathcal{N} \to \mathbb{N}_0 \, , \, a_i^{out} := N_n - \sum_{j \in \mathcal{N}} \delta[w_{ij}] + (1 - \delta[w_{ii}]), \tag{2.24}$$

which counts the number of each node's outgoing connections, because nodes in directed graphs can serve as both source and target for existing edges. The additional diagonal terms in (2.23) and (2.24) account here for the fact that in directed graphs a self-loop eventually contributes two directed edges and, thus, two in-degrees and two out-degrees. Similarly, for both directed and undirected graphs, we can furthermore define the *total node degree*,

$$a_i^{total} : \mathcal{N} \to \mathbb{N}_0 \, , \, a_i^{total} := \begin{cases} a_i^{in} + a_i^{out} & \text{if } \lambda_d = 1, \\ N_n - \sum_{j \in \mathcal{N}} \delta[w_{ij}] + (1 - \delta[w_{ii}]) & \text{if } \lambda_d = 0, \end{cases} \tag{2.25}$$

as a measure that provides a count of the total number of edges with which each node is embedded into the network. The ordered lists of node degrees then form vectors with N_n elements called the *node in-degree sequence* $\boldsymbol{a}^{in}$, *node out-degree sequence* $\boldsymbol{a}^{out}$ and *total node degree sequence* $\boldsymbol{a}^{total}$. Although the notion of node degree is commonly applied only to relational digraphs, owing to the presence of Kronecker's delta, the above definitions also encompass the more general case of weighted digraphs. The next section will expand upon this by taking the specific weights of edges into account.

Because in directed graphs each outgoing edge serves as an incoming edge to another node, or the same node in the case of a self-loop, the sum over all node in-degrees must necessarily be identical to that of all node out-degrees in any given graph, a fact which mathematically can be expresed in the form of

$$\left\| \boldsymbol{a}^{in} \right\|_1 = \left\| \boldsymbol{a}^{out} \right\|_1, \tag{2.26}$$

where

$$\|\boldsymbol{q}\|_p : \mathbb{Q}^n \to \mathbb{R} \, , \, \|\boldsymbol{q}\|_p := \left(\sum_{i=1}^{n} |q_i|^p \right)^{1/p} \tag{2.27}$$

for $p \in \mathbb{Q} : p \geq 1$ denotes the ℓ^p-norm of a vector $\boldsymbol{q} \in \mathbb{Q}^n, n \in \mathbb{N}$ with elements q_i. Furthermore, with (2.15) and (2.25), the ℓ^1-norm or *taxicab distance* [76, 81] of the total node degree sequence $\boldsymbol{a}^{total}$ of a given graph is naturally linked to its number of edges N_e. Before formalising this important link, however, we must note that, in the case of undirected graphs, the inclusion of self-loops in the form of an additional diagonal term in (2.25) deviates from the definition of the total node degree commonly employed in the applied graph-theoretical literature. As a direct consequence of our deviating convention – which, as we recall, defines each self-loop as contributing two edges in an undirected graph – we can formulate a consistency relation linking the sum over all node degrees with the number of edges of a graph more inclusively for all arbitrarily weighted graphs. Indeed, with (2.12) and (2.14), we easily find

$$\sum_{i \in \mathcal{N}} a_i^{total} = \begin{cases} 2N_n^2 - 2\sum_{i,j \in \mathcal{N}} \delta[w_{ij}] + 2N_l = 2A & \text{if } \lambda_d = 1, \\ N_n^2 - \sum_{i,j \in \mathcal{N}} \delta[w_{ij}] + N_l = A & \text{if } \lambda_d = 0 \end{cases} \tag{2.28}$$

which, together with (2.15), then yields the *handshaking lemma*

$$\left\| \boldsymbol{a}^{total} \right\|_1 = 2N_e \tag{2.29}$$

as the sought-after consistency relation which covers both directed and undirected self-looped weighted graphs.

Instead of considering the sum over all node degrees, further insight into a graph's structural makeup can be obtained by counting all nodes with a given degree $a \in \mathbb{N}_0$. Specifically, in terms of the node degree sequence, the function

$$p[\boldsymbol{a}^{total}; a] : \mathbb{N}_0 \to \mathbb{Q}\,,\; p[\boldsymbol{a}^{total}, a] := \frac{1}{N_n} \sum_{i \in \mathcal{N}} \delta[a_i^{total} - a] \tag{2.30}$$

will deliver the fraction of nodes with total node degree a and is called the *total node degree probability density function*, or, in short, a graph's *total node degree distribution*. This definition extends in the case of directed graphs naturally to the *node in-degree distribution* $p[\boldsymbol{a}^{in}; a]$ and *node out-degree distribution* $p[\boldsymbol{a}^{out}; a]$. A statistical characterisation of a graph's node degree sequences is then achieved by evaluating the k-moments of $p[\boldsymbol{a}^{total}; a]$, defined as

$$\left\langle (\boldsymbol{a}^{total})^k \right\rangle \in \mathbb{Q} : \left\langle (\boldsymbol{a}^{total})^k \right\rangle := \sum_{a = \min \boldsymbol{a}^{total}}^{\max \boldsymbol{a}^{total}} a^k p[\boldsymbol{a}^{total}; a] \tag{2.31}$$

for $k \in \mathbb{N}$, and, similarly for directed graphs, the k-moments

$$\left\langle (\boldsymbol{a}^{d})^k \right\rangle \in \mathbb{Q} : \left\langle (\boldsymbol{a}^{d})^k \right\rangle := \sum_{a = \min \boldsymbol{a}^{d}}^{\max \boldsymbol{a}^{d}} a^k p[\boldsymbol{a}^{d}; a] \tag{2.32}$$

of $p[\boldsymbol{a}^d; a]$ with $d \in \{in, out\}$. Here, the first moments

$$\langle \boldsymbol{a}^{total} \rangle \in \mathbb{Q} : \langle \boldsymbol{a}^{total} \rangle := \frac{1}{N_n} \sum_{a=\min \boldsymbol{a}^{total}}^{\max \boldsymbol{a}^{total}} \sum_{i \in \mathcal{N}} a\, \delta[a_i^{total} - a] = \frac{1}{N_n} \sum_{i \in \mathcal{N}} a_i^{total} \tag{2.33}$$

and

$$\langle \boldsymbol{a}^d \rangle \in \mathbb{Q} : \langle \boldsymbol{a}^d \rangle := \frac{1}{N_n} \sum_{i \in \mathcal{N}} a_i^d \tag{2.34}$$

play a particularly important role and are called *average node degree*, *average node in-degree* and *average node out-degree* respectively. Utilising (2.26) and (2.28), it can easily be shown that the average node degrees are subject to

$$\langle \boldsymbol{a}^{in} \rangle = \langle \boldsymbol{a}^{out} \rangle = \frac{1}{2} \langle \boldsymbol{a}^{total} \rangle = \frac{N_e}{N_n},$$

a relation which serves as an alternative form of the handshaking lemma (2.29) in the case of directed graphs.

It is important to note that the node degree distributions defined above suffice as an exhaustive statistical characterisation of a graph's structural makeup only under the stringent assumption that the individual connectivity patterns of its nodes are independent. Most real-world networks, however, display correlations between these patterns. For instance, a subset of nodes might preferentially connect to another subset of nodes, or nodes with a given degree might disfavour adjacency relations with nodes of a specific degree. In order to explore such correlations in greater detail, we will introduce the notion of *structural equivalence*, with two nodes being defined as structurally equivalent if both share the same relationships with all other nodes in a given graph. In the graph of Königsberg's bridges (Fig. 2.1), for example, node 2 is structurally equivalent to node 3, as both establish adjacency relations with nodes 1 and 4.

In order to quantify the structural equivalence and, thus, the level of similarities in the connectivity pattern of individual nodes in a graph, we first consider the subsets of nodes which serve as sources of edges to, and are targeted by, a given node, and we compare these subsets for each ordered pair of nodes. Specifically, we introduce for each node $i \in \mathcal{N}$ the *vector of source nodes* $\boldsymbol{n}_i^{in}$ and *vector of target nodes* $\boldsymbol{n}_i^{out}$, with elements

$$\begin{aligned} (\boldsymbol{n}_i^{in})_j &: \mathcal{N} \to \mathbb{B}\,,\ (\boldsymbol{n}_i^{in})_j := 1 - \delta[w_{ji}], \\ (\boldsymbol{n}_i^{out})_j &: \mathcal{N} \to \mathbb{B}\,,\ (\boldsymbol{n}_i^{out})_j := 1 - \delta[w_{ij}] \end{aligned} \tag{2.35}$$

taking on a non-zero value only in the case node $j \in \mathcal{N}$ is a source of an edge to node i or the target of an edge from node i, respectively. In the special case of undirected graphs, we have $\boldsymbol{n}_i^{in} = \boldsymbol{n}_i^{out} =: \boldsymbol{n}_i$. With this, the scalars

$$N_{ij}^{d\text{-}d'} : \mathcal{N} \times \mathcal{N} \to \mathbb{N}_0 \,, \; N_{ij}^{d\text{-}d'} := \boldsymbol{n}_i^d \cdot (\boldsymbol{n}_j^{d'})^\mathsf{T}, \tag{2.36}$$

where $d, d' \in \{in, out\}$ and $\boldsymbol{q}^\mathsf{T}$ denotes the transpose of a vector $\boldsymbol{q}$, then deliver the *number of shared source nodes* $N_{ij}^{in\text{-}in}$, *shared target nodes* $N_{ij}^{out\text{-}out}$ and *shared nearest neighbours* $N_{ij}^{in\text{-}out} = N_{ji}^{out\text{-}in}$ for each pair of nodes $i, j \in \mathcal{N}$. It can easily be shown that $N_{ij}^{in\text{-}in} = N_{ji}^{in\text{-}in}$ and $N_{ij}^{out\text{-}out} = N_{ji}^{out\text{-}out}$, and that $N_{ij}^{out\text{-}out} = N_{ij}^{in\text{-}in} = N_{ij}^{in\text{-}out} =: N_{ij}$ with $N_{ij} = N_{ji}$ for all $i, j \in \mathcal{N}$ in undirected graphs. By evaluating the statistical mean

$$\langle N_{ij}^{d\text{-}d'} \rangle \in \mathbb{Q} \colon \langle N_{ij}^{d\text{-}d'} \rangle := \frac{1}{N_n^2} \sum_{i,j \in \mathcal{N}} N_{ij}^{d\text{-}d'} \tag{2.37}$$

over all node pairs, we eventually obtain the *average number of shared source nodes* $\langle N_{ij}^{in\text{-}in} \rangle$, *shared target nodes* $\langle N_{ij}^{out\text{-}out} \rangle$ and *shared nearest neighbours* $\langle N_{ij}^{in\text{-}out} \rangle = \langle N_{ij}^{out\text{-}in} \rangle$ as first coarse quantifiers of the structural equivalence of nodes in a graph. For example, each of the four areas of Königsberg shares bridges with at average 1.6 other parts of the city with its neighbours.

Similar to the number of shared neighbours defined in (2.36), the scalars

$$S_{ij}^{d\text{-}d'} : \mathcal{N} \times \mathcal{N} \to \mathbb{R} \,, \; S_{ij}^{d\text{-}d'} := \left\| \boldsymbol{n}_i^d - \boldsymbol{n}_j^{d'} \right\|_2 \tag{2.38}$$

provide a viable measure for the *similarity of source nodes* $S_{ij}^{in\text{-}in}$, *target nodes* $S_{ij}^{out\text{-}out}$ and *nearest neighbours* $S_{ij}^{in\text{-}out} = S_{ji}^{out\text{-}in}$ by utilising the *Euclidean distance*, or ℓ^2-norm defined in (2.27), between the source and target node vectors for each pair of nodes $i, j \in \mathcal{N}$ [27]. Indeed, if two nodes $i, j \in \mathcal{N}$ target or are targeted by the same set of nodes in a graph, or if the targeted nodes of i are identical to the source nodes of j, the respective Euclidean distance is equal to zero and both nodes are said to exhibit structurally equivalent connections. The maximum value of $S_{ij}^{d\text{-}d'}$ is reached when both nodes have no common neighbours, in which case we have $N_{ij}^{d\text{-}d'} = 0$, and it can be shown that

$$\max_{i,j \in \mathcal{N}} S_{ij}^{d\text{-}d'} = a_i^d + a_j^{d'} + \delta[w_{ii}] + \delta[w_{jj}] - 2$$

by making use of (2.23) and (2.24) as well as the fact that both $\boldsymbol{n}_i^{in}$ and $\boldsymbol{n}_i^{out}$ are vectors over $\mathbb{B}$. As for the number of shared neighbours, the similarity of nearest neighbours satisfies $S_{ij}^{in\text{-}in} = S_{ji}^{in\text{-}in}$ and $S_{ij}^{out\text{-}out} = S_{ji}^{out\text{-}out}$, as well as $S_{ii}^{out\text{-}out} = 0$ and $S_{ii}^{in\text{-}in} = 0$ for all $i, j \in \mathcal{N}$. Moreover, in the case of undirected graphs, we find that $S_{ij}^{out\text{-}out} = S_{ij}^{in\text{-}in} = S_{ij}^{in\text{-}out} =: S_{ij}$ with $S_{ij} = S_{ji}$ and $S_{ii} = 0$ which, together with the fact that $S_{ij} \geq 0$ for all $i, j \in \mathcal{N}$, renders the Euclidean distance between the vectors of nearest neighbours naturally a distance metric. The latter, however, is generally not true for directed graphs. Inspired by (2.37), we finally take the statistical average

$$\langle S_{ij}^{d-d'} \rangle \in \mathbb{R} \colon \langle S_{ij}^{d-d'} \rangle := \frac{1}{N_n^2} \sum_{i,j \in \mathcal{N}} S_{ij}^{d-d'} \tag{2.39}$$

over all node pairs and eventually obtain another means to quantify the structural equivalence of a graph's or digraph's nodes by measuring the *average similarity of source nodes* $\langle S_{ij}^{in-in} \rangle$, *target nodes* $\langle S_{ij}^{out-out} \rangle$ and *nearest neighbours* $\langle S_{ij}^{in-out} \rangle = \langle S_{ji}^{out-in} \rangle$. Applying these measures again to our illustrative example of the Königsberg bridge graph, we find that $\langle S_{ij} \rangle$ is about 1.043, which suggests that, when compared to their neighbours, each area of the city draws bridges to, on average, one different part of the city.

A third commonly employed approach for assessing the structural equivalence of nodes is given by taking a closer look at potential correlations between the node degrees of connected nodes. Such correlations can be quantified by considering the *conditional node degree distribution*, defined as the conditional probability $p[\boldsymbol{a}^d; a'|a] : \mathbb{N}_0 \times \mathbb{N}_0 \to \mathbb{Q}$ that, given a node degree sequence $\boldsymbol{a}^d$ with $d \in \{in, out, total\}$, a node with degree a connects to a node of degree a'. While $p[\boldsymbol{a}^d; a'|a]$ satisfies both the normalisation requirement

$$\sum_{a'=\min \boldsymbol{a}^d}^{\max \boldsymbol{a}^d} p[\boldsymbol{a}^d; a'|a] = 1$$

and the *degree balance condition*

$$a \cdot p[\boldsymbol{a}^d; a'|a] \cdot p[\boldsymbol{a}^d; a] = a' \cdot p[\boldsymbol{a}^d; a|a'] \cdot p[\boldsymbol{a}^d; a'],$$

it must also be noted that as a numerical quantifier for structural equivalence, employing the conditional probability $p[\boldsymbol{a}^d; a'|a]$ often lacks statistical robustness, especially in cases where smaller networks or sparsely connected graphs are concerned.

For that reason, let us introduce as a final representative measure of structural equivalence the *average nearest neighbour degree* of node i in directed graphs. We define

$$a_i^{nn\ in-d},\ a_i^{nn\ out-d} : \mathcal{N} \to \mathbb{Q},$$

$$a_i^{nn\ in-d} := \begin{cases} \dfrac{1}{a_i^{in}} \left(\sum_{j \in \mathcal{N}} \left(1 - \delta[w_{ji}]\right) a_j^d + \left(1 - \delta[w_{ii}]\right) a_i^d \right) & \text{if } a_i^{in} \neq 0, \\ 0 \text{ otherwise,} \end{cases} \tag{2.40}$$

$$a_i^{nn\ out-d} := \begin{cases} \dfrac{1}{a_i^{out}} \left(\sum_{j \in \mathcal{N}} \left(1 - \delta[w_{ij}]\right) a_j^d + \left(1 - \delta[w_{ii}]\right) a_i^d \right) & \text{if } a_i^{out} \neq 0, \\ 0 \text{ otherwise,} \end{cases}$$

where $d \in \{in, out\}$. This measure allows for a statistically more robust quantification of the relation between the average in-degree and out-degree of source and target nodes in a given graph. Specifically, the scalars $a_i^{nn\ in\text{-}in}$ and $a_i^{nn\ in\text{-}out}$ respectively deliver the average node in-degree and out-degree of all nodes connecting to node i, while $a_i^{nn\ out\text{-}in}$ and $a_i^{nn\ out\text{-}out}$ yield the average node in-degree and out-degree of all nodes targeted by i. Similarly, in the special case of undirected graphs, we have

$$a_i^{nn} : \mathcal{N} \to \mathbb{Q}\,,$$
$$a_i^{nn} := \begin{cases} \frac{1}{a_i}\left(\sum_{j \in \mathcal{N}} \left(1 - \delta[w_{ij}]\right) a_j + \left(1 - \delta[w_{ii}]\right) a_i \right) & \text{if } a_i \neq 0, \\ 0 \text{ otherwise.} \end{cases} \tag{2.41}$$

In order to arrive at a more concise quantification of the relation between the average degree of a node and that of its nearest neighbours, we can then evaluate the ratio between the statistical mean across all elements of the vectors defined by (2.40) and (2.41) and the average node degree, eventually obtaining

$$\begin{aligned} \tau^{d\text{-}d'} \in \mathbb{Q} : \tau^{d\text{-}d'} &:= \frac{\langle a_i^{nn\ d\text{-}d'} \rangle}{\langle a^d \rangle} = \frac{1}{\langle a^d \rangle N_n} \sum_{i \in \mathcal{N}} a_i^{nn\ d\text{-}d'}\,, \\ \tau \in \mathbb{Q} : \tau &:= \frac{\langle a_i^{nn} \rangle}{\langle a^{total} \rangle} = \frac{1}{\langle a^{total} \rangle N_n} \sum_{i \in \mathcal{N}} a_i^{nn} \end{aligned} \tag{2.42}$$

as a measure of a graph's *assortativity*. If $\tau^{d\text{-}d'} < 1$ for digraphs, or $\tau < 1$ for undirected graphs, nodes tend to preferentially establish adjacency relations with nodes of a lower degree, and the graph is said to be *assortative*. In a *disassortative graph*, the opposite is true – that is, $\tau^{d\text{-}d'} > 1$ or $\tau > 1$. The graph of Königsberg's bridges, for example, yields $\tau = 16/15 \sim 1.07$ and thus tends to be slightly disassortative.

2.2.3 Weight-Based Measures

Up to now we considered the characterisation of a graph only in terms of the adjacency relations established by its nodes, irrespective of the weight assigned to each of its edges. Indeed, although all measures introduced above are generally defined for weighted digraphs, their functional dependence on $\delta[w_{ij}]$ only evaluates the presence or absence of an adjacency relation between two nodes i and j, thus discarding the actual weight w_{ij} carried by an associated edge. Although most graph-theoretical measures can easily be generalised to incorporate edge weights, it must be cautioned that a meaningful and coherent

Table 2.4 *Directed and weight-directed adjacency relations.*

	$\lambda_d = 0$	$\lambda_d = 1$
$\lambda_{wd} = 0$	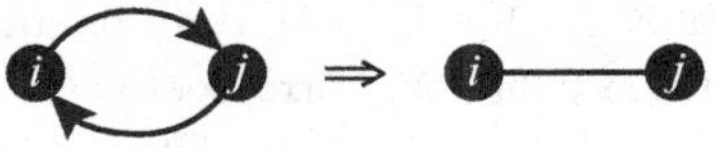	—
$\lambda_{wd} = 1$		

realisation of such measures encounters a number of subtleties, some of which will be addressed in this section.

The first of these subtleties concerns the very definition of a directed graph itself. According to (2.6), a graph is considered as being directed if there exists at least one edge $(i, j) \in \mathcal{E}$ for which $w_{ij} \neq 0$ and $w_{ji} = 0$, a definition which adheres to the classical notion of a directed edge in relational digraphs. As a necessary consequence, in a weighted graph, a bidirectional adjacency relation with $w_{ij} \neq 0$ and $w_{ji} \neq 0$, but $w_{ij} \neq w_{ji}$, is considered an undirected edge yet requires for its representation two differently weighted, directed edges. For all measures introduced so far, this subtle distinction is of little relevance as the mathematical definition of each of these measures solely relies on $\delta[w_{ij}]$. However, if edge weights are taken into account, the two cases $w_{ij} = w_{ji}$ and $w_{ij} \neq w_{ji}$ must be discerned. To that end, we say that a graph $\mathcal{G}$ *is weight-directed* if $w_{ij} \neq w_{ji}$ for at least one pair of nodes, and we define with

$$\lambda_{wd} \in \mathbb{B} : \lambda_{wd} := \begin{cases} 1 & \text{iff } \exists\, i, j \in \mathcal{N}, (i, j) \in \mathcal{E} : w_{ij} \neq 0 \land w_{ji} \neq w_{ij}, \\ 0 & \text{otherwise}, \end{cases} \tag{2.43}$$

a new Boolean measure complementing (2.6). With the requirement $w_{ij} \neq w_{ji}$, the notion of a weight-directed adjacency relation between two nodes i and j introduced in (2.43) is weaker than the notion of a directed adjacency relation defined in (2.6), for which either w_{ij} or w_{ji} must vanish. Thus, each directed graph is also weight-directed (see Table 2.4 for $\lambda_d = 1$ and $\lambda_{wd} = 1$), while a weight-directed graph is not necessarily directed but can also be undirected in the case all edges $(i, j) \in \mathcal{E}$ obey $w_{ij} \neq 0$ and $w_{ji} \neq 0$ (Table 2.4, $\lambda_d = 0$ and $\lambda_{wd} = 1$). Conversely, for an adjacency relation to be weight-undirected, the condition $w_{ij} = w_{ji}$ must be satisfied, which is certainly stronger than the requirement $w_{ij} \neq 0 \land w_{ji} \neq 0$ for an edge to be undirected. Thus, a weight-undirected graph is necessarily undirected, while an undirected graph can be weight-directed or, in the case all edges $(i, j) \in \mathcal{E}$ obey $w_{ij} = w_{ji}$, weight-undirected, as exemplified in Table 2.4 for $\lambda_d = 0$ and $\lambda_{wd} = 0$.

With the incorporation of edge weights, we also need to revisit our notions of symmetrical and asymmetrical edges introduced in (2.18) and (2.19). To illustrate this point, let us take a closer look at the adjacency relations between nodes i and j shown in Table 2.4 for $\lambda_d = 0$. Both relations will contribute to the number of symmetrical edges N_{se}, irrespective of the weight of the directed edges. However, as $w_{ij} \neq w_{ji}$ in the weight-directed case, the associated weighted adjacency relation between both nodes certainly carries an asymmetry. In order to quantify this asymmetry, we will generalise (2.18) by introducing the *number of symmetrical weighted edges*

$$N_{swe} \in \mathbb{N}_0 : N_{swe} := \frac{1}{2}\left(N_l + \sum_{i,j \in \mathcal{N}} \big(1 - \delta[w_{ij}w_{ji}]\big)\delta[w_{ij} - w_{ji}]\right) \tag{2.44}$$

as a count for the number of weighted edges between pairs of nodes (i, j) for which $w_{ij} = w_{ji} \neq 0$. Similarly, generalising (2.19), the *number of asymmetrical weighted edges*

$$N_{awe} \in \mathbb{N}_0 : N_{awe} := \frac{1}{2}\sum_{i,j \in \mathcal{N}} \big(2 - \delta[w_{ij}] - \delta[w_{ji}]\big)\big(1 - \delta[w_{ij} - w_{ji}]\big) \tag{2.45}$$

counts all weighted edges for which $w_{ij} \neq w_{ji}$. For relational digraphs or, more generally, multigraphs with $w_{ij} \in \mathbb{B}$ for $i \neq j$ and $w_{ii} = 2$ for self-loops, it can easily be demonstrated that the number of symmetrical and symmetrical weighted edges, as well as the number of asymmetrical and asymmetrical weighted edges, necessarily coincides. Indeed, for symmetrical edges in such graphs, we have $w_{ij} = w_{ji}$ such that $\delta[w_{ij} - w_{ji}] = 1$ which, with (2.18) and (2.44), directly yields $N_{swe} = N_{se}$. For an asymmetrical edge between two nodes i and j, we have either $w_{ij} = 0 \wedge w_{ji} = 1$ or $w_{ij} = 1 \wedge w_{ji} = 0$, as self-loops, by definition, cannot be asymmetrical. In the first case, noting that $\delta[w_{ij} - w_{ji}] = 0$, the sum on the right-hand side of (2.45) will then contribute $(2 - \delta[w_{ij}])/2 + (2 - \delta[w_{ij}])/2 = 1$ to the number of asymmetrical weighted edges, thus resulting in $N_{awe} = N_{ae}$. The second case is argued similarly.

With the notions of symmetrical and asymmetrical edges being sufficiently generalised to encompass arbitrarily weighted digraphs, it is then possible to also expand on the notion of the asymmetry index α introduced in (2.21). To that end, we define the *weighted asymmetry index*

$$\alpha_w \in \mathbb{Q}\,,\ \alpha_w \in [0, 1] : \alpha_w := \frac{N_{awe}}{A - N_{swe}} \tag{2.46}$$

as a measure of the ratio between weight-directed and weight-undirected edges. We find that $\alpha_w = 1$ in the case of fully weight-asymmetric graphs in which all edges are weight-directed, and that $\alpha_w = 0$ for graphs in which all edges are weight-undirected. Moreover, both asymmetry indices satisfy $\alpha \leq \alpha_w$ for any given weighted digraph, an inequality which can easily be shown by noting that each weight-directed adjacency relations with $w_{ij} \neq w_{ji}$ will contribute to the number of asymmetrical weighted edges N_{awe}, but not to the number of asymmetrical edges N_{ae} unless either $w_{ij} = 0$ or $w_{ji} = 0$.

With the arguments presented above, the list of subtle issues which need to be addressed when incorporating edge weights into the characterisation of graphs is certainly not yet exhausted. Having sensitised the interested reader to approach such generalisations cautiously, we can certainly bypass most of these subtleties by simply introducing, and properly formalising, new notions altogether, as we demonstrated here in the case of the number of symmetrical and asymmetrical edges as well as a graph's asymmetry index. For other measures, however, the inclusion of edge weights leads to more endearing challenges. To exemplify such a case, let us consider the notion of node connectivity itself. The open secret of Euler's now-famous solution to the Königsberg bridge problem lies in counting the number of bridges with which each part of the city is embedded into the network – that is, by assessing the number of edges with which each node in the corresponding graph is connected. The notion which, on established terminological grounds, should then formalise this solution is that of node connectivity, or node degree, introduced in (2.23)–(2.25) for generally weighted and directed graphs.

In the special case of undirected, unweighted and not self-looped graphs, we then arrive with (2.4) and (2.25) at the classical notion which defines the node degree $a_i = \sum_{j \in \mathcal{N}} a_{ij}$ as the sum over all rows or columns in the adjacency matrix defining a simple graph, a notion which is presented as the primary definition in the overwhelming majority of the graph-theoretical literature. However, application of this notion to the undirected multigraph of Königsberg's bridges, and thus its use for solving the associated problem, is not possible as for this graph no adjacency matrix, according to (2.4), can be defined. Indeed, the extension of the notion of node connectivity to arbitrary multigraphs constitutes a principal problem, as in such graphs an existing adjacency relation between two nodes i and j can be viewed as either $w_{ij} \in \mathbb{N}$ edges of weight one, or one edge of weight w_{ij}. By accounting for multiple edges in the definition of the node degree, the former point of view certainly allows for a generalisation to multigraphs but then becomes less meaningful in the case of generally weighted graphs with $w_{ij} \in \mathbb{Q}$. By considering individual weights in the definition of the node degree, the latter point of view can certainly be rendered coherent in its application to generally weighted graphs but then runs into conflict with commonly used and well-established terminology.

In order to formulate a satisfying compromise to this dilemma which not only circumnavigates terminological ambiguities while holding onto the generally accepted notion of node connectivity but is also valid for arbitrarily weighted digraphs with self-loops, let us introduce the *node in-adjacency*, *node out-adjacency* and *total node adjacency* by defining

$$
\begin{aligned}
A_i^{in} &: \mathcal{N} \to \mathbb{N}_0 \,,\; A_i^{in} := N_n - \sum_{j\in\mathcal{N}} \delta[w_{ji}], \\
A_i^{out} &: \mathcal{N} \to \mathbb{N}_0 \,,\; A_i^{out} := N_n - \sum_{j\in\mathcal{N}} \delta[w_{ij}], \\
A_i^{total} &: \mathcal{N} \to \mathbb{N}_0 \,,\; A_i := A_i^{in} + A_i^{out},
\end{aligned}
\tag{2.47}
$$

as well as with

$$
\langle A_i^d \rangle \in \mathbb{Q} \colon \langle A_i^d \rangle := \frac{1}{N_n} \sum_{i\in\mathcal{N}} A_i^d, \tag{2.48}
$$

where $d \in \{in, out, total\}$, the *average node in-adjacency* $\langle A_i^{in} \rangle$, *average node out-adjacency* $\langle A_i^{out} \rangle$ and *average total node adjacency* $\langle A_i^{total} \rangle$, respectively. These notions account only for the mere presence of adjacency relations established by each node $i \in \mathcal{N}$, irrespective of their weights or, in the case of self-loops and multiedges, the number of associated edges. In a relational digraph, the node adjacencies and degrees are identical, while for simple graphs we find $A_i^{in} = A_i^{out} = A_i^{total}/2$ and, with (2.25), the identity $A_i^{total} = 2a_i^{total}$. Furthermore, by recalling (2.35), we can show that $A_i^d = \|\boldsymbol{n}_i^d\|_1$ for $d \in \{in, out\}$ and $A_i^{total} = 2\|\boldsymbol{n}_i\|_1$ for undirected weighted graphs. In general, however, we have

$$
\begin{aligned}
A_i^d &= a_i^d - \big(1 - \delta[w_{ii}]\big), \\
A_i^{total} &= (2 - \lambda_d) a_i^{total} - 2\big(1 - \delta[w_{ii}]\big),
\end{aligned}
$$

as with (2.23)–(2.25), node degrees will provide the actual count of edges for each node and, thus, contribute two edges for each self-looped node.

With this arguably subtle conceptual distinction between the node adjacency count and node degree, we can now expand on the notion of node adjacencies by defining vectors with elements

$$
\begin{aligned}
s_i^{in} &: \mathcal{N} \to \mathbb{Q} \,,\; s_i^{in} := \sum_{j\in\mathcal{N}} w_{ji}, \\
s_i^{out} &: \mathcal{N} \to \mathbb{Q} \,,\; s_i^{out} := \sum_{j\in\mathcal{N}} w_{ij}, \\
s_i^{total} &: \mathcal{N} \to \mathbb{Q} \,,\; s_i^{total} := s_i^{in} + s_i^{out}
\end{aligned}
\tag{2.49}
$$

as measures of *node in-strength* $\boldsymbol{s}^{in}$, *node out-strength* $\boldsymbol{s}^{out}$ and *total node strength* $\boldsymbol{s}^{total}$ which apply not only to multigraphs but, indeed, to arbitrarily weighted graphs [14, 112]. In the special case of relational digraphs, we then easily find that $s_i^d = A_i^d$ for $d \in \{in, out\}$ and $s_i^{total} = A_i^{total}$ which, for simple graphs, establishes with $s_i^{total} = 2a_i^{total}$ the link to the historical notion of node degree. In general, however, these identities are certainly not satisfied, and (2.49) serves as measures quantifying how strongly embedded into a weighted network each node is, beyond the mere number of adjacency relations it establishes. Interestingly, we also find here that typically $s_i^{in} \neq s_i^{out}$ for undirected weighted graphs as, according to (2.6), only the existence of a reciprocal adjacency relation without further constraints imposed on its weight is required for a graph to be considered undirected. Finally, with the statistical average

$$\langle s_i^d \rangle \in \mathbb{Q}\colon \langle s_i^d \rangle := \frac{1}{N_n} \sum_{i \in \mathcal{N}} s_i^d \tag{2.50}$$

for $d \in \{in, out, total\}$ defining the *average node in-strength* $\langle s_i^{in} \rangle$, *average node out-strength* $\langle s_i^{out} \rangle$ and *average total node strength* $\langle s_i^{total} \rangle$, we obtain coarse scalar quantifiers describing the strength with which a typical node is embedded into the graph. Other degree-based measures, such as the node degree distribution, structural equivalence or assortativity introduced in Section 2.2.2, can be generalised to incorporate edge weights as well. However, we must caution that, somewhat unfortunately, such measures are rarely considered concisely in the graph-theoretical literature such that many variations, each adapted to serve a specific purpose, can be found, and the construction of a coherent framework of weighted measures remains an open challenge.

Before concluding our elaborations on weight-based measures, let us take a brief look at our multigraph of Königsberg's bridges. Recalling its weight matrix (2.2), we quickly obtain with (2.25), (2.47) and (2.49)

$$\begin{aligned} \boldsymbol{a}^{in} = \boldsymbol{a}^{out} = \boldsymbol{a}^{total} = \boldsymbol{A}^{in} = \boldsymbol{A}^{out} = \boldsymbol{A}^{total}/2 = (3, 2, 2, 3)^{\mathsf{T}}, \\ \boldsymbol{s}^{in} = \boldsymbol{s}^{out} = \boldsymbol{s}^{total}/2 = (5, 3, 3, 3)^{\mathsf{T}}. \end{aligned} \tag{2.51}$$

Thus, while nodes are embedded with both an even and odd number of multi-edges, the strength of all nodes measuring the number of bridges across which each area of Königsberg can be reached and connected to remains odd. The node strength, and not the node degree, then provides the correct mathematical key to Euler's now famous solution to this historical problem, highlighting once more the subtle conceptual difference between both measures.

2.2.4 Distance-Based Measures

All the measures considered so far in this section rely conceptually on only two types of links between nodes: adjacency relations, that is, edges which connect nodes with their nearest neighbours; and self-loops, that is, edges which connect nodes to themselves. However, the very notion of a link between nodes can certainly be generalised to include arbitrary pairs, or whole subsets, of nodes in a graph, and this opens up a new world of important graph-theoretical measures beyond those we already covered. We briefly encountered specific examples of this more-general notion of links between nodes in the form of Eulerian walks and Eulerian paths through the Königsberg bridge graph in Chapter 1. Many more examples with often intersecting and conflicting terminology can easily be found in the graph-theoretical literature.

In this section, we will primarily expand on the notion of links between arbitrary pairs of nodes and introduce some of the measures associated with such links. To that end, given a graph $\mathcal{G} = (\mathcal{N}, \mathcal{E})$, let us construct ordered sets of edges from elements of $\mathcal{E}$. If any ordered set

$$\mathcal{W}_{ij} := ((i_k, i_{k+1}) \in \mathcal{E} : k \in [1, m], m \in \mathbb{N}, i = i_1, j = i_{m+1}) \tag{2.52}$$

connects two not necessarily distinct nodes $i, j \in \mathcal{N}$ by sequentially following each of its elements, the set $\mathcal{W}_{ij}$ is called a *walk* of length m from i to j. Similarly, any ordered set

$$\mathcal{P}_{ij} := \left((i_k, i_{k+1}) \in \mathcal{E} : \left\{ \begin{array}{l} k \in [1, m], m \in \mathbb{N}, \\ i = i_1 \neq i_l, j = i_{m+1} \neq i_l \, \forall l \in [2, m], \\ i_l \neq i_{l'} \, \forall l, l' \in [2, m], l' > l \end{array} \right. \right) \tag{2.53}$$

of distinct edges connecting two not necessarily distinct nodes by visiting other nodes in $\mathcal{G}$ at most once defines a *path* $\mathcal{P}_{ij}$ from node i to node j. Nodes i and j are here typically referred to as *endnodes* of a walk or path. If a path $\mathcal{P}_{ij}$ with distinct endnodes visits all nodes of the graph, it is called a *Hamiltonian path*. In the case in which both endnoes coincide, a path $\mathcal{P}_{ii}$ defines a *cycle*, and it is a *Hamiltonian cycle* if it visits, with the exception of i, each node of the graph exactly once. Eulerian paths and walks introduced in Chapter 1 form somewhat of an exception to this terminology, with both being principally considered walks due to the lack of constraints imposed on the number of visited nodes. In general, each path is necessarily a walk, while the converse is true only for walks comprised of one edge. Moreover, while in a finite graph the number of possible walks between two arbitrary nodes is not subject to a principal upper bound, there can be only a finite number of unique paths between any two nodes. The *path length* of $\mathcal{P}_{ij}$, defined as the number of edges which need to be traversed in order to reach a target node j from a given source node i, is then given by the cardinality $|\mathcal{P}_{ij}| \in \mathbb{N}_0$ of the set $\mathcal{P}_{ij}$ and provides the conceptual basis for the notion of *distance* between two nodes.

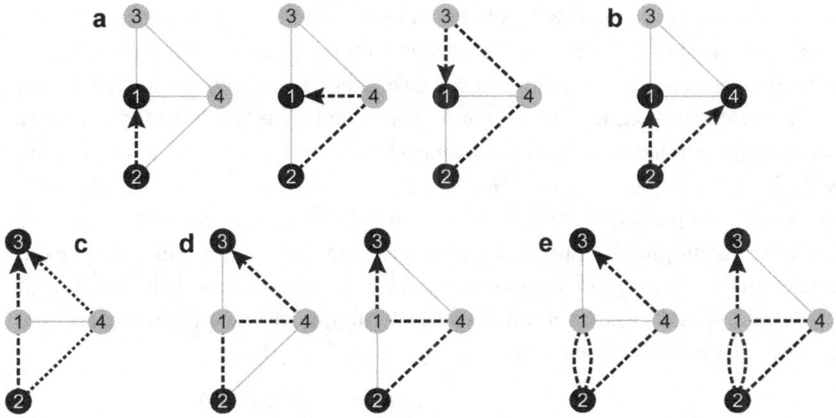

Figure 2.4 Examples of walks and paths through Königsberg's bridge graph. Departing from node 2, node 1 can be reached in a variety of ways by traversing one, two or three edges (**a**). The shortest paths from node 2 to nodes 1 and 4 have one edge, thus, nodes 1 and 4 comprise the set of nearest neighbours of node 2 (**b**). Node 3 can be reached from node 2 by multiple paths, specifically two paths of length two (**c**) and two paths of length three (**d**). By allowing for the repeated traversing of edges and revisiting of nodes, walks of arbitrary length can be constructed, with panel **e** showing examples of walks of lengths four and five.

Each adjacency relation $(i, j) \in \mathcal{E}$ which connects a node to one of its nearest neighbours forms a path $\mathcal{P}_{ij} = ((i, j))$ with $|\mathcal{P}_{ij}| = 1$, and each self-loop a cycle $\mathcal{P}_{ii} = ((i, i))$ with $|\mathcal{P}_{ii}| = 1$. Similarly, in a graph of order N_n, each Hamiltonian path will be of length $|\mathcal{P}_{ij}| = N_n - 1$, and each Hamiltonian cycle will be of length $|\mathcal{P}_{ii}| = N_n$. In general, however, multiple distinct paths $\mathcal{P}_{ij}$ of various lengths $1 \leq |\mathcal{P}_{ij}| \leq N_n$ connecting a given pair of endnodes i and j might exist. Resorting once more to the graph of Königsberg's bridges as an illustrative example, we find that, departing from node 2, node 1 can be reached following paths of different lengths, with the shortest of these possible paths having length one (Fig. 2.4a). This is also true for paths from node 2 to node 4, thus rendering both nodes 1 and 4 nearest neighbours of node 2 (Fig. 2.4b). Node 3, on the other hand, can be reached from node 2 only by following paths comprised of two or more edges. Indeed, there are only two paths of lengths both two (Fig. 2.4c) and three (Fig. 2.4d) connecting these nodes. In contrast, if we allow for the repeated traversing of edges and revisiting of nodes, walks between nodes 2 and 3 of arbitrary length larger than one can be constructed, as exemplified in Fig. 2.4e with walks of lengths four and five.

In order to arrive at a mathematically more rigorous representation of the number and length of connections between nodes, let us denote with $\mathscr{P}_{ij}$ the set of all existing distinct paths $\mathcal{P}_{ij}$ between an ordered pair of nodes $i, j \in \mathcal{N}$. If $\mathscr{P}_{ij} \neq \emptyset$, node i is said to be *connected* to node j, otherwise node j is said to be *disconnected* from node i. In the case a node i is both connected to and disconnected from node j, nodes i and j are called weakly connected, and they are strongly connected if both i is connected to j and j is connected to i – that is if $\mathscr{P}_{ij} \neq \emptyset$ and $\mathscr{P}_{ji} \neq \emptyset$ (see Section 2.1.2). Although, in general, multiple paths between pairs of connected nodes in a graph can be constructed, as we saw in the example of Königsberg's bridges (Fig. 2.4), there will always exist at least one *shortest path*, or *geodesic path*, comprised of the least number of edges. The length of such a not necessarily unique shortest path is called the *geodesic distance* between nodes i and j and is defined as

$$d_{ij} \colon \mathcal{N} \times \mathcal{N} \to \mathbb{N}_0 \, , \, d_{ij} := \begin{cases} \min\limits_{\mathcal{P}_{ij} \in \mathscr{P}_{ij}} \left|\mathcal{P}_{ij}\right| & \text{if } \mathscr{P}_{ij} \neq \emptyset, \\ 0 & \text{otherwise.} \end{cases} \tag{2.54}$$

Because in directed graphs the set $\mathscr{P}_{ij}$ of paths between two given nodes i and j will typically differ from the set $\mathscr{P}_{ji}$ of reciprocal paths connecting node j to node i, the geodesic distances d_{ij} are generally not symmetric. Only in the case of undirected graphs do we necesarily find $d_{ij} = d_{ji}$ for all $i, j \in \mathcal{N}$. If $\mathscr{P}_{ii} \neq \emptyset$ – that is, at least one path exists which links a node to itself – the shortest path is called a *closed geodesics*. In this case, according to (2.54), we have $\forall i \in \mathcal{L} : d_{ii} = 1$ and $\forall i \in \mathcal{N}, i \notin \mathcal{L} : d_{ii} \geq 2$, where $\mathcal{L}$ is the set of self-looped nodes introduced in (2.11). In the trivial case $d_{ii} = 1$, a closed geodesics is also called a *geodesic loop*, while closed geodesics with $d_{ii} > 1$ form *geodesic cycles*.

The geodesic distances between all pairs of nodes in a graph are typically represented as $N_n \times N_n$ *geodesic distance matrix* $\mathbf{d}$. The construction of this matrix, however, does not rely exclusively on an exhaustive search for possible paths between pairs of nodes, as suggested by (2.54), but it can be achieved in a computationally much less expensive fashion. In order to illustrate this point, let us first define with

$$A_{ij} \colon \mathcal{N} \times \mathcal{N} \to \mathbb{B} \, , \, A_{ij} := 1 - \delta[w_{ij}] = \begin{cases} 1 & \text{iff } (i, j) \in \mathcal{E}, \\ 0 & \text{otherwise} \end{cases} \tag{2.55}$$

the *matrix of adjacency relations* $\boldsymbol{A}$ of a graph, noting that the sum over rows and columns of $\boldsymbol{A}$ respectively yields the vectors of node in-adjacency A_i^{in} and node out-adjacency A_i^{out} introduced in (2.47). Similar to the adjacency matrix $\boldsymbol{a}$ defined in (2.4), each non-zero element of the Boolean matrix $\boldsymbol{A}$ marks the presence of an adjacency relation between two nodes in a graph. Indeed, in the special case of relational digraphs or simple graphs, we have $A_{ij} = a_{ij}$ for all $i, j \in \mathcal{N}$. For historical reasons, and in order to avoid terminological ambiguities, it is important to stress that the adjacency matrix (2.4) and the more general matrix of adjacency relations (2.55) are conceptually distinct objects which reflect the subtle distinction between node degree and node adjacency covered in Section 2.2.3.

With the mere presence or absence of adjacency relations in weighted graphs now formalised, we next consider matrix powers of $\boldsymbol{A}$. Using for illustrative purposes once again the Königsberg bridge graph as an example, we find

$$\boldsymbol{A} = \begin{pmatrix} 0 & 1 & 1 & 1 \\ 1 & 0 & 0 & 1 \\ 1 & 0 & 0 & 1 \\ 1 & 1 & 1 & 0 \end{pmatrix}, \boldsymbol{A}^2 = \begin{pmatrix} 3 & 1 & 1 & 2 \\ 1 & 2 & 2 & 1 \\ 1 & 2 & 2 & 1 \\ 2 & 1 & 1 & 3 \end{pmatrix},$$
$$\boldsymbol{A}^3 = \begin{pmatrix} 4 & 5 & 5 & 5 \\ 5 & 2 & 2 & 5 \\ 5 & 2 & 2 & 5 \\ 5 & 5 & 5 & 4 \end{pmatrix}, \boldsymbol{A}^4 = \begin{pmatrix} 15 & 9 & 9 & 14 \\ 9 & 10 & 10 & 9 \\ 9 & 10 & 10 & 9 \\ 14 & 9 & 9 & 15 \end{pmatrix}. \tag{2.56}$$

According to (2.55), the individual rows of $\boldsymbol{A}$ correspond to the vectors of target nodes $\boldsymbol{n}_i^{out}$ introduced in (2.35), thus marking all nearest neighbours of node i. Indeed, in the graph of Königsberg's bridges, nodes 2, 3 and 4 are nearest neighbours of node 1, nodes 1 and 4 are nearest neighbours of node 2 (see Fig. 2.4b) and so forth. The non-zero elements of A_{ij} will therefore deliver the complete set of shortest paths with a geodesic distance of one such that

$$\forall i, j \in \mathcal{N}: A_{ij} \neq 0 \Rightarrow d_{ij} = 1.$$

The matrix product of $\boldsymbol{A}$ with itself marks the set of all neighbours of nodes which themselves are neighbours of a given node, thus allowing to construct all walks comprised of two edges. Specifically, each element $(\boldsymbol{A}^2)_{ij}$ will count the number of possible walks of length two between i and j. In the case of Königsberg's bridge graph, we find with (2.56) that, for instance, $(\boldsymbol{A}^2)_{23} = 2$, confirming the existence of two walks of length two which connect node 2 to node 3 (Fig. 2.4c). In the case a path of length one does not already exist between two given nodes, such walks, with the exception of walks with identical source and target nodes, must necessarily also be shortest paths such that

$$\forall i, j \in \mathcal{N}, i \neq j: A_{ij} = 0 \wedge (\boldsymbol{A}^2)_{ij} \neq 0 \Rightarrow d_{ij} = 2.$$

In a similar fashion, the non-zero elements of the third matrix power $\boldsymbol{A}^3$ will count all walks of length three between two nodes which, if no walk of length two already exists, must then, in the case of distinct nodes, correspond to the number of shortest paths between those nodes.

This inductive argument can be applied to reach arbitrary matrix powers such that, in general, the mth power $(\boldsymbol{A}^m)_{ij}$ will deliver the number of walks of length m from node i to node j and must be the number of shortest paths between distinct nodes i and j if $(\boldsymbol{A}^k)_{ij} = 0$ for all $k \in [1, m-1]$. The non-diagonal elements of the geodesic distance matrix defined in (2.54) can then be expressed in an alternative fashion by

$$d_{ij} = \begin{cases} 1 & \text{if } A_{ij} = 1, \\ m & \text{if } \exists m \in \mathbb{N}, m < N_n : (\boldsymbol{A}^m)_{ij} \neq 0 \wedge \forall k \in [1, m-1] : (\boldsymbol{A}^k)_{ij} = 0, \\ 0 & \text{if } \forall k \in [1, N_n - 1] : (\boldsymbol{A}^k)_{ij} = 0 \end{cases} \tag{2.57}$$

for all $i, j \in \mathcal{N} : i \neq j$. A similarly concise expression for the diagonal elements of the geodesic distance matrix is, unfortunately, not that readily available. Although for geodesic loops we certainly have $d_{ii} = 1$ if $A_{ii} = 1$, the identification of geodesic cycles from walks in which both source and target node are identical requires the exclusion of already-traversed edges and thus cannot be achieved by considering powers of the matrix of adjacency relations alone. Indeed, while the non-zero diagonal elements of $\boldsymbol{A}^2$ in the case of the not self-looped multigraph of Königsberg's bridges correctly count the number of possible closed walks of length two, only some – and for some node pairs, none – of these walks are paths and, thus, are geodesic cycles. However, in the context of our operator graph-theoretical framework in Chapter 4, we will touch upon an alternative algebraic method with which geodesic cycles can be constructed, and their length measured, without resorting to a computationally demanding exhaustive search. Finally, we note that in (2.57), only powers up to $(\boldsymbol{A}^{N_n})$ need to be considered as, by definition, the length of possible paths in a graph is necessarily limited by the number N_n of its nodes. With this, recalling (2.57) and for diagonal elements (2.54), we eventually obtain

$$\boldsymbol{d} = \begin{pmatrix} 3 & 1 & 1 & 1 \\ 1 & 3 & 2 & 1 \\ 1 & 2 & 3 & 1 \\ 1 & 1 & 1 & 3 \end{pmatrix} \tag{2.58}$$

for the geodesic distance matrix of the graph of Königsberg's bridges.

The geodesic distance matrix (2.54) provides the conceptual and algebraic basis for the definition of a whole host of important graph-theoretical measures with which to further characterise and quantify the structural properties of networks. Focusing on only a small subset of these measures, let us begin by introducing the *geodesic node eccentricity*

$$\epsilon_i : \mathcal{N} \to \mathbb{N}_0 \,, \; \epsilon_i := \max_{j \in \mathcal{N}} d_{ij} \tag{2.59}$$

as a vectorial quantifier for the separation of each node from all other nodes in a graph. The maximum and minimum value of the node eccentricities,

$$
\begin{aligned}
\mathsf{d} \in \mathbb{N}_0 &: \mathsf{d} := \max_{i \in \mathcal{N}} \epsilon_i, \\
\mathsf{r} \in \mathbb{N}_0 &: \mathsf{r} := \min_{i \in \mathcal{N}} \epsilon_i,
\end{aligned}
\tag{2.60}
$$

then yield the *geodesic graph diameter*, the greatest geodesic distance between any pair of nodes, and *geodesic graph radius* respectively. A node i for which $\epsilon_i = \mathsf{r}$ is called a *central node*, and it is called a *peripheral node* if $\epsilon_i = \mathsf{d}$. Interestingly, in the case of the Königsberg bridge graph, we find with $\epsilon = (3, 3, 3, 3)$ that all nodes share the same geodesic eccentricity. When compared to the rows of d_{ij} in (2.58), this suggests that each node is farthest away from itself, and that in this graph each node must be considered as being both central and peripheral.

In order to further characterise how closely embedded into a graph a given node is, we will take the sum over individual rows and columns of the geodesic distance matrix and, inspired by the node strength (2.49), define with

$$
\begin{aligned}
d_i^{in} &: \mathcal{N} \to \mathbb{N}_0 \,,\; d_i^{in} := \sum_{j \in \mathcal{N}} d_{ji}, \\
d_i^{out} &: \mathcal{N} \to \mathbb{N}_0 \,,\; d_i^{out} := \sum_{j \in \mathcal{N}} d_{ij}, \\
d_i^{total} &: \mathcal{N} \to \mathbb{N}_0 \,,\; d_i^{total} := d_i^{in} + d_i^{out},
\end{aligned}
\tag{2.61}
$$

the *node in-distance* $\mathbf{d}^{in}$, *node out-distance* $\mathbf{d}^{out}$ and *total node distance* $\mathbf{d}^{total}$. The elements of these vectors provide a measure of the absolute total distance by which each node is separated from all other nodes and from itself in a given graph. The statistical averages

$$
\langle d_i^d \rangle \in \mathbb{Q} : \langle d_i^d \rangle := \frac{1}{N_n} \sum_{i \in \mathcal{N}} d_i^d
\tag{2.62}
$$

for $d \in \{in, out, total\}$ of the node distances over all nodes are called *average node in-distance* $\langle d_i^{in} \rangle$, *average node out-distance* $\langle d_i^{out} \rangle$ and *average total node distance* $\langle d_i^{total} \rangle$, and they define robust scalar quantifiers of the distance by which a typical node is separated from other nodes. Finally, the sum over the geodesic distance of each node pair in a graph yields the *geodesic graph distance*

$$
D \in \mathbb{N}_0 : D := \sum_{i,j \in \mathcal{N}} d_{ij} = \sum_{i \in \mathcal{N}} d_i^{in} = \sum_{i \in \mathcal{N}} d_i^{out},
\tag{2.63}
$$

and the statistical mean of the geodesic distances over all connected node pairs

$$
\langle D \rangle \in \mathbb{Q} : \langle D \rangle := \begin{cases} D/N_c & \text{if } N_c \neq 0, \\ 0 & \text{otherwise} \end{cases}
\tag{2.64}
$$

yields the *average geodesic graph distance*. Here, N_c denotes the *number of connected node pairs* and is defined by

$$N_c \in \mathbb{N}_0 : N_c := N_n^2 - \sum_{i,j \in \mathcal{N}} \delta[d_{ij}]. \tag{2.65}$$

It can easily be shown that, in general, $N_c \leq N_n^2$, with equality holding only in the case of connected graphs and strongly connected digraphs.

Although the notions introduced so far already deliver a fair characterisation of the typical separation of nodes in a graph, the applied graph-theoretical literature historically was, and still is, dominated by another and slightly variant set of distance-based measures. Firstly, dividing the geodesic graph distance D by the number of all possible node pairs in a graph, connected or not, we obtain the *average geodesic node distance*,

$$l \in \mathbb{Q} : l := \frac{D}{N_n^2}, \tag{2.66}$$

which is also called the *characteristic path length* and satisfies $l = \langle D \rangle$ in connected graphs and strongly connected digraphs. Secondly, the median of the normalised out-distances d_i^{out} by which each node is separated from all other nodes in a graph,

$$L \in \mathbb{Q} : L := \operatorname*{median}_{i \in \mathcal{N}} \left[\frac{d_i^{out}}{N_n} \right], \tag{2.67}$$

defines the *characteristic geodesic path length*. Lastly, the harmonic mean of geodesic distances d_{ij} between connected node pairs,

$$\ell \in \mathbb{Q} : \ell := N_c \left(\sum_{i,j \in \mathcal{N},\, d_{ij} \neq 0} \frac{1}{d_{ij}} \right)^{-1}, \tag{2.68}$$

provides the *geodesic connectivity length*, where N_c is the number of connected node pairs defined in (2.65). It is worth noting that many of these and similar distance-based measures are the source of interesting algebraic and number-theoretical identities when applied to exact graph models, an intriguing subject which, unfortunately, we cannot touch upon in the course of this book.

2.2.5 Network Motifs

The notion of geodesic distance between two nodes, introduced with (2.54) in the previous section, relies solely on the existence of at least one path connecting these nodes. Being defined as a set of edges which eventually connect a subset of nodes in a graph, each such path $\mathcal{P}_{ij}$ or, more generally, each walk

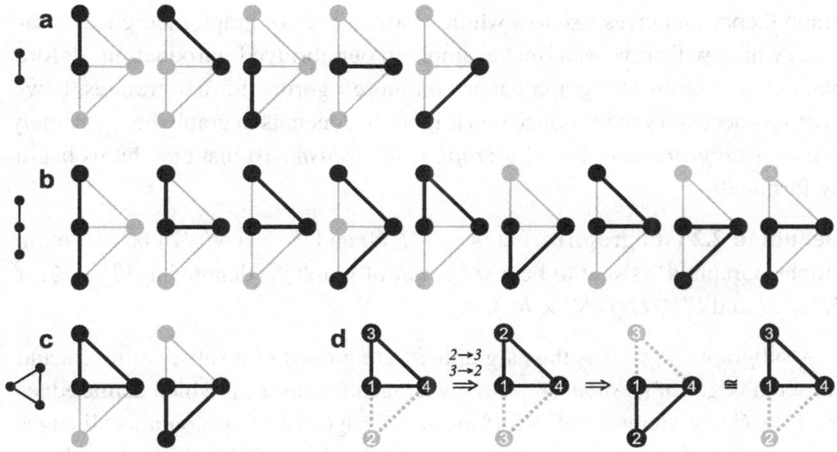

Figure 2.5 Examples of recurrent patterns in the graph of Königsberg's bridges. While paths of length one connecting two nodes occur five times (**a**), we find a total of nine realisations of paths of length two connecting three nodes (**b**). Triangular relations between three nodes, i.e. cycles of length three, occur two times (**c**) and generally form the basis for measuring the clustering property in graphs. All recurrent patterns shown in **a**–**c** are (vertex-induced) subgraphs of the Königsberg bridge graph and can be shown, by appropriate relabelling of their nodes (**d**), to be isomorphic to the network motifs illustrated as insets on the left.

$\mathcal{W}_{ij}$ itself can then be viewed as realisation of a graph which, as *graph pattern*, is embedded into a larger network. Indeed, by taking again a closer look at the graph of Königsberg's bridges, we easily discern a number of such recurrent patterns and find a total of five paths or walks of length one, each of which forms a complete graph of order 2 (Fig. 2.5a), and nine paths of length two which, as pattern, form a connected graph of order 3 with two edges (Fig. 2.5b). Embedded into the Königsberg bridge graph we also find two realisations of a graph pattern comprised of three edges which interconnects three nodes in form of a cycle (Fig. 2.5c). As we will see, this type of triangular pattern is of particular importance. By providing a measure describing the clustering of nodes in graphs, it resides at the very heart of a concept which became known as *small-world*, far beyond the confines of the applied graph-theoretical literature [108].

Due to their apparent importance not only for the conception of distance-based measures but for delineating finer structural characteristics of graphs in general, the identification of graph patterns along with the quantification of their occurrence naturally motivates another prominent branch of classical graph theory and gives rise to a whole new category of graph-theoretical measures which will serve as a final example in our abridged introduction. Before placing the notion of a graph pattern on more rigorous formal grounds, however, it is necessary to introduce two important concepts in graph theory, namely that of a *subgraph* and that of a *graph isomorphism*. To that end, let us begin by formulating

Definition 2.2 (subgraph) Let $\mathcal{G} = (\mathcal{N}, \mathcal{E})$ and $\mathcal{G}' = (\mathcal{N}', \mathcal{E}')$ be two finite graphs. Graph $\mathcal{G}'$ is said to be a *subgraph* of graph $\mathcal{G}$, denoted as $\mathcal{G}' \subseteq \mathcal{G}$, if $\mathcal{N}' \subseteq \mathcal{N}$ and $\mathcal{E}' \subseteq \mathcal{E} \cap (\mathcal{N}' \times \mathcal{N}')$.

A subgraph $\mathcal{G}' \subseteq \mathcal{G}$ is thus a graph $\mathcal{G}'$ comprised of a subset of nodes and subset of edges of its *supergraph* $\mathcal{G}$ such that all nodes i', j' which define edges $(i', j') \in \mathcal{E}'$ are elements of $\mathcal{N}'$. If the set of edges $\mathcal{E}'$ of $\mathcal{G}'$ contains all edges of $\mathcal{E}$ whose endnodes are both elements of $\mathcal{N}'$ – that is, if $\mathcal{E}' = \mathcal{E} \cap (\mathcal{N}' \times \mathcal{N}')$ – the graph $\mathcal{G}'$ is said to be a subgraph induced by the set $\mathcal{N}' \subseteq \mathcal{N}$ of nodes of $\mathcal{G}$ and is called *vertex-induced subgraph* or, in short, *induced subgraph* (see [59]). Similarly, a subgraph $\mathcal{G}' \subseteq \mathcal{G}$ is said to be induced by the subset of edges $\mathcal{E}' \subseteq \mathcal{E}$ and called an *edge-induced subgraph* of $\mathcal{G}$ if its set of nodes $\mathcal{N}'$ contains all nodes of $\mathcal{N}$ that are endnodes of edges in $\mathcal{E}'$. Each of the paths and cycles illustrated in Fig. 2.5a–c is an example of a vertex-induced subgraph of the Königsbergs bridge graph.

Instead of considering subsets of nodes and edges in a graph $\mathcal{G} = (\mathcal{N}, \mathcal{E})$, a new graph $\mathcal{G}' = (\mathcal{N}', \mathcal{E}')$ can also be generated by relabelling or reordering the set of nodes $\mathcal{N}$ of $\mathcal{G}$. The graph $\mathcal{G}'$ is then necessarily of the same order $|\mathcal{N}'| = |\mathcal{N}| \neq 0$ and has the same total adjacency count $|\mathcal{E}'| = |\mathcal{E}|$ as $\mathcal{G}$, and both graphs $\mathcal{G}$ and $\mathcal{G}'$ are said to be *isomorphic*. As exemplified in Fig. 2.5d, it can indeed be shown that the two subgraphs of triangular relations between nodes 1, 3, 4 and nodes 1, 2, 4 in the Königsberg bridge graph are isomorphic by simply relabelling nodes $2 \leftrightarrow 3$. In more rigorous terms, we formulate

Definition 2.3 (graph isomorphism) Let $\mathcal{G} = (\mathcal{N}, \mathcal{E})$ and $\mathcal{G}' = (\mathcal{N}', \mathcal{E}')$ be two finite graphs. The two graphs $\mathcal{G}$ and $\mathcal{G}'$ are said to be a *isomorphic*, denoted as $\mathcal{G} \cong \mathcal{G}'$ or $\mathcal{G} \leftrightarrow \mathcal{G}'$, if there exists a bijective mapping $f : \mathcal{N} \to \mathcal{N}'$ between the sets of nodes of both graphs such that

$$(i, j) \in \mathcal{E} \Leftrightarrow (f(i), f(j)) \in \mathcal{E}'$$

for $i, j \in \mathcal{N}$. The mapping f is called a *graph isomorphism* between $\mathcal{G}$ and $\mathcal{G}'$.

If there exists an isomorphism f between two finite graphs $\mathcal{G}'$ and $\mathcal{G}''$, and if $\mathcal{G}'$ is a subgraph of $\mathcal{G}$, then f is said to represent an *appearance* of $\mathcal{G}''$ in $\mathcal{G}$. Similarly, if $\mathcal{G} = (\mathcal{N}, \mathcal{E})$ and $\mathcal{G}'' = (\mathcal{N}'', \mathcal{E}'')$ are two graphs for which

$|\mathcal{N}| \geq |\mathcal{N}''|$, the graph $\mathcal{G}''$ is called an *occurrence* in $\mathcal{G}$ if there exists a subgraph $\mathcal{G}' = (\mathcal{N}', \mathcal{E}')$ in $\mathcal{G}$ with $\mathcal{N}' \subseteq \mathcal{N}$ such that $\mathcal{G}'$ and $\mathcal{G}''$ are isomorphic. In the graph of Königsberg's bridges, for example, not only are all of the subgraphs highlighted in black in Fig. 2.5a–c mutually isomorphic, but each of these subgraphs also constitutes an occurrence of the respective graphs illustrated as insets on the left-hand side.

With the definition of a subgraph and its occurrence in a supergraph at our disposal, we can now further confine the notion of a graph pattern. To that end, let $\mathcal{G}$ and $\mathcal{H}$ be two finite graphs. The graph $\mathcal{G}$ is said to *admit* graph $\mathcal{H}$ if $\mathcal{H}$ has at least one occurrence in $\mathcal{G}$. The set of all occurrences of $\mathcal{H}$ in $\mathcal{G}$ is denoted by $\mathcal{O}_{\mathcal{H}}^{\mathcal{G}}$, and its cardinality

$$F_{\mathcal{H}}^{\mathcal{G}} \in \mathbb{N}_0 : F_{\mathcal{H}}^{\mathcal{G}} := \left|\mathcal{O}_{\mathcal{H}}^{\mathcal{G}}\right| \tag{2.69}$$

is called the *frequency* of $\mathcal{H}$ in $\mathcal{G}$. If the frequency of a graph $\mathcal{H}$ in $\mathcal{G}$ exceeds a given threshold, $\mathcal{H}$ is called a *recurrent graph pattern* or a *frequent subgraph* in $\mathcal{G}$. Unfortunately, and similar to a graph's connectedness which distinguishes between sparse and dense graphs (see Section 2.2.1), there are no strict rules guiding the definition of a threshold above which a graph pattern becomes a frequent subgraph. However, many instances in the applied graph-theoretical literature evaluate the frequency of occurrence of a given graph pattern $\mathcal{H}$ in $\mathcal{G} = (\mathcal{N}, \mathcal{E})$ by comparing it with the statistical average $\langle F_{\mathcal{H}}^{\mathcal{R}} \rangle$ of the frequency of $\mathcal{H}$ in random graphs $\mathcal{R} = (\mathcal{N}^{\mathcal{R}}, \mathcal{E}^{\mathcal{R}})$ of order $|\mathcal{N}^{\mathcal{R}}| = |\mathcal{N}|$ and total adjacency count $|\mathcal{E}^{\mathcal{R}}| = |\mathcal{E}|$, specifically the Erdős–Rényi random graph model which we will formally introduce in the next section. In the case of $F_{\mathcal{H}}^{\mathcal{G}} > \langle F_{\mathcal{H}}^{\mathcal{R}} \rangle$ or, alternatively, if the probability that $F_{\mathcal{H}}^{\mathcal{G}} \leq \langle F_{\mathcal{H}}^{\mathcal{R}} \rangle$ is small, a recurrent graph pattern $\mathcal{H}$ is called *significant*, and $\mathcal{H}$ becomes a *network motif* for $\mathcal{G}$.

Some examples of simple graphs and relational digraphs $\mathcal{H} = (\mathcal{N}, \mathcal{E})$ which commonly serve as graph patterns in the analysis of network motifs are listed in Table 2.5. Such graph patterns are here typically categorised according to their order $|\mathcal{N}|$ and total adjacency count $|\mathcal{E}|$. In order to further distinguish individual graph patterns in each category, undirected graph patterns are labelled according to their not-ordered list of total node degrees such that $(2, 2, 2)$, for example, will refer to a pattern with three nodes, each of which has a total node degree of 2. In a similar fashion, directed patterns can be labelled by using the not-ordered list of associated node in-degrees and out-degrees such that the pattern $(12, 12, 22)$, for example, refers to a graph of three nodes in which two nodes have in-degree 1 and out-degree 2, and one node a node in-degree and out-degree of 2. As illustrated in Table 2.5, there is only one connected simple graph pattern of order 2, and a total of two not-isomorphic patterns of

Table 2.5 *Simple graph and relational digraph patterns $\mathcal{H} = (\mathcal{N}, \mathcal{E})$.*

$\lvert\mathcal{N}\rvert$	$\lvert\mathcal{E}\rvert$	Undirected	Directed			
1	0	(0)	(00)			
2	1	(1,1)	(01,10)			
	2		(11,11)			
3	2	(1,1,2)	(01,10,11)	(10,10,02)	(01,01,20)	
	3	(2,2,2)	(10,11,12)	(01,11,21)	(11,11,11)	(11,02,20)
	4		(11,12,21)	(12,12,20)	(02,21,21)	(11,11,22)
	5		(12,21,22)			
	6		(22,22,22)			

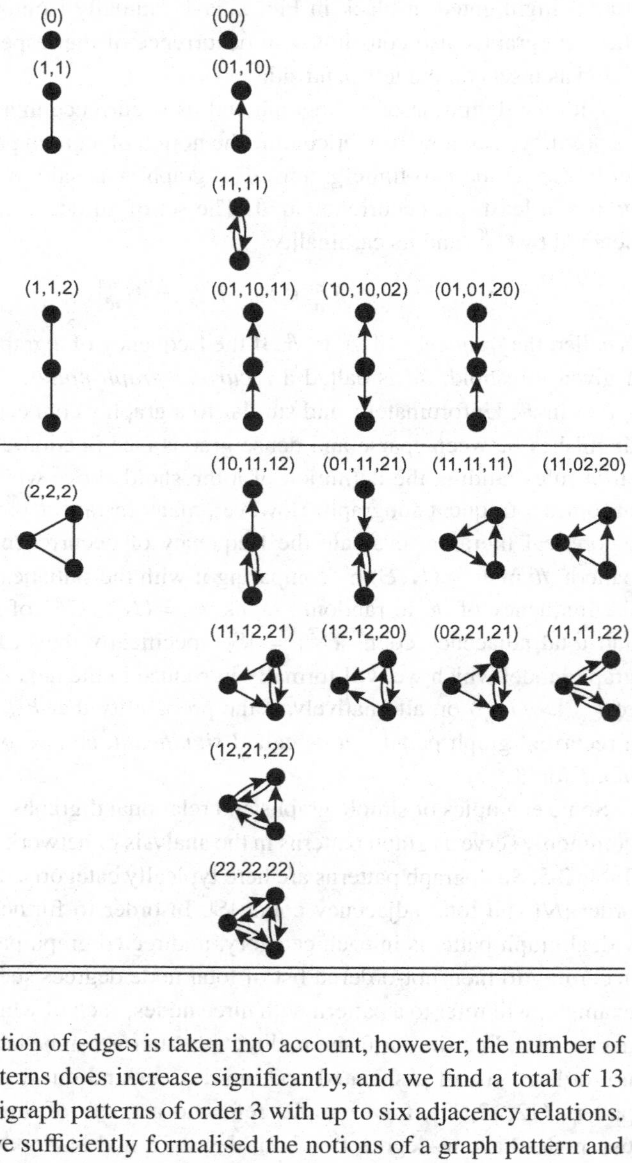

order 3. If the direction of edges is taken into account, however, the number of not-isomorphic patterns does increase significantly, and we find a total of 13 distinct relational digraph patterns of order 3 with up to six adjacency relations.

Now that we have sufficiently formalised the notions of a graph pattern and network motif, let us examine more closely in the remainder of this section some of the motifs which feature prominently in the applied graph-theoretical literature, and which will be further investigated in Part II of this book. Let us begin with the lowest-order patterns (0) and (00), illustrated in Table 2.5. Naturally, the frequencies of these patterns must be identical and equivalent to the number of nodes N_n of a graph such that

$$F^{\mathscr{G}}_{(0)} = F^{\mathscr{G}}_{(00)} = N_n. \tag{2.70}$$

Similarly, for undirected graphs, the frequency of the sole pattern (1, 1) of order 2 must necessarily correspond to the number of edges between distinct nodes in the graph, such that

$$F^{\mathscr{G}}_{(11)} = N_e - N_l. \tag{2.71}$$

In relational digraphs, the two possible patterns (01, 10) and (11, 11) of order 2 will distinguish between asymmetrical edges and symmetrical edges which are not self-loops. Noting that each symmetrical edge can be described by two asymmetrical edges, we then find

$$\begin{aligned} F^{\mathscr{G}}_{(11,11)} &= N_{se} - N_l, \\ F^{\mathscr{G}}_{(01,10)} &= 2(N_{se} - N_l) + N_{ae}, \end{aligned} \tag{2.72}$$

where N_{se} and N_{ae} are defined in (2.18) and (2.19).

The graph patterns (1, 1, 2) and (01, 10, 11) of order 3 shown in Table 2.5 respectively describe undirected and directed paths of length 2 between two distinct nodes. Thus, their frequencies must be proportional to the total number of possible unique paths $\mathcal{P}_{ij}$ with $|\mathcal{P}_{ij}| = 2$ between all ordered pairs of nodes $i, j \in \mathcal{N} : i \neq j$. In the undirected case, each occurrence of the pattern (1, 1, 2) contributes two such paths, one from node i to node j and a reciprocal second from j to i, and we have

$$F^{\mathscr{G}}_{(1,1,2)} = \frac{1}{2} \sum_{\substack{i,j \in \mathcal{N} \\ i \neq j}} |\mathscr{P}^2_{ij}|, \tag{2.73}$$

where $\mathscr{P}^m_{ij} \subseteq \mathscr{P}_{ij}$ denotes the subset of all paths $\mathcal{P}_{ij} \in \mathscr{P}_{ij}$ between $i, j \in \mathcal{N}$ for which $|\mathcal{P}_{ij}| = m$, that is the set of all paths of length m in a given graph. In contrast, each occurrence of the graph pattern (01, 10, 11) in a directed graph counts as only one directed path of length 2, thus yielding

$$F^{\mathscr{G}}_{(01,10,11)} = \sum_{\substack{i,j \in \mathcal{N} \\ i \neq j}} |\mathscr{P}^2_{ij}| \tag{2.74}$$

for the pattern's frequency.

Finally, the undirected graph pattern (2, 2, 2) of order 3 resembles a closed path of length 3, such that each individual occurrence contributes a total of six cycles, one cycle for each of the two edges emanating from a node in the pattern, and we have

$$F^{\mathcal{G}}_{(2,2,2)} = \frac{1}{6} \sum_{i \in \mathcal{N}} |\mathcal{P}^3_{ii}|. \tag{2.75}$$

On the other hand, the directed graph pattern $(11, 11, 11)$ will count only one cycle of length 3 for each node and eventually yield

$$F^{\mathcal{G}}_{(11,11,11)} = \frac{1}{3} \sum_{i \in \mathcal{N}} |\mathcal{P}^3_{ii}| \tag{2.76}$$

for the frequency of its occurrence.

Equations (2.73)–(2.76) can certainly be generalised to encompass graph patterns which describe paths and cycles of arbitrary length. To that end, and for reasons of notational simplicity, let us denote with $\bar{F}^d_n$ and $\bar{F}^{ud}_n$ the frequencies of patterns of order n isomorphic to directed and undirected paths comprised of $n-1$ edges visiting n distinct nodes, and denote with $\mathring{F}^d_n$ and $\mathring{F}^{ud}_n$ the frequencies of patterns of order n isomorphic to directed and undirected cycles comprised of n edges visiting n distinct nodes, respectively. In the case of undirected graphs, for each existing path $\mathcal{P}_{ij} \in \mathcal{P}^{n-1}_{ij}$ with $n > 1$ between distinct nodes i and j, there necessarily exists an isomorphic reciprocal path between nodes j and i such that

$$\bar{F}^{ud}_n \in \mathbb{N}_0 : \bar{F}^{ud}_n := \frac{1}{2} \sum_{\substack{i,j \in \mathcal{N} \\ i \neq j}} |\mathcal{P}^{n-1}_{ij}|. \tag{2.77}$$

In a similar fashion, we find a total of $2n$ closed paths isomorphic to a given cycle $\mathcal{P}_{ii} \in \mathcal{P}^n_{ii}$ of length $n > 1$, one for each of the two edges emanating from any of the n nodes comprising a cycle of length n, and obtain with

$$\mathring{F}^{ud}_n \in \mathbb{N}_0 : \mathring{F}^{ud}_n := \frac{1}{2n} \sum_{i \in \mathcal{N}} |\mathcal{P}^n_{ii}| \tag{2.78}$$

the generalisation of (2.75). Recalling that $|\mathcal{P}^1_{ij}| = A_{ij}$ for all $i, j \in \mathcal{N}$, where A_{ij} denotes the matrix of adjacency relations introduced in (2.55), we find that this yields with (2.14) and (2.15) a frequency

$$\bar{F}^{ud}_2 \equiv F^{\mathcal{G}}_{(11)} = \frac{1}{2} \sum_{\substack{i,j \in \mathcal{N} \\ i \neq j}} |\mathcal{P}^1_{ij}| = \frac{1}{2} \sum_{\substack{i,j \in \mathcal{N} \\ i \neq j}} A_{ij} = \frac{1}{2}(A - 2N_l) = N_e - N_l$$

for the undirected pattern of order $n = 2$ and one edge, and thus we have our earlier result (2.71).

The frequency of occurrences of paths and cycles in directed and eventually self-looped graphs can be approached correspondingly. Indeed, there does exist at most one directed path $\mathcal{P}_{ij} \in \mathscr{P}_{ij}^{n-1}$ of length $n-1 \geq 1$ between two given distinct nodes i and j which visits a fixed ordered set of n nodes. This then yields, as a generalisation of (2.74), the expression

$$\bar{F}_n^d \in \mathbb{N}_0 : \bar{F}_n^d := \sum_{\substack{i,j \in \mathcal{N} \\ i \neq j}} |\mathscr{P}_{ij}^{n-1}|, \tag{2.79}$$

which, with (2.20) and (2.15), results in

$$\bar{F}_2^d \equiv F_{(01,10)}^{\mathcal{G}} = \sum_{\substack{i,j \in \mathcal{N} \\ i \neq j}} |\mathscr{P}_{ij}^1| = 2N_{se} + N_{ae} - 2N_l = N_e - 2N_l$$

for the frequency of patterns of order $n = 2$ isomorphic to paths of length 2, as expected. Finally, there are n isomorphic closed paths contributing to the pattern that represents a directed cycle $\mathcal{P}_{ii} \in \mathscr{P}_{ii}^n$, which leaves

$$\mathring{F}_n^d \in \mathbb{N}_0 : \mathring{F}_n^d := \frac{1}{n} \sum_{i \in \mathcal{N}} |\mathscr{P}_{ii}^n| \tag{2.80}$$

for $n > 1$ as a generalisation of (2.76). For $n = 2$, given that $|\mathscr{P}_{ii}^2|$ corresponds to the number of bidirectional adjacency relations between two distinct nodes and, thus, to the number of symmetrical edges each node $i \in \mathcal{N}$ establishes with other nodes in the graph, (2.80) delivers with

$$\mathring{F}_2^d \equiv F_{(11,11)}^{\mathcal{G}} = \frac{1}{2} \sum_{i \in \mathcal{N}} |\mathscr{P}_{ii}^2| = \frac{1}{2} \sum_{i \in \mathcal{N}} (A^2)_{ii} - N_l = N_{se} - N_l$$

the frequency of graph patterns isomorphic to cycles of length 2.

Before concluding our brief excursion into the far-reaching and undoubtedly intriguing subject of network motifs, let us consider in greater detail graph patterns which form triangular relationships between nodes. As mentioned earlier, such patterns constitute the conceptual basis for an important structural network characteristic commonly referred to as *clustering* in the graph-theoretical literature. The notion of clustering was first introduced under the name *transitivity* in studies of undirected social networks for simply measuring the extent to which nodes, in this case people or groups of people, are linked, or clustered, together in triangular relationships [61]. Here, nodes 1, 2 and 3 are said to be *transitive* if, for an existing link between nodes 1 and 2 as well as between nodes 2 and 3, nodes 1 and 3 are also linked. In mathematically more rigorous terms, the *graph transitivity* C, also called the *global clustering coefficient*, is then defined as the ratio between the number of existing cycles of length 3 in an undirected graph, given by the sum over $|\mathscr{P}_{ii}^3|$ for all $i \in \mathcal{N}$, and the total number of paths of length 2 between distinct nodes, given by the sum over $|\mathscr{P}_{ij}^2|$ for all $i, j \in \mathcal{N}$ with $i \neq j$. Utilising the frequencies $\mathring{F}_3^{ud}$ and $\bar{F}_2^{ud}$

of the associated graph patterns given in (2.77) and (2.78), respectively, we thus can define

$$C \in \mathbb{Q}\,,\, C \in [0,1]\colon C := \begin{cases} 3\,\mathring{F}_3^{ud}/\bar{F}_2^{ud} & \text{if } \bar{F}_2^{ud} \neq 0, \\ 0 & \text{otherwise,} \end{cases} \tag{2.81}$$

as a first measure of the clustering in simple graphs.

With some modifications, the above notion of transitivity can certainly be applied to also measure how likely it is for the nearest neighbours of a given node to be connected [109]. To that end, given a simple graph $\mathcal{G} = (\mathcal{N}, \mathcal{E})$, let us consider the vertex-induced subgraph $\mathcal{G}_i = (\mathcal{N}^{\mathcal{G}_i}, \mathcal{E}^{\mathcal{G}_i})$ comprised of the subset $\mathcal{N}^{\mathcal{G}_i} \subseteq \mathcal{N}$ of all nearest neighbours of node i such that $|\mathcal{N}^{\mathcal{G}_i}| = a_i^{total}$, with a_i^{total} denoting the total node degree (2.25) for undirected graphs. The node or *local clustering coefficient* C_i is then defined as the ratio between the actual number of edges between distinct nodes in $\mathcal{G}_i$, given by the sum of $|\mathcal{P}^1_{i'j'}|$ over all $i', j' \in \mathcal{N}^{\mathcal{G}_i} : i' \neq j'$, and the maximum number $N_e^{\max}$ of possible edges for simple graphs of order $|\mathcal{N}^{\mathcal{G}_i}|$ introduced in (2.16), that is,

$$C_i \in \mathbb{Q}\,,\, C_i \in [0,1]\colon C_i := \begin{cases} 2F^{\mathcal{G}_i}_{(11)}/a_i(a_i-1) & \text{if } a_i \neq 0, \\ 0 & \text{otherwise.} \end{cases} \tag{2.82}$$

The statistical mean of all local clustering coefficients

$$\langle C_i \rangle \in \mathbb{Q}\,,\, \langle C_i \rangle \in [0,1]\colon \langle C_i \rangle := \frac{1}{N_n} \sum_{i \in \mathcal{N}} C_i \tag{2.83}$$

is called the *clustering coefficient* of $\mathcal{G}$ and serves alongside C as a scalar measure, characterising this important structural peculiarity found in simple or, more generally, undirected, not self-looped graphs. In the case of the multigraph of Königsberg's bridges, for example, we find $C = 0.25$ and $\langle C_i \rangle = 0.83$.

The clustering coefficients defined in (2.81) and (2.82) can easily be generalised to apply also in the case of directed graphs – with the caveat, however, that now we have various distinct graph patterns to account for. Illustrating such a generalisation only for the global clustering coefficient, with two triangular patterns (11, 11, 11) and (11, 02, 20) comprised of three nodes and three edges, and three patterns (01, 10, 11), (10, 10, 02) and (01, 01, 20) comprised of order three with two edges (see Table 2.5), we can indeed construct a total of six measures for digraphs akin to (2.81), four of which carry relevance as a measure of a digraph's global clustering property [85]. These are

$$C^d_{(k)} \in \mathbb{Q}\,,\, C^d_{(k)} \in [0,1]\,,\, k \in [1,4]\colon \tag{2.84}$$

$$C^d_{(1)} := \begin{cases} 3F^{\mathcal{G}}_{(11,11,11)}/F^{\mathcal{G}}_{(01,10,11)} & \text{if } F^{\mathcal{G}}_{(01,10,11)} \neq 0, \\ 0 & \text{otherwise,} \end{cases}$$

$$C^d_{(2)} := \begin{cases} F^{\mathscr{G}}_{(11,02,20)}/F^{\mathscr{G}}_{(01,01,20)} & \text{if } F^{\mathscr{G}}_{(01,01,20)} \neq 0, \\ 0 & \text{otherwise,} \end{cases}$$

$$C^d_{(3)} := \begin{cases} 2F^{\mathscr{G}}_{(11,02,20)}/F^{\mathscr{G}}_{(01,10,11)} & \text{if } F^{\mathscr{G}}_{(01,10,11)} \neq 0, \\ 0 & \text{otherwise,} \end{cases}$$

$$C^d_{(4)} := \begin{cases} F^{\mathscr{G}}_{(11,02,20)}/F^{\mathscr{G}}_{(10,10,02)} & \text{if } F^{\mathscr{G}}_{(10,10,02)} \neq 0, \\ 0 & \text{otherwise,} \end{cases}$$

where the coefficients in the terms on the right-hand side of $C^d_{(1)}$ and $C^d_{(3)}$ account for isomorphic representations of the associated patterns.

Finally, we introduce the normalised sum over all possible directed patterns of order 3 with two and three edges as the *total global clustering coefficient* C^d for digraphs [43]. In terms of the matrix of adjacency relations A_{ij} defined in (2.55), this coefficient is given by

$C^d \in \mathbb{Q}\,,\ C^d \in [0,1]$:

$$C^d := \begin{cases} \frac{1}{N^d} \sum_{i \in \mathcal{N}} \sum_{\substack{j \in \mathcal{N} \\ j \neq i}} \sum_{\substack{k \in \mathcal{N} \\ k \neq i \\ k \neq j}} \left(A_{ij} + A_{ji}\right)\left(A_{ik} + A_{ki}\right)\left(A_{jk} + A_{kj}\right) & \text{if } N^d \geq 1, \\ 0 \text{ otherwise} \end{cases} \tag{2.85}$$

with the normalisation term

$$N^d := 2 \sum_{i \in \mathcal{N}} \left(a_i^{total}(a_i^{total} - 1) - 2a_i^b\right),$$

where a_i^{total} denotes the total node degree for directed graphs (2.25) and

$$a_i^b := \sum_{\substack{j \in \mathcal{N} \\ j \neq i}} A_{ij} A_{ji}$$

the number of cycles of order 2 with two edges drawn by each node i in a graph. The so-defined global clustering coefficient carries special importance and is commonly used as the measure which quantifies the small-world property of graphs. The expectation value of C^d will be calculated explicitly for a variety of finite random graph models in Section 6.3, and then utilised in Section 6.3.3 for assessing to which extent biological neural networks are small-worlds.

2.2.6 Spectral Measures

The final major category of graph measures, which we will briefly touch upon in this abridged introduction into classical graph theory, concerns the spectral properties of a graph. These measures are commonly employed in the delineation of general structural characteristics of larger networks as they draw interesting links to distance-based meaures and a number of specific network motifs. At the very heart of this category resides the notion of a *graph spectrum*, historically defined for simple graphs as the set of eigenvalues of a graph's adjacency matrix [110]. In generalising this notion, let $\mathcal{G}$ be a not self-looped weighted directed graph of order n with matrix of adjacency relations $\boldsymbol{A}$ given in (2.55). The spectrum of $\mathcal{G}$ is then defined by the ordered set

$$\Sigma(\mathcal{G}) := (\mu_i \in \mathbb{C}\colon i \in [1,n], |\mu_1| \leq |\mu_2| \leq \cdots \leq |\mu_n|) \tag{2.86}$$

of all n typically complex eigenvalues μ_i of $\boldsymbol{A}$, with $|\mu_i|$ denoting their absolute value. In the case of undirected graphs only, each eigenvalue is ensured to be real due to the symmetric nature of the Boolean matrix $\boldsymbol{A}$. The eigenvalue μ_n with the largest absolute value is, however, always real according to the Perron–Frobenius theorem, and it can be shown that for connected graphs, $|\mu_i| < \mu_n$ for all $i \in [1, n-1]$. Moreover, in connected undirected graphs, we find either that

$$\min \boldsymbol{a}^{total} < \langle \boldsymbol{a}^{total} \rangle < \mu_n < \max \boldsymbol{a}^{total},$$

where $\boldsymbol{a}^{total}$ denotes the total node degree sequence, or that

$$\mu_n = \min \boldsymbol{a}^{total} = \max \boldsymbol{a}^{total},$$

with a complete simple graph being an example of the latter case.

Beyond this rather general relationship between node degree sequence and maximum eigenvalue μ_n, an access to the finer details of a graph's structural makeup can be gained by considering the full spectrum $\Sigma[\mathcal{G}]$ of $\mathcal{G}$. In order to illustrate this approach, let us restrict here to finite not self-looped undirected graphs $\mathcal{G} = (\mathcal{N}, \mathcal{E})$ of order n. As the eigenvalues of the mth power of $\boldsymbol{A}$ are identical to the mth power of μ_i, we find that the sum over all diagonal elements of $\boldsymbol{A}^m$ is given by

$$\sum_{i \in \mathcal{N}} (\boldsymbol{A}^m)_{ii} = \sum_{i=1}^{n} \mu_i^m = n \left\langle \Sigma(\mathcal{G})^m \right\rangle, \tag{2.87}$$

and thus is proportional to the mth moment

$$\left\langle \Sigma(\mathcal{G})^m \right\rangle \in \mathbb{R}\colon \left\langle \Sigma(\mathcal{G})^m \right\rangle := \int_{\min \Sigma(\mathcal{G})}^{\max \Sigma(\mathcal{G})} \mu^m p[\Sigma(\mathcal{G}); \mu] \, d\mu \tag{2.88}$$

of the *spectral density*

$$p[\Sigma(\mathcal{G}); \mu]\colon \mathbb{R} \to \mathbb{R}\,,\ p[\Sigma(\mathcal{G}); \mu] := \frac{1}{n} \sum_{i=1}^{n} \delta(\mu - \mu_i) \tag{2.89}$$

of $\mathcal{G}$ [44, 51]. Here $\delta(x)$ denotes the *Dirac delta function*, defined as

$$\int_a^b f(x)\delta(x-x_0)\,dx = \begin{cases} f(x_0) & \text{if } x_0 \in [a,b], \\ 0 & \text{otherwise} \end{cases} \tag{2.90}$$

for $a, b, x_0 \in \mathbb{C}$ and complex functions $f(x) : \mathbb{C} \to \mathbb{C}$.

Relations (2.87) and (2.88) indeed have far-reaching consequences. Recalling Section 2.2.4, the elements $(\boldsymbol{A}^m)_{ij}$ count the number of walks $\mathcal{W}_{ij}$ of length m between two nodes i and j in the graph, such that the sum over $(\boldsymbol{A}^m)_{ii}$ will provide the total number of closed walks of length m. For instance, in the case $m = 1$, we necessarily find for not self-looped undirected graphs

$$\sum_{i=1}^{n} \mu_i = \sum_{i \in \mathcal{N}} A_{ii} = 0,$$

and thus an important constraint on the spectrum $\Sigma(\mathcal{G})$ of $\mathcal{G}$. Similarly, for $m = 2$ we obtain with (2.71) the relations

$$\sum_{i=1}^{n} \mu_i^2 = \sum_{i_1, i_2 \in \mathcal{N}} A_{i_1 i_2} A_{i_2 i_1} = 2N_{(11)}^{\mathcal{G}} = 2N_e,$$

$$\sum_{\substack{i,j=1 \\ i \neq j}}^{n} \mu_i \mu_j = \sum_{i=1}^{n} \left(\mu_i \sum_{j=1}^{n} \mu_j \right) - \sum_{i=1}^{n} \mu_i^2 = -2N_e,$$

and for $m = 3$

$$\sum_{i=1}^{n} \mu_i^3 = \sum_{i_1, i_2, i_3 \in \mathcal{N}} A_{i_1 i_2} A_{i_2 i_3} A_{i_3 i_1} = 6F_{(2,2,2)}^{\mathcal{G}},$$

$$\sum_{\substack{i,j,l=1 \\ i \neq j, i \neq l, j \neq l}}^{n} \mu_i \mu_j \mu_l = 2 \sum_{i=1}^{n} \mu_i^3 = 12F_{(2,2,2)}^{\mathcal{G}},$$

with $F_{(2,2,2)}^{\mathcal{G}}$ being the frequency of the triangular graph pattern (2, 2, 2) (see Table 2.5) given in (2.75). Continuing with this argument, it can eventually be shown that, in general, sums over products of m eigenvalues from $\Sigma(\mathcal{G})$ are linked to the frequency of closed walks of length m, and thus to the number of occurrence of specific patterns in a graph [18, 100].

In this section, unfortunately, we could present only a tiny fraction of the measures which are commonly employed in the characterisation and quantification of network properties throughout the vast applied graph-theoretical literature. Many more measures exist and continue to be conceived in this ever-growing branch of graph theory, some of which adapted to delineate exclusively specific network properties, others being general and suited for a

Table 2.6 *Measuring the Königsberg bridge graph.*

General measures				
$\lambda_d = 0$	$\lambda_w = 1$	$\lambda_l = 0$	$N_n = 4$	$N_a = 5$
$N_e = 5$	$N_e^{\max} = 6$	$N_l = 0$	$A = 10$	$N_{se} = 5$
	$N_{ae} = 0$	$\alpha = 0$	$\rho = 5/6 \approx 0.83$	
Degree-based measures				
$\lVert \boldsymbol{a}^{total} \rVert_1 = 10$		$\langle \boldsymbol{a}^{total} \rangle = 5/2 = 2.5$		$\tau = 16/15 \approx 1.07$
	$\langle N_{ij} \rangle = 13/8 = 1.625$		$\langle S_{ij} \rangle = (\sqrt{2}+4\sqrt{3})/8 \approx 1.04$	
Weight-based measures				
$\lambda_{wd} = 0$		$\langle s_i^{in} \rangle = \langle s_i^{out} \rangle = 7/2 = 3.5$		$\langle s_i^{total} \rangle = 7$
$N_{swe} = 5$		$N_{awe} = 0$		$\alpha_w = 0$
Distance-based measures				
$\epsilon = (3, 3, 3, 3)$		$\mathsf{d} = 3$		$\mathsf{r} = 3$
$\boldsymbol{d}^{total} = (12, 14, 14, 12)$		$\langle d_i^{total} \rangle = 13$		$D = 26$
$N_c = 16$		$\langle D \rangle = 13/8 = 1.625$		$l = 13/8 = 1.625$
	$L = 13/8 = 1.625$		$\ell = 48/37 \approx 1.297$	
Network motifs				
$C = 3/4 = 0.75$		$C_i = (2/3, 1, 1, 2/3)$		$\langle C_i \rangle = 5/6 \approx 0.833$
Spectral measures				
$\Sigma(\mathcal{G}) = (-1, 0, (1-\sqrt{17})/2, (1+\sqrt{17})/2)$			$\langle \Sigma(\mathcal{G})^2 \rangle = 2.5$	$\langle \Sigma(\mathcal{G})^3 \rangle = 3$

comparative analysis of networks across different research fields. By focusing on a number of important concepts, by highlighting some of the challenges and subtleties surrounding the definition of existing measures and the conception of new measures, and by exemplifying the use of some of these measures with the application to the network which lies at the historical origins of classical graph theory, the Königsberg bridge graph (see Table 2.6 for a summary), this abridged presentation should provide not only a solid foundation but also stimulating insights and motivation to embark on the undoubtedly stony road towards a generalisation of widely used graph-theoretical notions. Many of the notions and measures presented here will be revisited in Part II of this book in the context of our operator graph-theoretical framework.

2.3 Graph Models

The application of graph-theoretical measures, such as those introduced in the previous section, to network representations of real-world systems serves

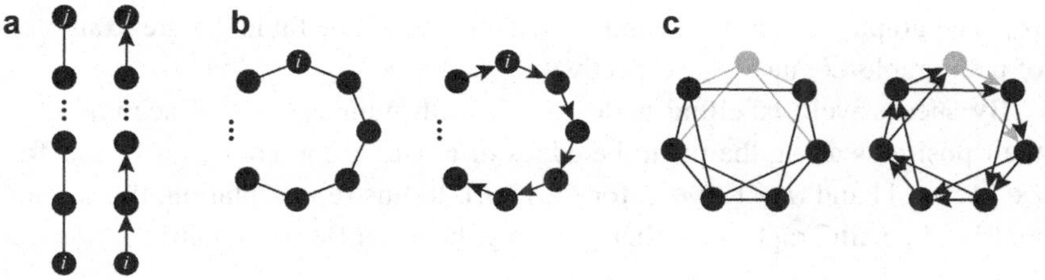

Figure 2.6 Examples of exact graph models. **a:** Path graph $\mathcal{P}_n$ and path digraph $\mathcal{P}_n^d$ connecting two distinct terminal nodes i and j. **b:** Cycle graph $\mathcal{C}_n$ and cycle digraph $\mathcal{C}_n^d$ connecting each node i with itself through a closed path spanning the whole network. **c:** Graphs $\mathcal{C}_{7,2}$ (left) and $\mathcal{C}_{7,2}^d$ (right) exemplifying undirected and directed k-ring graphs of order n.

today across many research fields as an indispensable tool for characterising the phenomena observed in these systems. Following such an approach, one typically collects a whole host of quantified properties, not dissimilar to the ones presented in Table 2.6 for the Königsberg bridge graph, which then can be employed in a comparative analysis as a means to identify common features shared among real-world systems, or to delineate and identify essential features for the construction of simplified models of those systems. Such network models are typically defined through a low-dimensional parameter space alongside a set of strict rules governing their construction and structural makeup. Depending on whether these rules involve some form of random process or not, one generally distinguishes *random graph models* from nonrandom or *exact graph models*. Both types of graph models find widespread applications in the description of a great range of real-world phenomena. In this section, we will introduce the most prominent of these network models and present some of their defining structural characteristics.

2.3.1 Path Graphs

Let us begin with one of the most simple exact graph models, namely that of a path graph. We already encountered realisations of this model in the previous section in the form of specific graph patterns, and in Section 2.2.4 as a conceptual basis for the notion of geodesic distance between nodes. In general, a connected simple graph $\mathcal{P}_n = (\mathcal{N}, \mathcal{E})$ of order $n = |\mathcal{N}| \geq 2$ with $|\mathcal{E}| = 2(n-1)$ is called a *path graph* of order n if $n-2$ of its nodes establish exactly two adjacency relations with neighbouring nodes, and the remaining two *terminal nodes* are each subject to exactly one adjacency relation (Fig. 2.6a, left). A path graph $\mathcal{P}_n$ thus represents a path of length $n-1$ between distinct nodes such that each path $\mathcal{P}_{ij} \in \mathcal{P}_{ij}^{n-1}$ with $i \neq j$ in a simple graph is isomorphic to

$\mathcal{P}_n$. The graph patterns (1, 1) and (1, 1, 2) illustrated in Table 2.5 are examples of path graphs $\mathcal{P}_2$ and $\mathcal{P}_3$, respectively.

By successively labelling nodes of $\mathcal{P}_n$ with numbers $i \in \mathbb{N}$ according to their positions along the path, the edges of a path graph are $(i, i+1) \in \mathcal{E}$ for $i \in [1, n-1]$ and $(i-1, i) \in \mathcal{E}$ for $i \in [2, n]$. In this representation, the weight matrix of a path graph $\mathcal{P}_n$ is then given by the $n \times n$ Boolean matrix

$$\boldsymbol{w} = \begin{pmatrix} 0 & 1 & 0 & \cdots & 0 & 0 \\ 1 & 0 & 1 & \cdots & 0 & 0 \\ 0 & 1 & 0 & \cdots & 0 & 0 \\ & \vdots & & \ddots & & \vdots \\ 0 & 0 & 0 & \cdots & 0 & 1 \\ 0 & 0 & 0 & \cdots & 1 & 0 \end{pmatrix}. \tag{2.91}$$

Noting that, by definition, a path graph does not contain any self-looped nodes, the weight matrix, adjacency matrix and matrix of adjacency relations of $\mathcal{P}_n$ are necessarily identical, and alternatively formalised by

$$w_{ij} = a_{ij} = A_{ij} = \delta[i+1-j] + \delta[i-1-j] \tag{2.92}$$

for $i, j \in [1, n]$ in terms of the generalised Kronecker delta function (2.13).

The relatively simple algebraic forms of (2.91) and (2.92) eventually allow explicit expression of many graph measures. Some of these expressions are listed in Table 2.7. For instance, the total adjacency of $\mathcal{P}_n$ is given by

$$A = \sum_{i,j=1}^{n} (\delta[i+1-j] + \delta[i-1-j]) = \sum_{i=2}^{n} 1 + \sum_{i=1}^{n-1} 1 = 2(n-1), \tag{2.93}$$

while for the total node degrees and their average (2.33), we find

$$a_i^{total} = \sum_{j=1}^{n} (\delta[i+1-j] + \delta[i-1-j]) = \begin{cases} 1 & \text{if } i \in \{1, n\}, \\ 2 & \text{if } i \in [2, n-1], \end{cases} \tag{2.94}$$

$$\langle \boldsymbol{a}^{total} \rangle = \frac{1}{n}\left(1 + \sum_{j=2}^{n-1} 2 + 1\right) = 2\frac{n-1}{n}. \tag{2.95}$$

Furthermore, we easily obtain

$$\boldsymbol{d} = \begin{pmatrix} 0 & 1 & 2 & \cdots & n-2 & n-1 \\ 1 & 0 & 1 & \cdots & n-3 & n-2 \\ 2 & 1 & 0 & \cdots & n-4 & n-3 \\ & \vdots & & \ddots & & \vdots \\ n-2 & n-3 & n-4 & \cdots & 0 & 1 \\ n-1 & n-2 & n-3 & \cdots & 1 & 0 \end{pmatrix} \tag{2.96}$$

for a path graph's geodesic distance matrix by recognising that between any two distinct nodes $i, j \in \mathcal{N}$ of $\mathcal{P}_n$ there exists only one shortest path of length $d_{ij} = |i-j|$. With this, we can then also deduce explicit expressions for a number of distance-dependent measures, such as the average total node distance

$$\langle d_i^{total} \rangle = \frac{2}{n} \sum_{i,j=1}^{n} |i-j| = \frac{4}{n} \sum_{\substack{i,j=1 \\ i>j}}^{n} (i-j) = \frac{2}{3}(n^2-1) \tag{2.97}$$

and, noting that $N_c = n(n-1)$, the geodesic connectivity length

$$\ell = n(n-1)\left(\sum_{\substack{i,j=1 \\ i>j}}^{n} \frac{1}{|i-j|} \right)^{-1} = \frac{n(n-1)}{2n(H_n-1)}, \tag{2.98}$$

where $H_n \colon \mathbb{N} \to \mathbb{Q}$, $H_n := \sum_{k=1}^{n} 1/k$ denotes the nth harmonic number.

The model of a path graph introduced above can certainly be generalised to cover directed edges as well. Such a *path digraph* $\mathcal{P}_n^d = (\mathcal{N}, \mathcal{E})$ of order $n = |\mathcal{N}| \geq 2$ and with $|\mathcal{E}| = n-1$ directed adjacency relations requires all but two of its nodes to be weakly connected by exactly one incoming and one outgoing directed edge, while one of the remaining two terminal nodes is weakly connected by only one outgoing, the other by only one incoming edge (Fig. 2.6a, right). A path digraph then describes a directed path such that each $\mathcal{P}_{ij} \in \mathcal{P}_{ij}^{n-1}$ of length $n-1$ from node i to a distinct node j in a relational digraph is isomorphic to $\mathcal{P}_n^d$, and the directed graph patterns $(01, 10)$ and $(01, 10, 11)$ in Table 2.5 present realisations of $\mathcal{P}_n^d$ for $n = 2$ and $n = 3$, respectively. By appropriately labelling the nodes in $\mathcal{N}$, the weight matrix of $\mathcal{P}_n^d$ is given by the upper triangular part of (2.91) such that

$$w_{ij} = a_{ij} = A_{ij} = \delta[i+1-j] \tag{2.99}$$

for $i, j \in [1, n]$. With this, it can furthermore be shown that the geodesic distance matrix of $\mathcal{P}_n^d$ finds a suitable representation in form of an upper triangular matrix comprised of all elements $d_{ij} \colon i, j \in [1, n], j > i$ of (2.96). As in the undirected case, such a representation, in conjunction with (2.99), can eventually be leveraged to deduce exact expressions for a whole host of a directed path graph's characteristics. Leaving this task as an entertaining exercise for the involved reader, we present a small selection of results in Table 2.7.

2.3.2 Cycle Graphs

Due to its simplicity, the model of a path graph introduced in the previous section constitutes the basis for the construction of a great number of other exact

Table 2.7 *Measuring exact graph models.*

	$\mathscr{P}_n$	$\mathscr{P}_n^d$	$\mathscr{C}_n$	$\mathscr{C}_n^d$	$\mathscr{C}_{n,k}$	$\mathscr{C}_{n,k}^d$	$\mathscr{L}_{m,n}^{(4,4)}$
	$n \in \mathbb{N} : n \geq 2$	$n \in \mathbb{N} : n \geq 2$	$n \in \mathbb{N} : n \geq 3$	$n \in \mathbb{N} : n \geq 2$	$n \in \mathbb{N} : n \geq 3$ $k \in \mathbb{N} : 1 \leq k \leq \lfloor n/2 \rfloor$	$n \in \mathbb{N} : n \geq 2$ $k \in \mathbb{N} : 1 \leq k \leq n-1$	$m,n \in \mathbb{N} : m,n \geq 2$
λ_d	0	1	0	1	0	1	0
λ_l	0	0	0	0	0	0	0
N_n	n	n	n	n	n	n	mn
N_a	$2(n-1)$	$n-1$	$2n$	n	$2nk$	nk	$4mn-2m-2n$
N_e	$n-1$	$n-1$	n	n	nk	nk	$2mn-m-n$
A	$2(n-1)$	$n-1$	$2n$	n	$2nk$	nk	$4mn-2m-2n$
ρ	$2/n$	$1/n$	$2/(n-1)$	$1/(n-1)$	$2k/(n-1)$	$k/(n-1)$	$2(2mn-m-n)/mn(mn-1)$
α	0	1	0	1	0	1	0
$\langle \boldsymbol{a}^d \rangle$	$2(n-1)/n$	$(n-1)/n$	2	1	$2k$	k	$4-2(m+n)/mn$
$\langle \boldsymbol{a}^{total} \rangle$	$2(n-1)/n$	$2(n-1)/n$	2	2	$2k$	$2k$	$4-2(m+n)/mn$
$\langle A_i^d \rangle$	$2(n-1)/n$	$(n-1)/n$	2	1	$2k$	k	$4-2(m+n)/mn$
$\langle A_i^{total} \rangle$	$4(n-1)/n$	$2(n-1)/n$	4	2	$4k$	$2k$	$8-4(m+n)/mn$
d	$n-1$	$n-1$	n	n	$1+\lfloor (n-1)/k \rfloor$	$1+\lfloor (n-1)/k \rfloor$	$m+n-2$
r	$\lfloor n/2 \rfloor$	0	n	n	$1+\lfloor (n-1)/k \rfloor$	$1+\lfloor (n-1)/k \rfloor$	4
$\langle d_i^d \rangle$	$(n^2-1)/3$	$(n^2-1)/6$	Eq. (2.115)	$n(n+1)/2$	Eq. (2.115)	Eq. (2.122)	$4+(mn-1)(m+n)/3$
$\langle d_i^{total} \rangle$	$2(n^2-1)/3$	$(n^2-1)/3$	Eq. (2.115)	$n(n+1)$	Eq. (2.115)	Eq. (2.122)	$8+2(mn-1)(m+n)/3$
N_c	$n(n-1)$	$n(n-1)/2$	n^2	n^2	n^2	n^2	$(mn)^2$
D	$n(n^2-1)/3$	$n(n^2-1)/6$	Eq. (2.104)	$n^2(n+1)/2$	Eq. (2.116)	Eq. (2.123)	$4mn+mn(mn-1)(m+n)/3$
$\langle D \rangle$	$(n+1)/3$	$(n+1)/3$	Eq. (2.105)	$(n+1)/2$	Eq. (2.117)	Eq. (2.123)	$4/mn+(mn-1)(m+n)/3mn$
l	$(n^2-1)/3n$	$(n^2-1)/6n$	Eq. (2.105)	$(n+1)/2$	Eq. (2.117)	Eq. (2.123)	$4/mn+(mn-1)(m+n)/3mn$
ℓ	$(n-1)/2(H_n-1)$	$(n-1)/2(H_n-1)$	Eq. (2.106)	n/H_n	Eq. (2.118)	Eq. (2.124)	numerical

graph models. For instance, given a path graph of order n, we can conceive a new graph of the same order but not isomorphic to $\mathscr{P}_n$ by simply adding one undirected edge between its two terminal nodes. The resulting graph then forms a cycle through all its n nodes, and it is called a circle or *cycle graph* (Fig. 2.6b, left). Formulated in mathematically more rigorous terms, a cycle graph $\mathscr{C}_n = (\mathcal{N}, \mathcal{E})$ of order n is defined as a connected simple graph with $n = |\mathcal{N}| \geq 3$ nodes and $|\mathcal{E}| = 2n$ adjacency relations in which each node establishes exactly one adjacency relations with each of two distinct neighbouring nodes. A path of length n in $\mathscr{C}_n$ is thus necessarily a Hamiltonian cycle and represents a cycle of length n such that each closed path $\mathcal{P}_{ii} \in \mathscr{P}^n_{ii}$ in a simple graph will be isomorphic to $\mathscr{C}_n$. We already encountered an example of a cycle graph of order 3 in Section 2.2.5 in the form of the graph pattern $(2, 2, 2)$ which, by describing triangular relationships between nodes, plays an important role in measuring the clustering properties of undirected graphs. The graph $\mathscr{C}_3$ also constitutes the lowest-order cycle graph. This can easily be argued by noting that, firstly, although a self-loop itself is a cycle, a graph with one self-looped node is not simple; and secondly, the path between two nodes connected by an undirected edge in a simple graph is not a cycle.

Cycle graphs allow for an algebraically convenient representation in terms of $n \times n$ circulant matrices if, starting from a fixed reference node, all nodes are successively labelled with numbers $i \in \mathbb{N}$ according to their positions along the circular path. In this case, we find that $(i, i \bmod n + 1) \in \mathcal{E}$ as well as $(i \bmod n + 1, i) \in \mathcal{E}$ for $i \in [1, n]$, and the weight matrix of $\mathscr{C}_n$ takes the form

$$\boldsymbol{w} = \operatorname{circ}\left[(0, 1, \overbrace{0, \ldots, 0}^{n-3}, 1)\right]. \tag{2.100}$$

As cycle graphs, by definition, are not self-looped graphs, we furthermore have

$$w_{ij} = a_{ij} = A_{ij} = \delta[i \bmod n + 1 - j] + \delta[j \bmod n + 1 - i] \tag{2.101}$$

for $i, j \in [1, n]$. Both (2.100) and (2.101) then easily provide many graph-theoretical measures in algebraically exact terms (see Table 2.7). Most interesting here in regards to the geodesic distance between nodes is not that just any two distinct nodes $i, j \in \mathcal{N}$ of $\mathscr{C}_n$ are connected by at most two shortest path of length $d_{ij} = \min\{|i - j|, n - |i - j|\}$, but that each node of a cycle graph also draws two unique geodesic cycles of length $d_{ii} = n$. The $n \times n$ matrix

$$\boldsymbol{d} = \begin{cases} \operatorname{circ}\left[\left(n, \overbrace{1, 2, \ldots, \tfrac{n}{2} - 1}^{n/2-1}, \tfrac{n}{2}, \overbrace{\tfrac{n}{2} - 1, \ldots, 2, 1}^{n/2-1}\right)\right] & n \text{ even}, \\ \operatorname{circ}\left[\left(n, \underbrace{1, 2, \ldots, \tfrac{n-1}{2}}_{(n-1)/2}, \underbrace{\tfrac{n-1}{2}, \ldots, 2, 1}_{(n-1)/2}\right)\right] & n \text{ odd} \end{cases} \tag{2.102}$$

with non-zero diagonal elements then provides a representation of the geodesic distance matrix of $\mathscr{C}_n$. Due to the circulant nature of $\boldsymbol{d}$, both the in-distance and out-distance (2.61) of each node are identical, eventually yielding

$$\langle d_i^d \rangle = \frac{1}{2}\langle d_i^{total} \rangle = \begin{cases} n(n+4)/4 & n \text{ even,} \\ n(n+4)/4 - 1/4 & n \text{ odd} \end{cases} \tag{2.103}$$

with $d \in \{in, out\}$ for their averages. Moreover, with (2.102), one easily finds

$$D = \begin{cases} n^2(n+4)/4 & n \text{ even,} \\ n^2(n+4)/4 - n/4 & n \text{ odd} \end{cases} \tag{2.104}$$

for a cycle graph's geodesic graph distance,

$$\langle D \rangle = l = \begin{cases} (n+4)/4 & n \text{ even,} \\ (n+4)/4 - 1/4n & n \text{ odd} \end{cases} \tag{2.105}$$

for its average geodesic graph distance and characteristic path length by noting that $N_c = n^2$, as well as

$$\ell = \begin{cases} n^2/(3 + 2nH_{n/2-1}) & n \text{ even,} \\ n^2/(1 + 2nH_{(n-1)/2}) & n \text{ odd} \end{cases} \tag{2.106}$$

for the geodesic connectivity length of $\mathscr{C}_n$. It is important to stress here that the distinction between cycle graphs of even and odd order is a direct consequence of the existence of one additional shortest path of length $n/2$ between nodes i and $(i + n/2 - 1) \bmod n + 1$ in the case $\mathscr{C}_n$ has an even number of nodes.

Similar to the construction of a path digraph in the previous section, we can expand on the notion of a cycle graph by replacing each undirected edge in $\mathscr{C}_n$ with a directed edge in such a way that both the in-degree and out-degree of all nodes is exactly one, and eventually obtain a connected relational digraph called a *cycle digraph* $\mathscr{C}_n^d = (\mathcal{N}, \mathcal{E})$ of order $n = |\mathcal{N}| \geq 2$ and $|\mathcal{E}| = n$ as illustrated in Fig. 2.6b (right). The weight matrix of $\mathscr{C}_n^d$ is given by the $n \times n$ circulant matrix

$$\boldsymbol{w} = \text{circ}\left[(0, 1, \overbrace{0, \ldots, 0}^{n-2})\right], \tag{2.107}$$

and we have

$$w_{ij} = a_{ij} = A_{ij} = \delta[i \bmod n + 1 - j] \tag{2.108}$$

for $i, j \in [1, n]$. Moreover, as each path in a cycle digraph follows only one direction, the geodesic distance matrix of $\mathscr{C}_n^d$ must take the circulant form

$$\boldsymbol{d} = \text{circ}\left[(n, 1, 2, \ldots, n-1)\right] \tag{2.109}$$

for all n, thus yielding

$$d_i^{in} = d_i^{out} = \frac{1}{2} d_i^{total} = \sum_{j=1}^{n} j = \frac{1}{2} n(n+1) \tag{2.110}$$

$\forall i \in \mathcal{N}$. Explicit algebraic expressions for other measures characterising cycle graphs $\mathcal{C}_n^d$ can be obtained in an equally straightforward fashion by leveraging the circulant nature of both $\boldsymbol{w}$ and $\boldsymbol{d}$. Leaving this again as an exercise for the reader, we list in Table 2.7 a small selection of results.

Instead, let us conclude with a brief look at graph patterns isomorphic to $\mathcal{C}_n^d$. We already encountered with (11, 11) and (11, 11, 11) illustrated in Table 2.5 two such patterns which, representing relational digraphs isomorphic to $\mathcal{C}_2^d$ and $\mathcal{C}_3^d$, play a defining role in quantifying the bidirectional connectivity and clustering properties in directed graphs (see Section 2.2.5). The utilisation of graph patterns isomorphic to $\mathcal{C}_n^d$ for discerning a directed graph's structural makeup is, however, not restricted to cycle graphs of lowest order alone. Indeed, in a cycle digraph $\mathcal{C}_n^d = (\mathcal{N}, \mathcal{E})$ of arbitrary order n, each node $i \in \mathcal{N}$ does allow for exactly one Hamiltonian cycle, such that $\mathcal{P}_{ii} \in \mathscr{P}_{ii}^n = \mathscr{P}_{ii}$ and $\sum_{i \in \mathcal{N}} |\mathscr{P}_{ii}| = n$. As we will demonstrate in Section 6.4.4, this property of directed cycle graphs serves as a valuable asset in algebraically formalising the percolation transition in random graph models.

2.3.3 Ring Graphs

Similar to path graphs, cycle graphs, owing to their conceptual simplicity, also serve as indispensable building blocks in the construction of a large variety of other exact graph models. One undoubtedly important generalisation of the model of cycle graphs $\mathcal{C}_n$ is obtained by adding $2(k-1)$ adjacency relations $(i, (i+l) \bmod n + 1)$ and $((i+l) \bmod n + 1, i)$ with $l \in [1, k-1]$ for each of its nodes $i \in [1, n]$ to the set of edges. The resulting graph, exemplified in Fig. 2.6c (left), is called a ring graph and plays a defining role in the construction of the small-world random graph model of Watts and Strogatz introduced later in this section. Formally, a *k-ring graph* $\mathcal{C}_{n,k} = (\mathcal{N}, \mathcal{E})$ of order n is defined as a connected simple graph with $n = |\mathcal{N}| \geq 3$ nodes and $|\mathcal{E}| = 2kn, k \in \mathbb{N} : k \leq \lfloor (n-1)/2 \rfloor$ adjacency relations such that each node has exactly $2k$ nearest neighbours. By appropriately labelling nodes, the weight matrix can be represented in form of the $n \times n$ circulant matrix

$$\boldsymbol{w} = \text{circ}\Big[(0, \overbrace{1, \ldots, 1}^{k}, \overbrace{0, \ldots, 0}^{n-2k-1}, \overbrace{1, \ldots, 1}^{k})\Big]. \tag{2.111}$$

Naturally, the cycle graph $\mathscr{C}_n$ of order n is isomorphic to the 1-ring graph $\mathscr{C}_{n,1}$ and, thus, represents a special case of a k-ring graph. Moreover, as a k-ring graph, by definition, does not contain any self-looped nodes, we find

$$w_{ij} = a_{ij} = A_{ij} = \sum_{l=1}^{k} \Big(\delta[(i+l-1) \bmod n + 1 - j] + \delta[(j+l-1) \bmod n + 1 - i]\Big) \tag{2.112}$$

for $i, j \in [1, n]$ as a suitable algebraic expression for the elements of its defining weight and adjacency matrix as well as its matrix of adjacency relations.

Some of the general and degree-based measures characterising k-ring graphs are listed in Table 2.7. The evaluation of distance-based measures for $\mathscr{C}_{n,k}$ is somewhat more involved, however, because the additional adjacency relations allow for shortcuts which significantly reduce the length of geodesic paths between pairs of its nodes. Indeed, as we successively labelled nodes of $\mathscr{C}_{n,k}$ with numbers $i \in \mathbb{N}$ according to their position along the ring, it can be shown that

$$\min_{\mathcal{P}_{ij} \in \mathscr{P}_{ij}} |\mathcal{P}_{ij}| = \begin{cases} \min\left\{1 + \left\lfloor \frac{|i-j|-1}{k} \right\rfloor, 1 + \left\lfloor \frac{n-|i-j|-1}{k} \right\rfloor\right\} & \text{if } i \neq j, \\ 1 + \left\lfloor \frac{n-1}{k} \right\rfloor & \text{if } i = j \end{cases}$$

yields the length of the shortest path $\mathcal{P}_{ij}$ between two nodes $i, j \in \mathcal{N}$, and that the geodesic distance matrix of $\mathscr{C}_{n,k}$ will eventually take the circulant form

$$\begin{aligned} \boldsymbol{d} = \operatorname{circ}\Bigg[\Bigg(1 + \left\lfloor \tfrac{n-1}{k} \right\rfloor, \overbrace{1, \ldots, 1}^{k}, \overbrace{2, \ldots, 2}^{k}, \ldots, \overbrace{\left\lfloor \tfrac{n-2}{2k} \right\rfloor, \ldots, \left\lfloor \tfrac{n-2}{2k} \right\rfloor}^{k}, \qquad \qquad (2.113) \\ \underbrace{1 + \left\lfloor \tfrac{n-2}{2k} \right\rfloor, \ldots, 1 + \left\lfloor \tfrac{n-2}{2k} \right\rfloor}_{n-1-2k\lfloor (n-2)/2k \rfloor}, \underbrace{\left\lfloor \tfrac{n-2}{2k} \right\rfloor, \ldots, \left\lfloor \tfrac{n-2}{2k} \right\rfloor}_{k}, \ldots, \underbrace{2, \ldots, 2}_{k}, \underbrace{1, \ldots, 1}_{k}\Bigg)\Bigg] \end{aligned}$$

for n even, and

$$\begin{aligned} \boldsymbol{d} = \operatorname{circ}\Bigg[\Bigg(1 + \left\lfloor \tfrac{n-1}{k} \right\rfloor, \overbrace{1, \ldots, 1}^{k}, \overbrace{2, \ldots, 2}^{k}, \ldots, \overbrace{\left\lfloor \tfrac{n-3}{2k} \right\rfloor, \ldots, \left\lfloor \tfrac{n-3}{2k} \right\rfloor}^{k}, \qquad \qquad (2.114) \\ \underbrace{1 + \left\lfloor \tfrac{n-3}{2k} \right\rfloor, \ldots, 1 + \left\lfloor \tfrac{n-3}{2k} \right\rfloor}_{n-1-2k\lfloor (n-3)/2k \rfloor}, \underbrace{\left\lfloor \tfrac{n-3}{2k} \right\rfloor, \ldots, \left\lfloor \tfrac{n-3}{2k} \right\rfloor}_{k}, \ldots, \underbrace{2, \ldots, 2}_{k}, \underbrace{1, \ldots, 1}_{k}\Bigg)\Bigg] \end{aligned}$$

for n odd. With (2.113) and (2.114), we then obtain

$$\langle d_i^d \rangle = \frac{1}{2} \langle d_i^{total} \rangle = \begin{cases} n + \left\lfloor \frac{n-1}{k} \right\rfloor + (n-k-1) \left\lfloor \frac{n-2}{2k} \right\rfloor - k \left\lfloor \frac{n-2}{2k} \right\rfloor^2 & n \text{ even}, \\ n + \left\lfloor \frac{n-1}{k} \right\rfloor + (n-k-1) \left\lfloor \frac{n-3}{2k} \right\rfloor - k \left\lfloor \frac{n-3}{2k} \right\rfloor^2 & n \text{ odd} \end{cases} \tag{2.115}$$

for the average node distances with $d \in \{in, out\}$, which yields

$$D = n \langle d_i^{in} \rangle = n \langle d_i^{out} \rangle \tag{2.116}$$

for the geodesic graph distance,

$$\langle D\rangle = l = \langle d_i^{in}\rangle/n = \langle d_i^{out}\rangle/n \tag{2.117}$$

for the average geodesic graph and node distance, and

$$\ell = \begin{cases} n\left(\frac{1}{1+\lfloor(n-1)/k\rfloor} + \frac{n+2k-1}{1+\lfloor(n-2)/2k\rfloor} - 2k + 2kH_{\lfloor(n-2)/2k\rfloor}\right)^{-1} & n \text{ even,} \\ n\left(\frac{1}{1+\lfloor(n-1)/k\rfloor} + \frac{n+2k-1}{1+\lfloor(n-3)/2k\rfloor} - 2k + 2kH_{\lfloor(n-3)/2k\rfloor}\right)^{-1} & n \text{ odd} \end{cases} \tag{2.118}$$

as a challenging expression for the geodesic connectivity length (2.68) of $\mathscr{C}_{n,k}$.

Finally, let us explore the construction of a ring digraph by directing each edge of $\mathscr{C}_{n,k}$ clockwise or counter-clockwise around the ring (Fig. 2.6c, right). Both approaches necessarily yield isomorphic graphs, such that we can define a *k-ring digraph* $\mathscr{C}^d_{n,k} = (\mathcal{N}, \mathcal{E})$ of order n as a connected relational digraph with $n = |\mathcal{N}| \geq 2$ nodes and $|\mathcal{E}| = kn, k \in \mathbb{N} : k \leq n-1$ adjacency relations in which each node has an in-degree and out-degree of k, and whose weight matrix can be represented in the form of the $n \times n$ circulant matrix

$$\boldsymbol{w} = \text{circ}\left[(0, \overbrace{1, \ldots, 1}^{k}, \overbrace{0, \ldots, 0}^{n-k-1})\right] \tag{2.119}$$

with elements given by

$$w_{ij} = a_{ij} = A_{ij} = \sum_{l=1}^{k} \delta[(i + l - 1) \bmod n + 1 - j] \tag{2.120}$$

for $i, j \in [1, n]$ in terms of Kronecker's delta. As paths in $\mathscr{C}^d_{n,k}$ follow only one direction, the geodesic distance matrix of a k-ring digraph can be represented in the arguably simpler form

$$\boldsymbol{d} = \text{circ}\Big[\Big(1 + \left\lfloor \tfrac{n-1}{k} \right\rfloor, \overbrace{1, \ldots, 1}^{k}, \overbrace{2, \ldots, 2}^{k}, \ldots \tag{2.121}$$

$$\ldots, \underbrace{\left\lfloor \tfrac{n-1}{k} \right\rfloor, \ldots, \left\lfloor \tfrac{n-1}{k} \right\rfloor}_{k}, \underbrace{1 + \left\lfloor \tfrac{n-1}{k} \right\rfloor, \ldots, 1 + \left\lfloor \tfrac{n-1}{k} \right\rfloor}_{n-1-k\lfloor(n-1)/k\rfloor}\Big)\Big]$$

valid for n both even and odd. Moreover, with this, we then quickly find

$$\langle d_i^d\rangle = \frac{1}{2}\langle d_i^{total}\rangle = \frac{1}{2}\left(1 + \left\lfloor \frac{n-1}{k} \right\rfloor\right)\left(2n - k\left\lfloor \frac{n-1}{k} \right\rfloor\right) \tag{2.122}$$

for the average node distances, and

$$D = n^2\langle D\rangle = n^2 l = n\langle d_i^{in}\rangle = n\langle d_i^{out}\rangle, \tag{2.123}$$

$$\ell = n\left(\frac{k+n}{1 + \lfloor(n-1)/k\rfloor} - k + kH_{\lfloor(n-1)/k\rfloor}\right)^{-1} \tag{2.124}$$

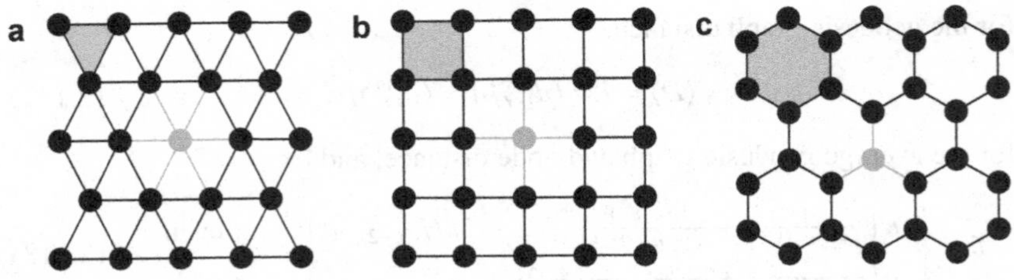

Figure 2.7 Examples of finite lattice graphs. **a:** Regular triangular grid graph $\mathcal{L}^{(3,6)}_{m,n}$ in which each node not residing at the boundary has six nearest neighbours (grey). **b:** Square grid graph $\mathcal{L}^{(4,4)}_{m,n}$ in which each node not residing at the boundary has four nearest neighbours. **c:** Hexagonal grid graph $\mathcal{L}^{(6,3)}_{m,n}$ in which each node not residing at the boundary has three nearest neighbours. These simple planar graphs correspond to the only possible regular tessellations in the Euclidean plane with identical convex regular polygons (grey area).

for the geodesic graph distance, average geodesic graph and node distance as well as geodesic connectivity length of $\mathcal{C}^d_{n,k}$ (Table 2.7). Due to these and other interesting characteristics complementing its simplicity, the ring graph resides at the conceptual heart of many other graph models both exact and random, such as the model of small-world networks which will be introduced in Section 2.3.6 and feature prominently in the context of our operator graph-theoretical framework in Part II.

2.3.4 Lattice Graphs

As a final representative example of exact graph models, let us here briefly touch upon the important class of *lattice graphs*. Lattice graphs, sometimes also called mesh or grid graphs, are simple planar graphs which form regular tilings, or tessellations, of the Euclidean plane with congruent convex regular polygons. It can easily be shown that there are no such tessellations for identical p-gons with $p \geq 7$; in fact, only three such regular tessellations exist in the Euclidean plane, those composed of triangles, squares or hexagons. Indeed, given a regular p-gon, the interior angle between the two edges at any of its corners, or nodes, is given by $\alpha = \pi - 2\pi/p$. Denoting with q the number of p-gons joined at each of a p-gon's nodes, we also have $q\alpha = 2\pi$. Eliminating the angle α in both of these relations, we then find

$$1/p + 1/q = 1/2 \tag{2.125}$$

as the necessary and sufficient condition governing the tessellation of the plane with identical regular polygons. Because $p, q \in \mathbb{N}\colon p, q > 0$, this diophantine equation eventually allows for only three distinct solutions (p, q), the triangle $(3, 6)$, square $(4, 4)$ and hexagon $(6, 3)$. The lattice graphs associated with these solutions are illustrated in Fig. 2.7 and respectively called *triangular grid graph, square grid graph* and *hexagonal grid graph*. In the remainder of this section, we will focus primarily on the square grid graph due to its instrumental role in some of the applications presented in Part II.

Before formulating a viable representation of square grid graphs, however, let us introduce another important notion in classical graph theory, namely that of the *Cartesian product*, sometimes simply called the *product*, of two graphs. Given two connected simple graphs $\mathcal{G}_1 = (\mathcal{N}_1, \mathcal{E}_1)$ and $\mathcal{G}_2 = (\mathcal{N}_2, \mathcal{E}_2)$ with $\mathcal{N}_1 \cap \mathcal{N}_2 = \emptyset$, the Cartesian graph product $\mathcal{G}_1 \Box \mathcal{G}_2 = (\mathcal{N}, \mathcal{E})$ is defined as a connected simple graph with a set of nodes $\mathcal{N}$ given by the Cartesian product $\mathcal{N}_1 \times \mathcal{N}_2$ such that

$$\mathcal{N} = \Big\{(i_1, i_2) \colon i_1 \in \mathcal{N}_1 \wedge i_2 \in \mathcal{N}_2\Big\},$$

and a set of edges $\mathcal{E}$ comprised of pairs of adjacent nodes $((i_1, i_2), (j_1, j_2))$ with $i_1, j_1 \in \mathcal{N}_1$ and $i_2, j_2 \in \mathcal{N}_2$ such that

$$\Big((i_1, i_2), (j_1, j_2)\Big) \in \mathcal{E} \Leftrightarrow \Big(i_1 = j_1 \wedge (i_2, j_2) \in \mathcal{E}_2\Big) \vee \Big(i_2 = j_2 \wedge (i_1, j_1) \in \mathcal{E}_1\Big).$$

Utilising this notion, a finite square grid graph $\mathcal{L}_{m,n}^{(4,4)}$ of spatial dimension $m \times n$ with $m, n \in \mathbb{N} \colon m, n \geq 2$ is then a connected simple planar graph of order $|\mathcal{N}| = mn$ with $|\mathcal{E}| = 2(2mn - m - n)$ adjacency relations, which is defined by the Cartesian product of a path graph $\mathcal{P}_m$ of order m with a path graph $\mathcal{P}_n$ of order n such that $\mathcal{L}_{m,n}^{(4,4)} := \mathcal{P}_m \Box \mathcal{P}_n$. The construction of square grid graphs is illustrated in Fig. 2.8a alongside some representative examples which include the *square graph* $\mathcal{L}_{2,2}^{(4,4)} := \mathcal{P}_2 \Box \mathcal{P}_2$, the *domino graph* $\mathcal{L}_{2,3}^{(4,4)} := \mathcal{P}_2 \Box \mathcal{P}_3$ and the *ladder graph* $\mathcal{L}_{2,n}^{(4,4)} := \mathcal{P}_2 \Box \mathcal{P}_n$ in Fig. 2.8b–d.

Due to its conception as a Cartesian graph product, each node of a grid graph $\mathcal{L}_{m,n}^{(4,4)}$ is uniquely identified by an ordered set of two coordinates (k, l) with $k, l \in \mathbb{N} : k \in [1, m], l \in [1, n]$. In order to arrive at a viable formalisation of its weight matrix and, for that matter, other graph measures, it is certainly more convenient to label each node of $\mathcal{L}_{m,n}^{(4,4)}$ consecutively by integer numbers $i \in \mathbb{N} : i \in [1, mn]$. To that end, let us introduce the two mappings

$$(k, l) \to i \colon \mathbb{N} \times \mathbb{N} \to \mathbb{N}\,,\ i = m(l - 1) + k \tag{2.126}$$

and

$$i \to (k, l) \colon \mathbb{N} \to \mathbb{N} \times \mathbb{N}\,,\ (k, l) = \left(i - m\left\lfloor \frac{i-1}{m} \right\rfloor, 1 + \left\lfloor \frac{i-1}{m} \right\rfloor\right) \tag{2.127}$$

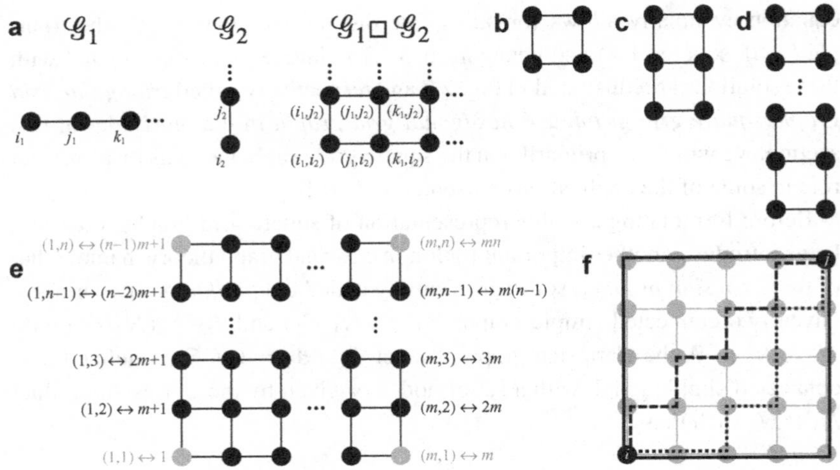

Figure 2.8 Construction of square grid graphs. **a:** Cartesian graph product $\mathscr{G}_1 \square \mathscr{G}_2$ of two simple graphs $\mathscr{G}_1$ and $\mathscr{G}_2$ of order m and n, respectively. If both $\mathscr{G}_1$ and $\mathscr{G}_2$ are path graphs, $\mathscr{G}_1 \square \mathscr{G}_2$ yields square grid graphs $\mathscr{L}_{m,n}^{(4,4)}$, such as for $(m,n) = (2,2)$ the square graph (**b**), for $(m,n) = (2,3)$ the domino graph graph (**c**), or for $(m,n) = (2,n)$ the ladder graph (**d**). **e:** Relabelling of nodes in a general square grid graph $\mathscr{L}_{m,n}^{(4,4)}$ according to (2.126) and (2.127), with the four corner nodes marked in grey. **f:** Each pair of distinct nodes in a grid graph $\mathscr{L}_{m,n}^{(4,4)}$ is connected by multiple shortest paths (black solid, dashed and dotted), as exemplified here for the two corner nodes $i = 1$ and $j = mn$.

for translating between finite grid coodinates and node labels (Fig. 2.8e). By employing these mappings, it can then be shown that the elements of the weight matrix of a finite grid graph $\mathscr{L}_{m,n}^{(4,4)}$ are given by

$$\begin{aligned} w_{ij} = {} & \delta[i+1-j] + \delta[i-1-j] + \delta[i+m-j] + \delta[i-m-j] \\ & - \delta[i+1-j]\,\delta\Big[i-m-m\Big\lfloor \tfrac{i-1}{m} \Big\rfloor\Big] - \delta[i-1-j]\,\delta\Big[j-m-m\Big\lfloor \tfrac{j-1}{m} \Big\rfloor\Big] \end{aligned} \tag{2.128}$$

with $i, j \in [1, mn]$, where the last two terms ensure that the boundary conditions restricting the dimension of the square grid graph are respected.

With (2.128), and by recalling that $w_{ij} = a_{ij} = A_{ij}$ for simple graphs, most general and degree-based measures characterising $\mathscr{L}_{m,n}^{(4,4)}$ can be exactly evaluated in a straightforward fashion (see Table 2.7 for a small selection of results). Distance-dependent measures, on the other hand, require more reflection as the 2-dimensional nature of the square grid graph typically allows for a multitude of shortest paths connecting two of its nodes (Fig. 2.8f). Indeed, it can be shown that the distance between two distinct nodes with coordinates (k, l) and (k', l') is here governed by the ℓ^1-norm $|k - k'| + |l - l'|$, defined in (2.27), and equals the length of any shortest path which can be drawn between these nodes. As an interesting historical sidenote, it is worth mentioning that this norm is commonly referred to as Manhattan or taxicab distance due to its relevance as a distance measure on the streets of Manhattan, for which $\mathscr{L}^{(4,4)}_{m,n}$ itself provides a viable graph-theoretical model [76, 81]. Employing again the coordinate mapping (2.127) and recognising that each node of a grid graph allows for at least two geodesic cycles of length four, we eventually obtain

$$d_{ij} = \begin{cases} \left| i - j - m\left(\left\lfloor \frac{i-1}{m} \right\rfloor - \left\lfloor \frac{j-1}{m} \right\rfloor\right)\right| + \left|\left\lfloor \frac{i-1}{m} \right\rfloor - \left\lfloor \frac{j-1}{m} \right\rfloor\right| & \text{for } i \neq j, \\ 4 & \text{for } i = j \end{cases} \tag{2.129}$$

with $i, j \in [1, mn]$ for the elements of the geodesic distance matrix of a grid graph $\mathscr{L}^{(4,4)}_{m,n}$. The geodesic distance d_{ij} will reach its maximum either for a geodesic cycle or a path connecting node i to one of the four corner nodes $j \in \{1, m, (n-1)m, mn\}$ (see Fig. 2.8e, grey), thus yielding

$$\epsilon_i = \max\left\{d_{ii}, d_{i1}, d_{im}, d_{i,(n-1)m+1}, d_{i,mn}\right\} \tag{2.130}$$

with $\mathsf{r} = 4 \leq \epsilon_i \leq m + n - 2 = \mathsf{d}$ for the geodesic node eccentricities, geodesic graph radius and diameter of $\mathscr{L}^{(4,4)}_{m,n}$. Finally, using the 2-dimensional coordinate representation of its nodes, the sum over the geodesic distances between all possible pairs of nodes in a grid graph can be shown to evaluate to

$$\begin{aligned} D = \sum_{k=1}^{m}\sum_{l=1}^{n}\Bigg\{ & \sum_{k'=1}^{k-1}\left(\sum_{l'=1}^{l-1}(k-k'+l-l') + \sum_{l'=l+1}^{n}(k-k'+l'-l) + k-k'\right) \\ & + \sum_{k'=k+1}^{m}\left(\sum_{l'=1}^{l-1}(k'-k+l-l') + \sum_{l'=l+1}^{n}(k'-k+l'-l) + k'-k\right) \\ & + \sum_{l'=1}^{l-1}(l-l') + \sum_{l'=l+1}^{n}(l'-l) + 4\Bigg\} \\ = {} & 4mn + mn(mn-1)(m+n)/3, \end{aligned} \tag{2.131}$$

from which, with $N_c = (mn)^2$, the average geodesic graph distance $\langle D \rangle$ and characteristic path length l follow. For other distance-dependent measures, however, similarly explicit expressions are not that readily available.

2.3.5 Erdős–Rényi and Gilbert Random Graphs

Having covered some of the more prominent exact graph models in the previous sections, let us now proceed onto the second major type of graph models, namely that of random graphs. Due to both their conceptual transparency and frequency of use as descriptive vessel for a vast range of natural phenomena,

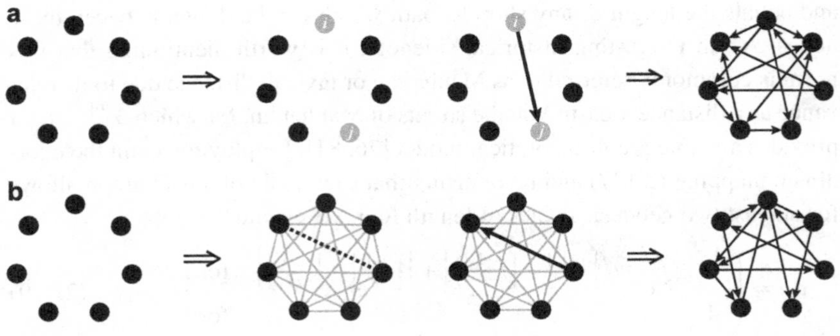

Figure 2.9 Examples of random graph models and their construction. **a:** Erdős–Rényi random digraph $\mathscr{R}^{dER}_{n,k}$. Given a set of nodes $\mathcal{N}$ (left), adjacency relations (i,j) are added to the set of edges $\mathcal{E}$ by selecting uniformly at random pairs of source and target nodes $i,j \in \mathcal{N}$ (middle) until $|\mathcal{E}|=k$ (right). **b:** Gilbert random digraph $\mathscr{R}^{dG}_{n,p}$. Given a set of nodes $\mathcal{N}$ (left), an adjacency relation (i,j) is added to $\mathcal{E}$ with probability p (middle) until all possible ordered pairs of nodes $i,j \in \mathcal{N}$ were considered (right).

the undoubtedly most important of these models are simply comprised of pairs of uniform-randomly connected nodes. Historically, two variations of such random graphs have emerged which, albeit closely related, show subtle difference in their construction and statistical properties. The first variation, introduced by Erdős and Rényi [38], defines a random graph as a relational digraph $\mathscr{G} = (\mathcal{N}, \mathcal{E})$ with a fixed set of nodes $\mathcal{N}$ from which directed edges $(i, j) \in \mathcal{E}$ are constructed by selecting uniformly at random nodes $i, j \in \mathcal{N} : i \neq j$ until $|\mathcal{E}| = k$ distinct adjacency relations are obtained (Fig. 2.9a). In what follows, we will refer to this model as the *Erdős–Rényi random digraph* $\mathscr{R}^{dER}_{n,k}$ of order $n \in \mathbb{N}$ with $k \in \mathbb{N}_0$ edges. Similarly, an undirected version of this model, the *Erdős–Rényi random graph* $\mathscr{R}^{ER}_{n,k}$ of order n with k edges, is defined as a simple graph whose set of edges $\mathcal{E}$ is comprised of reciprocal node pairs (i, j) and (j, i) which are constructed by uniform-randomly selecting distinct nodes i and j from a given set of nodes $\mathcal{N}$ until $|\mathcal{E}| = 2k$ is satisfied.

Contemporaneously and independently of Erdős and Rényi, a second variation of the original concept of a random graph was introduced by Gilbert [49]. Here, given a set of nodes $\mathcal{N}$ of cardinality $n = |\mathcal{N}|$, a relational digraph is constructed by considering all possible ordered pairs of distinct nodes $i, j \in \mathcal{N}$ and adding, with a fixed probability $p \in \mathbb{Q} : 0 \leq p \leq 1$, adjacency relations (i, j) to its set of edges $\mathcal{E}$ (Fig. 2.9b). In the remainder of this book, we will refer to this model as the *Gilbert random digraph* $\mathscr{R}^{dG}_{n,p}$ of order n and connection probability p. Finally, by adding with probability p both (i, j) and (j, i) for each pair of nodes $i, j \in \mathcal{N} : j > i$ to the set of edges $\mathcal{E}$, we eventually obtain a simple graph which defines the model of a *Gilbert random graph* $\mathcal{R}^G_{n,p}$ of order n and connection probability p.

In contrast to Erdős–Rényi random graphs, owing to the probabilistic nature of selecting edges from the set of all possible node pairs, the cardinality of $\mathcal{E}$ in individual realisations of a given Gilbert random graph or digraph model is not fixed but varies around the statistical expectation value $\langle|\mathcal{E}|\rangle = pn(n-1)$. It can then be argued that the model of Erdős–Rényi random graphs $\mathcal{R}^{ER}_{n,k}$ and digraphs $\mathcal{R}^{dER}_{n,k}$ will exhibit properties similar to that of Gilbert random graphs $\mathcal{R}^G_{n,p}$ with a connection probability $p = 2k/n(n-1)$ and digraphs $\mathcal{R}^{dG}_{n,p}$ with $p = k/n(n-1)$ respectively. Conversely, properties of $\mathcal{R}^G_{n,p}$ and $\mathcal{R}^{dG}_{n,p}$ will match closely those of respective realisations of $\mathcal{R}^{ER}_{n,k}$ with $k = \lfloor pn(n-1)/2 + 1/2 \rfloor$ undirected edges and $\mathcal{R}^{dER}_{n,k}$ with $k = \lfloor pn(n-1)+1/2 \rfloor$ directed edges. However, these apparent similarities in the characteristics of both types of random graph models for appropriately chosen model parameters apply only to the statistical expectation value of graph-theoretical measures over many – ideally, an infinite number of – realisations (see Table 2.8). This is an important subtlety which has to be considered especially at finite scales – for instance, when dealing with computational realisations of Erdős–Rényi and Gilbert random graphs as models of the same phenomenon – and can be shown to become negligible solely in the asymptotic limit $pn^2 \to \infty$ for $n \to \infty$.

Despite their conceptual proximity as models of uniform-randomly interconnected nodes, it is the Gilbert type of random graphs which dominates in the graph-theoretical literature alongside a vast number of computational applications, as it is both algebraically and computationally arguably easier to deal with than the Erdős–Rényi type. We will briefly touch upon this subject again in Section 5.1.3. Indeed, with $\langle|\mathcal{E}|\rangle = pn(n-1)$, we have $pn(n-1)/2$ and $pn(n-1)$ for the statistical expectation value of the number of edges $\langle N_e \rangle$ in realisations of $\mathcal{R}^G_{n,p}$ and $\mathcal{R}^{dG}_{n,p}$, respectively. In Gilbert random digraphs, we find that $\langle N_{se} \rangle = p^2 n(n-1)/2$ of these edges will be, on average, symmetric, while asymmetrical edges occur with a probability $p(1-p)$, thus yielding $\langle N_{ae} \rangle = p(1-p)n(n-1)$. The expected asymmetry index of $\mathcal{R}^{dG}_{n,p}$ is then

$$\langle \alpha \rangle := \frac{\langle N_{ae} \rangle}{\langle A \rangle - \langle N_{se} \rangle} = 2\,\frac{p(1-p)n(n-1)}{pn(n-1) - p^2 n(n-1)/2} = 2\,\frac{1-p}{2-p}, \tag{2.132}$$

which eventually delivers the interesting relation

$$\langle A \rangle = \frac{2}{n(n-1)}\,\frac{\langle \alpha \rangle - 1}{\langle \alpha \rangle - 2} \tag{2.133}$$

between the statistical expectation values of the total adjacency and asymmetry index in realisations of $\mathcal{R}^{dG}_{n,p}$ for fixed n and p, a result which proves to be somewhat more challenging to demonstrate for Erdős–Rényi digraphs.

A similar probabilistic approach can be utilised for deducing the expected degree distribution in Gilbert random graphs $\mathcal{R}^G_{n,p}$. To that end, we first note that the probability for a given node to be embedded into the network with exactly a edges is $p^a(1-p)^{n-1-a}$, and that there are a total of $\binom{n-1}{a}$ distinct configurations of a edges among $n-1$ possible edges. This then yields for the total node degree distribution (2.30) in $\mathcal{R}^G_{n,p}$ the binomial distribution

$$p[\boldsymbol{a}^{total}; a] = \binom{n-1}{a} p^a(1-p)^{n-1-a}, \tag{2.134}$$

which takes for $p\to 0$ with $pn = const$ the form of a Poisson distribution,

$$\lim_{\substack{p\to 0\\ np=const}} p[\boldsymbol{a}^{total}; a] = \frac{(pn)^a}{a!} \mathrm{e}^{-pn}, \tag{2.135}$$

and can be further approximated by the normal, or Gaussian, distribution

$$\lim_{n\to\infty} p[\boldsymbol{a}^{total}; a] = \frac{1}{\sqrt{2\pi pn}} \exp\left[-\frac{(a-pn)^2}{2pn}\right] \tag{2.136}$$

in the asymptotic limit $n\to\infty$.

In Table 2.8 we list some of the measures which characterise both Erdős–Rényi and Gilbert random graphs. Although other measures can be obtained and similarly expressed in algebraically explicit terms by using probabilistic arguments not unlike those employed above, many of these results are valid only under stringent assumptions, such as for large network size or small connectedness. However, as we will exemplify in Chapter 6, the representation of random graph models within our operator graph-theoretical framework will remedy at least some of these limitations and eventually provide the toolset for an algebraically more rigorous study of these important random graph models at finite scales.

2.3.6 Watts–Strogatz Random Graphs

The Erdős–Rényi and Gilbert random graphs introduced in the previous section certainly dominate as descriptive models of natural phenomena in a wide range of fields in the applied graph-theoretical literature. However, many real-world networks exhibit properties which deviate from the simplistic random connectivity pattern captured by these models. Indeed, it has been found that, among others, metabolic [19, 62] and food networks [83], technical networks such as that established by World Wide Web hyperlinks [4], economic networks [32, 66], networks of various transportation systems [55, 94], the electric

Table 2.8 *Measuring random graph models.*

	$\mathcal{R}^{ER}_{n,k}$	$\mathcal{R}^{dER}_{n,k}$	$\mathcal{R}^{G}_{n,p}$	$\mathcal{R}^{dG}_{n,p}$	$\mathcal{R}^{WS}_{n,k,q}$	$\mathcal{R}^{BA}_{n,k,n_0,k_0}$
	$n\in\mathbb{N}$ $k\in\mathbb{N}_0: 0\le k\le n(n-1)/2$	$n\in\mathbb{N}$ $k\in\mathbb{N}_0: 0\le k\le n(n-1)$	$n\in\mathbb{N}$ $p\in\mathbb{Q}: 0\le p\le 1$	$n\in\mathbb{N}$ $p\in\mathbb{Q}: 0\le p\le 1$	$n\in\mathbb{N}: n\ge 3$ $k\in\mathbb{N}: 1\le k\le\lfloor n/2\rfloor$ $q\in\mathbb{Q}: 1\le q\le 1$	$n\in\mathbb{N}: n\ge 2$ $k\in\mathbb{N}: 1\le k\le n_0$ $n_0\in\mathbb{N}: 2\le n_0\le n$ $k_0\in\mathbb{N}: 1\le k_0\le n_0(n_0-1)/2$
λ_d	0	1	0	1	0	0
λ_l	0	0	0	0	0	0
N_n	n	n	n	n	n	n
N_a	$2k$	k	–	–	$2nk$	$2k_0 + 2k(n - n_0)$
$\langle N_a\rangle$	–	–	$pn(n-1)$	$pn(n-1)$	–	–
N_e	k	k	–	–	kn	$k_0 + k(n - n_0)$
$\langle N_e\rangle$	–	–	$pn(n-1)/2$	$pn(n-1)$	–	–
A	$2k$	k	–	–	$2nk$	$2k_0 + 2k(n - n_0)$
$\langle A\rangle$	–	–	$pn(n-1)$	$pn(n-1)$	–	–
ρ	$2k/n(n-1)$	$k/n(n-1)$	–	–	$2k/(n-1)$	$(2k_0 + 2k(n-n_0))/n(n-1)$
$\langle\rho\rangle$	–	–	p	p	–	–
α	0	–	0	–	0	0
$\langle\alpha\rangle$	–	$1 - \dfrac{k}{2n(n-1)-k}$	–	$2(1-p)/(2-p)$	–	–
$\langle \boldsymbol{a}^d\rangle$	$2k/n$	$2k/n$	$p(n-1)$	$p(n-1)$	$2k$	$(2k_0 + 2k(n-n_0))/n$
$\langle \boldsymbol{a}^{total}\rangle$	$2k/n$	$4k/n$	$p(n-1)$	$2p(n-1)$	$2k$	$(2k_0 + 2k(n-n_0))/n$
$\langle A_i^d\rangle$	$2k/n$	$2k/n$	$p(n-1)$	$p(n-1)$	$2k$	$(2k_0 + 2k(n-n_0))/n$
$\langle A_i^{total}\rangle$	$4k/n$	$4k/n$	$2p(n-1)$	$2p(n-1)$	$4k$	$(4k_0 + 4k(n-n_0))/n$
$p[\boldsymbol{a}^{total}; a]$	$\binom{n-1}{a}\dfrac{\rho^a}{(1-\rho)^{-(n-1-a)}}$	$\binom{n-1}{a}\dfrac{(2\rho)^a}{(1-2\rho)^{-(n-1-a)}}$	$\binom{n-1}{a}p^a(1-p)^{n-1-a}$ (spans $\mathcal{R}^{G}_{n,p}$ and $\mathcal{R}^{dG}_{n,p}$)		Eq. (2.137)	$\sim a^{-3}$

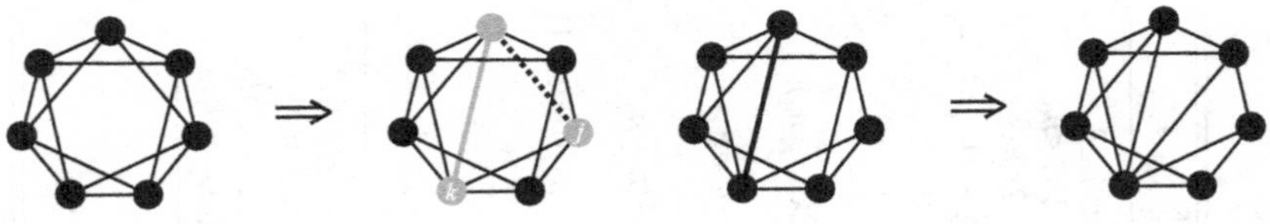

Figure 2.10 Example of a Watts–Strogatz small-world random graph $\mathcal{R}^{WS}_{n,k,q}$ and its construction. Given a k-ring graph $\mathcal{C}_{n,k}$ (left), the target node j of an edge (i,j) is rewired with probability q towards a new target node $k \in \mathcal{N}$ (middle) until all edges of $\mathcal{C}_{n,k}$ were considered (right).

power grid [5] as well as various social networks [91, 99, 107] not only maintain a low average number of links between arbitrary pairs of connected nodes, as typical for Erdős–Rényi and Gilbert random graphs, but at the same time also display an abundance of triangular graph patterns, that is, a local clustering of nodes. Both properties result in a high degree of local redundancy which exceeds that found in simple random graph models. Due to their practical importance across many research fields, graphs which encompass both a high clustering of network connections and a small average geodesic distance between nodes as their primary structural characteristics now comprise their own model class and are called *small-world networks*.

The first and undoubtedly most prominent model of small-world networks was introduced in a seminal paper by Watts and Strogatz [109]. A *Watts–Strogatz random graph* $\mathcal{R}^{WS}_{n,k,q} = (\mathcal{N}, \mathcal{E})$ of order n is defined as a simple graph with $n = |\mathcal{N}| \geq 3$ nodes subject to $|\mathcal{E}| = 2nk$ adjacency relations with $k \in \mathbb{N}: 1 \leq k < \lfloor n/2 \rfloor$, and it is constructed by rewiring the edges of a k-ring graph $\mathcal{C}_{n,k}$ with a given probability $q \in \mathbb{Q}: 0 \leq q \leq 1$. This rewiring is done by considering all nodes i of $\mathcal{C}_{n,k}$ and choosing for each edge $(i, (i+l) \bmod n + 1)$ with $l \in [0, k-1]$ uniformly at random a new target node $k \neq i$ from the subset of nodes which are not already nearest neighbours of i, as illustrated in Fig. 2.10. The abundance of triangular relationships between nodes in the initial ring graph $\mathcal{C}_{n,k}$ provides the baseline for a high clustering coefficient, while the subsequent rewiring introduces shortcuts which quickly lead to a significant shortening of the average geodesic distance between pairs of nodes. However, it is important to stress here that the defining characteristics of a small-world network occur, for any n and k, only in a very narrow range of the possible rewiring probability q, and for $q \ll 1$. Indeed, if $q \rightarrow 1$, the initial symmetry and high clustering of nodes in $\mathcal{C}_{n,k}$ will have all but disappeared, leaving $\mathcal{R}^{WS}_{n,k,1}$ to display properties identical to an Erdős–Rényi random graph $\mathcal{R}^{ER}_{n,nk}$ in the statistical limit over many realisations.

Due to the more sophisticated nature of the Watts–Strogatz model, at least when compared to the simple random graphs introduced in the previous section, only a small fraction of graph measures for its characterisation is readily available in an algebraically explicit form which applies to the whole parameter spectrum of this model. Some of these measures are listed in Table 2.8. For example, it can be shown that

$$p[\mathbf{a}^{total}; a] = \begin{cases} 0 & \text{for } a < k, \\ \sum_{l=0}^{\min\{a-k,k\}} \binom{k}{l} (1-q)^l q^{k-l} \frac{(qk)^{a-k-l}}{(a-k-l)!} \mathrm{e}^{-qk} & \text{for } a \geq k \end{cases} \tag{2.137}$$

describes the total node degree distribution in Watts–Strogatz random graphs of arbitrary order and for all rewiring probabilities [13]. In the limit of the initial k-ring graph $\mathscr{C}_{n,k}$, this expression then yields

$$\lim_{q \to 0} p[\mathbf{a}^{total}; a] = \delta[a - 2k], \tag{2.138}$$

and for $q \to 1$, as expected, a Poisson distribution

$$\lim_{q \to 1} p[\mathbf{a}^{total}; a] = \frac{(2k)^a}{a!} \mathrm{e}^{-2k} \tag{2.139}$$

similar to that presented in (2.135) for realisations of an Erdős–Rényi random graph in the asymptotic limit $n \to \infty, pn = const.$ For many other measures, however, we are less lucky and often find explicit expressions only under stringent conditions or for excessively narrow parameter regimes. In Part II, we will attempt to remedy this situation not only by proposing an algebraically rigorous construction of the adjacency matrix of $\mathscr{R}^{WS}_{n,k,q}$ within our operator graph-theoretical framework, but by extending with the conception of a canonical model for Watts–Strogatz random digraphs $\mathscr{R}^{dWS}_{n,k,q}$ the very notion of a small-world network originally proposed by Watts and Strogatz.

2.3.7 Barabási–Albert Random Graphs

The short list of random networks introduced so far included solely models of *static graphs* with a predefined number of nodes whose defining structural characteristics are present only after the completion of the network's construction. However, natural phenomena, alongside many artificial or human-made systems, and their associated graphs, often evolve over time. As an illustrative example of such *evolving graphs*, let us take a brief look at the network spanned by citations of academic papers [91] in a field such as high energy physics [73] or computer science [6]. Given a choice of references in the literature to cite from, researchers tend towards choosing already highly cited published work. Thus, if a new node in form of a new research paper is added to a given citation network, it will preferentially establish adjacency relations

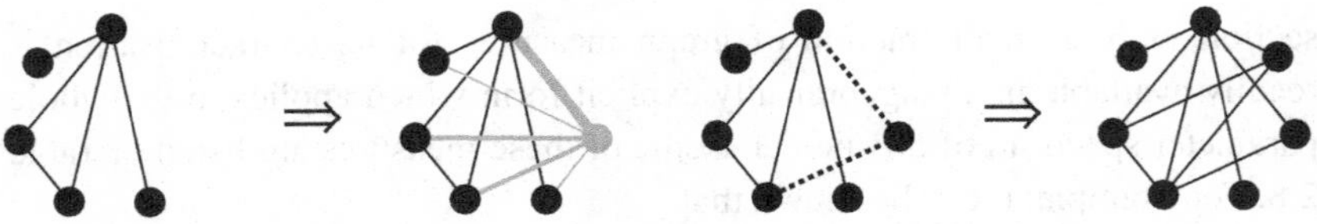

Figure 2.11 Example of a Barabási–Albert scale-free random graph $\mathcal{R}^{BA}_{n,k,n_0,k_0}$ and its construction. Starting with a small connected network with n_0 nodes and k_0 undirected edges (left), at each step in the construction a new node with k edges is added such that each new link to an already existing node is established with a probability which depends on the actual degree of the target node (middle; thicker grey lines indicate higher probability for adding an edge), until the graph size has reached n nodes (right).

with highly connected nodes already present in the network. This common practice leads to the emergence of a scale-free topological structure in which the node degree distribution follows an approximate power law behaviour, a universal property which was found also to reside at the very heart of many critical phenomena observed in complex self-organising systems in nature.

Networks which exhibit an approximate power law node degree distribution are called *scale-free graphs*. Due to the widespread occurrence of this structural feature, a large number of models of scale-free graphs and variations thereof were proposed over the past few decades. We will focus here on one of the historically first and most prominent of these models, namely the evolving *Barabási–Albert random graph* model of growth and preferential attachment [12]. The construction of a simple Barabási–Albert random graph $\mathcal{R}^{BA}_{n,k,n_0,k_0} = (\mathcal{N}, \mathcal{E})$ of order $n = |\mathcal{N}| \geq 2$ starts with a connected simple graph comprised of $n_0 \in \mathbb{N} : 2 \leq n_0 \leq n$ nodes and k_0 edges. This initial network is then recursively evolved in $n - n_0$ discrete steps by embedding, at each step, a new node with a fixed number $k \in \mathbb{N} : 1 \leq k \leq n_0$ of adjacency relations into the existing network in such a way that the newly added node j establishes a link to an already existing node i randomly with a probability given by a_i^{total}/A, that is, a probability linearly proportional to the total degree a_i^{total} of its potential target node i, as illustrated in Fig. 2.11.

After the completion of $n - n_0$ steps, the constructed graph $\mathcal{R}^{BA}_{n,k,n_0,k_0}$ will then be comprised of n nodes and a total of $|\mathcal{E}| = 2k_0 + 2k(n - n_0)$ adjacency relations. This results in an average total node degree of

$$\langle \boldsymbol{a}^{total} \rangle = (2k_0 + 2k(n - n_0))/n \tag{2.140}$$

for Barabási–Albert graphs of order n, which, for large n and $n_0, k_0 \ll n$, is approximated by $2k$. Moreover, it can be explicitly shown that for large networks, the node degree distribution will approach with $p[\boldsymbol{a}^{total}; a] \sim a^{-\gamma}$ a power law behaviour independent of n_0, k_0 and k, and with $\gamma = 3$ in the asymptotic limit $n \to \infty$ and for $n_0, k_0 \ll n$ [36, 70]. However, other graph measures for characterising $\mathscr{R}^{BA}_{n,k,n_0,k_0}$ will mostly elude an explicit formalisation beyond approximations without imposing stringently limiting assumptions, with Table 2.8 listing a few exceptions.

Finally, it is important to note that although the Barabási–Albert model of scale-free graphs received an exorbitant amount of attention since its original conception thanks to both its conceptional beauty and simplicity, the fixed exponent $\gamma = 3$ of its node degree distribution only rarely describes the behaviour observed in real-world scale-free graphs. For that reason, a whole host of modifications and generalisations has been proposed, ranging from preferential attachment models with constant offset terms and nonlinear attachment probability (e.g., see [36, 69, 70]), to models which allow for rewiring or removal of already-existing edges at each step (e.g., see [2, 35, 71, 103]), to models in which the addition of edges is guided by some specified fitness function (e.g., see [16, 17]) or principal of hierarchical organisation (e.g., see [92]), to mention but a few. Many of these variations of the original Barabási–Albert model serve as descriptive vessels for rather isolated real-world phenomena, and therefore, they will not be considered further. Instead, in Part II, we will focus within our operator graph-theoretical framework on the algebraic representations of the preferential attachment concept at the very heart of most scale-free graph models, on the basis of which the deduction of more specialised variations of the Barabási–Albert model should then, at least in principle, be possible.

2.4 Finite Graph Theory

Let us conclude our abridged introduction into classical graph theory by briefly reflecting on an intriguing yet often avoided line of thought which not only motivates the search for a more concise post-classical notion of a graph, but draws its delicate branches far beyond the subjects touched upon in this book. As already stressed in Chapter 1, graphs and networks, in their capacity of serving as descriptive models for real-world phenomena, are abstract and genuinely discrete mathematical objects of an inherently finite nature. In respecting this defining structural tenet, the overwhelming majority of measures and graph models employed throughout the literature, some of which we presented in the course of this chapter, are defined on algebraic rigorous grounds and naturally provide descriptions and characterisations of networks valid at finite scales. However, this algebraic formalisation also often hinders the further treatment of these descriptions and characterisations and forces the investigator to resort to analytic methods. Here, many graph-theoretical notions, when considered analytically under certain limiting asumptions, might unfortunately lead to conclusions which, albeit mathematically sound, can challenge the intuitive mind at best, or are wholly contradictory in nature at worst.

To illustrate this delicate point, let us consider the average geodesic graph distance $\langle D \rangle$ of a path graph $\mathcal{P}_n$ and a cycle graph $\mathcal{C}_n$. Recalling the corresponding algebraic expressions listed in Table 2.7, we immediately find

$$\langle D \rangle_{\mathcal{P}_n} = (n+1)/3 \overset{n\to\infty}{\to} \infty,$$

$$\langle D \rangle_{\mathcal{C}_n} = \left\{ \begin{array}{ll} (n+4)/4 & \text{for } n \text{ even,} \\ (n+4)/4 - 1/4n & \text{for } n \text{ odd} \end{array} \right\} \overset{n\to\infty}{\to} \infty$$

in the asymptotic limit. This result is certainly meaningful, as for each pair of nodes in either graph, another pair of nodes separated by a greater distance can be found. But what about the ratio of both measures? Looked at from a naive point of view, the only difference between $\mathcal{P}_n$ and $\mathcal{C}_n$ for finite n is one additional edge connecting both terminal nodes of the path graph, a subtlety which should become irrelevant in the asymptotic limit of infinite order as only one of these terminal nodes can ever be reached. Indeed, $\mathcal{P}_{n\to\infty}$ and $\mathcal{C}_{n\to\infty}$ can be considered as locally isomorphic in the sense that any subgraph of $\mathcal{C}_{n\to\infty}$ of arbitrary yet finite order is isomorphic to a path graph of the same order. For that reason, one would intuitively expect that the ratio between the average geodesic graph distances of both graphs approaches one. However, utilising the algebraic expressions presented in Section 2.3, we find with

$$\frac{\langle D \rangle_{\mathcal{P}_n}}{\langle D \rangle_{\mathcal{C}_n}} = \left\{ \begin{array}{ll} 4(n+1)/3(n+4) & \text{for } n \text{ even} \\ 4(n^2+n)/3(n^2+4n-1) & \text{for } n \text{ odd} \end{array} \right\} \overset{n\to\infty}{\to} \frac{4}{3} \tag{2.141}$$

a somewhat surprising result.

Certainly, it could be argued that the deviation from our naive expectation is a direct consequence of the fact that each pair of distinct nodes in a finite path graph is connected by exactly one and thus necessarily geodesic path, while in a finite cycle graph for each pair of nodes, two paths exist, with at least one of them being geodesic. The limit $n\to\infty$, however, will retain for only one of these paths a finite length, eventually rendering the geodesic distances between all pairs of distinct nodes in both $\mathcal{P}_{n\to\infty}$ and $\mathcal{C}_{n\to\infty}$ identical, and, thus, their ratio will differ from (2.141). We could then adjust our argument by noting that this is not the case for geodesic cycles. Indeed, closed paths can exist only in the cycle graph and will have infinite length in the asymptotic limit. But even after disregarding all geodesic cycles in $\mathcal{C}_{n\to\infty}$, the ratio of the average geodesic graph distance between distinct nodes in both graphs will remain with 4/3 distinct from our naive, albeit justified expectation informed by considering these models at finite scales.

Many more examples of this nature with similar and equally surprising observations can be constructed when exploring in a comparative fashion various exact graph models in their asymptotic limits. This leaves us not afar from concluding that such limits should be treated and interpreted with great care, or not at all, at least in cases where exact graph models are concerned. Unfortunately, however, the overwhelming majority of network models employed as descriptive vessels for real-world phenomena in the applied graph-theoretical literature, that of random graphs, cannot be made subject to such a privileged dismissive approach. Indeed, due to inherent mathematical challenges associated with models submitting to some form of random aspect in their conception, the theory of random graphs studies properties of networks almost exclusively in the asymptotic limit of infinite graph size by utilising probabilistic arguments. This approach inevitably entails stringent limitations on the validity of analytical expressions for various graph-theoretical properties and, in some cases, will lead to surprising or even counter-intuitive results not unlike those exemplified above for exact graph models.

Let us drive this latter point a bit further by utilising the delineation of properties of the Gilbert model as an illustrative example, although similar arguments can certainly be constructed for other random graph models as well. In most generic terms, any given graph measure can here be viewed as quantifying a specific property of $\mathcal{R}^G_{n,p}$ as a function $M(n, p)$ of the model's parameters n and p. On statistical grounds, one can then define the probability $\rho(M(n, p) = M)$ that $M(n, p)$ takes a specific value M in realisations of $\mathcal{R}^G_{n,p}$. Naturally, this probability will depend on n and p as well, and if $\rho(M(n, p) = M)\rightarrow 1$ as the order $n\rightarrow\infty$, the random graph model $\mathcal{R}^G_{n,p}$ is said to *exhibit* the property $M(n, p) = M$. The main goal of random graph theory is to study the emergence of $M(n, p)$ as a function of the connection probability p in graphs of order n in the asymptotic limit $n\rightarrow\infty$ (for a thorough introduction into random graph theory, we refer to the work of Erdős and Rényi [38, 39, 40], and the classic treatise of Bollobás [22]).

One of the seminal original contributions of Erdős and Rényi in this regard is the observation that many properties emerge rather suddenly in $\mathcal{R}^G_{n,p}$ as the connection probability is steadily increased from $p = 0$ to $p = 1$. Indeed, it was found that in the asymptotic limit at a given connection probability p, either none of the realisations of $\mathcal{R}^G_{n,p}$ will exhibit a given property $M(n, p) = M$, or almost all of the realisations will. The transition between what was subsequently termed the *subcritical phase* and *supercritical phase* is rapid and typically characterised by a critical connectivity threshold or *critical probability*

$p_c(M(n, p) = M; n)$ which, for most properties, depends not only on the considered property itself but also on the order n of the random graph model.

Due to this dependence of the critical probability on n, the emergence of properties characterising a random graph model are commonly studied as function of a connection probability $p = p(n)$ which itself is assumed to depend on the order of the graph. If $p(n)$ increases slower than $p_c(M(n, p) = M; n)$ in the asymptotic limit $n \to \infty$, the graph model $\mathcal{R}^G_{n,p}$ is said to not have property $M(n, p) = M$. Conversely, $\mathcal{R}^G_{n,p}$ will exhibit property $M(n, p) = M$ if $p(n)$ increases faster than $p_c(M(n, p) = M; n)$. In more rigorous terms, we thus have

$$\frac{p(n)}{p_c(M(n, p) = M; n)} \overset{n\to\infty}{\longrightarrow} 0 \Leftrightarrow \lim_{n\to\infty} \rho(M(n, p) = M) = 0$$

for the subcritical phase in which almost certainly no realisation of the random graph model $\mathcal{R}^G_{n,p}$ will have the property $M(n, p) = M$, and

$$\frac{p(n)}{p_c(M(n, p) = M; n)} \overset{n\to\infty}{\longrightarrow} \infty \Leftrightarrow \lim_{n\to\infty} \rho(M(n, p) = M) = 1$$

for the supercritical phase in which almost all realisation of $\mathcal{R}^G_{n,p}$ will exhibit property $M(n, p) = M$. The connection probability $p(n) \sim p_c(M(n, p) = M; n)$ marks the *critical transition* for the investigated property $M(n, p) = M$.

At their critical transition, the properties characterising a graph model typically undergo abrupt and, in some cases, significant changes. However, this finding stands in stark contrast to the behaviour observed in real-world systems and, in this regard, should ideally, or at least arguably, be considered as an undesirable feature of mathematical models conceived with the purpose of describing physical reality. Let us take a closer look at this crucial aspect of random graph theory by exploring the Gilbert random graph model with respect to the property of having at least one subgraph of order m with k edges. Due to the uniform-random assignment of edges in $\mathcal{R}^G_{n,p}$, such subgraphs are certainly formed with probability p^k. Moreover, as no constraints were imposed on the set of nodes of the subgraph other than its cardinality, we must consider the $\binom{n}{m}$ ways in which m nodes can be chosen from a set of n nodes, and all of the $m!$ possible permutations for each fixed subset of m nodes. Disregarding here that some of these subgraphs will necessarily be isomorphic, we then find that the expectation value of the number of subgraphs with m nodes and k edges is roughly given by

$$\langle N_{m,k} \rangle \propto \binom{n}{m} m! p^k \sim n^m p^k,$$

where on the right-hand side we utilised Stirling's approximation for $n \to \infty$ and $m \ll n$. In the asymptotic limit $n^m p^k \to 0$ – that is, $pn^{m/k} \to 0$ for $n \to \infty$ –

the expectation value $\langle N_{m,k}\rangle \to 0$, and almost no realisation of the random graph model will contain a subgraph with m nodes and k edges. On the other hand, if $n^m p^k \to \infty$ – that is, $pn^{m/k} \to \infty$ for $n \to \infty$ – then $\langle N_{m,k}\rangle \to \infty$, and almost all realisations of $\mathcal{R}^G_{n,p}$ will certainly contain a subgraph with m nodes and k edges. Finally, for $n^m p^k = c = const$, that is $p = p(n) = cn^{-m/k}$, the expected number of subgraphs in the asymptotic limit $n \to \infty$ is with $\langle N_{m,k}\rangle = c^k$ finite, and the property of $\mathcal{R}^G_{n,p}$ for having subgraphs with m nodes and k edges does emerge. This last case is of particular importance, as it defines with

$$p_c\big(\langle N_{m,k}\rangle = 1; n\big) = n^{-m/k} \tag{2.142}$$

the connection probability at the critical threshold for the emergence of the property of finding at least one subgraph of order m with k edges in the asymptotic limit $n \to \infty$ of the Gilbert random graph model.

Let us explore this rather general result more closely by taking a look at specific classes of subgraphs, starting with subgraphs which are isomorphic to tree graphs. Being defined as simple planar graphs with only one face (see Section 2.1.2), all tree graphs of order m do have $k = m - 1$ edges and no subgraph isomorphic to a cycle. Moreover, as nodes of a tree graph, with the exception of those terminating the tree's branches, will have a total degree greater than or equal to two, the average total node degree of a tree graph is given by $\langle \boldsymbol{a}^{total}\rangle = 2 - 2/m$. Recalling (2.142), we then have

$$p_c\big(\langle N_{m,m-1}\rangle = 1; n\big) = n^{-m/(m-1)}$$

as the critical threshold for the emergence of a tree of order m in $\mathcal{R}^G_{n,p}$. Thus, as long as $p(n) \propto n^{-z}$ with $z > 1$, almost all realisations of a Gilbert random graph will be comprised of isolated trees, devoid of any cycles, with an average node degree of $\langle \boldsymbol{a}^{total}\rangle = p(n)n \propto n^{1-z} \to 0$ for $n \to \infty$. The emergence of subgraphs isomorphic to cycle graphs of order m in $\mathcal{R}^G_{n,p}$ – that is, subgraphs with m nodes, a total of $k = m$ edges and an average total node degree of two – can be approached in a similar fashion, eventually yielding

$$p_c\big(\langle N_{m,m}\rangle = 1; n\big) = n^{-1}$$

for its critical probability. Thus, as long as $p(n) \propto n^{-z}$ with $z = 1$, we not only find $\langle \boldsymbol{a}^{total}\rangle = const$, but the asymptotic probability for realisations of $\mathcal{R}^G_{n,p}$ having cycles of arbitrary order will jump from 0 to 1. Finally, for subgraphs isomorphic to a complete graph of order m with $k = m(m-1)/2$, we obtain

$$p_c\big(\langle N_{m,m(m-1)/2}\rangle = 1; n\big) = n^{-2/(m-1)}.$$

Thus, if we choose $p(n) \propto n^{-z}$ with $z = 2/3$, for example, complete subgraphs of order four will start to appear in almost all realisations of the Gilbert random graph, and for $p(n) \propto n^{-z}$ with $z \to 0$, random graphs almost certainly will have the property of containing complete subgraphs of arbitrary yet finite order.

Although these specific results appear conceptually sound when looked at in isolation, something interesting happens if we choose $p(n) \propto n^{-z}$ for $z \to 1^+$. As we saw above, almost all realisations of the random graph model will now almost certainly contain subgraphs isomorphic to trees and cycles of arbitrary order – that is, the asymptotic probability of occurrence of these subgraphs will jump abruptly from 0 to 1. Moreover, as Bollobás demonstrated [22], at this critical transition, almost all nodes will belong to trees as long as $\langle \boldsymbol{a}^{total} \rangle = const < 1$, with the largest connected tree scaling in size proportional to $\ln n$. If $\langle \boldsymbol{a}^{total} \rangle = 1$, however, the characteristic of the random graph changes significantly, and a connected subgraph emerges whose order scales with $n^{2/3}$. As this connected subgraph contains the largest fraction of the nodes in the graph, it is commonly referred to as the *giant component*, and its emergence marks an abrupt change in the topological properties of the random graph model from a loose collection of small isolated trees and cycles to a giant connected subgraph encompassing almost the entire network.

This sudden change in one of the key structural characteristics of $\mathcal{R}^G_{n,p}$ is even more worrisome, at least when viewed from a perspective grounded in physical reality, if one considers that it occurs upon an incremental smooth change of $z \to 1^+$ and $\langle \boldsymbol{a}^{total} \rangle \to 1^-$. Indeed, in real-world systems, incremental changes even of parameters which are identified as being critical in their corresponding models will always be accompanied by smooth changes in the properties of the system itself due to the limitations imposed by the very nature of physical interactions between a system's constituents. We thus will argue that abrupt changes in mathematical models describing properties of physical systems should not be reckoned a desirable feature, and we will carefully assert that such changes, if they occur, will inevitably point to a limit of the considered model or, worse, a limitation of the utilised mathematical framework used to formalise physical reality alltogether.

The emergence of a giant component cited above is but one of many discontinuous changes in properties of random graph models. Already in one of the original papers on random graphs, Erdős and Rényi showed that for $p(n) < (1 - \varepsilon) \ln n/n$ with arbitrarily small $\varepsilon = const > 0$, almost all realisation of the random graph mode $\mathcal{R}^G_{n,p}$ will be disconnected in the asymptotic limit, that is, will almost certainly contain only isolated nodes, trees and cycles of small order [39]. For $p(n) > (1 + \varepsilon) \ln n/n$, on the other hand, almost all realisations will be connected. The connection probability $p_c = \ln n/n$ thus defines the critical threshold for the property of $\mathcal{R}^G_{n,p}$ being connected. Certainly, this sudden change in the connectedness of a random graph for $\varepsilon \to 0^+$ is subject to the same conceptional reservations as those outlined above for the emergence of trees, cycles and a giant component in random graphs. But something else happens for $p(n) = (1+\varepsilon)\ln n/n$ – that is in the supercritical phase for the property of $\mathcal{R}^G_{n,p}$ to be connected – if we take $\varepsilon\to\infty$. Intuitively, one would expect in a random graph of arbitrary large order a wide range of node degrees as reflecting the random nature of the graph's very construction, with a minimum node degree significantly smaller than the maximum degree some node will exhibit. Indeed, recalling (2.136), we immediately find that the variance of total node degrees in the asymptotic limit of $\mathcal{R}^G_{n,p}$ will increase linearly with n for any given connection probability p. Random graph theory paints a quite different picture, however [22]. Here, Bollobás showed that

$$\min \boldsymbol{a}^{total} = (1 + c_{\min})(1 + \varepsilon)\ln n$$

and

$$\max \boldsymbol{a}^{total} = (1 + c_{\max})(1 + \varepsilon)\ln n,$$

where $c_{\min}$ denotes the unique root satisfying $-1 < c_{\min} < 0$ and $c_{\max}$ the unique positive root of $1 + (1+\varepsilon)c = (1+\varepsilon)(1+c)\ln(1+c)$. For $\varepsilon\to\infty$, both $c_{\min}$ and $c_{\max}$ will converge to zero, leaving us with

$$\lim_{\varepsilon\to\infty} \min \boldsymbol{a}^{total} = \lim_{\varepsilon\to\infty} \min \boldsymbol{a}^{total} = np$$

and, thus, the unexpected result that all nodes will asymptotically approach the same degree – that is, all realisations of the random graph model $\mathcal{R}^G_{n,p}$ will become almost certainly np-regular and homogeneous.

Surprising conclusions of this kind arguably pose significant challenges not just for the intuitive mind but, more importantly, for the mathematical framework which we became accustomed to utilise in the formalisation of physical reality. There is little doubt that random graph theory with its asymptotic notion of random networks has provided us with invaluable insights into a whole host of physical phenomena. But it would be futile to disregard our cautious earlier assertion that it is precisely this asymptotic notion which also suffers both conceptually and mathematically from inherent limitations when it comes to its utilisation, especially where real-world networks are concerned. Perhaps it is time to reflect and search for a more coherent graph-theoretical framework – a *finite graph theory* which, at its conceptual core, is more attuned to the very finite and discrete makeup of our physical world by avoiding, or outright prohibiting, unrealistic limitcases and asymptotic considerations. After a brief introduction into operator theory in the next chapter, we will propose exactly such an operator graph-theoretical framework.

3

Operator Calculus: The Mapping between Vector Spaces

Leonard Euler's ingenious approach to the conundrum which surrounded the seven bridges of Königsberg at his time provided us not only with the definite solution to this intriguing problem, but also planted the seed from which the mathematical field of graph theory we touched upon in the previous chapter germinated. Although Euler's now-historic negative resolution ended the tedious explorative search for a viable path through the city by inspired inhabitants and visitors of this Prussian town, this brute-force approach certainly merits further investigation in light of many modern-day problems which rely on such an approach due to the lack of better options. Is it possible to formulate this active exploration of the network of Königsberg's bridges and search for an Eulerian path in mathematical terms? The affirmative answer to this question leads us to another well-established field of mathematics, operator theory. This chapter will provide an introduction – unfortunately, only a stringently limited one – into the very basics of *operator calculus*, the algebraic tool utilised to describe operations on and mappings between finite vector spaces. The application of this formalism to graph-theoretical objects will then establish the conceptual framework for *operator graph theory*, the central objective of this book, presented in the following chapter.

3.1 Vector Spaces

Let us return to Königsberg with its seven bridges and explore in some more algebraic terms the active search for those walks through the city which cross each of its bridges exactly once. In order to do so, we certainly require keeping track of both the visited areas of the city and the crossed bridges connecting these areas. Whether an area is being visited or a bridge has been crossed defines a specific state in which a node or edge in the associated graph can be found. The states of all nodes and edges can eventually be collected to form two *state vectors* which respectively carry four and seven elements in the case of the Königsberg bridge graph. When following a specific walk through the city, individual node and edge states are changed by means of algebraic operations. These operations can then be viewed as a mathematical representation of the incremental steps which comprise a walk, and provide an illustrative example of what we will call *maps* or *operators* and will explore in greater detail in the next section. By successively applying walk-generating operations, or operators, and assessing the resulting changes in the states of both nodes and edges of the graph, the solution to the Königsberg bridge problem amounts to finding an ordered set of operators which yields state vectors marking every node as visited at least once and each edge as having been traversed. If such an ordered set is found, it will represent a sought-after Eulerian path through the city and, thus, a positive solution to our problem.

Before formalising this approach, however, we require a more rigorous definition of the involved mathematical objects. The finite state vectors introduced above are but two examples of algebraic objects which form sets called *vector spaces* and adhere to a number of general rules encompassed in the mathematical field of linear algebra. Let us therefore begin by formulating the following

Definition 3.1 (vector space) A *vector space* or *linear space* $\mathcal{V}$ over a field $\mathcal{F}$ is a set of objects called *vectors* that is closed under the operations of finite *vector addition* $+ \colon \mathcal{V} \times \mathcal{V} \to \mathcal{V}$ and *scalar multiplication* $\cdot \colon \mathcal{F} \times \mathcal{V} \to \mathcal{V}$, and satisfies commutativity of vector addition,

$$\boldsymbol{u} + \boldsymbol{v} = \boldsymbol{v} + \boldsymbol{u},$$

associativity of vector addition,

$$(\boldsymbol{u} + \boldsymbol{v}) + \boldsymbol{w} = \boldsymbol{u} + (\boldsymbol{v} + \boldsymbol{w}),$$

the existence of an unique identity element $\mathbf{0} \in \mathcal{V}$ of vector addition,

$$\mathbf{0} + \boldsymbol{v} = \boldsymbol{v} + \mathbf{0} = \boldsymbol{v},$$

the existence of an unique inverse element $(-\boldsymbol{v}) \in \mathcal{V}$ of vector addition,

$$\boldsymbol{v} + (-\boldsymbol{v}) = (-\boldsymbol{v}) + \boldsymbol{v} = \mathbf{0},$$

associativity of scalar multiplication with respect to field multiplication,

$$a \cdot (b \cdot \boldsymbol{v}) = (ab) \cdot \boldsymbol{v},$$

distributivity of scalar multiplication with respect to field addition,

$$(a + b) \cdot \boldsymbol{v} = a \cdot \boldsymbol{v} + b \cdot \boldsymbol{v},$$

distributivity of scalar multiplication with respect to vector addition,

$$a \cdot (\boldsymbol{u} + \boldsymbol{v}) = a \cdot \boldsymbol{u} + a \cdot \boldsymbol{v},$$

and the existence of an unique identity element $1 \in \mathcal{F}$ of scalar multiplication,

$$1 \cdot \boldsymbol{v} = \boldsymbol{v},$$

for all $\boldsymbol{u}, \boldsymbol{v}, \boldsymbol{w} \in \mathcal{V}$ and $a, b \in \mathcal{F}$.

The most common instances of vector spaces with countless applications reaching far beyond the realms of mathematics include the n-dimensional Euclidean space $\mathbb{R}^n$, called *real vector space*, and the n-dimensional complex space $\mathbb{C}^n$, called *complex vector space*. The Boolean set $\mathbb{B} = \{0, 1\}$ gives rise to another important class of vector spaces which not only resides at the very core of computer science and technology, but also plays an instrumental role in graph theory as means to represent, among others, the existence, or absence, of adjacency relations between nodes. Indeed, by defining the operations of Boolean addition $+^{\mathbb{B}} : \mathbb{B} \times \mathbb{B} \to \mathbb{B}$ and Boolean multiplication $\cdot^{\mathbb{B}} : \mathbb{B} \times \mathbb{B} \to \mathbb{B}$ in the form of two truth tables

$+^{\mathbb{B}}$	0	1
0	0	1
1	1	0

$\cdot^{\mathbb{B}}$	0	1
0	0	0
1	0	1

(3.1)

corresponding to the logical XOR and AND operation, respectively, it can easily be demonstrated that $\mathbb{B}$ obeys the field axioms of associativity, commutativity and distributivity under Boolean addition and multiplication, that the identity element of addition is 0 and that of multiplication is 1, that each element of $\mathbb{B}$ is its own inverse under addition and that 1 is its own inverse element under multiplication. The Boolean set $\mathbb{B}$ thus forms with its two elements the smallest field in mathematics, called the *Galois field* $GF(2)$ or $\mathbb{Z}_2$. Defining vector addition and scalar multiplication by considering the operations (3.1) as applying element-wise, the set of vectors in $\mathbb{B}^n$ or, generally, any $\mathbb{B}^{m\times n} = \mathbb{B}^m \times \mathbb{B}^n$ then comprises a vector space over $\mathbb{B}$ which is commonly referred to as *Boolean vector space*. Vectors in $\mathbb{B}^{m\times n}$ and its subspaces will prominently feature as viable representation of many graph-theoretical objects and notions throughout this and later chapters alongside vectors in $\mathbb{Z}^{m\times n}$, $\mathbb{N}^{m\times n}$ or $\mathbb{N}_0^{m\times n}$ and their subspaces. Unfortunately, however, the latter do generally not form vector spaces, as neither the set of integers $\mathbb{Z}$ nor the sets of natural numbers $\mathbb{N}$ and $\mathbb{N}_0$ satisfy all required field axioms. In order to bypass eventual limitations resulting from this lack of algebraic structure, we will often represent such vectors as elements of an $(m \times n)$-dimensional *rational vector space* $\mathbb{Q}^{m\times n}$ over $\mathbb{Q}$ in the remainder of this book.

With the notion of a vector space at hand, let us now return to the graph of Königberg's bridges, $\mathcal{G} = (\mathcal{N}^{\mathcal{G}}, \mathcal{E}^{\mathcal{G}})$. Labelling the nodes $i \in \mathcal{N}^{\mathcal{G}}$ of $\mathcal{G}$ according to Fig. 3.1a, the elements of a node state vector $\boldsymbol{s}^n \in \mathbb{B}^4$ which marks individual nodes as being visited or not are given by

$$s_i^n : \mathcal{N}^{\mathcal{G}} \to \mathbb{B} \, , \; s_i^n := \begin{cases} 1 & \text{if node } i \text{ in } \mathcal{G} \text{ is being visited,} \\ 0 & \text{otherwise.} \end{cases} \tag{3.2}$$

The set of all possible state vectors then spans a Boolean vector space $\mathbb{B}^4$ over $\mathbb{B}$ which we will denote with $\mathcal{S}^n(\mathcal{G})$. As only one node can be visited at any given step along a walk through $\mathcal{G}$, the algebraic construction of walks needs to ensure that each $\boldsymbol{s}^n$ contains exactly one non-zero element. In a similar fashion, by appropriately labelling all adjacency relations $(i, j) \in \mathcal{E}^{\mathcal{G}}$ of $\mathcal{G}$ (Fig. 3.1a, grey) and utilising the resulting index set $\mathcal{I}(\mathcal{E}^{\mathcal{G}}) \subset \mathbb{N}$, the elements of an edge state vector $\boldsymbol{s}^e \in \mathbb{B}^7$ which distinguishes whether or not an edge is available for becoming part of a walk through $\mathcal{G}$ can be defined by

$$s_i^e : \mathcal{I}(\mathcal{E}^{\mathcal{G}}) \to \mathbb{B} \, , \; s_i^e = \begin{cases} 1 & \text{if edge } i \text{ in } \mathcal{G} \text{ is traversable,} \\ 0 & \text{otherwise.} \end{cases} \tag{3.3}$$

The set of all possible edge state vectors then forms a Boolean vector space $\mathbb{B}^7$ over $\mathbb{B}$, which we will denote with $\mathcal{S}^e(\mathcal{G})$. As only one edge can be traversed at any given step along a walk through $\mathcal{G}$, the algebraic construction of walks needs to ensure that only the state of the traversed edge in $\boldsymbol{s}^e$ is updated.

Before proceeding with the algebraic formalisation of operations which generate such walks and deliver the required state vector changes, however, it is necessary to take a closer look at the definition of our edge state vector (3.3). Although on a formal level it certainly suffices to simply index all elements of the edge set $\mathcal{E}^{\mathcal{G}}$ and assign each indexed node pair $(i, j) \in \mathcal{E}^{\mathcal{G}}$ to an element of $\boldsymbol{s}^e \in \mathcal{S}^e(\mathcal{G})$, it is possible, and conceptually often more convenient, to consider $\boldsymbol{s}^e$ itself as the node state vector of another graph called the *line graph* $\mathcal{L}(\mathcal{G})$ of $\mathcal{G}$. An operation, such as that of traversing one edge along a walk in our illustrative exercise, which results in a change of edge states in $\mathcal{G}$ will then necessarily be associated with an operation which results in a change of node states in the line graph $\mathcal{L}(\mathcal{G})$ of $\mathcal{G}$.

In order to make full use of the advantages such an alternative interpretation of our edge state vector carries, it is necessary to explore in greater detail the notion of a line graph and its scope. To that end, let $\mathcal{G} = (\mathcal{N}^{\mathcal{G}}, \mathcal{E}^{\mathcal{G}})$ be a simple graph. The line graph or *edge-to-vertex dual* $\mathcal{L}(\mathcal{G}) = (\mathcal{N}^{\mathcal{L}(\mathcal{G})}, \mathcal{E}^{\mathcal{L}(\mathcal{G})})$ of $\mathcal{G}$ is

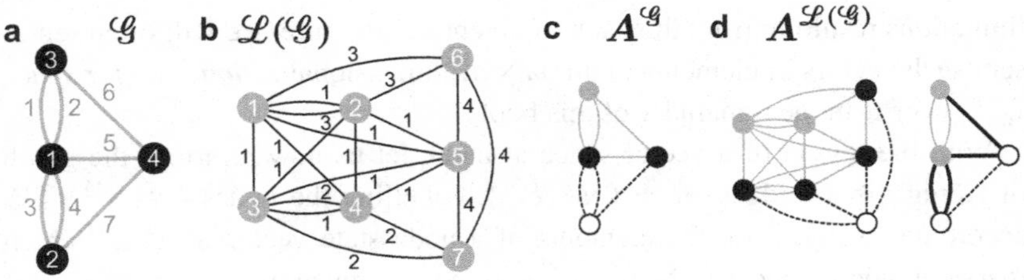

Figure 3.1 Node and edge states in the Königsberg bridge graph. **a:** Multigraph of Königsberg's bridges $\mathcal{G}$, with each node representing an area of the Prussian town, and each edge a bridge connecting two areas. By appropriately labelling nodes and edges of $\mathcal{G}$, vectors $\boldsymbol{s}^n$ and $\boldsymbol{s}^e$ can be constructed which respectively assign a state value to each node according to (3.2) and each edge according to (3.3). The set of all possible node state vectors $\boldsymbol{s}^n$ then forms a vector space $\mathcal{S}^n(\mathcal{G}) = \mathbb{B}^4$ over $\mathbb{B}$, that of all possible edge state vectors a vector space $\mathcal{S}^e(\mathcal{G}) = \mathbb{B}^7$ over $\mathbb{B}$. **b:** Line graph $\mathcal{L}(\mathcal{G})$ of $\mathcal{G}$ in which each node represents a bridge connected by an area of the city. As bridge pairs (1,2) and (3,4) are each connected by two areas, $\mathcal{L}(\mathcal{G})$ is a multigraph. **c:** Application of matrix operator $A^{\mathcal{G}}$ according to (3.8), exemplified here for the node state vector $\boldsymbol{s}^n = (0,1,0,0)$. The resulting state vector yields all nearest neighbours of node 2 in $\mathcal{G}$ (black). **d:** Application of matrix operator $A^{\mathcal{L}(\mathcal{G})}$ according to (3.9), exemplified here for the state vector $\bar{\boldsymbol{s}}^n = (0,0,0,0,0,0,1)$ of nodes in $\mathcal{L}(\mathcal{G})$. The obtained vector marks in $\mathcal{L}(\mathcal{G})$ all nearest neighbours of node 7 (left; black), and thus all edges in $\mathcal{G}$ which share a common node with the edge between nodes 2 and 4 (right; black solid).

then defined as the graph obtained by associating with each node $k \in \mathcal{N}^{\mathcal{L}(\mathcal{G})}$ an adjacency relation $(i, j) \in \mathcal{E}^{\mathcal{G}} : i, j \in \mathcal{N}^{\mathcal{G}}$ and with each adjacency relation $(k, l) \in \mathcal{E}^{\mathcal{L}(\mathcal{G})}$: $k, l \in \mathcal{N}^{\mathcal{L}(\mathcal{G})}$ a node $i \in \mathcal{N}^{\mathcal{G}}$ in such a way that two distinct nodes $k, l \in \mathcal{N}^{\mathcal{L}(\mathcal{G})}$ are adjacent in $\mathcal{L}(\mathcal{G})$ if and only if their associated edges in $\mathcal{G}$ share a common node $i \in \mathcal{N}^{\mathcal{G}}$ [53]. Although this definition is generally applied only to simple graphs $\mathcal{G}$, it can be easily extended to also include undirected multigraphs by considering an edge of weight $w \in \mathbb{N}: w \geq 2$ in $\mathcal{G}$ as w edges each of which carries a weight of 1. Because every pair of edges between two given nodes will share these two nodes in $\mathcal{G}$, the corresponding node pairs in the associated line graph $\mathcal{L}(\mathcal{G})$ will each be subject to two adjacency relations, thus rendering the line graph of a multigraph itself a multigraph. Moreover, all nodes in $\mathcal{L}(\mathcal{G})$ must necessarily be self-looped with weight 2, as each edge in $\mathcal{G}$ shares two nodes, namely its endpoints in $\mathcal{G}$, with itself. This also applies to adjacency relations connecting a node with itself, that is, self-loops in $\mathcal{G}$. However, adhering to the commonly used conception of a line graph, we will discard all self-loops present in $\mathcal{L}(\mathcal{G})$ and consider only not self-looped line graphs of simple and not self-looped undirected multigraphs.

The line graph $\mathcal{L}(\mathcal{G})$ of the Königsberg bridge graph is shown in Fig. 3.1b together with labels for its nodes which correspond to those of edges in $\mathcal{G}$, and labels for its edges which correspond to those of nodes in $\mathcal{G}$ (see Fig. 3.1a). With this, each component of the state vector $\boldsymbol{s}^e$ for edges in $\mathcal{G}$ can then be assigned to a node in the line graph of $\mathcal{G}$ such that

$$\bar{s}_i^n : \mathcal{N}^{\mathcal{L}(\mathcal{G})} \to \mathbb{B}\ ,\ \bar{s}_i^n := \begin{cases} 1 & \text{if node } i \text{ in } \mathcal{L}(\mathcal{G}) \text{ can be visited,} \\ 0 & \text{otherwise} \end{cases} \tag{3.4}$$

defines the elements of a state vector $\bar{\boldsymbol{s}}^n \in \mathbb{B}^7$ for nodes in $\mathcal{L}(\mathcal{G})$. The set of all such state vectors eventually forms a Boolean vector space $\mathcal{S}^n(\mathcal{L}(\mathcal{G}))$ isomorphic to $\mathcal{S}^e(\mathcal{G})$. In a similar fashion, it is certainly also possible to construct a vector space $\mathcal{S}^e(\mathcal{L}(\mathcal{G}))$ from edge state vectors $\bar{\boldsymbol{s}}^e \in \mathbb{B}^{19}$ in $\mathcal{L}(\mathcal{G})$ with

$$\bar{s}_i^e : \mathcal{I}(\mathcal{E}^{\mathcal{L}(\mathcal{G})}) \to \mathbb{B}\ ,\ \bar{s}_i^e := \begin{cases} 1 & \text{if edge } i \text{ in } \mathcal{L}(\mathcal{G}) \text{ is being traversed,} \\ 0 & \text{otherwise} \end{cases} \tag{3.5}$$

by utilising the index set $\mathcal{I}(\mathcal{E}^{\mathcal{L}(\mathcal{G})})$ of the 19 distinct edges comprising the set of adjacency relations of $\mathcal{L}(\mathcal{G})$. Unlike for $\mathcal{S}^e(\mathcal{G})$ and $\mathcal{S}^n(\mathcal{L}(\mathcal{G}))$, however, an isomorphism between $\mathcal{S}^n(\mathcal{G})$ and $\mathcal{S}^e(\mathcal{L}(\mathcal{G}))$ cannot easily be drawn, as each single node in $\mathcal{G}$ is associated with multiple edges between distinct node pairs in $\mathcal{L}(\mathcal{G})$. To address the Königsberg bridge problem in the remainder of this chapter, we will for reasons of conceptual clarity consider only $\boldsymbol{s}^n \in \mathcal{S}^n(\mathcal{G})$ as the state vector of nodes in $\mathcal{G}$ and $\bar{\boldsymbol{s}}^n \in \mathcal{S}^n(\mathcal{L}(\mathcal{G}))$ as the state vector of nodes in $\mathcal{L}(\mathcal{G})$, noting that the latter is identical to the edge state vector $\boldsymbol{s}^e \in \mathcal{S}^e(\mathcal{G})$ in $\mathcal{G}$. The Königsberg bridge problem itself can then be restated as a search for the existence of a walk which visits each node in $\mathcal{G}$ at least once, and each node in $\mathcal{L}(\mathcal{G})$ exactly once.

3.2 Operations on Vector Spaces

Having introduced state vectors $\boldsymbol{s}^n \in \mathbb{B}^4$ for nodes and $\boldsymbol{s}^e \in \mathbb{B}^7$ for edges in the graph $\mathcal{G}$ of Königsberg's bridges together with their respective vector spaces $\mathcal{S}^n(\mathcal{G})$ and $\mathcal{S}^e(\mathcal{G}) \cong \mathcal{S}^n(\mathcal{L}(\mathcal{G}))$, we can now explore the construction of algebraic operations which update these state vectors along a given walk through the city itself. This will not only bring us one step closer to formalising an alternative approach for addressing the Königsberg bridge problem through active search, but also, and more importantly, serve as an exercise which illustrates the general notion of an operator and its action on a vector space. To that end, let us begin by denoting with

$$A_{ij}^{\mathcal{G}} : \mathcal{N}^{\mathcal{G}} \times \mathcal{N}^{\mathcal{G}} \to \mathbb{B}\ ,\ A_{ij}^{\mathcal{G}} := 1 - \delta[w_{ij}] \tag{3.6}$$

the elements of the matrix of adjacency relations $\boldsymbol{A}^{\mathcal{G}}$ of the Königsberg bridge graph $\mathcal{G}$ with weight matrix (2.2) we already encountered in (2.56), and with

$$A_{ij}^{\mathcal{L}(\mathcal{G})} \colon \mathcal{N}^{\mathcal{L}(\mathcal{G})} \times \mathcal{N}^{\mathcal{L}(\mathcal{G})} \to \mathbb{B} \, , \, A_{ij}^{\mathcal{L}(\mathcal{G})} := \begin{pmatrix} 0 & 1 & 1 & 1 & 1 & 1 & 0 \\ 1 & 0 & 1 & 1 & 1 & 1 & 0 \\ 1 & 1 & 0 & 1 & 1 & 0 & 1 \\ 1 & 1 & 1 & 0 & 1 & 0 & 1 \\ 1 & 1 & 1 & 1 & 0 & 1 & 1 \\ 1 & 1 & 0 & 0 & 1 & 0 & 1 \\ 0 & 0 & 1 & 1 & 1 & 1 & 0 \end{pmatrix} \tag{3.7}$$

the elements of the matrix of adjacency relations $\boldsymbol{A}^{\mathcal{L}(\mathcal{G})}$ of its edge-to-vertex dual $\mathcal{L}(\mathcal{G})$ depicted in Fig. 3.1b. Given a node state row vector $\boldsymbol{s}^n$ with only one non-zero element $s_i^n = 1$, the matrix product $\boldsymbol{s}^n \cdot \boldsymbol{A}^{\mathcal{G}}$ will then yield a node state row vector with elements

$$\left(\boldsymbol{s}^n \cdot \boldsymbol{A}^{\mathcal{G}}\right)_j \colon \mathcal{N}^{\mathcal{G}} \to \mathbb{B} \, , \, \left(\boldsymbol{s}^n \cdot \boldsymbol{A}^{\mathcal{G}}\right)_j := \begin{cases} 1 & \text{iff } (i, j) \in \mathcal{E}^{\mathcal{G}} \, , \\ 0 & \text{otherwise,} \end{cases} \tag{3.8}$$

marking all nearest neighbours of node i in $\mathcal{G}$ (Fig. 3.1c). In a similar fashion, given a node state row vector $\bar{\boldsymbol{s}}^n$ in $\mathcal{L}(\mathcal{G})$ with one non-zero element $\bar{s}_i^n = 1$, the matrix product $\bar{\boldsymbol{s}}^n \cdot \boldsymbol{A}^{\mathcal{L}(\mathcal{G})}$ returns a row vector with components

$$\left(\bar{\boldsymbol{s}}^n \cdot \boldsymbol{A}^{\mathcal{L}(\mathcal{G})}\right)_j \colon \mathcal{N}^{\mathcal{L}(\mathcal{G})} \to \mathbb{B} \, , \, \left(\bar{\boldsymbol{s}}^n \cdot \boldsymbol{A}^{\mathcal{L}(\mathcal{G})}\right)_j := \begin{cases} 1 & \text{iff } (i, j) \in \mathcal{E}^{\mathcal{L}(\mathcal{G})}, \\ 0 & \text{otherwise,} \end{cases} \tag{3.9}$$

marking each nearest neighbour of node $i \in \mathcal{N}^{\mathcal{L}(\mathcal{G})}$ and, thus, all edges which are adjacent to – that is, share a common node with – the edge being traversed in $\mathcal{G}$, as illustrated in Fig. 3.1d.

The matrices $\boldsymbol{A}^{\mathcal{G}}$ and $\boldsymbol{A}^{\mathcal{L}(\mathcal{G})}$ present our first two concrete examples of algebraic operations which, through right-hand matrix multiplication, modify the elements of a given vector. As such, the mappings $\boldsymbol{A}^{\mathcal{G}} : \widetilde{\mathcal{S}}^n(\mathcal{G}) \to \mathcal{S}^n(\mathcal{G})$ and $\boldsymbol{A}^{\mathcal{L}(\mathcal{G})} \colon \widetilde{\mathcal{S}}^n(\mathcal{L}(\mathcal{G})) \to \mathcal{S}^n(\mathcal{L}(\mathcal{G}))$ then define operators which, by acting on vectors in the subsets $\widetilde{\mathcal{S}}^n(\mathcal{G}) \subset \mathcal{S}^n(\mathcal{G})$ and $\widetilde{\mathcal{S}}^n(\mathcal{L}(\mathcal{G})) \subset \mathcal{S}^n(\mathcal{L}(\mathcal{G}))$ comprised of Boolean vectors with exactly one non-zero element, respectively yield vectors in finite vector spaces $\mathcal{S}^n(\mathcal{G})$ and $\mathcal{S}^n(\mathcal{L}(\mathcal{G}))$. Formulated in the most generic terms, we can conceive of an operator as simply defining a mapping between two not necessarily distinct sets of objects by acting on elements of one set to produce elements of the other set. Familiar instances of such mappings are found in the mathematical field of functional analysis. Here, each real-valued function $f(x)$ can be construed as an operator $f \colon \mathbb{R} \to \mathbb{R}$ which maps the field of real numbers into itself. Operations such as differentiation and indefinite integration of $f(x)$ are examples of integro-differential operators which respectively map the set of all differentiable functions into the set of all functions and the set of integrable functions into the set of all differentiable functions. Similarly, in areas such as discrete mathematics, classical number theory and computer science, the instrumental floor and ceiling functions

$$\begin{aligned} \lfloor q \rfloor &: \mathbb{Q} \to \mathbb{Z}\,,\ \lfloor q \rfloor := \max\{n \in \mathbb{Z} : n \leq q\}, \\ \lceil q \rceil &: \mathbb{Q} \to \mathbb{Z}\,,\ \lceil q \rceil := \min\{n \in \mathbb{Z} : n \geq q\}, \end{aligned} \tag{3.10}$$

the signum function

$$\operatorname{sgn}[q] : \mathbb{Q} \to \{-1, 0, 1\}\,,\ \operatorname{sgn}[q] := \begin{cases} -1 & \text{if } q < 0, \\ 0 & \text{if } q = 0, \\ 1 & \text{if } q > 0 \end{cases} \tag{3.11}$$

or the Kronecker delta function (2.13) represent instances of operators which map the field of rational numbers $\mathbb{Q}$ into $\mathbb{Z}$, $\{-1, 0, 1\}$, or $\mathbb{B}$, respectively. Last but certainly not least, logical operations such as XOR or AND in (3.1), and all assignment or access operations utilised in computer programming, offer perhaps somewhat less transparent instances of operators which map, not unlike functions, between sets of objects which are represented in the registers and memory of the computer hardware as vectors in abstract Boolean vector spaces.

This small exposé of examples could be extended indefinitely and eventually will reach into all fields of modern science and its countless real-world applications. Due to the vast scope the notion of an operator as general descriptor for the relationship between objects, for transformation and dynamic change relishes in, let us tailor its definition to the subject matter presented in this book before we exemplify its utilisation by addressing the Königsberg bridge problem itself. To that end, we begin by formulating

Definition 3.2 (linear map) Let $\mathcal{V}$ and $\mathcal{V}'$ be finite vector spaces over a field $\mathcal{F}$. An $\mathcal{F}$*-linear map*, or simply *linear map*, $\mathfrak{M}$ is a morphism

$$\mathfrak{M} : \mathcal{V} \to \mathcal{V}'$$

between vector spaces satisfying linearity under addition,

$$\mathfrak{M}[\boldsymbol{u} + \boldsymbol{v}] = \mathfrak{M}[\boldsymbol{u}] + \mathfrak{M}[\boldsymbol{v}],$$

and homogeneity of degree 1 under scalar multiplication,

$$\mathfrak{M}[a \cdot \boldsymbol{u}] = a \cdot \mathfrak{M}[\boldsymbol{u}],$$

where $\boldsymbol{u}, \boldsymbol{v} \in \mathcal{V}$ and $a \in \mathcal{F}$.

The property of homogeneity of degree 1 under scalar multiplication that a linear map is required to satisfy here simply ensures that the identity element

$\mathbf{0}^{\mathcal{V}} \in \mathcal{V}$ of vector addition in $\mathcal{V}$ is mapped into the identity element $\mathbf{0}^{\mathcal{V}'} \in \mathcal{V}'$ of vector addition in $\mathcal{V}'$, such that

$$\mathfrak{M}[\mathbf{0}^{\mathcal{V}}] = \mathfrak{M}[0 \cdot \boldsymbol{v}] = 0 \cdot \mathfrak{M}[\boldsymbol{v}] = 0 \cdot \boldsymbol{v}' = \mathbf{0}^{\mathcal{V}'},$$

for all $\boldsymbol{v} \in \mathcal{V}$, $\boldsymbol{v}' \in \mathcal{V}'$, where $0 \in \mathcal{F}$ denotes the identity element of addition in $\mathcal{F}$. Furthermore, as both $\mathcal{V}$ and $\mathcal{V}'$ are finite vector spaces over $\mathcal{F}$, each linear map $\mathfrak{M}\colon \mathcal{V} \to \mathcal{V}'$ can be represented in terms of finite-dimensional matrices. To show this, we choose a set of basis vectors $\boldsymbol{v}_i \in \mathcal{V}\colon i \in [1, m]$ in $\mathcal{V}$, and with $\boldsymbol{v}'_j \in \mathcal{V}'\colon j \in [1, n]$ a set of basis vectors for $\mathcal{V}'$, where m and n respectively denote the dimension of $\mathcal{V}$ and $\mathcal{V}'$. Each vector $\boldsymbol{v} \in \mathcal{V}$ is then given by $\boldsymbol{v} = \sum_{i=1}^{m} v_i \cdot \boldsymbol{v}_i$, and each vector $\boldsymbol{v}' \in \mathcal{V}'$ by $\boldsymbol{v}' = \sum_{j=1}^{n} v'_j \cdot \boldsymbol{v}'_j$ for some $v_i, v'_j \in \mathcal{F}$, and we have

$$\mathfrak{M}[\boldsymbol{v}] = \mathfrak{M}\left[\sum_{i=1}^{m} v_i \cdot \boldsymbol{v}_i\right] = \sum_{i=1}^{m} v_i \cdot \mathfrak{M}[\boldsymbol{v}_i] = \sum_{i=1}^{m}\sum_{j=1}^{n} v_i \cdot (\mathfrak{M}\boldsymbol{v}_i)_j \cdot \boldsymbol{v}'_j.$$

Here $(\mathfrak{M}\boldsymbol{v}_i)_j \in \mathcal{F}$ defines the elements $\mathfrak{M}_{ij}$ of an $m \times n$ matrix which eventually represents the linear map $\mathfrak{M}$ in the chosen bases of $\mathcal{V}$ and $\mathcal{V}'$. As most graph-theoretical objects will find a natural representation in terms of vectors and matrices, we will predominantly utilise such matrix representations of linear maps and their generalisation in the remainder of this book. Finally, if both finite vector spaces $\mathcal{V}$ and $\mathcal{V}'$ in Definition 3.2 are identical, a linear map $\mathfrak{M}\colon \mathcal{V} \to \mathcal{V}$ is called an *endomorphism* of the vector space $\mathcal{V}$.

Although linear maps present arguably the most prominent examples of mappings between sets in the mathematical literature, some of the algebraic objects we already encountered and will continue to encounter, such as $\boldsymbol{A}^{\mathcal{G}}$ in (3.6) or $\boldsymbol{A}^{\mathcal{L}(\mathcal{G})}$ in (3.7), do require a generalisation of this notion. Indeed, it can easily be shown that the domain of $\boldsymbol{A}^{\mathcal{G}}$, defined by the subset $\widetilde{\mathcal{S}}^n(\mathcal{G}) \subset \mathbb{B}^4$ of Boolean vectors with exactly one non-zero element, does not by itself form a vector space according to Definition 3.1, as, for instance, the sum of any two of its vectors will not yield a vector in $\widetilde{\mathcal{S}}^n(\mathcal{G})$. A similar argument holds for the domain $\widetilde{\mathcal{S}}^n(\mathcal{L}(\mathcal{G}))$ of $\boldsymbol{A}^{\mathcal{L}(\mathcal{G})}$, thus rendering both $\boldsymbol{A}^{\mathcal{G}}$ and $\boldsymbol{A}^{\mathcal{L}(\mathcal{G})}$ not linear maps in the strict sense of Definition 3.2. However, as these examples also demonstrate, it certainly is possible to construct viable mappings between subsets $\widetilde{\mathcal{V}} \subseteq \mathcal{V}$ and $\widetilde{\mathcal{V}}' \subseteq \mathcal{V}'$ of two vector spaces $\mathcal{V}$ and $\mathcal{V}'$ which do not necessitate $\widetilde{\mathcal{V}}$ or $\widetilde{\mathcal{V}}'$ to be closed under the operations of vector addition and scalar multiplication of their respective encompassing vector superspaces – that is to construct mappings in which $\widetilde{\mathcal{V}}$ and $\widetilde{\mathcal{V}}'$ themselves do not form vector subspaces of $\mathcal{V}$ and $\mathcal{V}'$. To go even further, it is also possible to conceive of mappings between two vector spaces $\mathcal{V}$ and $\mathcal{V}'$ which are defined over different fields, in which case much care in formalising properties such as linearity under vector addition and homogeneity under scalar multiplication is required to avoid ambiguities, as we will briefly exemplify in the next section. Both of these generalisations eventually lead us to broaden our notion of a linear map to that of an *operator*. Specifically, let us formulate the following

Definition 3.3 (operator) Let $\mathscr{F}$ be a tuple of fields, and let $\mathcal{V}$ and $\mathcal{V}'$ be two finite vector spaces over distinct elements of $\mathscr{F}$. With $\mathcal{F} \in \mathscr{F}$, an *$\mathcal{F}$-linear operator* $\mathfrak{O}$ is a mapping

$$\mathfrak{O}\colon \widetilde{\mathcal{V}} \subseteq \mathcal{V} \to \widetilde{\mathcal{V}}' \subseteq \mathcal{V}'$$

between subsets $\widetilde{\mathcal{V}} \subseteq \mathcal{V}$ and $\widetilde{\mathcal{V}}' \subseteq \mathcal{V}'$ that preserves linearity under addition,

$$\mathfrak{O}[\boldsymbol{u} + \boldsymbol{v}] = \mathfrak{O}[\boldsymbol{u}] + \mathfrak{O}[\boldsymbol{v}],$$

and satisfies homogeneity of degree 1 under scalar multiplication,

$$\mathfrak{O}[a \cdot^{\mathcal{F}} \boldsymbol{u}] = a \cdot^{\mathcal{F}} \mathfrak{O}[\boldsymbol{u}],$$

where $\boldsymbol{u}, \boldsymbol{v} \in \widetilde{\mathcal{V}}$, $a \in \mathcal{F}$, and $\cdot^{\mathcal{F}}$ denotes the operation of multiplication in the field $\mathcal{F} \in \mathscr{F}$. In the case that linearity under addition and homogeneity of degree 1 under scalar multiplication are not both preserved, the mapping $\mathfrak{O}$ is generally called an *operator*.

This definition captures the notion of a mapping between sets of objects in its most encompassing and general sense. If $\mathscr{F}$ has two identical elements $\mathcal{F}$ – that is both $\mathcal{V}$ and $\mathcal{V}'$ are finite vector spaces over $\mathcal{F}$ – an $\mathcal{F}$-linear operator is simply referred to as a *linear operator*. Furthermore, in the special case in which $\widetilde{\mathcal{V}} \subseteq \mathcal{V}$ and $\widetilde{\mathcal{V}}' \subseteq \mathcal{V}'$ are themselves finite vector spaces over a field $\mathcal{F}$, an $\mathcal{F}$-linear operator is a linear map. Naturally, each linear map is an $\mathcal{F}$-linear operator and each $\mathcal{F}$-linear operator an operator, while the converse is generally not true. Finally, if an operator, $\mathcal{F}$-linear operator or linear map allows for a representation in terms of matrices and no ambiguity can arise, we will refer to the associated mapping collectively as a *matrix operator* in the remainder of this book. The matrices $\boldsymbol{A}^{\mathscr{G}}$ and $\boldsymbol{A}^{\mathscr{L}(\mathscr{G})}$ introduced at the beginning of this section provide concrete examples of two such matrix operators.

With a sufficiently concise notational framework established, let us now explore in more rigorous terms the algebraic formalisation of walks through the Königsberg bridge graph $\mathscr{G}$. Although the matrix operators $\boldsymbol{A}^{\mathscr{G}}$ and $\boldsymbol{A}^{\mathscr{L}(\mathscr{G})}$, when respectively applied according to (3.8) and (3.9), can here certainly be utilised to obtain state vectors marking all nodes which could eventually be visited, and all edges which could eventually be traversed in a next step along a walk through $\mathscr{G}$, the construction of walk-generating operators which deliver not only complete walks but also valid state vector updates requires more careful consideration. Firstly, recalling (2.52) in Section 2.2.4, a walk through a graph is generally defined as an ordered set of adjacency relations in which each pair of subsequent adjacency relations shares at least one common node. Given an initial node, this set then fully determines the ordered set of consecutively visited nodes along the walk. In order to accommodate the approach developed here, let

$$\mathcal{W} := \left(i_k \in \mathcal{N}^{\mathcal{L}(\mathcal{G})} : k \in [1,m], m \in \mathbb{N}\right) \tag{3.12}$$

denote an arbitrary ordered set of not necessarily distinct adjacency relations. We will refer to $\mathcal{W}$ as *potential walk* and to $\mathcal{W}_k$ as the edge $i_k \in \mathcal{N}^{\mathcal{L}(\mathcal{G})} = \mathcal{E}^{\mathcal{G}}$ traversed at step k along $\mathcal{W}$. If each ordered pair $(\mathcal{W}_k, \mathcal{W}_{k+1}), k \in [1, m-1]$ of consecutive edges in $\mathcal{W}$ shares at least one common node in $\mathcal{G}$, the set $\mathcal{W}$ represents a walk of length $|\mathcal{W}| = m$ through $\mathcal{G}$. Given a potential walk $\mathcal{W}$ of length m, let $\mathcal{W}' = (\mathcal{W}_k : k \in [1, m'])$ then be an ordered subset of $\mathcal{W}$ formed by the first $m' \leq m$ elements of $\mathcal{W}$ such that m' is the maximum length rendering $\mathcal{W}'$ a walk. In the case the subset $\mathcal{W}'$ is comprised of distinct adjacency relations, we will refer to its defining set $\mathcal{W}$ as an Eulerian walk of length m' if $m' < m$, and to $\mathcal{W}$ as an Eulerian path if $m' = m$.

Secondly, as reaching the node targeted in step $k + 1$ along a potential walk necessitates that $\mathcal{W}_k$ is traversable, the operator updating the node state vector $\boldsymbol{s}_k^n$ at step k will depend not only on $\mathcal{W}_k$ but also on the actual state $\boldsymbol{s}_k^e$ of all edges. In a similar fashion, whether a potential walk can be continued by traversing edge $\mathcal{W}_k$ necessitates that $\mathcal{W}_k$ can be traversed and that the node visited at step k is an endpoint of $\mathcal{W}_k$, thus rendering the operator updating the edge state vector $\boldsymbol{s}_k^e$ at step k along $\mathcal{W}$ dependent on both $\mathcal{W}_k$ and $\boldsymbol{s}_k^n$. In order to formalise this mutual dependence of node and edge state vector updates in algebraic terms, we introduce the 4×7 matrix

$$\boldsymbol{B} := \begin{pmatrix} 1 & 1 & 1 & 1 & 1 & 0 & 0 \\ 0 & 0 & 1 & 1 & 0 & 0 & 1 \\ 1 & 1 & 0 & 0 & 0 & 1 & 0 \\ 0 & 0 & 0 & 0 & 1 & 1 & 1 \end{pmatrix}, \tag{3.13}$$

whose elements $B_{ij}: \mathcal{N}^{\mathcal{G}} \times \mathcal{N}^{\mathcal{L}(\mathcal{G})} \to \mathbb{B}$ mark all those nodes $j \in \mathcal{N}^{\mathcal{L}(\mathcal{G})}$ which are associated with edges in $\mathcal{G}$ having $i \in \mathcal{N}^{\mathcal{G}}$ as one of their endnodes. Similarly, the transpose $\boldsymbol{B}^{\top}$ defines a matrix whose elements B_{ji} associate with each edge the endnodes of this edge in $\mathcal{G}$. Both $\boldsymbol{B}$ and $\boldsymbol{B}^{\top}$ are then matrix operators which map between subsets of the two finite vector spaces $\mathcal{S}^n(\mathcal{G})$ and $\mathcal{S}^n(\mathcal{L}(\mathcal{G}))$.

Lastly, as at any step along a potential walk $\mathcal{W}$ of length m through $\mathcal{G}$, only one node can be visited and at most one edge can be traversed; the operators updating the state vectors $\boldsymbol{s}_k^n$ and $\boldsymbol{s}_k^e$ need to ensure that $\exists!\, i \in \mathcal{N}^{\mathcal{G}} : (s_k^n)_i = 1$

for each $k \in [1, m]$, and that $(s_k^e)_j +^{\mathbb{B}} (s_{k+1}^e)_j = 1$ for at most one $j \in \mathcal{N}^{\mathcal{L}(\mathcal{G})}$ at each step $k \in [1, m-1]$. In order to express these requirements later in a more convenient form, we introduce here with

$$(\delta_i^n)_j \colon [1, n] \subset \mathbb{N} \to \mathbb{B} \,, \; (\delta_i^n)_j := \begin{cases} 1 & \text{if } i = j, \\ 0 & \text{otherwise} \end{cases} \tag{3.14}$$

the *Kronecker delta vector* $\boldsymbol{\delta}_i^n \in \mathbb{B}^n$, and denote with

$$\operatorname{diag}[\boldsymbol{v}] : \mathcal{V} \to \mathcal{V} \times \mathcal{V} \tag{3.15}$$

the diagonal matrix representation of a vector $\boldsymbol{v}$ in an arbitrary vector space $\mathcal{V}$.

We now have all necessary algebraic tools at our disposal to construct walk-generating operators which not only update both the node and edge state vectors associated with the Königsberg bridge problem along a given ordered set of adjacency relations $\mathcal{W}$ in the desired fashion, but also distinguish whether $\mathcal{W}$ forms an Eulerian walk or, ideally, an Eulerian path through the Königsberg bridge graph. Indeed, by utilising (3.13), we easily find that the matrix product $\boldsymbol{s}_k^n \cdot \boldsymbol{B} \cdot \operatorname{diag}[\boldsymbol{s}_k^e]$ yields a vector marking all edges which, given the actual edge state vector $\boldsymbol{s}_k^e$, can be traversed from the node visited at step k. Right-hand matrix multiplication of this vector with $\operatorname{diag}[\boldsymbol{\delta}_{\mathcal{W}_k}^7]$ will then select from these edges the next edge $\mathcal{W}_k$ along our potential walk and, through further right-hand matrix multiplication with $\boldsymbol{B}^\mathsf{T}$, deliver either a zero vector or a vector with two non-zero elements marking the two endnodes of $\mathcal{W}_k$. In both cases, element-wise Boolean addition with the current node state vector $\boldsymbol{s}_k^n$ ensures that the new state vector $\boldsymbol{s}_{k+1}^n$ has only one non-zero element. Taken together, this eventually leaves

$$\boldsymbol{s}_{k+1}^n = \mathfrak{O}^n(\mathcal{W}_k, \boldsymbol{s}_k^e)[\boldsymbol{s}_k^n] = \boldsymbol{s}_k^n \cdot \mathfrak{O}^n(\mathcal{W}_k, \boldsymbol{s}_k^e) \tag{3.16}$$

with

$$\mathfrak{O}^n(i, \boldsymbol{s}^e) := \boldsymbol{I}^4 +^{\mathbb{B}} \boldsymbol{B} \cdot \operatorname{diag}[\boldsymbol{s}^e] \cdot \operatorname{diag}[\boldsymbol{\delta}_i^7] \cdot \boldsymbol{B}^\mathsf{T} \tag{3.17}$$

as algebraic representation of an operation which results in incremental updates of all node states along steps $k \geq 1$ of $\mathcal{W}$. Here, $\boldsymbol{s}_1^n \in \widetilde{\mathcal{S}}^n(\mathcal{G})$ denotes the initial node state vector marking the node in $\mathcal{G}$ from which $\mathcal{W}$ starts, and $\boldsymbol{I}^n$ the $(n \times n)$-dimensional identity matrix. With this, $\mathfrak{O}^n(i, \boldsymbol{s}^e) \colon \widetilde{\mathcal{S}}^n(\mathcal{G}) \to \widetilde{\mathcal{S}}^n(\mathcal{G})$ defines a 4×4 matrix operator in $\widetilde{\mathcal{S}}^n(\mathcal{G})$ which depends on both the actual edge state vector $\boldsymbol{s}^e$ and the edge $i \in \mathcal{N}^{\mathcal{L}(\mathcal{G})}$ being traversed at any given step along our potential walk $\mathcal{W}$.

The formalisation of the incremental update of all edge states along the steps of a given potential walk $\mathcal{W}$ can be approached in a similar fashion by conceiving of a 7×7 matrix operator $\mathfrak{O}^e(i, \boldsymbol{s}^n) \colon \mathcal{S}^n(\mathcal{L}(\mathcal{G})) \to \mathcal{S}^n(\mathcal{L}(\mathcal{G}))$ which

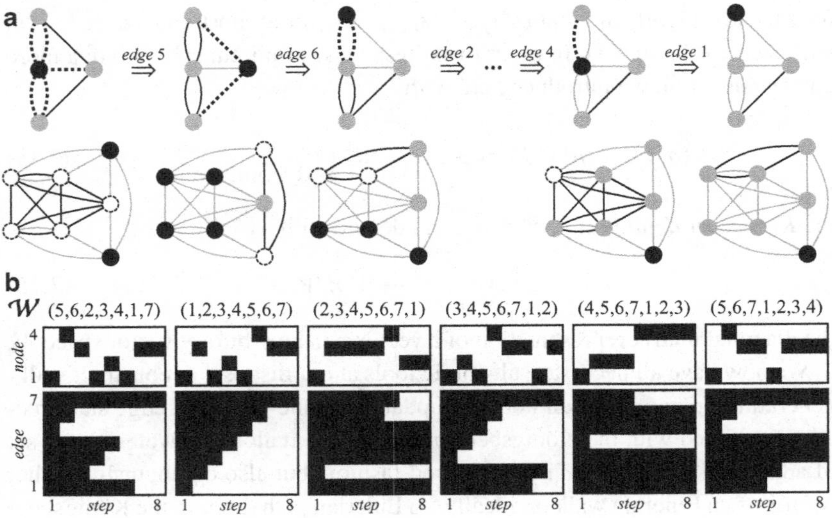

Figure 3.2 State vector changes during walks through the Königsberg bridge graph $\mathcal{G}$. **a:** Representative example of node state changes in $\mathcal{G}$ and its line graph $\mathcal{L}(\mathcal{G})$ following the potential walk $\mathcal{W} = (5,6,2,3,4,1,7)$. Black nodes in $\mathcal{G}$ indicate visited areas along $\mathcal{W}$, black nodes in $\mathcal{L}(\mathcal{G})$ traversable bridges, and dashed edges and nodes all bridges which can be crossed from the area being actually visited. **b:** Rasterplots of node state changes in $\mathcal{G}$ and $\mathcal{L}(\mathcal{G})$ for a small selection of potential walks $\mathcal{W}$ through $\mathcal{G}$, with black indicating non-zero states. Exploring in this manner each possible combination of distinct edges of $\mathcal{G}$ will always leave at least one node of $\mathcal{L}(\mathcal{G})$ in a non-zero state, and eventually will resolve the problem of Königsberg's bridges in the negative.

necessarily will depend on the actual node state vector s^n and the edge $i \in \mathcal{N}^{\mathcal{L}(\mathcal{G})}$ being traversed. We eventually find

$$s^e_{k+1} = \mathfrak{O}^e(\mathcal{W}_k, s^n_k)[s^e_k] = s^e_k \cdot \mathfrak{O}^e(\mathcal{W}_k, s^n_k) \tag{3.18}$$

with

$$\mathfrak{O}^e(i, s^n) := I^7 +^{\mathbb{B}} \operatorname{diag}[\delta^7_i] \cdot B^\top \cdot \operatorname{diag}[s^n] \cdot B \cdot \operatorname{diag}[\delta^7_i], \tag{3.19}$$

where the initial edge state vector $s^e_1 = (1,1,1,1,1,1,1)$ marks all edges as being traversable. It is important to stress here that, due to their general dependence on edge and node states, neither $\mathfrak{O}^n(i, s^e)$ nor $\mathfrak{O}^e(i, s^n)$ satisfy linearity under vector addition, and thus, they are operators in the strict sense of Definition 3.3. Moreover, owing to their construction, both of these operators ensure that the state of at most two nodes, namely those serving as endnodes of the traversed edge, and the state of at most one edge, namely that being traversed, are updated at each step, and that both state vectors remain unchanged if $\mathcal{W}$ contains an edge which can no longer be traversed or cannot be reached from the node being visited. This latter property of our walk-generating operators, then, provides not only a viable termination condition when addressing the Königsberg bridge problem but, as we will see later, also a viable means to distinguish potential walks into Eulerian walks and Eulerian paths.

Let us conclude this section by exemplifying the application of $\mathfrak{O}^n(i, \boldsymbol{s}^e)$ and $\mathfrak{O}^e(i, \boldsymbol{s}^n)$. To that end, let $\mathcal{W} = (5, 6, 2, 3, 4, 1, 7)$ be a potential walk. The node state updates in both $\mathcal{G}$ and $\mathcal{L}(\mathcal{G})$ along $\mathcal{W}$ resulting from (3.16) and (3.18) are illustrated in Fig. 3.2a. Reaching step 7, we find $(s_7^n)_3 = 1$, with only node 7 in $\mathcal{L}(\mathcal{G})$ being marked as traversable. As the associated edge in $\mathcal{G}$ is not connected to node 3, no further state updates can occur, and one not-traversed edge will remain. This renders $\mathcal{W}$ an Eulerian walk of length 6 which, by definition, cannot be an Eulerian path. A similar result is reached when considering other potential walks as well (see Fig. 3.2b). Indeed, with some investment, it can be shown that any potential walk $\mathcal{W}$ comprised of conceivable combinations of distinct edges will deliver at least one non-zero element in $\boldsymbol{s}^e$, eventually leaving us to conclude that the Königsberg bridge problem has no positive solution. Certainly, with $7! = 5{,}040$ possible combinations of seven bridges and, thus, potential walks to explore, the algebraic formalisation (3.16)–(3.19) of the active search for an Eulerian path through the city by means of walk-generating operators acting on state vectors does very little to cope with the combinatorial complexity inherent to an approach based on exhaustive search. However, as we will explore in greater detail in Section 3.4, it is possible, at least in principle, to curb this complexity somewhat by exploiting the algebraic properties of combinations of $\mathfrak{O}^n(i, \boldsymbol{s}^e)$ and $\mathfrak{O}^e(i, \boldsymbol{s}^n)$.

3.3 Mappings between Vector Spaces

The previous section introduced with (3.19) an operator $\mathfrak{O}^e(i, \boldsymbol{s}^n)$ which acts as mapping within a vector space $\mathcal{S}^n(\mathcal{L}(\mathcal{G}))$, and with (3.17) an operator $\mathfrak{O}^n(i, \boldsymbol{s}^e)$ which acts within a fixed subset $\widetilde{\mathcal{S}}^n(\mathcal{G}) \subset \mathcal{S}^n(\mathcal{G})$ of a vector space. Matrix operators such as $\boldsymbol{A}^{\mathcal{G}}$ in (3.6) and $\boldsymbol{A}^{\mathcal{L}(\mathcal{G})}$ in (3.7) map through right-hand matrix multiplication between distinct subsets of vector spaces $\mathcal{S}^n(\mathcal{G})$ and $\mathcal{S}^n(\mathcal{L}(\mathcal{G}))$ respectively, and with $\boldsymbol{B}$ in (3.13) and its transpose $\boldsymbol{B}^\top$ we found matrix representations of two operators which through right-hand matrix multiplication map between subsets of two distinct finite vector spaces $\mathcal{S}^n(\mathcal{G})$ and $\mathcal{S}^n(\mathcal{L}(\mathcal{G}))$. Especially these latter types of operators, namely those which act as mappings between different vector spaces or as mappings between distinct subsets of vector spaces, play a central role in a whole variety of graph-theoretical contexts. Indeed, as we will see in later chapters when exploring the algebraic formalisation of measuring various graph properties or the modification of node and edge sets during the algebraic construction and transformation of graphs, such more general operators are instrumental in establishing our operator graph-theoretical framework. Before proceeding, we therefore should take a closer look at the various notions introduced in Definition 3.3, and exemplify their distinctive nature along with some of the conceptual subtleties associated with their usage.

To that end, let us focus on a number of already-introduced simple functions of relevance for later chapters, starting with the floor and ceiling of rational numbers defined in (3.10). Both of these functions map the field of rational numbers $\mathbb{Q}$ into the the ring of integers $\mathbb{Z}$, which, although being closed under addition and multiplication, does itself not form a vector space in the strict sense of Definition 3.1 because the set of integers is not a field. More importantly however, neither of these functions satisfies linearity under addition as

$$\begin{aligned} \lfloor p \rfloor + \lfloor q \rfloor \leq \lfloor p + q \rfloor \leq \lfloor p \rfloor + \lfloor q \rfloor + 1, \\ \lceil p \rceil + \lceil q \rceil - 1 \leq \lceil p + q \rceil \leq \lceil p \rceil + \lceil q \rceil \end{aligned} \tag{3.20}$$

for $p, q \in \mathbb{Q}$, and homogeneity of degree 1 under scalar multiplication as

$$\begin{aligned} \lfloor n \cdot q \rfloor = n \cdot \lfloor q \rfloor + \lfloor n \cdot \{q\} \rfloor, \\ \lceil n \cdot q \rceil = n \cdot \lceil q \rceil + \lceil n \cdot \{q\} \rceil - n \end{aligned} \tag{3.21}$$

for $n \in \mathbb{N} \subset \mathbb{Z}$ and $q \in \mathbb{Q} \setminus \mathbb{Z}$, where $\{q\} = q - \lfloor q \rfloor$ denotes the fractional part of q. Adhering to Definition 3.3 and generalising (3.10) with an eye on later applications within a graph-theoretical context, the floor and ceiling functions then define operators

$$\begin{aligned} \lfloor . \rfloor &: \mathbb{Q}^{m \times n} \to \mathbb{Z}^{m \times n} \subset \mathbb{Q}^{m \times n}, \\ \lceil . \rceil &: \mathbb{Q}^{m \times n} \to \mathbb{Z}^{m \times n} \subset \mathbb{Q}^{m \times n} \end{aligned} \tag{3.22}$$

which act as mappings from the vector space $\mathbb{Q}^{m \times n}$ over $\mathbb{Q}$ into its subset $\mathbb{Z}^{m \times n}$ and, when applied to $\boldsymbol{A} \in \mathbb{Q}^{m \times n}$, yield matrices $\lfloor \boldsymbol{A} \rfloor, \lceil \boldsymbol{A} \rceil \in \mathbb{Z}^{m \times n}$ with elements

$$\begin{aligned} \lfloor \boldsymbol{A} \rfloor_{ij} &: [1, m] \times [1, n] \subset \mathbb{N}^2 \to \mathbb{Z}\,, \; \lfloor \boldsymbol{A} \rfloor_{ij} := \max\{n_{ij} \in \mathbb{Z} \colon n_{ij} \leq A_{ij}\}, \\ \lceil \boldsymbol{A} \rceil_{ij} &: [1, m] \times [1, n] \subset \mathbb{N}^2 \to \mathbb{Z}\,, \; \lceil \boldsymbol{A} \rceil_{ij} := \min\{n_{ij} \in \mathbb{Z} \colon n_{ij} \geq A_{ij}\}. \end{aligned} \tag{3.23}$$

We will refer to these operators as *floor operator* and *ceiling operator*.

Similarly, by defining with $\mathbb{B}_{-1} := \{-1, 0, 1\}$ an extension of the Boolean set $\mathbb{B}$, the signum function (3.11) can be thought of as representing an operator

$$\operatorname{sgn} \colon \mathbb{Q}^{m \times n} \to \mathbb{B}_{-1}^{m \times n} \subset \mathbb{Q}^{m \times n}, \tag{3.24}$$

referred to as the *signum operator*, which maps each $\boldsymbol{A} \in \mathbb{Q}^{m\times n}$ into a matrix in $\mathbb{B}_{-1}^{m\times n} \subset \mathbb{Q}^{m\times n}$ with elements given by

$$\mathrm{sgn}\,[\boldsymbol{A}]_{ij}]\colon [1,m]\times[1,n]\subset\mathbb{N}^2 \to \mathbb{B}_{-1}\,,\ \mathrm{sgn}\,[\boldsymbol{A}]_{ij} := \mathrm{sgn}\,[A_{ij}], \tag{3.25}$$

and which satisfies neither linearity under addition nor homogeneity of degree 1 under scalar multiplication. However, both of these useful properties can certainly be salvaged if we appropriately adapt the domain of the signum operator. In order to demonstrate this, we note that, not unlike the Boolean set $\mathbb{B}$, the set $\mathbb{B}_{-1}$ under addition and multiplication given by

$+^{\mathbb{B}_{-1}}$	−1	0	1
−1	1	−1	0
0	−1	0	1
1	0	1	−1

$\cdot^{\mathbb{B}_{-1}}$	−1	0	1
−1	1	0	−1
0	0	0	0
1	−1	0	1

(3.26)

satisfies all field axioms with additive identity 0 and multiplicative identity 1, and thus forms a field isomorphic to the Galois field $GF(3)$. By then restricting the domain of the signum operator (3.24), (3.25) to the vector space $\mathbb{B}_{-1}^{m\times n}$ over $\mathbb{B}_{-1}$, the mapping

$$\begin{aligned} &\mathrm{sgn}^{\mathbb{B}_{-1}}\colon \mathbb{B}_{-1}^{m\times n} \to \mathbb{B}_{-1}^{m\times n}\,, \\ &\mathrm{sgn}^{\mathbb{B}_{-1}}[\boldsymbol{A}]_{ij}\colon [1,m]\times[1,n]\subset\mathbb{N}^2 \to \mathbb{B}_{-1}\,,\ \mathrm{sgn}^{\mathbb{B}_{-1}}[\boldsymbol{A}]_{ij} := \mathrm{sgn}[A_{ij}] \end{aligned} \tag{3.27}$$

will preserve both linearity under vector addition, defined by element-wise application of $+^{\mathbb{B}_{-1}}$, and homogeneity of degree 1 under scalar multiplication, defined by element-wise application of $\cdot^{\mathbb{B}_{-1}}$, as

$$\begin{aligned} \mathrm{sgn}^{\mathbb{B}_{-1}}[\boldsymbol{A} +^{\mathbb{B}_{-1}} \boldsymbol{B}] &= \mathrm{sgn}^{\mathbb{B}_{-1}}[\boldsymbol{A}] +^{\mathbb{B}_{-1}} \mathrm{sgn}^{\mathbb{B}_{-1}}[\boldsymbol{B}] \in \mathbb{B}_{-1}^{m\times n}, \\ \mathrm{sgn}^{\mathbb{B}_{-1}}[a \cdot^{\mathbb{B}_{-1}} \boldsymbol{A}] &= a \cdot^{\mathbb{B}_{-1}} \mathrm{sgn}^{\mathbb{B}_{-1}}[\boldsymbol{A}] \in \mathbb{B}_{-1}^{m\times n} \end{aligned}$$

for all $\boldsymbol{A}, \boldsymbol{B} \in \mathbb{B}_{-1}^{m\times n}$ and $a \in \mathbb{B}_{-1}$. This, in turn, renders the *Boolean signum operator* $\mathrm{sgn}^{\mathbb{B}_{-1}}$ not only a $\mathbb{B}_{-1}$-linear operator according to Definition 3.3 but, according to Definition 3.2, indeed an albeit-trivial linear map acting on the vector space $\mathbb{B}_{-1}^{m\times n}$ over $\mathbb{B}_{-1}$ which simply returns its argument.

This interesting line of reasoning can also be applied to the Kronecker delta function $\delta[q]$, introduced for rational arguments $q \in \mathbb{Q}$ in (2.13). We eventually obtain the *Kronecker delta operator*

$$\boldsymbol{\delta}\colon \mathbb{Q}^{m\times n} \to \mathbb{B}^{m\times n} \subset \mathbb{Q}^{m\times n}, \tag{3.28}$$

which returns for each $\boldsymbol{A} \in \mathbb{Q}^{m\times n}$ a matrix $\boldsymbol{\delta}[\boldsymbol{A}] \in \mathbb{B}^{m\times n}$ with elements

$$\boldsymbol{\delta}[\boldsymbol{A}]_{ij}\colon [1,m]\times[1,n]\subset\mathbb{N}^2 \to \mathbb{B}\,,\ \boldsymbol{\delta}[\boldsymbol{A}]_{ij} := \delta[A_{ij}], \tag{3.29}$$

and with

$$\begin{aligned}\bar{\boldsymbol{\delta}}: \mathbb{Q}^{m\times n} &\to \mathbb{B}^{m\times n} \subset \mathbb{Q}^{m\times n}, \\ \bar{\boldsymbol{\delta}}[\boldsymbol{A}]_{ij}: [1,m]\times[1,n] \subset \mathbb{N}^2 &\to \mathbb{B}, \bar{\boldsymbol{\delta}}[\boldsymbol{A}]_{ij} := 1 - \delta[A_{ij}],\end{aligned} \tag{3.30}$$

a mapping which we will refer to as the *inverse Kronecker delta operator*. Similar to the signum operator, neither of these operators is linear under addition, as generally $\delta[p+q] \neq \delta[p]+\delta[q]$, or homogeneous under scalar multiplication, as generally $p \cdot \delta[q] \notin \mathbb{B}$ for $p, q \in \mathbb{Q}$. Recalling that vectors in $\mathbb{B}^{m\times n} \subset \mathbb{Q}^{m\times n}$ form with (3.1) a Boolean vector space over $\mathbb{B}$, it is however possible to define the *Boolean Kronecker delta operator* $\boldsymbol{\delta}^{\mathbb{B}}: \mathbb{B}^{m\times n} \to \mathbb{B}^{m\times n}$ and its inverse $\bar{\boldsymbol{\delta}}^{\mathbb{B}}$ by restricting the domain of $\boldsymbol{\delta}$ and $\bar{\boldsymbol{\delta}}$ to $\mathbb{B}^{m\times n}$. With this, both operators then act as mappings in $\mathbb{B}^{m\times n}$, and it can easily be shown that $\bar{\boldsymbol{\delta}}^{\mathbb{B}}$ satisfies linearity under Boolean addition $+^{\mathbb{B}}$ and homogeneity of degree 1 under scalar Boolean multiplication $.^{\mathbb{B}}$ as given in (3.1). This renders $\bar{\boldsymbol{\delta}}^{\mathbb{B}}$ not only a $\mathbb{B}$-linear operator but a linear map – indeed, an endomorphism – of the Boolean vector space $\mathbb{B}^{m\times n}$ over $\mathbb{B}$, while $\boldsymbol{\delta}^{\mathbb{B}}$ alongside $\boldsymbol{\delta}$ and $\bar{\boldsymbol{\delta}}$ remain to adhere to only the most general notion of an operator introduced in Definition 3.3.

It is interesting to note here that although $\mathbb{B}^{m\times n}$ as subset of $\mathbb{Q}^{m\times n}$ itself forms a finite vector space, the property of $\mathbb{B}$-linearity of the linear map $\bar{\boldsymbol{\delta}}^{\mathbb{B}}$ is not inherited by the operator $\bar{\boldsymbol{\delta}}$ when expanding its codomain to $\mathbb{Q}^{m\times n}$ because the Boolean field $\mathbb{B}$ over which $\mathbb{B}^{m\times n}$ is defined does not form a subfield of $\mathbb{Q}$. In general, such an inheritance is not even guaranteed if $\mathcal{F}'$ is a subfield of $\mathcal{F}$, in which case a finite vector space $\mathcal{V}$ over $\mathcal{F}$ is necessarily also a vector space over $\mathcal{F}'$. While here an $\mathcal{F}$-linear operator $\mathfrak{O}: \mathcal{V} \to \mathcal{V}$ will also be $\mathcal{F}'$-linear, the opposite is generally not true, as the example of conjugation of complex numbers, which is a $\mathbb{R}$-linear but not $\mathbb{C}$-linear operator acting as an endomorphism in the complex vector space, demonstrates. In a similar fashion, if $\mathcal{V}' \subseteq \mathcal{V}$ is a vector subspace over $\mathcal{F}'$ of its embedding vector space $\mathcal{V}$ over $\mathcal{F}$, and if $\mathcal{F}'$ is a subfield of $\mathcal{F}$, then an $\mathcal{F}$-linear operator $\mathfrak{O}: \mathcal{V} \to \mathcal{V}$ will also be $\mathcal{F}'$-linear and act as such on the subspace $\mathcal{V}'$, while the opposite for an $\mathcal{F}'$-linear operator $\mathfrak{O}' : \mathcal{V}' \to \mathcal{V}'$ is generally not true.

To illustrate this point in more detail, let us consider as a final example with

$$\mathrm{Tr}: \mathbb{Q}^{n\times n} \to \mathbb{Q}\,,\ \mathrm{Tr}\,[\boldsymbol{A}] := \sum_{i=1}^{n} A_{ii} \tag{3.31}$$

the *trace operator* which delivers the sum over all diagonal elements of square matrices $\boldsymbol{A} \in \mathbb{Q}^{n\times n}$. With

$$\begin{aligned}\mathrm{Tr}\,[\boldsymbol{A}+\boldsymbol{B}] &= \mathrm{Tr}\,[\boldsymbol{A}] + \mathrm{Tr}\,[\boldsymbol{B}], \\ \mathrm{Tr}\,[c\cdot\boldsymbol{A}] &= c\cdot\mathrm{Tr}\,[\boldsymbol{A}]\end{aligned} \tag{3.32}$$

for all $\boldsymbol{A}, \boldsymbol{B} \in \mathbb{Q}^{n\times n}, c \in \mathbb{Q}$, the trace is certainly a linear map in the vector space $\mathbb{Q}^{n\times n}$ over $\mathbb{Q}$. For the sake of our argument, let now $\mathrm{Tr}^{\mathbb{R}}\colon \mathbb{R}^{n\times n} \to \mathbb{R}$ and $\mathrm{Tr}^{\mathbb{Z}}\colon \mathbb{Z}^{n\times n} \to \mathbb{Z}$ define trace operators which respectively act on the vector space $\mathbb{R}^{n\times n}$ over $\mathbb{R}$ and its subset $\mathbb{Z}^{n\times n}$. Then $\mathrm{Tr}^{\mathbb{R}}$ is both a $\mathbb{R}$-linear operator and a $\mathbb{Q}$-linear operator in $\mathbb{R}^{n\times n}$, as $\mathbb{Q}$ is a subfield of the field of real numbers, while $\mathrm{Tr}^{\mathbb{Z}}$ remains as only an operator in $\mathbb{Z}^{n\times n} \subset \mathbb{R}^{n\times n}$ according to Definition 3.3 because $\mathbb{Z}^{n\times n}$ is not a vector space over a field, nor is $\mathbb{Z}$ a field. On the other hand, the *Boolean trace operator*

$$\mathrm{Tr}^{\mathbb{B}}\colon \mathbb{B}^{n\times n} \to \mathbb{B}\ ,\ \mathrm{Tr}^{\mathbb{B}}[\boldsymbol{B}] := \sum_{i=1}^{n}{}^{\mathbb{B}}\, B_{ii} = B_{11} +^{\mathbb{B}} \cdots +^{\mathbb{B}} B_{nn} \tag{3.33}$$

defines a linear map in the vector space $\mathbb{B}^{n\times n}$ over $\mathbb{B}$ because

$$\begin{aligned} \mathrm{Tr}^{\mathbb{B}}\left[\boldsymbol{A} +^{\mathbb{B}} \boldsymbol{B}\right] &= \mathrm{Tr}^{\mathbb{B}}[\boldsymbol{A}] +^{\mathbb{B}} \mathrm{Tr}^{\mathbb{B}}[\boldsymbol{B}], \\ \mathrm{Tr}^{\mathbb{B}}\left[c \cdot^{\mathbb{B}} \boldsymbol{A}\right] &= c \cdot^{\mathbb{B}} \mathrm{Tr}[\boldsymbol{A}] \end{aligned} \tag{3.34}$$

for all $\boldsymbol{A}, \boldsymbol{B} \in \mathbb{B}^{n\times n}, c \in \mathbb{B}$. However, as $\mathbb{B}$ is not a subfield of $\mathbb{Q}$, and as $\mathbb{B}^{n\times n}$ does not comprise a vector subspace of $\mathbb{Q}^{n\times n}$ over $\mathbb{Q}$, the trace operator (3.31) defined in $\mathbb{Q}^{n\times n}$ will not be $\mathbb{B}$-linear.

All of the linear maps, linear operators and operators introduced above present concrete examples of mappings between different vector spaces or between subsets of vector spaces within the notational framework established in Definitions 3.2 and 3.3. It certainly is possible, and sometimes useful, to weaken the notions of a linear map and linear operator distinguished in this section and the previous section by considering mappings between finite modules over a ring instead of finite vector spaces over a field. A *module* over a ring $\mathcal{R}$ is here defined as a set of objects closed under vector addition and scalar multiplication which obeys the rules listed in Definition 3.1, but with scalars being elements of a given ring $\mathcal{R}$ and not a field $\mathcal{F}$. As the set of integers $\mathbb{Z}$ is a classical example of a ring, a mapping such as $\mathrm{Tr}^{\mathbb{Z}}$ would then be considered a linear map $\mathbb{Z}^{n\times n} \to \mathbb{Z}$, and the operator $\mathrm{Tr}^{\mathbb{R}}$ not only would be $\mathbb{R}$-linear and $\mathbb{Q}$-linear, but it would inherit $\mathbb{Z}$-linearity as well. Although many graph-theoretical formalisations would arguably benefit from such a realignment of our notions, however, we will continue to adhere to those presented and most commonly employed across the mathematical literature.

3.4 Algebras of Operators

What happens if we concatenate two of the floor or ceiling operators introduced in the previous section? As the codomain $\mathbb{Z}^{m\times n}$ of these operators is a subset of $\mathbb{Q}^{m\times n}$, such a combination is certainly feasible and will yield

$$\begin{aligned} \big\lfloor \lfloor \boldsymbol{A} \rfloor \big\rfloor &= \lfloor \boldsymbol{A} \rfloor \text{ and } \big\lceil \lceil \boldsymbol{A} \rceil \big\rceil = \lceil \boldsymbol{A} \rceil, \\ \big\lceil \lfloor \boldsymbol{A} \rfloor \big\rceil &= \lfloor \boldsymbol{A} \rfloor \text{ and } \big\lfloor \lceil \boldsymbol{A} \rceil \big\rfloor = \lceil \boldsymbol{A} \rceil \end{aligned} \tag{3.35}$$

for all $\boldsymbol{A} \in \mathbb{Q}^{m\times n}$. In a similar fashion, the successive application of two signum operators (3.25) results in

$$\operatorname{sgn} \circ \operatorname{sgn}[\boldsymbol{A}] := \operatorname{sgn}[\operatorname{sgn}[\boldsymbol{A}]] = \operatorname{sgn}[\boldsymbol{A}], \tag{3.36}$$

where, for notational convenience, we introduced the symbol $\circ$ to denote the *composition of operators*. In the case of the Kronecker delta operators $\boldsymbol{\delta}$ and $\bar{\boldsymbol{\delta}}$ defined in (3.29) and (3.30), respectively, it can easily be shown that

$$\begin{aligned} \boldsymbol{\delta} \circ \boldsymbol{\delta}[\boldsymbol{A}] &:= \boldsymbol{\delta}[\boldsymbol{\delta}[\boldsymbol{A}]] = \bar{\boldsymbol{\delta}}[\boldsymbol{A}] \text{ and } \bar{\boldsymbol{\delta}} \circ \bar{\boldsymbol{\delta}}[\boldsymbol{A}] := \bar{\boldsymbol{\delta}}[\bar{\boldsymbol{\delta}}[\boldsymbol{A}]] = \bar{\boldsymbol{\delta}}[\boldsymbol{A}], \\ \boldsymbol{\delta} \circ \bar{\boldsymbol{\delta}}[\boldsymbol{A}] &:= \boldsymbol{\delta}[\bar{\boldsymbol{\delta}}[\boldsymbol{A}]] = \boldsymbol{\delta}[\boldsymbol{A}] \text{ and } \bar{\boldsymbol{\delta}} \circ \boldsymbol{\delta}[\boldsymbol{A}] := \bar{\boldsymbol{\delta}}[\boldsymbol{\delta}[\boldsymbol{A}]] = \boldsymbol{\delta}[\boldsymbol{A}], \end{aligned} \tag{3.37}$$

while for the trace operator (3.31), we find

$$\operatorname{Tr} \circ \operatorname{Tr}[\boldsymbol{A}] := \operatorname{Tr}[\operatorname{Tr}[\boldsymbol{A}]] = \operatorname{Tr}[\boldsymbol{A}] \tag{3.38}$$

for all $\boldsymbol{A} \in \mathbb{Q}^{n\times n}$ as the trace of a scalar returns the scalar itself.

Composition rules such as those presented in (3.35)–(3.38) bestow a given set of operators with an additional structure, called an *algebraic structure*. Such a structure can indeed be defined for any set of objects $\mathcal{A}$ as a collection of *finitary operations* on $\mathcal{A}$ – that is operations with only a finite number of operands from $\mathcal{A}$. In most universal and abstract terms, a set $\mathcal{A}$ endowed with an algebraic structure is then referred to as *algebra* [31]. Perhaps the most widely known and utilised examples of algebras include the sets of complex, real and rational numbers along with the vector spaces defined over these fields, with scalar and matrix multiplication providing the composition of elements in these sets and, thus, defining their respective algebraic structures. Other well-known examples include the set of continuous linear operators acting on topological vector spaces, such as the gradient, Laplacian or d'Alembertian, which features prominently as algebra of differential operators in the field of functional analysis, while operators formalising physical quantum states, their creation and annihilation serve as illustrative examples of finitary operations comprising algebras within the confines of quantum field and string theory. In order to distinguish subtle variations that the notion of an algebra experiences across different branches of mathematics and theoretical physics, and to tailor its use for the subject matter presented in this book, let us begin by formulating the following

Definition 3.4 (algebra) Let $\mathcal{A}$ be a set of objects, and let O be a set of finitary operations on $\mathcal{A}$. The set O is called an *algebraic structure* on $\mathcal{A}$ and the tuple $\mathscr{A} = (\mathcal{A}, \mathcal{O})$ an *algebra* with algebraic structure $\mathcal{O}$. Let $\mathcal{A}$ be a vector space over a field $\mathcal{F}$ with $+ \colon \mathcal{A} \times \mathcal{A} \to \mathcal{A}$ denoting the operation of vector addition and $\cdot \colon \mathcal{F} \times \mathcal{A} \to \mathcal{A}$ the operation of scalar multiplication. An algebra $\mathscr{A} = (\mathcal{A}, \mathcal{O})$ is called an *algebra over* $\mathcal{F}$, or simply $\mathcal{F}$*-algebra*, if its algebraic structure $\mathcal{O}$ contains the finitary operation of multiplication $\circ \colon \mathcal{A} \times \mathcal{A} \to \mathcal{A}$ on $\mathcal{A}$ and satisfies compatibility with scalar multiplication,

$$a \cdot (\boldsymbol{u} \circ \boldsymbol{v}) = (a \cdot \boldsymbol{u}) \circ \boldsymbol{v} = \boldsymbol{u} \circ (a \cdot \boldsymbol{v}),$$

as well as left-distributivity,

$$\boldsymbol{u} \circ (\boldsymbol{v} + \boldsymbol{w}) = \boldsymbol{u} \circ \boldsymbol{v} + \boldsymbol{u} \circ \boldsymbol{w},$$

and right-distributivity,

$$(\boldsymbol{u} + \boldsymbol{v}) \circ \boldsymbol{w} = \boldsymbol{u} \circ \boldsymbol{w} + \boldsymbol{v} \circ \boldsymbol{w},$$

with respect to vector addition for all $\boldsymbol{u}, \boldsymbol{v}, \boldsymbol{w} \in \mathcal{A}$ and $a \in \mathcal{F}$.

This definition is certainly rather general and encompasses each set of objects $\mathcal{A}$ for which a sufficiently rich set of finitary operations $\mathcal{O}$ can be defined. Naturally, each $\mathcal{F}$-algebra $\mathscr{A} = (\mathcal{A}, \mathcal{O})$ is here an algebra, and its algebraic structure $\mathcal{O}$ must contain at least three elements, namely multiplication and addition on $\mathcal{A}$ as well as the operation of scalar multiplication with elements of $\mathcal{F}$. The operation of multiplication on $\mathcal{A}$ is also called a *bilinear product*, as it satisfies both linearity with respect to addition, that is left-distributivity and right-distributivity, and linearity with respect to scalar multiplication. Furthermore, we will strictly adhere here to the common convention that the operation of multiplication in an $\mathcal{F}$-algebra is not required to be associative – that is, it does not necessarily satisfy

$$(\boldsymbol{u} \circ \boldsymbol{v}) \circ \boldsymbol{w} = \boldsymbol{u} \circ (\boldsymbol{v} \circ \boldsymbol{w}) = \boldsymbol{u} \circ \boldsymbol{v} \circ \boldsymbol{w} \tag{3.39}$$

for all $\boldsymbol{u}, \boldsymbol{v}, \boldsymbol{w} \in \mathcal{A}$ – and $\mathcal{A}$ is not required to possess a multiplicative identity. If the latter is the case and (3.39) is satisfied, an algebra is typically referred to as *associative algebra with identity*. Similarly, if

$$\boldsymbol{u} \circ \boldsymbol{v} = \boldsymbol{v} \circ \boldsymbol{u} \tag{3.40}$$

for all $\boldsymbol{u}, \boldsymbol{v} \in \mathcal{A}$, an algebra is called a *commutative algebra*. Most algebras we will encounter later within an operator graph-theoretical context are associative but, unfortunately, not commutative.

The class of algebras of particular importance in this context is obtained if the set $\mathcal{A}$ is comprised of objects which themselves operate on finite vector spaces or subsets thereof – that is, if $\mathcal{A}$ itself is a set of linear maps, linear operators or operators. In this case, the finitary operation acting as multiplication on $\mathcal{A}$ can be viewed as composition of operators, and $\mathcal{A}$ is said to form an *algebra of operators*. Indeed, utilising the various examples of operators introduced in the previous section, $\mathcal{A}$ could be any of the sets $\{\lfloor . \rfloor, \lceil . \rceil\}$, $\{\operatorname{sgn}\}$, $\{\delta, \bar{\delta}\}$ or $\{\operatorname{Tr}\}$ and eventually form, together with its respective operation of composition (3.35)–(3.38) as the sole finitary operation, an algebra of operators. As such finite sets of discrete operators and their rules of composition will be prominently employed in the manipulation of graph-theoretical objects later on, let us recognise the special notion of an algebra of operators and its connotations by formulating

Definition 3.5 (operator algebra) Let $\mathscr{A} = (\mathcal{A}, O)$ be an algebra. If $\mathcal{A}$ is a finite set of operators and O contains a finitary operation of multiplication $\circ\colon \mathcal{A} \times \mathcal{A} \to \mathcal{A}$ on $\mathcal{A}$ acting as composition of operators, then $\mathscr{A}$ is called an *algebra of operators* with algebraic structure O. Let $\mathcal{F}$ be a field, and let $\cdot\colon \mathcal{F} \times \mathcal{A} \to \mathcal{A}$ denote the operation of scalar multiplication. An algebra of operators $\mathscr{A}$ is called *operator algebra* if the operation of multiplication is compatible with scalar multiplication by satisfying

$$a \cdot (\mathfrak{A} \circ \mathfrak{B}) = (a \cdot \mathfrak{A}) \circ \mathfrak{B} = \mathfrak{A} \circ (a \cdot \mathfrak{B}),$$

with $\mathfrak{A}, \mathfrak{B} \in \mathcal{A}$ and $a \in \mathcal{F}$. If in an operator algebra $\mathscr{A} = (\mathcal{A}, O)$ the set of operators $\mathcal{A}$ forms a vector space over $\mathcal{F}$ with $+ : \mathcal{A} \times \mathcal{A} \to \mathcal{A}$ denoting the operation of vector addition, and if the operation of multiplication $\circ$ is both left-distributive and right-distributive by satisfying

$$\mathfrak{A} \circ (\mathfrak{B} + \mathfrak{C}) = \mathfrak{A} \circ \mathfrak{B} + \mathfrak{A} \circ \mathfrak{C},$$
$$(\mathfrak{A} + \mathfrak{B}) \circ \mathfrak{C} = \mathfrak{A} \circ \mathfrak{C} + \mathfrak{B} \circ \mathfrak{C}$$

for all $\mathfrak{A}, \mathfrak{B}, \mathfrak{C} \in \mathcal{A}$, then $\mathscr{A}$ is called an *operator algebra over* $\mathcal{F}$ or simply an $\mathcal{F}$*-operator algebra*.

In this definition, we distinguish between the notion of an operator algebra and the more specific type of an $\mathcal{F}$-operator algebra, as the latter requires that the set of operators $\mathcal{A}$ itself is endowed with an additional structure which renders the algebra closed under vector addition. Such a closure, however, is generally not ensured and often necessitates, as we will exemplify below, the enlargement of the set of operators $\mathcal{A}$, even if $\mathcal{A}$ is comprised of operators which themselves preserve linearity under vector addition. In contrast, compatibility with scalar multiplication is a direct consequence of homogeneity of degree 1 under scalar multiplication, thus endowing an operator algebra with an additional structure which is directly inherited from a defining property of the operators it is comprised of. Naturally, any $\mathcal{F}$-operator algebra is an operator algebra, and each operator algebra an algebra of operators, while the converse is generally not true. Furthermore, in an operator algebra $\mathscr{A} = (\mathcal{A}, O)$, the set of finitary operations O must contain at least two elements, the operation of multiplication on $\mathcal{A}$ and scalar multiplication with elements of $\mathcal{F}$, while the algebraic structure of an $\mathcal{F}$-operator algebra will be comprised of at least three elements, namely multiplication and addition on $\mathcal{A}$ as well as the operation of scalar multiplication. Finally, we note that, as in the case of an $\mathcal{F}$-algebra introduced in Definition 3.4, we will adhere here to the commonly used convention that an algebra of operators is not necessarily associative or commutative, or that $\mathcal{A}$ is required to possess a multiplicative identity element.

With the notational framework of Definition 3.5 firmly in place, let us now exemplify its finer nuances by exploring potential algebraic structures of sets of operators we introduced in the previous section. Recalling (3.21) and (3.35), the set $\mathcal{A} := \{\lfloor\,.\,\rfloor, \lceil\,.\,\rceil\}$ of floor and ceiling operators certainly forms an algebra of operators but not an operator algebra, as, for instance, with

$$a \cdot \big\lfloor \lfloor \boldsymbol{A} \rfloor \big\rfloor = a \cdot \lfloor \boldsymbol{A} \rfloor \neq \big\lfloor a \cdot \lfloor \boldsymbol{A} \rfloor \big\rfloor \neq \big\lfloor \lfloor a \cdot \boldsymbol{A} \rfloor \big\rfloor = \lfloor a \cdot \boldsymbol{A} \rfloor$$

for $\boldsymbol{A} \in \mathbb{Q}^{m\times n}$ and $a \in \mathbb{Q}$ compatibility with scalar multiplication is generally not satisfied. The same conclusion is reached for the signum operator because

$$a \cdot (\mathrm{sgn} \circ \mathrm{sgn})[\boldsymbol{A}] = a \cdot \mathrm{sgn}[\boldsymbol{A}] \neq \mathrm{sgn} \circ (a \cdot \mathrm{sgn})[\boldsymbol{A}] = \mathrm{sgn}\,[a \cdot \mathrm{sgn}[\boldsymbol{A}]]$$

unless $a \in \mathbb{B}_{-1}$. Interestingly, this latter exception implies that the $\mathbb{B}_{-1}$-linear map $\mathrm{sgn}^{\mathbb{B}_{-1}}$ introduced in (3.27) is indeed compatible with element-wise scalar multiplication $\cdot^{\mathbb{B}_{-1}}$ over the field $\mathbb{B}_{-1}$, and thus renders the set $\mathcal{A} = \{\,\mathrm{sgn}^{\mathbb{B}_{-1}}\,\}$ an operator algebra (albeit trivial) with algebraic structure $O = \{\circ, \cdot^{\mathbb{B}_{-1}}\}$ comprised of the two finitary operations defined in (3.26) and (3.36).

However, the operator algebra $\mathscr{A} := (\{\mathrm{sgn}^{\mathbb{B}_{-1}}\}, \{\circ, \cdot^{\mathbb{B}_{-1}}\})$ does not yet exhaust the algebraic structures the signum operator can be made subject of. In order to demonstrate the extension of $\mathscr{A}$ into a $\mathbb{B}_{-1}$-operator algebra, let

$$\begin{aligned} \overline{\mathrm{sgn}}^{\,\mathbb{B}_{-1}} &: \mathbb{B}_{-1}^{m\times n} \to \mathbb{B}_{-1}^{m\times n}\,, \\ \overline{\mathrm{sgn}}^{\,\mathbb{B}_{-1}}[\boldsymbol{A}]_{ij} &: [1,m]\times[1,n] \subset \mathbb{N}^2 \to \mathbb{B}_{-1}\,,\ \overline{\mathrm{sgn}}^{\,\mathbb{B}_{-1}}[\boldsymbol{A}]_{ij} := -\,\mathrm{sgn}\,[A_{ij}] \end{aligned} \tag{3.41}$$

for $\boldsymbol{A} \in \mathbb{B}_{-1}^{m\times n}$ define the $\mathbb{B}_{-1}$-linear *inverse Boolean signum operator*. As the signum operator (3.27) and its inverse (3.41) act element-wise on their arguments in $\mathbb{B}_{-1}^{m\times n}$, each of these operators naturally allows for a representation in terms of a $m \times n$ matrix. Together with the *zero operator*

$$\mathbf{0}\colon \mathbb{Q}^{m\times n} \to \mathbb{Q}^{m\times n}\,,\ \mathbf{0}[\boldsymbol{A}] := \boldsymbol{0}^{m\times n}, \tag{3.42}$$

which maps its argument $\boldsymbol{A} \in \mathbb{Q}^{m\times n}$ into the $(m \times n)$-dimensional all-zeroes matrix $\boldsymbol{0}^{m\times n}$ with elements $(\boldsymbol{0}^{m\times n})_{ij} = 0\ \forall i \in [1,m], j \in [1,n]$, it can then be shown that the set $\mathcal{A} = \{\mathbf{0}, \overline{\text{sgn}}^{\mathbb{B}_{-1}}, \text{sgn}^{\mathbb{B}_{-1}}\}$ itself forms an abstract vector space over $\mathbb{B}_{-1}$ with vector addition and scalar multiplication defined in (3.26), with $\mathbf{0}$ being the identity element of vector addition, and with $\mathbf{0}$, $\text{sgn}^{\mathbb{B}_{-1}}$, $\overline{\text{sgn}}^{\mathbb{B}_{-1}}$ providing the respective inverse elements of $\mathbf{0}$, $\overline{\text{sgn}}^{\mathbb{B}_{-1}}$, $\text{sgn}^{\mathbb{B}_{-1}}$ under vector addition. Expanding the scope of the composition rule (3.36) to include $\mathbf{0}$ and $\overline{\text{sgn}}^{\mathbb{B}_{-1}}$, we obtain with

$\circ$	$\mathbf{0}$	$\overline{\text{sgn}}^{\mathbb{B}_{-1}}$	$\text{sgn}^{\mathbb{B}_{-1}}$
$\mathbf{0}$	$\mathbf{0}$	$\mathbf{0}$	$\mathbf{0}$
$\overline{\text{sgn}}^{\mathbb{B}_{-1}}$	$\mathbf{0}$	$\text{sgn}^{\mathbb{B}_{-1}}$	$\overline{\text{sgn}}^{\mathbb{B}_{-1}}$
$\text{sgn}^{\mathbb{B}_{-1}}$	$\mathbf{0}$	$\overline{\text{sgn}}^{\mathbb{B}_{-1}}$	$\text{sgn}^{\mathbb{B}_{-1}}$

(3.43)

the operation of multiplication acting as composition $\circ$ on $\mathcal{A}$ which, together with its identity element $\text{sgn}^{\mathbb{B}_{-1}}$, eventually renders $\mathcal{A} = \{\mathbf{0}, \overline{\text{sgn}}^{\mathbb{B}_{-1}}, \text{sgn}^{\mathbb{B}_{-1}}\}$ an associative and commutative $\mathbb{B}_{-1}$-operator algebra $\mathscr{A} = (\mathcal{A}, O)$ with algebraic structure $O = \{\circ, +^{\mathbb{B}_{-1}}, \cdot^{\mathbb{B}_{-1}}\}$ and multiplicative identity.

The set $\mathcal{A} = \{\boldsymbol{\delta}, \bar{\boldsymbol{\delta}}\}$ of Kronecker delta operators, on the other hand, allows only for an algebra of operators with algebraic structure $O = \{\circ\}$ solely comprised of the operation of composition (3.37), as we find that, in general,

$$a \cdot (\boldsymbol{\delta} \circ \boldsymbol{\delta})[\boldsymbol{A}] = a \cdot \bar{\boldsymbol{\delta}}[\boldsymbol{A}] \neq \boldsymbol{\delta} \circ (a \cdot \boldsymbol{\delta})[\boldsymbol{A}] = \boldsymbol{\delta}[a \cdot \boldsymbol{\delta}[\boldsymbol{A}]]$$

for $\boldsymbol{A} \in \mathbb{Q}^{m\times n}$ and $a \in \mathbb{Q}$, unless $a = 1$. Unlike in the case of signum operators, however, this exception is here not sufficient for the construction of an operator algebra even if we restrict the domain of the Kronecker delta operators to $\mathbb{B}^{m\times n}$ – that is, if we consider the set $\{\boldsymbol{\delta}^{\mathbb{B}}$ and $\bar{\boldsymbol{\delta}}^{\mathbb{B}}\}$ instead of $\mathcal{A}$ – because also here we generally observe that

$$a \cdot^{\mathbb{B}} (\boldsymbol{\delta}^{\mathbb{B}} \circ \boldsymbol{\delta}^{\mathbb{B}})[\boldsymbol{A}] = a \cdot^{\mathbb{B}} \bar{\boldsymbol{\delta}}^{\mathbb{B}}[\boldsymbol{A}] \neq \boldsymbol{\delta}^{\mathbb{B}} \circ (a \cdot^{\mathbb{B}} \boldsymbol{\delta}^{\mathbb{B}})[\boldsymbol{A}] = \boldsymbol{\delta}^{\mathbb{B}}[a \cdot^{\mathbb{B}} \boldsymbol{\delta}^{\mathbb{B}}[\boldsymbol{A}]]$$

for $\boldsymbol{A} \in \mathbb{B}^{m\times n}$ and $a \in \mathbb{B}$, unless $a = 1$.

Finally, let us take a closer look at the trace operator introduced in (3.31). Due to (3.32) and the fact that its codomain is the field of rational numbers $\mathbb{Q}$, it is certainly possible to construct a $\mathbb{Q}$-operator algebra by introducing with

$$\overline{\text{Tr}}\colon \mathbb{Q}^{n\times n} \to \mathbb{Q}\,,\ \overline{\text{Tr}}[\boldsymbol{A}] := -\sum_{i=1}^{n} A_{ii}, \tag{3.44}$$

the *inverse trace operator*, and with

$$\mathbf{0}\colon \mathbb{Q}^{m\times n} \to \mathbb{Q}\,,\ \mathbf{0}[\boldsymbol{A}] := 0, \tag{3.45}$$

an operator which, akin to (3.42), returns zero when applied to any $\boldsymbol{A} \in \mathbb{Q}^{n \times n}$. With the multiplication rules summarised in

$\circ$	$\mathbf{0}$	$\overline{\mathrm{Tr}}$	Tr
$\mathbf{0}$	$\mathbf{0}$	$\mathbf{0}$	$\mathbf{0}$
$\overline{\mathrm{Tr}}$	$\mathbf{0}$	Tr	$\overline{\mathrm{Tr}}$
Tr	$\mathbf{0}$	$\overline{\mathrm{Tr}}$	Tr

(3.46)

the set of operators $\mathcal{A} = \{\mathbf{0}, \overline{\mathrm{Tr}}, \mathrm{Tr}\}$ then forms a commutative and associative $\mathbb{Q}$-operator algebra $\mathscr{A} = (\mathcal{A}, \mathcal{O})$ with algebraic structure $\mathcal{O} = \{\circ, +, \cdot\}$ and multiplicative identity given by Tr, where the last two elements of $\mathcal{O}$ denote the operations of addition and multiplication in $\mathbb{Q}$. Similarly, it can be shown that the set $\mathcal{A} = \{\mathbf{0}, \overline{\mathrm{Tr}}^{\mathbb{B}}, \mathrm{Tr}^{\mathbb{B}}\}$ with algebraic structure $\mathcal{O} = \{\circ, +^{\mathbb{B}}, \cdot^{\mathbb{B}}\}$ defines a both commutative and associative $\mathbb{B}$-operator algebra with multiplicative identity $\mathrm{Tr}^{\mathbb{B}}$ and additive identity $\mathbf{0}$, acting on the vector space of Boolean square matrices $\mathbb{B}^{n \times n}$ over $\mathbb{B}$.

The construction of algebraic structures exercised above for sets of operators which will feature prominently throughout the remainder of this book should suffice as the first illustration of an approach which is generally employed in the applied mathematical literature not only to arrive at a more abstract representation of a given problem, but to open up a whole new dimension for its exploration. What, then, about the problem associated with the bridges of Königsberg? Can we construct an algebraic structure for its walk-generating operators and, more importantly, levarage such an eventual structure for simplifying or even reducing the combinatorial complexity associated with the active search for Eulerian paths? With $\mathfrak{D}^n(i, \boldsymbol{s}^e)$ defined in (3.17) and $\mathfrak{D}^e(i, \boldsymbol{s}^n)$ defined in (3.19), it certainly is possible to define two disjoint sets $\mathcal{A}^n$ and $\mathcal{A}^e$ of walk-generating operators which respectively act on the subset $\widetilde{\mathcal{S}}^n(\mathcal{G})$ of the Boolean vector space $\mathcal{S}^n(\mathcal{G})$ and the Boolean vector space $\mathcal{S}^n(\mathcal{L}(\mathcal{G}))$. Following (3.16) and (3.18), the composition of elements in either of these sets is naturally given by right-hand matrix multiplication, such that

$$\mathfrak{D}^n(i', \boldsymbol{s}'^e) \circ \mathfrak{D}^n(i, \boldsymbol{s}^e)[\boldsymbol{s}^n] := \mathfrak{D}^n(i', \boldsymbol{s}'^e)\big[\mathfrak{D}^n(i, \boldsymbol{s}^e)[\boldsymbol{s}^n]\big] = \boldsymbol{s}^n \cdot \mathfrak{D}^n(i, \boldsymbol{s}^e) \cdot \mathfrak{D}^n(i', \boldsymbol{s}'^e)$$

and

$$\mathfrak{D}^e(i', \boldsymbol{s}'^n) \circ \mathfrak{D}^e(i, \boldsymbol{s}^n)[\boldsymbol{s}^e] := \mathfrak{D}^e(i', \boldsymbol{s}'^n)\big[\mathfrak{D}^e(i, \boldsymbol{s}^n)[\boldsymbol{s}^e]\big] = \boldsymbol{s}^e \cdot \mathfrak{D}^e(i, \boldsymbol{s}^n) \cdot \mathfrak{D}^e(i', \boldsymbol{s}'^n)$$

for all $i, i' \in \mathcal{N}^{\mathcal{L}(\mathcal{G})}$ as well as $\boldsymbol{s}^n, \boldsymbol{s}'^n \in \widetilde{\mathcal{S}}^n(\mathcal{G})$ and $\boldsymbol{s}^e, \boldsymbol{s}'^e \in \mathcal{S}^n(\mathcal{L}(\mathcal{G}))$. With some investment, it can then be shown that the 4×4 matrix operators updating node states in $\mathcal{G}$ satisfy composition rules such as

$$\mathfrak{D}^n(1, \boldsymbol{s}^{e1}) \circ \mathfrak{D}^n(1, \boldsymbol{s}^{e1}) = \mathfrak{D}^n(1, \boldsymbol{s}^{e1}) = \boldsymbol{I}^4,$$

$$\mathfrak{O}^n(1, s^{e1}) \circ \mathfrak{O}^n(2, s^{e1}) = \mathfrak{O}^n(1, s^{e1}) = I^4,$$

$$\mathfrak{O}^n(1, s^{e1}) \circ \mathfrak{O}^n(3, s^{e1}) = \begin{pmatrix} 0 & 0 & 1 & 0 \\ 1 & 0 & 0 & 0 \\ 0 & 1 & 0 & 0 \\ 0 & 0 & 0 & 1 \end{pmatrix},$$

$$\vdots$$

$$\mathfrak{O}^n(7, s^{e128}) \circ \mathfrak{O}^n(7, s^{e128}) = \mathfrak{O}^n(1, s^{e1}) = I^4,$$

where $s^{e1} = (1, 1, 1, 1, 1, 1, 1)$ to $s^{e128} = (0, 0, 0, 0, 0, 0, 0)$ denote all possible edge state vectors. By considering all possible node state vectors, a similar collection of specific composition rules can also be constructed for the 7×7 matrix operators comprising $\mathcal{A}^e$.

Although these rules would certainly allow for a simplification of state updates along walks through our Königsberg bridge graph $\mathcal{G}$, their sheer number unfortunately renders such an approach little inviting. Indeed, as each operator describing a possible node and edge state update in $\mathcal{G}$ and its edge-to-vertex dual $\mathcal{L}(\mathcal{G})$ depends not only on the chosen potential walk comprised of edges $i \in \mathcal{N}^{\mathcal{L}(\mathcal{G})}$ but also on the actual state of nodes and edges, we find a total of $|\mathcal{A}^e| = 7 \cdot 4 = 28$ edge state operators and $|\mathcal{A}^n| = 7 \cdot 2^7 = 896$ node state operators, eventually yielding 784 possible composition rules for $\mathcal{A}^e$ and a staggering number of 802,816 such rules for operators in $\mathcal{A}^n$. To make matters worse, for reaching closure with respect to operator composition, further elements need to be added to both $\mathcal{A}^n$ and $\mathcal{A}^e$ which are not directly linked to the set of node and edge state update operators defined by the original problem, as the composition $\mathfrak{O}^n(1, s_1^e) \circ \mathfrak{O}^n(3, s_1^e)$ from earlier exemplifies. Albeit with this addition, the set $\mathcal{A} = \{\widetilde{\mathcal{A}}^n, \widetilde{\mathcal{A}}^e\}$, where $\widetilde{\mathcal{A}}^n \supset \mathcal{A}^n$, $\widetilde{\mathcal{A}}^e \supset \mathcal{A}^e$ and $\widetilde{\mathcal{A}}^n \cap \widetilde{\mathcal{A}}^e = \emptyset$, will define an algebra of operators $(\mathcal{A}, O)$ with algebraic structure $O = \{\circ\}$ given by right-hand matrix multiplication as finitary operations of multiplication, the naive operator-inspired solution of the Königsberg bridge problem presented in this chapter will undoubtedly remain a cumbersome endeavour and, more importantly, presents little help in quelling its combinatorial complexity. Specifically, the solution of this original problem in the formalism developed so far would require to investigate each of the state vectors

$$\begin{aligned} s^n &= \bigcirc_{k=1}^{7} \mathfrak{O}^n(\mathcal{W}_k, s_k^e)[s_1^n] = \mathfrak{O}^n(\mathcal{W}_7, s_7^e) \circ \ldots \circ \mathfrak{O}^n(\mathcal{W}_1, s_1^e)[s_1^n], \\ s^e &= \bigcirc_{k=1}^{7} \mathfrak{O}^e(\mathcal{W}_k, s_k^n)[s_1^e] = \mathfrak{O}^e(\mathcal{W}_7, s_7^n) \circ \ldots \circ \mathfrak{O}^e(\mathcal{W}_1, s_1^n)[s_1^e], \end{aligned} \tag{3.47}$$

where consecutive node and edge state vectors along a given potential walk are defined by (3.16) and (3.18), for $s_1^e = s^{e1}$ and all four possible initial node state vectors $s_1^n \in \widetilde{\mathcal{S}}^n(\mathcal{G})$, and for each of the 5,040 possible permutations of seven bridges from which potential walks $\mathcal{W}$ – indeed, Eulerian walks – can be constructed. With a grand total of 20,160 edge state vectors to investigate, only a potential walk for which $s^e = s^{e128}$ in (3.47) would then deliver an Eulerian path and, thus, a positive resolution of the Königsberg bridge problem.

Where does this leave us? Although the combination of state vectors and walk-generating operators clearly provided us with an alternative approach to tackle the problem of Königsberg's bridges, it would be futile to conclude that this approach is anything more than just an algebraic exercise. However, let us carefully argue here that the primary reason for this undoubtedly rather disappointing conclusion regarding the exhaustive search approach might be linked to the classical conception of a graph itself which, referring to Definition 2.1, views a graph as a mere static collection of nodes and edges. In contrast, the algebraic formalisation of the active search for viable walks and paths through a graph certainly necessitates a more dynamic vantage point, introduced in this chapter through the utilisation of state vectors which are subject to changes when exposed to a set of walk-generating operators. As we have seen, such a naive combination of a primarily static notion with an inherently dynamic approach, albeit arguably powerful, can easily result in a combinatorial overhead which might void any generalisability and potential advantages such a combination might bring along.

Despite the somewhat bitter taste this argument leaves in regards to the Königsberg bridge problem, it also presents us with a strong motivation to search for a more dynamic perspective which challenges the very foundation of classical and contemporary graph theory, the notion of a graph itself. Indeed, by envisioning relations between objects forming a graph themselves as operations not unlike those which bestow an algebraic structure on a given set of objects, a whole new notion of a graph can be conceptualised which not only encompasses its classical counterpart but, more importantly, sets the framework for a more dynamic formalisation which will allow to embed graph-theoretical notions into a rigorous operator-algebraic setting. The conceptual foundation of such an *operator graph-theoretical framework* will finally be introduced and explored in greater detail in the next chapter.

3.5 Special Operators

Before proceeding on our journey towards an exploration of the central subject matter of this book, namely the fusion of finite graph theory and operator calculus, let us conclude this chapter by complementing the set of operators introduced in Section 3.3 with a number of special mappings which will prove useful in a graph-theoretical context later. With the floor and ceiling operators in (3.22), the signum operator in (3.24) and its inverse, as well as the Kronecker delta operator and its inverse in (3.28) and (3.30), we found mappings which act on vector spaces $\mathbb{Q}^{m\times n}$, $\mathbb{B}_{-1}^{m\times n}$ or $\mathbb{B}^{m\times n}$. All of these operators naturally allow for a representation in terms of $m \times n$ matrices if we assume the operator's actions to be element-wise on its argument. Similarly, the trace operator (3.31) and its inverse (3.44) act as linear maps on vector spaces comprised of square matrices. Other and more fundamental operators which define linear maps in $\mathbb{Q}^{n\times n}$ and its subsets include scalar multiplication, matrix addition and matrix multiplication. These operators render, as algebraic structure, the vector spaces of their respective domains associative yet generally not commutative algebras with additive identity given by the $(n \times n)$-dimensional zero matrix $\boldsymbol{0}^{n\times n}$ and multiplicative identity $\boldsymbol{I}^n$.

The linear maps which endow $\mathbb{Q}^{n\times n}$ with an algebraic structure can easily be generalised to operate on vector spaces $\mathbb{Q}^{m\times n}$ over $\mathbb{Q}$. Indeed, with

$$\begin{aligned}\cdot\colon \mathbb{Q} \times \mathbb{Q}^{m\times n} &\to \mathbb{Q}^{m\times n}\,,\\ (a\cdot \boldsymbol{A})_{ij}\colon [1,m]\times[1,n]\subset \mathbb{N}^2 \to \mathbb{Q}\,,\ (a\cdot\boldsymbol{A})_{ij} &:= a\cdot A_{ij}\end{aligned} \tag{3.48}$$

as scalar multiplication, and

$$\begin{aligned}+\colon \mathbb{Q}^{m\times n} \times \mathbb{Q}^{m\times n} &\to \mathbb{Q}^{m\times n}\,,\\ (\boldsymbol{A}+\boldsymbol{B})_{ij}\colon [1,m]\times[1,n]\subset \mathbb{N}^2 \to \mathbb{Q}\,,\ (\boldsymbol{A}+\boldsymbol{B})_{ij} &:= A_{ij}+B_{ij}\end{aligned} \tag{3.49}$$

as matrix addition, we have two mappings which act as $\mathbb{Q}$-linear operators on $\mathbb{Q}^{m\times n}$. The generalisation of matrix multiplication is somewhat more involved as it defines a linear map which typically acts between three distinct vector spaces according to

$$\begin{aligned}\cdot\colon \mathbb{Q}^{m\times l} \times \mathbb{Q}^{l\times n} &\to \mathbb{Q}^{m\times n}\,,\\ (\boldsymbol{A}\cdot\boldsymbol{B})_{ij}\colon [1,m]\times[1,n]\subset \mathbb{N}^2 \to \mathbb{Q}\,,\ (\boldsymbol{A}\cdot\boldsymbol{B})_{ij} &:= \sum_{k=1}^{l} A_{ik}\cdot B_{kj}\end{aligned} \tag{3.50}$$

for $\boldsymbol{A} \in \mathbb{Q}^{m\times l}$ and $\boldsymbol{B} \in \mathbb{Q}^{l\times n}$. It is important to note here that, adhering to standard convention, we will continue to use the symbol $\cdot$ for both the scalar and matrix multiplication operator in $\mathbb{Q}^{m\times n}$ and its subsets. But for notational consistency, we will indicate each ground field distinct from $\mathbb{Q}$ by a superscript on the respective operator notation such that, for example,

$$(\boldsymbol{A} \cdot^{\mathbb{B}} \boldsymbol{B})_{ij} := {\sum_{k=1}^{l}}^{\mathbb{B}} A_{ik} \cdot^{\mathbb{B}} B_{kj} = (A_{i1} \cdot^{\mathbb{B}} B_{1j}) +^{\mathbb{B}} \ldots +^{\mathbb{B}} (A_{il} \cdot^{\mathbb{B}} B_{lj}) \tag{3.51}$$

denotes matrix multiplication of elements in vector spaces $\mathbb{B}^{m\times n}$ over $\mathbb{B}$.

Another fundamental linear map which not only acts as composition operator similar to matrix multiplication on the vector space of $m \times n$ matrices but indeed presents an endomorphism of the vector space $\mathbb{Q}^{m\times n}$ is given by the commutative, associative and distributive *Hadamard product*

$$\begin{aligned} \odot\colon \mathbb{Q}^{m\times n} \times \mathbb{Q}^{m\times n} &\to \mathbb{Q}^{m\times n}\,, \\ (\boldsymbol{A} \odot \boldsymbol{B})_{ij}\colon [1,m]\times[1,n] \subset \mathbb{N}^2 \to \mathbb{Q}\,,\ (\boldsymbol{A} \odot \boldsymbol{B})_{ij} &:= A_{ij} \cdot B_{ij}. \end{aligned} \tag{3.52}$$

In contrast, the bilinear and associative but not commutative *Kronecker product*

$$\begin{aligned} &\otimes\colon \mathbb{Q}^{m\times n} \times \mathbb{Q}^{k\times l} \to \mathbb{Q}^{mk\times nl}\,, \\ &(\boldsymbol{A} \otimes \boldsymbol{B})_{ij}\colon [1,mk]\times[1,nl] \subset \mathbb{N}^2 \to \mathbb{Q}\,, \\ &(\boldsymbol{A} \otimes \boldsymbol{B})_{ij} := A_{\lfloor (i-1)/k\rfloor+1\,,\,\lfloor (j-1)/l\rfloor+1} \cdot B_{i-k\lfloor (i-1)/k\rfloor\,,\,j-l\lfloor (j-1)/l\rfloor} \end{aligned} \tag{3.53}$$

generally acts between three vector spaces of different dimension. Examples of linear maps which operate between two distinct vector spaces over $\mathbb{Q}$ include the *transposition operator*

$$\begin{aligned} .^{\mathsf{T}}\colon \mathbb{Q}^{m\times n} &\to \mathbb{Q}^{n\times m}\,, \\ (\boldsymbol{A}^{\mathsf{T}})_{ij}\colon [1,n]\times[1,m] \subset \mathbb{N}^2 \to \mathbb{Q}\,,\ (\boldsymbol{A}^{\mathsf{T}})_{ij} &:= A_{ji}, \end{aligned} \tag{3.54}$$

which generates the transpose of a matrix $\boldsymbol{A} \in \mathbb{Q}^{m\times n}$, the *diagonal operator*

$$\begin{aligned} &\operatorname{diag}\colon \mathbb{Q}^{n} \to \mathbb{Q}^{n\times n}\,, \\ &\operatorname{diag}[\boldsymbol{q}]_{ij}\colon [1,n]\times[1,n] \subset \mathbb{N}^2 \to \mathbb{Q}\,,\ \operatorname{diag}[\boldsymbol{q}]_{ij} := \begin{cases} q_i & \text{if } i = j, \\ 0 & \text{otherwise,} \end{cases} \end{aligned} \tag{3.55}$$

which constructs the diagonal $n \times n$ matrix in $\mathbb{Q}^{n\times n}$ from a vector $\boldsymbol{q} \in \mathbb{Q}^n$, and the *circulant operator*

$$\begin{aligned} &\operatorname{circ}\colon \mathbb{Q}^{n} \to \mathbb{Q}^{n\times n}\,, \\ &\operatorname{circ}[\boldsymbol{q}]_{ij}\colon [1,n]\times[1,n] \subset \mathbb{N}^2 \to \mathbb{Q}\,,\ \operatorname{circ}[\boldsymbol{q}]_{ij} := q_{1+(n(i-1)+j-i) \bmod n}, \end{aligned} \tag{3.56}$$

which results in a circulant $n \times n$ matrix $\boldsymbol{A} \in \mathbb{Q}^{n\times n}$ when applied to a vector $\boldsymbol{q} \in \mathbb{Q}^n$. The definitions of these operators can also be adapted to specifically target only subspaces or subsets of $\mathbb{Q}^{m\times n}$ and $\mathbb{Q}^n$.

An operator which, not dissimilar to the signum or Kronecker delta operator, modifies individual elements of its argument in $\mathbb{Q}^{m\times n}$ is defined by

$$\begin{aligned} |.|\colon \mathbb{Q}^{m\times n} &\to \mathbb{Q}^{m\times n}\,, \\ |\boldsymbol{A}|_{ij}\colon [1,m]\times[1,n] \subset \mathbb{N}^2 \to \mathbb{Q}\,,\ |\boldsymbol{A}|_{ij} &:= |A_{ij}| \end{aligned} \tag{3.57}$$

and will be called *abs-operator*. Because with $|a + b| \leq |a| + |b|$ for $a, b \in \mathbb{Q}$ the absolute value is generally subadditive, the abs-operator is not linear. Only by restricting to the trivial case of a Boolean vector space $\mathbb{B}^{m\times n}$ over $\mathbb{B}$, the abs-operator can be shown to define a linear map, indeed, an endomorphism of $\mathbb{B}^{m\times n}$. In contrast, from (3.26), it easily follows that $|a +^{\mathbb{B}_{-1}} b| \geq |a| +^{\mathbb{B}_{-1}} |b|$ for $a, b \in \mathbb{B}_{-1}$, which renders the restriction of (3.57) to the vector space $\mathbb{B}_{-1}^{m\times n}$ over $\mathbb{B}_{-1}$ superadditive, and thus again nonlinear.

The property of nonlinearity generally holds as well for

$$\begin{aligned} \min\colon \mathbb{Q}^{m\times n} &\to \mathbb{Q}\,,\ \min\,[\boldsymbol{A}] := \min_{\substack{i\in[1,m]\\ j\in[1,n]}} A_{ij}, \\ \max\colon \mathbb{Q}^{m\times n} &\to \mathbb{Q}\,,\ \max\,[\boldsymbol{A}] := \max_{\substack{i\in[1,m]\\ j\in[1,n]}} A_{ij}, \end{aligned} \tag{3.58}$$

which we will respectively refer to as *min-operator* and *max-operator*, while generalising the trace operator introduced in (3.31) yields the mapping

$$\mathrm{T}\colon \mathbb{Q}^{m\times n} \to \mathbb{Q}\,,\ \mathrm{T}\,[\boldsymbol{A}] := \sum_{i=1}^{m}\sum_{j=1}^{n} A_{ij}, \tag{3.59}$$

which acts $\mathbb{Q}$-linearly on $\mathbb{Q}^{m\times n}$ by delivering the total sum of all elements of its matrix argument, and will be referred to as *total sum operator*. It can be shown that $\mathrm{T}[\boldsymbol{A}+\boldsymbol{B}] = \mathrm{T}[\boldsymbol{A}] + \mathrm{T}[\boldsymbol{B}]$ and $\mathrm{T}[q\cdot\boldsymbol{A}] = q\cdot\mathrm{T}[\boldsymbol{A}]$ for all $\boldsymbol{A},\boldsymbol{B}\in\mathbb{Q}^{m\times n}$ and $q\in\mathbb{Q}$. Moreover, we find the useful identities $\mathrm{T}[\boldsymbol{A}] = \boldsymbol{1}^{m\mathrm{T}}\cdot\boldsymbol{A}\cdot\boldsymbol{1}^{n}$ for $\boldsymbol{A}\in\mathbb{Q}^{m\times n}$, where $\boldsymbol{1}^{n}$ denotes the all-ones column vector in $\mathbb{Q}^{n}$ defined as vector with all elements being 1, as well as $\mathrm{Tr}[\boldsymbol{A}] = \mathrm{T}[\boldsymbol{I}^{n}\odot\boldsymbol{A}]$ for $\boldsymbol{A}\in\mathbb{Q}^{n\times n}$, while $\mathrm{T}[\boldsymbol{a}] = \mathrm{Tr}\,[\,\mathrm{diag}[\boldsymbol{a}]]$ for $\boldsymbol{a}\in\mathbb{Q}^{n}$. Last but not least,

$$\begin{aligned} &\mathrm{id}\colon \mathbb{Q}^{m\times n} \to \mathbb{Q}^{m\times n}\,, \\ &\mathrm{id}\,[\boldsymbol{A}]_{ij}\colon [1,m]\times[1,n]\subset\mathbb{N}^2 \to \mathbb{Q}\,,\ \mathrm{id}\,[\boldsymbol{A}]_{ij} := A_{ij} \end{aligned} \tag{3.60}$$

defines the *identity operator* which will play an instrumental role in the generation and transformation of graphs in later sections.

With this small complementary sample of special operators and linear maps, we conclude our condensed introduction into the conceptual and mathematical preliminaries required to formulate a new exciting perspective which will present classical finite graph theory in the more dynamic light of operator calculus. Once more accompanied by the historic yet illustrious puzzle surrounding the seven bridges of Königsberg, the next chapter will propose exactly such a perspective with the inherently discrete and finite framework termed *operator graph theory*. On this journey, we will not only conceptualise our original motivation for such a fusion, but develop the necessary algebraical and notational toolset to exemplify and explore in a number of concrete applications the potential usefulness of this fusion in Part II.

4

Operator Graph Theory: The Mathematics of Finite Networks

Over the course of nearly three centuries, the field of graph theory has rapidly matured from its initial conception as an abstract model for solving a rather specific mathematical problem into an indispensable and powerful vessel for describing countless real-world phenomena, with applications now reaching far beyond applied mathematics. Its static formalisation, which is built around the classical notion of a graph as being comprised of a mere fixed collection of discrete discernible nodes and edges, however, puts a number of limitations in place which arguably, or undoubtedly, hamper an advantageous utilisation of graph-theoretical concepts, especially in circumstances which require a more dynamic perspective. Is it possible to overcome these limitations by challenging the classical notion of a graph? In this chapter, we will propose exactly such a challenge by considering a graph's nodes and their relations as the result of operations performed on a set of suitable objects. This subtle yet consequential change in the conception of a graph not only delivers a more dynamic vantage point, but eventually generalises the very notion of a graph by structurally equating it with an abstract algebra. Although the mathematical framework embedding this notion, *operator graph theory*, is still under active development, this chapter will introduce its basic notions and formalisations and candidly argue in expository form for its potential merits and usefulness.

4.1 From Operations on Graphs to Operator Graphs

In the previous chapter, we introduced and explored the general notion of an operator as mapping between two vector spaces or subsets thereof. By constructing a set of appropriate operators which act on state vectors of the nodes and edges comprising a graph, we then exemplified an operator-inspired approach addressing the now-historic problem of Königsberg's seven bridges.

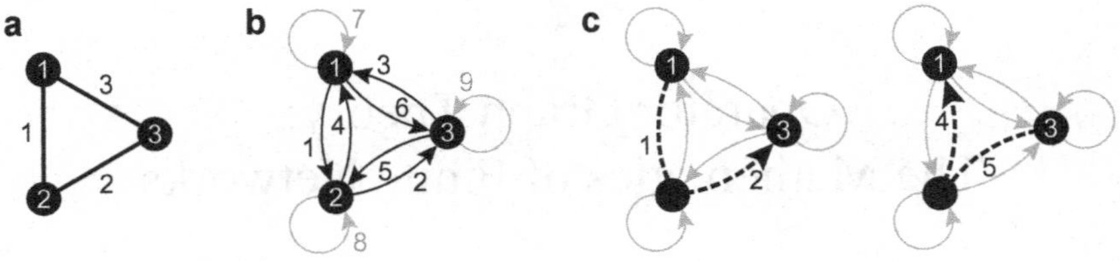

Figure 4.1 Triangle graph $\mathscr{C}_3$ and its operator graph. **a:** Classical representation of $\mathscr{C}_3$, a simple cycle graph with 3 nodes and 3 undirected edges. **b:** Operator representation of $\mathscr{C}_3$ in which each undirected edge of $\mathscr{C}_3$ is replaced by two directed adjacency relations (black), and three directed adjacency relations rendering each node adjacent to itself (grey) are added to ensure closure of the associated algebra of edge-generating operators under composition. **c:** Operator graph-theoretical representation of all Eulerian walks of length 2 (dashed) generated by the ordered sets $\mathcal{W}_1 = (1,2)$ and $\mathcal{W}_2 = (2,1)$ of edges in $\mathscr{C}_3$. In all illustrated operator representations, the node n_0 and all edge operators associated with n_0 are omitted.

Although the presented approach is certainly feasible and generalisable, we also found that its practical application is challenged by the manageability of the algebraic structure which governs the set of operators at the heart of this formulation. This led us to suggest that the encountered difficulties are rooted in the discordant fusion of an inherently static concept, that of a classical graph, with a naturally dynamic notion, that of operations or mappings between objects. Is it possible to harmonise this arguably powerful fusion by conceiving classical graph-theoretical structures themselves from a more dynamic vantage point?

Before returning with this question to the graph of Königsberg's bridges, let us consider the more elementary example of the triangle graph depicted in Fig. 4.1a. Mirroring the approach developed in Chapter 3, the search for Eulerian paths requires here the introduction of two vectors in order to keep track of the three states for the set of three nodes, and of the $2^3 = 8$ states the set of three edges can be found in. The update of these node and edge state vectors along the three edges of the graph then follows interdependent update rules similar to those presented in (3.16) and (3.18), with respectively $3 \cdot 8 = 24$ and $3 \cdot 3 = 9$ operators of the form (3.17) and (3.19) which are subject to a minimum of $24^2 = 576$ and $9^2 = 81$ composition rules akin to (3.47) if we disregard closure of the respective sets of operators under operator composition. Aiming at avoiding such a cumbersome approach, is it possible to keep track of both visited nodes and traversed edges without the introduction of state vectors?

Certainly, as an Eulerian path demands that each edge is traversed exactly once, every node of a connected simple graph must necessarily be visited at least once along each such walk. Similarly, edge state vectors will be rendered somewhat unnecessary if we restrict our search to potential walks constructed solely from permutations of the graph's edges, and we assess whether any such walk is an Eulerian walk of length 3 targeting one of the graph's nodes, in which case it must necessarily be an Eulerian path. This line of reasoning eventually provides the conceptual basis for an alternative approach which will not require the introduction of state vectors for nodes and edges along with the management of a sizeable number of state-dependent operators, but instead will focus on considering specific combinations of the graph's edges, and on determining their validity as Eulerian walks.

In order to arrive at an algebraic formalisation of this alternative approach, let us first take a look at walks of arbitrary length in the undirected triangle graph by utilising its classical representation $\mathscr{C}_3 = (\mathcal{N}^{\mathscr{C}_3}, \mathcal{E}^{\mathscr{C}_3})$. Labelling the nodes of $\mathscr{C}_3$ according to Fig. 4.1a, the weight and adjacency matrix as well as the matrix of adjacency relations of this simple graph are given by

$$\boldsymbol{w} = \boldsymbol{a} = \boldsymbol{A} = \begin{pmatrix} 0 & 1 & 1 \\ 1 & 0 & 1 \\ 1 & 1 & 0 \end{pmatrix}. \tag{4.1}$$

Referring to the presentation of distance-dependent measures in Section 2.2.4, the mth power of $\boldsymbol{A}$ then delivers the number $N_m^{\mathcal{W}}(i,i')$ of walks of length m between each pair (i,i') of not necessarily distinct nodes, that is

$$N_m^{\mathcal{W}}(i,i') = N_m^{\mathcal{W}}(i',i) = (\boldsymbol{A}^m)_{ii'} = (\boldsymbol{A}^m)_{i'i}, \tag{4.2}$$

with the result for walks up to length 4 listed in Table 4.1. By tracking successive powers of $\boldsymbol{A}$, it is also possible to discern the number of shortest paths between two distinct nodes and, thus, obtain their geodesic distance according to (2.57). But what about the number of Eulerian walks of length $m \leq 3$ or, more specifically, Eulerian paths of length $m = 3$? The naive approach (4.2) is certainly of little help here and demands some further exploration.

To that end, instead of using mere integer labels, let us distinguish each of the three nodes $i \in \mathcal{N}^{\mathscr{C}_3}$ of $\mathscr{C}_3$ by a unique row vector $\boldsymbol{n}_i := \boldsymbol{\delta}_i^3, i \in [1,3]$, where $\boldsymbol{\delta}_k^n$ denotes the Kronecker delta vector (3.14). Furthermore, introducing the *Kronecker delta matrix* $\boldsymbol{\delta}_{kl}^{m\times n} \in \mathbb{B}^{m\times n}$ with elements

$$(\boldsymbol{\delta}_{kl}^{m\times n})_{ij}\colon [1,m]\times[1,n] \subset \mathbb{N}^2 \to \mathbb{B}\,,\ (\boldsymbol{\delta}_{kl}^{m\times n})_{ij} := \begin{cases} 1 & \text{if } i = k \wedge j = l, \\ 0 & \text{otherwise} \end{cases} \tag{4.3}$$

as a generalisation of (3.14), let us replace each of the three undirected edges comprising $\mathscr{C}_3$ with two directed adjacency relations by assigning with

$$\mathfrak{E}_1 = \mathfrak{E}_4^{\mathsf{T}} := \boldsymbol{\delta}_{1,2}^{3\times3}\,,\ \mathfrak{E}_2 = \mathfrak{E}_5^{\mathsf{T}} := \boldsymbol{\delta}_{2,3}^{3\times3}\,,\ \mathfrak{E}_3 = \mathfrak{E}_6^{\mathsf{T}} := \boldsymbol{\delta}_{3,1}^{3\times3} \tag{4.4}$$

Table 4.1 *Number of walks* $N_m^{\mathcal{W}}(i,i')$ *and Eulerian walks* $\bar{N}_m^{\mathcal{W}}(i,i')$ *in* $\mathscr{C}_3$.

(i,i')	$N_1^{\mathcal{W}}$	$N_2^{\mathcal{W}}$	$N_3^{\mathcal{W}}$	$N_4^{\mathcal{W}}$	$\cdots$	$\bar{N}_1^{\mathcal{W}}$	$\bar{N}_2^{\mathcal{W}}$	$\bar{N}_3^{\mathcal{W}}$
(1,1)	0	2	2	6		0	0	2
(1,2)	1	1	3	5		1	1	0
(1,3)	1	1	3	5		1	1	0
(2,2)	0	2	2	6		0	0	2
(2,3)	1	1	3	5		1	1	0
(3,3)	0	2	2	6		0	0	2

a unique Boolean matrix to each of the six directed edges $\mathfrak{E}_j$, $j \in [1,6]$ illustrated in Fig. 4.1b (black). The sums

$$\bar{\mathfrak{E}}_j := \mathfrak{E}_j + \mathfrak{E}_{j+3} \tag{4.5}$$

for $j \in [1,3]$ will then correspond to matrix representations of the three undirected edges $\{(1,2),(2,1)\}$, $\{(2,3),(3,2)\}$ and $\{(1,3),(3,1)\}$ comprising $\mathcal{E}^{\mathscr{C}_3}$. With an eye on the purpose of our little exercise, it is important to note here that this association of undirected edge in $\mathscr{C}_3$ with directed edges is certainly necessary in order to distinguish eventual links between ordered pairs of nodes when constructing walks through $\mathscr{C}_3$. For example, although combining the undirected edges 1 and 2 in the original graph (Fig. 4.1a) establishes a bidirectional link between nodes 1 and 3, node 3 can be reached only from node 1 via edges 1 and 2 by following the ordered composition of edge 1 with edge 2, while the converse, that is traversing edge 1 after edge 2, can result only in a walk from node 3 to node 1 (see Fig. 4.1c, dashed).

With nodes of $\mathscr{C}_3$ represented in terms of vectors $\boldsymbol{n}_i \in \mathbb{B}^3$ and edges in terms of matrices $\mathfrak{E}_j \in \mathbb{B}^{3\times3}$, we now have all the necessary algebraic tools at our disposal to explore an alternative and more operator-inspired formalisation of our simple triangle graph. In order to arrive at such a formalisation, we introduce the all-zeroes row vector $\boldsymbol{n}_0 := \boldsymbol{0}^3$ as a fourth node, and define with

$$\hat{\mathcal{N}}^{\mathscr{C}_3} := \left\{\boldsymbol{n}_i : i \in [0,3]\right\} \subset \mathbb{B}^3 \tag{4.6}$$

the set of nodes associated with $\mathcal{N}^{\mathscr{C}_3}$ of $\mathscr{C}_3$. It can then easily be shown that each $\mathfrak{E}_j$ acts through right-hand matrix multiplication on $\boldsymbol{n}_i \in \hat{\mathcal{N}}^{\mathscr{C}_3}$ such that

$$\mathfrak{E}_j : \hat{\mathcal{N}}^{\mathscr{C}_3} \to \hat{\mathcal{N}}^{\mathscr{C}_3}\,,\ \mathfrak{E}_j[\boldsymbol{n}_i] := \boldsymbol{n}_i \cdot \mathfrak{E}_j \tag{4.7}$$

for all $j \in [1,6]$ represents, according to Definition 3.3, a matrix operator in the subset $\hat{\mathcal{N}}^{\mathscr{C}_3}$ of the Boolean vector space $\mathbb{B}^3$. Moreover, right-hand matrix multiplication of these *edge-generating operators* also provides a finitary operation defining operator composition. To ensure closure under this composition, however, we require the introduction of the four additional matrix operators

$$\mathfrak{E}_0 := \mathbf{0}^{3\times3}\,,\; \mathfrak{E}_7 := \delta_{1,1}^{3\times3}\,,\; \mathfrak{E}_8 := \delta_{2,2}^{3\times3}\,,\; \mathfrak{E}_9 := \delta_{3,3}^{3\times3}\,, \tag{4.8}$$

which, with the exception of $\mathfrak{E}_0$, correspond to directed adjacency relations rendering the nodes of $\mathscr{C}_3$ adjacent to themselves (Fig. 4.1b, grey). The set

$$\hat{\mathcal{E}}^{\mathscr{C}_3} := \left\{\mathfrak{E}_j : j \in [0,9]\right\} \subset \mathbb{B}^{3\times3} \tag{4.9}$$

of edge operators together with

$$\circ : \hat{\mathcal{E}}^{\mathscr{C}_3} \times \hat{\mathcal{E}}^{\mathscr{C}_3} \to \hat{\mathcal{E}}^{\mathscr{C}_3}\,,\; \mathfrak{E}_{j_2} \circ \mathfrak{E}_{j_1} := \mathfrak{E}_{j_1} \cdot \mathfrak{E}_{j_2} \tag{4.10}$$

as operator composition then forms an associative algebra of operators

$$\mathscr{E}^{\mathscr{C}_3} := (\hat{\mathcal{E}}^{\mathscr{C}_3}, \mathcal{O}^{\mathscr{C}_3}) \tag{4.11}$$

with algebraic structure $\mathcal{O}^{\mathscr{C}_3} := \{\,\circ\,\}$ which encompasses a description of all undirected adjacency relations in our triangle graph and, thus, serves as a viable replacement for the set of edges $\mathcal{E}^{\mathscr{C}_3}$ in the classical definition of $\mathscr{C}_3$.

This algebra of edge-generating matrix operators together with the set of nodes $\hat{\mathcal{N}}^{\mathscr{C}_3}$ introduced in (4.6) provides us finally with all the building blocks necessary for defining a graph, and eventually leads us to propose the tuple $(\hat{\mathcal{N}}^{\mathscr{C}_3}, \mathscr{E}^{\mathscr{C}_3})$ as a suitable representation of the triangle graph $\mathscr{C}_3$ within an operator graph-theoretical context. Let us denote this representation with $\hat{\mathscr{C}}_3$ in order to distinguish it from its classical counterpart. With nodes and edges of $\hat{\mathscr{C}}_3$ being vectors and matrices in subsets of Boolean vector spaces, right-hand matrix multiplication naturally serves as an operation which fully defines both the action of operators $\mathfrak{E}_j \in \hat{\mathcal{E}}^{\mathscr{C}_3}$ on $\boldsymbol{n}_i \in \hat{\mathcal{N}}^{\mathscr{C}_3}$ according to (4.7), and the composition of operators in $\hat{\mathcal{E}}^{\mathscr{C}_3}$ according to (4.10). Table 4.2 lists the result of these operations in a form not unlike that used for conveying the composition rules (3.43) or (3.46) of signum and trace operators we encountered in the previous chapter, with highlighted entries marking operations on and between elements of $\hat{\mathcal{N}}^{\mathscr{C}_3}$ and $\hat{\mathcal{E}}^{\mathscr{C}_3}$ which are associated with the nodes and edges in the classical conception of our triangle graph $\mathscr{C}_3$.

How can we now leverage this alternative operator-based representation $\hat{\mathscr{C}}_3$ in our search for Eulerian walks and paths through $\mathscr{C}_3$? Let us here again start by taking a look at walks of arbitrary length m between two nodes. Adhering to (3.12) and denoting with $\mathscr{L}(\mathscr{C}_3)$ the line graph of $\mathscr{C}_3$, each ordered set

$$\mathcal{W} = \left(j_k \in \mathcal{N}^{\mathscr{L}(\mathscr{C}_3)} : k \in [1,m], m \in \mathbb{N}\right)$$

of not necessarily distinct adjacency relations describes a potential walk of length m through $\mathscr{C}_3$. Employing the operator graph-theoretical formulation introduced above, any such potential walk $\mathcal{W}$ can be uniquely represented as

Table 4.2 *Action and composition of operators representing $\hat{\mathscr{C}}_3$.*

$\mathfrak{E}_j[\boldsymbol{n}_i]$	$j = 0$	1	2	3	4	5	6	7	8	9
$i = 0$	$\boldsymbol{n}_0$	$\boldsymbol{n}_0$	$\boldsymbol{n}_0$	$\boldsymbol{n}_0$	$\boldsymbol{n}_0$	$\boldsymbol{n}_0$	$\boldsymbol{n}_0$	$\boldsymbol{n}_0$	$\boldsymbol{n}_0$	$\boldsymbol{n}_0$
1	$\boldsymbol{n}_0$	$\boldsymbol{n}_2$	$\boldsymbol{n}_0$	$\boldsymbol{n}_0$	$\boldsymbol{n}_0$	$\boldsymbol{n}_0$	$\boldsymbol{n}_3$	$\boldsymbol{n}_1$	$\boldsymbol{n}_0$	$\boldsymbol{n}_0$
2	$\boldsymbol{n}_0$	$\boldsymbol{n}_0$	$\boldsymbol{n}_3$	$\boldsymbol{n}_0$	$\boldsymbol{n}_1$	$\boldsymbol{n}_0$	$\boldsymbol{n}_0$	$\boldsymbol{n}_0$	$\boldsymbol{n}_2$	$\boldsymbol{n}_0$
3	$\boldsymbol{n}_0$	$\boldsymbol{n}_0$	$\boldsymbol{n}_0$	$\boldsymbol{n}_1$	$\boldsymbol{n}_0$	$\boldsymbol{n}_2$	$\boldsymbol{n}_0$	$\boldsymbol{n}_0$	$\boldsymbol{n}_0$	$\boldsymbol{n}_3$
$\mathfrak{E}_{j_2}\circ\mathfrak{E}_{j_1}$	$j_2 = 0$	1	2	3	4	5	6	7	8	9
$j_1 = 0$	$\mathfrak{E}_0$	$\mathfrak{E}_0$	$\mathfrak{E}_0$	$\mathfrak{E}_0$	$\mathfrak{E}_0$	$\mathfrak{E}_0$	$\mathfrak{E}_0$	$\mathfrak{E}_0$	$\mathfrak{E}_0$	$\mathfrak{E}_0$
1	$\mathfrak{E}_0$	$\mathfrak{E}_0$	$\mathfrak{E}_6$	$\mathfrak{E}_0$	$\mathfrak{E}_7$	$\mathfrak{E}_0$	$\mathfrak{E}_0$	$\mathfrak{E}_0$	$\mathfrak{E}_1$	$\mathfrak{E}_0$
2	$\mathfrak{E}_0$	$\mathfrak{E}_0$	$\mathfrak{E}_0$	$\mathfrak{E}_4$	$\mathfrak{E}_0$	$\mathfrak{E}_8$	$\mathfrak{E}_0$	$\mathfrak{E}_0$	$\mathfrak{E}_0$	$\mathfrak{E}_2$
3	$\mathfrak{E}_0$	$\mathfrak{E}_5$	$\mathfrak{E}_0$	$\mathfrak{E}_0$	$\mathfrak{E}_0$	$\mathfrak{E}_0$	$\mathfrak{E}_9$	$\mathfrak{E}_3$	$\mathfrak{E}_0$	$\mathfrak{E}_0$
4	$\mathfrak{E}_0$	$\mathfrak{E}_8$	$\mathfrak{E}_0$	$\mathfrak{E}_0$	$\mathfrak{E}_0$	$\mathfrak{E}_0$	$\mathfrak{E}_2$	$\mathfrak{E}_4$	$\mathfrak{E}_0$	$\mathfrak{E}_0$
5	$\mathfrak{E}_0$	$\mathfrak{E}_0$	$\mathfrak{E}_9$	$\mathfrak{E}_0$	$\mathfrak{E}_3$	$\mathfrak{E}_0$	$\mathfrak{E}_0$	$\mathfrak{E}_0$	$\mathfrak{E}_5$	$\mathfrak{E}_0$
6	$\mathfrak{E}_0$	$\mathfrak{E}_0$	$\mathfrak{E}_0$	$\mathfrak{E}_7$	$\mathfrak{E}_0$	$\mathfrak{E}_1$	$\mathfrak{E}_0$	$\mathfrak{E}_0$	$\mathfrak{E}_0$	$\mathfrak{E}_6$
7	$\mathfrak{E}_0$	$\mathfrak{E}_1$	$\mathfrak{E}_0$	$\mathfrak{E}_0$	$\mathfrak{E}_0$	$\mathfrak{E}_0$	$\mathfrak{E}_6$	$\mathfrak{E}_7$	$\mathfrak{E}_0$	$\mathfrak{E}_0$
8	$\mathfrak{E}_0$	$\mathfrak{E}_0$	$\mathfrak{E}_2$	$\mathfrak{E}_0$	$\mathfrak{E}_4$	$\mathfrak{E}_0$	$\mathfrak{E}_0$	$\mathfrak{E}_0$	$\mathfrak{E}_8$	$\mathfrak{E}_0$
9	$\mathfrak{E}_0$	$\mathfrak{E}_0$	$\mathfrak{E}_0$	$\mathfrak{E}_3$	$\mathfrak{E}_0$	$\mathfrak{E}_5$	$\mathfrak{E}_0$	$\mathfrak{E}_0$	$\mathfrak{E}_0$	$\mathfrak{E}_9$

ordered composition $\bar{\mathfrak{E}}_{j_m} \circ \cdots \circ \bar{\mathfrak{E}}_{j_1}$ of m operators $\bar{\mathfrak{E}}_{j_k}$, $j_k \in [1,3]$ defined in (4.5). By then applying this composition to the node $\boldsymbol{n}_i \in \hat{\mathcal{N}}^{\mathscr{C}_3}$ from which our potential walk $\mathcal{W}$ emanates, we obtain

$$\boldsymbol{n}_{i'} = \bigcirc_{k=1}^{m} \bar{\mathfrak{E}}_{j_k}[\boldsymbol{n}_i] = \bar{\mathfrak{E}}_{j_m} \circ \cdots \circ \bar{\mathfrak{E}}_{j_1}[\boldsymbol{n}_i], \tag{4.12}$$

with $\boldsymbol{n}_{i'} \in \hat{\mathcal{N}}^{\mathscr{C}_3}$ for some $i' \in [0,3]$. By applying the composition rules listed in Table 4.2, the right-hand side of (4.12) can be simplified and eventually delivers the node $\boldsymbol{n}_{i'}$ targeted by our potential walk $\mathcal{W}$. In the case $i' \in [1,3]$, this approach will distinguish the set $\mathcal{W}$ and its corresponding composition of edge-generating operators as walk of length m from node i to node i' in $\mathscr{C}_3$, while for $i' = 0$ the potential walk $\mathcal{W}$ does not constitute an actual walk through $\mathscr{C}_3$ as $\boldsymbol{n}_0$ is not associated with a node in $\mathscr{C}_3$. In order to illustrate the application of (4.12), let us consider as examples the two potential walks $\mathcal{W}_1 = (1,2)$ and $\mathcal{W}_2 = (2,1)$ between nodes 1 and 3. We easily find

$$\begin{aligned}
\bar{\mathfrak{E}}_2 \circ \bar{\mathfrak{E}}_1[\boldsymbol{n}_1] &= (\mathfrak{E}_2 + \mathfrak{E}_5) \circ (\mathfrak{E}_1 + \mathfrak{E}_4)[\boldsymbol{n}_1] \\
&= \mathfrak{E}_2 \circ \mathfrak{E}_1[\boldsymbol{n}_1] + \mathfrak{E}_2 \circ \mathfrak{E}_4[\boldsymbol{n}_1] + \mathfrak{E}_5 \circ \mathfrak{E}_1[\boldsymbol{n}_1] + \mathfrak{E}_5 \circ \mathfrak{E}_4[\boldsymbol{n}_1] \\
&= \mathfrak{E}_6[\boldsymbol{n}_1] + \mathfrak{E}_0[\boldsymbol{n}_1] + \mathfrak{E}_0[\boldsymbol{n}_1] + \mathfrak{E}_0[\boldsymbol{n}_1] = \boldsymbol{n}_3, \\
\bar{\mathfrak{E}}_2 \circ \bar{\mathfrak{E}}_1[\boldsymbol{n}_3] &= \mathfrak{E}_6[\boldsymbol{n}_3] + \mathfrak{E}_0[\boldsymbol{n}_3] + \mathfrak{E}_0[\boldsymbol{n}_3] + \mathfrak{E}_0[\boldsymbol{n}_3] = \boldsymbol{n}_0
\end{aligned}$$

for $\mathcal{W}_1$ and

$$\bar{\mathfrak{E}}_1 \circ \bar{\mathfrak{E}}_2[\boldsymbol{n}_1] = \mathfrak{E}_0[\boldsymbol{n}_1] + \mathfrak{E}_0[\boldsymbol{n}_1] + \mathfrak{E}_0[\boldsymbol{n}_1] + \mathfrak{E}_3[\boldsymbol{n}_1] = \boldsymbol{n}_0,$$
$$\bar{\mathfrak{E}}_1 \circ \bar{\mathfrak{E}}_2[\boldsymbol{n}_3] = \mathfrak{E}_0[\boldsymbol{n}_3] + \mathfrak{E}_0[\boldsymbol{n}_3] + \mathfrak{E}_0[\boldsymbol{n}_3] + \mathfrak{E}_3[\boldsymbol{n}_3] = \boldsymbol{n}_1,$$

for $\mathcal{W}_2$, and we can conclude that $\mathcal{W}_1$ is indeed a walk of length 2 from node 1 to 3, and $\mathcal{W}_2$ a walk from node 3 to node 1 (see Fig. 4.1c, dashed).

So far, this approach allows us only to distinguish whether or not a potential walk $\mathcal{W}$ forms an actual walk through $\mathcal{C}_3$. However, as (4.12) yields for each composition of edges and nodes of $\mathcal{C}_3$ a unique Boolean vector in $\hat{\mathcal{N}}^{\mathcal{C}_3}$, it certainly can also be exploited for counting the number of walks between nodes. In order to do so, we recall that only if $\mathcal{W}$ is a walk, its defining composition of edge-generating operators will result in a vector $\boldsymbol{n}_{i'}$, $i' \in [1,3]$ with $\mathrm{T}[\boldsymbol{n}_{i'}] = 1$ which is associated with a node in the classical definition of $\mathcal{C}_3$. On the other hand, for $i' = 0$, the combination of edges cannot describe a valid walk through $\mathcal{C}_3$ as, by construction, the all-zeroes vector $\boldsymbol{n}_0 = \boldsymbol{0}^3$ does not correspond to a node of $\mathcal{C}_3$. By then summing (4.12) over all possible ordered compositions of m edges and applying the result to a node i in $\mathcal{C}_3$, we obtain a vector

$$N_m^{\mathcal{W}}(i) = \sum_{(j_1,\dots,j_m)\in\mathfrak{T}_m([1,3])} \bigodot_{k=1}^{m} \bar{\mathfrak{E}}_{j_k}[\boldsymbol{n}_i] \tag{4.13}$$

whose ith element contains the number $N_m^{\mathcal{W}}(i,i')$ of all possible walks of length m from node i to node i' in $\mathcal{C}_3$. Here, we denoted with $\mathfrak{T}_m(\mathcal{S})$ the set of ordered m-tuples over a finite set $\mathcal{S}$, that is the set of all m-permutations with repetition over $\mathcal{S}$ with $|\mathfrak{T}_m(\mathcal{S})| = |\mathcal{S}|^m$ elements. In (4.13), the set $\mathcal{S} = [1,3] \subset \mathbb{N}$ results in a total of $|\mathfrak{T}_m([1,3])| = 3^m$ different compositions which, by employing the rules listed in Table 4.2, can be simplified to yield

$$\begin{aligned}
N_1^{\mathcal{W}}(i) &= (\mathfrak{E}_1+\mathfrak{E}_2+\mathfrak{E}_3+\mathfrak{E}_4+\mathfrak{E}_5+\mathfrak{E}_6)[\boldsymbol{n}_i],\\
N_2^{\mathcal{W}}(i) &= 24\,\mathfrak{E}_0[\boldsymbol{n}_i] + (\mathfrak{E}_1+\mathfrak{E}_2+\mathfrak{E}_3+\mathfrak{E}_4+\mathfrak{E}_5+\mathfrak{E}_6)[\boldsymbol{n}_i] + 2\,(\mathfrak{E}_7+\mathfrak{E}_8+\mathfrak{E}_9)[\boldsymbol{n}_i],\\
N_3^{\mathcal{W}}(i) &= 192\,\mathfrak{E}_0[\boldsymbol{n}_i] + 3\,(\mathfrak{E}_1+\mathfrak{E}_2+\mathfrak{E}_3+\mathfrak{E}_4+\mathfrak{E}_5+\mathfrak{E}_6)[\boldsymbol{n}_i] + 2\,(\mathfrak{E}_7+\mathfrak{E}_8+\mathfrak{E}_9)[\boldsymbol{n}_i],\\
N_4^{\mathcal{W}}(i) &= 1248\,\mathfrak{E}_0 + 6\,(\mathfrak{E}_7+\mathfrak{E}_8+\mathfrak{E}_9)[\boldsymbol{n}_i] + 5\,(\mathfrak{E}_1+\mathfrak{E}_2+\mathfrak{E}_3+\mathfrak{E}_4+\mathfrak{E}_5+\mathfrak{E}_6)[\boldsymbol{n}_i],\\
&\vdots
\end{aligned}$$

and eventually deliver an alternative to (4.2) for counting the number $N_m^{\mathcal{W}}(i,i')$ of walks of length m between two arbitrary nodes i and i' of $\mathcal{C}_3$.

In contrast to (4.2), however, here we can go one step further by recognising that with a slight change to the sum, the right-hand side of (4.13) also covers the number of Eulerian walks between nodes in $\mathcal{C}_3$. Indeed, by restricting the sum over compositions of edge-generating operators to $\mathfrak{S}_m([1,3])$, where $\mathfrak{S}_m(\mathcal{S})$ denotes the set of ordered m-subsets over a finite set $\mathcal{S}$, that is, the set of all m-permutations over $\mathcal{S}$ with a total of $|\mathfrak{S}_m(\mathcal{S})| = |\mathcal{S}|!/(|\mathcal{S}|-m)!$ elements, we obtain a vector

$$\bar{N}_m^{\mathcal{W}}(i) = \sum_{(j_1,\ldots,j_m)\in\mathfrak{S}_m([1,3])} \bigodot_{k=1}^{m} \bar{\mathfrak{E}}_{j_k}[\boldsymbol{n}_i] \tag{4.14}$$

whose i'th element counts the number $\bar{N}_m^{\mathcal{W}}(i,i')$ of all possible Eulerian walks of length m from node i to node i' in $\mathscr{C}_3$. Naturally, as $m \leq |\mathcal{S}|$, only Eulerian walks up to length $m = 3$ are here possible such that (4.14) yields

$$\begin{aligned}
\bar{N}_1^{\mathcal{W}}(i) &= (\mathfrak{E}_1+\mathfrak{E}_2+\mathfrak{E}_3+\mathfrak{E}_4+\mathfrak{E}_5+\mathfrak{E}_6)[\boldsymbol{n}_i],\\
\bar{N}_2^{\mathcal{W}}(i) &= 18\,\mathfrak{E}_0[\boldsymbol{n}_i] + (\mathfrak{E}_1+\mathfrak{E}_2+\mathfrak{E}_3+\mathfrak{E}_4+\mathfrak{E}_5+\mathfrak{E}_6)[\boldsymbol{n}_i],\\
\bar{N}_3^{\mathcal{W}}(i) &= 42\,\mathfrak{E}_0[\boldsymbol{n}_i] + 2\,(\mathfrak{E}_7+\mathfrak{E}_8+\mathfrak{E}_9)[\boldsymbol{n}_i].
\end{aligned}$$

After applying the rules which govern the action of edge-generating operators on the nodes comprising our triangle graph, we eventually obtain for $\bar{N}_m^{\mathcal{W}}(i,i')$ the values listed in Table 4.1. More importantly, however, with (4.14) we finally reach the goal of our little exercise as $\bar{N}_3^{\mathcal{W}}(i)$ discerns Eulerian walks of length 3 and, thus, also delivers the desired number of Eulerian paths in $\mathscr{C}_3$. Indeed, with $\bar{N}_3^{\mathcal{W}}(1,1) = \bar{N}_3^{\mathcal{W}}(2,2) = \bar{N}_3^{\mathcal{W}}(3,3) = 2$ (see Table 4.1, grey), we are left to conclude that there exists a total of 6 Eulerian paths, in fact Hamiltonian cycles, in our simple triangle graph $\mathscr{C}_3$. Albeit expected, this result would have been difficult to obtain in algebraically explicit terms by considering powers of the graph's adjacency matrix alone.

It must certainly be argued here that the operator graph-theoretical approach presented above still requires the consideration of all possible combinations of edge-generating operators (4.5) in order to deliver the number of walks through $\mathscr{C}_3$ according to (4.13), and all of their possible permutations to arrive at the number of Eulerian walks and Eulerian paths according to (4.14). However, with a total of only 10 operators (4.4) and (4.8) defining $\hat{\mathscr{C}}_3$ and their accompanying $100 + 40$ composition rules in Table 4.2, this approach arguably bestows a more hospitable view on the inherent combinatorial complexity associated with exhaustive search problems in graph structures, especially when compared to the required minimum of 24 + 9 operators and 576 + 81 composition rules in the operator-inspired approach based on node and edge state vectors we explored in the previous chapter. Before we return to the bridges of Königsberg and gauge the viability and benefits of its operator graph-theoretical representation in tackling the search for Eulerian paths, however, we must first address the generalisability of the approach presented above, in particular with regard to its applicability to directed graphs and multigraphs. Such a generalisability might not be guaranteed as, for instance, each of the w edges of weight 1

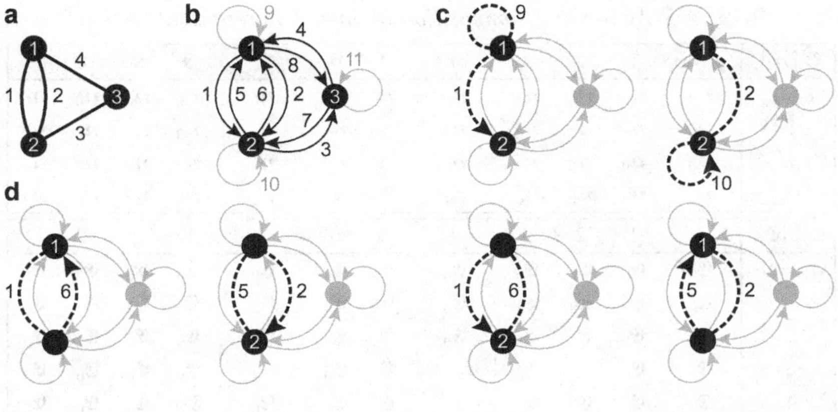

Figure 4.2 Triangle multigraph $\mathcal{C}'_3$ and its operator graph representation. **a:** Classical representation of a triangle multigraph $\mathcal{C}'_3$ with 3 nodes and 4 undirected edges. **b:** Operator representation of $\mathcal{C}'_3$ with eight directed adjacency relations between distinct nodes (black), and three directed adjacency relations which render each node adjacent to itself (grey). **c:** Non-associativity of the composition of edge-generating operators. Illustrated are $\mathfrak{E}_1\circ(\mathfrak{E}_5\circ\mathfrak{E}_2) = \mathfrak{E}_1\circ\mathfrak{E}_9$ (left) and $(\mathfrak{E}_1\circ\mathfrak{E}_5)\circ\mathfrak{E}_2 = \mathfrak{E}_{10}\circ\mathfrak{E}_2$ (right). **d:** Operator graph-theoretical representation of Eulerian walks of length 2 generated by the ordered sets $\mathcal{W}_1 = (1,2)$ (left) and $\mathcal{W}_2 = (2,1)$ (right) of undirected edges of $\mathcal{C}'_3$. In all illustrated operator representations, node $\boldsymbol{n}_0$ and all edge-generating operators associated with $\boldsymbol{n}_0$ are omitted.

representing a multiedge of weight $w \in \mathbb{N}: w > 1$ in a multigraph will be subject to the same matrix representation yet also require a distinction from the operators representing the remaining $w - 1$ edges in order to allow for the systematic construction and consideration of all possible walks.

In order to illustrate the subtleties associated with this latter point, let us take a closer look at the undirected triangle multigraph $\mathcal{C}'_3$ with four edges depicted in Fig. 4.2a. Akin to $\mathcal{C}_3$, we find that an operator representation $\hat{\mathcal{C}}'_3$ of $\mathcal{C}'_3$ is furnished by a tuple $(\hat{\mathcal{N}}^{\mathcal{C}'_3}, \mathcal{E}^{\mathcal{C}'_3})$ comprised of a set of nodes $\hat{\mathcal{N}}^{\mathcal{C}'_3}$ and an algebra of matrix operators $\mathcal{E}^{\mathcal{C}'_3} := (\hat{\mathcal{E}}^{\mathcal{C}'_3}, O^{\mathcal{C}'_3})$ which serves as formalisation of the graph's set of edges. Here, the set $\hat{\mathcal{N}}^{\mathcal{C}'_3}$ is given by (4.6) as both graphs $\mathcal{C}_3$ and $\mathcal{C}'_3$ share identical sets of nodes. In contrast, with one additional undirected edge connecting node 1 and 2 in $\mathcal{C}'_3$, the set of edge operators

$$\hat{\mathcal{E}}^{\mathcal{C}'_3} := \left\{\mathfrak{E}_j\colon\ j \in [0, 11]\right\} \subset \mathbb{B}^{3\times 3} \tag{4.15}$$

now has 12 elements

$$\begin{aligned}\mathfrak{E}_0 &:= \boldsymbol{0}^{3\times 3},\ \mathfrak{E}_1 = \mathfrak{E}_5^{\mathsf{T}} = \mathfrak{E}_2 = \mathfrak{E}_6^{\mathsf{T}} := \boldsymbol{\delta}_{1,2}^{3\times 3},\\ \mathfrak{E}_3 &= \mathfrak{E}_7^{\mathsf{T}} := \boldsymbol{\delta}_{2,3}^{3\times 3},\ \mathfrak{E}_4 = \mathfrak{E}_8^{\mathsf{T}} := \boldsymbol{\delta}_{3,1}^{3\times 3},\end{aligned} \tag{4.16}$$

Table 4.3 *Action and composition of operators representing* $\hat{\mathscr{C}}'_3$.

$\mathfrak{E}_j[n_i]$	$j=0$	1	2	3	4	5	6	7	8	9	10	11
$i=0$	n_0	n_0	n_0	n_0	n_0	n_0	n_0	n_0	n_0	n_0	n_0	n_0
1	n_0	n_2	n_2	n_0	n_0	n_0	n_0	n_0	n_3	n_1	n_0	n_0
2	n_0	n_0	n_0	n_3	n_0	n_1	n_1	n_0	n_0	n_0	n_2	n_0
3	n_0	n_0	n_0	n_0	n_1	n_0	n_0	n_2	n_0	n_0	n_0	n_3

$\mathfrak{E}_{j_2}\circ\mathfrak{E}_{j_1}$	$j_2=0$	1	2	3	4	5	6	7	8	9	10	11
$j_1=0$	$\mathfrak{E}_0$	$\mathfrak{E}_0$	$\mathfrak{E}_0$	$\mathfrak{E}_0$	$\mathfrak{E}_0$	$\mathfrak{E}_0$	$\mathfrak{E}_0$	$\mathfrak{E}_0$	$\mathfrak{E}_0$	$\mathfrak{E}_0$	$\mathfrak{E}_0$	$\mathfrak{E}_0$
1	$\mathfrak{E}_0$	$\mathfrak{E}_0$	$\mathfrak{E}_0$	$\mathfrak{E}_8$	$\mathfrak{E}_0$	$\mathfrak{E}_9$	$\mathfrak{E}_9$	$\mathfrak{E}_0$	$\mathfrak{E}_0$	$\mathfrak{E}_0$	$\mathfrak{E}_1$	$\mathfrak{E}_0$
2	$\mathfrak{E}_0$	$\mathfrak{E}_0$	$\mathfrak{E}_0$	$\mathfrak{E}_8$	$\mathfrak{E}_0$	$\mathfrak{E}_9$	$\mathfrak{E}_9$	$\mathfrak{E}_0$	$\mathfrak{E}_0$	$\mathfrak{E}_0$	$\mathfrak{E}_2$	$\mathfrak{E}_0$
3	$\mathfrak{E}_0$	$\mathfrak{E}_0$	$\mathfrak{E}_0$	$\mathfrak{E}_0$	$\frac{1}{2}(\mathfrak{E}_5+\mathfrak{E}_6)$	$\mathfrak{E}_0$	$\mathfrak{E}_0$	$\mathfrak{E}_{10}$	$\mathfrak{E}_0$	$\mathfrak{E}_0$	$\mathfrak{E}_0$	$\mathfrak{E}_3$
4	$\mathfrak{E}_0$	$\mathfrak{E}_7$	$\mathfrak{E}_7$	$\mathfrak{E}_0$	$\mathfrak{E}_0$	$\mathfrak{E}_0$	$\mathfrak{E}_0$	$\mathfrak{E}_0$	$\mathfrak{E}_{11}$	$\mathfrak{E}_4$	$\mathfrak{E}_0$	$\mathfrak{E}_0$
5	$\mathfrak{E}_0$	$\mathfrak{E}_{10}$	$\mathfrak{E}_{10}$	$\mathfrak{E}_0$	$\mathfrak{E}_0$	$\mathfrak{E}_0$	$\mathfrak{E}_0$	$\mathfrak{E}_0$	$\mathfrak{E}_3$	$\mathfrak{E}_5$	$\mathfrak{E}_0$	$\mathfrak{E}_0$
6	$\mathfrak{E}_0$	$\mathfrak{E}_{10}$	$\mathfrak{E}_{10}$	$\mathfrak{E}_0$	$\mathfrak{E}_0$	$\mathfrak{E}_0$	$\mathfrak{E}_0$	$\mathfrak{E}_0$	$\mathfrak{E}_3$	$\mathfrak{E}_6$	$\mathfrak{E}_0$	$\mathfrak{E}_0$
7	$\mathfrak{E}_0$	$\mathfrak{E}_0$	$\mathfrak{E}_0$	$\mathfrak{E}_{11}$	$\mathfrak{E}_0$	$\mathfrak{E}_4$	$\mathfrak{E}_4$	$\mathfrak{E}_0$	$\mathfrak{E}_0$	$\mathfrak{E}_0$	$\mathfrak{E}_7$	$\mathfrak{E}_0$
8	$\mathfrak{E}_0$	$\mathfrak{E}_0$	$\mathfrak{E}_0$	$\mathfrak{E}_0$	$\mathfrak{E}_9$	$\mathfrak{E}_0$	$\mathfrak{E}_0$	$\frac{1}{2}(\mathfrak{E}_1+\mathfrak{E}_2)$	$\mathfrak{E}_0$	$\mathfrak{E}_0$	$\mathfrak{E}_0$	$\mathfrak{E}_8$
9	$\mathfrak{E}_0$	$\mathfrak{E}_1$	$\mathfrak{E}_2$	$\mathfrak{E}_0$	$\mathfrak{E}_0$	$\mathfrak{E}_0$	$\mathfrak{E}_0$	$\mathfrak{E}_0$	$\mathfrak{E}_8$	$\mathfrak{E}_9$	$\mathfrak{E}_0$	$\mathfrak{E}_0$
10	$\mathfrak{E}_0$	$\mathfrak{E}_0$	$\mathfrak{E}_0$	$\mathfrak{E}_3$	$\mathfrak{E}_0$	$\mathfrak{E}_5$	$\mathfrak{E}_6$	$\mathfrak{E}_0$	$\mathfrak{E}_0$	$\mathfrak{E}_0$	$\mathfrak{E}_{10}$	$\mathfrak{E}_0$
11	$\mathfrak{E}_0$	$\mathfrak{E}_0$	$\mathfrak{E}_0$	$\mathfrak{E}_0$	$\mathfrak{E}_4$	$\mathfrak{E}_0$	$\mathfrak{E}_0$	$\mathfrak{E}_7$	$\mathfrak{E}_0$	$\mathfrak{E}_0$	$\mathfrak{E}_0$	$\mathfrak{E}_{11}$

$$\mathfrak{E}_9 := \delta^{3\times3}_{1,1},\ \mathfrak{E}_{10} := \delta^{3\times3}_{2,2},\ \mathfrak{E}_{11} := \delta^{3\times3}_{3,3},$$

as illustrated in Fig. 4.2b, with the sums

$$\bar{\mathfrak{E}}_j := \mathfrak{E}_j + \mathfrak{E}_{j+4} \tag{4.17}$$

for $j \in [1,4]$ corresponding to the matrix representations of the four undirected edges of $\mathscr{C}'_3$. Akin to $\hat{\mathscr{C}}_3$, it can then be shown that each $\mathfrak{E}_j \in \hat{\mathcal{E}}^{\mathscr{C}'_3}$ acts through right-hand matrix multiplication as operator $\mathfrak{E}_j\colon \hat{\mathcal{N}}^{\mathscr{C}'_3} \to \hat{\mathcal{N}}^{\mathscr{C}'_3}$ over $\hat{\mathcal{N}}^{\mathscr{C}'_3}$ and is subject to the finitary operation of composition $\circ\colon \hat{\mathcal{E}}^{\mathscr{C}'_3} \times \hat{\mathcal{E}}^{\mathscr{C}'_3} \to \hat{\mathcal{E}}^{\mathscr{C}'_3}$ which renders $\hat{\mathcal{E}}^{\mathscr{C}'_3}$ closed. The governing rules, listed in Table 4.3, eventually provide a complete operator representation of our triangle multigraph $\mathscr{C}'_3$.

Owing to the fact that both $\bar{\mathfrak{E}}_1$ and $\bar{\mathfrak{E}}_2$ share identical nodes as part of the same undirected edge in $\mathscr{C}'_3$, the associated pairs of edge-generating operators $\mathfrak{E}_1$, $\mathfrak{E}_2$ and $\mathfrak{E}_5$, $\mathfrak{E}_6$ will necessarily share identical matrices within the confines of our approach. Adhering to this defining representation of our operators in terms of Boolean matrices (4.16), and recalling that the operation of operator composition is naturally provided by right-hand matrix multiplication, the generated algebra of operators $\mathscr{E}^{\mathscr{C}'_3}$ is then associative. However, this associative nature of $\mathscr{E}^{\mathscr{C}_3'}$ is unfortunately less evident if we ignore for a moment the matrix form of our operators and restrict solely to the arguably more abstract level of formal composition rules listed in Table 4.3. To illustrate this delicate point, let us consider the composition $\mathfrak{E}_1 \circ \mathfrak{E}_5 \circ \mathfrak{E}_2$ as an example. While employing (4.16) immediately yields

$$\mathfrak{E}_1 \circ (\mathfrak{E}_5 \circ \mathfrak{E}_2) = (\mathfrak{E}_1 \circ \mathfrak{E}_5) \circ \mathfrak{E}_2 = \delta_{1,2}^{3\times3} \cdot \delta_{2,1}^{3\times3} \cdot \delta_{1,2}^{3\times3} = \delta_{1,2}^{3\times3}, \tag{4.18}$$

the naked application of our formal composition rules does suggest that

$$\mathfrak{E}_1 \circ (\mathfrak{E}_5 \circ \mathfrak{E}_2) = \mathfrak{E}_1 \circ \mathfrak{E}_9 = \mathfrak{E}_1 \neq (\mathfrak{E}_1 \circ \mathfrak{E}_5) \circ \mathfrak{E}_2 = \mathfrak{E}_{10} \circ \mathfrak{E}_2 = \mathfrak{E}_2. \tag{4.19}$$

Certainly, as $\mathfrak{E}_1$ and $\mathfrak{E}_2$ are both represented by $\delta_{1,2}^{3\times3}$, the expressions on either side of the inequality in (4.19) are identical and relinquish a result in coherence with (4.18). On a more conceptual level, however, each of the operators $\mathfrak{E}_1$ and $\mathfrak{E}_2$ distinguishes its own directed adjacency relation in our graph such that the expressions on both sides of the inequality in (4.19) represent different walks in $\hat{\mathscr{C}}_3'$, as shown in Fig. 4.2c. In order to accomodate both justified perspectives, we recognise that edge-generating operators, per definition, act on nodes from the left according to

$$\mathfrak{E}_1 \circ \mathfrak{E}_5 \circ \mathfrak{E}_2[\boldsymbol{n}] = \mathfrak{E}_1\Big[\mathfrak{E}_5[\mathfrak{E}_2[\boldsymbol{n}]]\Big],$$

and then define without loss of generality the operation of operator composition as strictly acting from the right such that

$$\mathfrak{E}_1 \circ \mathfrak{E}_5 \circ \mathfrak{E}_2[\boldsymbol{n}] = \mathfrak{E}_1 \circ (\mathfrak{E}_5 \circ \mathfrak{E}_2)[\boldsymbol{n}] = \mathfrak{E}_1 \circ \mathfrak{E}_9[\boldsymbol{n}] = \mathfrak{E}_1[\boldsymbol{n}]$$

according to the left-hand side of inequaility (4.19). This distinction, or choice of convention, we will adhere to for the remainder of this book indeed becomes a requirement for the construction of walks within our framework, but at the expense that the representation which allows for such a distinction is rendered non-associative. For notational purposes, we will therefore refer to the latter as *non-associative representation*, while the set of vectors and matrices defining the nodes and edges together with their actions through matrix multiplication will naturally furnish an *associative representation* of a graph.

The example of our triangle graph $\mathscr{C}_3'$ hints at yet another delicate point when approaching multigraphs within the operator graph-theoretical context developed so far. What is the result of combining the undirected edges 4 and 3 in $\mathscr{C}_3'$? Utilising our associative operator representation, we easily find

$$\mathfrak{E}_7 \circ \mathfrak{E}_8 = \delta_{1,3}^{3\times3} \cdot \delta_{3,2}^{3\times3} = \delta_{1,2}^{3\times3},$$

which, according to (4.16), defines both edge-generating operators $\mathfrak{E}_1$ and $\mathfrak{E}_2$. However, a possible continuation of the considered walk certainly depends on

Table 4.4 *Number of walks $N_m^{\mathcal{W}}(i,i')$ and Eulerian walks $\bar{N}_m^{\mathcal{W}}(i,i')$ in $\mathscr{C}_3'$.*

(i,i')	$N_1^{\mathcal{W}}$	$N_2^{\mathcal{W}}$	$N_3^{\mathcal{W}}$	$N_4^{\mathcal{W}}$	$\cdots$	$\bar{N}_1^{\mathcal{W}}$	$\bar{N}_2^{\mathcal{W}}$	$\bar{N}_3^{\mathcal{W}}$	$\bar{N}_4^{\mathcal{W}}$
(1,1)	0	5	4	30		0	2	4	0
(1,2)	2	1	12	14		2	1	0	6
(1,3)	1	2	6	16		1	2	2	0
(2,2)	0	5	4	30		0	2	4	0
(2,3)	1	2	6	16		1	2	2	0
(3,3)	0	2	4	12		0	0	4	0

the distinction of these directed edges, especially when constructing Eulerian walks which allow only for each edge to be traversed at most once. In order to accommodate all possible options for continuing a walk in our non-associative operator representation of $\mathscr{C}_3'$, let us define the composition of $\mathfrak{E}_7$ and $\mathfrak{E}_8$ as superposition of $\mathfrak{E}_1$ and $\mathfrak{E}_2$ such that

$$\mathfrak{E}_7 \circ \mathfrak{E}_8 = (\mathfrak{E}_1 + \mathfrak{E}_2)/2,$$

a choice which, perhaps somewhat intriguingly, is inspired by the superposition of states in quantum theory. With a similar superposition rule applying to the result of the composition $\mathfrak{E}_4 \circ \mathfrak{E}_3$ (see Table 4.3), we then have all the required tools at our disposal for our exploration of walks through $\mathscr{C}_3'$ using its non-associative operator graph-theoretical representation $\hat{\mathscr{C}}_3'$ introduced above.

Let us here begin by exemplifying the application of (4.12) to potential walks comprised of the two edges connecting nodes 1 and 2 in our multigraph. Considering $\mathcal{W}_1 = (1,2)$, we easily obtain

$$\bar{\mathfrak{E}}_2 \circ \bar{\mathfrak{E}}_1[\boldsymbol{n}_1] = (\mathfrak{E}_2+\mathfrak{E}_6) \circ (\mathfrak{E}_1+\mathfrak{E}_5)[\boldsymbol{n}_1] = \mathfrak{E}_{10}[\boldsymbol{n}_1] + \mathfrak{E}_9[\boldsymbol{n}_1] = \boldsymbol{n}_1,$$
$$\bar{\mathfrak{E}}_2 \circ \bar{\mathfrak{E}}_1[\boldsymbol{n}_2] = \mathfrak{E}_{10}[\boldsymbol{n}_2] + \mathfrak{E}_9[\boldsymbol{n}_2] = \boldsymbol{n}_2,$$

while $\mathcal{W}_2 = (2,1)$ delivers

$$\bar{\mathfrak{E}}_1 \circ \bar{\mathfrak{E}}_2[\boldsymbol{n}_1] = (\mathfrak{E}_1+\mathfrak{E}_5) \circ (\mathfrak{E}_2+\mathfrak{E}_6)[\boldsymbol{n}_1] = \mathfrak{E}_{10}[\boldsymbol{n}_1] + \mathfrak{E}_9[\boldsymbol{n}_1] = \boldsymbol{n}_1,$$
$$\bar{\mathfrak{E}}_1 \circ \bar{\mathfrak{E}}_2[\boldsymbol{n}_2] = \mathfrak{E}_{10}[\boldsymbol{n}_2] + \mathfrak{E}_9[\boldsymbol{n}_2] = \boldsymbol{n}_2.$$

This covers all four possible walks of length 2 involving edges 1 and 2 in $\mathscr{C}_3'$ (see Fig. 4.2d). In order to arrive at the total count of walks through $\mathscr{C}_3'$, we will mirror the approach used for $\mathscr{C}_3$ and employ (4.13) with $\mathfrak{T}_m([1,4])$, eventually obtaining vectors

$$N_1^{\mathcal{W}}(i) = (\mathfrak{E}_1+\mathfrak{E}_2+\mathfrak{E}_3+\mathfrak{E}_4+\mathfrak{E}_5+\mathfrak{E}_6+\mathfrak{E}_7+\mathfrak{E}_8)[\boldsymbol{n}_i],$$
$$N_2^{\mathcal{W}}(i) = 42\,\mathfrak{E}_0[\boldsymbol{n}_i] + 5\,(\mathfrak{E}_9+\mathfrak{E}_{10})[\boldsymbol{n}_i] + 2\,(\mathfrak{E}_3+\mathfrak{E}_4+\mathfrak{E}_7+\mathfrak{E}_8+\mathfrak{E}_{11})[\boldsymbol{n}_i]$$
$$+(\mathfrak{E}_1+\mathfrak{E}_2+\mathfrak{E}_5+\mathfrak{E}_6)[\boldsymbol{n}_i]/2,$$

$$N_3^{\mathcal{W}}(i) = 452\,\mathfrak{E}_0[\boldsymbol{n}_i] + 6\,(\mathfrak{E}_1{+}\mathfrak{E}_2{+}\mathfrak{E}_3{+}\mathfrak{E}_4{+}\mathfrak{E}_5{+}\mathfrak{E}_6{+}\mathfrak{E}_7{+}\mathfrak{E}_8)[\boldsymbol{n}_i] + 4\,(\mathfrak{E}_9{+}\mathfrak{E}_{10}{+}\mathfrak{E}_{11})[\boldsymbol{n}_i],$$

$$N_4^{\mathcal{W}}(i) = 3932\,\mathfrak{E}_0[\boldsymbol{n}_i] + 30\,(\mathfrak{E}_9{+}\mathfrak{E}_{10})[\boldsymbol{n}_i] + 16\,(\mathfrak{E}_3{+}\mathfrak{E}_4{+}\mathfrak{E}_7{+}\mathfrak{E}_8)[\boldsymbol{n}_i] + 12\,\mathfrak{E}_{11}[\boldsymbol{n}_i] + 7\,(\mathfrak{E}_1{+}\mathfrak{E}_2{+}\mathfrak{E}_5{+}\mathfrak{E}_6)[\boldsymbol{n}_i],$$

$$\vdots$$

whose ith elements yield the number $N_m^{\mathcal{W}}(i,i')$ of all possible walks of length m from node i to i'. In a similar fashion, using (4.14) with $\mathfrak{S}_m([1,4])$, we find

$$\bar{N}_1^{\mathcal{W}}(i) = (\mathfrak{E}_1{+}\mathfrak{E}_2{+}\mathfrak{E}_3{+}\mathfrak{E}_4{+}\mathfrak{E}_5{+}\mathfrak{E}_6{+}\mathfrak{E}_7{+}\mathfrak{E}_8)[\boldsymbol{n}_i],$$

$$\bar{N}_2^{\mathcal{W}}(i) = 34\,\mathfrak{E}_0[\boldsymbol{n}_i] + 2\,(\mathfrak{E}_3{+}\mathfrak{E}_4{+}\mathfrak{E}_7{+}\mathfrak{E}_8{+}\mathfrak{E}_9{+}\mathfrak{E}_{10})[\boldsymbol{n}_i] + (\mathfrak{E}_1{+}\mathfrak{E}_2{+}\mathfrak{E}_5{+}\mathfrak{E}_6)[\boldsymbol{n}_i]/2,$$

$$\bar{N}_3^{\mathcal{W}}(i) = 172\,\mathfrak{E}_0[\boldsymbol{n}_i] + 4\,(\mathfrak{E}_9{+}\mathfrak{E}_{10}{+}\mathfrak{E}_{11})[\boldsymbol{n}_i] + 2\,(\mathfrak{E}_3{+}\mathfrak{E}_4{+}\mathfrak{E}_7{+}\mathfrak{E}_8)[\boldsymbol{n}_i],$$

$$\bar{N}_4^{\mathcal{W}}(i) = 372\,\mathfrak{E}_0[\boldsymbol{n}_i] + 3\,(\mathfrak{E}_1{+}\mathfrak{E}_2{+}\mathfrak{E}_5{+}\mathfrak{E}_6)[\boldsymbol{n}_i],$$

and thus the number $\bar{N}_m^{\mathcal{W}}(i,i')$ of all possible Eulerian walks up to length 4, including the desired number of Eulerian paths $\bar{N}_4^{\mathcal{W}}(i,i')$. The numerical results of this evaluation, listed in Table 4.4, correctly show that $\mathscr{C}_3'$ contains a total of 12 Eulerian paths, six of which connect node 1 with node 2 (Table 4.4, grey) and six of which reciprocally connect node 2 with node 1.

This leaves us with the challenging task of exploring the application of our operator graph-theoretical formalism to the problem of finding Eulerian paths in the undirected multigraph $\mathscr{G}$ of Königsberg's bridges with its four nodes and seven edges. Inspired by the approach presented above, let

$$\hat{\mathcal{N}}^{\mathscr{G}} := \{\boldsymbol{n}_i \colon i \in [0,4]\} \tag{4.20}$$

define the set of nodes in the operator representation $\hat{\mathscr{G}}$ associated with $\mathscr{G}$, where $\boldsymbol{n}_i, i \in [1,4]$ correspond to the four nodes of $\mathscr{G}$ (Fig. 4.3a). Similarly, let

$$\hat{\mathcal{E}}^{\mathscr{G}} := \{\mathfrak{E}_j \colon j \in [0,20]\} \tag{4.21}$$

denote the set of 21 edge operators representing directed adjacency relations in $\hat{\mathscr{G}}$, where $\mathfrak{E}_j, j \in [1,14]$ correspond with

$$\bar{\mathfrak{E}}_j := \mathfrak{E}_j + \mathfrak{E}_{j+7} \tag{4.22}$$

for $j \in [1,7]$ to the seven undirected edges of $\mathscr{G}$, and the remaining seven operators $\mathfrak{E}_0, \mathfrak{E}_j, j \in [15,20]$ ensure closure under composition (Fig. 4.3b). The rules which govern the action of operators $\mathfrak{E}_j \colon \hat{\mathcal{N}}^{\mathscr{G}} \to \hat{\mathcal{N}}^{\mathscr{G}}$ over $\hat{\mathcal{N}}^{\mathscr{G}}$ and their composition $\circ \colon \hat{\mathcal{E}}^{\mathscr{G}} \times \hat{\mathcal{E}}^{\mathscr{G}} \to \hat{\mathcal{E}}^{\mathscr{G}}$, and render $\hat{\mathcal{E}}^{\mathscr{G}}$ closed, are listed in Tables 4.5 and 4.6 respectively. With this, a non-associative operator representation of the Königsberg bridge graph $\mathscr{G}$ is then furnished by the tuple $\hat{\mathscr{G}} = (\hat{\mathcal{N}}^{\mathscr{G}}, \mathcal{E}^{\mathscr{G}})$,

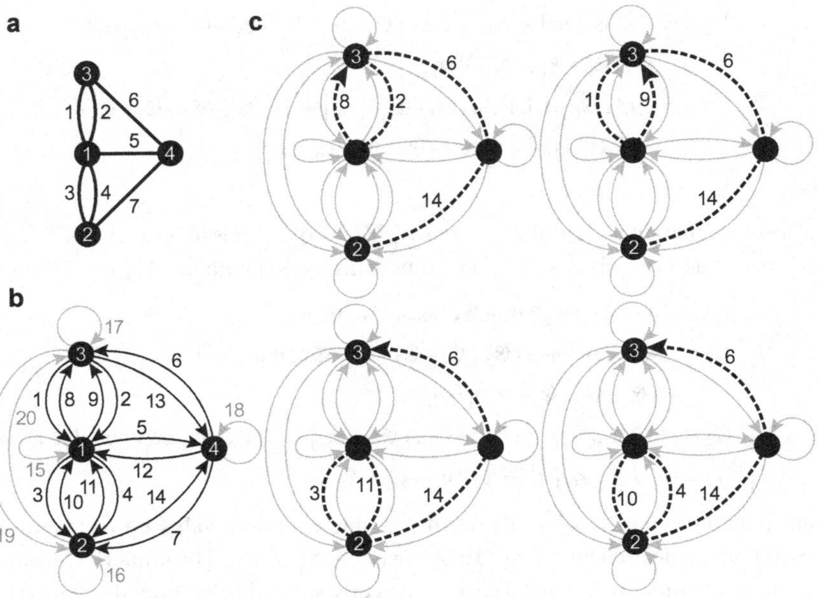

Figure 4.3 The multigraph of Königsberg's bridges and its operator representation. **a:** Classical representation of the Königsberg bridge graph $\mathscr{G}$. **b:** Operator representation of $\mathscr{G}$ with 14 directed adjacency relations between distinct nodes (black) and 7 additional adjacency relations to ensure closure of the associated algebra (grey). **c:** Operator graph-theoretical representation of all possible Eulerian walks of length 4 from node 2 to node 3. In all illustrated operator representations, node $\boldsymbol{n}_0$ and all edge-generating operators associated with $\boldsymbol{n}_0$ are omitted.

where $\mathscr{E}^{\mathscr{G}} := (\hat{\mathcal{E}}^{\mathscr{G}}, O^{\mathscr{G}})$ denotes the algebra of edge operators with algebraic structure given by $O^{\mathscr{G}} = \{\circ\}$.

Similar to our triangle graphs before, let us now employ this abstract representation for determining the number of walks $N_m^{\mathcal{W}}(i,i') = N_m^{\mathcal{W}}(i',i)$ and Eulerian walks $\bar{N}_m^{\mathcal{W}}(i,i') = \bar{N}_m^{\mathcal{W}}(i',i)$ of length m between pairs of nodes i,i' by using (4.13) with $\mathfrak{T}_m([1,7])$, and (4.14) with $\mathfrak{S}_m([1,7])$. The numerical results of this assessment are listed in Table 4.7. Naturally, the number of walks increases factorially with length and is not subject to an upper bound. In contrast, as $\mathscr{G}$ is comprised of seven edges, we only have to explore Eulerian walks up to length $m = 7$, and we find after a lengthy yet straightforward calculation that

$$\bar{N}_1^{\mathcal{W}}(i) = \textstyle\sum_{j=1}^{14} \mathfrak{E}_j[\boldsymbol{n}_i],$$
$$\vdots$$

Table 4.5 *Action of operators* $\mathfrak{C}_j : \hat{\mathcal{N}}^{\mathcal{G}} \to \hat{\mathcal{N}}^{\mathcal{G}}$ *in* $\hat{\mathcal{G}}$.

$\mathfrak{C}_j[\boldsymbol{n}_i]$	$j=0$	1	2	3	4	5	6	7	8	9	10
$i=0$	$\boldsymbol{n}_0$	$\boldsymbol{n}_0$	$\boldsymbol{n}_0$	$\boldsymbol{n}_0$	$\boldsymbol{n}_0$	$\boldsymbol{n}_0$	$\boldsymbol{n}_0$	$\boldsymbol{n}_0$	$\boldsymbol{n}_0$	$\boldsymbol{n}_0$	$\boldsymbol{n}_0$
1	$\boldsymbol{n}_0$	$\boldsymbol{n}_0$	$\boldsymbol{n}_0$	$\boldsymbol{n}_2$	$\boldsymbol{n}_2$	$\boldsymbol{n}_4$	$\boldsymbol{n}_0$	$\boldsymbol{n}_0$	$\boldsymbol{n}_3$	$\boldsymbol{n}_3$	$\boldsymbol{n}_0$
2	$\boldsymbol{n}_0$	$\boldsymbol{n}_0$	$\boldsymbol{n}_0$	$\boldsymbol{n}_0$	$\boldsymbol{n}_0$	$\boldsymbol{n}_0$	$\boldsymbol{n}_0$	$\boldsymbol{n}_0$	$\boldsymbol{n}_0$	$\boldsymbol{n}_0$	$\boldsymbol{n}_1$
3	$\boldsymbol{n}_0$	$\boldsymbol{n}_1$	$\boldsymbol{n}_1$	$\boldsymbol{n}_0$	$\boldsymbol{n}_0$	$\boldsymbol{n}_0$	$\boldsymbol{n}_0$	$\boldsymbol{n}_0$	$\boldsymbol{n}_0$	$\boldsymbol{n}_0$	$\boldsymbol{n}_0$
4	$\boldsymbol{n}_0$	$\boldsymbol{n}_0$	$\boldsymbol{n}_0$	$\boldsymbol{n}_0$	$\boldsymbol{n}_0$	$\boldsymbol{n}_0$	$\boldsymbol{n}_3$	$\boldsymbol{n}_2$	$\boldsymbol{n}_0$	$\boldsymbol{n}_0$	$\boldsymbol{n}_0$

$\mathfrak{C}_j[\boldsymbol{n}_i]$	$j=11$	12	13	14	15	16	17	18	19	20
$i=0$	$\boldsymbol{n}_0$	$\boldsymbol{n}_0$	$\boldsymbol{n}_0$	$\boldsymbol{n}_0$	$\boldsymbol{n}_0$	$\boldsymbol{n}_0$	$\boldsymbol{n}_0$	$\boldsymbol{n}_0$	$\boldsymbol{n}_0$	$\boldsymbol{n}_0$
1	$\boldsymbol{n}_0$	$\boldsymbol{n}_0$	$\boldsymbol{n}_0$	$\boldsymbol{n}_0$	$\boldsymbol{n}_1$	$\boldsymbol{n}_0$	$\boldsymbol{n}_0$	$\boldsymbol{n}_0$	$\boldsymbol{n}_0$	$\boldsymbol{n}_0$
2	$\boldsymbol{n}_1$	$\boldsymbol{n}_0$	$\boldsymbol{n}_0$	$\boldsymbol{n}_4$	$\boldsymbol{n}_0$	$\boldsymbol{n}_2$	$\boldsymbol{n}_0$	$\boldsymbol{n}_0$	$\boldsymbol{n}_0$	$\boldsymbol{n}_3$
3	$\boldsymbol{n}_0$	$\boldsymbol{n}_0$	$\boldsymbol{n}_4$	$\boldsymbol{n}_0$	$\boldsymbol{n}_0$	$\boldsymbol{n}_0$	$\boldsymbol{n}_3$	$\boldsymbol{n}_0$	$\boldsymbol{n}_2$	$\boldsymbol{n}_0$
4	$\boldsymbol{n}_0$	$\boldsymbol{n}_1$	$\boldsymbol{n}_0$	$\boldsymbol{n}_0$	$\boldsymbol{n}_0$	$\boldsymbol{n}_0$	$\boldsymbol{n}_0$	$\boldsymbol{n}_4$	$\boldsymbol{n}_0$	$\boldsymbol{n}_0$

$$\begin{aligned}
\bar{N}_4^{\mathcal{W}}(i) &= 13272\,\mathfrak{C}_0[\boldsymbol{n}_i] + 16\,\mathfrak{C}_{15}[\boldsymbol{n}_i] + 12\,(\mathfrak{C}_{16}+\mathfrak{C}_{17})[\boldsymbol{n}_i] \\
&\quad +8\textstyle\sum_{j=1}^{14}\mathfrak{C}_j[\boldsymbol{n}_i] + 8\,\mathfrak{C}_{18}[\boldsymbol{n}_i] + 4\,(\mathfrak{C}_{19}+\mathfrak{C}_{20})[\boldsymbol{n}_i], \\
\bar{N}_5^{\mathcal{W}}(i) &= 80384\,\mathfrak{C}_0[\boldsymbol{n}_i] + 32\,(\mathfrak{C}_5+\mathfrak{C}_{12}+\mathfrak{C}_{15})[\boldsymbol{n}_i] + 24\,(\mathfrak{C}_{19}+\mathfrak{C}_{20})[\boldsymbol{n}_i] \\
&\quad +16\textstyle\sum_{j=16}^{18}\mathfrak{C}_j[\boldsymbol{n}_i] + 6\sum_{j=1}^{4}(\mathfrak{C}_j+\mathfrak{C}_{j+7})[\boldsymbol{n}_i] + 4\sum_{j=6}^{7}(\mathfrak{C}_j+\mathfrak{C}_{j+7})[\boldsymbol{n}_i], \\
\bar{N}_6^{\mathcal{W}}(i) &= 322304\,\mathfrak{C}_0[\boldsymbol{n}_i] + 16\,(\mathfrak{C}_{19}+\mathfrak{C}_{20})[\boldsymbol{n}_i] \\
&\quad +32\textstyle\sum_{j=6}^{7}(\mathfrak{C}_j+\mathfrak{C}_{j+7})[\boldsymbol{n}_i] + 12\sum_{j=1}^{4}(\mathfrak{C}_j+\mathfrak{C}_{j+7})[\boldsymbol{n}_i], \\
\bar{N}_7^{\mathcal{W}}(i) &= 645120\,\mathfrak{C}_0[\boldsymbol{n}_i]
\end{aligned}$$

with the help of the composition rules listed in Table 4.6. Considering as an illustrative example node $i = 2$ as departure point of our walks, the expressions obtained above then deliver

$$\begin{aligned}
\bar{N}_1^{\mathcal{W}}(2) &= 2\,\boldsymbol{n}_1 + \boldsymbol{n}_4, \\
&\ \vdots \\
\bar{N}_4^{\mathcal{W}}(2) &= 13400\,\boldsymbol{n}_0 + 16\,\boldsymbol{n}_1 + 12\,\boldsymbol{n}_2 + 4\,\boldsymbol{n}_3 + 8\,\boldsymbol{n}_4, \\
\bar{N}_5^{\mathcal{W}}(2) &= 80584\,\boldsymbol{n}_0 + 12\,\boldsymbol{n}_1 + 16\,\boldsymbol{n}_2 + 24\,\boldsymbol{n}_3 + 4\,\boldsymbol{n}_4, \\
\bar{N}_6^{\mathcal{W}}(2) &= 322488\,\boldsymbol{n}_0 + 24\,\boldsymbol{n}_1 + 16\,\boldsymbol{n}_3 + 32\,\boldsymbol{n}_4, \\
\bar{N}_7^{\mathcal{W}}(2) &= 645120\,\boldsymbol{n}_0,
\end{aligned}$$

and eventually discern 16 Eulerian walks of length 4 targeting node 1, a total of 12 *Eulerian cycles*, i.e. Eulerian walks with identical endnodes, of length 4, the four walks of length 4 targeting node 3 shown in Fig. 4.3c and so forth. Indeed, remaining with the southernmost river bank of the river Pregel as the

Table 4.6 *Composition rules for operators* $\mathfrak{E}_j \in \hat{\mathcal{E}}^{\mathcal{G}}$ *in* $\hat{\mathcal{G}}$.

$\mathfrak{E}_{j_2} \circ \mathfrak{E}_{j_1}$	$j_2 = 0$	1	2	3	4	5	6	7	8	9	10	11	12	13	14	15	16	17	18	19	20
$j_1 = 0$	$\mathfrak{E}_0$	$\mathfrak{E}_0$	$\mathfrak{E}_0$	$\mathfrak{E}_0$	$\mathfrak{E}_0$	$\mathfrak{E}_0$	$\mathfrak{E}_0$	$\mathfrak{E}_0$	$\mathfrak{E}_0$	$\mathfrak{E}_0$	$\mathfrak{E}_0$	$\mathfrak{E}_0$	$\mathfrak{E}_0$	$\mathfrak{E}_0$	$\mathfrak{E}_0$	$\mathfrak{E}_0$	$\mathfrak{E}_0$	$\mathfrak{E}_0$	$\mathfrak{E}_0$	$\mathfrak{E}_0$	$\mathfrak{E}_0$
1	$\mathfrak{E}_0$	$\mathfrak{E}_0$	$\mathfrak{E}_0$	$\mathfrak{E}_{19}$	$\mathfrak{E}_{19}$	$\mathfrak{E}_{13}$	$\mathfrak{E}_0$	$\mathfrak{E}_0$	$\mathfrak{E}_{17}$	$\mathfrak{E}_{17}$	$\mathfrak{E}_0$	$\mathfrak{E}_0$	$\mathfrak{E}_0$	$\mathfrak{E}_0$	$\mathfrak{E}_0$	$\mathfrak{E}_1$	$\mathfrak{E}_0$	$\mathfrak{E}_0$	$\mathfrak{E}_0$	$\mathfrak{E}_0$	$\mathfrak{E}_0$
2	$\mathfrak{E}_0$	$\mathfrak{E}_0$	$\mathfrak{E}_0$	$\mathfrak{E}_{19}$	$\mathfrak{E}_{19}$	$\mathfrak{E}_{13}$	$\mathfrak{E}_0$	$\mathfrak{E}_0$	$\mathfrak{E}_{17}$	$\mathfrak{E}_{17}$	$\mathfrak{E}_0$	$\mathfrak{E}_0$	$\mathfrak{E}_0$	$\mathfrak{E}_0$	$\mathfrak{E}_0$	$\mathfrak{E}_2$	$\mathfrak{E}_0$	$\mathfrak{E}_0$	$\mathfrak{E}_0$	$\mathfrak{E}_0$	$\mathfrak{E}_0$
3	$\mathfrak{E}_0$	$\mathfrak{E}_0$	$\mathfrak{E}_0$	$\mathfrak{E}_0$	$\mathfrak{E}_0$	$\mathfrak{E}_0$	$\mathfrak{E}_0$	$\mathfrak{E}_0$	$\mathfrak{E}_0$	$\mathfrak{E}_0$	$\mathfrak{E}_{15}$	$\mathfrak{E}_{15}$	$\mathfrak{E}_0$	$\mathfrak{E}_0$	$\mathfrak{E}_5$	$\mathfrak{E}_0$	$\mathfrak{E}_3$	$\mathfrak{E}_0$	$\mathfrak{E}_0$	$\mathfrak{E}_0$	$\frac{1}{2}(\mathfrak{E}_8+\mathfrak{E}_9)$
4	$\mathfrak{E}_0$	$\mathfrak{E}_0$	$\mathfrak{E}_0$	$\mathfrak{E}_0$	$\mathfrak{E}_0$	$\mathfrak{E}_0$	$\mathfrak{E}_0$	$\mathfrak{E}_0$	$\mathfrak{E}_0$	$\mathfrak{E}_0$	$\mathfrak{E}_{15}$	$\mathfrak{E}_{15}$	$\mathfrak{E}_0$	$\mathfrak{E}_0$	$\mathfrak{E}_5$	$\mathfrak{E}_0$	$\mathfrak{E}_4$	$\mathfrak{E}_0$	$\mathfrak{E}_0$	$\mathfrak{E}_0$	$\frac{1}{2}(\mathfrak{E}_8+\mathfrak{E}_9)$
5	$\mathfrak{E}_0$	$\mathfrak{E}_0$	$\mathfrak{E}_0$	$\mathfrak{E}_0$	$\mathfrak{E}_0$	$\mathfrak{E}_0$	$\frac{1}{2}(\mathfrak{E}_8+\mathfrak{E}_9)$	$\frac{1}{2}(\mathfrak{E}_3+\mathfrak{E}_4)$	$\mathfrak{E}_0$	$\mathfrak{E}_0$	$\mathfrak{E}_0$	$\mathfrak{E}_0$	$\mathfrak{E}_{15}$	$\mathfrak{E}_0$	$\mathfrak{E}_0$	$\mathfrak{E}_0$	$\mathfrak{E}_0$	$\mathfrak{E}_0$	$\mathfrak{E}_5$	$\mathfrak{E}_0$	$\mathfrak{E}_0$
6	$\mathfrak{E}_0$	$\mathfrak{E}_{12}$	$\mathfrak{E}_{12}$	$\mathfrak{E}_0$	$\mathfrak{E}_0$	$\mathfrak{E}_0$	$\mathfrak{E}_0$	$\mathfrak{E}_0$	$\mathfrak{E}_0$	$\mathfrak{E}_0$	$\mathfrak{E}_0$	$\mathfrak{E}_0$	$\mathfrak{E}_0$	$\mathfrak{E}_{18}$	$\mathfrak{E}_0$	$\mathfrak{E}_0$	$\mathfrak{E}_0$	$\mathfrak{E}_6$	$\mathfrak{E}_0$	$\mathfrak{E}_7$	$\mathfrak{E}_0$
7	$\mathfrak{E}_0$	$\mathfrak{E}_0$	$\mathfrak{E}_0$	$\mathfrak{E}_0$	$\mathfrak{E}_0$	$\mathfrak{E}_0$	$\mathfrak{E}_0$	$\mathfrak{E}_0$	$\mathfrak{E}_0$	$\mathfrak{E}_0$	$\mathfrak{E}_{12}$	$\mathfrak{E}_{12}$	$\mathfrak{E}_0$	$\mathfrak{E}_0$	$\mathfrak{E}_{18}$	$\mathfrak{E}_0$	$\mathfrak{E}_7$	$\mathfrak{E}_0$	$\mathfrak{E}_0$	$\mathfrak{E}_0$	$\mathfrak{E}_6$
8	$\mathfrak{E}_0$	$\mathfrak{E}_{15}$	$\mathfrak{E}_{15}$	$\mathfrak{E}_0$	$\mathfrak{E}_0$	$\mathfrak{E}_0$	$\mathfrak{E}_0$	$\mathfrak{E}_0$	$\mathfrak{E}_0$	$\mathfrak{E}_0$	$\mathfrak{E}_0$	$\mathfrak{E}_0$	$\mathfrak{E}_0$	$\mathfrak{E}_5$	$\mathfrak{E}_0$	$\mathfrak{E}_0$	$\mathfrak{E}_0$	$\mathfrak{E}_8$	$\mathfrak{E}_0$	$\frac{1}{2}(\mathfrak{E}_3+\mathfrak{E}_4)$	$\mathfrak{E}_0$
9	$\mathfrak{E}_0$	$\mathfrak{E}_{15}$	$\mathfrak{E}_{15}$	$\mathfrak{E}_0$	$\mathfrak{E}_0$	$\mathfrak{E}_0$	$\mathfrak{E}_0$	$\mathfrak{E}_0$	$\mathfrak{E}_0$	$\mathfrak{E}_0$	$\mathfrak{E}_0$	$\mathfrak{E}_0$	$\mathfrak{E}_0$	$\mathfrak{E}_5$	$\mathfrak{E}_0$	$\mathfrak{E}_0$	$\mathfrak{E}_0$	$\mathfrak{E}_9$	$\mathfrak{E}_0$	$\frac{1}{2}(\mathfrak{E}_3+\mathfrak{E}_4)$	$\mathfrak{E}_0$
10	$\mathfrak{E}_0$	$\mathfrak{E}_0$	$\mathfrak{E}_0$	$\mathfrak{E}_{16}$	$\mathfrak{E}_{16}$	$\mathfrak{E}_{14}$	$\mathfrak{E}_0$	$\mathfrak{E}_0$	$\mathfrak{E}_{20}$	$\mathfrak{E}_{20}$	$\mathfrak{E}_0$	$\mathfrak{E}_0$	$\mathfrak{E}_0$	$\mathfrak{E}_0$	$\mathfrak{E}_0$	$\mathfrak{E}_{10}$	$\mathfrak{E}_0$	$\mathfrak{E}_0$	$\mathfrak{E}_0$	$\mathfrak{E}_0$	$\mathfrak{E}_0$
11	$\mathfrak{E}_0$	$\mathfrak{E}_0$	$\mathfrak{E}_0$	$\mathfrak{E}_{16}$	$\mathfrak{E}_{16}$	$\mathfrak{E}_{14}$	$\mathfrak{E}_0$	$\mathfrak{E}_0$	$\mathfrak{E}_{20}$	$\mathfrak{E}_{20}$	$\mathfrak{E}_0$	$\mathfrak{E}_0$	$\mathfrak{E}_0$	$\mathfrak{E}_0$	$\mathfrak{E}_0$	$\mathfrak{E}_{11}$	$\mathfrak{E}_0$	$\mathfrak{E}_0$	$\mathfrak{E}_0$	$\mathfrak{E}_0$	$\mathfrak{E}_0$
12	$\mathfrak{E}_0$	$\mathfrak{E}_0$	$\mathfrak{E}_0$	$\mathfrak{E}_7$	$\mathfrak{E}_7$	$\mathfrak{E}_{18}$	$\mathfrak{E}_0$	$\mathfrak{E}_0$	$\mathfrak{E}_6$	$\mathfrak{E}_6$	$\mathfrak{E}_0$	$\mathfrak{E}_0$	$\mathfrak{E}_0$	$\mathfrak{E}_0$	$\mathfrak{E}_0$	$\mathfrak{E}_{12}$	$\mathfrak{E}_0$	$\mathfrak{E}_0$	$\mathfrak{E}_0$	$\mathfrak{E}_0$	$\mathfrak{E}_0$
13	$\mathfrak{E}_0$	$\mathfrak{E}_0$	$\mathfrak{E}_0$	$\mathfrak{E}_0$	$\mathfrak{E}_0$	$\mathfrak{E}_0$	$\mathfrak{E}_{17}$	$\mathfrak{E}_{19}$	$\mathfrak{E}_0$	$\mathfrak{E}_0$	$\mathfrak{E}_0$	$\mathfrak{E}_0$	$\frac{1}{2}(\mathfrak{E}_1+\mathfrak{E}_2)$	$\mathfrak{E}_0$	$\mathfrak{E}_0$	$\mathfrak{E}_0$	$\mathfrak{E}_0$	$\mathfrak{E}_0$	$\mathfrak{E}_{13}$	$\mathfrak{E}_0$	$\mathfrak{E}_0$
14	$\mathfrak{E}_0$	$\mathfrak{E}_0$	$\mathfrak{E}_0$	$\mathfrak{E}_0$	$\mathfrak{E}_0$	$\mathfrak{E}_0$	$\mathfrak{E}_{20}$	$\mathfrak{E}_{16}$	$\mathfrak{E}_0$	$\mathfrak{E}_0$	$\mathfrak{E}_0$	$\mathfrak{E}_0$	$\frac{1}{2}(\mathfrak{E}_{10}+\mathfrak{E}_{11})$	$\mathfrak{E}_0$	$\mathfrak{E}_0$	$\mathfrak{E}_0$	$\mathfrak{E}_0$	$\mathfrak{E}_0$	$\mathfrak{E}_{14}$	$\mathfrak{E}_0$	$\mathfrak{E}_0$
15	$\mathfrak{E}_0$	$\mathfrak{E}_0$	$\mathfrak{E}_0$	$\mathfrak{E}_3$	$\mathfrak{E}_4$	$\mathfrak{E}_5$	$\mathfrak{E}_0$	$\mathfrak{E}_0$	$\mathfrak{E}_8$	$\mathfrak{E}_9$	$\mathfrak{E}_0$	$\mathfrak{E}_0$	$\mathfrak{E}_0$	$\mathfrak{E}_0$	$\mathfrak{E}_0$	$\mathfrak{E}_{15}$	$\mathfrak{E}_0$	$\mathfrak{E}_0$	$\mathfrak{E}_0$	$\mathfrak{E}_0$	$\mathfrak{E}_0$
16	$\mathfrak{E}_0$	$\mathfrak{E}_0$	$\mathfrak{E}_0$	$\mathfrak{E}_0$	$\mathfrak{E}_0$	$\mathfrak{E}_0$	$\mathfrak{E}_0$	$\mathfrak{E}_0$	$\mathfrak{E}_0$	$\mathfrak{E}_0$	$\mathfrak{E}_{10}$	$\mathfrak{E}_{11}$	$\mathfrak{E}_0$	$\mathfrak{E}_0$	$\mathfrak{E}_{14}$	$\mathfrak{E}_0$	$\mathfrak{E}_{16}$	$\mathfrak{E}_0$	$\mathfrak{E}_0$	$\mathfrak{E}_0$	$\mathfrak{E}_{20}$
17	$\mathfrak{E}_0$	$\mathfrak{E}_1$	$\mathfrak{E}_2$	$\mathfrak{E}_0$	$\mathfrak{E}_0$	$\mathfrak{E}_0$	$\mathfrak{E}_0$	$\mathfrak{E}_0$	$\mathfrak{E}_0$	$\mathfrak{E}_0$	$\mathfrak{E}_0$	$\mathfrak{E}_0$	$\mathfrak{E}_0$	$\mathfrak{E}_{13}$	$\mathfrak{E}_0$	$\mathfrak{E}_0$	$\mathfrak{E}_0$	$\mathfrak{E}_{17}$	$\mathfrak{E}_0$	$\mathfrak{E}_{19}$	$\mathfrak{E}_0$
18	$\mathfrak{E}_0$	$\mathfrak{E}_0$	$\mathfrak{E}_0$	$\mathfrak{E}_0$	$\mathfrak{E}_0$	$\mathfrak{E}_0$	$\mathfrak{E}_6$	$\mathfrak{E}_7$	$\mathfrak{E}_0$	$\mathfrak{E}_0$	$\mathfrak{E}_0$	$\mathfrak{E}_0$	$\mathfrak{E}_{12}$	$\mathfrak{E}_0$	$\mathfrak{E}_0$	$\mathfrak{E}_0$	$\mathfrak{E}_0$	$\mathfrak{E}_0$	$\mathfrak{E}_{18}$	$\mathfrak{E}_0$	$\mathfrak{E}_0$
19	$\mathfrak{E}_0$	$\mathfrak{E}_0$	$\mathfrak{E}_0$	$\mathfrak{E}_0$	$\mathfrak{E}_0$	$\mathfrak{E}_0$	$\mathfrak{E}_0$	$\mathfrak{E}_0$	$\mathfrak{E}_0$	$\mathfrak{E}_0$	$\frac{1}{2}(\mathfrak{E}_1+\mathfrak{E}_2)$	$\frac{1}{2}(\mathfrak{E}_1+\mathfrak{E}_2)$	$\mathfrak{E}_0$	$\mathfrak{E}_0$	$\mathfrak{E}_{13}$	$\mathfrak{E}_0$	$\mathfrak{E}_{19}$	$\mathfrak{E}_0$	$\mathfrak{E}_0$	$\mathfrak{E}_0$	$\mathfrak{E}_{17}$
20	$\mathfrak{E}_0$	$\frac{1}{2}(\mathfrak{E}_{10}+\mathfrak{E}_{11})$	$\frac{1}{2}(\mathfrak{E}_{10}+\mathfrak{E}_{11})$	$\mathfrak{E}_0$	$\mathfrak{E}_0$	$\mathfrak{E}_0$	$\mathfrak{E}_0$	$\mathfrak{E}_0$	$\mathfrak{E}_0$	$\mathfrak{E}_0$	$\mathfrak{E}_0$	$\mathfrak{E}_0$	$\mathfrak{E}_0$	$\mathfrak{E}_{14}$	$\mathfrak{E}_0$	$\mathfrak{E}_0$	$\mathfrak{E}_0$	$\mathfrak{E}_{20}$	$\mathfrak{E}_0$	$\mathfrak{E}_{16}$	$\mathfrak{E}_0$

Table 4.7 *Number of walks $N_m^W(i, i')$ and Eulerian walks $\bar{N}_m^W(i, i')$ in $\mathcal{G}$.*

(i, i')	N_1^W	N_2^W	N_3^W	N_4^W	...	$\bar{N}_1^W$	$\bar{N}_2^W$	$\bar{N}_3^W$	$\bar{N}_4^W$	$\bar{N}_5^W$	$\bar{N}_6^W$	$\bar{N}_7^W$
(1,1)	0	9	8	99		0	4	8	16	32	0	0
(1,2)	2	1	22	27		2	1	6	16	12	24	0
(1,3)	2	1	22	27		2	1	6	16	12	24	0
(1,4)	1	4	11	52		1	4	4	8	32	0	0
(2,2)	0	5	4	55		0	2	4	12	16	0	0
(2,3)	0	5	4	55		0	5	4	4	24	16	0
(2,4)	1	2	11	30		1	2	6	8	4	32	0
(3,3)	0	5	4	55		0	2	4	12	16	0	0
(3,4)	1	2	11	30		1	2	6	8	4	32	0
(4,4)	0	3	8	33		0	0	8	8	16	0	0

starting point of our walks through the city, this approach yields a total of 40 Eulerian walks crossing at least 4 bridges, 56 walks crossing at least 5 bridges, and 72 Eulerian walks which leave one bridge untraversed. Moreover, with a subtle modification of (4.14) which we leave as exercise to the interested reader, one obtains all those Eulerian walks of length m which cannot be continued to length $m + 1$. In coherence with the result of our tedious manual search presented in Chapter 1, we find here 6 walks emanating from the southernmost river bank which leave three bridges uncrossed, 12 walks which leave two bridges uncrossed, and 72 walks with one bridge remaining untraversed.

Most importantly, however, our result for $m = 7$ suggests that there are no Eulerian walks of length 7 between any pair of nodes in $\mathcal{G}$ (Table 4.7, grey), thus leaving us without much surprise to conclude our search for Eulerian paths in the Königsberg bridge graph in the negative. Certainly, the drawing of this conclusion still requires us to evaluate all 5,040 possible permutations of undirected edges according to (4.14). But with only 105 + 441 rules in Tables 4.5 and 4.6 to consider, the operator graph-theoretical representation explored in this chapter does relish in a more than three orders of magnitude advantage over the number of composition rules which govern the operator-inspired state vector approach of Chapter 3.

But we are not at the end of our explorative journey yet. The representation of a graph's nodes in terms of Boolean vectors, the association of a graph's edges with matrices serving as operators in a subset of a Boolean vector space, and the construction of walks through a graph by composition of these edge-generating matrix operators present an approach which, albeit tailored to address the problem of active search for specific paths, remains but a choice among many other and equally suitable possibilities. Indeed, the principal idea behind the approach exemplified above, namely to consider a graph as being comprised of algebraic objects and operators acting on these objects, is rather flexible in regards to its concrete realisation. Given such a degree of flexibility, is it possible to achieve further leverage by also eliminating the necessity of a combinatorially expensive search through all possible combinations of edges when searching for paths with specific properties?

Let us conclude this section by exploring an alternative operator representation of the Königsberg bridge graph which, on the expense of abandoning the distinction of individual walks through a graph, indeed delivers an affirmative answer to this question. To that end, we begin by noting that, without loss of generality, in each not self-looped undirected graph with n nodes labelled successively by numbers $i \in \mathbb{N}: i \in [1, n]$, an edge is uniquely identified by a pair (i_1, i_2) with $i_1, i_2 \in [1, n]: i_1 < i_2$, and thus can be suitably represented in form of a Boolean vector $\boldsymbol{\delta}^n_{i_1} + \boldsymbol{\delta}^n_{i_2} \in \mathbb{B}^n$ with exactly two non-zero elements. By assigning to each node i a vector $\boldsymbol{\delta}^n_i \in \mathbb{B}^n$ as before, the element-wise Boolean addition of a node and edge vector according to (3.1) then distinguishes the three possible results

$$(\boldsymbol{\delta}^n_{i_1} + \boldsymbol{\delta}^n_{i_2}) +^{\mathbb{B}} \boldsymbol{\delta}^n_i = \begin{cases} \boldsymbol{\delta}^n_{i_1} & \text{if } i = i_2, \\ \boldsymbol{\delta}^n_{i_2} & \text{if } i = i_1, \\ \boldsymbol{\delta}^n_{i_1} + \boldsymbol{\delta}^n_{i_2} + \boldsymbol{\delta}^n_i & \text{if } i \neq i_1, i_2. \end{cases}$$

Naturally, in the first two cases, we find the vector representation of the target node of the considered edge, while the third case yields a Boolean vector with three non-zero elements formalising the fact that node i and edge (i_1, i_2) are not adjacent to each other. Furthermore, whether a given node and edge are adjacent or not can easily be discerned by employing a scalar obtained from the Boolean product of node and edge vectors, such that

$$\left((\boldsymbol{\delta}^n_{i_1} + \boldsymbol{\delta}^n_{i_2}) \cdot^{\mathbb{B}} (\boldsymbol{\delta}^n_i)^{\mathsf{T}}\right) \cdot^{\mathbb{B}} \left((\boldsymbol{\delta}^n_{i_1} + \boldsymbol{\delta}^n_{i_2}) +^{\mathbb{B}} \boldsymbol{\delta}^n_i\right) = \begin{cases} \boldsymbol{\delta}^n_{i_1} & \text{if } i = i_2, \\ \boldsymbol{\delta}^n_{i_2} & \text{if } i = i_1, \\ \boldsymbol{0}^n & \text{if } i \neq i_1, i_2. \end{cases}$$

Interestingly, the left-hand side of this expression can be viewed as eventually defining the action of an edge-generating operator $\boldsymbol{\delta}^n_{i_1} + \boldsymbol{\delta}^n_{i_2}$ on nodes given in terms of Boolean vectors $\boldsymbol{\delta}^n_i$.

In a similar fashion, Boolean addition of two arbitrary edge-generating operators $\boldsymbol{\delta}^n_{i_1} + \boldsymbol{\delta}^n_{i_2}$ and $\boldsymbol{\delta}^n_{i_3} + \boldsymbol{\delta}^n_{i_4}$ distinguishes with

$$(\boldsymbol{\delta}^n_{i_1} + \boldsymbol{\delta}^n_{i_2}) +^{\mathbb{B}} (\boldsymbol{\delta}^n_{i_3} + \boldsymbol{\delta}^n_{i_4}) = \begin{cases} \boldsymbol{0}^n & \text{if } (i_1 = i_3, i_2 = i_4) \vee (i_1 = i_4, i_2 = i_3), \\ \boldsymbol{\delta}^n_{i_1} + \boldsymbol{\delta}^n_{i_{2+k}} & \text{if } i_1 \neq i_{2+k}, i_2 = i_{5-k} \text{ for } k = 1 \vee k = 2, \\ \boldsymbol{\delta}^n_{i_2} + \boldsymbol{\delta}^n_{i_{2+k}} & \text{if } i_1 = i_{5-k}, i_2 \neq i_{2+k} \text{ for } k = 1 \vee k = 2, \\ \sum_{k=1}^4 \boldsymbol{\delta}^n_{i_k} & \text{if } i_1 \neq i_2 \neq i_3 \neq i_4 \end{cases}$$

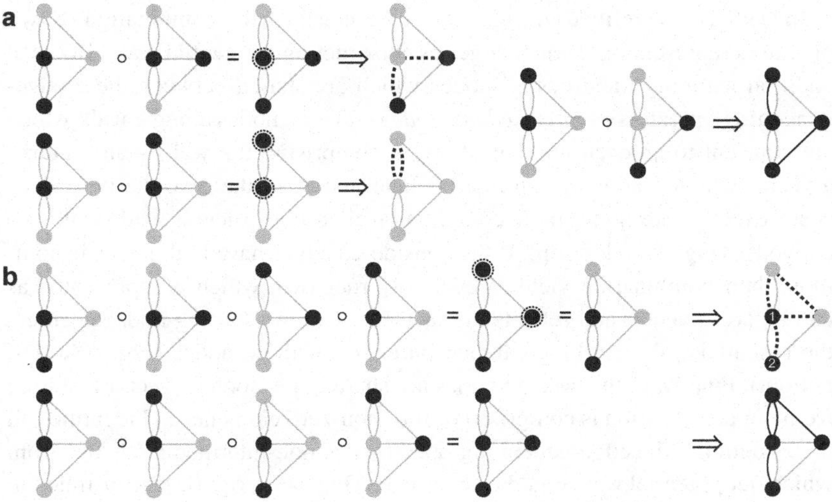

Figure 4.4 Composition of edge-generating operators through Boolean addition. **a:** Examples of the composition of two edges in the multigraph of Königsberg's bridges. Each undirected edge is here defined by a pair of nodes (black). If the combined edges share one or more nodes (dotted circles), Boolean addition identifies these nodes as intermediate nodes in a potential walk through the graph, and returns a vector marking only those nodes which allow for a continuation of this walk. **b:** Examples of compositions of four edge-generating operators. If an even number of edges share a common node, Boolean addition ensures their identification as intermediate nodes. If the resulting Boolean vector has no or two non-zero elements, the considered composition comprises either a cycle or, as shown here, a walk (top; walk from node 2 to node 1), otherwise a potential walk (bottom).

whether both edges connect the same pair of distinct nodes, share exactly one node, or have no node in common. In the case both edges share one node, the left-hand side yields a vector with two non-zero elements which again represents an undirected edge, thus providing the basis for defining an operation of operator composition through Boolean addition. In contrast, if both or no nodes are shared by the two combined edges, the resulting vector in $\mathbb{B}^n$ will no longer correspond to an undirected edge in our classical graph, but will instead govern the extension of the set of edge-generating operators in its operator representation to ensure closure under this composition. Interestingly, it is also this particular property of our operator composition to deliver Boolean vectors with an even number of non-zero elements which eventually provides the key for addressing the Königsberg bridge problem from a somewhat different angle.

Indeed, as exemplified in Fig. 4.4a, if we consider the combination of two operators representing distinct edges as constructing a potential walk, Boolean addition naturally identifies all nodes which are shared between these edge-generating operators as *intermediate nodes* – that is, nodes along a walk which are adjacent to an even number of edges comprising the walk – and returns a vector which marks all non-intermediate nodes. In the case the two edges share exactly one node, their combination then constructs a walk with two endnodes (Fig. 4.4a, left top). If the considered edges have both nodes in common, their combination yields a cycle of order two, which is represented as an all-zeroes vector and reflects the fact that, with no starting node specified, the potential walk can be continued on either of these nodes (Fig. 4.4a, left bottom). Finally, in the case no nodes are shared, the Boolean vector resulting from our composition is comprised of four non-zero elements and identifies all nodes defining the edge-generating operators as non-intermediate nodes from which our potential walk could be continued (Fig. 4.4a, right). As illustrated in Fig. 4.4b, this argument can easily be generalised, and it eventually leaves us to conclude that each potential walk comprised of a composition of m operators $\delta^n_{i_1}+\delta^n_{i_2}$ representing distinct edges $\{(i_1,i_2),(i_2,i_1)\}$ in a not self-looped undirected multigraph is an Eulerian walk of length m if and only if the resulting Boolean vector is an all-zeroes vector, in which case the Eulerian walk is a cycle, or has exactly two non-zero elements marking the walk's endnodes.

In order to leverage this necessary and sufficient condition for the construction of Eulerian walks in the Königsberg bridge problem, let us first explore a suitable operator representation. To that end, we introduce with

$$\hat{\mathcal{N}}^{\mathcal{G}} := \left\{\boldsymbol{n}_i \colon i \in [0,4]\right\} \subset \mathbb{B}^4 \tag{4.23}$$

a set of nodes $\boldsymbol{n}_0 := \boldsymbol{0}^4$, $\boldsymbol{n}_i := \boldsymbol{\delta}^4_i$ for $i \in [1,4]$, and with

$$\hat{\mathcal{E}}^{\mathcal{G}} := \left\{\mathfrak{E}_j \colon j \in [0,9]\right\} \subset \mathbb{B}^4 \tag{4.24}$$

the set of 10 edge operators

$$\begin{aligned}
\mathfrak{E}_0 := \boldsymbol{0}^4 \,,\ \mathfrak{E}_1 = \mathfrak{E}_2 := \boldsymbol{\delta}^4_1+\boldsymbol{\delta}^4_3 \,,\ \mathfrak{E}_3 = \mathfrak{E}_4 := \boldsymbol{\delta}^4_1+\boldsymbol{\delta}^4_2, \\
\mathfrak{E}_5 := \boldsymbol{\delta}^4_1+\boldsymbol{\delta}^4_4 \,,\ \mathfrak{E}_6 := \boldsymbol{\delta}^4_3+\boldsymbol{\delta}^4_4 \,,\ \mathfrak{E}_7 := \boldsymbol{\delta}^4_2+\boldsymbol{\delta}^4_4, \\
\mathfrak{E}_8 := \boldsymbol{\delta}^4_2+\boldsymbol{\delta}^4_3 \,,\ \mathfrak{E}_9 := \boldsymbol{\delta}^4_1+\boldsymbol{\delta}^4_2+\boldsymbol{\delta}^4_3+\boldsymbol{\delta}^4_4 = \boldsymbol{I}^4
\end{aligned}$$

illustrated in Fig. 4.5a which act according to

$$\begin{aligned}
&\mathfrak{E}_j[\boldsymbol{n}_i] : \hat{\mathcal{N}}^{\mathcal{G}} \to \hat{\mathcal{N}}^{\mathcal{G}}, \\
&\mathfrak{E}_j[\boldsymbol{n}_i] := \begin{cases} (\mathfrak{E}_j \cdot^{\mathbb{B}} \boldsymbol{n}_i^{\mathsf{T}}) \cdot^{\mathbb{B}} (\mathfrak{E}_j +^{\mathbb{B}} \boldsymbol{n}_i) & \text{if } j \in [1,8], \\ \boldsymbol{n}_0 & \text{if } j \in \{0,9\} \end{cases}
\end{aligned} \tag{4.25}$$

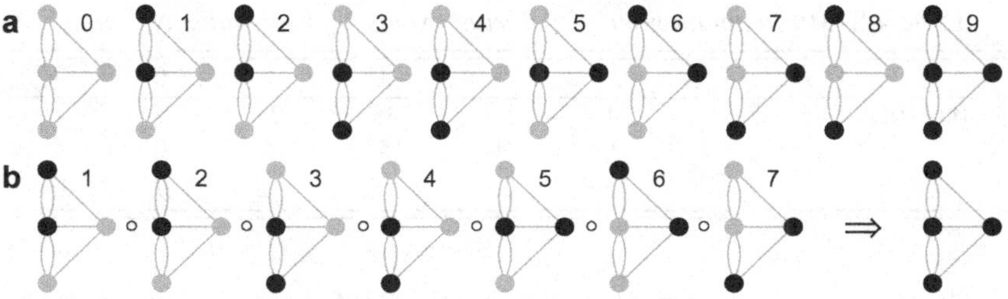

Figure 4.5 Alternative operator representation $\hat{\mathscr{G}}$ of the multigraph of Königsberg's bridges $\mathscr{G}$. **a:** Illustration of the 10 edge operators defining $\hat{\mathscr{G}}$, with operators 1 to 7 representing the undirected edges of $\mathscr{G}$, and operators 0, 8 and 9 ensuring closure of the associated algebra under composition. **b:** Composition of the seven operators representing the undirected edges of $\mathscr{G}$ distinguishes whether any potential walk of length 7 is a walk and, thus, an Eulerian path or not. As the resulting vector has four non-zero elements (indictated in black), no such potential walk can be a walk and, therefore, an Eulerian path. In all illustrated representations, node n_0 and all edge operators associated with it are omitted.

over $\hat{\mathcal{N}}^{\mathscr{G}}$. It can easily be shown that this set of edge operators is closed under operator composition

$$\circ : \hat{\mathcal{E}}^{\mathscr{G}} \times \hat{\mathcal{E}}^{\mathscr{G}} \to \hat{\mathcal{E}}^{\mathscr{G}}, \; \mathfrak{E}_{j_2} \circ \mathfrak{E}_{j_1} := \mathfrak{E}_{j_1} +^{\mathbb{B}} \mathfrak{E}_{j_2} \tag{4.26}$$

and forms an algebra $\mathscr{E}^{\mathscr{G}} := (\hat{\mathcal{E}}^{\mathscr{G}}, O^{\mathscr{G}})$ with algebraic structure $O^{\mathscr{G}} = \{ \circ \}$. The tuple $\hat{\mathscr{G}} = (\hat{\mathcal{N}}^{\mathscr{G}}, \mathscr{E}^{\mathscr{G}})$ then defines, as alternative to (4.20) and (4.21), an operator representation of the Königsberg bridge graph $\mathscr{G}$.

With this alternative representation in place, let us now consider arbitrary compositions of operators associated with edges of $\mathscr{G}$. Specifically, let

$$\begin{aligned} \tilde{N}^{C}_{m} \in \mathbb{N}_0 : \tilde{N}^{C}_{m} &:= \sum_{(j_1,\dots,j_m)\in\mathfrak{C}_m([1,7])} \delta\left[\mathrm{T}\left[\bigodot_{k=1}^{m} \mathfrak{E}_{j_k}\right]\right], \\ \tilde{N}^{W}_{m} \in \mathbb{N}_0 : \tilde{N}^{W}_{m} &:= \sum_{(j_1,\dots,j_m)\in\mathfrak{C}_m([1,7])} \delta\left[\mathrm{T}\left[\bigodot_{k=1}^{m} \mathfrak{E}_{j_k}\right] - 2\right] \end{aligned} \tag{4.27}$$

define the total number of distinct compositions which satisfy the necessary and sufficient condition for the construction of Eulerian cycles and Eulerian walks of length m formulated above. Here, the Kronecker delta operator δ and total sum operator T ensure that only Boolean vectors with no or two non-zero entries are counted. Moreover, as Boolean addition is both commutative and associative, we can restrict the sum to $\mathfrak{C}_m([1,7])$, where $\mathfrak{C}_m(\mathcal{S})$ denotes the set of all m-combinations over a finite set $\mathcal{S}$, that is the set of all unordered subsets of m distinct elements of $\mathcal{S}$, with a total of $|\mathfrak{C}_m(\mathcal{S})| = \binom{|\mathcal{S}|}{m}$ elements.

Table 4.8 *Minimum number of Eulerian cycles $\tilde{N}^C_m$ and walks $\tilde{N}^W_m$ in $\mathscr{G}$.*

	$m = 1$	2	3	4	5	6	7
$\lvert\mathfrak{C}_m([1,7])\rvert$	7	21	35	35	21	7	1
$\tilde{N}^C_m$	0	2	4	5	4	0	0
$\tilde{N}^W_m$	7	15	26	26	15	7	0

The results of the numerical evaluation of (4.27) for $1 \leq m \leq 7$ are listed in Table 4.8. As these results show, $\tilde{N}^W_m$ does not deliver the number of Eulerian walks of a given length m (see Table 4.7 for comparison), but instead yields the number of distinct unordered sets of edges each of which must contain at least one permutation of edges representing an Eulerian walk. The measure $\tilde{N}^W_m$ thus provides both the minimum number of Eulerian walks through $\mathscr{G}$, and with $\tilde{N}^W_m \geq 1$ a necessary condition for the existence of at least one Eulerian walk. A similar argument can be constructed for Eulerian cycles using $\tilde{N}^C_m$. The results for $m = 7$ – that is, $\tilde{N}^W_m = 0$ and $\tilde{N}^C_m = 0$ – then leave us to confirm our earlier conclusion that the Königsberg bridge graph does not allow for the construction of an Eulerian walk of length 7 and, thus, by definition cannot have an Eulerian path.

Certainly, the alternative operator representation of undirected multigraphs considered above inspired an approach for the solution of the Königsberg bridge problem which is more in tune with Euler's original solution, both in its computational simplicity and conceptual beauty. Indeed, closer inspection reveals that the composition of appropriately constructed edge-generating operators through Boolean addition distinguishes nodes with even degree – that is, intermediate nodes – and nodes with odd degree which necessarily must serve as start or endpoint of walks through the graph. Moreover, with only one possible combination of all operators $\mathfrak{E}_j, j \in [1,k]$ representing a graph's complete set of k edges to consider, we eventually find

$$\lambda_{ew} \in 2\mathbb{N}_0 : \lambda_{ew} := \mathrm{T}\left[\sum_{j=1}^{k}{}^{\mathbb{B}}\, \mathfrak{E}_j\right] \tag{4.28}$$

as a measure which ascertains the existence of Eulerian walks and cycles in general connected not self-looped undirected multigraphs $\mathscr{G}$, specifically

$$\lambda_{ew} = \begin{cases} 0 & \Leftrightarrow \exists \text{ Eulerian cycle of length } k \text{ in } \mathscr{G}, \\ 2 & \Leftrightarrow \exists \text{ Eulerian path in } \mathscr{G}, \\ l \in 2\mathbb{N} : l > 2 & \Leftrightarrow \nexists \text{ Eulerian path or cycle of length } k \text{ in } \mathscr{G}. \end{cases}$$

Encouraged by this propitious operator-inspired conclusion of the Königsberg bridge problem almost three centuries after Euler, we will now dedicate the remainder of this chapter to a more rigorous formalisation of the operator graph-theoretical approach motivated here by introducing, at the conceptual and algebraic levels, the general notion of an operator graph, and by exploring how this notion can be utilised not only to viably represent but also to generate, transform and measure graphs.

4.2 Operator Graph Theory

By tailoring the representation of a graph's nodes and edges, we exemplified in the previous section an operator-inspired approach for the construction of arbitrary walks through a graph which eventually delivered an alternative solution to an intriguing problem at the very heart of classical graph theory. In this approach, we described each node $i \in \mathcal{N}$ of a not self-looped undirected graph $\mathcal{G} = (\mathcal{N}, \mathcal{E})$ by a vector $\boldsymbol{n} \in \mathbb{B}^{|\mathcal{N}|}$ with $\mathrm{T}[\boldsymbol{n}] = 1$, and each pair of connected nodes $(i, j) \in \mathcal{E}$ by either a vector $\mathfrak{E} \in \mathbb{B}^{|\mathcal{N}|}$ with $\mathrm{T}[\mathfrak{E}] = 2$ or a matrix $\mathfrak{E} \in \mathbb{B}^{|\mathcal{N}|\times|\mathcal{N}|}$ with $\mathrm{T}[\mathfrak{E}] = 1$. These representations not only allowed us to discern the existence of Eulerian walks according to (4.27), but also provided us with an arguably efficient and generalisable means to identify individual walks out of the set of potential walks through $\mathcal{G}$ according to (4.13) and (4.14). More importantly, in such representations, the edges of a graph are no longer considered as mere static pairs of nodes, but indeed can be interpreted as operators which actively generate links between nodes by acting as mappings on the graph's set of nodes. By then replacing the set of edges in the classical definition $\mathcal{G}$ of a graph with the set of such edge-generating operators, we bestow the set of nodes of $\mathcal{G}$ itself with an algebraic structure which defines what we referred to as *operator representation* $\hat{\mathcal{G}}$ of a graph $\mathcal{G}$.

Certainly, such a representation furnishes both a necessary and sufficient description of the defining structural makeup of a graph as collection of discrete and discernible interconnected objects and, thus, is reminiscent of the classical notion of a graph according to Definition 2.1. It also carries the potential of accommodating a more dynamic perspective, as we demonstrated in Section 4.1, thus generalising in a subtle yet distinctive way the intuitional conception and mathematical model upon which classical graph theory is built. In order to arrive at an algebraically more rigorous formalisation of this generalisation from which we can develop an operator graph-theoretical framework akin to classical graph theory, let us begin by formulating the following

Definition 4.1 (operator representation) Let $\mathbb{G}$ denote the set of all finite graphs $\mathcal{G} = (\mathcal{N}, \mathcal{E})$. Let $\hat{\mathcal{N}} \neq \emptyset$ be a finite set of objects, and let $\hat{\mathcal{E}}$ be a set of

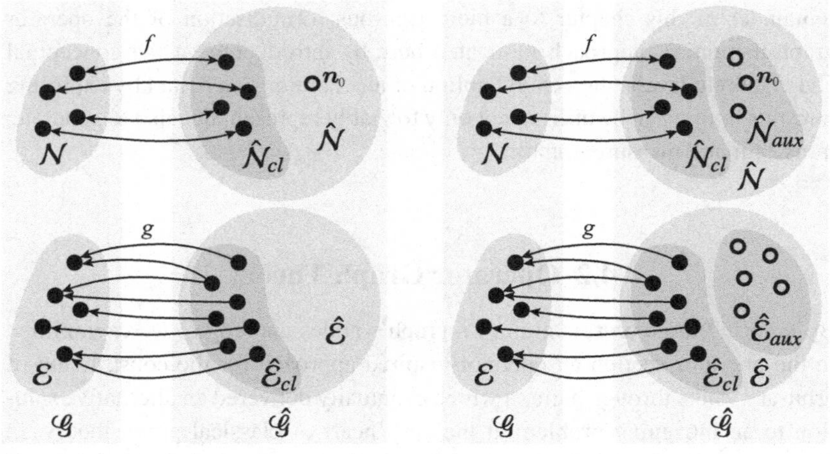

Figure 4.6 Classical representation of a graph $\mathcal{G} = (\mathcal{N}, \mathcal{E})$, and construction of a minimal operator (left) and operator representation (right) $\hat{\mathcal{G}} = (\hat{\mathcal{N}}, \hat{\mathcal{E}})$ of $\mathcal{G}$.

unary operations acting as operators over $\hat{\mathcal{N}}$ such that $\mathfrak{E}[\boldsymbol{n}] \in \hat{\mathcal{N}}$ for all $\boldsymbol{n} \in \hat{\mathcal{N}}$ and $\mathfrak{E} \in \hat{\mathcal{E}}$. The ordered tuple $\hat{\mathcal{G}} = (\hat{\mathcal{N}}, \hat{\mathcal{E}})$ defines an *operator representation* of $\mathcal{G}$ with set of nodes $\hat{\mathcal{N}}$ and set of edge operators $\hat{\mathcal{E}}$ if there exist a subset $\hat{\mathcal{N}}_{cl} \subset \hat{\mathcal{N}}$: $\hat{\mathcal{N}}_{cl} \neq \emptyset$ and a bijective mapping $f\colon \hat{\mathcal{N}}_{cl} \to \mathcal{N}$ such that

$$\boldsymbol{n} \in \hat{\mathcal{N}}_{cl} \Leftrightarrow f(\boldsymbol{n}) \in \mathcal{N},$$

if there exist a subset $\hat{\mathcal{E}}_{cl} \subseteq \hat{\mathcal{E}}$ and a mapping $g\colon \hat{\mathcal{E}}_{cl} \to \mathcal{E}$ such that

$$\mathfrak{E} \in \hat{\mathcal{E}}_{cl} : \mathfrak{E}[\boldsymbol{n}_i] = \boldsymbol{n}_j \Rightarrow \exists\, g(\mathfrak{E}) \in \mathcal{E} : g(\mathfrak{E}) = (f(\boldsymbol{n}_i), f(\boldsymbol{n}_j)),$$
$$(i, j) \in \mathcal{E} \Rightarrow \exists\, \mathfrak{E} \in \hat{\mathcal{E}}_{cl}\colon \mathfrak{E}[f^{-1}(i)] = f^{-1}(j)$$

for $\boldsymbol{n}_i, \boldsymbol{n}_j \in \hat{\mathcal{N}}_{cl}$ and $i, j \in \mathcal{N}$, and if there exists a node $\boldsymbol{n}_0 \in \hat{\mathcal{N}} \setminus \hat{\mathcal{N}}_{cl}$ such that

$$\mathfrak{E} \in \hat{\mathcal{E}}_{cl} : \mathfrak{E}[\boldsymbol{n}_i] = \boldsymbol{n}_j \Rightarrow \mathfrak{E}[\boldsymbol{n}_{i'}] = \boldsymbol{n}_0 \;\forall \boldsymbol{n}_{i'} \in \hat{\mathcal{N}}_{cl}\colon \boldsymbol{n}_{i'} \neq \boldsymbol{n}_i$$

for $\boldsymbol{n}_i, \boldsymbol{n}_j \in \hat{\mathcal{N}}_{cl}$ and $\mathfrak{E}[\boldsymbol{n}_0] = \boldsymbol{n}_0 \;\forall \mathfrak{E} \in \hat{\mathcal{E}}$. If $\hat{\mathcal{E}} \setminus \hat{\mathcal{E}}_{cl} = \emptyset$ and $\hat{\mathcal{N}} \setminus \hat{\mathcal{N}}_{cl} = \{\boldsymbol{n}_0\}$, an operator representation of $\mathcal{G}$ is called a *minimal operator representation* of $\mathcal{G}$.

The relation between the classical representation $\mathcal{G} = (\mathcal{N}, \mathcal{E})$ of a graph $\mathcal{G}$ in terms of a set of nodes $\mathcal{N}$ and set of edges $\mathcal{E}$ on one hand, and the notion of an operator or minimal operator representation $\hat{\mathcal{G}} = (\hat{\mathcal{N}}, \hat{\mathcal{E}})$ of $\mathcal{G}$ in terms of a set of nodes $\hat{\mathcal{N}}$ and set of edge operators $\hat{\mathcal{E}}$ on the other, is illustrated in Fig. 4.6. Before proceeding any further, let us motivate Definition 4.1 by exploring this relation in greater detail. According to the classical conception of a graph introduced with Definition 2.1, each link or edge between two nodes $i, j \in \mathcal{N}$

of a finite graph $\mathcal{G} = (\mathcal{N}, \mathcal{E})$ is given by an ordered pair $(i, j) \in \mathcal{E}$. The set of all edges $\mathcal{E}$ together with their algebraic representation in the form of a weight matrix (2.3) or, in the case of relational digraphs, an adjacency matrix (2.4) then provides all necessary and sufficient details for a complete description of $\mathcal{G}$. Instead of considering an edge as simply a node pair marking the mere static existence of a link between two nodes, however, it certainly is also possible to interpret each $(i, j) \in \mathcal{E}$ from a somewhat more dynamic vantage point by arguing that node i can realise a connection to node j, or that node j is the result of an operation acting on node i.

In order to formalise such a dynamic perspective, let us first and without loss of generality consider that the set of nodes $\mathcal{N}$ of $\mathcal{G}$ is being ordered such that we can refer to each node i by its order in $\mathcal{N}$, and assign to each $i \in \mathcal{N}$ a unique element $\boldsymbol{n}_i$ of a suitable vector space through a surjective and injective mapping f such that $f(\boldsymbol{n}_i) = i$. The set of all $\boldsymbol{n}_i$ then replaces the set of all nodes $\mathcal{N}$ in the classical representation of $\mathcal{G}$ and will be denoted with

$$\hat{\mathcal{N}}_{cl} = \left\{\boldsymbol{n}_i : i \in [1, |\mathcal{N}|]\right\}. \tag{4.29}$$

By utilising the bijective mapping f, each edge $(i, j) \in \mathcal{E}$ is furthermore associated with a unique ordered pair $(\boldsymbol{n}_i, \boldsymbol{n}_j)$, and thus defines through $\mathfrak{E}[\boldsymbol{n}_i] = \boldsymbol{n}_j$ an operator $\mathfrak{E}$ in the strict sense of Definition 3.3. This assignment of edge-generating operators $\mathfrak{E}$ to elements of $\mathcal{E}$ is here realised through a mapping g such that for each $\mathfrak{E}$ there exists at least one $g(\mathfrak{E}) \in \mathcal{E}$, and for each $(i, j) \in \mathcal{E}$ there exists at least one $\mathfrak{E} : \mathfrak{E}[f^{-1}(i)] = f^{-1}(j)$, where f^{-1} denotes the inverse of the bijection f. As we will see later, the generally not surjective and not injective nature of g allows for the accommodation of both directed and undirected graphs as well as multigraphs and even arbitrarily weighted graphs within the same framework. The set of all $\mathfrak{E}$ then replaces the set of all edges $\mathcal{E}$ in the classical representation of $\mathcal{G}$ and will be denoted with

$$\hat{\mathcal{E}}_{cl} = \left\{\mathfrak{E}_j : j \in [1, j_{\max}]\right\}, \tag{4.30}$$

where the number $j_{\max}$ of edge operators, albeit being strongly related to the total adjacency of $\mathcal{G}$, also depends on the type of the graph and the chosen representation of $\boldsymbol{n}_i \in \hat{\mathcal{N}}_{cl}$.

Lastly, although each $\mathfrak{E} \in \hat{\mathcal{E}}_{cl}$ by definition realises only one edge between two specific nodes $\boldsymbol{n}_i, \boldsymbol{n}_j \in \hat{\mathcal{N}}_{cl}$, and thus is initially conceived with the one-element subsets $\{\boldsymbol{n}_i\}$ and $\{\boldsymbol{n}_j\}$ of $\hat{\mathcal{N}}_{cl}$ as domain and codomain, its action as operator can certainly be expanded to encompass all elements of $\hat{\mathcal{N}}_{cl}$. Doing so, however, requires the introduction of an auxiliary node $\boldsymbol{n}_0$ that will serve as the target for all edges which are generated by $\mathfrak{E}$ but are not associated with $(\boldsymbol{n}_i, \boldsymbol{n}_j)$. Specifically, if $\mathfrak{E} \in \hat{\mathcal{E}}_{cl}$ represents the edge-generating operator such that $\mathfrak{E}[\boldsymbol{n}_i] = \boldsymbol{n}_j$ for $\boldsymbol{n}_i, \boldsymbol{n}_j \in \hat{\mathcal{N}}_{cl}$, we define $\mathfrak{E}[\boldsymbol{n}_{i'}] = \boldsymbol{n}_0 \; \forall \boldsymbol{n}_{i'} \in \hat{\mathcal{N}}_{cl} \colon \boldsymbol{n}_{i'} \neq \boldsymbol{n}_i$ and $\mathfrak{E}[\boldsymbol{n}_0] = \boldsymbol{n}_0$. We will refer to $\boldsymbol{n}_0$ conveniently as *null-node*, as neither it nor its adjacent edges are part of $\mathcal{G}$. With this, each edge operator $\mathfrak{E} \in \hat{\mathcal{E}}_{cl}$ then acts as mapping $\mathfrak{E} \colon \hat{\mathcal{N}}_{cl} \cup \{\boldsymbol{n}_0\} \to \hat{\mathcal{N}}_{cl} \cup \{\boldsymbol{n}_0\}$ over the complete set of nodes $\hat{\mathcal{N}}_{cl} \cup \{\boldsymbol{n}_0\}$, such that the sets $\hat{\mathcal{N}}_{cl}$ and $\hat{\mathcal{E}}_{cl}$ along with $\boldsymbol{n}_0$ eventually provide all the necessary and sufficient algebraic structures for a complete description of a given graph $\mathcal{G}$. Indeed, by replacing the set of nodes $\mathcal{N}$ which comprises $\mathcal{G}$ according to Definition 2.1 with the union $\hat{\mathcal{N}}_{cl} \cup \{\boldsymbol{n}_0\}$ of the set of nodes in (4.29) and null-node, and set of edges $\mathcal{E}$ of $\mathcal{G}$ with the set of edge operators $\hat{\mathcal{E}}_{cl}$ in (4.30), the tuple

$$\hat{\mathcal{G}} = \left(\hat{\mathcal{N}}_{cl} \cup \{\boldsymbol{n}_0\}, \hat{\mathcal{E}}_{cl}\right) \tag{4.31}$$

furnishes what we introduced as minimal operator representation of a finite graph $\mathcal{G}$ in Definition 4.1.

Let us briefly illustrate the notational framework presented above by demonstrating how each classical representation of a finite relational digraph itself can be made to define a minimal operator representation. To that end, given $\mathcal{G} = (\mathcal{N}, \mathcal{E})$, we successively label the elements of $\mathcal{N}$ by numbers $i \in \mathbb{N}$ such that each element of $\mathcal{E}$ defines a vector $(i, j) \in \mathbb{N}^2$. The set

$$\hat{\mathcal{N}}_{cl} = \left\{\boldsymbol{n}_i := i \colon i \in [1, |\mathcal{N}|] \subset \mathbb{N}\right\} \tag{4.32}$$

then serves as a representation for the set of nodes $\mathcal{N}$. Moreover, complementing $\hat{\mathcal{N}}_{cl}$ with a null-node $\boldsymbol{n}_0 = 0$, each element of $\mathcal{E} \subset \mathbb{N}^2$ is naturally associated with an operator $\mathfrak{E} \colon \mathbb{N}_0 \to \mathbb{N}_0$ whose action on $\boldsymbol{n} \in \hat{\mathcal{N}}_{cl} \cup \{\boldsymbol{n}_0\} \subset \mathbb{N}_0$ can be algebraically expressed as

$$\mathfrak{E}[\boldsymbol{n}] := \delta\left[\boldsymbol{n} - \mathfrak{E} \cdot (1, 0)^{\mathsf{T}}\right] \cdot \left(\mathfrak{E} \cdot (0, 1)^{\mathsf{T}}\right). \tag{4.33}$$

The first term ensures here that $\mathfrak{E}$ acts only in a non-trivial fashion on its associated source node, while the last term returns the target node of $\mathfrak{E}$. The set

$$\hat{\mathcal{E}}_{cl} = \left\{\mathfrak{E}_j \in \mathbb{N}^2 \colon j \in [1, |\mathcal{E}|]\right\} := \mathcal{E}, \tag{4.34}$$

albeit being formally identical to $\mathcal{E}$, then replaces as the set of edge-generating operators the set of all ordered node pairs in the classical representation of $\mathcal{G}$, and together with $\hat{\mathcal{N}}_{cl} \cup \{\boldsymbol{n}_0\}$ eventually defines a minimal operator representation $\hat{\mathcal{G}}$ of a relational digraph $\mathcal{G}$.

Mirroring this approach, minimal operator representations not only for relational digraphs but also for graphs with self-looped nodes and multigraphs, and indeed for generally weighted graphs and digraphs, can be constructed. Each of these representations remains, at the most abstract level, satisfied by a set of objects and a set of operations between these objects, independent of the specific type of graph being considered, and thus adheres formally and structurally to the very conception of a finite graph as a set of discrete and discernible interconnected objects. More importantly, as each edge in such a representation acts as unary operation over the set of nodes $\hat{\mathcal{N}}_{cl} \cup \{\boldsymbol{n}_0\}$, the set of edge operators $\hat{\mathcal{E}}_{cl}$ naturally defines an algebraic structure on $\hat{\mathcal{N}}_{cl} \cup \{\boldsymbol{n}_0\}$ which, in turn, renders the tuple $\hat{\mathcal{G}} = (\hat{\mathcal{N}}_{cl} \cup \{\boldsymbol{n}_0\}, \hat{\mathcal{E}}_{cl})$ and, thus, a graph itself an abstract algebra according to Definition 3.4. Indeed, this perspective has intriguing consequences. By expanding on the algebraic structure of $\hat{\mathcal{G}}$ through the introduction of complementary operators, or by enriching a graph's set of edge operators through the introduction of additional finitary operations, the algebra representing a graph can be tailored to address specific and eventually challenging graph-theoretical problems. We already encountered one example of this representational flexibility in our active search for Eulerian walks and paths in the previous section. There, by supplementing a graph's defining set of edge-generating operators with a set of auxiliary operators, and by introducing the binary operation of composition of edge operators, we arrived not only at a rigorous but also a generalisable algebraic formulation of this search.

Inspired by this promising perspective of our operator graph-theoretical approach, let us devise a generalisation of the notion of a minimal operator representation $\hat{\mathcal{G}} = (\hat{\mathcal{N}}_{cl} \cup \{\boldsymbol{n}_0\}, \hat{\mathcal{E}}_{cl})$ explored so far. As illustrated in Fig. 4.6, in such a minimal representation, both $\hat{\mathcal{N}}_{cl}$ and $\hat{\mathcal{E}}_{cl}$ are by construction directly associated with the defining structural makeup of a classical graph $\mathcal{G} = (\mathcal{N}, \mathcal{E})$. The presence of the null-node $\boldsymbol{n}_0$ ensures here that each element of $\hat{\mathcal{E}}_{cl}$ acts as operator over the whole set $\hat{\mathcal{N}}_{cl} \cup \{\boldsymbol{n}_0\}$. However, $\boldsymbol{n}_0$ itself does not represent a node of $\mathcal{G}$, but instead can be viewed as element of a set of auxiliary nodes $\hat{\mathcal{N}}_{aux}$ with $\hat{\mathcal{N}}_{cl} \cap \hat{\mathcal{N}}_{aux} = \emptyset$ which is comprised of objects not associated with elements of $\mathcal{N}$ and satisfies

$$\boldsymbol{n} \in \hat{\mathcal{N}}_{aux} \Leftrightarrow \mathfrak{E}[\boldsymbol{n}] \in \hat{\mathcal{N}}_{aux}\, \forall \mathfrak{E} \in \hat{\mathcal{E}}_{cl}. \tag{4.35}$$

In a similar fashion, the set of edge-generating operators $\hat{\mathcal{E}}_{cl}$, whose elements are all associated with the edges comprising $\mathcal{G}$, can be supplemented by a set of auxiliary edge operators $\hat{\mathcal{E}}_{aux}$ with $\hat{\mathcal{E}}_{cl} \cap \hat{\mathcal{E}}_{aux} = \emptyset$ such that

$$\mathfrak{E} \in \hat{\mathcal{E}}_{aux} \Leftrightarrow \mathfrak{E}[\boldsymbol{n}] \in \hat{\mathcal{N}}_{aux}\, \forall \boldsymbol{n} \in \hat{\mathcal{N}}_{aux}. \tag{4.36}$$

Finally, both (4.35) and (4.36), together with

$$\boldsymbol{n} \in \hat{\mathcal{N}}_{cl}\,,\ \mathfrak{E} \in \hat{\mathcal{E}}_{cl} \cup \hat{\mathcal{E}}_{aux} \Rightarrow \mathfrak{E}[\boldsymbol{n}] \in \hat{\mathcal{N}}_{cl} \cup \hat{\mathcal{N}}_{aux}, \tag{4.37}$$

ensure that all elements of the combined set $\hat{\mathcal{E}} = \hat{\mathcal{E}}_{cl} \cup \hat{\mathcal{E}}_{aux}$ of edge operators act as unary operations over the combined set $\hat{\mathcal{N}} = \hat{\mathcal{N}}_{cl} \cup \hat{\mathcal{N}}_{aux}$ of nodes. With this, the tuple $\hat{\mathcal{G}} = (\hat{\mathcal{N}}, \hat{\mathcal{E}})$ then defines what we introduced in Definition 4.1 as operator representation of a finite graph $\mathcal{G}$. If $\hat{\mathcal{E}}_{aux} = \emptyset$ and $\hat{\mathcal{N}}_{aux} = \{n_0\}$, we naturally recover a minimal operator representation of $\mathcal{G}$.

Given a minimal operator representation, complementing the set of edge operators $\hat{\mathcal{E}}_{cl}$ with $\hat{\mathcal{E}}_{aux}$ is certainly not the only way to enrich a graph's algebraic structure. This was illustrated in Section 4.1 with the search for Eulerian paths through the definition of a composition of edge operators which acts as the binary operation of multiplication over $\hat{\mathcal{E}} = \hat{\mathcal{E}}_{cl} \cup \hat{\mathcal{E}}_{aux}$. Interestingly, not only does this composition introduce an algebraic structure on $\hat{\mathcal{E}}$ which renders $\hat{\mathcal{E}}$ itself an algebra, specifically an algebra of operators $\mathscr{E}$ (see Definition 3.5), but by complementing this algebraic structure with other finitary operations, such as scalar multiplication or vector addition, the properties of the resulting algebra $\mathscr{E}$ can be tailored towards a specific and consequential purpose. Due to the special nature and, as we will see later, general importance of operator representations of graphs with such additional algebraic properties, let us expand on the notion of an operator representation of a finite graph with

Definition 4.2 (operator graph) Let $\hat{\mathcal{G}} = (\hat{\mathcal{N}}, \hat{\mathcal{E}})$ be an operator representation of a finite graph $\mathcal{G} \in \mathbb{G}$. If the set of edge operators $\hat{\mathcal{E}}$ of $\hat{\mathcal{G}}$ forms an algebra of operators $\mathscr{E} = (\hat{\mathcal{E}}, O)$ whose algebraic structure O contains the finitary operation of multiplication acting as composition of operators in $\hat{\mathcal{E}}$, the ordered tuple $\hat{\mathcal{G}} = (\hat{\mathcal{N}}, \mathscr{E})$ defines an *operator graph.* If the algebra of edge operators $\mathscr{E}$ is an $\mathcal{F}$-operator algebra over a field $\mathcal{F}$, an operator graph $\hat{\mathcal{G}}$ is called an *operator graph over* $\mathcal{F}$ or an $\mathcal{F}$*-operator graph.*

The notion of an operator graph introduced here encompasses, together with that of an operator representation of a finite graph in Definition 4.1, not only the central propositional notion of this book but also, and more importantly, the conceptual foundation for our operator graph-theoretical framework. Within this framework, each finite graph can give rise to a whole host of algebraically different representations, depending on and tailored for the specific problems being addressed. Table 4.9 summarises some of these representations for the Königsberg bridge graph we encountered earlier in our search for Eulerian paths. Between the static classical representation of a given graph on the one hand, and a number of descriptively equivalent yet algebraically distinct operator representations on the other, it certainly can be argued that the flexibility inherent to an algebraic formalisation of the latter type leads to some notable advantages at the conceptual level, especially when dealing with finite graphs of arbitrary type.

In order to argue our case, let us once more consider a relational digraph as an illustrative example. Here, the tuple $(\mathcal{N}, \mathcal{E})$ provides, classically, the necessary and sufficient information for a complete structural description of the

Table 4.9 *Representations of the Königsberg bridge graph* $\mathscr{G}$.

Classical representation	$\mathscr{G} = (\mathcal{N}, \mathcal{E})$
$\mathcal{N} := \{1,2,3,4\}$	
$\mathcal{E} := \{(1,2),(1,3),(1,4),(2,1),(2,4),(3,1),(3,4),(4,1),(4,2),(4,3)\}$	
$w := \begin{pmatrix} 0 & 2 & 2 & 1 \\ 2 & 0 & 0 & 1 \\ 2 & 0 & 0 & 1 \\ 1 & 1 & 1 & 0 \end{pmatrix}$	
Minimal operator representation	$\hat{\mathscr{G}} = (\hat{\mathcal{N}}, \hat{\mathcal{E}})$
$\hat{\mathcal{N}} = \hat{\mathcal{N}}_{cl} \cup \{\boldsymbol{n}_0\} := \{\boldsymbol{n}_i : i \in [0,4]\}$ with $\boldsymbol{n}_i \in \mathbb{B}^4$ defined in (4.23) $\hat{\mathcal{E}} = \hat{\mathcal{E}}_{cl} := \{\mathfrak{E}_j :\ j \in [1,14]\}$ with $\mathfrak{E}_j \in \mathbb{B}^{4\times 4}$ defined as $\mathfrak{E}_1 = \mathfrak{E}_2 := \delta^{4\times4}_{3,1}$, $\mathfrak{E}_3 = \mathfrak{E}_4 := \delta^{4\times4}_{1,2}$, $\mathfrak{E}_5 := \delta^{4\times4}_{1,4}$, $\mathfrak{E}_6 := \delta^{4\times4}_{4,3}$, $\mathfrak{E}_7 := \delta^{4\times4}_{4,2}$, $\mathfrak{E}_8 := \mathfrak{E}_9 = \delta^{4\times4}_{1,3}$, $\mathfrak{E}_{10} := \mathfrak{E}_{11} = \delta^{4\times4}_{2,1}$, $\mathfrak{E}_{12} := \delta^{4\times4}_{4,1}$, $\mathfrak{E}_{13} := \delta^{4\times4}_{3,4}$, $\mathfrak{E}_{14} := \delta^{4\times4}_{2,4}$ $\mathfrak{E} : \hat{\mathcal{N}} \to \hat{\mathcal{N}}\ ,\ \mathfrak{E}[\boldsymbol{n}] := \boldsymbol{n} \cdot \mathfrak{E}$ for all $\mathfrak{E} \in \hat{\mathcal{E}}, \boldsymbol{n} \in \hat{\mathcal{N}}$	
$\hat{\mathcal{N}} = \hat{\mathcal{N}}_{cl} \cup \{\boldsymbol{n}_0\} := \{\boldsymbol{n}_i : i \in [0,4]\}$ with $\boldsymbol{n}_i \in \mathbb{B}^4$ defined in (4.23) $\hat{\mathcal{E}} = \hat{\mathcal{E}}_{cl} := \{\mathfrak{E}_j :\ j \in [1,7]\}$ with $\mathfrak{E}_j \in \mathbb{B}^4$ defined as $\mathfrak{E}_1 = \mathfrak{E}_2 := \delta^4_1 + \delta^4_3$, $\mathfrak{E}_3 = \mathfrak{E}_4 := \delta^4_1 + \delta^4_2$, $\mathfrak{E}_5 := \delta^4_1 + \delta^4_4$, $\mathfrak{E}_6 := \delta^4_3 + \delta^4_4$, $\mathfrak{E}_7 := \delta^4_2 + \delta^4_4$ $\mathfrak{E} : \hat{\mathcal{N}} \to \hat{\mathcal{N}}\ ,\ \mathfrak{E}[\boldsymbol{n}] := (\mathfrak{E} \cdot \boldsymbol{n}^{\mathsf{T}}) \cdot \big(\mathfrak{E} \odot (\boldsymbol{I}^4 - \boldsymbol{n})\big)$ for all $\mathfrak{E} \in \hat{\mathcal{E}}, \boldsymbol{n} \in \hat{\mathcal{N}}$	
Operator graph representation	$\hat{\mathscr{G}} = (\hat{\mathcal{N}}, \mathscr{E})$
$\hat{\mathcal{N}} := \{\boldsymbol{n}_i : i \in [0,4]\}$ $\mathscr{E} := (\hat{\mathcal{E}}, O)$ $\hat{\mathcal{E}} := \{\mathfrak{E}_j :\ j \in [0,20]\}$ $O := \{\circ\}$ $\mathfrak{E} : \hat{\mathcal{N}} \to \hat{\mathcal{N}}$, defined for all $\mathfrak{E} \in \hat{\mathcal{E}}$ in Table 4.5 $\circ : \hat{\mathcal{E}} \times \hat{\mathcal{E}} \to \hat{\mathcal{E}}$, defined in Table 4.6	
$\hat{\mathcal{N}} := \{\boldsymbol{n}_i : i \in [0,4]\}$ with $\boldsymbol{n}_i \in \mathbb{B}^4$ defined in (4.23) $\mathscr{E} := (\hat{\mathcal{E}}, O)$ $\hat{\mathcal{E}} := \{\mathfrak{E}_j : j \in [0,9]\}$ with $\mathfrak{E}_j \in \mathbb{B}^4$ defined in (4.24) $O := \{\circ\}$ $\mathfrak{E}_j : \hat{\mathcal{N}} \to \hat{\mathcal{N}}\ ,\ \mathfrak{E}_j[\boldsymbol{n}_i] := \begin{cases} (\mathfrak{E}_j \cdot^{\mathbb{B}} \boldsymbol{n}_i^{\mathsf{T}}) \cdot^{\mathbb{B}} (\mathfrak{E}_j +^{\mathbb{B}} \boldsymbol{n}_i) & j \in [1,8], \\ \boldsymbol{n}_0 & j \in \{0,9\} \end{cases}$ $\circ : \hat{\mathcal{E}} \times \hat{\mathcal{E}} \to \hat{\mathcal{E}}\ ,\ \mathfrak{E}_{j_2} \circ \mathfrak{E}_{j_1} := \mathfrak{E}_{j_1} +^{\mathbb{B}} \mathfrak{E}_{j_2}$	

given graph. The mathematical formalisation of the entirety of edges – that is, of set $\mathcal{E}$ – in terms of a single adjacency matrix then serves merely as an algebraic convenience for defining and assessing a whole host of graph measures, some of which we presented in Section 2.2. This situation changes, however, if we face graphs with self-looped nodes, multigraphs or generally weighted graphs, in which case a complete classical representation does indeed necessitate a complementary algebraic structure in the form of a weight matrix that serves as the descriptor for the presence of multiple or weighted edges. Consequently, the central notion at the very heart of graph theory, namely that of a graph as set of distinct objects interconnected by edges which themselves are given by pairs of these objects, no longer suffices because edges are now bestowed with additional properties, such as a weight. This conceptual nuisance becomes even more challenging if we assign multiple properties to edges, such as a transition delay when dealing with technical or biological networks, or if we endow nodes and edges with state variables, as demonstrated in Chapter 3.

On a classical level, each such additional property characterising the nodes and edges of a graph will require a tailored algebraic object not unlike a weight matrix which, in turn, will render the defining formalisation of a graph dependent on the type of graph being considered, or the specific problem being addressed. In other words, a graph will eventually no longer be fully described by a set of nodes and edges alone, but will necessitate supplementary algebraic structures such as a weight matrix, matrix of edge delays, state vectors for nodes or edges, and so forth. This nuisance stands in stark contrast to the conception of a graph proposed in Definitions 4.1 and 4.2 because each operator representation does, by definition, remain at its most abstract level satisfied by a set of objects $\hat{\mathcal{N}}$ and set of operations $\hat{\mathcal{E}}$ between these objects, irrespective of the specific type of graph being considered, and thus will adhere, formally and structurally, to the very conception of a finite graph as a set of discrete interconnected objects. Eventual properties of a graph's nodes and edges are here algebraically formalised and managed by the representation of elements of $\hat{\mathcal{N}}$ and $\hat{\mathcal{E}}$ itself. Albeit conceptually subtle, it is this difference in the algebraic representation of a graph and its defining constituents which ultimately will distinguish our operator graph-theoretical framework from classical graph theory, and it bestows the former with a flexibility which we will thoroughly explore and utilise in the remainder of this book.

Certainly, this representational flexibility not only is tied to the choice of algebraic objects describing the nodes and edges of a graph but also is a direct consequence of the presence of auxiliary nodes and edge operators. Indeed, as we will see later, the sets $\hat{\mathcal{N}}_{aux}$ and $\hat{\mathcal{E}}_{aux}$ serve to tailor a graph's representation within our operator graph-theoretical framework towards a specific purpose by providing the necessary structural supplements which allow us to furnish a graph with a consequential and useful algebraic structure. These additional nodes and edge operators, however, will no longer be associated with nodes

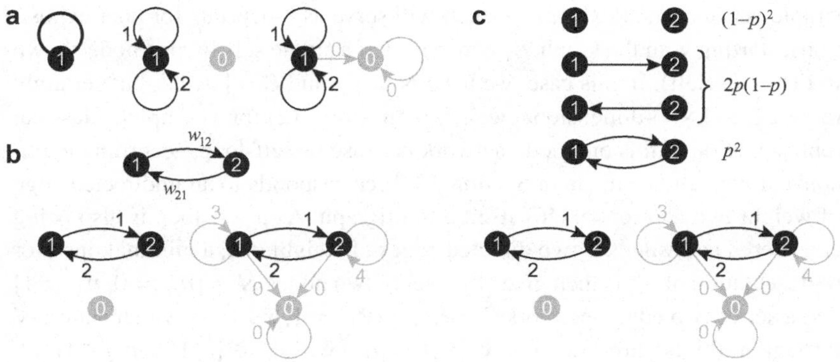

Figure 4.7 Classical and operator representations of self-loops, weighted and random edges. **a:** Graph $\mathscr{C}_1$ comprised of a single self-looped node. As each self-loop carries a weight of two (left), $\mathscr{C}_1$ requires a weight matrix for its classical representation, while both the operator representation (middle) and operator graph (right) consider two directed edges for each self-loop and add a null-node as well as one auxiliary edge operator to the algebraic formalisation of $\hat{\mathscr{C}}_1$. **b:** Classical (top) and operator (bottom) representations of a complete weighted digraph $\mathscr{C}_2^{dw}$ comprised of two nodes. **c:** Gilbert random digraph $\mathscr{R}_{2,p}^{dG}$. The classical representation of this graph (top) encompasses three distinct realisations which occur with distinct probabilities, while its operator representation (bottom left) and operator graph (bottom right) resemble that of the weighted graph in **b** and describe all possible realisations at once. In all examples, the null-node n_0 and set of auxiliary edge operators are marked in grey.

and edges in the classical representation of a given graph. Worse still, despite acting on $\hat{\mathcal{N}} = \hat{\mathcal{N}}_{cl} \cup \hat{\mathcal{N}}_{aux}$ as unary operations according to (4.35) and (4.37), elements of $\hat{\mathcal{E}}_{aux}$ might not even correspond to potential edges describing links or relation between two elements of $\hat{\mathcal{N}}$. In the operator graph representation of Königsberg's bridge graph (4.23)–(4.26), for example, only $\{\mathfrak{E}_j\colon j \in [1,7]\} \subset \hat{\mathcal{E}}$ correspond to operators associated with the seven edges comprising the graph. While $\mathfrak{E}_8$ still represents an edge operator which links between two nodes, here n_2 and n_3, it no longer corresponds to an actual edge in the associated classical graph, and $\mathfrak{E}_0$ or $\mathfrak{E}_9$ with their zero and four non-zero elements serve solely as auxiliary operators which ensure closure of the set $\hat{\mathcal{E}}$ under operator composition (4.26). But it is the addition of exactly these auxiliary edge operators which allowed us in the previous section to discern the existence and number of Eulerian walks and paths, and thus eventually enabled an alternative formulation and somewhat different take on the solution of this now-historic graph-theoretical problem.

Before concluding this section, let us briefly illustrate some other implications of this representational flexibility by taking a closer look at a number of simple yet important examples which will serve as blueprints for later expositions, starting with the graph $\mathscr{C}_1$ comprised of a single self-looped node shown in Fig. 4.7a (left). In this case, we have $\mathcal{N} = \{1\}$ and $\mathcal{E} = \{(1,1)\}$, but certainly require the (1×1)-dimensional weight matrix $\boldsymbol{w} = (2)$ for a complete classical representation of this one-node network because its self-loop, according to our conventional choice made in Section 2.1.1, corresponds to an undirected edge of weight two and renders $\mathscr{C}_1$ itself a multigraph. As a self-loop is also being considered equivalent to two directed edges of weight one, a minimal operator representation of $\mathscr{C}_1$ is then given by a set of two nodes $\hat{\mathcal{N}} = \{\boldsymbol{n}_0 := 0, \boldsymbol{n}_1 := 1\}$ and a set of two edge operators $\hat{\mathcal{E}} = \hat{\mathcal{E}}_{cl} = \{\mathfrak{E}_1 := 1, \mathfrak{E}_2 := 1\}$ which act on $\hat{\mathcal{N}}$ through multiplication such that $\mathfrak{E}_j[\boldsymbol{n}_i] := \boldsymbol{n}_i \cdot \mathfrak{E}_j$ for $i \in \{0,1\}$ and $j \in \{1,2\}$. By furthermore complementing the set of edge operators $\hat{\mathcal{E}}$ with $\mathfrak{E}_0 := 0$, by extending the action of edge operators on $\hat{\mathcal{N}}$ to include $\mathfrak{E}_0$, and by rendering $\hat{\mathcal{E}}$ an algebra of operators $\mathscr{E}$ with the introduction of an operator composition

$$\mathfrak{E}_{j_2} \circ \mathfrak{E}_{j_1} := \begin{cases} \mathfrak{E}_{j_1} \cdot \mathfrak{E}_{j_2} & \text{if } j_1 \neq j_2, \\ \mathfrak{E}_0 & \text{otherwise,} \end{cases}$$

we can even define an operator graph $\hat{\mathscr{C}}_1 = (\hat{\mathcal{N}}, \mathscr{E})$ which serves as a viable algebraic representation of $\mathscr{C}_1$ and, thus, a self-looped node. However, it must be cautioned here that, firstly, the null-node $\boldsymbol{n}_0$ in this representation is indeed required only if $\mathscr{C}_1$ itself is a subgraph or graph pattern of a graph with two or more nodes and, secondly, that the choice of operator composition is solely guided by the purpose of this representation to construct paths such that each edge of $\hat{\mathcal{E}}_{cl}$ is traversed at most once. More importantly still, noting that $\hat{\mathcal{E}}_{cl} = \{\mathfrak{E}_1, \mathfrak{E}_2\}$ for $\hat{\mathscr{C}}_1$, we find that the classical properties of a self-loop are recovered by considering the properties of both edge operator associated with a self-loop. For instance, we obtain with

$$\boldsymbol{w} = \sum_{\mathfrak{E} \in \hat{\mathcal{E}}_{cl}} \mathfrak{E} = \mathfrak{E}_1 + \mathfrak{E}_2 = (2) \tag{4.38}$$

the correct weight matrix of $\mathscr{C}_1$ and, thus, the expected weight of a self-loop in a relational digraph.

Arbitrarily weighted directed and undirected edges can be represented in a similar fashion. In order to exemplify this, let us take a look at $\mathscr{C}_2^{dw}$, a weighted digraph comprised of a pair of nodes connected with each other through two directed edges of weight $w_{12}, w_{21} \in \mathbb{Q}$ (Fig. 4.6b). Classically, a complete representation of $\mathscr{C}_2^{dw}$ is furnished by the set of nodes $\mathcal{N} = \{1,2\}$, the set of edges $\mathcal{E} = \{(1,2),(2,1)\}$ and the weight matrix

$$\boldsymbol{w} = \begin{pmatrix} 0 & w_{12} \\ w_{21} & 0 \end{pmatrix}.$$

A minimal operator representation $\hat{\mathscr{C}}_2^{dw}$ of $\mathscr{C}_2^{dw}$ can dispense of the weight matrix as a necessary supplement to $\mathcal{E}$ by formalising both of the graph's weighted directed edges in terms of 2×2 matrix operators which act on row vectors in $\mathbb{Q}^2$ such that $\hat{\mathscr{C}}_2^{dw} = (\hat{\mathcal{N}}, \hat{\mathcal{E}})$ with

$$\hat{\mathcal{N}} = \left\{ \boldsymbol{n}_0 := \boldsymbol{0}^2, \boldsymbol{n}_1 := \boldsymbol{\delta}_1^2, \boldsymbol{n}_2 := \boldsymbol{\delta}_2^2 \right\} \subset \mathbb{Q}^2,$$
$$\hat{\mathcal{E}} = \hat{\mathcal{E}}_{cl} = \left\{ \mathfrak{E}_1 := \begin{pmatrix} 0 & w_{12} \\ 0 & 0 \end{pmatrix}, \mathfrak{E}_2 := \begin{pmatrix} 0 & 0 \\ w_{21} & 0 \end{pmatrix} \right\} \subset \mathbb{Q}^{2\times 2} \tag{4.39}$$

and $\mathfrak{E}[\boldsymbol{n}] := \boldsymbol{n} \cdot \bar{\boldsymbol{\delta}}[\mathfrak{E}]$ for all $\mathfrak{E} \in \hat{\mathcal{E}}$ and $\boldsymbol{n} \in \hat{\mathcal{N}}$. Moreover, right-hand matrix multiplication puts a viable operation of operator composition at our disposal which renders the extended set of edge operators $\hat{\mathcal{E}} = \hat{\mathcal{E}}_{cl} \cup \hat{\mathcal{E}}_{aux}$ with

$$\hat{\mathcal{E}}_{aux} = \left\{ \mathfrak{E}_0 := \boldsymbol{0}^{2\times 2}, \mathfrak{E}_3 := \begin{pmatrix} w_{12}w_{21} & 0 \\ 0 & 0 \end{pmatrix}, \mathfrak{E}_4 := \begin{pmatrix} 0 & 0 \\ 0 & w_{12}w_{21} \end{pmatrix} \right\} \subset \mathbb{Q}^{2\times 2},$$

an algebra of operators $\mathscr{E}$ closed under

$$\mathfrak{E}_{j_2} \circ \mathfrak{E}_{j_1} := \begin{cases} \mathfrak{E}_{j_1} \cdot \mathfrak{E}_{j_2} & \text{if } j_1, j_2 \in \{1, 2\}, \\ \mathfrak{E}_0 & \text{otherwise,} \end{cases} \tag{4.40}$$

and thus $\hat{\mathscr{C}}_2^{dw} = (\hat{\mathcal{N}}, \mathscr{E})$ is an operator graph representation of $\mathscr{C}_2^{dw}$. Again, we must caution here that this specific choice of operator composition targets the construction of paths from edges associated with $\hat{\mathcal{E}}_{cl}$. But we will note that, beyond that purpose, through the consideration of arbitrary weights $w_{12}, w_{21} \in \mathbb{Q}$, and by including the operations of vector addition in $\mathbb{Q}^{2\times 2}$ and scalar multiplication over $\mathbb{Q}$, the algebra of edge operators $\mathscr{E}$ can indeed be moulded into a $\mathbb{Q}$-operator algebra which eventually provides as a $\mathbb{Q}$-operator graph the algebraic blueprint for formalising generally weighted digraphs.

With (4.39) defining an operator representation of weighted directed edges in mind, let us then explore as a third and final example the Gilbert random digraph $\mathscr{R}_{2,p}^{dG}$ which, as a graph pattern, resides at the very heart of the construction of all random graphs. Although Section 2.3 briefly described some specific properties of a few random graph models (see Table 2.8), it must be stressed that, generally, the very nature of these models often prevents algebraic characterisations beyond statistical averages obtained from, and only valid for, a large number of concrete computational realisations. Indeed, as illustrated in Fig. 4.6c, already the two randomly connected nodes of $\mathscr{R}_{2,p}^{dG}$ allow for a total of three different not-isomorphic realisations which find both of its nodes as being either disconnected, connected through one directed edge, or mutually connected with two directed edges, and which respectively occur with a probability of $(1-p)^2$, $2p(1-p)$ and p^2. Certainly, only a given concrete realisation lends itself classically to a description in terms of a tuple $(\mathcal{N}, \mathcal{E})$ and associated adjacency matrix, thus leaving a satisfying classical representation of a random graph model in the hands of a sufficiently large and eventually unmanageable set of possible distinct realisations.

This arguably somewhat hopeless situation changes, however, if we discard the notion of an edge as being described by a fixed pair of nodes and instead view an edge as operator which performs a certain action on its argument with a given probability. In order to algebraically formalise this perspective, let us introduce the *binomial randomisation operator* $\mathfrak{r}^p$ by defining

$$\begin{aligned} \mathfrak{r}^p &: \mathbb{Q}^{m\times n} \to \mathbb{Q}^{m\times n}, \\ \mathfrak{r}^p[\boldsymbol{A}]_{ij} &: [1,m]\times[1,n] \subset \mathbb{N}^2 \to \mathbb{Q}, \\ \mathfrak{r}^p[\boldsymbol{A}]_{ij} &:= \begin{cases} A_{ij} & \text{with probability } p, \\ 0 & \text{otherwise} \end{cases} \end{aligned} \tag{4.41}$$

for arbitrary matrices $\boldsymbol{A} \in \mathbb{Q}^{m\times n}$ and $p \in \mathbb{Q}$, $p \in [0,1]$. It is important to note here that $\mathfrak{r}^p$ acts element-wise on its matrix argument, and that all of these element-wise actions are independent. Moreover, the application of $\mathfrak{r}^p$ must be interpreted within a statistical context such that, for instance, the expectation value of resulting matrix elements is given by

$$\langle \mathfrak{r}^p[\boldsymbol{A}]_{ij} \rangle = pA_{ij}, \tag{4.42}$$

which then leaves us with

$$\begin{aligned} \langle \mathfrak{r}^p[\boldsymbol{A}] \rangle &= p \cdot \boldsymbol{A}, \\ \left\langle \mathrm{T}\left[\mathfrak{r}^p[\boldsymbol{A}]\right] \right\rangle &= p\,\mathrm{T}[\boldsymbol{A}] \end{aligned} \tag{4.43}$$

for general matrices $\boldsymbol{A} \in \mathbb{Q}^{m\times n}$. Finally, as we will demonstrate more thoroughly in Chapter 5, the set of binomial randomisation operators itself forms an algebra with a number of interesting properties which render it useful not only as a tool in an algebraic rigorous formalisation of the generation of random graphs, but also for exactly measuring specific characteristics of random graph models without the need to consider statistical averages over large numbers of concrete realisations. For the purpose of our example, we will restrict ourselves here to noting that these properties include the definition of a composition of binomial randomisation operators according to

$$\mathfrak{r}^q \circ \mathfrak{r}^p[\boldsymbol{A}] = \mathfrak{r}^q\left[\mathfrak{r}^p[\boldsymbol{A}]\right] = \mathfrak{r}^{pq}[\boldsymbol{A}]. \tag{4.44}$$

Furthermore, by utilising the base decomposition of vector spaces over $\mathbb{Q}$, it can easily be shown that the matrix product satisfies

$$\left(\mathfrak{r}^p[\boldsymbol{A}]\right) \cdot \left(\mathfrak{r}^q[\boldsymbol{B}]\right) = \mathfrak{r}^p \circ \mathfrak{r}^q[\boldsymbol{A} \cdot \boldsymbol{B}] = \mathfrak{r}^{pq}[\boldsymbol{A} \cdot \boldsymbol{B}] \tag{4.45}$$

with $\boldsymbol{A} \in \mathbb{Q}^{m\times l}$ and $\boldsymbol{B} \in \mathbb{Q}^{l\times n}$, and that

$$\left(\mathfrak{r}^p[\boldsymbol{A}]\right) \odot \left(\mathfrak{r}^q[\boldsymbol{B}]\right) = \mathfrak{r}^p \circ \mathfrak{r}^q[\boldsymbol{A} \odot \boldsymbol{B}] = \mathfrak{r}^{pq}[\boldsymbol{A} \odot \boldsymbol{B}] \tag{4.46}$$

for $\boldsymbol{A}, \boldsymbol{B} \in \mathbb{Q}^{m\times n}$, where $\odot$ denotes the Hadamard product introduced in (3.52).

Guided by the operator representation (4.39) of the weighted digraph $\mathscr{C}_2^{dw}$, we can then, with the help of (4.41), construct the sets

$$\begin{aligned} \hat{\mathcal{N}} &= \left\{\boldsymbol{n}_0 := \boldsymbol{0}^2, \boldsymbol{n}_1 := \boldsymbol{\delta}_1^2, \boldsymbol{n}_2 := \boldsymbol{\delta}_2^2\right\} \subset \mathbb{B}^2, \\ \hat{\mathcal{E}} &= \hat{\mathcal{E}}_{cl} = \left\{\mathfrak{E}_1 := \mathfrak{r}^p[\boldsymbol{\delta}_{1,2}^{2\times 2}], \mathfrak{E}_2 := \mathfrak{r}^p[\boldsymbol{\delta}_{2,1}^{2\times 2}]\right\} \subset \mathbb{B}^{2\times 2} \end{aligned} \tag{4.47}$$

of nodes and edge operators which, together with $\mathfrak{E}[\boldsymbol{n}] := \boldsymbol{n} \cdot \mathfrak{E}$ for all $\mathfrak{E} \in \hat{\mathcal{E}}$ and $\boldsymbol{n} \in \hat{\mathcal{N}}$, furnish a minimal operator representation of the Gilbert random digraph $\mathscr{R}_{2,p}^{dG}$ in terms of the tuple $\hat{\mathscr{R}}_{2,p}^{dG} = (\hat{\mathcal{N}}, \hat{\mathcal{E}})$, as illustrated in Fig. 4.6c. Both edge-generating operators $\mathfrak{E}_1$ and $\mathfrak{E}_2$ act here as 2×2 matrix operators which establish independently, and with probability p, directed links from node 1 to node 2 and from node 2 to node 1 respectively. Interestingly, in the probabilistic sense of (4.43), we find

$$\langle \mathfrak{E}_1 \rangle = p \cdot \boldsymbol{\delta}_{1,2}^{2\times 2} = \begin{pmatrix} 0 & p \\ 0 & 0 \end{pmatrix}, \langle \mathfrak{E}_2 \rangle = p \cdot \boldsymbol{\delta}_{2,1}^{2\times 2} = \begin{pmatrix} 0 & 0 \\ p & 0 \end{pmatrix}, \tag{4.48}$$

which suggests that, within our operator graph-theoretical framework, there exists an algebraic connection between $\mathscr{R}_{2,p}^{dG}$ and the weighted digraph $\mathscr{C}_2^{dw}$ with both edge weights being equal to p, a connection which we will indeed amply exploit later in the construction and measurement of random graph models. However, it is important to stress here that (4.48) holds only in the probabilistic sense, and that both $\mathfrak{E}_1$ and $\mathfrak{E}_2$ are uniform-randomly drawn from the sets of matrix operators $\{\boldsymbol{0}^{2\times 2}, \boldsymbol{\delta}_{1,2}^{2\times 2}\}$ and $\{\boldsymbol{0}^{2\times 2}, \boldsymbol{\delta}_{2,1}^{2\times 2}\}$ according to

$$\mathfrak{E}_1 = \left\{ \begin{array}{ll} \boldsymbol{\delta}_{1,2}^{2\times 2} & \text{with probability } p, \\ \boldsymbol{0}^{2\times 2} & \text{otherwise} \end{array} \right\}, \quad \mathfrak{E}_2 = \left\{ \begin{array}{ll} \boldsymbol{\delta}_{2,1}^{2\times 2} & \text{with probability } p, \\ \boldsymbol{0}^{2\times 2} & \text{otherwise} \end{array} \right\}$$

where concrete realisations of $\mathscr{R}_{2,p}^{dG}$ are concerned.

Building on this algebraic similarity to $\mathscr{C}_2^{dw}$, it is certainly possible to also devise a viable operator graph for $\mathscr{R}_{2,p}^{dG}$. To that end, we employ the operator composition (4.40), and find that

$$\begin{aligned} \mathfrak{E}_2 \circ \mathfrak{E}_1 &= \mathfrak{E}_1 \cdot \mathfrak{E}_2 = \mathfrak{r}^p[\boldsymbol{\delta}_{1,2}^{2\times 2}] \cdot \mathfrak{r}^p[\boldsymbol{\delta}_{2,1}^{2\times 2}] = \mathfrak{r}^p \circ \mathfrak{r}^p[\boldsymbol{\delta}_{1,2}^{2\times 2} \cdot \boldsymbol{\delta}_{2,1}^{2\times 2}] = \mathfrak{r}^{p^2}[\boldsymbol{\delta}_{1,1}^{2\times 2}], \\ \mathfrak{E}_1 \circ \mathfrak{E}_2 &= \mathfrak{E}_2 \cdot \mathfrak{E}_1 = \mathfrak{r}^p[\boldsymbol{\delta}_{2,1}^{2\times 2}] \cdot \mathfrak{r}^p[\boldsymbol{\delta}_{1,2}^{2\times 2}] = \mathfrak{r}^p \circ \mathfrak{r}^p[\boldsymbol{\delta}_{2,1}^{2\times 2} \cdot \boldsymbol{\delta}_{1,2}^{2\times 2}] = \mathfrak{r}^{p^2}[\boldsymbol{\delta}_{2,2}^{2\times 2}]. \end{aligned}$$

Here, we used (4.44) and (4.45) to simplify the right-hand sides of these compositions. By then introducing the set of auxiliary edge operators

$$\hat{\mathcal{E}}_{aux} = \left\{\mathfrak{E}_0 := \boldsymbol{0}^{2\times 2}, \mathfrak{E}_3 := \mathfrak{E}_2 \circ \mathfrak{E}_1 = \mathfrak{r}^{p^2}[\boldsymbol{\delta}_{1,1}^{2\times 2}], \mathfrak{E}_4 := \mathfrak{E}_1 \circ \mathfrak{E}_2 = \mathfrak{r}^{p^2}[\boldsymbol{\delta}_{2,2}^{2\times 2}]\right\}$$

and the algebraic structure $O := \{\circ\}$, the tuple $(\hat{\mathcal{N}}, \mathscr{E})$ with $\mathscr{E} = (\hat{\mathcal{E}}_{cl} \cup \hat{\mathcal{E}}_{aux}, O)$ defines an operator graph $\hat{\mathscr{R}}_{2,p}^{dG}$ representing our Gilbert random digraph. Indeed, as we will show in Chapter 5, by exploiting the properties governing the set of binomial randomisation operators $\mathfrak{r}^p$, the algebraic structure O can be further extended, and $\mathscr{E}$ shaped into an operator algebra which renders $(\hat{\mathcal{N}}, \mathscr{E})$ an operator graph with an algebraic structure rich enough to serve as a blueprint for the construction of all random graph models introduced in Section 2.3.

With the operator representations of the classical graphs $\mathscr{C}_1$, $\mathscr{C}_2^{dw}$ and $\mathscr{R}_{2,p}^{dG}$ explored in this section, we hope to have illustrated some of the subtle conceptual differences that distinguish a more operator-inspired perspective from the classical description of finite graphs and networks. Before exemplifying the arguably advantageous consequences of such a perspective in dealing with various graph-theoretical questions and problems in Part II, however, we need to complement the notions of an operator representation of a graph and operator graph introduced in Definitions 4.1 and 4.2 with some additional notational conventions which encompass not only the generation and modification of graphs but also their characterisation through measurements. The remaining sections of this chapter are dedicated to the introduction of and motivation behind these notions, which, in conjunction with the material presented in this section, eventually will form the basis of *operator graph theory* as a workable framework for the mathematics of finite networks.

4.3 Transforming Operator Graphs

The previous section introduced the central notions of an operator representation of a graph (Definition 4.1) and an operator graph (Definition 4.2) as a collection of objects and operators acting on these objects. The inherently dynamic nature of such a representation of classical graph structures along with its algebraic formalisation certainly allows us to go one step further and conceive of operations which act, not unlike classical graph isomorphisms (Definition 2.3), in a transforming manner on a graph's nodes and edges themselves, either individually or at the level of the whole set. Recalling that only the subset $\hat{\mathcal{N}}_{cl} \subset \hat{\mathcal{N}}$ of nodes and subset $\hat{\mathcal{E}}_{cl} \subseteq \hat{\mathcal{E}}$ of edge operators defining an operator representation are associated with the nodes and edges comprising a classical graph, we will broadly distinguish here such operations into two types: those which act as bijective mappings over these subsets, and those which do not. While the former, more specific type can be visualised as a simple rewiring of edges, the latter and more general type encompasses operations such as the replacement, addition or removal of nodes and edges in a given graph. Before taking a closer look at such general operations, however, let us first formalise and explore in this section transformations associated with the rewiring of a graph's edges. To that end, we begin by formulating

Definition 4.3 (operator graph transformation) Let $\hat{\mathscr{G}} = (\hat{\mathcal{N}}, \hat{\mathcal{E}})$ be an operator representation of a finite graph $\mathscr{G} \in \mathbb{G}$, and $\hat{\mathscr{G}}' = (\hat{\mathcal{N}}', \hat{\mathcal{E}}')$ be that of $\mathscr{G}' \in \mathbb{G}$. Let $\hat{\mathfrak{M}}_{\mathcal{N}}: \hat{\mathcal{N}} \to \hat{\mathcal{N}}'$ be a surjective mapping from the set of nodes of $\hat{\mathscr{G}}$ onto the set of nodes of $\hat{\mathscr{G}}'$, and let $\hat{\mathfrak{M}}_{\mathcal{E}} : \hat{\mathcal{E}} \to \hat{\mathcal{E}}'$ be a surjective mapping from the set of edge operators of $\hat{\mathscr{G}}$ onto the set of edge operators of $\hat{\mathscr{G}}'$. The ordered tuple $\hat{\mathfrak{M}} = (\hat{\mathfrak{M}}_{\mathcal{N}}, \hat{\mathfrak{M}}_{\mathcal{E}})$ is called an *operator graph transformation*,

$$\hat{\mathfrak{M}}: \mathbb{G} \to \mathbb{G}\, ,\; \hat{\mathfrak{M}}[\hat{\mathscr{G}}] = \hat{\mathscr{G}}',$$

if $\hat{\mathfrak{M}}_{\mathcal{N}}$ acts as bijection between $\hat{\mathcal{N}}_{cl} \subset \hat{\mathcal{N}}$ and $\hat{\mathcal{N}}'_{cl} \subset \hat{\mathcal{N}}'$, and $\hat{\mathfrak{M}}_{\mathcal{E}}$ as bijection between $\hat{\mathcal{E}}_{cl} \subseteq \hat{\mathcal{E}}$ and $\hat{\mathcal{E}}'_{cl} \subseteq \hat{\mathcal{E}}'$, such that

$$\begin{aligned} \boldsymbol{n} \in \hat{\mathcal{N}}_{cl} &\Leftrightarrow \hat{\mathfrak{M}}_{\mathcal{N}}[\boldsymbol{n}] \in \hat{\mathcal{N}}'_{cl}, \\ \mathfrak{E} \in \hat{\mathcal{E}}_{cl} &\Leftrightarrow \hat{\mathfrak{M}}_{\mathcal{E}}[\mathfrak{E}] \in \hat{\mathcal{E}}'_{cl} \end{aligned}$$

and

$$\begin{aligned} \boldsymbol{n} \in \hat{\mathcal{N}}_{aux} &\Rightarrow \hat{\mathfrak{M}}_{\mathcal{N}}[\boldsymbol{n}] \in \hat{\mathcal{N}}'_{aux}, \\ \mathfrak{E} \in \hat{\mathcal{E}}_{aux} &\Rightarrow \hat{\mathfrak{M}}_{\mathcal{E}}[\mathfrak{E}] \in \hat{\mathcal{E}}'_{aux}. \end{aligned}$$

The operator representation $\hat{\mathscr{G}}'$ is called an *operator graph transform*, or simply *transform*, of the operator representation $\hat{\mathscr{G}}$.

The action of a transformation between operator representations $\hat{\mathscr{G}}$ and $\hat{\mathscr{G}}'$ of two finite graphs is illustrated in Fig. 4.8. It is important to note here that due to the bijective nature of the mapping $\hat{\mathfrak{M}}_{\mathcal{N}}$ between the subsets $\hat{\mathcal{N}}_{cl}$ and $\hat{\mathcal{N}}'_{cl}$, and the bijectivity of the mapping $\hat{\mathfrak{M}}_{\mathcal{E}}$ between subsets $\hat{\mathcal{E}}_{cl}$ and $\hat{\mathcal{E}}'_{cl}$, an operator graph transformation $\hat{\mathfrak{M}}$ necessarily preserves the cardinality of the classical subsets of nodes and edge-generating operators representing $\hat{\mathscr{G}}$ such that

$$\left|\hat{\mathcal{N}}_{cl}\right| = \left|\hat{\mathcal{N}}'_{cl}\right|\, ,\; \left|\hat{\mathcal{E}}_{cl}\right| = \left|\hat{\mathcal{E}}'_{cl}\right|. \tag{4.49}$$

Each transformation $\hat{\mathfrak{M}}$ can thus be viewed as acting over $\mathbb{G}_{n,k}$, where $\mathbb{G}_{n,k} \subset \mathbb{G}$ denotes the subset of all finite graphs of order $n \in \mathbb{N}$ with $k \in \mathbb{N}_0$ edges.

We already encountered specific examples of such operator graph transformations, albeit not in algebraically formalised terms or yet embedded into our operator graph-theoretical framework, in Chapters 2 and 3. Indeed, the very construction of a Watts–Strogatz random graph through rewiring of edges in a k-ring graph presented in Section 2.3.6 can be viewed as a transformation which realises structurally distinct graphs over the same set of nodes and a fixed number of edges. Similarly, the matrix operators $\mathfrak{O}^n(i, s^e)$ and $\mathfrak{O}^e(i, s^n)$

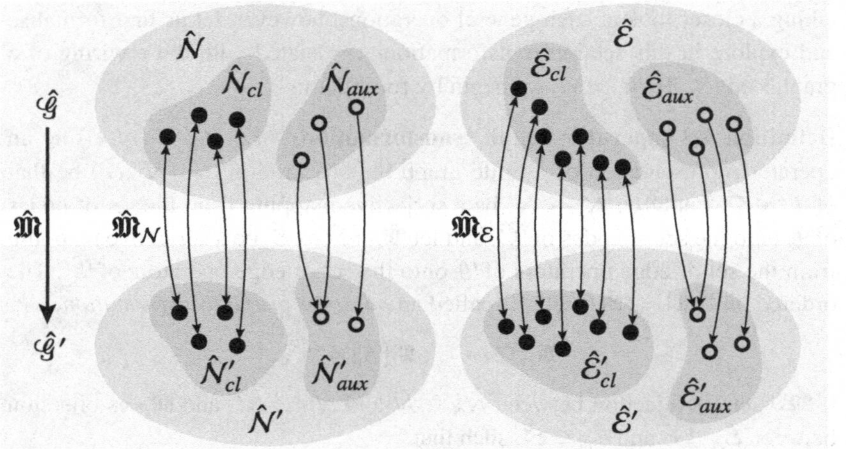

Figure 4.8 Operator graph transformation $\hat{\mathfrak{M}} = (\hat{\mathfrak{M}}_{\mathcal{N}},\hat{\mathfrak{M}}_{\mathcal{E}})$ between operator representations $\hat{\mathscr{G}} = (\hat{\mathcal{N}},\hat{\mathcal{E}})$ and $\hat{\mathscr{G}}' = (\hat{\mathcal{N}}',\hat{\mathcal{E}}')$ of two finite graphs.

introduced in Section 3.2 served to find and mark visited nodes and edges during the construction of walks through the Königsberg bridge graph and, thus, act as transformations which do not result in a change of the graph's structural makeup as defined by number of nodes, number of edges and, most importantly, set of connected node pairs. Interestingly, this algebraic realisation of an active search with its eventual preservation of the graph's defining structural characteristics beyond the number of nodes and edges hints at a further distinction of operator graph transformations. Before proceeding with the exploration of concrete examples illustrating graph transformations and their algebraic representation, let us therefore complement Definition 4.3 with

Definition 4.4 (operator graph isomorphism) Let $\hat{\mathscr{G}} = (\hat{\mathcal{N}}, \hat{\mathcal{E}})$ be an operator representation of a finite graph $\mathscr{G} \in \mathbb{G}$. Let $\hat{\mathfrak{M}} = (\hat{\mathfrak{M}}_{\mathcal{N}}, \hat{\mathfrak{M}}_{\mathcal{E}})$ be an operator graph transformation of $\hat{\mathscr{G}}$ with transform $\hat{\mathscr{G}}' = (\hat{\mathcal{N}}', \hat{\mathcal{E}}')$ such that $\hat{\mathscr{G}}' = \hat{\mathfrak{M}}[\hat{\mathscr{G}}]$. If the mapping $\hat{\mathfrak{M}}_{\mathcal{N}} : \hat{\mathcal{N}} \to \hat{\mathcal{N}}'$ satisfies

$$\hat{\mathfrak{E}} \in \hat{\mathcal{E}}_{cl} : \hat{\mathfrak{E}}[\boldsymbol{n}_i] = \boldsymbol{n}_j \Rightarrow \exists \hat{\mathfrak{E}}' \in \hat{\mathcal{E}}'_{cl} : \hat{\mathfrak{E}}'\Big[\hat{\mathfrak{M}}_{\mathcal{N}}[\boldsymbol{n}_i]\Big] = \hat{\mathfrak{M}}_{\mathcal{N}}[\boldsymbol{n}_j],$$
$$\hat{\mathfrak{E}}' \in \hat{\mathcal{E}}'_{cl} : \hat{\mathfrak{E}}'\Big[\boldsymbol{n}'_i\Big] = \boldsymbol{n}'_j \Rightarrow \exists \hat{\mathfrak{E}} \in \hat{\mathcal{E}}_{cl} : \hat{\mathfrak{E}}\Big[\hat{\mathfrak{M}}^{-1}_{\mathcal{N}}[\boldsymbol{n}'_i]\Big] = \hat{\mathfrak{M}}^{-1}_{\mathcal{N}}[\boldsymbol{n}'_j]$$

for $\boldsymbol{n}_i, \boldsymbol{n}_j \in \hat{\mathcal{N}}_{cl}$ and $\boldsymbol{n}'_i, \boldsymbol{n}'_j \in \hat{\mathcal{N}}'_{cl}$, the transformation $\hat{\mathfrak{M}}$ is called an *operator graph isomorphism*, and both operator representations $\hat{\mathscr{G}}$, $\hat{\mathscr{G}}'$ are said to be *isomorphic* and denoted as $\hat{\mathscr{G}} \triangleq \hat{\mathscr{G}}'$.

Because $\hat{\mathfrak{M}}_{\mathcal{N}}$ in an operator graph transformation acts bijectively between subsets $\hat{\mathcal{N}}_{cl}$ and $\hat{\mathcal{N}}'_{cl}$ in operator representations of two graphs $\mathcal{G}, \mathcal{G}' \in \mathbb{G}$, the condition in Definition 4.4 is algebraically equivalent to the necessary and sufficient condition for the existence of a classical isomorphism between $\mathcal{G}$ and $\mathcal{G}'$. It is important to point out, however, that the notion of an operator graph isomorphism also displays a subtle yet consequential conceptual difference to its classical counterpart. Indeed, recalling Definition 2.3, a classical isomorphism is given by a bijective map solely between the sets of nodes of two graphs, with the mapping between both graphs' set of edges being a necessary and sufficient consequence of this bijection. An operator graph transformation, on the other hand, treats the functional relation between the sets of nodes and edge operators in two operator representations separately by requiring two mappings $\hat{\mathfrak{M}}_{\mathcal{N}}$ and $\hat{\mathfrak{M}}_{\mathcal{E}}$. Although Definition 4.4 certainly presents here the condition for a classical isomorphism in an operator graph-theoretical context by demanding that for each $\mathfrak{E} \in \hat{\mathcal{E}}_{cl}$ there exists an $\mathfrak{E}' \in \hat{\mathcal{E}}'_{cl}$ and vice versa, it does so by recognising not only that the transformation $\hat{\mathfrak{M}}$ acts through $\hat{\mathfrak{M}}_{\mathcal{N}}$ on the set of nodes and, independently, through $\hat{\mathfrak{M}}_{\mathcal{E}}$ on the set of edge operators, but also that the nodes in an operator representation of a graph are no longer arbitrarily labelled yet conceptually identical but are instead distinct objects with discernible algebraic representations. This renders the notion of an operator graph isomorphism more refined by imposing stronger conditions on the set of nodes and edge operators of two isomorphic operator representations and, thus, the mapping $\hat{\mathfrak{M}} = (\hat{\mathfrak{M}}_{\mathcal{N}}, \hat{\mathfrak{M}}_{\mathcal{E}})$, such that each operator graph isomorphism naturally defines a classical graph isomorphism while the converse is generally not true. We will encounter below an example of such a not-isomorphic operator graph transform which yields a classically isomorphic graph.

Interestingly, this conceptual divorce of an operator graph isomorphism from the notion of a classical graph isomorphism allows – in fact, necessitates – going one step further and distinguishing isomorphisms which leave the operator representation of a given graph altogether unaltered. Specifically, let us formulate the following

Definition 4.5 (operator graph identity) Let $\hat{\mathcal{G}} = (\hat{\mathcal{N}}, \hat{\mathcal{E}})$ be an operator representation of a finite graph $\mathcal{G} \in \mathbb{G}$. Let $\hat{\mathfrak{M}} = (\hat{\mathfrak{M}}_{\mathcal{N}}, \hat{\mathfrak{M}}_{\mathcal{E}})$ be an operator graph isomorphism of $\hat{\mathcal{G}}$ with transform $\hat{\mathcal{G}}' = (\hat{\mathcal{N}}', \hat{\mathcal{E}}')$ such that $\hat{\mathcal{G}}' = \hat{\mathfrak{M}}[\hat{\mathcal{G}}]$. If the mapping $\hat{\mathfrak{M}}_{\mathcal{E}}\colon \hat{\mathcal{E}} \to \hat{\mathcal{E}}'$ satisfies

$$\mathfrak{E}[\boldsymbol{n}_i] = \boldsymbol{n}_j \Leftrightarrow \hat{\mathfrak{M}}_{\mathcal{E}}[\mathfrak{E}]\big[\hat{\mathfrak{M}}_{\mathcal{N}}[\boldsymbol{n}_i]\big] = \hat{\mathfrak{M}}_{\mathcal{N}}[\boldsymbol{n}_j]$$

for $\boldsymbol{n}_i, \boldsymbol{n}_j \in \hat{\mathcal{N}}_{cl}$ and $\mathfrak{E} \in \hat{\mathcal{E}}_{cl}$, the isomorphism $\hat{\mathfrak{M}}$ is called an *operator graph identity*, and both operator representations $\hat{\mathcal{G}}$, $\hat{\mathcal{G}}'$ are said to be *identical* and denoted as $\hat{\mathcal{G}} \triangleq \hat{\mathcal{G}}'$.

The necessary and sufficient condition which renders an operator graph isomorphism an operator graph identity according to Definition 4.5 can be visualised in form of the diagram

$$\begin{array}{ccc}
\boldsymbol{n}_i \in \hat{\mathcal{N}}_{cl} & \xrightarrow{\hat{\mathfrak{M}}_{\mathcal{N}}} & \hat{\mathfrak{M}}_{\mathcal{N}}[\boldsymbol{n}_i] \in \hat{\mathcal{N}}'_{cl} \\
\Big\downarrow & \mathfrak{E} \in \hat{\mathcal{E}}_{cl} \xrightarrow{\hat{\mathfrak{M}}_{\mathcal{E}}} \hat{\mathfrak{M}}_{\mathcal{E}}[\mathfrak{E}] \in \hat{\mathcal{E}}'_{cl} & \Big\downarrow \\
\boldsymbol{n}_j \in \hat{\mathcal{N}}_{cl} & \xrightarrow[\hat{\mathfrak{M}}_{\mathcal{N}}]{} & \hat{\mathfrak{M}}_{\mathcal{N}}[\boldsymbol{n}_j] \in \hat{\mathcal{N}}'_{cl}
\end{array}$$

from which

$$\hat{\mathfrak{M}}_{\mathcal{N}}\Big[\mathfrak{E}[\boldsymbol{n}]\Big] = \hat{\mathfrak{M}}_{\mathcal{E}}[\mathfrak{E}]\Big[\hat{\mathfrak{M}}_{\mathcal{N}}[\boldsymbol{n}]\Big] \tag{4.50}$$

for $\boldsymbol{n} \in \hat{\mathcal{N}}_{cl}$ and $\mathfrak{E} \in \hat{\mathcal{E}}_{cl}$ follows. Certainly, operator graph identities yield identical classical graphs and, thus, are generally associated with mappings between different operator graph representations of the same graph.

In order to illustrate a simple operator graph transformation along with its algebraic formalisation and variations, let us consider the directed version $\mathscr{C}_3^d$ of the triangle graph depicted in Fig. 4.9 (left) as an example. With

$$\begin{aligned}
\hat{\mathcal{N}}^{\mathscr{C}_3^d} &= \left\{\boldsymbol{n}_i := \boldsymbol{\delta}_i^3 : i \in [1,3]\right\} \cup \left\{\boldsymbol{n}_0 := \boldsymbol{0}^3\right\} \subset \mathbb{B}^3, \\
\hat{\mathcal{E}}^{\mathscr{C}_3^d} = \hat{\mathcal{E}}_{cl}^{\mathscr{C}_3^d} &= \left\{\mathfrak{E}_1 := \boldsymbol{\delta}_{1,2}^{3\times3}, \mathfrak{E}_2 := \boldsymbol{\delta}_{2,3}^{3\times3}, \mathfrak{E}_3 := \boldsymbol{\delta}_{3,1}^{3\times3}\right\} \subset \mathbb{B}^{3\times3}
\end{aligned} \tag{4.51}$$

and the action of edge operators on nodes given by right-hand matrix multiplication, the tuple $\hat{\mathscr{C}}_3^d = (\hat{\mathcal{N}}^{\mathscr{C}_3^d}, \hat{\mathcal{E}}^{\mathscr{C}_3^d})$ comprises a minimal operator representation of $\mathscr{C}_3^d$. It can then easily be shown that

$$\hat{\mathfrak{M}} = \left(\hat{\mathfrak{M}}_{\mathcal{N}} : \hat{\mathfrak{M}}_{\mathcal{N}}[\boldsymbol{n}] := \boldsymbol{n} \cdot \boldsymbol{M} \ , \ \hat{\mathfrak{M}}_{\mathcal{E}} := \mathrm{id}\right) \tag{4.52}$$

with $\boldsymbol{M} := (\boldsymbol{\delta}_{1,2}^{3\times3} + \boldsymbol{\delta}_{2,3}^{3\times3} + \boldsymbol{\delta}_{3,1}^{3\times3})$ defines an operator graph transformation according to Definition 4.3 by acting on $\boldsymbol{n} \in \hat{\mathcal{N}}^{\mathscr{C}_3^d}$ through right-hand matrix multiplication and, trivially, as identity mapping on $\mathfrak{E} \in \hat{\mathcal{E}}^{\mathscr{C}_3^d}$. The results of an independent application of $\hat{\mathfrak{M}}_{\mathcal{N}}$ and $\hat{\mathfrak{M}}_{\mathcal{E}}$ as well as their combination $\hat{\mathfrak{M}}$ are distinguished in Fig. 4.9a. We note here that the application of $\hat{\mathfrak{M}}_{\mathcal{N}}$ alone does naturally result in a different action of edge operators by altering the vectors representing the nodes of $\hat{\mathscr{C}}_3^d$. Indeed, the operator $\hat{\mathfrak{M}}_{\mathcal{N}}$ defines a bijective mapping which leads with

$$\hat{\mathfrak{M}}_{\mathcal{N}} : \hat{\mathcal{N}}_{cl}^{\mathscr{C}_3^d} \to \hat{\mathcal{N}}_{cl}^{\hat{\mathfrak{M}}[\mathscr{C}_3^d]} \ , \ \hat{\mathfrak{M}}_{\mathcal{N}}[\boldsymbol{n}_i] = \boldsymbol{n}_{1+i \bmod 3}$$

for $i \in [1,3]$ to a simple cyclic reordering of the graph's three nodes. Together with the trivial action of $\hat{\mathfrak{M}}_{\mathcal{E}}$ on the graph's edge-generating operators, the

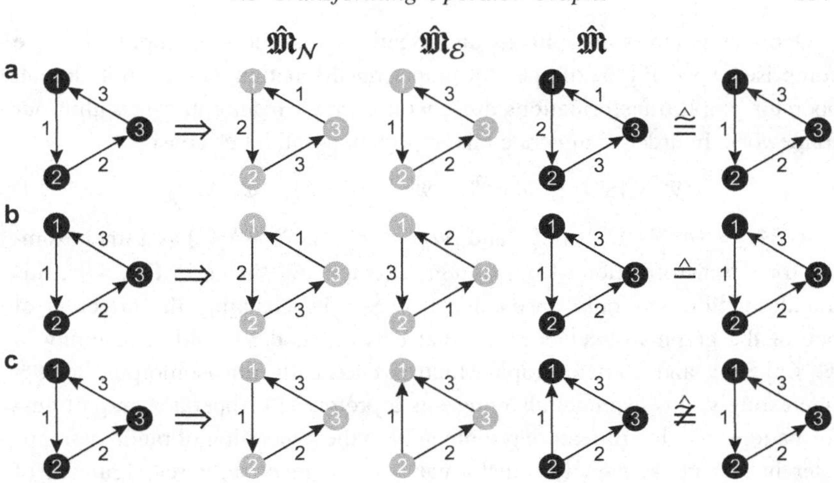

Figure 4.9 Examples of operator graph transformations of the triangle digraph $\mathscr{C}_3^d$. **a:** Action of the operator $\hat{\mathfrak{M}}$ defined in (4.52) yielding $\hat{\mathfrak{M}}[\mathscr{C}_3^d] \hat{\cong} \mathscr{C}_3^d$. **b:** Action of the operator $\hat{\mathfrak{M}}$ defined in (4.53) yielding $\hat{\mathfrak{M}}[\mathscr{C}_3^d] \hat{=} \mathscr{C}_3^d$. **c:** Action of the operator $\hat{\mathfrak{M}}$ defined in (4.54) yielding $\hat{\mathfrak{M}}[\mathscr{C}_3^d] \hat{\ncong} \mathscr{C}_3^d$. In all cases, the results of the independent actions of $\hat{\mathfrak{M}}_{\mathcal{N}}$ and $\hat{\mathfrak{M}}_{\mathcal{E}}$ as well as $\hat{\mathfrak{M}}=(\hat{\mathfrak{M}}_{\mathcal{N}},\hat{\mathfrak{M}}_{\mathcal{E}})$ on the classical sets of nodes and edge-generating operators of $\mathscr{C}_3^d$ are illustrated.

transformation (4.52) eventually describes an operator graph isomorphism of $\hat{\mathscr{C}}_3^d$ such that $\hat{\mathfrak{M}}[\hat{\mathscr{C}}_3^d] \hat{\cong} \hat{\mathscr{C}}_3^d$, and thus necessarily a classical graph isomorphism of $\mathscr{C}_3^d$ according to Definition 2.3.

Staying for a moment longer with the triangle digraph and its operator representation (4.51), we can also construct an example of a transformation which acts in a modifying manner over both $\hat{\mathcal{N}}^{\mathscr{C}_3^d}$ and $\hat{\mathcal{E}}^{\mathscr{C}_3^d}$. Specifically, let

$$\hat{\mathfrak{M}} = \Big(\hat{\mathfrak{M}}_{\mathcal{N}} \colon \hat{\mathfrak{M}}_{\mathcal{N}}[\boldsymbol{n}] := \boldsymbol{n} \cdot \boldsymbol{M} \,,\, \hat{\mathfrak{M}}_{\mathcal{E}} \colon \hat{\mathfrak{M}}_{\mathcal{E}}[\mathfrak{E}] := \boldsymbol{M}^{\mathsf{T}} \cdot \mathfrak{E} \cdot \boldsymbol{M}\Big) \tag{4.53}$$

with $\boldsymbol{M} := (\delta_{1,2}^{3\times3} + \delta_{2,3}^{3\times3} + \delta_{3,1}^{3\times3})$ for all $\boldsymbol{n} \in \hat{\mathcal{N}}^{\mathscr{C}_3^d}$ and $\mathfrak{E} \in \hat{\mathcal{E}}^{\mathscr{C}_3^d}$. It is then straightforward to show that

$$\hat{\mathfrak{M}}_{\mathcal{N}}\big[\mathfrak{E}[\boldsymbol{n}]\big] = \hat{\mathfrak{M}}_{\mathcal{N}}[\boldsymbol{n} \cdot \mathfrak{E}] = (\boldsymbol{n} \cdot \mathfrak{E}) \cdot \boldsymbol{M},$$
$$\hat{\mathfrak{M}}_{\mathcal{E}}[\mathfrak{E}]\big[\hat{\mathfrak{M}}_{\mathcal{N}}[\boldsymbol{n}]\big] = \hat{\mathfrak{M}}_{\mathcal{N}}[\boldsymbol{n}] \cdot \hat{\mathfrak{M}}_{\mathcal{E}}[\mathfrak{E}] = (\boldsymbol{n} \cdot \boldsymbol{M}) \cdot (\boldsymbol{M}^{\mathsf{T}} \cdot \mathfrak{E} \cdot \boldsymbol{M})$$

which, together with the associativity of matrix multiplication and the fact that $\boldsymbol{M} \cdot \boldsymbol{M}^{\mathsf{T}} = \boldsymbol{M}^{\mathsf{T}} \cdot \boldsymbol{M} = \boldsymbol{I}^3$, satisfies identity (4.50). This in turn renders (4.53) an example of not only an operator graph isomorphism of $\hat{\mathscr{C}}_3^d$ but indeed an operator graph identity such that $\hat{\mathfrak{M}}[\hat{\mathscr{C}}_3^d] \hat{=} \hat{\mathscr{C}}_3^d$, as depicted in Fig. 4.9b.

Operator graph isomorphisms and identities like those exemplified above comprise a special type of operator graph transformation, but certainly not all operator graph transformations are operator graph isomorphisms within our framework. In order to illustrate this important point, let us consider

$$\hat{\mathfrak{M}} = \left(\hat{\mathfrak{M}}_{\mathcal{N}} := \text{id}\ ,\ \hat{\mathfrak{M}}_{\mathcal{E}} : \hat{\mathfrak{M}}_{\mathcal{E}}[\mathfrak{E}] := M_L \cdot \mathfrak{E} \cdot M_R\right) \tag{4.54}$$

with $M_L := (\delta^{3\times3}_{2,1}+\delta^{3\times3}_{2,2}+\delta^{3\times3}_{3,3})$ and $M_R := (\delta^{3\times3}_{1,1}+\delta^{3\times3}_{2,1}+\delta^{3\times3}_{3,3})$ as a final example for a transformation of our triangle digraph. As shown in Fig. 4.9c, this transformation acts only on elements of $\hat{\mathcal{E}}^{\mathscr{C}^d_3}$ by changing the direction of one of the graph's directed edges, that between nodes 1 and 2, resulting in $\hat{\mathfrak{M}}[\hat{\mathscr{C}}^d_3] \ncong \hat{\mathscr{C}}^d_3$ and, thus, a graph which is classically not isomorphic to $\mathscr{C}^d_3$. Interestingly, this example also presents a prototype of operator graph transformations which will feature prominently in the generation of random graphs later in this book, namely transformations that result in a reassignment of source and target nodes of existing edges in a graph.

In order to demonstrate such a reassignment of nodes from a somehwat different angle, let us take a closer look at the cycle digraph $\mathscr{C}^d_4$ of order 4 depicted in Fig. 4.10 (top left), for which the sets

$$\begin{aligned} \hat{\mathcal{N}}^{\mathscr{C}^d_4} &= \left\{\boldsymbol{n}_i := \boldsymbol{\delta}^4_i : i \in [1,4]\right\} \cup \left\{\boldsymbol{n}_0 := \boldsymbol{0}^4\right\} \subset \mathbb{B}^4, \\ \hat{\mathcal{E}}^{\mathscr{C}^d_4} &= \hat{\mathcal{E}}^{\mathscr{C}^d_4}_{cl} = \left\{\mathfrak{E}_1 := \delta^{4\times4}_{1,2}, \mathfrak{E}_2 := \delta^{4\times4}_{2,3}, \mathfrak{E}_3 := \delta^{4\times4}_{3,4}, \mathfrak{E}_4 := \delta^{4\times4}_{4,1}\right\} \subset \mathbb{B}^{4\times4} \end{aligned} \tag{4.55}$$

of nodes and edge-generating operators furnish a minimal operator representation $\hat{\mathscr{C}}^d_4 = (\hat{\mathcal{N}}^{\mathscr{C}^d_4}, \hat{\mathcal{E}}^{\mathscr{C}^d_4})$. The operator

$$\hat{\mathfrak{M}} = \left(\hat{\mathfrak{M}}_{\mathcal{N}} := \text{id}\ ,\ \hat{\mathfrak{M}}_{\mathcal{E}} : \hat{\mathfrak{M}}_{\mathcal{E}}[\mathfrak{E}] := \mathfrak{E} \cdot M\right) \tag{4.56}$$

with $M := (\delta^{4\times4}_{1,2}+\delta^{4\times4}_{2,3}+\delta^{4\times4}_{3,4}+\delta^{4\times4}_{4,1})$, which acts in a modifying manner through right-hand matrix multiplication solely on elements of $\hat{\mathcal{E}}^{\mathscr{C}^d_4}$, then provides an operator graph transformation that changes the target nodes of each directed edge while leaving their respective source nodes unaltered. The result of this mapping is an operator representation $\hat{\mathfrak{M}}[\hat{\mathscr{C}}^d_4] \ncong \hat{\mathscr{C}}^d_4$ of a directed graph with two bidirectional adjacency relations connecting node 1 with node 3 and node 2 with node 4 which, classically, corresponds to a disconnected bipartite graph with two undirected edges.

But with this change of our original cycle graph from a strongly connected directed graph to a disconnected simple bipartite graph, we certainly have not yet exhausted the list of interesting properties of (4.56). Indeed, $\hat{\mathfrak{M}}$ not only presents a viable operator graph transformation for $\hat{\mathscr{C}}^d_4$ but also can be applied to the graph transform $\hat{\mathfrak{M}}[\hat{\mathscr{C}}^d_4]$ itself, and it delivers with

$$\hat{\mathfrak{M}}^2[\hat{\mathscr{C}}^d_4] := \hat{\mathfrak{M}} \circ \hat{\mathfrak{M}}[\hat{\mathscr{C}}^d_4] = \hat{\mathfrak{M}}\left[\hat{\mathfrak{M}}[\hat{\mathscr{C}}^d_4]\right] \ncong \hat{\mathscr{C}}^d_4$$

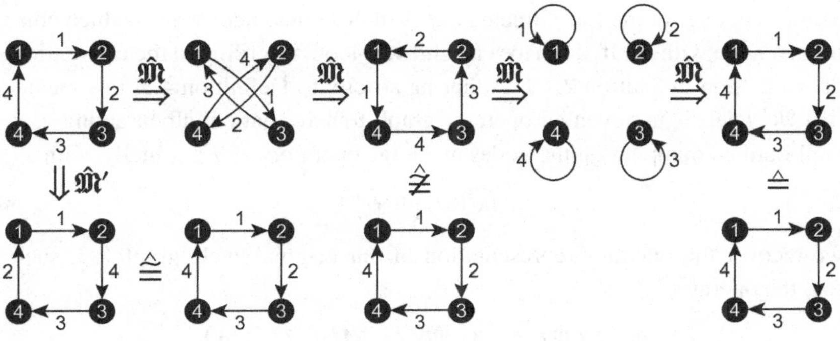

Figure 4.10 Examples of operator graph transformations of $\mathscr{C}_4^d$ which reassign source and target nodes of edges through repeated application of $\hat{\mathfrak{M}}$ in (4.56). While $\hat{\mathfrak{M}}[\hat{\mathscr{C}}_4^d] \hat{\not\cong} \hat{\mathscr{C}}_4^d$, and $\hat{\mathfrak{M}}^3[\hat{\mathscr{C}}_4^d]$ itself does not represent a graph, we also find that $\hat{\mathfrak{M}}^2[\hat{\mathscr{C}}_4^d] \hat{\cong} \hat{\mathscr{C}}_4^d$ and $\hat{\mathfrak{M}}^4[\hat{\mathscr{C}}_4^d] \hat{=} \hat{\mathscr{C}}_4^d$. In all operator representations illustrated, only elements of $\hat{\mathcal{N}}_{cl}$ and $\hat{\mathcal{E}}_{cl}$ are shown.

a second transform which, as illustrated in Fig. 4.10, once again represents a directed cycle graph that is not isomorphic to $\hat{\mathfrak{M}}[\hat{\mathscr{C}}_4^d]$. This repeated application of $\hat{\mathfrak{M}}$, however, carries another and perhaps somewhat more surprising consequence. A closer inspection reveals that

$$\hat{\mathfrak{M}}^2 = \left(\hat{\mathfrak{M}}_{\mathcal{N}} := \text{id}\, ,\, \hat{\mathfrak{M}}_{\mathcal{E}} \colon \hat{\mathfrak{M}}_{\mathcal{E}}[\boldsymbol{\mathfrak{E}}] := \boldsymbol{\mathfrak{E}} \cdot M\right)$$

with $M := (\delta_{1,3}^{4\times4} + \delta_{2,4}^{4\times4} + \delta_{3,1}^{4\times4} + \delta_{4,2}^{4\times4})$ defines a transformation which, despite describing a classical graph isomorphism under the bijection $1\leftrightarrow1$, $2\leftrightarrow4$, $3\leftrightarrow3$, $4\leftrightarrow2$ of nodes in $\mathscr{C}_4^d$, is not an operator graph isomorphism of $\hat{\mathscr{C}}_4^d$. This can easily be seen by recognising that $\hat{\mathfrak{M}}^2$ acts solely on the set of edge operators of $\hat{\mathscr{C}}_4^d$ such that, for example, for edge $\boldsymbol{\mathfrak{E}}_1$ connecting node $\boldsymbol{n}_1$ to node $\boldsymbol{n}_2$ in $\hat{\mathscr{C}}_4^d$ there does not exist an edge in $\hat{\mathfrak{M}}^2[\hat{\mathscr{C}}_4^d]$ between node $\hat{\mathfrak{M}}_{\mathcal{N}}[\boldsymbol{n}_1] = \boldsymbol{n}_1$ and node $\hat{\mathfrak{M}}_{\mathcal{N}}[\boldsymbol{n}_2] = \boldsymbol{n}_2$. For the latter to be true would require, in accordance with the independent actions of $\hat{\mathfrak{M}}_{\mathcal{N}}$ and $\hat{\mathfrak{M}}_{\mathcal{E}}$ in an operator graph transformation, a non-trivial mapping of the set of nodes $\hat{\mathcal{N}}^{\mathscr{C}_4^d}$ in our cycle digraph which echoes the bijection of nodes defining the classical isomorphism. Modifying $\hat{\mathfrak{M}}^2$ in this respect, an operator graph isomorphism of $\hat{\mathscr{C}}_4^d$ is eventually given by

$$\hat{\mathfrak{M}}' = \left(\hat{\mathfrak{M}}_{\mathcal{N}} \colon \hat{\mathfrak{M}}_{\mathcal{N}}[\boldsymbol{n}] := \boldsymbol{n} \cdot M'\, ,\, \hat{\mathfrak{M}}_{\mathcal{E}} \colon \hat{\mathfrak{M}}_{\mathcal{E}}[\boldsymbol{\mathfrak{E}}] := \boldsymbol{\mathfrak{E}} \cdot M\right) \tag{4.57}$$

with $M' := (\delta_{1,1}^{4\times4} + \delta_{2,4}^{4\times4} + \delta_{3,3}^{4\times4} + \delta_{4,2}^{4\times4})$, as illustrated in Fig. 4.10 (bottom left).

Running with the idea of a successive application of (4.56) a little longer, what happens if we apply $\hat{\mathfrak{M}}$ once more to the graph generated by $\hat{\mathfrak{M}}^2[\hat{\mathscr{C}}_4^d]$? Unfortunately, $\hat{\mathfrak{M}}^3[\hat{\mathscr{C}}_4^d]$ does here not represent a graph in the classical sense at all, as neither of the four directed edges in this construct, each of which connects a node with itself, describes a valid self-loop according to the convention decided upon in Section 2.1.1. Adhering strictly to Definition 4.3, this means that $\hat{\mathfrak{M}}^3$ itself is not even an operator graph transformation, albeit acting as a well-defined mapping on the nodes and edge operators of $\hat{\mathscr{C}}_4^d$. Finally, with

$$\hat{\mathfrak{M}}^4[\hat{\mathscr{C}}_4^d] \triangleq \hat{\mathscr{C}}_4^d$$

we recover the operator representation of our original cycle graph $\mathscr{C}_4^d$, such that the operator

$$\hat{\mathfrak{M}}^4 = \left(\hat{\mathfrak{M}}_{\mathcal{N}} := \mathrm{id}\, ,\, \hat{\mathfrak{M}}_{\mathcal{E}} := \boldsymbol{M}^4 = \boldsymbol{I}^4 = \mathrm{id}\right)$$

acts as identity mapping on both the set of nodes and edge operators and, thus, describes a transformation of $\hat{\mathscr{C}}_4^d$ which not only is an operator graph identity but also represents the trivial classical isomorphism between identical graphs.

As already hinted at earlier, operator graph transformations such as (4.54) or (4.56) that act solely on the set of edge operators of a given graph by altering the direction of adjacency relations, or by reassigning their source and target nodes, play an instrumental role in the algebraic formalisation and generation of random graphs. For example, each computational realisation of an undirected Erdős–Rényi random graph $\mathscr{R}_{n,k}^{ER}$ can be envisioned as a transformation acting on an exact graph of order n with k edges – such as a disconnected graph with n isolated nodes, one of which carries a total of k self-loops – by randomising independently both target and source nodes of each edge. In a similar fashion, realisations of a Watts–Strogatz random graph $\mathscr{R}_{n,k,q}^{WS}$ can be generated by envisioning an operator that acts on an appropriate ring graph of order n by randomising independently and with probability q either the target node or source node of each edge while keeping the total number of edges unchanged. Although at first glance, such a perspective appears arguably best suited for computational purposes and, thus, as somewhat arbitrary and complicating matters for a mathematically more rigorous approach, we will advocate in Chapter 5 for its potential effectiveness by algebraically formalising the generation of generally non-isomorphic random graphs. Furthermore, we will also demonstrate that, consequently, such an approach dispenses with the necessity of computationally studying large numbers of realisations of a given random graph model when measuring its properties.

In order to place the groundwork for such a formalisation, let us conclude this section by considering as a first concrete step towards the algebraic rigorous treatment of random graphs the generation of random digraphs in which all nodes share the same out-degree or in-degree by respectively mapping the source or target nodes of edges in a directed k-ring graph. Recalling Section 2.3.3 and, with (2.119), the defining weight matrix of a ring digraph, a viable minimal operator representation of $\mathscr{C}^d_{n,k}$ is furnished by the tuple $\hat{\mathscr{C}}^d_{n,k} = (\hat{\mathcal{N}}^{\mathscr{C}^d_{n,k}}, \hat{\mathcal{E}}^{\mathscr{C}^d_{n,k}})$ with the sets of nodes and edge-generating operators given by

$$\hat{\mathcal{N}}^{\mathscr{C}^d_{n,k}} = \left\{\boldsymbol{n}_i := \boldsymbol{\delta}^n_i : i \in [1,n]\right\} \cup \left\{\boldsymbol{n}_0 := \boldsymbol{0}^n\right\} \subset \mathbb{B}^n, \tag{4.58}$$

$$\hat{\mathcal{E}}^{\mathscr{C}^d_{n,k}} = \hat{\mathcal{E}}_{cl}^{\mathscr{C}^d_{n,k}} = \left\{\mathfrak{E}_j := \boldsymbol{\delta}^{n\times n}_{1+\lfloor (j-1)/k\rfloor, 1+(\lfloor (j-1)/k\rfloor (1-k)+j) \bmod n} : j \in [1,nk]\right\} \subset \mathbb{B}^{n\times n}.$$

Here, the set $\hat{\mathcal{E}}^{\mathscr{C}^d_{n,k}}$ is comprised of $n \times n$ Boolean matrices, each being associated with a single directed edge between the nodes of $\mathscr{C}^d_{n,k}$. A reassignment of the node targeted by an edge operator $\mathfrak{E} \in \hat{\mathcal{E}}^{\mathscr{C}^d_{n,k}}$ then amounts to changing the column of the sole non-zero element of $\mathfrak{E}$, while a change of its row will result in the reassignment of the corresponding edge's source node. As in our little exercise such reassignments should occur uniform-randomly, we certainly require a randomisation operator not unlike $\mathfrak{r}^p$ introduced in (4.41). However, $\mathfrak{r}^p$ itself is here ill-suited as it cannot ensure, due to its probabilistic conception, that a resulting edge operator still carries exactly one non-zero element and, thus, the total number of edges in the original ring graph is preserved.

To remedy this shortcoming and allow for an algebraic formalisation of a uniform-random reassignment of source or target nodes of edges in a given ring digraph, let us, inspired by (4.41), introduce with

$$\bar{\mathfrak{r}}^k : \mathbb{Q}^{m\times n} \to \mathbb{Q}^{m\times n}, \tag{4.59}$$

$$\bar{\mathfrak{r}}^k[\boldsymbol{A}]_{ij} : [1,m] \times [1,n] \subset \mathbb{N}^2 \to \mathbb{Q},$$

$$\bar{\mathfrak{r}}^k[\boldsymbol{A}]_{ij} := \begin{cases} A_{ij} & \text{for } j \in C^{\text{rand}}_k(\{j' \in [1,n] : A_{ij'} \neq 0\}) \text{ and each given } i, \\ 0 & \text{otherwise} \end{cases}$$

a *column randomisation operator* which selects from each row of a given matrix $\boldsymbol{A} \in \mathbb{Q}^{m\times n}$ with $(\bar{\boldsymbol{\delta}}[\boldsymbol{A}] \cdot \boldsymbol{1}^n)_i \geq k$ for all $i \in [1,m]$ exactly k non-zero elements such that $\bar{\boldsymbol{\delta}}[\bar{\mathfrak{r}}^k[\boldsymbol{A}]] \cdot \boldsymbol{1}^n = k \cdot \boldsymbol{1}^m$. Here, $\boldsymbol{1}^n$ denotes the all-ones column vector with n elements, and $C^{\text{rand}}_k(\mathcal{S}) \in \mathfrak{C}_k(\mathcal{S})$ an unordered k-subset of a finite set $\mathcal{S}$ comprised of uniform-randomly chosen elements of $\mathcal{S}$. It can then easily be shown that the tuple of matrix operators

$$\hat{\mathfrak{M}} = \left(\hat{\mathfrak{M}}_{\mathcal{N}} := \text{id}, \hat{\mathfrak{M}}_{\mathcal{E}} : \hat{\mathfrak{M}}_{\mathcal{E}}[\mathfrak{E}] := \mathfrak{E} \cdot \boldsymbol{M}\right) \tag{4.60}$$

with

$$\boldsymbol{M} := \bar{\mathfrak{r}}^1\left[\text{circ}\,[(\overbrace{1,\ldots,1}^{n-k},\overbrace{0,\ldots,0}^{k})]\right]$$

defines an operator graph transformation which leaves the set of nodes $\hat{\mathcal{N}}^{\mathscr{C}^d_{n,k}}$ unchanged but acts through right-hand matrix multiplication on elements of $\hat{\mathcal{E}}^{\mathscr{C}^d_{n,k}}$ by assigning, in a uniform-randomly fashion, a new column to the sole non-zero matrix element of each $\mathfrak{E} \in \hat{\mathcal{E}}^{\mathscr{C}^d_{n,k}}$, hereby randomising the target

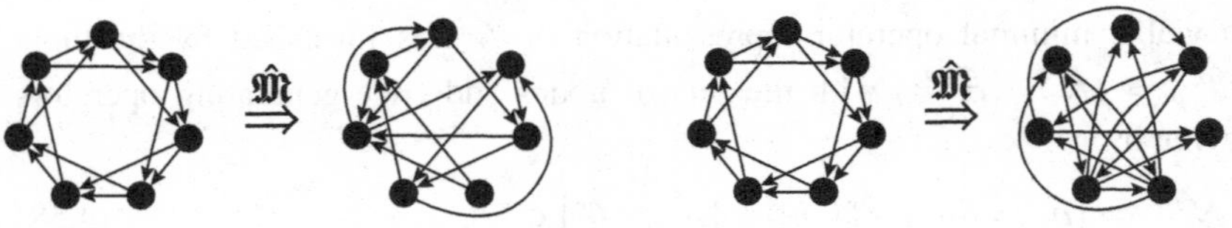

Figure 4.11 Representative examples for the generation of directed random multigraphs by randomising target nodes (left) and source nodes (right) of edges in the ring graph $\mathscr{C}_{7,2}$ through the application of a realisation of transformations (4.60) and (4.61). In both cases, we generally find $\hat{\mathfrak{M}}[\hat{\mathscr{C}}_{7,2}]\ncong\mathscr{C}_{7,2}$. In all examples shown, only elements of $\hat{\mathcal{N}}_{cl}$ and $\hat{\mathcal{E}}_{cl}$ are illustrated.

nodes of all directed edges in the given ring graph $\mathscr{C}^{d}_{n,k}$. Similarly, if the action of the matrix operator $\hat{\mathfrak{M}}_{\mathcal{E}}$ is defined through left-hand matrix multiplication, the operator graph transform

$$\hat{\mathfrak{M}} = \left(\hat{\mathfrak{M}}_{\mathcal{N}} := \mathrm{id}\,,\, \hat{\mathfrak{M}}_{\mathcal{E}}\colon \hat{\mathfrak{M}}_{\mathcal{E}}[\mathfrak{E}] := M^{\top}\cdot\mathfrak{E}\right) \tag{4.61}$$

uniform-randomly reassigns the row index of the sole non-zero matrix element of each $\mathfrak{E}$, thus resulting in a randomisation of the source nodes of all directed edges in $\mathscr{C}^{d}_{n,k}$. In both cases, the resulting directed random multigraphs comprise a special subset of the Erdős–Rényi random digraph model $\mathscr{R}^{dER}_{n,nk}$ of order n with nk edges and no self-loops in which each node has, respectively, the same out-degree or in-degree k. Representative examples of concrete realisations of these operator graph transformations for the ring digraph $\mathscr{C}^{d}_{7,2}$ are illustrated in Fig. 4.11.

Certainly, the specific form of the argument of the column randomisation operator $\bar{\mathfrak{r}}^{1}$ in (4.60) and (4.61) ensures that none of the generated realisations of random graphs will contain self-looped nodes. However, it is important to note that neither of these transformations here prevents the eventual assignment of multiple directed edges connecting two given distinct nodes, thus, $\hat{\mathfrak{M}}[\hat{\mathscr{C}}^{d}_{n,k}]$ will generally result in the generation of a directed multigraph. Indeed, the algebraic formalisation of operator graph transformations which deliver random graphs or digraphs without multiple edges is somewhat more involved and will be thoroughly explored in the next chapter. Similarly, the generation of realisations of random graphs from exact graph models in which both source and target nodes are independently assigned necessitates a generalisation of the notion of an operator graph transformation that we will formally introduce in the last section of this chapter.

Finally, and most importantly, we note that due to the very nature of the utilised column randomisation operator $\bar{\mathfrak{r}}^{k}$, each concrete transform $\hat{\mathfrak{M}}[\hat{\mathscr{C}}^{d}_{n,k}]$ will generally represent a different realisation of the targeted random graph model, which in the case of (4.60) and (4.61) is comprised of a specific subset of Erdős–Rényi random digraphs $\mathcal{R}^{dER}_{n,nk}$. The algebraic formalisation of $\hat{\mathfrak{M}}[\hat{\mathscr{C}}^{d}_{n,k}]$ in terms of $\bar{\mathfrak{r}}^{k}$ itself, however, can be viewed as describing all possible realisations of a specific random graph model at once. This is indeed an interesting prospect which, as we will demonstrate in Chapters 5 and 6, will prove instrumental in the derivation of exact expressions for many algebraically well-defined graph measures – and, thus, the characterisation of various random graph models as a whole – beyond numerical results obtained from statistical assessments over large numbers of concrete computational realisations.

4.4 Measuring Operator Graphs

In Section 2.2, we presented a small subset of the vast and ever-growing number of available quantities which are commonly employed in the applied graph-theoretical literature for delineating and quantifying structural properties of finite graphs in general and real-world networks in particular. Most if not all of these quantities, which we conveniently termed *graph measures*, can be defined as algebraic constructs of a graph's weight matrix or, in the case of relational digraphs, an adjacency matrix. Therefore, somewhat necessarily, these constructs rely on the classical representation of the set of edges in terms of a finite-dimensional matrix. But what if such a matrix representation is not available or exceeds the limitations of our computational hardware? While the latter situation, albeit not an uncommon occurrence, is certainly malleable, the unavailability of a workable matrix representation is more principal in nature. Let us take the Erdős–Rényi random graph model as an illustrative example. Although this model is well-defined (see Section 2.3.5), the adjacency matrix of an Erdős–Rényi random graph remains as an abstract notion only, until a concrete realisation out of a large set of possible realisations of the model is at hand. This, naturally, puts stringent limitations on the availability and accessibility of measures that provide an algebraic characterisation of random graph models beyond the scope of statistical and, thus, numerical explorations of a large number of computational realisations.

In order to examine the characterisation of graphs within an operator graph-theoretical context, and assess whether such a formalisation can indeed circumvent some of the limitations inherent to the classical conception of measuring graphs, let us first look briefly at the general process of measuring a physical quantity and, with that, the epistemological notion of an *observable*. In most general terms, a physical observable is synonymous with a real-valued operator which acts on the set of all possible states in which a given physical system can exist. The result of the application of such an operator then provides a quantification, either numerical or algebraical, of the actual state of the physical system with respect to the concrete property delineated by the observable. Certainly, in order for an operator to serve as a physically meaningful observable, the result of its application must be independent of not only the specific representation of the operator itself but also the specific representation of the physical system it acts upon. This translates mathematically into the requirement of invariance with respect to transformations in the space of representations of an operator and in the state space describing the physical system. Only if both of these conditions are satisfied can an observable then measure a specific property of a physical system and eventually be identified with the associated measure itself.

Recognising the epistemological significance of the concept of a physical observable, we will adopt this notion here for the purpose of describing and quantifying properties of finite networks within our operator graph-theoretical framework. In order to remain consistent within the boundaries of an algebraic – that is, an inherently discrete and finite – approach, we furthermore will without loss of generality assume that the codomain of an operator formalising a physical observable is given by a vector space over the field of rational numbers $\mathbb{Q}$ or one of its subsets. With this, we then formulate the following

Definition 4.6 (operator graph observable) Let $\hat{\mathcal{G}}$ be an operator representations of a finite graph $\mathcal{G} \in \mathbb{G}$. Let $\mathcal{V}$ be a vector space over $\mathbb{Q}$. An operator

$$\hat{O}\colon \mathbb{G} \to \widetilde{\mathcal{V}} \subseteq \mathcal{V}\,,\; \hat{O}[\hat{\mathcal{G}}] = O$$

is called an *operator graph observable*, or simply *graph observable*, if there exists an orthogonal endomorphism $f\colon \mathcal{V} \to \mathcal{V}$ such that

$$\hat{O}[\hat{\mathcal{G}}] = f\big(\hat{O}[\hat{\mathcal{G}}']\big)$$

for an operator representation $\hat{\mathcal{G}}' \triangleq \hat{\mathcal{G}}$.

Adhering to this definition, a scalar graph measure is thus to be understood as the result of the action of a graph observable – that is, an operator – on an operator representation $\hat{\mathcal{G}}$ of a finite graph $\mathcal{G}$ which remains invariant under operator graph isomorphisms. Similarly, a graph measure with a codomain in a higher-dimensional rational vector space is the result of the action of a graph observable which remains up to orthogonal transformations of its codomain invariant under operator graph isomorphisms. As for any given finite graph, a variety of representations – classical or operator graph-theoretical – can be conceived, this invariance naturally extends to the set of all possible representations of a graph but necessarily renders the algebraic formalisation of an operator serving as a graph observable also dependent on the chosen representation. In order to then distinguish operators involved in the representation, transformation or construction of graphs, we will generally denote in the remainder of this book a graph observable associated with the classical graph measure O by $\hat{O}$ such that $\hat{O}[\hat{\mathcal{G}}] = O$.

For most graph measures, some of which we introduced in Section 2.2, an operator can readily be constructed. As already noted above, the concrete algebraic form of a graph observable certainly depends on the representation of the graph but typically acts on the set of nodes $\mathcal{N}$, set of edges $\mathcal{E}$ or weight matrix $\boldsymbol{w}$ in a classical representation of $\mathcal{G}$; or, in the case of an operator representations or operator graph $\hat{\mathcal{G}}$, on the subsets $\hat{\mathcal{N}}_{cl} \subset \hat{\mathcal{N}}$ and $\hat{\mathcal{E}}_{cl} \subseteq \hat{\mathcal{E}}$ of its nodes and edge operators. With (4.38) we already encountered an example of what could be construed as the representations of a graph observable for the weight matrix of a graph comprised of a single self-looped node. This expression can easily be generalised, and it eventually delivers the operator

$$\hat{\boldsymbol{w}} : \mathbb{G} \to \mathbb{Q}^{n \times n} \, , \; \hat{\boldsymbol{w}}[\hat{\mathcal{G}}] = \boldsymbol{w} := \sum_{\mathfrak{E} \in \hat{\mathcal{E}}_{cl}} \mathfrak{E} \tag{4.62}$$

as a weight matrix observable for an operator representation $\hat{\mathcal{G}} = (\hat{\mathcal{N}}, \hat{\mathcal{E}})$ of a generally weighted digraph $\mathcal{G}$ of order $n = |\hat{\mathcal{N}}_{cl}|$ in which the set $\hat{\mathcal{E}}$ is comprised of matrices in the rational vector space $\mathbb{Q}^{n \times n}$ such that each $\mathfrak{E} \in \hat{\mathcal{E}}_{cl}$ satisfies $\mathrm{T}[\bar{\delta}[\mathfrak{E}]] = 1$ and represents a single-weighted directed edge of $\mathcal{G}$. In a similar fashion, restricting to simple graphs $\mathcal{G}$, the operator

$$\hat{\boldsymbol{a}} : \mathbb{G} \to \mathbb{B}^{n \times n} \subset \mathbb{Q}^{n \times n} \, , \; \hat{\boldsymbol{a}}[\hat{\mathcal{G}}] = \boldsymbol{a} := \sum_{\mathfrak{E} \in \hat{\mathcal{E}}_{cl}} \left(\mathfrak{E} \otimes \mathfrak{E}^{\mathsf{T}} - \mathrm{diag}\,[\mathfrak{E}] \right) \tag{4.63}$$

can be shown to represent the adjacency matrix observable for operator representations $\hat{\mathcal{G}}$ in which each edge-generating operator $\mathfrak{E} \in \hat{\mathcal{E}}_{cl}$ is given by a vector in $\mathbb{B}^n$ and satisfies $\mathrm{T}[\mathfrak{E}] = 2$.

To briefly illustrate the application of $\hat{\boldsymbol{w}}$, let us revisit the operator representation (4.55) of the cycle digraph $\hat{\mathcal{C}}_4^d$ and its transform $\hat{\mathfrak{M}}'[\hat{\mathcal{C}}_4^d]$ with $\hat{\mathfrak{M}}'$ given by (4.57). Observing that, here, $\mathrm{T}[\bar{\delta}[\mathfrak{E}]] = 1$ for all $\mathfrak{E} \in \hat{\mathcal{E}}_{cl}^{\hat{\mathcal{C}}_4^d}$ and $\mathfrak{E} \in \hat{\mathcal{E}}_{cl}^{\hat{\mathfrak{M}}'[\hat{\mathcal{C}}_4^d]}$, equation (4.62) then yields

$$\hat{\boldsymbol{w}}[\hat{\mathcal{C}}_4^d] = \begin{pmatrix} 0 & 1 & 0 & 0 \\ 0 & 0 & 1 & 0 \\ 0 & 0 & 0 & 1 \\ 1 & 0 & 0 & 0 \end{pmatrix} , \; \hat{\boldsymbol{w}}\left[\hat{\mathfrak{M}}'[\hat{\mathcal{C}}_4^d]\right] = \begin{pmatrix} 0 & 0 & 0 & 1 \\ 1 & 0 & 0 & 0 \\ 0 & 1 & 0 & 0 \\ 0 & 0 & 1 & 0 \end{pmatrix}$$

and eventually defines an observable $\hat{\boldsymbol{w}} : \mathbb{G} \to \mathbb{B}^{4 \times 4} \subset \mathbb{Q}^{4 \times 4}$ which returns, and thus measures, the given graph's weight matrix. Furthermore, by noting that the operator graph transformation $\hat{\mathfrak{M}}'$ comprises an operator graph isomorphism of $\hat{\mathscr{C}}_4^d$, we easily find the specific orthogonal endomorphism

$$f : \mathbb{B}^{4\times 4} \to \mathbb{B}^{4\times 4}\,,\; f := \begin{pmatrix} 0 & 0 & 1 & 0 \\ 0 & 0 & 0 & 1 \\ 1 & 0 & 0 & 0 \\ 0 & 1 & 0 & 0 \end{pmatrix},$$

which ensures that, according to Definition 4.6, with

$$\hat{\mathfrak{w}}[\hat{\mathscr{C}}_4^d] = f\left(\hat{\mathfrak{w}}\left[\hat{\mathfrak{M}}'[\hat{\mathscr{C}}_4^d]\right]\right),$$

the necessary condition is satisfied such that $\hat{\mathfrak{w}}$ can indeed be considered as a viable weight matrix observable for $\hat{\mathscr{C}}_4^d$.

Because most measures employed in the graph-theoretical literature are naturally defined as functions of a graph's weight or adjacency matrix (see Section 2.2), the operators introduced with (4.62) and (4.63) certainly provide two important graph observables which, as we will see below and in Part II of this book, will prove instrumental for the conception and formalisation of other graph observables. Another such instrumental observable is given by an operator which, through acting on the operator representation $\hat{\mathscr{G}} = (\hat{\mathcal{N}}, \hat{\mathcal{E}})$ of an arbitrary graph $\mathscr{G}$, returns the number of nodes N_n comprising $\mathscr{G}$. Recalling that only the subset $\hat{\mathcal{N}}_{cl}$ of $\hat{\mathcal{N}}$ is associated with the nodes of a classical graph, this observable can be algebraically formalised through

$$\hat{N}_n : \mathbb{G} \to \mathbb{N}\,,\; \hat{N}_n[\hat{\mathscr{G}}] = N_n := \left|\hat{\mathcal{N}}_{cl}\right|. \tag{4.64}$$

In a similar fashion, we find that

$$\hat{N}_l \;:\; \mathbb{G} \to \mathbb{N}_0\,,\; \hat{N}_l[\hat{\mathscr{G}}] = N_l := \mathrm{Tr}\left[\bar{\delta}\left[\sum_{\mathfrak{E}\in\hat{\mathcal{E}}_{cl}} \mathfrak{E}\right]\right] = \mathrm{Tr}\left[\bar{\delta}[\hat{\mathfrak{w}}[\hat{\mathscr{G}}]]\right], \tag{4.65}$$

and

$$\hat{A} \;:\; \mathbb{G} \to \mathbb{N}_0\,,\; \hat{A}[\hat{\mathscr{G}}] = A := \left|\hat{\mathcal{E}}_{cl}\right| \tag{4.66}$$

define observables that measure the number of self-loops N_l and the total adjacency A in generally weighted digraphs in which each edge-generating operator $\mathfrak{E} \in \hat{\mathcal{E}}_{cl}$ is represented as a matrix in $\mathbb{Q}^{N_n \times N_n}$ such that $\mathrm{T}\left[\bar{\delta}[\mathfrak{E}]\right] = 1$. It is worth noting here that with Definition 4.3 and (4.49), the observables $\hat{N}_n$ and $\hat{A}$ then necessarily satisfy

$$\hat{N}_n[\hat{\mathscr{G}}] = \hat{N}_n\left[\hat{\mathfrak{M}}[\hat{\mathscr{G}}]\right],\; \hat{A}[\hat{\mathscr{G}}] = \hat{A}\left[\hat{\mathfrak{M}}[\hat{\mathscr{G}}]\right] \tag{4.67}$$

for all graphs $\mathscr{G} \in \mathbb{G}$ and arbitrary operator graph transformations $\hat{\mathfrak{M}}$.

As a final exercise illustrating the conception and formalisation of graph observables, let us consider the scalar Boolean measures which discern the type of a graph. Without loss of generality, we will restrict ourselves here again to operator representations in which each edge operator in $\hat{\mathcal{E}}_{cl}$ is represented as a matrix in $\mathbb{Q}^{N_n \times N_n}$ with exactly one non-zero element. Together with (2.6), (2.7) and (2.8), it can then easily be shown that

$$\hat{\lambda}_d : \mathbb{G} \to \mathbb{B} , \hat{\lambda}_d[\hat{\mathcal{G}}] = \lambda_d := \bar{\delta}\Big[\mathrm{T}\left[\bar{\delta}[\hat{w}[\hat{\mathcal{G}}]] +^{\mathbb{B}} \left(\bar{\delta}[\hat{w}[\hat{\mathcal{G}}]]\right)^{\mathsf{T}}\right]\Big], \tag{4.68}$$

$$\hat{\lambda}_w : \mathbb{G} \to \mathbb{B} , \hat{\lambda}_w[\hat{\mathcal{G}}] = \lambda_w := \bar{\delta}\Big[\mathrm{T}\left[\hat{w}[\hat{\mathcal{G}}] - \bar{\delta}[\hat{w}[\hat{\mathcal{G}}]]\right]\Big], \tag{4.69}$$

$$\hat{\lambda}_l : \mathbb{G} \to \mathbb{B} , \hat{\lambda}_l[\hat{\mathcal{G}}] = \lambda_l := \bar{\delta}\Big[\mathrm{Tr}\left[\bar{\delta}[\hat{w}[\hat{\mathcal{G}}]]\right]\Big] \tag{4.70}$$

with $\hat{w}[\hat{\mathcal{G}}]$ given by (4.62) defining viable observables which distinguish whether the graph $\mathcal{G}$ represented by $\hat{\mathcal{G}}$ is directed, is weighted or is self-looped, respectively. Interestingly, yet not surprisingly, these operators dispose of the necessity of evaluating the conditional statements which define their associated classical measures (see Section 2.2.1 and Table 2.1). Thus, they can be readily utilised not only for the characterisation of graphs on a more formal algebraic level but also, and more importantly, for expressing other graph measures which rely on similar conditional statements.

A classic example of the latter type is given by the number of edges (2.15) in a graph, as this measure is defined differently for undirected and directed graphs. Using (4.68), a realisation of the graph observable which delivers a graph's number of edges is furnished by

$$\begin{aligned} &\hat{N}_e : \mathbb{G} \to \mathbb{N}_0, \\ &\hat{N}_e[\hat{\mathcal{G}}] = N_e := \frac{1}{2}\Big(1 + \bar{\delta}\Big[\mathrm{T}\left[\bar{\delta}[\hat{w}[\hat{\mathcal{G}}]] +^{\mathbb{B}} \left(\bar{\delta}[\hat{w}[\hat{\mathcal{G}}]]\right)^{\mathsf{T}}\right]\Big]\Big)\hat{A}[\hat{\mathcal{G}}] \end{aligned} \tag{4.71}$$

and applies to suitable operator representations of both undirected and directed weighted graphs irrespective of the presence of self-loops. However, it must be stressed that operators (4.65) and (4.68)–(4.71) represent graph observables of classical measures as functions of a graph's weight matrix and, thus, will generally not apply correctly to graphs with multiple weighted edges connecting distinct nodes or graphs with multiple self-loops. For instance, in the case a given node establishing two adjacency relations of opposite weight to the same target, the corresponding element in the weight matrix will be zero despite the presence of two edges. An appropriately constructed operator graph representation will certainly allow for correct treatment of such a pathological case or, for that matter, other similar eventualities, but at the expense of a necessary adaptation of the considered measure and its associated observable to the specific graph being assessed.

We leave the exciting and often challenging search for such adaptations, and the algebraic formalisation of graph observables for other graph measures introduced in Section 2.2, as a creative exercise to the interested reader. In Part II, we will present and evaluate some of these graph observables, but we also will encounter a number of new observables which are associated with measures that address a variety of specific applied graph-theoretical problems. We already met two such special measures earlier in this chapter during our investigative exploration of the Königsberg bridge problem. The first, defined in (4.14), delivers the number of all possible Eulerian walks of fixed length between two given nodes in not self-looped undirected finite multigraphs $\mathcal{G}$ for operator representations $\hat{\mathcal{G}}$ in which each edge operator of $\hat{\mathcal{E}}_{cl}$ is given by a Boolean matrix with exactly one non-zero element. Inspired by this result, but restricting ourselves to Eulerian walks with a length equal to the number of edges N_e of $\mathcal{G}$, we can then easily formalise a graph observable

$$\hat{N}^{\mathcal{P}} : \mathbb{G} \to \mathbb{N}_0,$$
$$\hat{N}^{\mathcal{P}}[\hat{\mathcal{G}}] = \sum_{i,j \in \mathcal{N}} \bar{N}^{\mathcal{W}}_{N_e}(i,j) := \mathrm{T}\left[\sum_{\mathfrak{n} \in \hat{\mathcal{N}}_{cl}} \mathfrak{n} \cdot \left(\sum_{\mathfrak{s} \in \mathfrak{S}(\hat{\mathcal{E}}_{cl})} \prod_{\mathfrak{E} \in \mathfrak{s}} \mathfrak{E} \right) \right], \tag{4.72}$$

which delivers the total number of Eulerian paths in a finite directed multigraph. In this expression, the second sum runs over all $|\hat{\mathcal{E}}_{cl}|!$ permutations of elements in the set of edge operators, and the product denotes right-hand matrix multiplication over all edge operators in each such N_e-permutation.

For the second special graph measure (4.28) we encountered in this chapter, a viable observable can be conceived in a similar fashion. Indeed, given an operator representation $\hat{\mathcal{G}}$ of a not self-looped undirected multigraph $\mathcal{G} \in \mathbb{G}$ in which each edge operator is represented as a Boolean vector marking two connected nodes such that for all $\mathfrak{E} \in \hat{\mathcal{E}}_{cl} : \mathrm{T}[\mathfrak{E}] = 2$, the observable

$$\hat{\lambda}_{ew} : \mathbb{G} \to 2\mathbb{N}_0 \, , \; \hat{\lambda}_{ew}[\hat{\mathcal{G}}] = \lambda_{ew} := \mathrm{T}\left[\sum_{\mathfrak{E} \in \hat{\mathcal{E}}_{cl}}^{\mathbb{B}} \mathfrak{E} \right] \tag{4.73}$$

delineates whether an Eulerian path or cycle can exist at all in $\mathcal{G}$. We stress here again that the algebraic form of each such graph observable necessarily depends on chosen operator representation of a graph and, thus, is specific to a given representation of a graph's set of nodes and set of edge operators. In this chapter, we primarily employed representations in which nodes are vectors in subsets of a Boolean vector space, and edge operators are formalised either in terms of matrices or vectors forming subsets of vector spaces over $\mathbb{B}$ or $\mathbb{Q}$. Both of these algebraic representations will continue to play an important role in the applications presented in Part II of this book and, thus, will remain the primary focus of our presentation.

4.5 Generating Operator Graphs

In Section 4.3, we explored numerous transformations between operator representations of finite graphs, many of which resulted in the generation of transforms that describe classically distinct graphs. The arguably most taunting example of such an operator graph transformation led to the generation of directed Erdős–Rényi random multigraphs from ring digraphs, and thus the algebraically formalised transformation of an exact graph model into realisations of a random graph model. Viewed from a general perspective, this transformation is then no longer a simple mapping between graphs of the same type, but indeed can be construed as a generator of a new type of graphs. Unfortunately, Definition 4.3 also puts stringent limitations into place regarding the specific properties of the graphs, the principal graph types or the graph models which can be generated. More importantly, given these limitations, the conception of operator graph transformations in which both source and target nodes of edge-generating operators are altered typically requires exorbitant care in order to confine the type of graphs being generated, especially in cases where random graphs are concerned. The operator (4.60), for example, maps a relational digraph into a realisation of an Erdős–Rényi random digraph model which, in general, will also be a multigraph. Although with a simple modification, which we leave as exercise for the reader, the generation of multiple directed edges in this example can be prevented and, thus, the graph type can be preserved, the algebraic formalisation of operator graph transformations which target specific graph types or models, or deliver particular graph characteristics, is often challenging or outright impossible.

Departing from the tightly knit notion of an operator graph transformation, however, some of the challenges and complications accompanying the generation of graphs can be alleviated by considering more general mappings between the sets of nodes and edge operators which comprise their operator representations. As we recall that in each such representation, only the subsets $\hat{\mathcal{N}}_{cl} \subset \hat{\mathcal{N}}$ and $\hat{\mathcal{E}}_{cl} \subseteq \hat{\mathcal{E}}$ of nodes and edge-generating operators are directly linked to a graph's classical description, these more general mappings should, or ideally must, include operations which add nodes and edge operators to and remove nodes and edge operators from their respective classical subsets. In order to accommodate such a demand, let us formulate the following

Definition 4.7 (operator graph generator) Let $\hat{\mathcal{G}} = (\hat{\mathcal{N}}, \hat{\mathcal{E}})$ be an operator representation of a finite graph $\mathcal{G} \in \mathbb{G}$, and $\hat{\mathcal{G}}' = (\hat{\mathcal{N}}', \hat{\mathcal{E}}')$ be that of $\mathcal{G}' \in \mathbb{G}$. An ordered tuple $\hat{\mathfrak{G}} = (\hat{\mathfrak{G}}_{\mathcal{N}}, \hat{\mathfrak{G}}_{\mathcal{E}})$ of operators is called an *operator graph generator*

$$\hat{\mathfrak{G}} \colon \mathbb{G} \to \mathbb{G}\,,\; \hat{\mathfrak{G}}[\hat{\mathcal{G}}] = \hat{\mathcal{G}}'$$

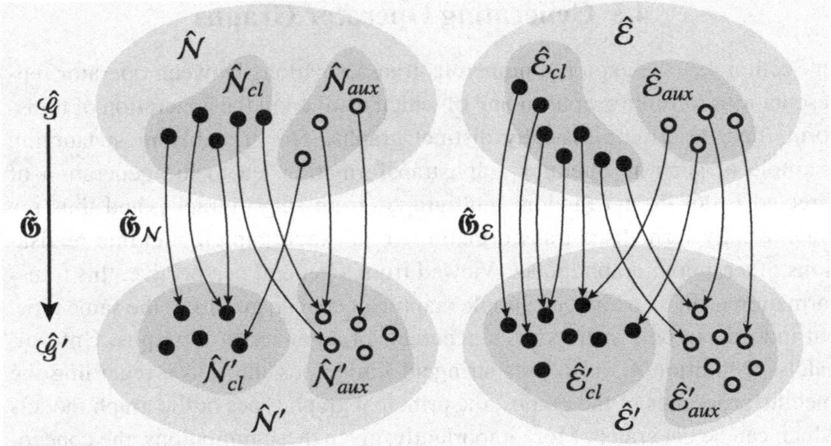

Figure 4.12 Generation of an operator representation $\hat{\mathcal{G}}' = (\hat{\mathcal{N}}',\hat{\mathcal{E}}')$ of a finite graph $\mathcal{G}'$ from an operator representation $\hat{\mathcal{G}} = (\hat{\mathcal{N}},\hat{\mathcal{E}})$ of a finite graph $\mathcal{G}$ using an operator graph generator $\hat{\mathfrak{G}} = (\hat{\mathfrak{G}}_{\mathcal{N}},\hat{\mathfrak{G}}_{\mathcal{E}})$.

if both $\hat{\mathfrak{G}}_{\mathcal{N}} : \hat{\mathcal{N}} \to \hat{\mathcal{N}}'$ and $\hat{\mathfrak{G}}_{\mathcal{E}} : \hat{\mathcal{E}} \to \hat{\mathcal{E}}'$ are surjective mappings such that

$$n \in \hat{\mathcal{N}} \Rightarrow \hat{\mathfrak{G}}_{\mathcal{N}}[n] \in \hat{\mathcal{N}}',$$
$$\mathfrak{E} \in \hat{\mathcal{E}} \Rightarrow \hat{\mathfrak{G}}_{\mathcal{E}}[\mathfrak{E}] \in \hat{\mathcal{E}}'.$$

The operator representation $\hat{\mathcal{G}}$ is called the *operator graph seed*, or simply *seed*, of the operator representation $\hat{\mathcal{G}}'$.

Not unlike the notion of an operator representation of a graph, the scope of an operator graph generator that we introduced with this definition is extremely broad. It certainly includes as special cases all mappings that serve as transformations, isomorphisms or identities between operator representations of two finite graphs if we restrict $\hat{\mathfrak{G}}_{\mathcal{N}}$ to act as a bijection between $\hat{\mathcal{N}}_{cl}$ and $\hat{\mathcal{N}}'_{cl}$, and $\hat{\mathfrak{G}}_{\mathcal{E}}$ to act as a bijection between $\hat{\mathcal{E}}_{cl}$ and $\hat{\mathcal{E}}'_{cl}$. However, as shown in Fig. 4.12, by weakening this assumption of a bijective relationship between the classical subsets of nodes and edge-generating operators of $\hat{\mathcal{G}}$ and $\hat{\mathcal{G}}'$, the notion of an operator graph generator naturally also covers, at least at the conceptional level, the computational and algebraic realisations of graph-generating algorithms which will allow for the modification of finite sets of objects and their respective relations as a whole, beyond their individual elements.

Let us illustrate this important generalisation by recalling the graph mapping (4.60) as an example. Here, realisations of a specific random graph model were obtained by simply rewiring the edges in a given ring graph through a transformation of the elements of $\hat{\mathcal{E}}_{cl}$. If instead we considered the probabilistic removal of edges in a complete graph through the mapping of edge-generating operators of $\hat{\mathcal{E}}_{cl}$ into the auxiliary set $\hat{\mathcal{E}}_{aux}$, the addition of edges to a fully disconnected graph comprised solely of isolated nodes through the mapping of edge operators from $\hat{\mathcal{E}}_{aux}$ to $\hat{\mathcal{E}}_{cl}$, or a combination of both of these mappings in a ring graph and its graph complement, the generated graphs would not only be realisations of directed random multigraphs, but would respectively include viable realisations of the Gilbert, Erdős–Rényi, or Watts–Strogatz random graph models (see Section 2.3 and Figs. 2.9 and 2.10). In a similar fashion, the very definition of scale-free random graphs in form of the Barabási–Albert model (see Section 2.3.7 and Fig. 2.11) relies on the process of growth and preferential attachment, which itself could be realised by assigning nodes and edge operators from $\hat{\mathcal{N}}_{aux}$ and $\hat{\mathcal{E}}_{aux}$ to the respective subsets $\hat{\mathcal{N}}_{cl}$ and $\hat{\mathcal{E}}_{cl}$ that define the classical representation of a graph. With this, the notion of an operator graph generator in Definition 4.7 then not only covers conceptually all important algorithms that are commonly employed in the computational realisation of various prominent random graph models, but indeed provides a solid foundation on which to algebraically formalise such algorithms.

In order to arrive at such a formalisation, however, we must widen our perspective somewhat on the notion of an operator representation of a graph and make full use of its flexibility. So far, we primarily utilised only minimal representations whose sets of nodes $\hat{\mathcal{N}} = \hat{\mathcal{N}}_{cl} \cup \{\boldsymbol{n}_0\}$ and edge-generating operators $\mathcal{E} = \hat{\mathcal{E}}_{cl}$ were explicitly constructed to describe only a given classical graph $\mathscr{G}$ with its fixed sets of nodes and edges. Let us now consider

$$\begin{aligned} \hat{\mathcal{N}}^{\mathscr{G}} &= \left\{\boldsymbol{n}_0 := \boldsymbol{0}^N \,,\, \boldsymbol{n}_i := \boldsymbol{\delta}_i^N : i \in [1,N]\right\} \subseteq \mathbb{B}^N, \\ \hat{\mathcal{E}}^{\mathscr{G}} &= \left\{\mathfrak{E}_j := \boldsymbol{\delta}^{N\times N}_{1+\lfloor (j+\lfloor (j-1)/N \rfloor)/N \rfloor, 1+(j+\lfloor (j-1)/N \rfloor) \bmod N} : j \in [1, N(N-1)]\right\} \subseteq \mathbb{B}^{N\times N} \end{aligned} \tag{4.74}$$

as a set of nodes and set of edge operators in sufficiently large vector spaces $\mathbb{B}^N$ and $\mathbb{B}^{N\times N}$ over $\mathbb{B}$, respectively, and implicitly define for $n \leq N$ the subsets

$$\begin{aligned} \hat{\mathcal{N}}^{\mathscr{G}}_{cl} &:= \left\{\boldsymbol{n}_i \in \hat{\mathcal{N}}^{\mathscr{G}} : i \in [1,n]\right\}, \hat{\mathcal{N}}^{\mathscr{G}}_{aux} := \hat{\mathcal{N}}^{\mathscr{G}} \setminus \hat{\mathcal{N}}^{\mathscr{G}}_{cl}, \\ \hat{\mathcal{E}}^{\mathscr{G}}_{cl} &:= \left\{\mathfrak{E} \in \hat{\mathcal{E}}^{\mathscr{G}} : \exists!\, \boldsymbol{n} \in \hat{\mathcal{N}}^{\mathscr{G}}_{cl}, \mathfrak{E}[\boldsymbol{n}] \in \hat{\mathcal{N}}^{\mathscr{G}}_{cl}\right\}, \hat{\mathcal{E}}^{\mathscr{G}}_{aux} := \hat{\mathcal{E}}^{\mathscr{G}} \setminus \hat{\mathcal{E}}^{\mathscr{G}}_{cl} \end{aligned} \tag{4.75}$$

such that $\hat{\mathscr{G}} = (\hat{\mathcal{N}}^{\mathscr{G}}_{cl} \cup \hat{\mathcal{N}}^{\mathscr{G}}_{aux}, \hat{\mathcal{E}}^{\mathscr{G}}_{cl} \cup \hat{\mathcal{E}}^{\mathscr{G}}_{aux})$ comprises an operator representation of a not self-looped digraph $\mathscr{G}$ of order $1 \leq n \leq N$. With (4.74) and (4.75), it can easily be shown that the nodes of $\mathscr{G}$ are represented by elements of $\hat{\mathcal{N}}^{\mathscr{G}}$ which span an n-dimensional subspace $\mathbb{B}^n \subseteq \mathbb{B}^N$, and that each element of $\hat{\mathcal{E}}^{\mathscr{G}}$ which acts as an operator over this subspace describes a specific directed edge of $\mathscr{G}$. As (4.74) furthermore ensures that for each ordered pair of distinct nodes $\boldsymbol{n}, \boldsymbol{n}' \in \hat{\mathcal{N}}^{\mathscr{G}} : \boldsymbol{n}, \boldsymbol{n}' \neq \boldsymbol{n}_0$, there is exactly one edge operator $\mathfrak{E} \in \hat{\mathcal{E}}^{\mathscr{G}}$

with $\boldsymbol{n}' = \mathfrak{E}[\boldsymbol{n}]$, the tuple $\hat{\mathcal{G}}$ naturally provides an operator representation of a complete relational digraph $\mathcal{K}_n^d$ of order $n \geq 1$ which we will denote by $\hat{\mathcal{K}}_n^d$. In a similar fashion, for $n = 0$, the subsets in (4.75) also define with

$$\begin{aligned} \hat{\mathcal{N}}_{cl}^{\mathcal{K}_0^d} &:= \left\{\boldsymbol{n}_0 \in \hat{\mathcal{N}}^{\mathcal{G}}\right\}, \ \hat{\mathcal{N}}_{aux}^{\mathcal{K}_0^d} := \hat{\mathcal{N}}^{\mathcal{G}} \setminus \hat{\mathcal{N}}_{cl}^{\mathcal{G}}, \\ \hat{\mathcal{E}}_{cl}^{\mathcal{K}_0^d} &:= \emptyset, \ \hat{\mathcal{E}}_{aux}^{\mathcal{K}_0^d} := \hat{\mathcal{E}}^{\mathcal{G}} \setminus \hat{\mathcal{E}}_{cl}^{\mathcal{G}} = \hat{\mathcal{E}}^{\mathcal{G}} \end{aligned} \tag{4.76}$$

an operator representation $\hat{\mathcal{K}}_0^d = (\hat{\mathcal{N}}_{cl}^{\mathcal{K}_0^d} \cup \hat{\mathcal{N}}_{aux}^{\mathcal{K}_0^d}, \hat{\mathcal{E}}_{cl}^{\mathcal{K}_0^d} \cup \hat{\mathcal{E}}_{aux}^{\mathcal{K}_0^d})$ of what we will for presentational purposes refer to as *null-digraph* and denote by $\mathcal{K}_0^d$.

The complete set $\hat{\mathcal{E}}^{\mathcal{K}_n^d} = \hat{\mathcal{E}}_{cl}^{\mathcal{K}_n^d} \cup \hat{\mathcal{E}}_{aux}^{\mathcal{K}_n^d}$ of edge operators in each representation $\hat{\mathcal{K}}_n^d$ for $2 \leq n \leq N$ contains all mappings between pairs of distinct nodes in $\hat{\mathcal{N}}^{\mathcal{K}_n^d} \setminus \{\boldsymbol{n}_0\} = (\hat{\mathcal{N}}_{cl}^{\mathcal{K}_n^d} \cup \hat{\mathcal{N}}_{aux}^{\mathcal{K}_n^d}) \setminus \{\boldsymbol{n}_0\}$, and for $\hat{\mathcal{K}}_n^d$ with $n \in \{0, 1\}$, no elements at all. With an eye on Definition 4.7, it is then certainly possible to conceive of two surjective mappings $\hat{\mathfrak{G}}_{\mathcal{N}}: \hat{\mathcal{N}}^{\mathcal{K}_n^d} \to \hat{\mathcal{N}}^{\mathcal{G}'}$ and $\hat{\mathfrak{G}}_{\mathcal{E}}: \hat{\mathcal{E}}^{\mathcal{K}_n^d} \to \hat{\mathcal{E}}^{\mathcal{G}'}$ in order to respectively generate the set $\hat{\mathcal{N}}^{\mathcal{G}'}$ of nodes and set $\hat{\mathcal{E}}^{\mathcal{G}'}$ of edge operators of an operator representation $\hat{\mathcal{G}}' = (\hat{\mathcal{N}}^{\mathcal{G}}, \hat{\mathcal{E}}^{\mathcal{G}})$, and to tailor both of these mappings such that, through subsequent utilisation of an implicit definition not unlike (4.75), only specific nodes and edge-generating operators appear in the classical subsets $\hat{\mathcal{N}}_{cl}^{\mathcal{G}'}$ and $\hat{\mathcal{E}}_{cl}^{\mathcal{G}'}$ of $\hat{\mathcal{G}}'$. Indeed, as $\hat{\mathcal{K}}_n^d$ represents all possible edges between distinct pairs of nodes in a graph of order n, any desired relational structure between n nodes can eventually be generated if $\hat{\mathfrak{G}}_{\mathcal{E}}$ maps only a specific subset of edges of its seed graph into $\hat{\mathcal{E}}_{cl}^{\mathcal{G}'}$, an approach which reflects the fact that all conceivable not self-looped relational digraphs can be constructed by simply removing edges from a complete relational digraph of the same order. Moreover, as $\hat{\mathcal{K}}_n^d$ for all $0 \leq n \leq N$ by definition share the same set of nodes, the addition of nodes to, or the removal of nodes from, $\hat{\mathcal{N}}_{cl}^{\mathcal{K}_n^d}$ through $\hat{\mathfrak{G}}_{\mathcal{N}}$ naturally provides the basis for the generation of operator representations of graphs $\mathcal{G}'$ with any desired order smaller than or equal to N. With the combination of both of these actions on the set of nodes and edge operators of $\hat{\mathcal{K}}_n^d$, we then have all the necessary algebraic tools at our disposal to eventually generate arbitrary relational digraphs by means of suitable operator graph generators $\hat{\mathfrak{G}} = (\hat{\mathfrak{G}}_{\mathcal{N}}, \hat{\mathfrak{G}}_{\mathcal{E}})$ from complete relational digraphs and null-digraphs.

Let us illustrate the flexibility of this approach with a few simple examples. As shown in Fig. 4.13 (left), the application of the operator graph generator

$$\hat{\mathfrak{G}} = \left(\hat{\mathfrak{G}}_{\mathcal{N}}: \hat{\mathfrak{G}}_{\mathcal{N}}[\boldsymbol{n}] := \boldsymbol{n} \cdot \delta_{1,1}^{N\times 1}, \ \hat{\mathfrak{G}}_{\mathcal{E}}: \hat{\mathfrak{G}}_{\mathcal{E}}[\mathfrak{E}] := \boldsymbol{0}^N \cdot \mathfrak{E} \cdot \boldsymbol{0}^{N\mathsf{T}}\right) \tag{4.77}$$

to the seed $\hat{\mathcal{K}}_N^d$ delivers $\hat{\mathfrak{G}}[\hat{\mathcal{K}}_N^d] = \hat{\mathcal{K}}_1$ with

$$\hat{\mathcal{N}}_{cl}^{\mathcal{K}_1} = \left\{\boldsymbol{n}_1 := \delta_1^1 = 1\right\} \subset \mathbb{B}, \ \hat{\mathcal{N}}_{aux}^{\mathcal{K}_1} = \left\{\boldsymbol{n}_0 := 0, \boldsymbol{n}_i := 0 : i \in [2, N]\right\} \subset \mathbb{B}$$

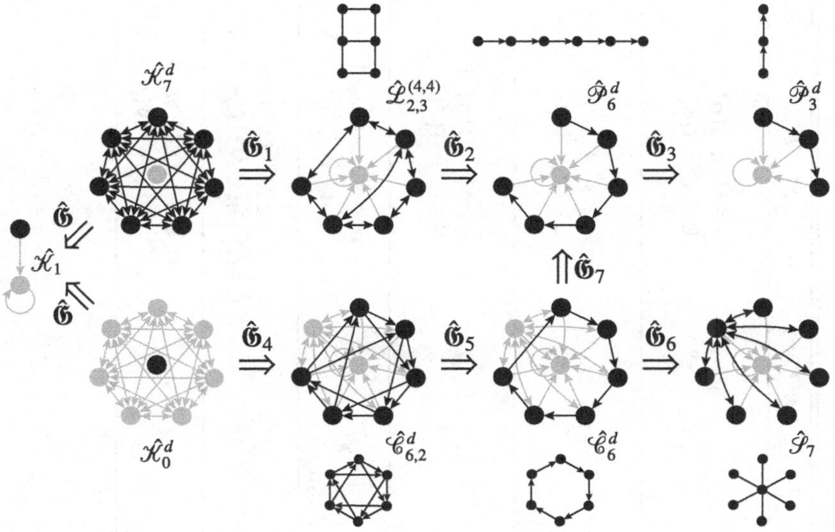

Figure 4.13 Examples of operator graph generators. Starting from an operator representation $\hat{\mathcal{K}}_7^d$ of the complete relational digraph $\mathcal{K}_7^d$ or the null-digraph $\hat{\mathcal{K}}_0^d$ as seeds, operator representations of various realisations of exact graph models can be generated. Illustrated are the generation of representations of the ladder graph $\mathcal{L}_{2,3}^{(4,4)}$ (domino graph), the path digraphs $\mathcal{P}_3^d$ and $\mathcal{P}_6^d$, the ring digraph $\mathcal{C}_{6,2}^d$, cycle digraph $\mathcal{C}_6^d$ and the undirected star graph $\mathcal{S}_7$ by means of the operator graph generator (4.77) and the generators listed in Table 4.10 for $N = 7$. In all cases, the complete operator representations of the associated classical graphs (insets) are shown, with black marking nodes and edge operators in $\hat{N}_{cl}$ and $\hat{\mathcal{E}}_{cl}$, and grey marking nodes and edge operators comprising $\hat{N}_{aux}$ and $\hat{\mathcal{E}}_{aux}$ respectively.

and

$$\hat{\mathcal{E}}_{cl}^{\mathcal{K}_1} = \emptyset\,,\; \hat{\mathcal{E}}_{aux}^{\mathcal{K}_1} = \left\{\mathfrak{E}_j := 0\colon\, j \in [1, N(N-1)]\right\} \subset \mathbb{B}$$

as a viable operator representation that describes, classically, the *trivial graph* $\mathcal{K}_1$ comprised of a single isolated node and no adjacency relations. The action of $\hat{\mathfrak{G}}$ thus formalises the removal of $N-1$ nodes and all edges from a complete digraph $\mathcal{K}_N^d$ of order N. Unsurprisingly, the same representation $\hat{\mathcal{K}}_1$ can also be obtained through the application of the generator (4.77) to the operator representation $\hat{\mathcal{K}}_0^d$ of the null-digraph. In this case, the generator $\hat{\mathfrak{G}}$ acts by removing node n_0 from $\hat{N}_{cl}^{\mathcal{K}_0^d}$ and by adding node n_1 in $\hat{N}_{aux}^{\mathcal{K}_0^d}$ to $\hat{N}_{cl}^{\mathcal{K}_1}$, after having mapped each node of the seed graph into the vector space $\mathbb{B}$.

Certainly, these actions of our generator $\hat{\mathfrak{G}}$ are not very enticing in the sense that the generated representation, irrespective of seed, describes in terms of structure a rather trivial classical graph. In order to provide a somewhat more

Table 4.10 *Examples of operator graph generators.*

Operator graph generator $\hat{\mathfrak{G}}$	$\hat{\mathcal{G}}$	$\hat{\mathfrak{G}}[\hat{\mathcal{G}}]=\hat{\mathcal{G}}'$	$\hat{\mathcal{N}}_{cl}^{\mathcal{G}'}, \hat{\mathcal{E}}_{cl}^{\mathcal{G}'}$
$\hat{\mathfrak{G}}_1 = \left(\hat{\mathfrak{G}}_{\mathcal{N}} : \hat{\mathfrak{G}}_{\mathcal{E}}[\boldsymbol{n}] := \boldsymbol{n} \cdot \boldsymbol{M} \, , \, \hat{\mathfrak{G}}_{\mathcal{E}} : \hat{\mathfrak{G}}_{\mathcal{E}}[\boldsymbol{\mathfrak{E}}] := (\boldsymbol{M})^{\mathsf{T}} \cdot (\boldsymbol{\mathfrak{E}} \odot^{\mathbb{B}} \boldsymbol{M}') \cdot \boldsymbol{M}\right), \, 2m \leq N$ $\boldsymbol{M} := \sum_{i=1}^{2m} \boldsymbol{\delta}_{i,i}^{N\times 2m}$ $\boldsymbol{M}' := \sum_{i=1}^{m-1} (\boldsymbol{\delta}_{i,i+1}^{N\times N} + \boldsymbol{\delta}_{i+1,i}^{N\times N} + \boldsymbol{\delta}_{i+m,i+m+1}^{N\times N} + \boldsymbol{\delta}_{i+m+1,i+m}^{N\times N}) + \sum_{i=1}^{m} (\boldsymbol{\delta}_{i,2m-i+1}^{N\times N} + \boldsymbol{\delta}_{2m-i+1,i}^{N\times N})$	$\hat{\mathcal{K}}_N^d$	$\hat{\mathcal{L}}_{2,m}^{(4,4)}$	$\boldsymbol{n} \in \hat{\mathcal{N}}^{\mathcal{G}'} : \mathrm{T}[\boldsymbol{n}]=1$ $\boldsymbol{\mathfrak{E}} \in \hat{\mathcal{E}}^{\mathcal{G}'} : \mathrm{T}[\boldsymbol{\mathfrak{E}}]=1$
$\hat{\mathfrak{G}}_2 = \left(\hat{\mathfrak{G}}_{\mathcal{N}} : \hat{\mathfrak{G}}_{\mathcal{E}}[\boldsymbol{n}] := \boldsymbol{n} \cdot \boldsymbol{M} \, , \, \hat{\mathfrak{G}}_{\mathcal{E}} : \hat{\mathfrak{G}}_{\mathcal{E}}[\boldsymbol{\mathfrak{E}}] := (\boldsymbol{M})^{\mathsf{T}} \cdot (\boldsymbol{\mathfrak{E}} \odot^{\mathbb{B}} \boldsymbol{M}') \cdot \boldsymbol{M}\right)$ $\boldsymbol{M} := \sum_{i=1}^{2m} \boldsymbol{\delta}_{i,i}^{2m\times 2m}$ $\boldsymbol{M}' := \sum_{i=1}^{2m-1} \boldsymbol{\delta}_{i,i+1}^{2m\times 2m}$	$\hat{\mathcal{L}}_{2,m}^{(4,4)}$	$\hat{\mathcal{P}}_{2m}^d$	$\boldsymbol{n} \in \hat{\mathcal{N}}^{\mathcal{G}'} : \mathrm{T}[\boldsymbol{n}]=1$ $\boldsymbol{\mathfrak{E}} \in \hat{\mathcal{E}}^{\mathcal{G}'} : \mathrm{T}[\boldsymbol{\mathfrak{E}}]=1$
$\hat{\mathfrak{G}}_3 = \left(\hat{\mathfrak{G}}_{\mathcal{N}} : \hat{\mathfrak{G}}_{\mathcal{E}}[\boldsymbol{n}] := \boldsymbol{n} \cdot \boldsymbol{M} \, , \, \hat{\mathfrak{G}}_{\mathcal{E}} : \hat{\mathfrak{G}}_{\mathcal{E}}[\boldsymbol{\mathfrak{E}}] := (\boldsymbol{M})^{\mathsf{T}} \cdot (\boldsymbol{\mathfrak{E}} \odot^{\mathbb{B}} \boldsymbol{M}') \cdot \boldsymbol{M}\right)$ $\boldsymbol{M} := \sum_{i=1}^{m} \boldsymbol{\delta}_{i,i}^{2m\times m}$ $\boldsymbol{M}' := \sum_{i=1}^{m-1} \boldsymbol{\delta}_{i,i+1}^{2m\times 2m}$	$\hat{\mathcal{P}}_{2m}^d$	$\hat{\mathcal{P}}_{m}^d$	$\boldsymbol{n} \in \hat{\mathcal{N}}^{\mathcal{G}'} : \mathrm{T}[\boldsymbol{n}]=1$ $\boldsymbol{\mathfrak{E}} \in \hat{\mathcal{E}}^{\mathcal{G}'} : \mathrm{T}[\boldsymbol{\mathfrak{E}}]=1$
$\hat{\mathfrak{G}}_4 = \left(\hat{\mathfrak{G}}_{\mathcal{N}} := \mathrm{id} \, , \, \hat{\mathfrak{G}}_{\mathcal{E}} : \hat{\mathfrak{G}}_{\mathcal{E}}[\boldsymbol{\mathfrak{E}}] := \boldsymbol{\mathfrak{E}} \odot^{\mathbb{B}} \boldsymbol{M}'\right), \, m < N \, , \, k \leq \lfloor \frac{m-1}{2} \rfloor$ $\boldsymbol{M}' := \boldsymbol{1}^{N\times N} - (\sum_{i=1}^{m} \boldsymbol{\delta}_{i,i}^{N\times N})^{\mathsf{T}} \cdot \boldsymbol{1}^{N\times N} \cdot (\sum_{i=1}^{m} \boldsymbol{\delta}_{i,i}^{N\times N}) - \sum_{i=m+1}^{N} \boldsymbol{\delta}_{i,i}^{N\times N} + \sum_{i=1}^{m} \sum_{l=1}^{k} \boldsymbol{\delta}_{i,1+(i+l-1) \bmod m}^{N\times N}$	$\hat{\mathcal{K}}_0^d$	$\hat{\mathcal{C}}_{m,k}^d$	$\boldsymbol{n}_i \in \hat{\mathcal{N}}^{\mathcal{G}'} : i \in [1,m]$ $\boldsymbol{\mathfrak{E}} \in \hat{\mathcal{E}}^{\mathcal{G}'} : \exists \boldsymbol{n} \in \hat{\mathcal{N}}_{cl}^{\mathcal{G}'}, \boldsymbol{\mathfrak{E}}[\boldsymbol{n}] \in \hat{\mathcal{N}}_{cl}^{\mathcal{G}'}$
$\hat{\mathfrak{G}}_5 = \left(\hat{\mathfrak{G}}_{\mathcal{N}} := \mathrm{id} \, , \, \hat{\mathfrak{G}}_{\mathcal{E}} : \hat{\mathfrak{G}}_{\mathcal{E}}[\boldsymbol{\mathfrak{E}}] := \boldsymbol{\mathfrak{E}} \odot^{\mathbb{B}} \boldsymbol{M}'\right), \, m < N \, , \, k \leq \lfloor \frac{m-1}{2} \rfloor$ $\boldsymbol{M}' := \boldsymbol{1}^{N\times N} - (\sum_{i=1}^{m} \boldsymbol{\delta}_{i,i}^{N\times N})^{\mathsf{T}} \cdot \boldsymbol{1}^{N\times N} \cdot (\sum_{i=1}^{m} \boldsymbol{\delta}_{i,i}^{N\times N}) - \sum_{i=m+1}^{N} \boldsymbol{\delta}_{i,i}^{N\times N} + \sum_{i=1}^{m} \sum_{l=1}^{k} \boldsymbol{\delta}_{i,i \bmod m}^{N\times N}$	$\hat{\mathcal{C}}_{m,k}^d$	$\hat{\mathcal{C}}_{m}^d$	$\boldsymbol{n}_i \in \hat{\mathcal{N}}^{\mathcal{G}'} : i \in [1,m]$ $\boldsymbol{\mathfrak{E}} \in \hat{\mathcal{E}}^{\mathcal{G}'} : \exists \boldsymbol{n} \in \hat{\mathcal{N}}_{cl}^{\mathcal{G}'}, \boldsymbol{\mathfrak{E}}[\boldsymbol{n}] \in \hat{\mathcal{N}}_{cl}^{\mathcal{G}'}$
$\hat{\mathfrak{G}}_6 = \left(\hat{\mathfrak{G}}_{\mathcal{N}} := \mathrm{id} \, , \, \hat{\mathfrak{G}}_{\mathcal{E}} : \hat{\mathfrak{G}}_{\mathcal{E}}[\boldsymbol{\mathfrak{E}}] := \boldsymbol{\mathfrak{E}} \odot^{\mathbb{B}} \boldsymbol{M}'\right), \, m < N$ $\boldsymbol{M}' := \sum_{i=1}^{m} (\boldsymbol{\delta}_{m,i}^{N\times N} + \boldsymbol{\delta}_{i,m}^{N\times N})$	$\hat{\mathcal{C}}_{m}^d$	$\hat{\mathcal{S}}_{m+1}$	$\boldsymbol{n}_i \in \hat{\mathcal{N}}^{\mathcal{G}'} : i \in [1,m+1],$ $\boldsymbol{\mathfrak{E}} \in \hat{\mathcal{E}}^{\mathcal{G}'} : \exists \boldsymbol{n} \in \hat{\mathcal{N}}_{cl}^{\mathcal{G}'}, \boldsymbol{\mathfrak{E}}[\boldsymbol{n}] \in \hat{\mathcal{N}}_{cl}^{\mathcal{G}'}$
$\hat{\mathfrak{G}}_7 = \left(\hat{\mathfrak{G}}_{\mathcal{N}} : \hat{\mathfrak{G}}_{\mathcal{E}}[\boldsymbol{n}] := \boldsymbol{n} \cdot \boldsymbol{M} \, , \, \hat{\mathfrak{G}}_{\mathcal{E}} : \hat{\mathfrak{G}}_{\mathcal{E}}[\boldsymbol{\mathfrak{E}}] := (\boldsymbol{M})^{\mathsf{T}} \cdot (\boldsymbol{\mathfrak{E}} \odot^{\mathbb{B}} \boldsymbol{M}') \cdot \boldsymbol{M}\right), \, m \leq N$ $\boldsymbol{M} := \sum_{i=1}^{m} \boldsymbol{\delta}_{i,i}^{N\times m}$ $\boldsymbol{M}' := \sum_{i=1}^{m-1} \boldsymbol{\delta}_{i,i+1}^{N\times N}$	$\hat{\mathcal{C}}_{m}^d$	$\hat{\mathcal{P}}_{m}^d$	$\boldsymbol{n} \in \hat{\mathcal{N}}^{\mathcal{G}'} : \mathrm{T}[\boldsymbol{n}]=1$ $\boldsymbol{\mathfrak{E}} \in \hat{\mathcal{E}}^{\mathcal{G}'} : \mathrm{T}[\boldsymbol{\mathfrak{E}}]=1$

interesting example, let us now consider the generator $\hat{\mathfrak{G}}_1$ defined in Table 4.10. As illustrated in Fig. 4.13, this operator formalises the construction of an undirected ladder graph $\mathcal{L}_{2,m}^{(4,4)}$ of order $2m$ from a complete relational digraph $\mathcal{K}_N^d$ of order $N \geq 2m$. It does so by removing $N - 2m$ nodes from the classical subset $\hat{\mathcal{N}}_{cl}^{\mathcal{K}_N^d}$ of $\hat{\mathcal{K}}_N^d$, and by mapping a total of $N(N-1)-6m+4$ edge-generating operators in $\hat{\mathcal{E}}_{cl}^{\mathcal{K}_N^d}$ into $\boldsymbol{0}^{2m\times 2m}$, eventually delivering

$$\begin{aligned} \hat{\mathcal{N}}_{cl}^{\mathcal{L}_{2,m}^{(4,4)}} &:= \left\{\boldsymbol{n} \in \hat{\mathcal{N}}^{\mathcal{L}_{2,m}^{(4,4)}} : \mathrm{T}[\boldsymbol{n}] = 1\right\}, \; \hat{\mathcal{N}}_{aux}^{\mathcal{L}_{2,m}^{(4,4)}} = \left\{\boldsymbol{n} \in \hat{\mathcal{N}}^{\mathcal{L}_{2,m}^{(4,4)}} : \boldsymbol{n} = \boldsymbol{0}^{2m}\right\}, \\ \hat{\mathcal{E}}_{cl}^{\mathcal{L}_{2,m}^{(4,4)}} &:= \left\{\mathfrak{E} \in \hat{\mathcal{E}}^{\mathcal{L}_{2,m}^{(4,4)}} : \mathrm{T}[\mathfrak{E}] = 1\right\}, \; \hat{\mathcal{E}}_{aux}^{\mathcal{L}_{2,m}^{(4,4)}} = \left\{\mathfrak{E} \in \hat{\mathcal{E}}^{\mathcal{L}_{2,m}^{(4,4)}} : \mathfrak{E} = \boldsymbol{0}^{2m\times 2m}\right\} \end{aligned} \tag{4.78}$$

with

$$\begin{aligned} \hat{\mathcal{N}}^{\mathcal{L}_{2,m}^{(4,4)}} &:= \left\{\boldsymbol{n} \cdot \boldsymbol{M} : \boldsymbol{n} \in \hat{\mathcal{N}}^{\mathcal{K}_N^d}\right\}, \\ \hat{\mathcal{E}}^{\mathcal{L}_{2,m}^{(4,4)}} &:= \left\{(\boldsymbol{M})^{\mathsf{T}} \cdot (\mathfrak{E} \odot^{\mathbb{B}} \boldsymbol{M}') \cdot \boldsymbol{M} : \mathfrak{E} \in \hat{\mathcal{E}}^{\mathcal{K}_N^d}\right\} \end{aligned}$$

as sets of nodes and edge operators that constitute a viable operator representation $\hat{\mathcal{L}}_{2,m}^{(4,4)}$ of $\mathcal{L}_{2,m}^{(4,4)}$. It is important to note here that the assignments (4.78) of nodes and edge operators of the generated representation $\hat{\mathcal{L}}_{2,m}^{(4,4)}$ to their respective classical and auxiliary subsets are reminiscent of the implicit definition (4.75), and that these assignments can easily be applied to other generated representations as well. For instance, by using $\mathcal{L}_{2,m}^{(4,4)}$ itself as a seed of a suitable generator, other graphs can be constructed through the removal of some, or all, of the nodes and edge operators which comprise $\hat{\mathcal{L}}_{2,m}^{(4,4)}$. This is exemplified in Fig. 4.13 (top), with the construction of path digraphs $\mathcal{P}_n^d$ through the actions of $\hat{\mathfrak{G}}_2$ and $\hat{\mathfrak{G}}_3$ in Table 4.10 on their respective seeds $\hat{\mathcal{L}}_{2,m}^{(4,4)}$ and $\hat{\mathfrak{G}}_2[\hat{\mathcal{L}}_{2,m}^{(4,4)}] = \hat{\mathcal{P}}_{2m}^d$.

The flexibility of our approach is, however, not yet exhausted by generating new operator representations through the explicit removal of nodes and edge-generating operators from the classical subsets in the generator's seed. Indeed, as already demonstrated with the action of $\hat{\mathfrak{G}}$ in (4.77) on the null-digraph $\hat{\mathcal{K}}_0^d$, it is certainly also possible to formalise the addition of nodes and edge operators to an appropriately defined seed graph through the reassignment of nodes and edge operators from the auxiliary subsets to their respective classical subsets. By employing the implicit definition (4.75), the generator $\hat{\mathfrak{G}}_4$ (Table 4.10), for example, acts by transferring $m \leq N$ nodes from the set of N auxiliary nodes and $mk \leq N(N-1)$ elements from the subset of $N(N-1)$ auxiliary edge operators, and in turn delivers a viable operator representation of a directed ring graph $\mathcal{C}_{m,k}^d$ (Fig. 4.13, bottom). Last but not least, while subsequent application of $\hat{\mathfrak{G}}_5$ to this representation results in a removal of some of the ring graph's edges and, thus, describes the generation of an operator representation of a cycle digraph $\mathcal{C}_m^d$ of order m from a seed $\hat{\mathcal{C}}_{m,k}^d$, the operator $\hat{\mathfrak{G}}_6$

transfers another node from the auxiliary set of nodes of its seed $\hat{\mathfrak{G}}_5[\hat{\mathscr{C}}^d_m]$ and eventually describes the generation of an operator representation of an undirected *star graph* $\mathscr{S}_n$ of order $n = m + 1$.

This small selection of operator graph generators along with their actions should suffice to illustrate the conceptual idea behind the realisation of various exact graph models within our operator graph-theoretical framework, and to demonstrate the algebraic formalisation and flexibility of this approach. The examples provided here certainly present only a few among an infinite number of possibilities for generating operator representations of classical relational digraphs and simple graphs. At first glance, such a construction of graphs by means of operators might appear arguably more challenging with respect to its algebraic formalisation when compared to the direct representation of a desired graph in terms of an adjacency matrix. However its potential benefits will become clearer when dealing with more elaborate graph models, in particular with random graph models for which, as previously noted, representations in terms of adjacency matrices are generally available only for concrete realisations and not for the model class itself. Indeed, each of the operator graph generators exemplified in this section can be more abstractly viewed as acting on a given graph model as a whole. Just as a graph can be operator graph-theoretically represented as a set of operators acting over a set of objects, this more abstract perspective motivates the intriguing idea to view the representation of a graph itself as the result of an operator acting as a generator on a seed graph. In this light, the properties of a graph are then fully determined by the algebraic properties of its generator and seed which, as we will demonstrate in greater detail in Part II, opens up a new dimension for characterising not only individual graphs but their encompassing model classes as a whole.

With such a promising outlook in hand, it is important to stress that the notion of an operator graph generator defined and exemplified in this section is not restricted to relational graphs alone. By considering (4.74) with an appropriately defined set of edge operators in a vector space over $\mathbb{Q}$, for instance, operator representations of arbitrary weighted graphs and digraphs with or without self-loops can be generated from complete weighted digraphs in a fashion similar to the one illustrated above for relational graphs. Moreover, noting that any multiedge comprised of k undirected edges between a given pair of nodes can be generated from a simple tree graph of order $k + 1$ by mapping all of the tree graph's $k - 1$ leave nodes to the same target node, the notion of a graph generator naturally encapsulates undirected and directed multigraphs as well.

In order to exemplify this generalisation of our approach, let us conclude this chapter by exploring the generation of a multigraph from the operator representation (4.75) of the complete relational digraph $\mathscr{K}^d_N$ and, to that end,

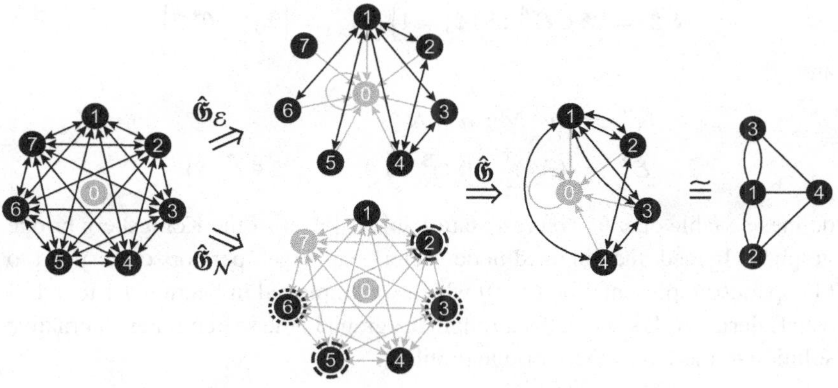

Figure 4.14 Generation of an operator representation of the Königsberg bridge graph. By mapping multiple nodes in the generator's seed to one target node, operator representations of multigraphs can be constructed from suitable relational digraphs. This approach is illustrated here with the generation of the undirected multigraph of Königsberg's bridges from $\hat{\mathscr{K}}_7^d$ by using $\hat{\mathfrak{G}} = (\hat{\mathfrak{G}}_{\mathcal{N}},\hat{\mathfrak{G}}_{\mathcal{E}})$ defined in (4.79) and (4.80).

pay one last deserved tribute to the beautiful Prussian town of Königsberg with its seven bridges across the river Pregel. In the graph of these bridges $\mathscr{G}$ (Fig. 4.14, right), nodes 1 and 2 as well as 1 and 3 are linked by two undirected adjacency relations. Utilising the vector representation (4.75) for nodes of $\hat{\mathscr{K}}_N^d$ and noting that $\mathscr{G}$ is of order 4, both of these undirected multiedges can be constructed by mapping with the matrix operator

$$\begin{aligned} &\hat{\mathfrak{G}}_{\mathcal{N}} \colon \hat{\mathcal{N}}^{\mathscr{K}_N^d} \to \hat{\mathcal{N}}^{\mathscr{G}} \ , \ \hat{\mathfrak{G}}_{\mathcal{N}}[\boldsymbol{n}] := \boldsymbol{n} \cdot \boldsymbol{M}, \\ &\boldsymbol{M} := \sum_{i=1}^{4} \boldsymbol{\delta}_{i,i}^{N\times 4} + \boldsymbol{\delta}_{5,2}^{N\times 4} + \boldsymbol{\delta}_{6,3}^{N\times 4} \end{aligned} \tag{4.79}$$

pairs of nodes $\boldsymbol{n}_2, \boldsymbol{n}_5$ and $\boldsymbol{n}_3, \boldsymbol{n}_6$ in $\hat{\mathcal{N}}^{\mathscr{K}_N^d}, N \geq 6$ to the same target nodes $\boldsymbol{n}_2$ and $\boldsymbol{n}_3$ in $\hat{\mathcal{N}}^{\mathscr{G}}$ (Fig. 4.14, bottom). By then applying

$$\begin{aligned} &\hat{\mathfrak{G}}_{\mathcal{E}} \colon \hat{\mathcal{E}}^{\mathscr{K}_N^d} \to \hat{\mathcal{E}}^{\mathscr{G}} \ , \ \hat{\mathfrak{G}}_{\mathcal{E}}[\mathfrak{E}] := (\boldsymbol{M})^{\mathsf{T}} \cdot (\mathfrak{E} \odot^{\mathbb{B}} \boldsymbol{M}') \cdot \boldsymbol{M}, \\ &\boldsymbol{M}' := \sum_{i=2}^{6} \left(\boldsymbol{\delta}_{1,i}^{N\times N} + \boldsymbol{\delta}_{i,1}^{N\times N} \right) + \sum_{i=2}^{3} \left(\boldsymbol{\delta}_{4,i}^{N\times N} + \boldsymbol{\delta}_{i,4}^{N\times N} \right), \end{aligned} \tag{4.80}$$

all edge operators which do not correspond to adjacency relations in the classical representation of the Königsberg bridge graph are mapped into $\boldsymbol{0}^{4\times 4}$ (see Fig. 4.14, top), and we eventually obtain with $\hat{\mathfrak{G}} = (\hat{\mathfrak{G}}_{\mathcal{N}}, \hat{\mathfrak{G}}_{\mathcal{E}})$ an operator graph generator that with

$$\hat{\mathcal{N}}_{cl}^{\mathscr{G}} := \left\{ \boldsymbol{n} \in \hat{\mathcal{N}}^{\mathscr{G}} : \ \mathrm{T}[\boldsymbol{n}] = 1 \right\}, \ \hat{\mathcal{N}}_{aux}^{\mathscr{G}} = \left\{ \boldsymbol{n}_0 := \boldsymbol{0}^4 \right\},$$

$$\hat{\mathcal{E}}^{\mathcal{G}}_{cl} := \left\{\mathfrak{E} \in \hat{\mathcal{E}}^{\mathcal{G}} : \mathrm{T}[\mathfrak{E}] = 1\right\}, \hat{\mathcal{E}}^{\mathcal{G}}_{aux} = \left\{\mathfrak{E}_0 := 0^{4\times 4}\right\}$$

and

$$\hat{\mathcal{N}}^{\mathcal{G}} := \left\{\boldsymbol{n} \cdot \boldsymbol{M} : \boldsymbol{n} \in \hat{\mathcal{N}}^{\mathcal{K}^d_N}\right\},$$
$$\hat{\mathcal{E}}^{\mathcal{G}} := \left\{(\boldsymbol{M})^{\mathsf{T}} \cdot (\mathfrak{E} \odot^{\mathbb{B}} \boldsymbol{M}') \cdot \boldsymbol{M} : \mathfrak{E} \in \hat{\mathcal{E}}^{\mathcal{K}^d_N}\right\}$$

defines a viable operator representation $\hat{\mathfrak{G}}[\mathcal{K}^d_N] = \hat{\mathcal{G}}$ of the Königsberg bridge graph $\mathcal{G}$. Indeed, the obtained node vectors and edge operators correspond to the operator representation (4.20) which we employed in Section 4.1 to delineate Eulerian walks and paths through this graph in the search for an alternative solution to the Königsberg bridge problem.

With this, we will now finally take our leave from Königsberg, the river Pregel and walks across its seven bridges which formed the first leg of our adventurous journey, and which not only served as the historically important exercise that illustrated the notions, and some of their limitations, at the very heart of classical graph theory, but guided us in the exploration of an alternative, more dynamic take on the idea of a graph as collection of interconnected discrete objects. This journey led us from Euler's seminal insights into what arguably could be asserted as the fundamental architectural premise of physical reality that each system is comprised of discrete interacting constituents, over the sometimes unwieldy waters of the notions and formalisations which constitute classical graph theory, to a wild ride across the treacherous depths of a more operator-inspired perspective, and eventually culminated in the proposition of the notational foundation for a novel, operator graph-theoretical framework. With the concepts of an operator representation and operator graph, we hope to have captured the very essence of the abstract notion of a graph and, with the introduction of operator graph transformations, observables and generators, also its inherently dynamic nature. We deliberately abstained here from a more rigorous mathematical presentation, and from providing hard proofs to various and sometimes certainly challenging statements. Our primary goal was instead to focus on simple examples in order not only to stimulate a broadening of the reader's perspective beyond the static view of classical graph theory, but also, and more importantly, to motivate the reader's creativity and offer the necessary push to dive into an ocean of infinite possibilities. After all, in mathematics, as in all natural sciences, the key to the solution of a problem often if not always can be found in its appropriate representation. The second part of this book will be dedicated to some of these problems, and to their representation in terms of the operator graph-theoretical framework introduced here.

PART II

APPLICATIONS

5
Generating Graphs

The first part of this book led us on, at times, a perhaps unwieldy journey from one of the undoubtedly most cherished fields of applied mathematics, classical graph theory, across the ghastly depths of an inherently dynamic formalisation of physical reality in terms of mappings and operators, to an inspired yet propositional attempt at a fusion of both of these perspectives. With the backing of what is hopefully a sufficiently motivated conceptional and notational framework at hand, it is time to bring this attempt to a test by continuing our adventurous journey with an excursion into the endless realm of applications and illustrative examples. Naturally, this second part of our journey must be strictly limited for reasons of available space and time, and we will start in this chapter with an exploration of graph generators and their algebraic, that is operator graph-theoretical, formulation. In this undertaking, we will primarily focus on the generation of random graphs, specifically the models introduced in Section 2.3, as such models enjoy, in one way or another, widespread and prominent employment throughout almost all fields of science and technology. Only the last section will see the exemplary generation of an exact graph model, the finite square grid graph, as preparation for a closer inspection of an intriguing yet unsolved problem at the very heart of condensed matter physics in the next chapter, and a playful excursion into game theory in Chapter 7.

5.1 Erdős–Rényi Random Graphs

Let us begin our excursion with the random graph model of Erdős and Rényi [38] which, at least by name, dominates graph-theoretical applications in a vast variety of research fields. Recalling its brief introduction in Section 2.3.5, the Erdős–Rényi random digraph model $\mathcal{R}^{dER}_{n,k}$ is classically defined as a relational digraph $(\mathcal{N}, \mathcal{E})$ of order $n \in \mathbb{N}$ with a fixed number $k \in \mathbb{N}_0$ of edges that is realised by uniform-randomly selecting ordered pairs of distinct nodes i and j from the set of nodes $\mathcal{N}$ and adding (i, j) to the set of edges $\mathcal{E}$ until $|\mathcal{E}| = k$. If for each ordered pair $(i, j) \in \mathcal{E}$ also $(j, i) \in \mathcal{E}$ such that $|\mathcal{E}| = 2k$, we obtain a realisation of the simple Erdős–Rényi random graph model $\mathscr{R}^{ER}_{n,k}$ of order n with k undirected edges.

Despite the undeniable simplicity of this model, especially in regard to computational realisations, its algebraic formalisation faces a number of challenges due to the *sine qua non* of constructing a fixed number of adjacency relations which, as we will demonstrate below, stringently limits the use of probabilistic arguments in formulating appropriate operator graph generators. Certainly, a satisfying answer to these challenges is provided by instead considering the closely related Gilbert random graph model, whose operator graph-theoretical formalisation we will study in greater detail in the next section. For the moment, however, let us explore how far the framework conceptualised in the previous chapter will carry us by constructing operator representations of both the simple and relational Erdős–Rényi random graph model, and by taking a closer look at the inherent limitations of these representations.

5.1.1 Undirected Erdős–Rényi Random Graphs

Among the plethora of algebraic objects which could serve in conceiving feasible operator representations of simple graphs and, consequently, simple Erdős–Rényi random graphs $\mathscr{R}^{ER}_{n,k}$, we will restrict ourselves here to the formulation which inspired the facile alternative solution to the problem of Königsberg's bridges at the end of Section 4.1, and expressed both nodes and edge operators of this historic graph in terms of vectors in a sufficiently large Boolean vector space. Specifically, recalling (4.23)–(4.25), let the n Boolean row vectors

$$\boldsymbol{n}_i := \boldsymbol{\delta}^n_i \in \mathbb{B}^n : i \in [1, n] \tag{5.1}$$

define the nodes of a simple graph of order n such that $\mathrm{T}[\boldsymbol{n}_i] = 1\ \forall i \in [1, n]$, and let the Boolean row vectors

$$\mathfrak{E}_j := \boldsymbol{\delta}^n_{j_1} + \boldsymbol{\delta}^n_{j_2} \in \mathbb{B}^n : j \in [1, k_{\max}] \tag{5.2}$$

with two non-zero elements for

$$\begin{aligned} j_1 &:= 1 + \left\lfloor n - \frac{1}{2} - \frac{1}{2}\sqrt{9 - 8j - 4n + 4n^2} \right\rfloor, \\ j_2 &:= n + j + \frac{1}{2} j_1 (j_1 - 2n + 1) \end{aligned} \tag{5.3}$$

represent all of the $k_{\max} = n(n-1)/2$ possible undirected adjacency relations between these nodes. However, in order to realise simple Erdős–Rényi

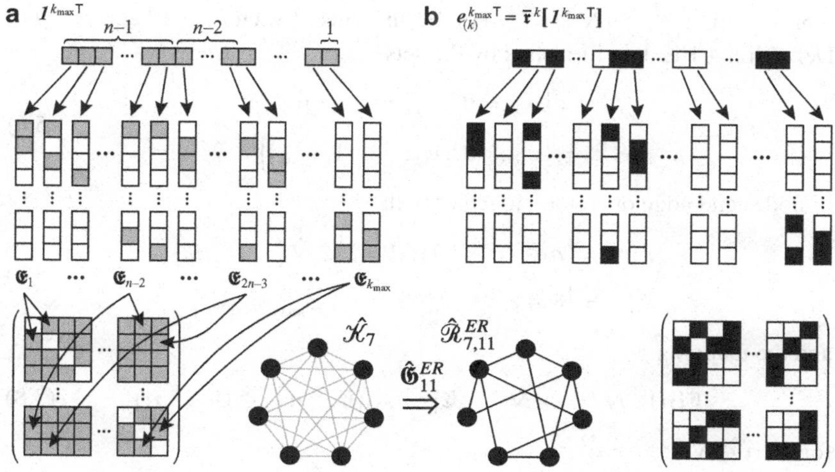

Figure 5.1 Generation of simple Erdős–Rényi random graphs $\mathscr{R}_{n,k}^{ER}$. **a:** Using (5.4), each of the $k_{\max}$ elements of the all-ones row vector $\mathbf{1}^{k_{\max}\,\mathsf{T}}$ can be uniquely mapped into a distinct vector in $\mathbb{B}^n$ with two non-zero elements that serves as representation of an undirected edge in the complete simple graph $\mathscr{K}_n$ by marking two symmetric non-zero elements in its matrix of adjacency relations (bottom). **b:** By uniform-randomly selecting k non-zero elements of $\mathbf{1}^{k_{\max}\,\mathsf{T}}$ through the utilisation of the column randomisation operator $\bar{\mathfrak{r}}^k$, the edge operators defining an operator representation of $\mathscr{R}_{n,k}^{ER}$ are constructed from the seed $\hat{\mathscr{K}}_n$ by means of the generator $\hat{\mathfrak{G}}_k^{ER}$ given in (5.10), eventually yielding a symmetric matrix of adjacency relations with randomly distributed non-zero elements (bottom). The inset illustrates a representative realisation of this graph generation for $n = 7, k = 11$.

random graphs by selecting from this set of $k_{\max}$ edges exactly k elements in a uniform-random fashion, we need to find a somewhat more suitable algebraic formalisation that allows us to perform this random selection at the level of individual edges itself. To that end, let us utilise the $k_{\max}$-dimensional all-ones column vector $\mathbf{1}^{k_{\max}}$, and represent each of the two terms on the right-hand side in (5.2) by the matrix product $\delta_{j'}^{n} = \mathbf{1}^{k_{\max}\,\mathsf{T}} \cdot \delta_{j,j'}^{k_{\max}\times n}$ such that

$$\mathfrak{E}_j := \mathbf{1}^{k_{\max}\,\mathsf{T}} \cdot (\delta_{j,j_1}^{k_{\max}\times n} + \delta_{j,j_2}^{k_{\max}\times n}) \in \mathbb{B}^n : j \in [1, k_{\max}]. \tag{5.4}$$

It can easily be shown that $\mathrm{T}[\mathfrak{E}_j] = 2\,\forall j \in [1, k_{\max}]$, and that the index

$$j := j_2 - \frac{1}{2} j_1 (j_1 - 2n + 1) - n \tag{5.5}$$

successively labels all $k_{\max}$ possible undirected adjacency relations between pairs of distinct nodes $j_1, j_2 \in [1, n]$: $j_2 > j_1$ in a *complete simple graph* $\mathscr{K}_n$ of order n, as illustrated in Fig. 5.1a. With (5.1) and (5.4), a viable operator representation $\hat{\mathscr{K}}_n = (\hat{\mathcal{N}}^{\mathscr{K}_n}, \hat{\mathcal{E}}^{\mathscr{K}_n})$ of $\mathscr{K}_n$ in terms of vectors in $\mathbb{B}^n$ according to Definition 4.1 is then furnished by the sets

$$\begin{aligned} \hat{\mathcal{N}}^{\mathscr{K}_n} &= \left\{ \boldsymbol{n}_0 := \boldsymbol{0}^n, \boldsymbol{n}_i \colon i \in [1,n] \right\} \subset \mathbb{B}^n, \\ \hat{\mathcal{E}}^{\mathscr{K}_n} &= \left\{ \mathfrak{E}_0 := \boldsymbol{0}^n, \mathfrak{E}_j \colon j \in [1, k_{\max}] \right\} \subset \mathbb{B}^n \end{aligned} \tag{5.6}$$

of nodes and edge operators, together with

$$\begin{aligned} \hat{\mathcal{N}}^{\mathscr{K}_n}_{cl} &:= \left\{ \boldsymbol{n} \in \hat{\mathcal{N}}^{\mathscr{K}_n} : \mathrm{T}[\boldsymbol{n}] = 1 \right\}, \ \hat{\mathcal{N}}^{\mathscr{K}_n}_{aux} := \left\{ \boldsymbol{n}_0 \right\}, \\ \hat{\mathcal{E}}^{\mathscr{K}_n}_{cl} &:= \left\{ \mathfrak{E} \in \hat{\mathcal{E}}^{\mathscr{K}_n} \colon \mathrm{T}[\mathfrak{E}] = 2 \right\}, \ \hat{\mathcal{E}}^{\mathscr{K}_n}_{aux} := \left\{ \mathfrak{E}_0 \right\} \end{aligned} \tag{5.7}$$

and the mapping

$$\mathfrak{E}[\boldsymbol{n}] : \hat{\mathcal{N}}^{\mathscr{K}_n} \to \hat{\mathcal{N}}^{\mathscr{K}_n}, \ \mathfrak{E}[\boldsymbol{n}] := (\mathfrak{E} \cdot^{\mathbb{B}} \boldsymbol{n}^{\mathsf{T}}) \cdot^{\mathbb{B}} (\mathfrak{E} +^{\mathbb{B}} \boldsymbol{n}) \tag{5.8}$$

for all $\boldsymbol{n} \in \hat{\mathcal{N}}^{\mathscr{K}_n}, \mathfrak{E} \in \hat{\mathcal{E}}^{\mathscr{K}_n}$.

By having represented all edge operators of $\hat{\mathscr{K}}_n$ with (5.4) suitably in terms of $\boldsymbol{1}^{k_{\max}}$, we can now make use of the column randomisation operator $\bar{\mathfrak{r}}^k$ introduced in (4.59) to algebraically formalise the uniform-random selection of these operators, and to ensure that only k edge-generating operators are chosen in each realisation of $\mathscr{R}^{ER}_{n,k}$. Indeed, as exemplified in Fig. 5.1b, the application of $\bar{\mathfrak{r}}^k$ to $\boldsymbol{1}^{k_{\max}\mathsf{T}}$ will, by definition, yield a $k_{\max}$-dimensional Boolean row vector with exactly k uniform-randomly chosen non-zero elements. For notational purposes, let us denote this vector by $\boldsymbol{e}^{k_{\max}\mathsf{T}}_{(k)}$ with

$$\boldsymbol{e}^{k_{\max}}_{(k)} := \left(\bar{\mathfrak{r}}^k [\boldsymbol{1}^{k_{\max}\mathsf{T}}] \right)^{\mathsf{T}} \tag{5.9}$$

and its jth element by $(\boldsymbol{e}^{k_{\max}\mathsf{T}}_{(k)})_j$. If we then replace the term $\boldsymbol{1}^{k_{\max}\mathsf{T}}$ in the representation (5.4) of each edge operator with a given $\boldsymbol{e}^{k_{\max}\mathsf{T}}_{(k)}$, we find

$$\begin{aligned} \boldsymbol{e}^{k_{\max}\mathsf{T}}_{(k)} \cdot (\boldsymbol{\delta}^{k_{\max}\times n}_{j,j_1} + \boldsymbol{\delta}^{k_{\max}\times n}_{j,j_2}) &= (\boldsymbol{e}^{k_{\max}\mathsf{T}}_{(k)})_j \cdot (\boldsymbol{\delta}^n_{j_1} + \boldsymbol{\delta}^n_{j_2}) \\ &= (\boldsymbol{e}^{k_{\max}\mathsf{T}}_{(k)})_j \cdot \boldsymbol{1}^{k_{\max}\mathsf{T}} \cdot (\boldsymbol{\delta}^{k_{\max}\times n}_{j,j_1} + \boldsymbol{\delta}^{k_{\max}\times n}_{j,j_2}) \\ &= (\boldsymbol{e}^{k_{\max}\mathsf{T}}_{(k)})_j \cdot \mathfrak{E}_j \end{aligned}$$

for any $j \in [1, k_{\max}]$. The non-zero elements of the Boolean vector $\boldsymbol{e}^{k_{\max}}_{(k)}$ thus mark the k edge-generating operators $\mathfrak{E} \in \hat{\mathcal{E}}^{\mathscr{K}_n} \colon \mathfrak{E} \neq \boldsymbol{0}^n$ which eventually describe a desired realisation of $\mathscr{R}^{ER}_{n,k}$, while the remaining $k_{\max} - k$ edge operators of $\hat{\mathscr{K}}_n$ will be mapped into the all-zeroes vector $\boldsymbol{0}^n =: \mathfrak{E}_0$. Following this approach and recalling Definition 4.7, the construction of an operator representation $\hat{\mathscr{R}}^{ER}_{n,k} = (\hat{\mathcal{N}}^{\mathscr{R}^{ER}_{n,k}}, \hat{\mathcal{E}}^{\mathscr{R}^{ER}_{n,k}})$ of a simple Erdős–Rényi random graph from a complete simple graph can therefore be formalised by introducing the tuple

$$\hat{\mathfrak{G}}^{ER}_k = \left(\hat{\mathfrak{G}}_{\mathcal{N}}, \hat{\mathfrak{G}}_{\mathcal{E}} \right) \tag{5.10}$$

with

$$\hat{\mathfrak{G}}_{\mathcal{N}} \colon \hat{\mathcal{N}}^{\mathcal{K}_n} \to \hat{\mathcal{N}}^{\mathcal{R}^{ER}_{n,k}},\ \hat{\mathfrak{G}}_{\mathcal{N}} := \mathrm{id},$$
$$\hat{\mathfrak{G}}_{\mathcal{E}} \colon \hat{\mathcal{E}}^{\mathcal{K}_n} \to \hat{\mathcal{E}}^{\mathcal{R}^{ER}_{n,k}},\ \hat{\mathfrak{G}}_{\mathcal{E}}[\mathfrak{E}_j] := (\boldsymbol{e}^{k_{\max}}_{(k)})_j \cdot \mathfrak{E}_j = \boldsymbol{e}^{k_{\max}\,\mathsf{T}}_{(k)} \cdot (\boldsymbol{\delta}^{k_{\max}\times n}_{j,j_1} + \boldsymbol{\delta}^{k_{\max}\times n}_{j,j_2})$$

as operator graph generator with seed $\hat{\mathcal{K}}_n$ such that $\hat{\mathfrak{G}}^{ER}_k[\hat{\mathcal{K}}_n] = \hat{\mathcal{R}}^{ER}_{n,k}$ with

$$\begin{aligned}\hat{\mathcal{N}}^{\mathcal{R}^{ER}_{n,k}} &:= \left\{\hat{\mathfrak{G}}_{\mathcal{N}}[\boldsymbol{n}] \colon \boldsymbol{n} \in \hat{\mathcal{N}}^{\mathcal{K}_n}\right\} = \hat{\mathcal{N}}^{\mathcal{K}_n} \subset \mathbb{B}^n,\\ \hat{\mathcal{E}}^{\mathcal{R}^{ER}_{n,k}} &:= \left\{\hat{\mathfrak{G}}_{\mathcal{E}}[\mathfrak{E}] \colon \mathfrak{E} \in \hat{\mathcal{E}}^{\mathcal{K}_n}\right\} \subset \mathbb{B}^n,\end{aligned} \tag{5.11}$$

and

$$\begin{aligned}\hat{\mathcal{N}}^{\mathcal{R}^{ER}_{n,k}}_{cl} &:= \left\{\boldsymbol{n} \in \hat{\mathcal{N}}^{\mathcal{R}^{ER}_{n,k}} \colon \mathrm{T}[\boldsymbol{n}] = 1\right\},\ \hat{\mathcal{N}}^{\mathcal{R}^{ER}_{n,k}}_{aux} := \left\{\boldsymbol{n}_0\right\},\\ \hat{\mathcal{E}}^{\mathcal{R}^{ER}_{n,k}}_{cl} &:= \left\{\mathfrak{E} \in \hat{\mathcal{E}}^{\mathcal{R}^{ER}_{n,k}} \colon \mathrm{T}[\mathfrak{E}] = 2\right\},\ \hat{\mathcal{E}}^{\mathcal{R}^{ER}_{n,k}}_{aux} := \hat{\mathcal{E}}^{\mathcal{R}^{ER}_{n,k}} \setminus \hat{\mathcal{E}}^{\mathcal{R}^{ER}_{n,k}}_{cl}\end{aligned} \tag{5.12}$$

implicitly define the respective classical and auxiliary subsets of nodes and edge operators of the generated operator representation $\hat{\mathcal{R}}^{ER}_{n,k}$.

With $\hat{\mathfrak{G}}^{ER}_k[\hat{\mathcal{K}}_n]$, we have finally arrived at an algebraic rigorous representation of the simple Erdős–Rényi random graph model. More importantly, while classically only individual realisations of this model allow for an algebraic formalisation in terms of concrete adjacency matrices, the two sets (5.11) furnish a parametrised representation of Erdős–Rényi random graphs as a whole, beyond such individual realisations. To illustrate this crucial perspective of our approach, and explore its potential advantages and limitations, let us derive and take a closer look at the adjacency matrix associated with $\hat{\mathcal{R}}^{ER}_{n,k}$. To that end, noting that an Erdős–Rényi random graph, by construction, does not contain any multiedges or self-looped nodes, we will utilise (4.63) which, with

$$\hat{\boldsymbol{a}}[\hat{\mathcal{G}}] = \sum_{\mathfrak{E}\in\hat{\mathcal{E}}_{cl}} \left(\mathfrak{E} \otimes \mathfrak{E}^{\mathsf{T}} - \mathrm{diag}\,[\mathfrak{E}]\right), \tag{5.13}$$

provides a viable adjacency matrix observable for operator representations $\hat{\mathcal{G}}$ formulated in terms of Boolean vectors. As (5.10) and (5.12) ensure that all $\mathfrak{E} \in \hat{\mathcal{E}}^{\mathcal{R}^{ER}_{n,k}}_{aux}$ are equal to $\boldsymbol{0}^n$ and, thus, will not contribute to the right-hand side of (5.13), the sum can be performed over all elements of $\hat{\mathcal{E}}^{\mathcal{R}^{ER}_{n,k}}$. By using the representation $\hat{\mathfrak{G}}_{\mathcal{E}}[\mathfrak{E}]$ of edge operators of $\hat{\mathcal{R}}^{ER}_{n,k}$, we then find

$$\begin{aligned}\hat{\boldsymbol{a}}[\hat{\mathcal{R}}^{ER}_{n,k}] &= \sum_{j=1}^{k_{\max}} \left(\mathfrak{E}_j \otimes \mathfrak{E}_j^{\mathsf{T}} - \mathrm{diag}\,[\mathfrak{E}_j]\right)\\ &= \sum_{j=1}^{k_{\max}} \Big(\left(\boldsymbol{e}^{k_{\max}\,\mathsf{T}}_{(k)} \cdot (\boldsymbol{\delta}^{k_{\max}\times n}_{j,j_1} + \boldsymbol{\delta}^{k_{\max}\times n}_{j,j_2})\right) \otimes \left(\boldsymbol{e}^{k_{\max}\,\mathsf{T}}_{(k)} \cdot (\boldsymbol{\delta}^{k_{\max}\times n}_{j,j_1} + \boldsymbol{\delta}^{k_{\max}\times n}_{j,j_2})\right)^{\mathsf{T}}\\ &\qquad - \mathrm{diag}\left[\boldsymbol{e}^{k_{\max}\,\mathsf{T}}_{(k)} \cdot (\boldsymbol{\delta}^{k_{\max}\times n}_{j,j_1} + \boldsymbol{\delta}^{k_{\max}\times n}_{j,j_2})\right]\Big),\end{aligned}$$

and eventually

$$\begin{aligned}
&\hat{\mathfrak{a}}[\hat{\mathscr{R}}_{n,k}^{ER}] \\
&= \sum_{j=1}^{k_{\max}} \Big(\big(e_{(k)}^{k_{\max}\,\mathsf{T}} \cdot \delta_{j,j_1}^{k_{\max}\times n}\big) \otimes \big(e_{(k)}^{k_{\max}\,\mathsf{T}} \cdot \delta_{j,j_1}^{k_{\max}\times n}\big)^{\mathsf{T}} + \big(e_{(k)}^{k_{\max}\,\mathsf{T}} \cdot \delta_{j,j_1}^{k_{\max}\times n}\big) \otimes \big(e_{(k)}^{k_{\max}\,\mathsf{T}} \cdot \delta_{j,j_2}^{k_{\max}\times n}\big)^{\mathsf{T}} \\
&\qquad + \big(e_{(k)}^{k_{\max}\,\mathsf{T}} \cdot \delta_{j,j_2}^{k_{\max}\times n}\big) \otimes \big(e_{(k)}^{k_{\max}\,\mathsf{T}} \cdot \delta_{j,j_1}^{k_{\max}\times n}\big)^{\mathsf{T}} + \big(e_{(k)}^{k_{\max}\,\mathsf{T}} \cdot \delta_{j,j_2}^{k_{\max}\times n}\big) \otimes \big(e_{(k)}^{k_{\max}\,\mathsf{T}} \cdot \delta_{j,j_2}^{k_{\max}\times n}\big)^{\mathsf{T}} \\
&\qquad - \operatorname{diag}\big[e_{(k)}^{k_{\max}\,\mathsf{T}} \cdot \delta_{j,j_1}^{k_{\max}\times n}\big] - \operatorname{diag}\big[e_{(k)}^{k_{\max}\,\mathsf{T}} \cdot \delta_{j,j_2}^{k_{\max}\times n}\big] \Big), \qquad (5.14)
\end{aligned}$$

after employing the bilinear property of the Kronecker matrix product.

At first sight, this result admittedly does not look overly inviting. However, as already hinted at in the previous chapter, the generation of graphs through the application of operators might provide room for simplifying manipulations by exploiting the algebraic properties which govern both the generating operators and the objects these operators act upon. To explore the extent to which such manipulations are possible in the case of our adjacency matrix observable for the simple Erdős–Rényi random graph model, let us take a closer look at the individual terms which make up the right-hand side of (5.14). For each given $j \in [1, k_{\max}]$ and $l \in \{1, 2\}$, the product $e_{(k)}^{k_{\max}\,\mathsf{T}} \cdot \delta_{j,j_l}^{k_{\max}\times n}$ yields an n-dimensional row vector whose j_lth element is non-zero if and only if the jth element of $e_{(k)}^{k_{\max}\,\mathsf{T}}$ is non-zero. Similarly, it can be shown that the n-dimensional column vector $(e_{(k)}^{k_{\max}\,\mathsf{T}} \cdot \delta_{j,j_l}^{k_{\max}\times n})^{\mathsf{T}}$ has at most one non-zero j_lth element. The Kronecker product between these two vectors must then result in an $(n \times n)$-dimensional matrix with at most one non-zero element on its diagonal such that

$$\big(e_{(k)}^{k_{\max}\,\mathsf{T}} \cdot \delta_{j,j_l}^{k_{\max}\times n}\big) \otimes \big(e_{(k)}^{k_{\max}\,\mathsf{T}} \cdot \delta_{j,j_l}^{k_{\max}\times n}\big)^{\mathsf{T}} = \operatorname{diag}\big[e_{(k)}^{k_{\max}\,\mathsf{T}} \cdot \delta_{j,j_l}^{k_{\max}\times n}\big].$$

This simplifies (5.14) significantly, and leaves us with

$$\begin{aligned}
\hat{\mathfrak{a}}[\hat{\mathscr{R}}_{n,k}^{ER}] = \sum_{j=1}^{k_{\max}} \Big(&\big(e_{(k)}^{k_{\max}\,\mathsf{T}} \cdot \delta_{j,j_1}^{k_{\max}\times n}\big) \otimes \big(e_{(k)}^{k_{\max}\,\mathsf{T}} \cdot \delta_{j,j_2}^{k_{\max}\times n}\big)^{\mathsf{T}} \\
&+ \big(e_{(k)}^{k_{\max}\,\mathsf{T}} \cdot \delta_{j,j_2}^{k_{\max}\times n}\big) \otimes \big(e_{(k)}^{k_{\max}\,\mathsf{T}} \cdot \delta_{j,j_1}^{k_{\max}\times n}\big)^{\mathsf{T}} \Big). \qquad (5.15)
\end{aligned}$$

It is interesting to note here that, for each given j, the two terms in the argument of the sum are transpose of each other, and that therefore the measured adjacency matrix observable must be that of an undirected graph.

But we are not quite finished yet. Further inspection of the first term of (5.15) reveals that it will contribute non-trivially to the sum only in the case the jth element of the vector $e_{(k)}^{k_{\max}\,\mathsf{T}}$ is non-zero. Indeed, we find

$$\big(e_{(k)}^{k_{\max}\,\mathsf{T}} \cdot \delta_{j,j_1}^{k_{\max}\times n}\big) \otimes \big(e_{(k)}^{k_{\max}\,\mathsf{T}} \cdot \delta_{j,j_2}^{k_{\max}\times n}\big)^{\mathsf{T}} = \begin{cases} \delta_{j_2 j_1}^{n\times n} & \text{iff } (e_{(k)}^{k_{\max}\,\mathsf{T}})_j \neq 0, \\ 0^{n\times n} & \text{otherwise,} \end{cases}$$

with a similar assessment holding for the second term in (5.15) as well. By recognising (5.5), and that with (5.3) the ordered index pairs (j_1, j_2) mark all non-zero elements in a strict upper triangular matrix, we then finally arrive at the comparably simple expression

$$\begin{aligned}\hat{\mathbf{a}}[\hat{\mathcal{R}}^{ER}_{n,k}] &= \sum_{j=1}^{k_{\max}} (\boldsymbol{e}^{k_{\max}\,\mathsf{T}}_{(k)})_j \cdot (\boldsymbol{\delta}^{n\times n}_{j_1 j_2} + \boldsymbol{\delta}^{n\times n}_{j_2 j_1}) \\ &= \sum_{\substack{j_1,j_2=1\\ j_2>j_1}}^{n} (\boldsymbol{e}^{k_{\max}\,\mathsf{T}}_{(k)})_{j_2-j_1(j_1-2n+1)/2-n} \cdot (\boldsymbol{\delta}^{n\times n}_{j_1 j_2} + \boldsymbol{\delta}^{n\times n}_{j_2 j_1})\end{aligned} \tag{5.16}$$

for the symmetric adjacency matrix observable of the simple Erdős–Rényi random graph model $\mathcal{R}^{ER}_{n,k}$.

The above result is certainly not surprising and could have been obtained through a more direct approach by noting that the sum of the two $\boldsymbol{\delta}$-terms on the right-hand side of (5.16) represents, for each given pair of distinct indices (j_1, j_2), the undirected edge between nodes j_1 and j_2 as $n \times n$ matrix, and that multiplication with the scalar $(\boldsymbol{e}^{k_{\max}\,\mathsf{T}}_{(k)})_j$ eventually selects k of these $n(n-1)/2$ possible undirected edges as contributions to the set of adjacency relations. However, within our operator graph-theoretical framework, the adjacency matrix $\boldsymbol{a} = \hat{\mathbf{a}}[\hat{\mathcal{G}}]$ takes the more general role of a graph observable applied to an operator representation $\hat{\mathcal{G}}$ of a graph $\mathcal{G}$ rather than that of an algebraic object defining $\mathcal{G}$ itself. The less direct route we followed in deducing (5.16) serves to highlight this subtle distinction, and to illustrate an easily verifiable application of the identities which govern the algebraical properties of the simpler components both the seed graph and graph generator are comprised of. But most importantly, the right-hand side of (5.16) does not represent a specific realisation of the random graph model $\mathcal{R}^{ER}_{n,k}$, but instead applies generally by encompassing all possible realisations of the simple Erdős–Rényi random graph model. This can easily be seen by noting that the adjacency matrix observable returns a function of the two parameters n and k defining $\mathcal{R}^{ER}_{n,k}$. A similar case can be made for any algebraically well-defined graph observable, as we will further exemplify in this and the next chapter.

In order to construct and manipulate such other graph observables, the set of identities that we utilised so far and allowed us to eventually arrive at (5.16) is not sufficient, however. Let us therefore dig a bit deeper into the relations satisfied by the algebraic objects which define our edge operators $\mathfrak{E}_j$, starting with $\boldsymbol{\delta}^n_i$ and the general Kronecker delta matrices $\boldsymbol{\delta}^{m\times n}_{ij}$. We find

$$\boldsymbol{\delta}^n_i +^{\mathbb{B}} \boldsymbol{\delta}^n_j = \begin{cases} \boldsymbol{\delta}^n_i + \boldsymbol{\delta}^n_j & \text{iff } i \neq j, \\ \boldsymbol{0}^n & \text{otherwise,} \end{cases} \tag{5.17}$$

$$\delta_i^n \cdot \delta_j^{n\mathsf{T}} = \delta_i^n \cdot^{\mathbb{B}} \delta_j^{n\mathsf{T}} = \begin{cases} 1 & \text{iff } i = j, \\ 0 & \text{otherwise,} \end{cases} \tag{5.18}$$

$$\delta_i^n \odot \delta_j^n = \delta_i^n \odot^{\mathbb{B}} \delta_j^n = \begin{cases} \delta_i^n & \text{iff } i = j, \\ \mathit{0}^n & \text{otherwise,} \end{cases} \tag{5.19}$$

$$\delta_i^m \otimes \delta_j^{n\mathsf{T}} = \delta_i^m \otimes^{\mathbb{B}} \delta_j^{n\mathsf{T}} = \delta_{ij}^{m\times n} \tag{5.20}$$

and, restricting to the matrix and Hadamard product to avoid introducing higher-dimensional generalised Kronecker delta matrices,

$$\delta_{ij}^{m\times n} +^{\mathbb{B}} \delta_{kl}^{m\times n} = \begin{cases} \delta_{ij}^{m\times n} + \delta_{kl}^{m\times n} & \text{iff } i \neq k \vee j \neq l, \\ \mathit{0}^{m\times n} & \text{otherwise,} \end{cases} \tag{5.21}$$

$$\delta_{ij}^{m\times n} \cdot \delta_{kl}^{n\times m'} = \delta_{ij}^{m\times n} \cdot^{\mathbb{B}} \delta_{kl}^{n\times m'} = \begin{cases} \delta_{il}^{m\times m'} & \text{iff } j = k, \\ \mathit{0}^{m\times m'} & \text{otherwise,} \end{cases} \tag{5.22}$$

$$\delta_{ij}^{m\times n} \odot \delta_{kl}^{m\times n} = \delta_{ij}^{m\times n} \odot^{\mathbb{B}} \delta_{kl}^{m\times n} = \begin{cases} \delta_{ij}^{m\times n} & \text{iff } i = k \wedge j = l, \\ \mathit{0}^{m\times n} & \text{otherwise.} \end{cases} \tag{5.23}$$

Moreover, it can easily be shown that

$$\sum_{k=1}^{m} (\delta_{ij}^{m\times n})_{kl} = (\delta_j^{n\mathsf{T}})_l\,, \quad \sum_{l=1}^{n} (\delta_{ij}^{m\times n})_{kl} = (\delta_i^m)_k \tag{5.24}$$

and, trivially, that

$$\sum_{k=1}^{m}\sum_{l=1}^{n} (\delta_{ij}^{m\times n})_{kl} = \mathrm{T}\,[\delta_{ij}^{m\times n}] = \sum_{k=1}^{m} (\delta_i^m)_k = \mathrm{T}\,[\delta_i^m] = 1. \tag{5.25}$$

Finally, we have

$$\mathrm{T}\left[\sum_{j=1}^{k_{\max}} (e_{(k)}^{k_{\max}\,\mathsf{T}})_j \cdot \delta_{j_1 j_2}^{n\times n}\right] = k \tag{5.26}$$

as for each $j \in [1, k_{\max}]$ and j_1, j_2 given by (5.3), the Kronecker delta matrix contributes 1 to the sum, but $e_{(k)}^{k_{\max}\,\mathsf{T}}$ ensures that only k contributions are selected. It is important to stress here that (5.26) delivers an exact result, despite the random nature of its element-wise selection process. The above list of relations can certainly be extended but should cover the most important identities which we will need for evaluating the various graph observables presented in the remainder of this book.

More interesting, yet arguably also more challenging, are algebraic relations satisfied by the column randomisation operator (4.59) that with (5.9) defines the term $e_{(k)}^{k_{\max}}$ in our representation of the Erdős–Rényi random graph model. Let us begin by taking a closer look at the simple composition $\bar{\mathfrak{r}}^{k'}[\bar{\mathfrak{r}}^{k}[A]]$ for arbitrary matrices $A \in \mathbb{Q}^{m\times n}$ with $(\bar{\delta}[A] \cdot \mathit{1}^n)_i \geq k\; \forall i \in [1, m]$. The application of $\bar{\mathfrak{r}}^k$ chooses uniform-randomly a total of k non-zero elements on each row of $\boldsymbol{A}$, from which subsequent application of $\bar{\mathfrak{r}}^{k'}$ then eventually selects a subset of k' elements for each row of the resulting matrix. For this composite selection to be defined at all, we necessarily require that $k' \leq k$. Moreover, as by definition both of these random selections are mutually independent, we can directly choose k' non-zero elements from each row of $\boldsymbol{A}$, without going through the intermediate process of realising $\bar{\mathfrak{r}}^k[\boldsymbol{A}]$ itself. This leaves us with

$$\bar{\mathfrak{r}}^{k'} \circ \bar{\mathfrak{r}}^k[\boldsymbol{A}] := \bar{\mathfrak{r}}^{k'}[\bar{\mathfrak{r}}^k[\boldsymbol{A}]] = \bar{\mathfrak{r}}^{k'}[\boldsymbol{A}] \tag{5.27}$$

for $k' \leq k$, and exhausts, with

$$\bar{\mathfrak{r}}^{k'} \circ \bar{\mathfrak{r}}^k[\boldsymbol{A}] = \bar{\mathfrak{r}}^k \circ \bar{\mathfrak{r}}^{k'}[\boldsymbol{A}] \tag{5.28}$$

if and only if $k' = k$, the commutative properties of compositions of $\bar{\mathfrak{r}}^k$. Unfortunately, it is precisely this unavailability of a generally applicable commutative rule for column randomisation operators which not only renders their composition unsuitable for defining a viable operation of multiplication, but also constitutes the primary reason for the algebraically more challenging nature of the Erdős–Rényi random graph model. A related and similarly dire conclusion holds for compositions of three or more $\bar{\mathfrak{r}}^k$ operators. Indeed, by employing (5.27), one can easily demonstrate that associativity

$$\bar{\mathfrak{r}}^{k''} \circ \left(\bar{\mathfrak{r}}^{k'} \circ \bar{\mathfrak{r}}^k\right)[\boldsymbol{A}] = \left(\bar{\mathfrak{r}}^{k''} \circ \bar{\mathfrak{r}}^{k'}\right) \circ \bar{\mathfrak{r}}^k[\boldsymbol{A}] \tag{5.29}$$

is satisfied if and only if $k'' \leq k' \leq k$, and that

$$(\bar{\mathfrak{r}}^k)^n[\boldsymbol{A}] := \Big(\overbrace{\bar{\mathfrak{r}}^k \circ \cdots \circ \bar{\mathfrak{r}}^k}^{n}\Big)[\boldsymbol{A}] = \bar{\mathfrak{r}}^k[\boldsymbol{A}] \tag{5.30}$$

for matrices $\boldsymbol{A} \in \mathbb{Q}^{m \times n}$ with at least k non-zero elements on each row.

What about algebraic identities that involve the sum of column randomisation operators? By defining for appropriate matrices $\boldsymbol{A} \in \mathbb{Q}^{m \times n}$ this sum as

$$(\bar{\mathfrak{r}}^k + \bar{\mathfrak{r}}^{k'})[\boldsymbol{A}] := \bar{\mathfrak{r}}^k[\boldsymbol{A}] + \bar{\mathfrak{r}}^{k'}[\boldsymbol{A}], \tag{5.31}$$

the operator $\bar{\mathfrak{r}}^k$ naturally satisfies with

$$\begin{gathered}(\bar{\mathfrak{r}}^k + \bar{\mathfrak{r}}^{k'})[\boldsymbol{A}] = (\bar{\mathfrak{r}}^{k'} + \bar{\mathfrak{r}}^k)[\boldsymbol{A}], \\ \left((\bar{\mathfrak{r}}^k + \bar{\mathfrak{r}}^{k'}) + \bar{\mathfrak{r}}^{k''}\right)[\boldsymbol{A}] = \left(\bar{\mathfrak{r}}^k + (\bar{\mathfrak{r}}^{k'} + \bar{\mathfrak{r}}^{k''})\right)[\boldsymbol{A}]\end{gathered} \tag{5.32}$$

the properties of additive commutativity and associativity. Although this definition is certainly meaningful, it must be cautioned that the right-hand side of (5.31) and, consequentially, both equations in (5.32) cannot be understood or utilised without resorting to probabilistic arguments. Indeed, assuming without loss of generality that $k' \leq k$, the two terms $\bar{\mathfrak{r}}^k[\boldsymbol{A}]$ and $\bar{\mathfrak{r}}^{k'}[\boldsymbol{A}]$ respectively contribute k and k' non-zero elements to each row of the resulting matrix. Recalling the mutual independence and uniform-random nature of this contribution, the sum $\bar{\mathfrak{r}}^k[\boldsymbol{A}] + \bar{\mathfrak{r}}^{k'}[\boldsymbol{A}]$ will then contain between k and $\min[k + k', n]$ non-zero elements on any given row, and thus generally can no longer be expressed in terms of a single $\bar{\mathfrak{r}}^{k''}$ for some $k \leq k'' \leq \min[k + k', n]$. As we will see shortly, this necessarily, and unfortunately, has some detrimental bearing on the distributive properties of our column randomisation operator.

Such a negative prospect is shared by an expression like $\bar{\mathfrak{r}}^k[\boldsymbol{A} + \boldsymbol{B}]$, which is meaningful only if $\boldsymbol{A}, \boldsymbol{B} \in \mathbb{Q}^{m \times n}$ and their sum results in at least k non-zero elements on each row. But even if these conditions are satisfied, a uniform-random selection still stringently depends on how many columns of each row in both matrices share non-zero elements. Although probabilistic arguments can also be leveraged here to evaluate $\bar{\mathfrak{r}}^k[\boldsymbol{A} + \boldsymbol{B}]$ by choosing elements from $\boldsymbol{A}$ and $\boldsymbol{B}$ depending on the distribution of their non-zero elements, the selection of exactly k of these elements requires exorbitant care. In some important special cases, however, an easy evaluation is possible. If, for example, both $\boldsymbol{A}$ and $\boldsymbol{B}$ are equal to an $(m \times n)$-dimensional all-ones matrix $\boldsymbol{1}^{m \times n}$, we have $\boldsymbol{A} + \boldsymbol{B} = 2 \cdot \boldsymbol{1}^{m \times n}$ and find $\bar{\mathfrak{r}}^k[\boldsymbol{1}^{m \times n} + \boldsymbol{1}^{m \times n}] = 2 \cdot \bar{\mathfrak{r}}^k[\boldsymbol{1}^{m \times n}]$. Here, we made use of the algebraic identity

$$\bar{\mathfrak{r}}^k[q \cdot \boldsymbol{A}] = q \cdot \bar{\mathfrak{r}}^k[\boldsymbol{A}] \tag{5.33}$$

for $q \in \mathbb{Q}$ which renders $\bar{\mathfrak{r}}^k$ an operator satisfying homogeneity of degree 1 under scalar multiplication (see Definition 3.3). Unfortunately, this example also demonstrates that, in general, we must with

$$\bar{\mathfrak{r}}^k[\boldsymbol{A} + \boldsymbol{B}] \neq \bar{\mathfrak{r}}^k[\boldsymbol{A}] + \bar{\mathfrak{r}}^k[\boldsymbol{B}] \tag{5.34}$$

dispense of linearity under addition. Indeed, employing (5.31), the right-hand side of this expression yields $\bar{\mathfrak{r}}^k[\boldsymbol{1}^{m \times n}] + \bar{\mathfrak{r}}^k[\boldsymbol{1}^{m \times n}] = (\bar{\mathfrak{r}}^k + \bar{\mathfrak{r}}^k)[\boldsymbol{1}^{m \times n}]$, resulting in a matrix with at least k and at most $\min[2k, n]$ non-zero elements taken from the set $\{1, 2\}$ on each given row. In contrast, with (5.33), the left-hand side of (5.34) certainly delivers $2 \cdot \bar{\mathfrak{r}}^k[\boldsymbol{1}^{m \times n}]$ and, thus, returns a matrix with exactly k elements valued 2 on each row.

This brings us finally to the distributive properties of our column randomisation operator $\bar{\mathfrak{r}}^k$ with respect to the operations of addition (5.31) and composition (5.27). Considering first right-distributivity, we have on the one hand

$$\begin{aligned}(\bar{\mathfrak{r}}^{k''} + \bar{\mathfrak{r}}^{k'}) \circ \bar{\mathfrak{r}}^k[\boldsymbol{A}] &= (\bar{\mathfrak{r}}^{k''} + \bar{\mathfrak{r}}^{k'})[\bar{\mathfrak{r}}^k[\boldsymbol{A}]] \\ &= \bar{\mathfrak{r}}^{k''}[\bar{\mathfrak{r}}^k[\boldsymbol{A}]] + \bar{\mathfrak{r}}^{k'}[\bar{\mathfrak{r}}^k[\boldsymbol{A}]] = \bar{\mathfrak{r}}^{k''}[\boldsymbol{A}] + \bar{\mathfrak{r}}^{k'}[\boldsymbol{A}]\end{aligned}$$

for matrices $\boldsymbol{A} \in \mathbb{Q}^{m \times n}$ that will be assumed to have a sufficient number of non-zero elements on each of their rows such that all terms in this and the following expression are well-defined. The last step requires here that $k', k'' \leq k$, and yields a matrix with a number of non-zero elements on any given row in the range $[\max[k', k''], \min[k' + k'', n]]$. On the other hand, it can be shown that

$$(\bar{\mathbf{r}}^{k''} \circ \bar{\mathbf{r}}^{k} + \bar{\mathbf{r}}^{k'} \circ \bar{\mathbf{r}}^{k})[A] = \bar{\mathbf{r}}^{k''} \circ \bar{\mathbf{r}}^{k}[A] + \bar{\mathbf{r}}^{k'} \circ \bar{\mathbf{r}}^{k}[A] = \bar{\mathbf{r}}^{k''}[A] + \bar{\mathbf{r}}^{k'}[A].$$

Comparing both of these expressions, we eventually find

$$(\bar{\mathbf{r}}^{k''} + \bar{\mathbf{r}}^{k'}) \circ \bar{\mathbf{r}}^{k}[A] = (\bar{\mathbf{r}}^{k''} \circ \bar{\mathbf{r}}^{k} + \bar{\mathbf{r}}^{k'} \circ \bar{\mathbf{r}}^{k})[A], \tag{5.35}$$

and can conclude that $\bar{\mathbf{r}}^{k}$ indeed satisfies right-distributivity. The situation is quite different, however, if we consider its left counterpart. With

$$\bar{\mathbf{r}}^{k} \circ (\bar{\mathbf{r}}^{k'} + \bar{\mathbf{r}}^{k''})[A] = \bar{\mathbf{r}}^{k}\big[(\bar{\mathbf{r}}^{k'} + \bar{\mathbf{r}}^{k''})[A]\big] = \bar{\mathbf{r}}^{k}\big[\bar{\mathbf{r}}^{k'}[A] + \bar{\mathbf{r}}^{k''}[A]\big],$$

we obtain a matrix which not only requires that $k', k'' \geq k$ but also will have exactly k non-zero elements on each of its rows. On the other hand, employing (5.27) and (5.31) directly yields

$$(\bar{\mathbf{r}}^{k} \circ \bar{\mathbf{r}}^{k'} + \bar{\mathbf{r}}^{k} \circ \bar{\mathbf{r}}^{k''})[A] = \bar{\mathbf{r}}^{k}[A] + \bar{\mathbf{r}}^{k}[A]$$

and, thus, a matrix with a number of non-zero elements on any given row in the range $[k, \min[2k, n]]$. This together with (5.34) leaves us with

$$\bar{\mathbf{r}}^{k} \circ (\bar{\mathbf{r}}^{k'} + \bar{\mathbf{r}}^{k''})[A] \neq (\bar{\mathbf{r}}^{k} \circ \bar{\mathbf{r}}^{k'} + \bar{\mathbf{r}}^{k} \circ \bar{\mathbf{r}}^{k''})[A], \tag{5.36}$$

and the unfortunate conclusion that the column randomisation operator, in general, does not satisfy left-distributivity. This finding only adds to the challenging algebraic nature of the Erdős–Rényi random graph model, to which we will return with further exploration later in this section.

5.1.2 Directed Erdős–Rényi Random Graphs

Before detailing some of the principal limitations inherent in the Erdős–Rényi random graph model, however, let us take a brief look at its directed variant. The construction and application of a viable operator graph generator for the Erdős–Rényi random digraph model $\mathcal{R}^{dER}_{n,k}$ here follow the same pattern as in its simple counterpart. The differences are that now the seed graph is given by the complete relational digraph $\mathcal{K}^{d}_{n}$ of order n, that we have to randomly select k edges from a pool of $n(n-1)$ directed adjacency relations, and that ensuring the construction of symmetric edges is no longer necessary. It is this latter distinguishing quality which renders the algebraic treatment of $\mathcal{R}^{dER}_{n,k}$ arguably less demanding. Moreover, with (4.74) and (4.75), we are already in possession of a suitable operator representation $\hat{\mathcal{K}}^{d}_{n}$ of $\mathcal{K}^{d}_{n}$ in which nodes and edge

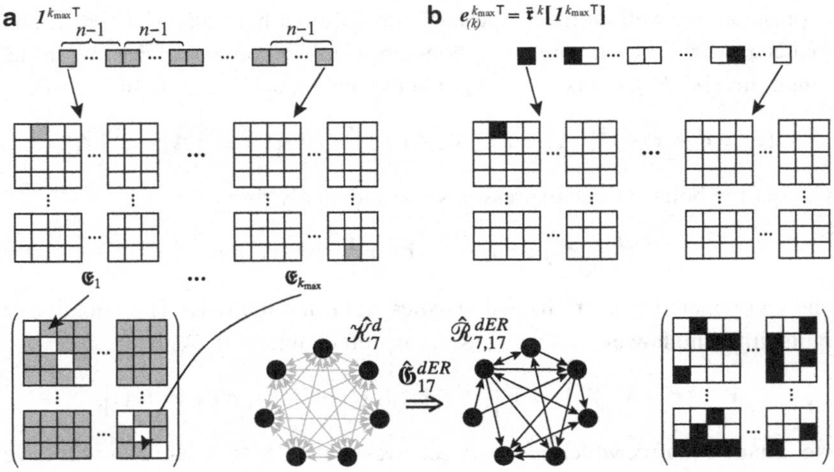

Figure 5.2 Generation of Erdős–Rényi random digraphs $\mathscr{R}_{n,k}^{dER}$. **a:** Using (5.39), each of the $k_{\max} = n(n-1)$ elements of $\mathbf{1}^{k_{\max}\mathsf{T}}$ can be uniquely mapped into a distinct matrix in $\mathbb{B}^{n\times n}$ that serves as representation of a directed edge in the complete relational digraph $\mathscr{K}_n^d$ by contributing a single non-zero element to its matrix of adjacency relations (bottom). **b:** By uniform-randomly selecting k non-zero elements of $\mathbf{1}^{k_{\max}\mathsf{T}}$ through the utilisation of the column randomisation operator $\bar{\mathfrak{r}}^k$, the edge operators defining an operator representation of $\mathscr{R}_{n,k}^{dER}$ are constructed from the seed $\hat{\mathscr{K}}_n^d$ by means of the generator $\hat{\mathfrak{G}}_k^{dER}$ in (5.40) and eventually yield a matrix of adjacency relations with randomly distributed non-zero elements (bottom). The inset shows a representative example of this graph generation for $n = 7, k = 17$.

operators are respectively formalised by suitable Boolean vectors and matrices. For notational convenience, we will use

$$\begin{aligned} j_1 &:= 1 + \left\lfloor \frac{j + \lfloor (j-1)/n \rfloor}{n} \right\rfloor, \\ j_2 &:= 1 + (j + \lfloor (j-1)/n \rfloor) \bmod n \end{aligned} \tag{5.37}$$

to index connected node pairs such that

$$j := n j_1 + j_2 - \left\lfloor \frac{n j_1 + j_2}{n+1} \right\rfloor - n \tag{5.38}$$

successively labels, and

$$\mathfrak{E}_j := (\mathbf{1}^{k_{\max}\mathsf{T}})_j \cdot \delta_{j_1 j_2}^{n\times n} \in \mathbb{B}^{n\times n} \; : \; j \in [1, k_{\max}] \tag{5.39}$$

represents, all $k_{\max} = n(n-1)$ directed edges of $\mathscr{K}_n^d$.

With (5.39) at hand, we can then generate a viable operator representation $\hat{\mathscr{R}}_{n,k}^{dER}$ of the Erdős–Rényi random digraph model. To that end, we need to select from the set of $k_{\max}$ edge operators comprising $\mathscr{K}_n^d$ exactly k elements in a uniform-random fashion. As illustrated in Fig. 5.2, and mirroring the approach followed in Section 5.1.1, this can be achieved by simply exploiting the action of the column randomisation operator $\bar{\mathfrak{r}}^k$ on the all-ones row vector $\boldsymbol{1}^{k_{\max}\mathsf{T}}$ employed in the definition of these edge operators. Avoiding here the introduction of generalisations of Kronecker delta matrices, however, we will confine ourselves to the algebraically more transparent approach of directly using the elements of $(\boldsymbol{e}_{(k)}^{k_{\max}})^{\mathsf{T}} := \bar{\mathfrak{r}}^k[\boldsymbol{1}^{k_{\max}\mathsf{T}}]$ to mark the selection of edge-generating operators. With this, we eventually find

$$\hat{\mathfrak{G}}_k^{dER} = \left(\hat{\mathfrak{G}}_{\mathcal{N}} := \mathrm{id}\ ,\ \hat{\mathfrak{G}}_{\mathcal{E}} \colon \hat{\mathfrak{G}}_{\mathcal{E}}[\mathfrak{E}_j] := (\boldsymbol{e}_{(k)}^{k_{\max}\mathsf{T}})_j \cdot \mathfrak{E}_j = (\boldsymbol{e}_{(k)}^{k_{\max}\mathsf{T}})_j \cdot \boldsymbol{\delta}_{j_1 j_2}^{n\times n}\right) \tag{5.40}$$

as a generator which constructs an operator representation $\hat{\mathscr{R}}_{n,k}^{dER}$ of the Erdős–Rényi random digraph model from a seed $\hat{\mathscr{K}}_n^d$ representing a complete relational digraph, such that $\hat{\mathfrak{G}}_k^{dER}[\hat{\mathscr{K}}_n^d] = \hat{\mathscr{R}}_{n,k}^{dER} := (\hat{\mathcal{N}}^{\mathscr{R}_{n,k}^{dER}}, \hat{\mathcal{E}}^{\mathscr{R}_{n,k}^{dER}})$ with

$$\begin{aligned} \hat{\mathcal{N}}^{\mathscr{R}_{n,k}^{dER}} &:= \hat{\mathcal{N}}^{\mathscr{K}_n^d} \subset \mathbb{B}^n, \\ \hat{\mathcal{E}}^{\mathscr{R}_{n,k}^{dER}} &:= \left\{\hat{\mathfrak{G}}_{\mathcal{E}}[\mathfrak{E}] \colon \mathfrak{E} \in \hat{\mathcal{E}}^{\mathscr{K}_n^d}\right\} \subset \mathbb{B}^{n\times n}, \end{aligned} \tag{5.41}$$

and the subsets

$$\begin{aligned} \hat{\mathcal{N}}_{cl}^{\mathscr{R}_{n,k}^{dER}} &:= \left\{\boldsymbol{n} \in \hat{\mathcal{N}}^{\mathscr{R}_{n,k}^{dER}} \colon \mathrm{T}[\boldsymbol{n}] = 1\right\},\ \hat{\mathcal{N}}_{aux}^{\mathscr{R}_{n,k}^{dER}} := \left\{\boldsymbol{n}_0\right\}, \\ \hat{\mathcal{E}}_{cl}^{\mathscr{R}_{n,k}^{dER}} &:= \left\{\mathfrak{E} \in \hat{\mathcal{E}}^{\mathscr{R}_{n,k}^{dER}} \colon \mathrm{T}[\mathfrak{E}] = 1\right\},\ \hat{\mathcal{E}}_{aux}^{\mathscr{R}_{n,k}^{dER}} := \hat{\mathcal{E}}^{\mathscr{R}_{n,k}^{dER}} \setminus \hat{\mathcal{E}}_{cl}^{\mathscr{R}_{n,k}^{dER}} \end{aligned} \tag{5.42}$$

distinguish the classical and auxiliary nodes and edge operators of $\hat{\mathscr{R}}_{n,k}^{dER}$.

To briefly demonstrate the feasibility of (5.40), let us conclude by evaluating the adjacency matrix of graphs generated by $\hat{\mathfrak{G}}_k^{dER}$. As the Erdős–Rényi random digraph model, by construction, realises only relational digraphs, we can adapt the weight matrix observable introduced in (4.62), and define with

$$\hat{\boldsymbol{a}} \colon \mathbb{G} \to \mathbb{B}^{n\times n}\ ,\ \hat{\boldsymbol{a}}[\hat{\mathscr{G}}] = \boldsymbol{a} := \sum_{\mathfrak{E}\in\hat{\mathcal{E}}_{cl}} \mathfrak{E} \tag{5.43}$$

an adjacency matrix observable suitable for operator representations of graphs whose edge operators are formalised in terms of $(n \times n)$-dimensional Boolean matrices with at most one non-zero element. Applied to $\hat{\mathscr{R}}_{n,k}^{dER} = \hat{\mathfrak{G}}_k^{dER}[\hat{\mathscr{K}}_n^d]$, we then directly obtain

$$\begin{aligned} \hat{\boldsymbol{a}}[\hat{\mathscr{R}}_{n,k}^{dER}] = \sum_{j=1}^{k_{\max}} \mathfrak{E}_j &= \sum_{j=1}^{k_{\max}} (\boldsymbol{e}_{(k)}^{k_{\max}\mathsf{T}})_j \cdot \boldsymbol{\delta}_{j_1 j_2}^{n\times n} \\ &= \sum_{\substack{j_1,j_2=1 \\ j_1\neq j_2}}^{n} (\boldsymbol{e}_{(k)}^{k_{\max}\mathsf{T}})_{nj_1+j_2-\lfloor(nj_1+j_2)/(n+1)\rfloor-n} \cdot \boldsymbol{\delta}_{j_1 j_2}^{n\times n} \end{aligned} \tag{5.44}$$

for the adjacency matrix of the Erdős–Rényi random digraph model. Unsurprisingly, this result is in its algebraic form similar to (5.16), and differs only in the absence of a second δ-term which reflects, in the case of simple graphs, the expected symmetry of the adjacency matrix. Finally, it is important to stress here again that although both (5.16) and (5.44) provide algebraically rather unexciting results, their presentation as first concrete applications of observables to operator representations of random graphs serves to motivate the potential of our novel operator graph-theoretical framework to provide parametrised algebraical expressions for a variety of graph measures which, unlike the adjacency matrices evaluated in this section, are not that readily available or even possible to acquire classically.

5.1.3 Algebraic Challenges of the Erdős–Rényi Model

In our formalisation of Erdős–Rényi random graphs and digraphs, we already hinted at a number of challenges and limitations which arguably complicate the algebraically rigorous treatment of these models, not only in the context of an operator graph-theoretical framework. Due to the principal nature of these complications, let us therefore conclude this section with a closer inspection of their origin, before introducing the conceptually similar yet algebraically quite different Gilbert random graph model for circumnavigating some of their consequences. With (5.10) and (5.40), we defined two graph generators which construct viable operator representations of simple and directed Erdős–Rényi random graphs from their respective exact seed graphs, eventually yielding parametrised algebraical descriptions which encompass all possible concrete realisations of both models. Utilising these descriptions in conjunction with the various algebraic identities which govern their generators and seeds should then, ideally, allow us to evaluate, manipulate and ultimately simplify graph observables to arrive at a characterisation in terms of a model's defining parameters. But, as we already noted earlier, it is also these algebraic identities, or lack thereof, which renders – at least in the case of the Erdős–Rényi random graph model – an evaluation of graph observables difficult, especially if these observables represent graph measures that are defined in terms of products or sums of the adjacency matrix.

In order to develop a sensitivity for these difficulties and, in turn, shed some light on the complicating subtlety at the very heart of the Erdős–Rényi model, let us take a fresh look at the approach we have chosen, in particular the representation of the two graph generators $\hat{\mathfrak{G}}_k^{ER}$ and $\hat{\mathfrak{G}}_k^{dER}$ in terms of the column randomisation operator $\vec{\mathfrak{r}}^k$. The presence of this operator, or some similar algebraic object serving the same principal purpose, is made necessary due to the conception of an Erdős–Rényi random graph at any given order as a set of edges with fixed cardinality. This stringent requirement of an exact number of edges defining each of the model's realisations immediately leads to one glaring problem. It conflicts, at least when searching for a concrete algebraic formalisation, with the random selection of individual edges in the sense that such a selection process must necessarily be performed element-wise on the set of all possible edges while at the same time also being subject to a constraint imposed on the set of already selected edges. We dealt with this subtle complication in both graph generators (5.10) and (5.40) by considering the vector $(e^{k_{\max}}_{(k)})^{\mathsf{T}} := \bar{\mathfrak{r}}^k[\mathit{1}^{k_{\max}\,\mathsf{T}}]$ formally as being realised independently of the construction of edge operators itself. Although this algebraic distinction between edge operators and their random selection will naturally have a bearing on the scope of eventual algebraic manipulations involving edge operators, it also carries the benefit of formalising this selection process in more direct and generalisable terms, away from specific details of the considered model.

But even with the introduction of an algebraic object such as $e^{k_{\max}}_{(k)}$, we only delegate the problem of conditional random selection of edges, without actually redressing it. Indeed, with (5.28), (5.34) and (5.36), the algebraic structure defined by addition and composition of column randomisation operators unfortunately satisfies neither linearity under addition nor commutativity and left-distributivity under composition. The reason for these little satisfying algebraic properties can be found in the conception of this operator itself. Albeit $\bar{\mathfrak{r}}^k$ selects non-zero elements from each row of its matrix argument in a uniform-random fashion, which necessarily renders their occurrence and, thus, each algebraic construct involving or depending on individual matrix elements probabilistic in nature, an additional condition has to be imposed for each row to ensure that only a fixed number k of non-zero elements are selected. Similar to the random selection of edges in the original conception of the Erdős–Rényi model, this additional constraint conflicts with the independence of the element-wise selection process itself – or at least, it presents a cause for challenges where algebraic formalisations are concerned. For example, what precisely is meant by the composition of two column randomisation operators which choose a distinct number of non-zero elements from an argument, or the sum of two vectors with distinct fixed numbers of non-zero elements that were randomly chosen from a common argument? The result of such operations either requires some supplementary probabilistic assessment, as evident for (5.31) and its variable number of non-zero elements on each row, or is not defined at all, as evident for (5.27) with $k < k'$.

It could be rightfully argued that the encountered challenges are a direct repercussion of our chosen approach, specifically the utilisation of the perhaps somewhat ill-defined and, therefore, taxing column randomisation operator $\bar{\mathfrak{r}}^k$, and that by algebraically formalising the construction of Erdős–Rényi random graphs in a different way, some of these challenges could be alleviated. However, as noted before, the ultimate source of the problem lies in the very conception of the Erdős–Rényi model itself, as it necessitates, by definition, a fixed number of randomly distributed edges. Whatever the concrete algebraic realisation of this selection process may look like, with $\bar{\mathfrak{r}}^k$ introduced in (4.59) arguably presenting an excessively crude way, it must account for this stringent curtailment in one way or another.

Having thus pinpointed the subtle reason behind the algebraic challenges encountered in the construction of the Erdős–Rényi model, let us then explore what a weakening of the restriction on the number of constructed edges in a random graph would entail. For entertaining such a change to the graph model at hand, it suffices to consider all-ones row vectors $\boldsymbol{1}^{n\top} \in \mathbb{B}^n$ for which $\bar{\mathfrak{r}}^k[\boldsymbol{1}^{n\top}]$, by definition, yields a Boolean vector with k non-zero elements such that

$$\mathrm{T}\left[\bar{\mathfrak{r}}^k[\boldsymbol{1}^{n\top}]\right] = k. \tag{5.45}$$

But what about the individual elements of the resulting vector? From a probabilistic perspective, ignoring for a moment the requirement (5.45) which defines (4.59), we immediately find

$$\left(\bar{\mathfrak{r}}^k[\boldsymbol{1}^{n\top}]\right)_i \to \left\{ \begin{array}{ll} 1 & \text{with probability } p := k/n, \\ 0 & \text{with probability } (1-p) \end{array} \right\} = \left(\mathfrak{r}^p[\boldsymbol{1}^{n\top}]\right)_i$$

as $\bar{\mathfrak{r}}^k$ acts in an element-wise independent and uniform-random fashion on its argument vector. The occurrence of non-zero elements can thus be expressed in terms of the binomial randomisation operator $\mathfrak{r}^p$ introduced in (4.41). Moreover, employing (4.43), we have

$$\left\langle \mathrm{T}\left[\mathfrak{r}^p[\boldsymbol{1}^{n\top}]\right]\right\rangle = np = k,$$

which leaves us to conclude that such a probabilistic perspective, at least in the statistical average over many realisations and for appropriately chosen p, naturally satisfies the requirement of delivering k non-zero elements. Both operators $\mathfrak{r}^k$ and $\mathfrak{r}^p$ are thus bound to deliver, in the statistical limit, the same result, with the advantage of the latter to circumvent the troublesome additional constraint imposed on the total number of occurring non-zero elements.

What about the composition of two column randomisation operators? Recalling (5.27), the expression $\bar{\mathfrak{r}}^{k'} \circ \bar{\mathfrak{r}}^k[\boldsymbol{1}^{n\top}]$ is not defined at all for $k' > k$, and for $k' \leq k$ delivers a vector with exactly k' non-zero elements, chosen from a set of k non-zero elements which themselves are randomly selected from the n elements of $\boldsymbol{1}^{n\top}$, such that

$$\mathrm{T}\left[\bar{\mathfrak{r}}^{k'} \circ \bar{\mathfrak{r}}^{k}[\mathbf{1}^{n\mathsf{T}}]\right] = k'. \tag{5.46}$$

Viewed element-wise probabilistically, we then obtain

$$\left(\bar{\mathfrak{r}}^{k'} \circ \bar{\mathfrak{r}}^{k}[\mathbf{1}^{n\mathsf{T}}]\right)_i \to \left\{ \begin{array}{ll} 1 & \text{with probability } pp' = k'/n, \\ 0 & \text{with probability } (1 - pp') \end{array} \right\} = \left(\mathfrak{r}^{p'} \circ \mathfrak{r}^{p}[\mathbf{1}^{n\mathsf{T}}]\right)_i$$

for $p' := k'/k$ and $p := k/n$. Recalling (4.43), and with (4.44) the identity that underlies the composition of binomial randomisation operators, not only does this result through

$$\left\langle \mathrm{T}\left[\mathfrak{r}^{p'} \circ \mathfrak{r}^{p}[\mathbf{1}^{n\mathsf{T}}]\right]\right\rangle = \left\langle \mathrm{T}\left[\mathfrak{r}^{p'p}[\mathbf{1}^{n\mathsf{T}}]\right]\right\rangle = np'p = k'$$

satisfy (5.46) in the statistical limit over many realisations, but it also, and more importantly, delivers with

$$\mathfrak{r}^{p'} \circ \mathfrak{r}^{p}[\mathbf{1}^{n\mathsf{T}}] = \mathfrak{r}^{p'p}[\mathbf{1}^{n\mathsf{T}}] = \mathfrak{r}^{pp'}[\mathbf{1}^{n\mathsf{T}}] = \mathfrak{r}^{p} \circ \mathfrak{r}^{p'}[\mathbf{1}^{n\mathsf{T}}]$$

an identity that will allow us to bypass the limitation imposed on commutativity that the composition of our column randomisation operators suffers from. Indeed, it can be shown that the commutative rule

$$\bar{\mathfrak{r}}^{p'} \circ \bar{\mathfrak{r}}^{p}[\boldsymbol{A}] = \bar{\mathfrak{r}}^{p} \circ \bar{\mathfrak{r}}^{p'}[\boldsymbol{A}] \tag{5.47}$$

holds for arbitrary $\boldsymbol{A} \in \mathbb{Q}^{m\times n}$ and $p, p' \in \mathbb{Q} : p, p' \in [0, 1]$.

Poised by this optimistic prospect, let us next take a closer look at the operation of addition of column randomisation operators, specifically its definition (5.31). Adhering to (4.59), $\bar{\mathfrak{r}}^{k}$ and $\bar{\mathfrak{r}}^{k'}$ will respectively select k and k' non-zero elements from each row of their common argument such that

$$\mathrm{T}\left[\bar{\mathfrak{r}}^{k}[\mathbf{1}^{n\mathsf{T}}] + \bar{\mathfrak{r}}^{k'}[\mathbf{1}^{n\mathsf{T}}]\right] = k + k'. \tag{5.48}$$

However, these elements will be uniform-randomly distributed such that the number of non-zero elements in the sum $\bar{\mathfrak{r}}^{k}[\mathbf{1}^{n\mathsf{T}}] + \bar{\mathfrak{r}}^{k'}[\mathbf{1}^{n\mathsf{T}}]$ must be at least k, can be at most $\min[n, k + k']$, and will generally differ between individual realisations due to the random nature of the selection process. Indeed, we find that $(\bar{\mathfrak{r}}^{k}[\mathbf{1}^{n\mathsf{T}}])_i = 1$ with probability $p := k/n$ and $(\bar{\mathfrak{r}}^{k'}[\mathbf{1}^{n\mathsf{T}}])_i = 1$ with probability $p' := k'/n$ for each $i \in [1, n]$. With this, we can then easily show that

$$\begin{aligned}
\left((\bar{\mathfrak{r}}^{k} + \bar{\mathfrak{r}}^{k'})[\mathbf{1}^{n\mathsf{T}}]\right)_i &= \left(\bar{\mathfrak{r}}^{k}[\mathbf{1}^{n\mathsf{T}}]\right)_i + \left(\bar{\mathfrak{r}}^{k'}[\mathbf{1}^{n\mathsf{T}}]\right)_i \\
&\to \left\{ \begin{array}{ll} 0 & \text{with probability } (1 - p)(1 - p'), \\ 1 & \text{with probability } p + p' - 2pp', \\ 2 & \text{with probability } pp' \end{array} \right\} \\
&= \left(\mathfrak{r}^{p}[\mathbf{1}^{n\mathsf{T}}]\right)_i + \left(\mathfrak{r}^{p'}[\mathbf{1}^{n\mathsf{T}}]\right)_i = \left((\mathfrak{r}^{p} + \mathfrak{r}^{p'})[\mathbf{1}^{n\mathsf{T}}]\right)_i
\end{aligned}$$

and that the expectation value

$$\left\langle \mathrm{T}\left[\mathfrak{r}^{p}[\mathbf{1}^{n\mathsf{T}}] + \mathfrak{r}^{p'}[\mathbf{1}^{n\mathsf{T}}]\right]\right\rangle = \left\langle \mathrm{T}\left[\mathfrak{r}^{p}[\mathbf{1}^{n\mathsf{T}}]\right]\right\rangle + \left\langle \mathrm{T}\left[\mathfrak{r}^{p'}[\mathbf{1}^{n\mathsf{T}}]\right]\right\rangle = np + np' = k + k'$$

satisfies (5.48), such that

$$(\mathfrak{r}^{p} + \mathfrak{r}^{p'})[\boldsymbol{A}] := \mathfrak{r}^{p}[\boldsymbol{A}] + \mathfrak{r}^{p'}[\boldsymbol{A}] \tag{5.49}$$

for general $\boldsymbol{A} \in \mathbb{Q}^{m \times n}$ eventually defines a both commutative and associative operation of addition for binomial randomisation operators which, in a statistical sense, will be compatible with (5.31).

Our promising approach ends here, unfortunately, as even employing the operator $\mathfrak{r}^{p}$ instead of $\bar{\mathfrak{r}}^{k}$ will not help to remedy the general lack of linearity under addition, or the stringently limited validity of left-distributivity due to the ever-present additive law of probability. Because the binomial randomisation operator, by conception, acts independently on the elements of its argument, we indeed find

$$\mathfrak{r}^{p}[\boldsymbol{A} + \boldsymbol{B}] \neq \mathfrak{r}^{p}[\boldsymbol{A}] + \mathfrak{r}^{p}[\boldsymbol{B}] \tag{5.50}$$

and

$$\mathfrak{r}^{p} \circ (\mathfrak{r}^{p'} + \mathfrak{r}^{p''})[\boldsymbol{A}] \neq (\mathfrak{r}^{p} \circ \mathfrak{r}^{p'} + \mathfrak{r}^{p} \circ \mathfrak{r}^{p''})[\boldsymbol{A}] \tag{5.51}$$

for general $p, p', p'' \in \mathbb{Q}\colon\ p, p', p'' \in [0, 1]$. However, at least the former of these two crucial properties can be salvaged in some special cases. One of these special cases is given by restricting the domain of $\mathfrak{r}^{p}$ to matrices $\boldsymbol{A}, \boldsymbol{B} \in \mathbb{Q}^{m \times n}$ which satisfy $\boldsymbol{A} \odot \boldsymbol{B} = \boldsymbol{0}^{m \times n}$. Recalling (5.19) and (5.23), we can then show that

$$\mathfrak{r}^{p}[\delta_i^n + \delta_j^n] = \mathfrak{r}^{p}[\delta_i^n] + \mathfrak{r}^{p}[\delta_j^n] \tag{5.52}$$

for $i \neq j$ and

$$\mathfrak{r}^{p}[\delta_{ij}^{m \times n} + \delta_{kl}^{m \times n}] = \mathfrak{r}^{p}[\delta_{ij}^{m \times n}] + \mathfrak{r}^{p}[\delta_{kl}^{m \times n}] \tag{5.53}$$

for $i \neq k \vee j \neq l$ and arbitrary $p \in \mathbb{Q}\colon\ p \in [0, 1]$. Interestingly, it is precisely this case that will be of relevance for the construction and algebraic assessment of the random graph models presented in the remainder of this chapter.

It is important to note in conclusion that with an algebraic structure comprised of scalar multiplication, operator addition and operator composition, the set of column randomisation operators $\bar{\mathfrak{r}}^{k}$ eventually realises a non-linear algebra of operators $\mathscr{A}^{\bar{\mathfrak{r}}} := (\{\bar{\mathfrak{r}}^{k}\colon k \in \mathbb{N}_0\}, \{\cdot, +, \circ\})$ with additive identity. On the other hand, the set of binomial randomisation operators $\mathfrak{r}^{p}$ yields a non-linear operator algebra $\mathscr{A}^{\mathfrak{r}} := (\{\mathfrak{r}^{p}\colon p \in \mathbb{Q}, p \in [0, 1]\}, \{\cdot, +, \circ\})$ with additive and multiplicative identity which is both commutative and associative with respect to operator addition and operator composition. These two algebras of

Table 5.1 *Comparison of algebraic properties of* $\bar{\mathbf{r}}^k$ *and* $\mathbf{r}^p$.

	Column randomisation operator	**Binomial randomisation operator**
	$\bar{\mathbf{r}}^k : \mathbb{Q}^{m\times n} \to \mathbb{Q}^{m\times n}$, $\bar{\mathbf{r}}^k[\boldsymbol{A}]_{ij} : [1,m]\times[1,n] \subset \mathbb{N}^2 \to \mathbb{Q}$	$\mathbf{r}^p : \mathbb{Q}^{m\times n} \to \mathbb{Q}^{m\times n}$, $\mathbf{r}^p[\boldsymbol{A}]_{ij} : [1,m]\times[1,n] \subset \mathbb{N}^2 \to \mathbb{Q}$
definition	$\bar{\mathbf{r}}^k[\boldsymbol{A}]_{ij} := \begin{cases} A_{ij} & \text{for } j \in C_k^{\text{rand}}(\{j' \in [1,n] : A_{ij'} \neq 0\}), \\ 0 & \text{otherwise} \end{cases}$	$\mathbf{r}^p[\boldsymbol{A}]_{ij} := \begin{cases} A_{ij} & \text{with probability } p, \\ 0 & \text{otherwise} \end{cases}$
	$\boldsymbol{A} \in \mathbb{Q}^{m\times n} : (\bar{\delta}[\boldsymbol{A}]\cdot \boldsymbol{I}^n)_i \geq k\ \forall i \in [1,m]$	$\boldsymbol{A} \in \mathbb{Q}^{m\times n}$, $p \in \mathbb{Q} : p \in [0,1]$
	Operator addition	
definition	$(\bar{\mathbf{r}}^k + \bar{\mathbf{r}}^{k'})[\boldsymbol{A}] := \bar{\mathbf{r}}^k[\boldsymbol{A}] + \bar{\mathbf{r}}^{k'}[\boldsymbol{A}]$	$(\mathbf{r}^p + \mathbf{r}^{p'})[\boldsymbol{A}] := \mathbf{r}^p[\boldsymbol{A}] + \mathbf{r}^{p'}[\boldsymbol{A}]$
identity	$\bar{\mathbf{r}}^0$	$\mathbf{r}^0$
commutativity	$(\bar{\mathbf{r}}^k + \bar{\mathbf{r}}^{k'})[\boldsymbol{A}] = (\bar{\mathbf{r}}^{k'} + \bar{\mathbf{r}}^k)[\boldsymbol{A}]$	$(\mathbf{r}^p + \mathbf{r}^{p'})[\boldsymbol{A}] = (\mathbf{r}^{p'} + \mathbf{r}^p)[\boldsymbol{A}]$
associativity	$\left((\bar{\mathbf{r}}^k + \bar{\mathbf{r}}^{k'}) + \bar{\mathbf{r}}^{k''}\right)[\boldsymbol{A}] = \left(\bar{\mathbf{r}}^k + (\bar{\mathbf{r}}^{k'} + \bar{\mathbf{r}}^{k''})\right)[\boldsymbol{A}]$	$\left((\mathbf{r}^p + \mathbf{r}^{p'}) + \mathbf{r}^{p''}\right)[\boldsymbol{A}] = \left(\mathbf{r}^p + (\mathbf{r}^{p'} + \mathbf{r}^{p''})\right)[\boldsymbol{A}]$
	Operator composition	
definition	$\bar{\mathbf{r}}^{k'} \circ \bar{\mathbf{r}}^k[\boldsymbol{A}] := \bar{\mathbf{r}}^{k'}[\boldsymbol{A}]$ iff $k' \leq k$	$\mathbf{r}^{p'} \circ \mathbf{r}^p[\boldsymbol{A}] := \mathbf{r}^{pp'}[\boldsymbol{A}]\ \forall p, p' \in \mathbb{Q} : p, p' \in [0,1]$
identity	dependant on argument	$\mathbf{r}^1$
commutativity	$\bar{\mathbf{r}}^{k'} \circ \bar{\mathbf{r}}^k[\boldsymbol{A}] = \bar{\mathbf{r}}^k \circ \bar{\mathbf{r}}^{k'}[\boldsymbol{A}]$ iff $k' = k$	$\mathbf{r}^{p'} \circ \mathbf{r}^p[\boldsymbol{A}] = \mathbf{r}^p \circ \mathbf{r}^{p'}[\boldsymbol{A}]$
associativity	$\bar{\mathbf{r}}^{k''} \circ (\bar{\mathbf{r}}^{k'} \circ \bar{\mathbf{r}}^k)[\boldsymbol{A}] = (\bar{\mathbf{r}}^{k''} \circ \bar{\mathbf{r}}^{k'}) \circ \bar{\mathbf{r}}^k[\boldsymbol{A}]$ iff $k'' \leq k' \leq k$	$\mathbf{r}^{p''} \circ (\mathbf{r}^{p'} \circ \mathbf{r}^p)[\boldsymbol{A}] = (\mathbf{r}^{p''} \circ \mathbf{r}^{p'}) \circ \mathbf{r}^p[\boldsymbol{A}]$
power	$(\bar{\mathbf{r}}^k)^n[\boldsymbol{A}] = \bar{\mathbf{r}}^k[\boldsymbol{A}]$	$(\mathbf{r}^p)^n[\boldsymbol{A}] = \mathbf{r}^{p^n}[\boldsymbol{A}]$
compatibility with scalar multiplication	$\left(a\cdot(\bar{\mathbf{r}}^{k'} \circ \bar{\mathbf{r}}^k)\right)[\boldsymbol{A}] = (a\cdot\bar{\mathbf{r}}^{k'}) \circ \bar{\mathbf{r}}^k[\boldsymbol{A}] = \bar{\mathbf{r}}^{k'} \circ (a\cdot\bar{\mathbf{r}}^k)[\boldsymbol{A}]$ $= a\cdot\bar{\mathbf{r}}^{k'}[\boldsymbol{A}]$, $a \in \mathbb{Q}$ iff $k' \leq k$	$\left(a\cdot(\mathbf{r}^{p'} \circ \mathbf{r}^p)\right)[\boldsymbol{A}] = (a\cdot\mathbf{r}^{p'}) \circ \mathbf{r}^p[\boldsymbol{A}] = \mathbf{r}^{p'} \circ (a\cdot\mathbf{r}^p)[\boldsymbol{A}]$ $= a\cdot\mathbf{r}^{pp'}[\boldsymbol{A}]$, $a \in \mathbb{Q}$
linearity	$\bar{\mathbf{r}}^k[\boldsymbol{A}+\boldsymbol{B}] \neq \bar{\mathbf{r}}^k[\boldsymbol{A}] + \bar{\mathbf{r}}^k[\boldsymbol{B}]$	$\mathbf{r}^p[\boldsymbol{A}+\boldsymbol{B}] \neq \mathbf{r}^p[\boldsymbol{A}] + \mathbf{r}^p[\boldsymbol{B}]$
homogeneity of degree 1	$\bar{\mathbf{r}}^k[a\cdot\boldsymbol{A}] = a\cdot\bar{\mathbf{r}}^k[\boldsymbol{A}]$, $a \in \mathbb{Q}$	$\mathbf{r}^p[a\cdot\boldsymbol{A}] = a\cdot\mathbf{r}^p[\boldsymbol{A}]$, $a \in \mathbb{Q}$
left-distributivity	$\bar{\mathbf{r}}^k \circ (\bar{\mathbf{r}}^{k'} + \bar{\mathbf{r}}^{k''})[\boldsymbol{A}] \neq (\bar{\mathbf{r}}^k \circ \bar{\mathbf{r}}^{k'} + \bar{\mathbf{r}}^k \circ \bar{\mathbf{r}}^{k''})[\boldsymbol{A}]$	$\mathbf{r}^p \circ (\mathbf{r}^{p'} + \mathbf{r}^{p''})[\boldsymbol{A}] \neq (\mathbf{r}^p \circ \mathbf{r}^{p'} + \mathbf{r}^p \circ \mathbf{r}^{p''})[\boldsymbol{A}]$
right-distributivity	$(\bar{\mathbf{r}}^{k''} + (\bar{\mathbf{r}}^{k'}) \circ \bar{\mathbf{r}}^k[\boldsymbol{A}] = (\bar{\mathbf{r}}^{k''} \circ \bar{\mathbf{r}}^k + \bar{\mathbf{r}}^{k'} \circ \bar{\mathbf{r}}^k)[\boldsymbol{A}]$ iff $k', k'' \leq k$	$(\mathbf{r}^{p''} + (\mathbf{r}^{p'}) \circ \mathbf{r}^p[\boldsymbol{A}] = (\mathbf{r}^{p''} \circ \mathbf{r}^p + \mathbf{r}^{p'} \circ \mathbf{r}^p)[\boldsymbol{A}]$

randomisation operators are distinguished in Table 5.1 by summarising some of their primary properties. As we will demonstrate in subsequent sections, this enriched set of algebraic properties of $\mathscr{A}^{\mathfrak{r}}$, in conjunction with the fact that this algebra relinquishes the stringent restriction that governs the applicability of the column randomisation operator, renders it a more suitable candidate for aiding the algebraic construction of a variety of random graphs.

5.2 Gilbert Random Graphs

After this brief excursion into the challenging nature of the Erdős–Rényi model, and a closer comparative look at the properties which define both column and binomial randomisation operators, let us now proceed by making use of the gained insights and algebraically formulate the alternative model of Gilbert random graphs [49]. As we recall from Section 2.3.5, a realisation $(\mathcal{N}, \mathcal{E})$ of the directed Gilbert random graph $\mathscr{R}^{dG}_{n,p}$ of order n and connection probability p is obtained through the consideration of all possible ordered pairs (i, j) of nodes $i, j \in \mathcal{N} : i \neq j$ from a set $\mathcal{N}$ with $|\mathcal{N}| = n \in \mathbb{N}$, and the independent assignment of each such pair with probability $p \in \mathbb{Q} : p \in [0, 1]$ to a set of edges $\mathcal{E}$ (see Fig. 2.9a). In a similar fashion, a simple Gilbert random graph $\mathscr{R}^{G}_{n,p}$ is realised by restricting to ordered node pairs (i, j) with $j > i$, and assigning the tuple $\{(i, j), (j, i)\}$ with probability p to $\mathcal{E}$.

Because of this purely element-wise probabilistic conception of Gilbert random graphs, and the principal absence of an overarching constraint imposed on the exact number of generated edges, the binomial randomisation operator (4.41) naturally presents itself here as a viable algebraic tool in the construction of this model. Restricting ourselves to the Boolean vector and matrix representations for nodes and edge operators utilised for the Erdős–Rényi model, we will in this section not only algebraically formalise the generation of undirected and directed Gilbert random graphs from complete simple graphs and complete relational digraphs, respectively, but also lay the groundwork for the generation of small-world and scale-free random graph models later in this chapter.

5.2.1 Undirected Gilbert Random Graphs

Aiming at the formalisation that proved suitable in the case of the undirected Erdős–Rényi model, let us start with the operator representation $\hat{\mathcal{K}}_n$ of the complete simple graph $\mathcal{K}_n$ of order n defined by (5.1)–(5.3) and (5.6)–(5.8). In order to realise from this representation an undirected Gilbert random graph $\mathscr{R}^{G}_{n,p}$, we then must select uniform-randomly with probability p individual

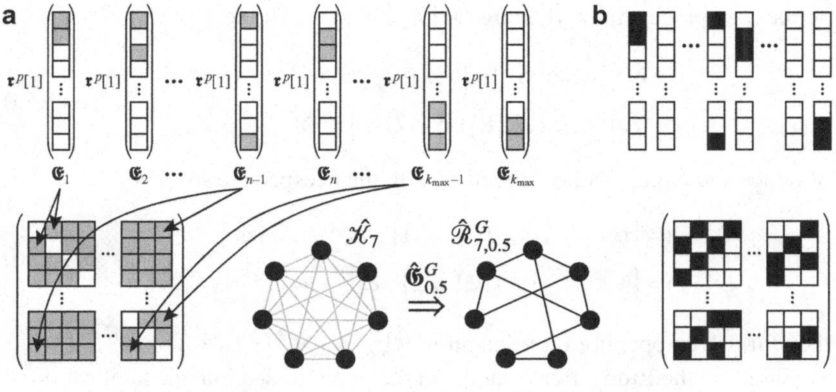

Figure 5.3 Generation of simple Gilbert random graphs $\mathscr{R}^G_{n,p}$. **a:** Assignment of scalar realisations $\mathfrak{r}^p[1]$ of the binomial randomisation operator to each of the $k_{\max}$ edge operators $\mathfrak{E}_j$ in an operator representation of the simple complete graph $\mathscr{K}_n$ that mark two symmetric non-zero elements in its matrix of adjacency relations (bottom). **b:** Independent realisations of $\mathfrak{r}^p[1]$ randomly select edge operators $\mathfrak{E}_j$ with probability p and eventually construct an operator representation of $\mathscr{R}^G_{n,p}$ with a symmetric matrix of adjacency relations comprised of randomly distributed non-zero elements (bottom) from the seed $\hat{\mathscr{K}}_n$ by means of the generator $\hat{\mathfrak{G}}^G_p$ in (5.10). The inset exemplifies a realisation of this graph generation for $n = 7, p = 0.5$.

elements from its set of $k_{\max} = n(n-1)/2$ edge operators $\hat{\mathcal{E}}^{\mathscr{K}_n}_{cl}$. This element-wise selection process can be algebraically formalised in a variety of ways by utilising the binomial randomisation operator $\mathfrak{r}^p$. For instance, the application of $\mathfrak{r}^p$ to the $k_{\max}$-dimensional row vector $e^{k_{\max}\mathsf{T}}$ could be employed to mark selected edges such that $\mathfrak{r}^p[e^{k_{\max}\mathsf{T}}] \cdot (\delta^{k_{\max}\times n}_{j,j_1} + \delta^{k_{\max}\times n}_{j,j_2})$ delivers all edge operators which eventually construct a Gilbert random graph. This approach mirrors that used in Section 5.1.1, the difference being that now the total number of edges is no longer fixed but can vary between different realisations of the same model, equalling $k = pk_{\max}$ only in the statistical average for an appropriately chosen probability $p := k/k_{\max}$.

Another yet conceptually equivalent approach is to apply $k_{\max}$ independent scalar realisations $\mathfrak{r}^p[1]$, one for each $\mathfrak{E} \in \hat{\mathcal{E}}^{\mathscr{K}_n}_{cl}$, such that $\mathfrak{r}^p[1] \cdot \mathfrak{E}$ formalises the random selection of edge-generating operators. This alternative approach, illustrated in Fig. 5.3, will be the focus of what follows, as it allows for an algebraically more transparent treatment. Specifically, let

$$\begin{aligned} &\hat{\mathfrak{G}}^G_p = \left(\hat{\mathfrak{G}}_{\mathcal{N}}\,,\, \hat{\mathfrak{G}}_{\mathcal{E}}\right), && (5.54)\\ &\hat{\mathfrak{G}}_{\mathcal{N}} : \hat{\mathcal{N}}^{\mathscr{K}_n} \to \hat{\mathcal{N}}^{\mathscr{R}^G_{n,p}}\,,\ \hat{\mathfrak{G}}_{\mathcal{N}} := \mathrm{id}\,,\\ &\hat{\mathfrak{G}}_{\mathcal{E}} : \hat{\mathcal{E}}^{\mathscr{K}_n} \to \hat{\mathcal{E}}^{\mathscr{R}^G_{n,p}}\,,\ \hat{\mathfrak{G}}_{\mathcal{E}}[\mathfrak{E}_j] := \mathfrak{r}^p[1]\cdot\mathfrak{E}_j = \mathfrak{r}^p[1]\cdot(\delta^n_{j_1} + \delta^n_{j_2}) \end{aligned}$$

define a graph generator yielding $\hat{\mathfrak{G}}_p^G[\hat{\mathcal{K}}_n] = \hat{\mathcal{R}}_{n,p}^G$. The sets

$$\begin{aligned} \hat{\mathcal{N}}^{\mathcal{R}_{n,p}^G} &:= \left\{\hat{\mathfrak{G}}_{\mathcal{N}}[\boldsymbol{n}] : \boldsymbol{n} \in \hat{\mathcal{N}}^{\mathcal{K}_n}\right\} = \hat{\mathcal{N}}^{\mathcal{K}_n} \subset \mathbb{B}^n, \\ \hat{\mathcal{E}}^{\mathcal{R}_{n,p}^G} &:= \left\{\hat{\mathfrak{G}}_{\mathcal{E}}[\mathfrak{E}] : \mathfrak{E} \in \hat{\mathcal{E}}^{\mathcal{K}_n}\right\} \subset \mathbb{B}^n \end{aligned} \tag{5.55}$$

of nodes and edge operators together with their respective subsets

$$\begin{aligned} \hat{\mathcal{N}}_{cl}^{\mathcal{R}_{n,p}^G} &:= \left\{\boldsymbol{n} \in \hat{\mathcal{N}}^{\mathcal{R}_{n,p}^G} : \mathrm{T}[\boldsymbol{n}] = 1\right\}, \; \hat{\mathcal{N}}_{aux}^{\mathcal{R}_{n,p}^G} := \left\{\boldsymbol{n}_0\right\}, \\ \hat{\mathcal{E}}_{cl}^{\mathcal{R}_{n,p}^G} &:= \left\{\mathfrak{E} \in \hat{\mathcal{E}}^{\mathcal{R}_{n,p}^G} : \mathrm{T}[\mathfrak{E}] = 2\right\}, \; \hat{\mathcal{E}}_{aux}^{\mathcal{R}_{n,p}^G} := \hat{\mathcal{E}}^{\mathcal{R}_{n,p}^G} \setminus \hat{\mathcal{E}}_{cl}^{\mathcal{R}_{n,p}^G} \end{aligned} \tag{5.56}$$

then furnish an operator representation $\hat{\mathcal{R}}_{n,p}^G := (\hat{\mathcal{N}}^{\mathcal{R}_{n,p}^G}, \hat{\mathcal{E}}^{\mathcal{R}_{n,p}^G})$ of $\mathcal{R}_{n,p}^G$.

Similar to the Erdős–Rényi model in the previous section, the application of the generator $\hat{\mathfrak{G}}_p^G$ to its seed $\hat{\mathcal{K}}_n$ can be interpreted as a parametrised algebraic representation of the Gilbert model as a whole, encompassing all of its concrete computational realisations. Indeed, by evaluating the observable (4.63) with $\mathfrak{E}_j = \mathfrak{r}^p[1] \cdot (\boldsymbol{\delta}_{j_1}^n + \boldsymbol{\delta}_{j_2}^n)$, we readily find

$$\begin{aligned} \hat{\mathfrak{a}}[\hat{\mathcal{R}}_{n,p}^G] = \sum_{j=1}^{k_{\max}} \Big(&(\mathfrak{r}_j^p[1])^2 \cdot \big(\boldsymbol{\delta}_{j_1}^n \otimes \boldsymbol{\delta}_{j_1}^{n\mathsf{T}} + \boldsymbol{\delta}_{j_1}^n \otimes \boldsymbol{\delta}_{j_2}^{n\mathsf{T}} + \boldsymbol{\delta}_{j_2}^n \otimes \boldsymbol{\delta}_{j_1}^{n\mathsf{T}} + \boldsymbol{\delta}_{j_2}^n \otimes \boldsymbol{\delta}_{j_2}^{n\mathsf{T}}\big) \\ &-\mathfrak{r}_j^p[1] \cdot \big(\operatorname{diag}[\boldsymbol{\delta}_{j_1}^n] - \operatorname{diag}[\boldsymbol{\delta}_{j_2}^n]\big)\Big) \end{aligned} \tag{5.57}$$

for the adjacency matrix of Gilbert random graphs at arbitrary order $n \in \mathbb{N}$ and connection probability $0 \leq p \leq 1$. Because the Kronecker product and diagonalisation operator in (4.63) involve for any given $j \in [1, k_{\max}]$ the same edge operator $\mathfrak{E}_j$, however, it is important to stress that the occurrence of $\mathfrak{r}^p[1]$ in the above expression marks only independent realisations over j, and not over individual terms in the sum's argument. Having indicated this subtlety by introducing a subscript on the randomisation operator, we recognise that

$$(\mathfrak{r}_j^p[1])^2 = \left\{ \begin{array}{ll} 1 & \text{with probability } p, \\ 0 & \text{with probability } (1-p) \end{array} \right\} = \mathfrak{r}_j^p[1] \tag{5.58}$$

differs from the scalar product $\mathfrak{r}_j^p[1] \cdot \mathfrak{r}_{j'}^p[1]$ or, more generally, $\mathfrak{r}_j^p[1] \cdot \mathfrak{r}_{j'}^q[1]$ involving distinct realisations $j \neq j'$, for which

$$\mathfrak{r}_j^p[1] \cdot \mathfrak{r}_{j'}^q[1] = \left\{ \begin{array}{ll} 1 & \text{with probability } pq, \\ 0 & \text{with probability } (1-pq) \end{array} \right. \tag{5.59}$$

in accordance with (4.45). Together with (5.20), the right-hand side of (5.57) can then easily be simplified, and it finally delivers

$$\hat{\mathfrak{a}}[\hat{\mathcal{R}}_{n,p}^G] = \sum_{j=1}^{k_{\max}} \mathfrak{r}_j^p[1] \cdot (\boldsymbol{\delta}_{j_1 j_2}^{n\times n} + \boldsymbol{\delta}_{j_2 j_1}^{n\times n}) = \sum_{\substack{j_1, j_2 = 1 \\ j_2 > j_1}}^{n} \mathfrak{r}_{j_1 j_2}^p[1] \cdot (\boldsymbol{\delta}_{j_1 j_2}^{n\times n} + \boldsymbol{\delta}_{j_2 j_1}^{n\times n}). \tag{5.60}$$

The presence of $n(n-1)/2$ distinct scalar realisations $\mathfrak{r}^p_{j_1 j_2}[1]$ ensures here that all adjacency relations are chosen uniform-randomly with probability p, and the presence of the two $\boldsymbol{\delta}$-terms that each of these relations contributes a symmetric pair of non-zero elements to the adjacency matrix, as expected for realisations of a simple Gilbert random graph.

5.2.2 Directed Gilbert Random Graphs

An operator representation of directed Gilbert random graphs $\mathscr{R}^{dG}_{n,p}$ can be obtained in a similar fashion by adapting the generator (5.54) for the undirected model to operate on the representation $\hat{\mathscr{K}}^d_n$ of the complete relational digraph $\mathscr{K}^d_n$ defined in (4.74) and (4.75). We now have to select uniform at random with probability p individual elements from the set $\hat{\mathcal{E}}^{\mathscr{K}^d_n}_{cl}$ of $k_{\max} = n(n-1)$ edge operators $\mathfrak{E}_j := \boldsymbol{\delta}^{n\times n}_{j_1 j_2}$, where $j \in [1, k_{\max}]$ and $j_1, j_2 \in [1, n]$ with $j_1 \neq j_2$ are respectively given by (5.38) and (5.37). To do so, we will again make use of $k_{\max}$ scalar realisations $\mathfrak{r}^p[1]$ of our binomial randomisation operator, such that $\mathfrak{r}^p[1] \cdot \mathfrak{E}_j$ algebraically formalises the selection of edge-generating operators that eventually realises a Gilbert random digraph.

In contrast to the construction of edges operators for simple Gilbert random graphs, however, the random selection of edge operators in the directed model allows for further simplification. Indeed, while the former requires the application of a single realisation of $\mathfrak{r}^p[1]$ to both non-zero elements of a Boolean vector $\boldsymbol{\delta}^n_{j_1} + \boldsymbol{\delta}^n_{j_2}$ representing an undirected edge in order to ensure the symmetry of adjacency relations between connected nodes (Fig. 5.3a), each edge operator $\mathfrak{E}_j$ of $\hat{\mathscr{K}}^d_n$ is represented by a Boolean matrix with at most one non-zero element such that $\mathfrak{r}^p[1] \cdot \mathfrak{E}_j = \mathfrak{r}^p[\mathfrak{E}_j]$ for all $\mathfrak{E}_j \in \hat{\mathcal{E}}^{\mathscr{K}^d_n}$. As illustrated in Fig. 5.4, we can exploit this algebraically more convenient form and obtain

$$\hat{\mathfrak{G}}^{dG}_k = \left(\hat{\mathfrak{G}}_{\mathcal{N}} := \mathrm{id}\,,\ \hat{\mathfrak{G}}_{\mathcal{E}}\colon \hat{\mathfrak{G}}_{\mathcal{E}}[\mathfrak{E}_j] := \mathfrak{r}^p[\mathfrak{E}_j] = \mathfrak{r}^p[\boldsymbol{\delta}^{n\times n}_{j_1 j_2}]\right) \tag{5.61}$$

as a generator for an operator representation $\hat{\mathscr{R}}^{dG}_{n,p} = \hat{\mathfrak{G}}^{dG}_p[\hat{\mathscr{K}}^d_n]$ of Gilbert random digraphs $\mathscr{R}^{dG}_{n,p}$ from a seed $\hat{\mathscr{K}}^d_n$ which represents the complete relational digraph $\mathscr{K}^d_n$. The sets of nodes and edge operators of $\hat{\mathscr{R}}^{dG}_{n,p} := (\hat{\mathcal{N}}^{\mathscr{R}^{dG}_{n,p}}, \hat{\mathcal{E}}^{\mathscr{R}^{dG}_{n,p}})$ are then given by

$$\begin{aligned} \hat{\mathcal{N}}^{\mathscr{R}^{dG}_{n,p}} &:= \hat{\mathcal{N}}^{\mathscr{K}^d_n} \subset \mathbb{B}^n, \\ \hat{\mathcal{E}}^{\mathscr{R}^{dG}_{n,p}} &:= \left\{\hat{\mathfrak{G}}_{\mathcal{E}}[\mathfrak{E}] : \mathfrak{E} \in \hat{\mathcal{E}}^{\mathscr{K}^d_n}\right\} \subset \mathbb{B}^{n\times n}, \end{aligned} \tag{5.62}$$

alongside

$$\begin{aligned} \hat{\mathcal{N}}^{\mathscr{R}^{dG}_{n,p}}_{cl} &:= \left\{\boldsymbol{n} \in \hat{\mathcal{N}}^{\mathscr{R}^{dG}_{n,p}} :\ \mathrm{T}[\boldsymbol{n}] = 1\right\},\ \hat{\mathcal{N}}^{\mathscr{R}^{dG}_{n,p}}_{aux} := \left\{\boldsymbol{n}_0\right\}, \\ \hat{\mathcal{E}}^{\mathscr{R}^{dG}_{n,p}}_{cl} &:= \left\{\mathfrak{E} \in \hat{\mathcal{E}}^{\mathscr{R}^{dG}_{n,p}} :\ \mathrm{T}[\mathfrak{E}] = 1\right\},\ \hat{\mathcal{E}}^{\mathscr{R}^{dG}_{n,p}}_{aux} := \hat{\mathcal{E}}^{\mathscr{R}^{dG}_{n,p}} \setminus \hat{\mathcal{E}}^{\mathscr{R}^{dG}_{n,p}}_{cl} \end{aligned} \tag{5.63}$$

as implicit definition of their respective classical and auxiliary subsets.

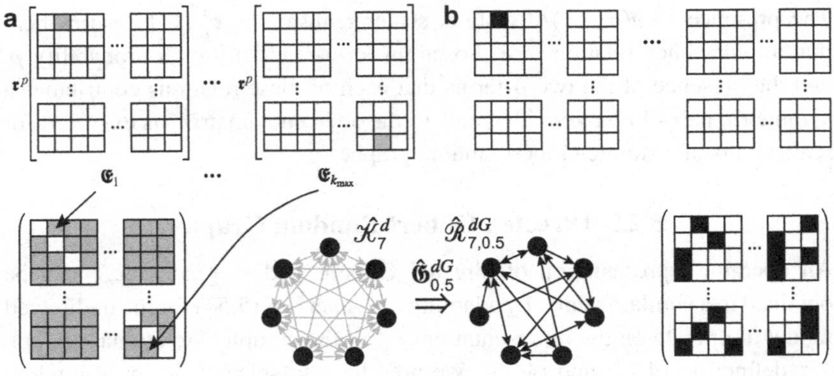

Figure 5.4 Generation of Gilbert random digraphs $\mathscr{R}_{n,p}^{dG}$. **a:** Application of binomial randomisation operators to the $k_{max} = n(n-1)$ edge operators $\mathfrak{E}_j \in \mathbb{B}^{n\times n}$, $j \in [1, k_{max}]$ representing the directed edges of the complete relational digraph $\mathscr{K}_n^d$ by contributing a single non-zero element to its matrix of adjacency relations (bottom). **b:** Independent realisations of $\mathfrak{r}^p[\mathfrak{E}_j]$ uniform-randomly select edge operators with probability p, and eventually construct an operator representation of $\mathscr{R}_{n,p}^{dG}$ with a matrix of adjacency relations comprised of randomly distributed non-zero elements (bottom) from the seed $\hat{\mathscr{K}}_n^d$ by means of the generator $\hat{\mathfrak{G}}_p^{dG}$ in (5.61). The inset exemplifies a realisation of this graph generation for $n = 7$, $p = 0.5$.

By having with (5.61) a viable generator at our disposal, an algebraically rigorous parametrised expression for the adjacency matrix of the Gilbert random digraph model can now be obtained in a straightforward fashion. Recalling the definition of the associated observable (5.43), we easily find

$$\hat{\mathfrak{a}}[\hat{\mathscr{R}}_{n,p}^{dG}] = \sum_{j=1}^{k_{max}} \mathfrak{r}^p[\delta_{j_1 j_2}^{n\times n}] = \mathfrak{r}^p\left[\sum_{\substack{j_1,j_2=1\\ j_1\neq j_2}}^{n} \delta_{j_1 j_2}^{n\times n}\right]. \tag{5.64}$$

Here we made use of the fact that, due to (5.37), each given j in the sum yields a distinct ordered index pair (j_1, j_2), in which case identity (5.53) and, thus, the property of linearity for the binomial randomisation operator applies. In order to simplify this expression further, let us introduce for notational convenience the Boolean matrix $\mathbf{\Delta}_{\mathcal{I}}^{m\times n} \in \mathbb{B}^{m\times n}$ with elements

$$(\mathbf{\Delta}_{\mathcal{I}}^{m\times n})_{ij}\colon [1,m]\times[1,n] \subset \mathbb{N}^2 \to \mathbb{B}\,,\ (\mathbf{\Delta}_{\mathcal{I}}^{m\times n})_{ij} := \begin{cases} 1 & \text{if } (i,j) \in \mathcal{I}, \\ 0 & \text{otherwise} \end{cases} \tag{5.65}$$

as a generalisation of the Kronecker delta matrix (4.3), where $\mathcal{I}$ denotes a finite set of ordered index pairs (i, j): $i \in [1, m]$, $j \in [1, n]$ labelling elements in an $(m \times n)$-dimensional matrix. By utilising the index set

$$\mathcal{I}_n^{dG} := \left\{(i,j) \colon i,j \in [1,n], i \neq j\right\} \tag{5.66}$$

to mark all non-diagonal elements of a square matrix, the right-hand side of (5.64) then finally yields

$$\hat{\mathfrak{a}}[\hat{\mathcal{R}}_{n,p}^{dG}] = \mathfrak{r}^p\left[\boldsymbol{\Delta}_{\mathcal{I}_n^{dG}}^{n\times n}\right] \tag{5.67}$$

for the adjacency matrix observable of directed Gilbert random graphs $\mathcal{R}_{n,p}^{dG}$ at arbitrary order n and connection probability p. It is important to note here that

$$\boldsymbol{\Delta}_{\mathcal{I}_n^{dG}}^{n\times n} = \boldsymbol{I}^{n\times n} - \boldsymbol{I}^n = \text{circ}\,[(0, \overbrace{1, \ldots, 1}^{n-1})] \tag{5.68}$$

describes a circulant matrix, and that $\boldsymbol{\Delta}_{\mathcal{I}_n^{dG}}^{n\times n}$ is subject to the algebraic identities

$$\boldsymbol{\Delta}_{\mathcal{I}_n^{dG}}^{n\times n} \odot \boldsymbol{\Delta}_{\mathcal{I}_n^{dG}}^{n\times n} = \boldsymbol{\Delta}_{\mathcal{I}_n^{dG}}^{n\times n} \odot^{\mathbb{B}} \boldsymbol{\Delta}_{\mathcal{I}_n^{dG}}^{n\times n} = \boldsymbol{\Delta}_{\mathcal{I}_n^{dG}}^{n\times n} \tag{5.69}$$

as well as the relations

$$\begin{aligned} \mathrm{T}\left[\boldsymbol{\Delta}_{\mathcal{I}_n^{dG}}^{n\times n}\right] &= n(n-1), \\ \left\langle \mathrm{T}\left[\mathfrak{r}^p[\boldsymbol{\Delta}_{\mathcal{I}_n^{dG}}^{n\times n}]\right]\right\rangle &= pn(n-1) \end{aligned} \tag{5.70}$$

involving the total sum operator (3.59). As we will demonstrate in Sections 6.3 and 6.4, it is precisely this circulant nature of the argument on which the binomial randomisation operator defining the adjacency matrix (5.67) acts that renders the model of Gilbert random digraphs algebraically accessible and will prove instrumental in obtaining algebraic expressions for a variety of graph observables describing $\mathcal{R}_{n,p}^{dG}$.

5.3 Watts–Strogatz Random Graphs

After having successfully embedded the prominent random graph models of Erdős–Rényi and Gilbert into our operator graph-theoretical framework, let us now proceed with the arguably more involved small-world random graph model introduced by Watts and Strogatz [109]. Recalling the brief presentation of this model from Section 2.3.6, a realisation of a Watts–Strogatz graph $\mathcal{R}_{n,k,q}^{WS}$ is obtained through the rewiring of all kn edges in a k-ring graph of order n by choosing, with a given probability $q \in \mathbb{Q}\colon 0 \leq q \leq 1$, for each adjacency relation $(i, (i + l) \bmod n + 1)$ with $i \in [1,n], l \in [0, k-1]$ uniformly at random a new target node while avoiding the assignment of multiple edges and self-loops. Despite its conceptual simplicity and beauty, however, this algorithmic definition is strictly limited to undirected small-world graphs and, by

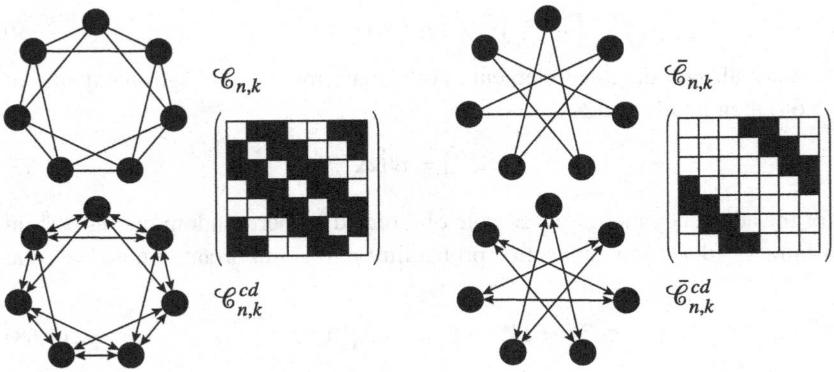

Figure 5.5 Illustration of an undirected k-ring graph $\mathscr{C}_{n,k}$ and complete relational k-ring digraph $\mathscr{C}^{cd}_{n,k}$ (left) along with their respective graph complements $\bar{\mathscr{C}}_{n,k}$ and $\bar{\mathscr{C}}^{cd}_{n,k}$ (right). The non-zero elements of their shared matrices of adjacency relations are marked by the index sets $\mathcal{I}^{\mathscr{C}}_{n,k}$ and $\mathcal{I}^{\bar{\mathscr{C}}}_{n,k}$ defined in (5.71) and (5.72). All graphs and matrices of adjacency relations are here exemplified for $n = 7$ and $k = 2$.

predominantly targeting their computational construction, poses a number of challenges for not only a mathematically more rigorous description but also a generalisation towards the inclusion of directed adjacency relations. In order to overcome these challenges, it is therefore necessary to first reflect on the possibility of a more canonical description of the original model by Watts and Strogatz, before exploring the generation of viable operator representations that encompass both undirected and directed small-world random graphs.

5.3.1 Canonical Model of Small-World Graphs and Digraphs

Let us begin by visualising changes in the adjacency relations between nodes during the algorithmic construction of a simple small-world graph according to the model of Watts and Strogatz. To that end, we define with

$$\mathcal{I}^{\mathscr{C}}_{n,k} := \left\{ \begin{array}{l} (i,j)\colon i,j \in [1,n], \\ 1 \leq (j-i+n) \bmod n \leq k \vee 1 \leq (i-j+n) \bmod n \leq k \end{array} \right\} \tag{5.71}$$

the index set marking all $2kn$ adjacency relations which describe the kn undirected edges of a k-ring graph $\mathscr{C}_{n,k}$, and with

$$\mathcal{I}^{\bar{\mathscr{C}}}_{n,k} := \left\{(i,j)\colon i,j \in [1,n], 1+k \leq |i-j| \leq n-k-1\right\} \tag{5.72}$$

the set of all ordered index pairs that mark the $n(n-1) - 2kn$ adjacency relations between nodes of the graph complement $\bar{\mathscr{C}}_{n,k}$ of $\mathscr{C}_{n,k}$ (see Fig. 5.5). Furthermore, let $\boldsymbol{A}_t$ denote the symmetric matrix of adjacency relations at step t in the construction of our small-world graph, with $(\boldsymbol{A}_0)_{ij} = 1\ \forall(i,j) \in \mathcal{I}^{\mathscr{C}}_{n,k}$ marking all non-zero elements that represent $\mathscr{C}_{n,k}$ at the initial step $t = 0$. At step $t > 0$, we then choose for $(i,j) \in \mathcal{I}^{\mathscr{C}}_{n,k} : 1 \leq (j - i + n) \bmod n \leq k$ with

$$\begin{cases} i = \lfloor (t-1)/k \rfloor + 1, \\ j = \big(t - (k-1)\lfloor (t-1)/k \rfloor\big) \bmod n + 1 \end{cases}$$

uniform-randomly a new target node j' from the set of available target nodes $\{j \in [1,n] : j \neq i \wedge (\boldsymbol{A}_t)_{ij} = 0\}$ and replace, or rewire, with probability q the original target node j of the considered adjacency relation such that

$$\left\{ \begin{array}{l} (\boldsymbol{A}_t)_{ij} = 1, \\ (\boldsymbol{A}_t)_{ij'} = 0 \end{array} \right\} \overset{\text{with probability } q}{\longrightarrow} \left\{ \begin{array}{l} (\boldsymbol{A}_{t+1})_{ij} = (\boldsymbol{A}_{t+1})_{ji} = 0, \\ (\boldsymbol{A}_{t+1})_{ij'} = (\boldsymbol{A}_{t+1})_{j'i} = 1 \end{array} \right\}.$$

The two conditions $j' \neq i$ and $(\boldsymbol{A}_t)_{ij'} = 0$ imposed on the selection of new target nodes ensure here that neither self-loops nor multiple edges are assigned. Eventually, after nk steps, all undirected edges of $\mathscr{C}_{n,k}$ are considered, and the generated matrix of adjacency relations $\boldsymbol{A}_{nk}$ describes a desired realisation of the Watts–Strogatz random graph model $\mathscr{R}^{WS}_{n,k,q}$.

Looking at this generation from a more statistical perspective, we find that, on average, a total of $N_e^{rew} := qkn$ edges is removed from the original k-ring graph and redistributed across $n(n-1)/2 - (1-q)kn$ undirected edges of which $N_e'^{\max} := n(n-1)/2 - kn$ belong to $\bar{\mathscr{C}}_{n,k}$ and the remaining $N_e^{\max} := qkn$ belong to $\mathscr{C}_{n,k}$. Because this redistribution is realised in a uniform-random fashion, and $kn - N_e^{rew}$ edges in the initial k-ring graph $\mathscr{C}_{n,k}$ remain unaffected by the rewiring process, it can then be argued that the construction of a Watts–Strogatz graph is equivalent to randomly selecting a total of

$$N_e' := N_e^{rew} \frac{N_e'^{\max}}{N_e^{\max} + N_e'^{\max}} = \frac{qkn(n-2k-1)}{n-1-2k(1-q)} \tag{5.73}$$

undirected edges from $\bar{\mathscr{C}}_{n,k}$, and

$$N_e := kn - N_e^{rew} + N_e^{rew} \frac{N_e^{\max}}{N_e^{\max} + N_e'^{\max}} = (1-q)kn + \frac{2q^2k^2n}{n-1-2k(1-q)} \tag{5.74}$$

edges from $\mathscr{C}_{n,k}$. Furthermore, as $N_e + N_e' = kn$, the total number of selected edges is independent of q and equal to the number of edges in $\mathscr{C}_{n,k}$. With this, we are now one step closer to conceiving a canonical model for Watts–Strogatz random graphs $\mathscr{R}^{WS}_{n,k,q}$ as the sum of a randomised k-ring graph, constructed from $\mathscr{C}_{n,k}$ by selecting uniform-randomly N_e of its edges, and a randomised graph complement of $\mathscr{C}_{n,k}$, comprised of N_e' randomly selected edges of $\bar{\mathscr{C}}_{n,k}$.

In order to arrive at a useable algebraic formalisation of this model, however, we still need to deal with the subtle obstacle presented by the strict conservation of the total number of edges in the original Watts–Strogatz model. As we recall from our exploration of the Erdős–Rényi random graph model in Section 5.1, the incorporation of a constraint which fixes the number of edges comprising a graph poses a number of challenges as such a constraint conflicts with the element-wise independent and probabilistic nature of the graph generation itself. For that reason, let us follow the path which naturally led us to the Gilbert random graph model in Section 5.2, and consider the conservation of the total number of edges as satisfied only in the statistical average over many realisations of the same model. In this case, the uniform-random selection of N_e undirected edges from the k-ring graph $\mathscr{C}_{n,k}$ corresponds to constructing a simple graph of order n whose adjacency relations are obtained by selecting from the set $I^{\mathscr{C}}_{n,k}$ of $2kn$ ordered index pairs with probability

$$p := \frac{N_e}{kn} = \frac{(n-1)(1-q) - 2k(1-2q)}{n-1-2k(1-q)} \tag{5.75}$$

distinct tuples $\{(i, j), (j, i)\}$ that satisfy $1 \leq (j - i + n) \bmod n \leq k$. Let us denote the so-generated *randomised k-ring graph* with $\mathscr{C}_{n,k,p}$. Similarly, choosing independently and uniform-randomly a total of N'_e undirected edges from the $n(n-1)/2 - kn$ edges describing the k-ring graph complement $\bar{\mathscr{C}}_{n,k}$ of $\mathscr{C}_{n,k}$ corresponds to constructing a simple randomised graph complement $\bar{\mathscr{C}}_{n,k,p'}$ of $\mathscr{C}_{n,k}$ whose undirected adjacency relations are obtained by selecting distinct tuples $\{(i, j), (j, i)\}$ of associated index pairs with probability

$$p' := \frac{N'_e}{n(n-1)/2 - kn} = \frac{2qk}{n-1-2k(1-q)} \tag{5.76}$$

from the set $I^{\bar{\mathscr{C}}}_{n,k}$. As exemplified in Fig. 5.6a, the sum

$$\mathscr{R}^{WS}_{n,k,q} := \mathscr{C}_{n,k,p} \triangledown \bar{\mathscr{C}}_{n,k,p'} \tag{5.77}$$

of both of these randomised graphs then eventually defines a canonical model for simple Watts–Strogatz random graphs $\mathscr{R}^{WS}_{n,k,q}$ of order n and rewiring probability q whose realisations are comprised of, at average, kn undirected edges.

Before generalising this model to small-world graphs with directed edges, let us briefly validate two important limit cases of the original Watts–Strogatz model. In the first of these cases, $q = 0$, no rewiring of edges occurs, and the initial k-ring graph should be preserved. Indeed, with (5.75) and (5.76), we have $p = 1$ and $p' = 0$ such that all of the nk edges comprising $\mathscr{C}_{n,k}$ but none of the edges in $\bar{\mathscr{C}}_{n,k}$ are selected and, thus, $\mathscr{R}^{WS}_{n,k,0} = \mathscr{C}_{n,k,1} \triangledown \bar{\mathscr{C}}_{n,k,0} = \mathscr{C}_{n,k}$. Similarly, for $q = 1$, we find $p = p' = 2k/(n-1)$ such that undirected edges

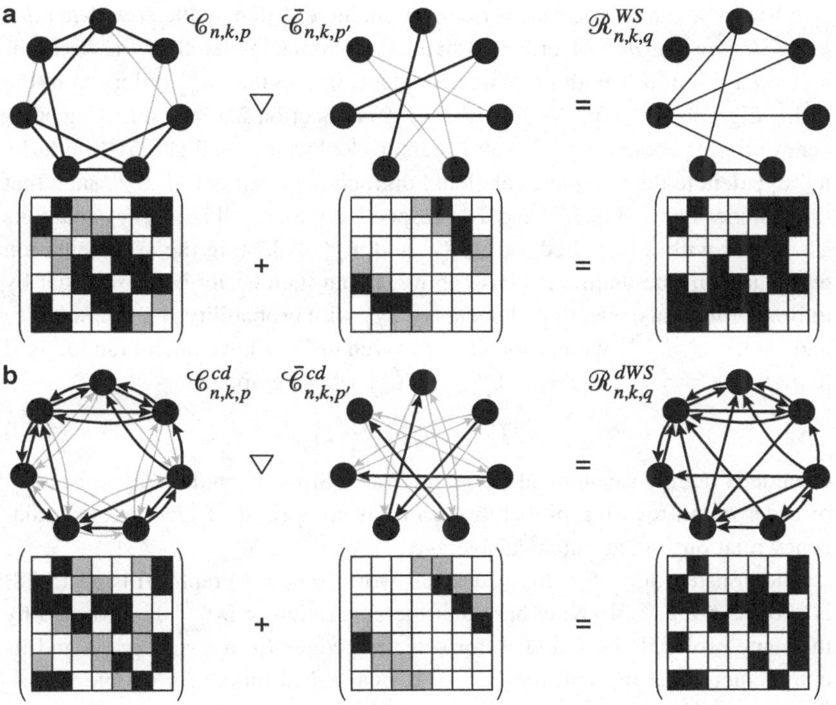

Figure 5.6 Canonical model of Watts–Strogatz random graphs. **a:** Generation of a simple Watts–Strogatz graph $\mathscr{R}^{WS}_{n,k,q}$ through the sum of a randomised k-ring graph $\mathscr{C}_{n,k,p}$ and a randomised graph complement $\bar{\mathscr{C}}_{n,k,p'}$ of $\mathscr{C}_{n,k}$. **b:** The sum of a randomised complete relational k-ring digraph $\mathscr{C}^{cd}_{n,k,p}$ and a randomised digraph complement $\bar{\mathscr{C}}^{cd}_{n,k,p'}$ of $\mathscr{C}^{cd}_{n,k}$ describing a canonical realisation of the directed Watts–Strogatz random graph model $\mathscr{R}^{dWS}_{n,k,q}$. The generation of both directed and undirected graphs (top) and their associated matrices of adjacency relations (bottom) is here exemplified for $n = 7$, $k = 2$ and $q = 0.2$, with selected and not-selected adjacency relations respectively marked in black and grey.

from both disjunct edge sets of $\mathscr{C}_{n,k}$ and $\bar{\mathscr{C}}_{n,k}$ are chosen with equal probability. In this case, our canonical model delivers with $\mathscr{R}^{WS}_{n,k,1} = \mathscr{C}_{n,k,p} \triangledown \bar{\mathscr{C}}_{n,k,p} = \mathscr{R}^{G}_{n,p}$ an undirected Gilbert random graph with connection probability p. Only in a very narrow range of the rewiring probability q between these two limit cases do the characteristic properties of a small-world network become apparent, a feature of the Watts–Strogatz model we touched upon in Section 2.3.6 and will further explore in the next chapter.

Our approach for constructing simple Watts–Strogatz random graphs naturally translates into a canonical model for small-world digraphs if we consider each undirected edge of $\mathscr{C}_{n,k}$ and $\bar{\mathscr{C}}_{n,k}$ as two directed edges. In order to arrive also here at a viable algebraic formalisation, let $\mathscr{C}^{cd}_{n,k}$ denote the *complete relational k-ring digraph* of order n obtained by replacing each of the kn undirected edges of $\mathscr{C}_{n,k}$ with two directed edges, noting that $\mathscr{C}^{cd}_{n,k}$ differs from the k-ring digraph $\mathscr{C}^{d}_{n,k}$ introduced with (2.119) in Section 2.3.3 by directing adjacency relations both clockwise and counter-clockwise (see Fig. 5.5). Similarly, let $\bar{\mathscr{C}}^{cd}_{n,k}$ denote the complete relational digraph complement of $\mathscr{C}^{cd}_{n,k}$, such that the disjunct index sets $\mathcal{I}^{\mathscr{C}}_{n,k}$ and $\mathcal{I}^{\bar{\mathscr{C}}}_{n,k}$ respectively mark all adjacency relations associated with directed edges in $\mathscr{C}^{cd}_{n,k}$ and $\bar{\mathscr{C}}^{cd}_{n,k}$. Adapting the argumentation entertained in the undirected case above, it can then easily be shown that by uniform-randomly selecting elements of $\mathcal{I}^{\mathscr{C}}_{n,k}$ with probability p given in (5.75) and elements of $\mathcal{I}^{\bar{\mathscr{C}}}_{n,k}$ with probability p' given in (5.76), we obtain randomised realisations $\mathscr{C}^{cd}_{n,k,p}$ of $\mathscr{C}^{cd}_{n,k}$ and $\bar{\mathscr{C}}^{cd}_{n,k,p'}$ of $\bar{\mathscr{C}}^{cd}_{n,k}$ whose graph sum

$$\mathscr{R}^{dWS}_{n,k,q} := \mathscr{C}^{cd}_{n,k,p} \triangledown \bar{\mathscr{C}}^{cd}_{n,k,p'} \tag{5.78}$$

eventually defines a canonical model for Watts–Strogatz random digraphs $\mathscr{R}^{dWS}_{n,k,q}$ of order n and rewiring probability q that is comprised of $2kn$ directed adjacency relations in the statistical average.

The construction of a directed small-world random graph utilising (5.78) is shown in Fig. 5.6b. Note here that the generation of $\mathscr{R}^{dWS}_{n,k,q}$ is governed by the same probabilities p and p' for selecting edges from a ring graph and its complement that apply in the case of the canonical model for simple Watts–Strogatz graphs. This is not surprising, however, as now $2qkn$ directed edges, at average, are being redistributed across $n(n-1) - 2(1-q)kn$ possible edges, which leaves us with $2N_e$ and $2N'_e$ directed adjacency relations that need to be respectively selected from $\mathscr{C}^{cd}_{n,k}$ and $\bar{\mathscr{C}}^{cd}_{n,k}$. Finally, similar to the undirected case and in coherence with the conception of the original Watts–Strogatz model, we find $\mathscr{R}^{dWS}_{n,k,0} = \mathscr{C}^{cd}_{n,k,1} \triangledown \bar{\mathscr{C}}^{cd}_{n,k,0} = \mathscr{C}^{cd}_{n,k}$ and $\mathscr{R}^{dWS}_{n,k,1} = \mathscr{C}^{cd}_{n,k,p} \triangledown \bar{\mathscr{C}}^{cd}_{n,k,p} = \mathscr{R}^{dG}_{n,p}$ with $p = 2k/(n-1)$, which validates our canonical model for small-world digraphs in the two important limit cases for $q = 0$ and $q = 1$.

5.3.2 Undirected Watts–Strogatz Random Graphs

With a canonical model for simple Watts–Strogatz random graphs formulated, let us continue by exploring an algebraic formalisation of its generation within the confines of our operator graph-theoretical framework. To that end, we recall that the two index sets $\mathcal{I}^{\mathscr{C}}_{n,k}$ and $\mathcal{I}^{\bar{\mathscr{C}}}_{n,k}$ defined in (5.71) and (5.72) respectively mark all distinct adjacency relations of a k-ring graph $\mathscr{C}_{n,k}$ and its graph complement $\bar{\mathscr{C}}_{n,k}$, such that $\mathcal{I}^{\mathscr{C}}_{n,k} \cap \mathcal{I}^{\bar{\mathscr{C}}}_{n,k} = \emptyset$, and the union $\mathcal{I}^{\mathscr{C}}_{n,k} \cup \mathcal{I}^{\bar{\mathscr{C}}}_{n,k}$ describes all adjacency relations which comprise the complete simple graph $\mathscr{K}_n$ of order n. Because both $\mathscr{C}_{n,k}$ and $\bar{\mathscr{C}}_{n,k}$ are necessary for realising simple Watts–Strogatz

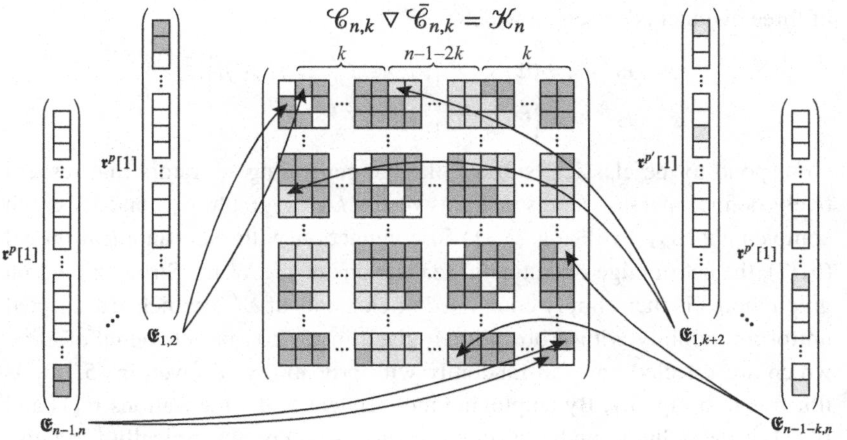

Figure 5.7 Generation of simple Watts–Strogatz random graphs $\mathscr{R}^{WS}_{n,k,q}$. By respectively combining independent scalar realisations $\mathfrak{r}^p[1]$ and $\mathfrak{r}^{p'}[1]$ of the binomial randomisation operator with each of the kn edge operators defining an operator representation of the k-ring graph $\mathscr{C}_{n,k}$ (left) and the $n(n-1)/2-kn$ edge operators defining an operator representation of its graph complement $\bar{\mathscr{C}}_{n,k}$ (right), the set of edge operators furnishing an operator representation $\hat{\mathscr{R}}^{WS}_{n,k,q}$ of the simple Watts–Strogatz random graph model can be constructed from the seed $\hat{\mathscr{K}}_n$ by means of the generator $\hat{\mathfrak{G}}^{WS}_q$ defined in (5.82).

random graphs according to (5.77), an operator representation $\hat{\mathscr{K}}_n$ of $\mathscr{K}_n$ certainly constitutes the natural choice for a generator seed. Akin to our models of undirected Erdős–Rényi and Gilbert random graphs, we will again represent here the nodes and edge operators of $\hat{\mathscr{K}}_n$ by the Boolean row vectors introduced in (5.1) and (5.2). However, for notational convenience, we now label each edge operator by an ordered index pair $(j_1, j_2) \in \mathcal{I}^{\mathscr{C}}_{n,k} \cup \mathcal{I}^{\bar{\mathscr{C}}}_{n,k}$, such that

$$\mathfrak{E}_{j_1 j_2} := \boldsymbol{\delta}^n_{j_1} + \boldsymbol{\delta}^n_{j_2} \in \mathbb{B}^n \tag{5.79}$$

for $j_1, j_2 \in [1, n] : j_2 > j_1$ defines the edge operators of $\hat{\mathscr{K}}_n$, and

$$\begin{aligned} \hat{\mathcal{E}}^{\mathscr{K}_n} &= \left\{ \mathfrak{E}_{00} := \boldsymbol{0}^n, \mathfrak{E}_{j_1 j_2} : (j_1, j_2) \in \mathcal{I}^{\mathscr{C}}_{n,k} \cup \mathcal{I}^{\bar{\mathscr{C}}}_{n,k} \wedge j_2 > j_1 \right\} \subset \mathbb{B}^n, \\ \hat{\mathcal{E}}^{\mathscr{K}_n}_{cl} &:= \left\{ \mathfrak{E} \in \hat{\mathcal{E}}^{\mathscr{K}_n} : \mathrm{T}[\mathfrak{E}] = 2 \right\}, \ \hat{\mathcal{E}}^{\mathscr{K}_n}_{aux} := \left\{ \mathfrak{E}_{00} \right\} \end{aligned} \tag{5.80}$$

defines their associated set and subsets.

As by construction of $\mathcal{I}^{\mathscr{C}}_{n,k}$ and $\mathcal{I}^{\bar{\mathscr{C}}}_{n,k}$ for each given pair of distinct indices $j_1, j_2 \in [1, n]$: $j_1 \neq j_2$ both (j_1, j_2) and (j_2, j_1) belong to either $\mathcal{I}^{\mathscr{C}}_{n,k}$ or $\mathcal{I}^{\bar{\mathscr{C}}}_{n,k}$, the set $\hat{\mathcal{E}}^{\mathscr{K}_n}$ of edge operators of $\hat{\mathscr{K}}_n$ can be expressed as the union

$$\hat{\mathcal{E}}^{\mathscr{K}_n} = \hat{\mathcal{E}}^{\mathscr{C}_{n,k}} \cup \hat{\mathcal{E}}^{\bar{\mathscr{C}}_{n,k}} \cup \left\{ \mathfrak{E}_{00} \right\} \tag{5.81}$$

of three disjunct edge sets in which

$$\hat{\mathcal{E}}^{\mathscr{C}_{n,k}} := \left\{\mathfrak{E}_{j_1 j_2} : (j_1, j_2) \in \mathcal{I}^{\mathscr{C}}_{n,k} \wedge j_2 > j_1\right\},$$
$$\hat{\mathcal{E}}^{\bar{\mathscr{C}}_{n,k}} := \left\{\mathfrak{E}_{j_1 j_2} : (j_1, j_2) \in \mathcal{I}^{\bar{\mathscr{C}}}_{n,k} \wedge j_2 > j_1\right\}$$

correspond to the classical subsets of edge-generating operators that respectively define operator representations of the k-ring graph $\mathscr{C}_{n,k}$ and its graph complement $\bar{\mathscr{C}}_{n,k}$. Utilising (5.81) in conjunction with our canonical model (5.77), the set of edge operators in realisations of the Watts–Strogatz random graph model is then simply comprised of elements of $\hat{\mathcal{E}}^{\mathscr{C}_{n,k}}$ which are selected uniform-randomly with probability p given in (5.75), and elements of $\hat{\mathcal{E}}^{\bar{\mathscr{C}}_{n,k}}$ which are selected uniform-randomly with probability p' given in (5.76), as illustrated in Fig. 5.7. By employing independent scalar realisations $\mathfrak{r}^p[1]$ and $\mathfrak{r}^{p'}[1]$ of the column randomisation operator (4.41) to algebraically formalise this random selection, we finally find

$$\hat{\mathfrak{G}}^{WS}_q = \left(\hat{\mathfrak{G}}_{\mathcal{N}}\,,\ \hat{\mathfrak{G}}_{\mathcal{E}}\right) \tag{5.82}$$

with

$$\hat{\mathfrak{G}}_{\mathcal{N}} : \hat{\mathcal{N}}^{\mathscr{K}_n} \to \hat{\mathcal{N}}^{\mathscr{R}^{WS}_{n,k,q}}\,,\ \hat{\mathfrak{G}}_{\mathcal{N}} := \mathrm{id}$$

and

$$\hat{\mathfrak{G}}_{\mathcal{E}} : \hat{\mathcal{E}}^{\mathscr{K}_n} \to \hat{\mathcal{E}}^{\mathscr{R}^{WS}_{n,k,q}}\,,$$
$$\hat{\mathfrak{G}}_{\mathcal{E}}[\mathfrak{E}_{j_1 j_2}] := \begin{cases} \mathfrak{r}^p[1]\cdot\mathfrak{E}_{j_1 j_2} = \mathfrak{r}^p[1]\cdot(\delta^n_{j_1} + \delta^n_{j_2}) & \text{if } (j_1, j_2) \in \mathcal{I}^{\mathscr{C}}_{n,k}\,,\ j_2 > j_1 \\ \mathfrak{r}^{p'}[1]\cdot\mathfrak{E}_{j_1 j_2} = \mathfrak{r}^{p'}[1]\cdot(\delta^n_{j_1} + \delta^n_{j_2}) & \text{if } (j_1, j_2) \in \mathcal{I}^{\bar{\mathscr{C}}}_{n,k}\,,\ j_2 > j_1 \end{cases}$$

as a suitable generator for the canonical model of simple Watts–Strogatz random graphs $\mathscr{R}^{WS}_{n,k,q}$ such that $\hat{\mathfrak{G}}^{WS}_q[\hat{\mathscr{K}}_n] = \hat{\mathscr{R}}^{WS}_{n,k,q} := (\hat{\mathcal{N}}^{\mathscr{R}^{WS}_{n,k,q}}, \hat{\mathcal{E}}^{\mathscr{R}^{WS}_{n,k,q}})$. Here,

$$\begin{aligned} \hat{\mathcal{N}}^{\mathscr{R}^{WS}_{n,k,q}} &:= \left\{\hat{\mathfrak{G}}_{\mathcal{N}}[\boldsymbol{n}] : \boldsymbol{n} \in \hat{\mathcal{N}}^{\mathscr{K}_n}\right\} = \hat{\mathcal{N}}^{\mathscr{K}_n} \subset \mathbb{B}^n, \\ \hat{\mathcal{E}}^{\mathscr{R}^{WS}_{n,k,q}} &:= \left\{\hat{\mathfrak{G}}_{\mathcal{E}}[\mathfrak{E}] : \mathfrak{E} \in \hat{\mathcal{E}}^{\mathscr{K}_n}\right\} \subset \mathbb{B}^n \end{aligned} \tag{5.83}$$

and

$$\begin{aligned} \hat{\mathcal{N}}^{\mathscr{R}^{WS}_{n,k,q}}_{cl} &:= \left\{\boldsymbol{n} \in \hat{\mathcal{N}}^{\mathscr{R}^{WS}_{n,k,q}} : \mathrm{T}[\boldsymbol{n}] = 1\right\},\ \hat{\mathcal{N}}^{\mathscr{R}^{WS}_{n,k,q}}_{aux} := \left\{\boldsymbol{n}_0\right\}, \\ \hat{\mathcal{E}}^{\mathscr{R}^{WS}_{n,k,q}}_{cl} &:= \left\{\mathfrak{E} \in \hat{\mathcal{E}}^{\mathscr{R}^{WS}_{n,k,q}} : \mathrm{T}[\mathfrak{E}] = 2\right\},\ \hat{\mathcal{E}}^{\mathscr{R}^{WS}_{n,k,q}}_{aux} := \hat{\mathcal{E}}^{\mathscr{R}^{WS}_{n,k,q}} \setminus \hat{\mathcal{E}}^{\mathscr{R}^{WS}_{n,k,q}}_{cl} \end{aligned} \tag{5.84}$$

define the sets of nodes and edge operators along with their respective classical and auxiliary subsets which eventually furnish a viable parametrised operator representation $\hat{\mathscr{R}}^{WS}_{n,k,q}$ of $\mathscr{R}^{WS}_{n,k,q}$.

Before applying this approach to the generation of directed Watts–Strogatz random graphs, let us conclude our algebraic formalisation of the undirected model by taking a brief look at its adjacency matrix observable. With (4.63), (5.81) and (5.83), we immediately obtain

$$\begin{aligned}\hat{\mathfrak{a}}[\hat{\mathscr{R}}^{WS}_{n,k,q}] = &\sum_{\substack{(j_1,j_2)\in\mathcal{I}^{\mathscr{C}}_{n,k}\\ j_2>j_1}} \Big(\mathbf{r}^p_{j_1j_2}[1]\cdot\big(\delta^n_{j_1}\otimes\delta^{n\mathsf{T}}_{j_1}+\delta^n_{j_1}\otimes\delta^{n\mathsf{T}}_{j_2}+\delta^n_{j_2}\otimes\delta^{n\mathsf{T}}_{j_1}+\delta^n_{j_2}\otimes\delta^{n\mathsf{T}}_{j_2}\big)\\ &\qquad -\mathbf{r}^p_{j_1j_2}[1]\cdot\big(\operatorname{diag}[\delta^n_{j_1}]-\operatorname{diag}[\delta^n_{j_2}]\big)\Big)\\ &+\sum_{\substack{(j_1,j_2)\in\mathcal{I}^{\bar{\mathscr{C}}}_{n,k}\\ j_2>j_1}} \Big(\mathbf{r}^{p'}_{j_1j_2}[1]\cdot\big(\delta^n_{j_1}\otimes\delta^{n\mathsf{T}}_{j_1}+\delta^n_{j_1}\otimes\delta^{n\mathsf{T}}_{j_2}+\delta^n_{j_2}\otimes\delta^{n\mathsf{T}}_{j_1}+\delta^n_{j_2}\otimes\delta^{n\mathsf{T}}_{j_2}\big)\\ &\qquad -\mathbf{r}^{p'}_{j_1j_2}[1]\cdot\big(\operatorname{diag}[\delta^n_{j_1}]-\operatorname{diag}[\delta^n_{j_2}]\big)\Big),\end{aligned}$$

where we again distinguish independent realisations of the randomisation operator by appropriate subscripts and recognise that, by definition, both sums run over distinct index pairs $(j_1, j_2) \in \mathcal{I}^{\mathscr{C}}_{n,k} \cup \mathcal{I}^{\bar{\mathscr{C}}}_{n,k}$, $j_2 > j_1$ such that (5.58) applies. By making use of (5.20), all terms containing Kronecker products in the last expression can be further simplified, eventually yielding

$$\hat{\mathfrak{a}}[\hat{\mathscr{R}}^{WS}_{n,k,q}] = \sum_{\substack{(j_1,j_2)\in\mathcal{I}^{\mathscr{C}}_{n,k}\\ j_2>j_1}} \mathbf{r}^p_{j_1j_2}[1]\cdot\big(\delta^{n\times n}_{j_1j_2}+\delta^{n\times n}_{j_2j_1}\big)+\sum_{\substack{(j_1,j_2)\in\mathcal{I}^{\bar{\mathscr{C}}}_{n,k}\\ j_2>j_1}} \mathbf{r}^{p'}_{j_1j_2}[1]\cdot\big(\delta^{n\times n}_{j_1j_2}+\delta^{n\times n}_{j_2j_1}\big) \tag{5.85}$$

for the adjacency matrix observable of the canonical model for Watts–Strogatz random graphs $\mathscr{R}^{WS}_{n,k,q}$, where p and p' are respectively defined by (5.75) and (5.76). In the limit case $q = 0$, we then find

$$\hat{\mathfrak{a}}[\hat{\mathscr{R}}^{WS}_{n,k,1}] = \sum_{\substack{(j_1,j_2)\in\mathcal{I}^{\mathscr{C}}_{n,k}\\ j_2>j_1}} \mathbf{r}^1_{j_1j_2}[1]\cdot\big(\delta^{n\times n}_{j_1j_2}+\delta^{n\times n}_{j_2j_1}\big) = \hat{\mathfrak{a}}[\hat{\mathscr{C}}_{n,k}],$$

and for $q = 1$ we recover, as expected, with

$$\hat{\mathfrak{a}}[\hat{\mathscr{R}}^{WS}_{n,k,1}] = \sum_{\substack{(j_1,j_2)\in\mathcal{I}^{\mathscr{C}}_{n,k}\cup\mathcal{I}^{\bar{\mathscr{C}}}_{n,k}\\ j_2>j_1}} \mathbf{r}^p_{j_1j_2}[1]\cdot\big(\delta^{n\times n}_{j_1j_2}+\delta^{n\times n}_{j_2j_1}\big) = \sum_{\substack{j_1,j_2=1\\ j_2>j_1}}^{n} \mathbf{r}^p_{j_1j_2}[1]\cdot\big(\delta^{n\times n}_{j_1j_2}+\delta^{n\times n}_{j_2j_1}\big)$$

the adjacency matrix observable $\hat{\mathfrak{a}}[\hat{\mathscr{R}}^G_{n,p}]$ of the simple Gilbert random graph model $\mathscr{R}^G_{n,p}$ in (5.60) for $p = 2k/(n-1)$.

5.3.3 Directed Watts–Strogatz Random Graphs

The algebraic approach which led to the construction of simple Watts–Strogatz random graphs also can easily be adapted to deliver relational digraphs if we consider each undirected edge as being comprised of two directed adjacency relations. In doing so, the operator representation $\hat{\mathscr{K}}^d_n$ of the complete relational digraph $\mathscr{K}^d_n$ of order n defined in (4.74) and (4.75) naturally presents itself as a suitable choice for a generator seed. For notational simplicity, we will label here the $n(n-1)$ edge operators of $\hat{\mathcal{K}}_n^d$ again by index pairs

$$(j_1, j_2) \in \{(i,j) : i, j \in [1,n] \wedge i \neq j\} = \mathcal{I}_{n,k}^{\mathscr{C}} \cup \mathcal{I}_{n,k}^{\bar{\mathscr{C}}}$$

such that

$$\begin{aligned} \hat{\mathcal{E}}^{\mathcal{K}_n^d} &= \left\{\mathfrak{E}_{00} := \boldsymbol{0}^n, \mathfrak{E}_{j_1 j_2} := \delta_{j_1 j_2}^{n\times n} : (j_1, j_2) \in \mathcal{I}_{n,k}^{\mathscr{C}} \cup \mathcal{I}_{n,k}^{\bar{\mathscr{C}}}\right\} \subset \mathbb{B}^{n\times n}, \\ \hat{\mathcal{E}}_{cl}^{\mathcal{K}_n^d} &:= \left\{\mathfrak{E} \in \hat{\mathcal{E}}^{\mathcal{K}_n^d} : \mathrm{T}[\mathfrak{E}] = 1\right\}, \hat{\mathcal{E}}_{aux}^{\mathcal{K}_n^d} := \left\{\mathfrak{E}_{00}\right\} \end{aligned} \tag{5.86}$$

define their associated set and subsets. Similar to (5.81), it can then be demonstrated that $\hat{\mathcal{E}}^{\mathcal{K}_n^d}$ is equivalent to the union

$$\hat{\mathcal{E}}^{\mathcal{K}_n^d} = \hat{\mathcal{E}}^{\mathscr{C}_{n,k}^{cd}} \cup \hat{\mathcal{E}}^{\bar{\mathscr{C}}_{n,k}^{cd}} \cup \left\{\mathfrak{E}_{00}\right\}. \tag{5.87}$$

of three disjunct edge sets in which

$$\begin{aligned} \hat{\mathcal{E}}^{\mathscr{C}_{n,k}^{cd}} &:= \left\{\mathfrak{E}_{j_1 j_2} : (j_1, j_2) \in \mathcal{I}_{n,k}^{\mathscr{C}}\right\}, \\ \hat{\mathcal{E}}^{\bar{\mathscr{C}}_{n,k}^{cd}} &:= \left\{\mathfrak{E}_{j_1 j_2} : (j_1, j_2) \in \mathcal{I}_{n,k}^{\bar{\mathscr{C}}}\right\} \end{aligned}$$

describe the classical subsets of edge-generating operators that furnish operator representations of the complete relational k-ring digraph $\mathscr{C}_{n,k}^{cd}$ of order n and its complete relational digraph complement $\bar{\mathscr{C}}_{n,k}^{cd}$. By recalling the canonical model (5.78) of $\mathscr{R}_{n,k,q}^{dWS}$ as a graph sum over randomised realisations of $\mathscr{C}_{n,k}^{cd}$ and $\bar{\mathscr{C}}_{n,k}^{cd}$, we eventually find

$$\hat{\mathfrak{G}}_q^{dWS} = \left(\hat{\mathfrak{G}}_{\mathcal{N}}, \hat{\mathfrak{G}}_{\mathcal{E}}\right) \tag{5.88}$$

with

$$\begin{aligned} &\hat{\mathfrak{G}}_{\mathcal{N}} : \hat{\mathcal{N}}^{\mathcal{K}_n^d} \to \hat{\mathcal{N}}^{\mathscr{R}_{n,k,q}^{dWS}}, \ \hat{\mathfrak{G}}_{\mathcal{N}} := \mathrm{id}, \\ &\hat{\mathfrak{G}}_{\mathcal{E}} : \hat{\mathcal{E}}^{\mathcal{K}_n^d} \to \hat{\mathcal{E}}^{\mathscr{R}_{n,k,q}^{dWS}}, \\ &\hat{\mathfrak{G}}_{\mathcal{E}}[\mathfrak{E}_{j_1 j_2}] := \begin{cases} \mathfrak{r}^{p}[\mathfrak{E}_{j_1 j_2}] = \mathfrak{r}^{p}[\delta_{j_1 j_2}^{n\times n}] & \text{if } (j_1, j_2) \in \mathcal{I}_{n,k}^{\mathscr{C}}, \\ \mathfrak{r}^{p'}[\mathfrak{E}_{j_1 j_2}] = \mathfrak{r}^{p'}[\delta_{j_1 j_2}^{n\times n}] & \text{if } (j_1, j_2) \in \mathcal{I}_{n,k}^{\bar{\mathscr{C}}} \end{cases} \end{aligned}$$

as a viable generator that delivers with $\hat{\mathfrak{G}}_q^{dWS}[\hat{\mathcal{K}}_n^d] = \hat{\mathscr{R}}_{n,k,q}^{dWS} := (\hat{\mathcal{N}}^{\mathscr{R}_{n,k,q}^{dWS}}, \hat{\mathcal{E}}^{\mathscr{R}_{n,k,q}^{dWS}})$ a parametrised operator representation of Watts–Strogatz random digraphs. Here p and p' are given by (5.75) and (5.76), and

$$\begin{aligned} \hat{\mathcal{N}}^{\mathscr{R}_{n,k,q}^{dWS}} &:= \left\{\hat{\mathfrak{G}}_{\mathcal{N}}[\boldsymbol{n}] : \boldsymbol{n} \in \hat{\mathcal{N}}^{\mathcal{K}_n^d}\right\} = \hat{\mathcal{N}}^{\mathcal{K}_n^d} \subset \mathbb{B}^n, \\ \hat{\mathcal{E}}^{\mathscr{R}_{n,k,q}^{dWS}} &:= \left\{\hat{\mathfrak{G}}_{\mathcal{E}}[\mathfrak{E}] : \mathfrak{E} \in \hat{\mathcal{E}}^{\mathcal{K}_n^d}\right\} \subset \mathbb{B}^{n\times n}, \end{aligned} \tag{5.89}$$

together with

$$\begin{aligned} \hat{\mathcal{N}}_{cl}^{\mathscr{R}_{n,k,q}^{dWS}} &:= \left\{\boldsymbol{n} \in \hat{\mathcal{N}}^{\mathscr{R}_{n,k,q}^{dWS}} : \mathrm{T}[\boldsymbol{n}] = 1\right\}, \hat{\mathcal{N}}_{aux}^{\mathscr{R}_{n,k,q}^{dWS}} := \left\{\boldsymbol{n}_0\right\}, \\ \hat{\mathcal{E}}_{cl}^{\mathscr{R}_{n,k,q}^{dWS}} &:= \left\{\mathfrak{E} \in \hat{\mathcal{E}}^{\mathscr{R}_{n,k,q}^{dWS}} : \mathrm{T}[\mathfrak{E}] = 1\right\}, \hat{\mathcal{E}}_{aux}^{\mathscr{R}_{n,k,q}^{dWS}} := \hat{\mathcal{E}}^{\mathscr{R}_{n,k,q}^{dWS}} \setminus \hat{\mathcal{E}}_{cl}^{\mathscr{R}_{n,k,q}^{dWS}} \end{aligned} \tag{5.90}$$

define the sets and subsets of nodes and edge operators that comprise $\hat{\mathscr{R}}_{n,k,q}^{dWS}$.

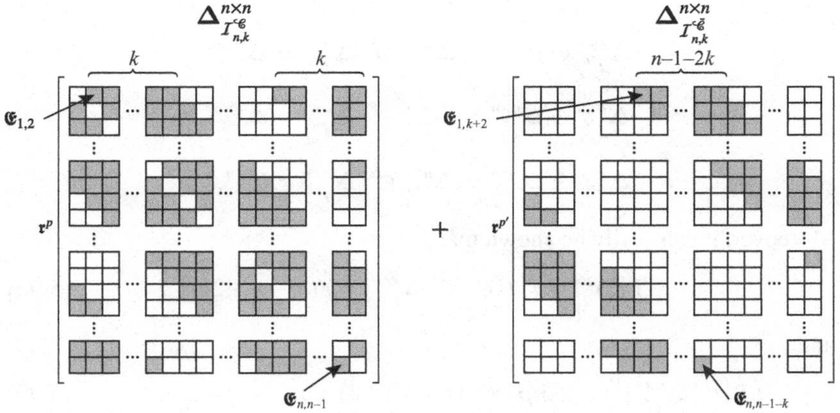

Figure 5.8 Construction of the adjacency matrix for the canonical model of Watts–Strogatz random digraphs $\mathscr{R}^{dWS}_{n,k,q}$ through the sum of the binomial randomisation operator $\mathfrak{r}^p$ acting on the circulant matrix (5.92) that describes all adjacency relations comprising a complete relational k-ring digraph $\mathscr{C}^{cd}_{n,k}$ of order n, and $\mathfrak{r}^{p'}$ acting on the circulant adjacency matrix that defines the complete relational digraph complement $\bar{\mathscr{C}}^{cd}_{n,k}$ of $\mathscr{C}^{cd}_{n,k}$. Each element marked in grey represents here a distinct adjacency relation associated with a directed edge.

Using this operator representation of our canonical model, an algebraic expression for the adjacency matrix of Watts–Strogatz random digraphs $\mathscr{R}^{dWS}_{n,k,q}$ at arbitrary order $n \geq 3$, $1 \leq k < \lfloor n/2 \rfloor$ and rewiring probability $0 \leq q \leq 1$ can now be obtained in a straightforward fashion. Indeed, by noting that each edge-generating operator of $\hat{\mathcal{E}}_{cl}^{\mathscr{R}^{dWS}_{n,k,q}}$ contributes a distinct non-zero matrix element to the sum on the right-hand side of (5.43) such that (5.53) applies, we immediately find

$$\hat{\mathfrak{a}}[\hat{\mathscr{R}}^{dWS}_{n,k,q}] = \mathfrak{r}^p\Big[\mathbf{\Delta}^{n\times n}_{\mathcal{I}^{\mathscr{C}}_{n,k}}\Big] + \mathfrak{r}^{p'}\Big[\mathbf{\Delta}^{n\times n}_{\mathcal{I}^{\bar{\mathscr{C}}}_{n,k}}\Big], \tag{5.91}$$

as illustrated in Fig. 5.8. Interestingly, the generalised Kronecker delta matrices

$$\begin{aligned} \mathbf{\Delta}^{n\times n}_{\mathcal{I}^{\mathscr{C}}_{n,k}} &= \operatorname{circ}\,[(0, \overbrace{1,\ldots,1}^{k}, \overbrace{0,\ldots,0}^{n-1-2k}, \overbrace{1,\ldots,1}^{k})], \\ \mathbf{\Delta}^{n\times n}_{\mathcal{I}^{\bar{\mathscr{C}}}_{n,k}} &= \operatorname{circ}\,[(0,0,\ldots,0,1,\ldots,1,0,\ldots,0)] \end{aligned} \tag{5.92}$$

on which the binomial randomisation operators $\mathfrak{r}^p$ and $\mathfrak{r}^{p'}$ respectively act represent here circulant matrices that satisfy the algebraic identities

$$\mathbf{\Delta}^{n\times n}_{\mathcal{I}^{\mathscr{C}}_{n,k}} + \mathbf{\Delta}^{n\times n}_{\mathcal{I}^{\bar{\mathscr{C}}}_{n,k}} = \mathbf{\Delta}^{n\times n}_{\mathcal{I}^{\mathscr{C}}_{n,k}} +^{\mathbb{B}} \mathbf{\Delta}^{n\times n}_{\mathcal{I}^{\bar{\mathscr{C}}}_{n,k}} = \mathbf{1}^{n\times n} - \mathbf{I}^{n} = \mathbf{\Delta}^{n\times n}_{\mathcal{I}^{dG}_{n}}, \tag{5.93}$$

$$\mathbf{\Delta}^{n\times n}_{\mathcal{I}^{\mathscr{C}}_{n,k}} +^{\mathbb{B}} \mathbf{\Delta}^{n\times n}_{\mathcal{I}^{\mathscr{C}}_{n,k}} = \mathbf{\Delta}^{n\times n}_{\mathcal{I}^{\bar{\mathscr{C}}}_{n,k}} +^{\mathbb{B}} \mathbf{\Delta}^{n\times n}_{\mathcal{I}^{\bar{\mathscr{C}}}_{n,k}} = \mathbf{0}^{n\times n}, \tag{5.94}$$

and

$$\begin{aligned}
\boldsymbol{\Delta}^{n\times n}_{\mathcal{I}^{\mathscr{C}}_{n,k}} \odot \boldsymbol{\Delta}^{n\times n}_{\mathcal{I}^{\mathscr{C}}_{n,k}} &= \boldsymbol{\Delta}^{n\times n}_{\mathcal{I}^{\mathscr{C}}_{n,k}} \odot^{\mathbb{B}} \boldsymbol{\Delta}^{n\times n}_{\mathcal{I}^{\mathscr{C}}_{n,k}} = \boldsymbol{\Delta}^{n\times n}_{\mathcal{I}^{\mathscr{C}}_{n,k}}, \\
\boldsymbol{\Delta}^{n\times n}_{\mathcal{I}^{\bar{\mathscr{C}}}_{n,k}} \odot \boldsymbol{\Delta}^{n\times n}_{\mathcal{I}^{\bar{\mathscr{C}}}_{n,k}} &= \boldsymbol{\Delta}^{n\times n}_{\mathcal{I}^{\bar{\mathscr{C}}}_{n,k}} \odot^{\mathbb{B}} \boldsymbol{\Delta}^{n\times n}_{\mathcal{I}^{\bar{\mathscr{C}}}_{n,k}} = \boldsymbol{\Delta}^{n\times n}_{\mathcal{I}^{\bar{\mathscr{C}}}_{n,k}}, \\
\boldsymbol{\Delta}^{n\times n}_{\mathcal{I}^{\mathscr{C}}_{n,k}} \odot \boldsymbol{\Delta}^{n\times n}_{\mathcal{I}^{\bar{\mathscr{C}}}_{n,k}} &= \boldsymbol{\Delta}^{n\times n}_{\mathcal{I}^{\mathscr{C}}_{n,k}} \odot^{\mathbb{B}} \boldsymbol{\Delta}^{n\times n}_{\mathcal{I}^{\bar{\mathscr{C}}}_{n,k}} = \boldsymbol{0}^{n\times n}.
\end{aligned} \tag{5.95}$$

Moreover, it can easily be shown that

$$\mathrm{T}\,[\boldsymbol{\Delta}^{n\times n}_{\mathcal{I}^{\mathscr{C}}_{n,k}}] = 2kn\,,\ \mathrm{T}\,[\boldsymbol{\Delta}^{n\times n}_{\mathcal{I}^{\bar{\mathscr{C}}}_{n,k}}] = n(n-1-2k) \tag{5.96}$$

and

$$\left\langle \mathrm{T}\left[\mathfrak{r}^p[\boldsymbol{\Delta}^{n\times n}_{\mathcal{I}^{\mathscr{C}}_{n,k}}]\right]\right\rangle = 2knp\,,\ \left\langle \mathrm{T}\left[\mathfrak{r}^p[\boldsymbol{\Delta}^{n\times n}_{\mathcal{I}^{\bar{\mathscr{C}}}_{n,k}}]\right]\right\rangle = n(n-1-2k)p. \tag{5.97}$$

These relations together with the circulant nature of the algebraic objects that realise all adjacency relations of Watts–Strogatz random digraphs through the action of binomial randomisation operators according to (5.91) will prove instrumental in evaluating other graph observables for this model, as we will demonstrate in greater detail in the next chapter.

5.4 Barabási–Albert Random Graphs

As another concrete example of random graphs which prominently feature in the wider applied graph-theoretical literature, let us consider the Barabási–Albert model of growth and preferential attachment [12] introduced in Section 2.3.7. This model constructs in a finite number of discrete steps an approximately scale-free simple graph whose node degrees approach a power law distribution. Specifically, starting from an undirected not self-looped connected graph of order n_0 with k_0 edges, a network is grown by adding at each step a new node with k edges to the existing network in such a way that new adjacency relations are established with a probability that is directly proportional to the node degree of the target node, as illustrated in Fig. 2.11. A newly added node is thus preferentially attached to already highly connected nodes, eventually approximating a power law node degree distribution which becomes independent of the model's parameters in the statistical limit of large networks.

Despite the apparent conceptual and algorithmic simplicity of the Barabási–Albert random graph model $\mathscr{R}^{BA}_{n,k,n_0,k_0}$, its algebraic formulation faces a number of challenges, not only within the confines of our operator graph-theoretical framework. For that reason, before presenting a viable formalisation of its generation, let us begin by developing a suitable canonical model for $\mathcal{R}^{BA}_{n,k,n_0,k_0}$. In Section 5.5, we will then explore a more general, and arguably simpler, approach concerning the algebraic construction of random graphs with arbitrary degree distributions which, naturally, includes the Barabási–Albert model and its extension to directed graphs as two important special cases.

5.4.1 A Canonical Model for Barabási–Albert Random Graphs

One of the problems that hinder a direct translation of the original model of Barabási and Albert into a rigorous algebraic language is that, during each step in the construction, not only the number of edges but also the actual order of the graph changes. As the target of this construction is ultimately a graph with a predefined number of nodes, however, we can easily abstract from the incremental growth of the network size by simply considering a graph of fixed order in which new edges are then successively embedded. To that end, let $\mathcal{R}^{BA}_t$ denote the graph of order n and $\boldsymbol{A}_t$ its associated $(n \times n)$-dimensional matrix of adjacency relations at step $t \in \mathbb{N}_0 : t \in [0, n - n_0]$ in the construction. At the initial step $t = 0$, the graph $\mathcal{R}^{BA}_0$ is comprised of a sole connected component with k_0 undirected edges connecting n_0 nodes, and $n - n_0$ isolated nodes with zero node degrees each. During step $t \geq 1$, new undirected edges are embedded into the graph by preferentially attaching one of the isolated nodes to k of the $n_0 + t - 1$ nodes comprising the connected component of $\mathcal{R}^{BA}_{t-1}$ such that the connected component of $\mathcal{R}^{BA}_t$ reaches order $n_0 + t$ and has a total of $k_0 + tk$ edges. At the final step, $t = n - n_0$, we eventually arrive at a graph $\mathcal{R}^{BA}_{n-n_0}$ that has one connected component spanning all of its n nodes with $k_0 + (n - n_0)k$ undirected edges, and that presents itself as a realisation of the Barabási–Albert random graph model $\mathcal{R}^{BA}_{n,k,n_0,k_0}$.

Before we can explore a more rigorous formalisation of this approach, however, we still need to deal with a second complication, namely that the number of undirected edges added at each step $t \geq 1$ is constant. Recalling our brief argumentation regarding the limitations of the Erdős–Rényi random graph model in Section 5.1.3, imposing such a strict condition is expected to conflict with the element-wise probabilistic nature of the random selection process of target nodes for the added edges. Indeed, although the column randomisation operator (4.59) certainly provides a viable means to algebraically formulate the conditional random attachment of a fixed number of edges, such a formulation would be limited with respect to its usability due to the little satisfying algebraic properties of $\bar{\mathfrak{r}}^k$ (see Table 5.1). In order to bypass these limitations, we will therefore follow the path which naturally led us to the Gilbert random

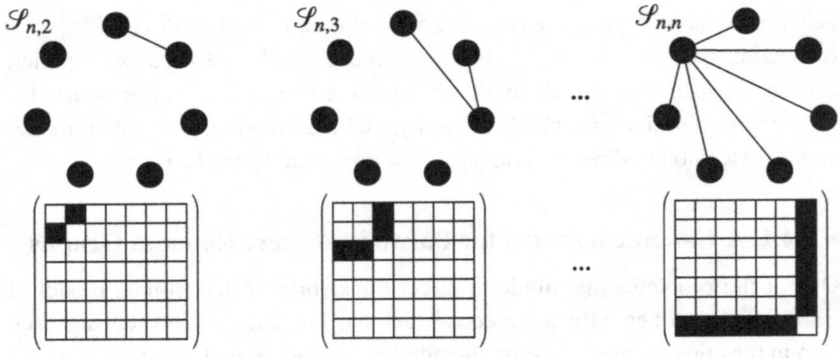

Figure 5.9 Examples of simple generalised star graphs $\mathcal{S}_{n,m}$ of order n with $m-1$ undirected edges, $n-m$ isolated nodes and connected components isomorphic to star graphs $\mathcal{S}_m$ for $n = 7$ and $m \in \{2,3,7\}$. The non-zero elements in the matrix of adjacency relations (bottom) associated with each $\mathcal{S}_{n,m}$ are marked by the elements of the index set $I_m^{\mathcal{S}}$ defined in (5.98).

graph model and a canonical model for Watts–Strogatz random graphs in the previous sections, and only consider at average and in the statistical limit over many realisations the attachment of k edges at each step in the construction of $\mathcal{R}^{BA}_{n,k,n_0,k_0}$. It is important to note here that this approach carries the possibility that at any step no edges will be added to the graph under construction and, thus, will result in a scale-free graph with isolated nodes, especially in cases where k is small. On the other hand, while in the original model of Barabási and Albert the minimum node degree is strictly bound and cannot be larger than k, it can also be argued that weakening the condition imposed on the number of added edges will widen the range of possible node degrees and, thus, foster the realisation of a scale-free node degree distribution, in particular where larger k or smaller networks are concerned.

Accepting this reasonable compromise, we are now finally in a position to formulate a canonical model for simple Barabási–Albert random graphs. To that end, let us introduce with

$$I_m^{\mathcal{S}} := \Big\{(i,m),(m,i) : i \in [1, m-1]\Big\} \tag{5.98}$$

for $1 < m \leq n$ an index set marking all $2(m-1)$ adjacency relations which describe the $m-1$ undirected edges from node m to nodes $i : i \in [1, m-1]$ in a simple *generalised star graph* $\mathcal{S}_{n,m}$ of order n with $n-m$ isolated nodes and a connected component isomorphic to the star graph $\mathcal{S}_m$ of order m (Fig. 5.9). Moreover, and without loss of generality, let us label the n_0 connected nodes of the initial graph $\mathcal{R}_0^{BA}$ successively with $i \in \mathbb{N} : i \in [1, n_0]$ such that non-zero

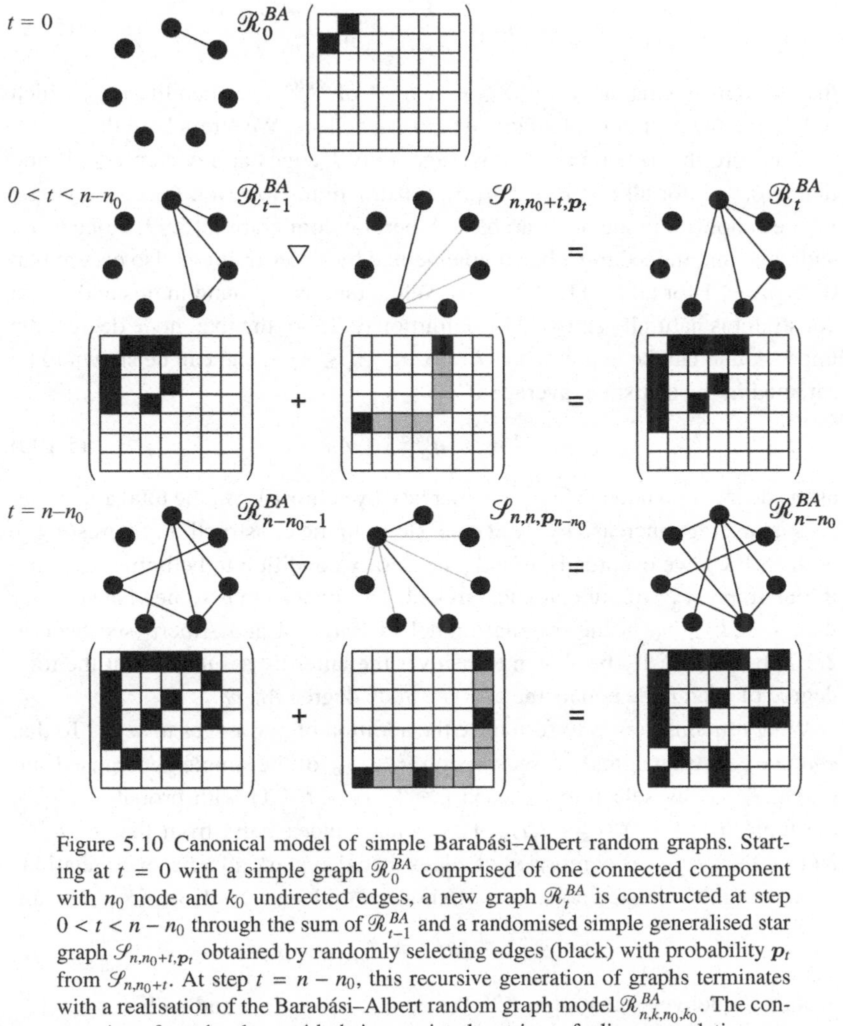

Figure 5.10 Canonical model of simple Barabási–Albert random graphs. Starting at $t = 0$ with a simple graph $\mathscr{R}_0^{BA}$ comprised of one connected component with n_0 node and k_0 undirected edges, a new graph $\mathscr{R}_t^{BA}$ is constructed at step $0 < t < n - n_0$ through the sum of $\mathscr{R}_{t-1}^{BA}$ and a randomised simple generalised star graph $\mathscr{S}_{n,n_0+t,\boldsymbol{p}_t}$ obtained by randomly selecting edges (black) with probability $\boldsymbol{p}_t$ from $\mathscr{S}_{n,n_0+t}$. At step $t = n - n_0$, this recursive generation of graphs terminates with a realisation of the Barabási–Albert random graph model $\mathscr{R}_{n,k,n_0,k_0}^{BA}$. The construction of graphs along with their associated matrices of adjacency relations are here exemplified for $n = 7$, $k = 1$, $n_0 = 2$ and $k_0 = 1$.

elements of its matrix of adjacency relations $\boldsymbol{A}_0$ are marked by ordered index pairs $(i, j)\colon 1 \leq i, j \leq n_0$ (Fig. 5.10, $t = 0$). At step $t \geq 1$ in the construction, we start by considering the graph $\mathscr{R}_{t-1}^{BA}$, obtained in the preceding step $t - 1$, and evaluate its total node degree sequence $\boldsymbol{a}_{t-1}^{total} := \boldsymbol{A}_{t-1} \cdot \boldsymbol{1}^n$ and total adjacency $A_{t-1} := \mathrm{T}[\boldsymbol{A}_{t-1}]$ by adapting (2.25) and (2.14) respectively, while recalling that for a simple graph the weight matrix and matrix of adjacency relations are identical. The vector

$$\boldsymbol{p}_t := \frac{k}{A_{t-1}} \cdot \boldsymbol{a}_{t-1}^{total} \tag{5.99}$$

then assigns to each node $1 \leq i \leq n_0 + t - 1$ of $\mathscr{R}_{t-1}^{BA}$ a probability $(\boldsymbol{p}_t)_i$ which will guide the preferential attachment of new edges. We stress here that (5.99) does ensure the selection of, at average, only k edges at any step $t \geq 1$, and that $(\boldsymbol{p}_t)_i = 0$ for all $i \in [n_0 + t, n]$ by construction. However, for conceiving a viable canonical model for Barabási–Albert random graphs, (5.99) alone is not sufficient and indeed must be complemented by a constraint to also ensure that $0 \leq (\boldsymbol{p}_t)_i \leq 1$ for all $i \in [1, n_0 + t - 1]$. While the lower bound in this additional constraint is naturally satisfied by definition (2.25) of the total node degree, the upper bound can be expressed as $k \max [\boldsymbol{a}_{t-1}^{total}] \leq A_{t-1}$, and can be shown to be satisfied in the statistical average if

$$k \max [\boldsymbol{a}_0^{total}] \leq A_0 \tag{5.100}$$

as the degree of a node in $\mathscr{R}_{t-1}^{BA}$ can increase by at most 1, yet the total adjacency sees an average increase by $2k$ at each step t in the construction. Interestingly, with (5.100), we eventually found a necessary condition to be imposed on the initial graph $\mathscr{R}_0^{BA}$ of our canonical model. This condition is somewhat stronger than $1 \leq k \leq n_0$ in the original model of Barabási and Albert (see Section 2.3.7) but can easily be shown to recover the latter by assuming that the total degree of each node equals the average node degree A_0/n_0.

What remains now is to formalise the addition of new edges to $\mathscr{R}_{t-1}^{BA}$. To that end, we construct a randomised version $\mathscr{S}_{n,n_0+t,\boldsymbol{p}_t}$ of the simple generalised star graph $\mathscr{S}_{n,n_0+t}$ by selecting for each $i \in [1, n_0 + t - 1]$ with probability $(\boldsymbol{p}_t)_i$ the tuple $\{(i, n_0 + t), (n_0 + t, i)\}$ of associated index pairs from the set $I_{n_0+t}^{\mathscr{S}}$. Noting that $\mathscr{S}_{n,n_0+t}$ is comprised of edges that also mark all adjacency relations connecting the isolated node $n_0 + t$ to nodes $i \in [1, n_0 + t - 1]$ in $\mathscr{R}_{t-1}^{BA}$, the sum

$$\mathscr{R}_t^{BA} := \mathscr{R}_{t-1}^{BA} \triangledown \mathscr{S}_{n,n_0+t,\boldsymbol{p}_t} \tag{5.101}$$

eventually delivers the graph $\mathscr{R}_t^{BA}$ at step $0 < t < n - n_0$, and with

$$\mathscr{R}_{n-n_0}^{BA} = \mathscr{R}_{n-n_0-1}^{BA} \triangledown \mathscr{S}_{n,n,\boldsymbol{p}_{n-n_0}} =: \mathscr{R}_{n,k,n_0,k_0}^{BA} \tag{5.102}$$

at step $t = n - n_0$ a desired realisation of $\mathscr{R}_{n,k,n_0,k_0}^{BA}$, as shown in Fig. 5.10. This finally allows us to define a canonical model of Barabási–Albert random graphs $\mathscr{R}_{n,k,n_0,k_0}^{BA}$ as the finite sequence of simple graphs $\mathscr{R}_t^{BA}$, $0 \leq t \leq n - n_0$, generated in $n - n_0$ discrete steps t according to (5.101) and (5.102) from a given initial graph $\mathscr{R}_0^{BA}$ of order n_0 that is comprised of a single connected component with k_0 edges, and whose total node degrees and adjacency satisfy (5.100).

5.4.2 Simple Barabási–Albert Random Graphs

After having conceived of a canonical model for simple Barabási–Albert random graphs, let us now formalise this model within our operator graph-theoretical framework. We begin by noting that, according to (5.101), the construction of $\mathcal{R}_t^{BA}$ at step $t \geq 1$ solely depends on $\mathcal{R}_{t-1}^{BA}$ as the variable component, to which then randomly selected edges of the generalised star graph $\mathcal{S}_{n,n_0+t}$ are added. An operator representation of $\mathcal{R}_{t-1}^{BA}$ thus naturally presents itself as seed of a graph generator that delivers an operator representation of $\mathcal{R}_t^{BA}$. Furthermore, our canonical model immediately allows us to define each of the simple graphs $\mathcal{R}_t^{BA}, 0 < t \leq n - n_0$ in explicit terms as sum

$$\mathcal{R}_t^{BA} := \mathcal{R}_0^{BA} \triangledown \mathcal{S}_{n,n_0+1,\boldsymbol{p}_1} \triangledown \ldots \triangledown \mathcal{S}_{n,n_0+t,\boldsymbol{p}_t} \tag{5.103}$$

over the initial graph $\mathcal{R}_0^{BA}$ and randomised generalised star graphs $\mathcal{S}_{n,n_0+s,\boldsymbol{p}_s}$ for $1 \leq s \leq t$. All undirected edges that are eventually added to $\mathcal{R}_0^{BA}$ thus belong to generalised star graphs $\mathcal{S}_{n,n_0+s}, s \geq 1$ which, by definition, do not share edges either with $\mathcal{R}_0^{BA}$ or among each other. It therefore suffices to construct an operator representation $\hat{\mathcal{R}}_0^{BA}$ of the initial graph $\mathcal{R}_0^{BA}$ as seed for the sequential generation of representations $\hat{\mathcal{R}}_t^{BA}$ of the simple graphs $\mathcal{R}_t^{BA}$ along each step $0 < t < n - n_0$, and for ultimately obtaining with $\hat{\mathcal{R}}_{n,k,n_0,k_0}^{BA} := \hat{\mathcal{R}}_{n-n_0}^{BA}$ a representation of $\mathcal{R}_{n,k,n_0,k_0}^{BA}$ at $t = n - n_0$.

In order to arrive at a suitable operator representation $\hat{\mathcal{R}}_0^{BA} := (\hat{\mathcal{N}}^{\mathcal{R}_0^{BA}}, \hat{\mathcal{E}}^{\mathcal{R}_0^{BA}})$, we recognise that the classical subset of its set of edge operators must certainly be comprised of all undirected adjacency relations that define $\mathcal{R}_0^{BA}$. Moreover, in order to accommodate the sequential generation of $\hat{\mathcal{R}}_t^{BA}$, the set $\hat{\mathcal{E}}^{\mathcal{R}_0^{BA}}$ should also contain all operators which represent edges that could eventually be added to $\mathcal{R}_0^{BA}$ and, in accordance with our canonical model, thus define the generalised star graphs $\mathcal{S}_{n,n_0+t}$ for $1 \leq t \leq n - n_0$. By assigning these latter edge operators to the auxiliary subset of $\hat{\mathcal{E}}^{\mathcal{R}_0^{BA}}$, we not only ensure their availability during the construction of $\hat{\mathcal{R}}_t^{BA}$ but also preserve $\hat{\mathcal{R}}_0^{BA}$ as representation which, classically, describes the given initial graph $\mathcal{R}_0^{BA}$.

With these conceptual preliminaries in place, let us now construct our seed graph $\hat{\mathcal{R}}_0^{BA}$. To that end, we again employ n-dimensional Boolean vectors to represent nodes and edge operators such that

$$\mathfrak{E}[\boldsymbol{n}] \colon \hat{\mathcal{N}}^{\mathcal{R}_0^{BA}} \to \hat{\mathcal{N}}^{\mathcal{R}_0^{BA}}, \; \mathfrak{E}[\boldsymbol{n}] := (\mathfrak{E} \cdot^{\mathbb{B}} \boldsymbol{n}^{\mathsf{T}}) \cdot^{\mathbb{B}} (\mathfrak{E} +^{\mathbb{B}} \boldsymbol{n})$$

defines the action of each edge operator $\mathfrak{E} \in \hat{\mathcal{E}}^{\mathcal{R}_0^{BA}}$. Furthermore, let

$$\mathcal{I}_0^{BA} := \left\{(i, j) : i, j \in [1, n_0], (\boldsymbol{A}_0)_{ij} = 1\right\}$$

denote the set of ordered index pairs which mark all non-zero elements in the symmetric matrix of adjacency relations $\boldsymbol{A}_0$ of $\mathscr{R}_0^{BA}$. It can then be shown that the sets and subsets

$$\begin{aligned} \hat{\mathcal{N}}^{\mathscr{R}_0^{BA}} &= \left\{\boldsymbol{n}_0 := \boldsymbol{0}^n, \boldsymbol{n}_i := \boldsymbol{\delta}_i^n : i \in [1,n]\right\} \subset \mathbb{B}^n, \\ \hat{\mathcal{N}}_{cl}^{\mathscr{R}_0^{BA}} &:= \left\{\boldsymbol{n}_i \in \hat{\mathcal{N}}^{\mathscr{R}_0^{BA}} : i \in [1,n]\right\}, \\ \hat{\mathcal{N}}_{aux}^{\mathscr{R}_0^{BA}} &:= \hat{\mathcal{N}}^{\mathscr{R}_0^{BA}} \setminus \hat{\mathcal{N}}_{cl}^{\mathscr{R}_0^{BA}} = \left\{\boldsymbol{n}_0\right\} \end{aligned} \tag{5.104}$$

of nodes and

$$\begin{aligned} \hat{\mathcal{E}}^{\mathscr{R}_0^{BA}} &= \left\{\mathfrak{E}_{00} := \boldsymbol{0}^n, \mathfrak{E}_{j_1 j_2} := \boldsymbol{\delta}_{j_1}^n + \boldsymbol{\delta}_{j_2}^n : (j_1,j_2) \in \mathcal{I}_0^{BA} \cup \bigcup_{s=1}^{n-n_0} \mathcal{I}_{n_0+s}^{\mathscr{S}} \wedge j_2 > j_1\right\} \subset \mathbb{B}^n, \\ \hat{\mathcal{E}}_{cl}^{\mathscr{R}_0^{BA}} &:= \left\{\mathfrak{E}_{j_1 j_2} \in \hat{\mathcal{E}}^{\mathscr{R}_0^{BA}} : (j_1,j_2) \in \mathcal{I}_0^{BA} \wedge j_2 > j_1\right\}, \\ \hat{\mathcal{E}}_{aux}^{\mathscr{R}_0^{BA}} &:= \hat{\mathcal{E}}^{\mathscr{R}_0^{BA}} \setminus \hat{\mathcal{E}}_{cl}^{\mathscr{R}_0^{BA}} = \left\{\mathfrak{E}_{00}, \mathfrak{E}_{j_1 j_2} \in \hat{\mathcal{E}}^{\mathscr{R}_0^{BA}} : (j_1,j_2) \in \bigcup_{s=1}^{n-n_0} \mathcal{I}_{n_0+s}^{\mathscr{S}} \wedge j_2 > j_1\right\} \end{aligned} \tag{5.105}$$

of edge operators furnish a viable operator representation $\hat{\mathscr{R}}_0^{BA}$ of $\mathscr{R}_0^{BA}$. The set $\hat{\mathcal{E}}^{\mathscr{R}_0^{BA}}$ is here comprised of the n-dimensional all-zeroes vector $\boldsymbol{0}^n$ and a total of $((n-n_0)(n+n_0-1)+\mathrm{T}[\boldsymbol{A}_0])/2$ Boolean vectors with two non-zero elements each. Of these vectors, $\mathrm{T}[\boldsymbol{A}_0]/2$ represent the undirected edges of $\mathscr{R}_0^{BA}$, and the remaining $n(n-1)/2 - n_0(n_0-1)/2$ all edges that form the simple generalised star graphs $\mathscr{S}_{n,n_0+t}$, $1 \le t \le n-n_0$ and are subject to random selection during the construction of $\hat{\mathscr{R}}_{n,k,n_0,k_0}^{BA}$ (see Fig. 5.11a). By reassigning operators associated with these edges from the classical to the auxiliary subset of $\hat{\mathcal{E}}^{\mathscr{R}_t^{BA}}$ through the action of an appropriately defined graph generator, we will be able to not only distinguish operator representations $\hat{\mathscr{R}}_t^{BA}$ at different steps in the construction of our random graph, but also algebraically formalise the incremental growth of the classical network through the attachment of new edges.

Let us illustrate this approach for step $t=1$ and define a graph generator $\hat{\mathfrak{G}}_1^{BA}$ which delivers $\hat{\mathscr{R}}_1^{BA}$ when acting upon its seed graph $\hat{\mathscr{R}}_0^{BA}$. In order to construct $\hat{\mathscr{R}}_1^{BA}$ according to our canonical model, we need to consider all edge operators $\mathfrak{E}_{j_1 j_2} \in \hat{\mathcal{E}}_{aux}^{\mathscr{R}_0^{BA}}$ with $(j_1, j_2) \in \mathcal{I}_{n_0+1}^{\mathscr{S}}$, $j_2 > j_1$ that represent the undirected edges of the generalised star graph $\mathscr{S}_{n,n_0+1}$, and then reassign each of these operators with probability $(\boldsymbol{p}_1)_{j_1}$ to the classical subset $\hat{\mathcal{E}}_{cl}^{\mathscr{R}_0^{BA}}$. Utilising scalar realisations of the binomial randomisation operator (4.41), we can easily demonstrate that

$$\hat{\mathfrak{G}}_1^{BA} = \left(\hat{\mathfrak{G}}_{\mathcal{N}1} := \mathrm{id}\,,\, \hat{\mathfrak{G}}_{\mathcal{E}1}\right) \tag{5.106}$$

with

$$\hat{\mathfrak{G}}_{\mathcal{E}1} : \hat{\mathcal{E}}^{\mathscr{R}_0^{BA}} \to \hat{\mathcal{E}}^{\mathscr{R}_1^{BA}}, \hat{\mathfrak{G}}_{\mathcal{E}1}[\mathfrak{E}_{j_1 j_2}] := \begin{cases} \mathfrak{r}^{(\boldsymbol{p}_1)_{j_1}}[1] \cdot \mathfrak{E}_{j_1 j_2} & \text{if } (j_1,j_2) \in \mathcal{I}_{n_0+1}^{\mathscr{S}}, \\ \mathfrak{E}_{j_1 j_2} & \text{otherwise} \end{cases}$$

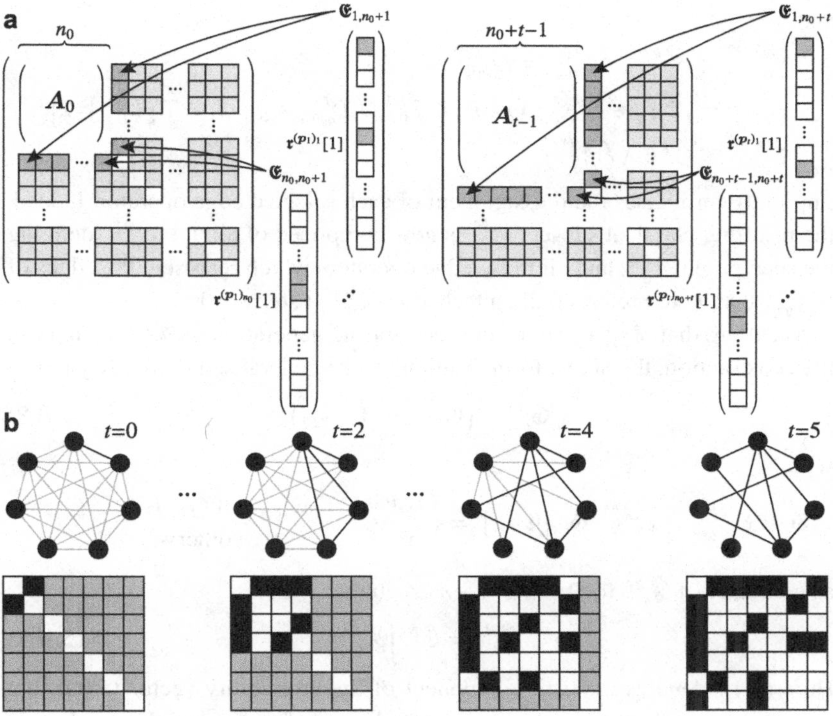

Figure 5.11 Generation of simple Barabási–Albert random graphs. **a:** Matrix of adjacency relations which marks all auxiliary edge operators in an operator representation of $\mathscr{R}^{BA}_{t-1}$ serving as generator seed at step $t = 1$ (left) and $1 < t \leq n - n_0$ (right). By combining independent scalar realisations $\mathfrak{r}^{p_t}[1]$ of the binomial randomisation operator with each of the edge operators associated with the simple generalised star graph $\mathscr{S}_{n,n_0+t}$ (dark grey), the generator (5.108) will then deliver $\hat{\mathscr{R}}^{BA}_t$ and provide the seed to be utilised at step $t + 1$. The classical subset of edge-generating operators of $\hat{\mathscr{R}}^{BA}_t$ defines here $\mathscr{R}^{BA}_t$ and its associated matrix of adjacency relations $\boldsymbol{A}_t$. The generation terminates with an operator representation of $\mathscr{R}^{BA}_{n,k,n_0,k_0}$ at step $t = n - n_0$. **b:** Representative steps in the realisation of a Barabási–Albert random graph for $n = 7$, $k = 1$, $n_0 = 2$ and $k_0 = 1$. Graph edges and non-zero elements in the matrix of adjacency relations that are associated with classical and auxiliary edge operators $\mathfrak{E} \neq \boldsymbol{0}^n$ are respectively marked in black and grey.

accommodates this preferential selection of edge operators, and that the generated operator representation $\hat{\mathscr{R}}^{BA}_1 = \hat{\mathfrak{G}}_{\mathcal{E}1}[\hat{\mathscr{R}}^{BA}_0] := (\hat{\mathcal{N}}^{\mathscr{R}^{BA}_1}, \hat{\mathcal{E}}^{\mathscr{R}^{BA}_1})$ with

$$\begin{aligned} \hat{\mathcal{N}}^{\mathscr{R}^{BA}_1} &:= \left\{ \hat{\mathfrak{G}}_{\mathcal{N}1}[\boldsymbol{n}] : \boldsymbol{n} \in \hat{\mathcal{N}}^{\mathscr{R}^{BA}_0} \right\} = \hat{\mathcal{N}}^{\mathscr{R}^{BA}_0} \subset \mathbb{B}^n, \\ \hat{\mathcal{E}}^{\mathscr{R}^{BA}_1} &:= \left\{ \hat{\mathfrak{G}}_{\mathcal{E}1}[\mathfrak{E}] : \mathfrak{E} \in \hat{\mathcal{E}}^{\mathscr{R}^{BA}_0} \right\} \subset \mathbb{B}^n \end{aligned} \tag{5.107}$$

and

$$\hat{\mathcal{N}}_{cl}^{\mathscr{R}_1^{BA}} := \hat{\mathcal{N}}_{cl}^{\mathscr{R}_0^{BA}}, \hat{\mathcal{N}}_{aux}^{\mathscr{R}_1^{BA}} := \hat{\mathcal{N}}_{aux}^{\mathscr{R}_0^{BA}},$$
$$\hat{\mathcal{E}}_{cl}^{\mathscr{R}_1^{BA}} := \left\{\mathfrak{E}_{j_1 j_2} \in \hat{\mathcal{E}}^{\mathscr{R}_0^{BA}} : (j_1, j_2) \in \mathcal{I}_0^{BA} \cup \mathcal{I}_{n_0+1}^{\mathscr{S}} \wedge j_2 > j_1 \wedge \mathrm{T}[\mathfrak{E}_{j_1 j_2}]=2\right\},$$
$$\hat{\mathcal{E}}_{aux}^{\mathscr{R}_1^{BA}} := \hat{\mathcal{E}}^{\mathscr{R}_1^{BA}} \setminus \hat{\mathcal{E}}_{cl}^{\mathscr{R}_1^{BA}}$$

implicitly formalises the reassignment of each selected edge operator. Indeed, the resulting classical subset $\hat{\mathcal{E}}_{cl}^{\mathscr{R}_1^{BA}}$ is now comprised of all $\mathfrak{E} \in \hat{\mathcal{E}}_{cl}^{\mathscr{R}_0^{BA}}$ defining the seed graph $\hat{\mathscr{R}}_0^{BA}$, and all those edge operators which represent the edges of $\mathscr{S}_{n,n_0+1}$ that were preferentially attached to $\mathscr{R}_0^{BA}$ at step $t = 1$.

Recalling that $\hat{\mathscr{R}}_{t-1}^{BA}$ provides the seed for the generation of $\hat{\mathscr{R}}_t^{BA}$ at step t in the construction, the above formalisation can be generalised to finally yield

$$\hat{\mathfrak{G}}_t^{BA} = \left(\hat{\mathfrak{G}}_{\mathcal{N}t} := \mathrm{id}\,,\, \hat{\mathfrak{G}}_{\mathcal{E}t}\right) \tag{5.108}$$

with

$$\hat{\mathfrak{G}}_{\mathcal{E}t}: \hat{\mathcal{E}}^{\mathscr{R}_{t-1}^{BA}} \to \hat{\mathcal{E}}^{\mathscr{R}_t^{BA}}, \hat{\mathfrak{G}}_{\mathcal{E}t}[\mathfrak{E}_{j_1 j_2}] := \begin{cases} \mathfrak{r}^{(\boldsymbol{p}_t)_{j_1}}[1] \cdot \mathfrak{E}_{j_1 j_2} & \text{if } (j_1, j_2) \in \mathcal{I}_{n_0+t}^{\mathscr{S}}, \\ \mathfrak{E}_{j_1 j_2} & \text{otherwise} \end{cases}$$

as generator of $\hat{\mathscr{R}}_t^{BA}$ for $1 \leq t \leq n - n_0$ such that

$$\hat{\mathscr{R}}_t^{BA} = \hat{\mathfrak{G}}_t^{BA}\left[\hat{\mathscr{R}}_{t-1}^{BA}\right]. \tag{5.109}$$

Here $(\boldsymbol{p}_t)_{j_1}$ denotes the j_1th component of the probability vector (5.99) that governs the preferential attachment of edges as function of the total node degree sequence observable

$$\hat{\boldsymbol{a}}^{total}[\hat{\mathscr{R}}_{t-1}^{BA}] = \boldsymbol{a}_{t-1}^{total} := \sum_{\mathfrak{E} \in \hat{\mathcal{E}}_{cl}^{\mathscr{R}_{t-1}^{BA}}} \mathfrak{E} \tag{5.110}$$

and total adjacency observable

$$\hat{A}[\hat{\mathscr{R}}_{t-1}^{BA}] = A_{t-1} := \mathrm{T}\left[\boldsymbol{a}_{t-1}^{total}\right] \tag{5.111}$$

of the seed graph $\hat{\mathscr{R}}_{t-1}^{BA}$. Furthermore, the generated sets

$$\begin{aligned} \hat{\mathcal{N}}^{\mathscr{R}_t^{BA}} &:= \left\{\hat{\mathfrak{G}}_{\mathcal{N}t}[\boldsymbol{n}] : \boldsymbol{n} \in \hat{\mathcal{N}}^{\mathscr{R}_{t-1}^{BA}}\right\} = \hat{\mathcal{N}}^{\mathscr{R}_0^{BA}} \subset \mathbb{B}^n, \\ \hat{\mathcal{E}}^{\mathscr{R}_t^{BA}} &:= \left\{\hat{\mathfrak{G}}_{\mathcal{E}t}[\mathfrak{E}] : \mathfrak{E} \in \hat{\mathcal{E}}^{\mathscr{R}_{t-1}^{BA}}\right\} \subset \mathbb{B}^n \end{aligned} \tag{5.112}$$

of nodes and edge operators together with their classical and auxiliary subsets

$$\hat{\mathcal{N}}_{cl}^{\mathscr{R}_t^{BA}} := \hat{\mathcal{N}}_{cl}^{\mathscr{R}_0^{BA}}, \hat{\mathcal{N}}_{aux}^{\mathscr{R}_t^{BA}} := \hat{\mathcal{N}}_{aux}^{\mathscr{R}_0^{BA}},$$
$$\hat{\mathcal{E}}_{cl}^{\mathscr{R}_t^{BA}} := \left\{\mathfrak{E}_{j_1 j_2} \in \hat{\mathcal{E}}^{\mathscr{R}_{t-1}^{BA}} : (j_1, j_2) \in \mathcal{I}_0^{BA} \cup \bigcup_{s=1}^{t} \mathcal{I}_{n_0+s}^{\mathscr{S}} \wedge j_2 > j_1 \wedge \mathrm{T}[\mathfrak{E}_{j_1 j_2}]=2\right\},$$
$$\hat{\mathcal{E}}_{aux}^{\mathscr{R}_t^{BA}} := \hat{\mathcal{E}}^{\mathscr{R}_t^{BA}} \setminus \hat{\mathcal{E}}_{cl}^{\mathscr{R}_t^{BA}}$$

define an operator representation $\hat{\mathcal{R}}_t^{BA} := (\hat{\mathcal{N}}^{\mathcal{R}_t^{BA}}, \hat{\mathcal{E}}^{\mathcal{R}_t^{BA}})$ for each $\mathcal{R}_t^{BA}$ and eventually deliver a desired operator representation $\hat{\mathcal{R}}_{n,k,n_0,k_0}^{BA} := \hat{\mathcal{R}}_{n-n_0}^{BA}$ of our Barabási–Albert random graph $\mathcal{R}_{n,k,n_0,k_0}^{BA}$ at the final step in the construction. An example of the application of (5.108) is illustrated in Fig. 5.11b.

Let us conclude our short exposition of the Barabási–Albert random graph model with an evaluation of its adjacency matrix observable. Adapting definition (4.63) and recognising with (5.109) and (5.112) the recursive nature of the graph generation, we immediately find

$$
\begin{aligned}
\hat{\mathfrak{a}}[\hat{\mathcal{R}}_t^{BA}] &:= \sum_{\mathfrak{C}\in\hat{\mathcal{E}}_{cl}^{\mathcal{R}_t^{BA}}} \left(\mathfrak{C}\otimes\mathfrak{C}^{\mathsf{T}} - \mathrm{diag}\,[\mathfrak{C}]\right) \\
&= \sum_{\mathfrak{C}\in\hat{\mathcal{E}}_{cl}^{\mathcal{R}_{t-1}^{BA}}} \left(\mathfrak{C}\otimes\mathfrak{C}^{\mathsf{T}} - \mathrm{diag}\,[\mathfrak{C}]\right) + \sum_{\substack{(j_1,j_2)\in\mathcal{I}_{n_0+t}^{\mathcal{S}}\\ j_2>j_1}} \left(\mathfrak{C}_{j_1 j_2}\otimes\mathfrak{C}_{j_1 j_2}^{\mathsf{T}} - \mathrm{diag}\,[\mathfrak{C}_{j_1 j_2}]\right) \\
&= \hat{\mathfrak{a}}[\hat{\mathcal{R}}_{t-1}^{BA}] + \sum_{j=1}^{n_0+t-1} \mathfrak{r}^{(\boldsymbol{p}_t)_j}[1]\cdot(\delta_{j,n_0+t}^{n\times n} + \delta_{n_0+t,j}^{n\times n})
\end{aligned}
\tag{5.113}
$$

for $1 \leq t \leq n - n_0$, where in the last step we made use of (5.98) to explicitly represent the sum over all ordered index pairs $(j_1, j_2) \in \mathcal{I}_{n_0+t}^{\mathcal{S}}$ with $j_2 > j_1$. It is important to stress here that each term $\mathfrak{r}^{(\boldsymbol{p}_t)_j}[1]$ for given t and j marks a single independent scalar realisation of the binomial randomisation operator, and thus governs the contribution of two non-zero elements associated with a single undirected edge to the adjacency matrix of $\mathcal{R}_t^{BA}$. Noting that $\hat{\mathfrak{a}}[\hat{\mathcal{R}}_0^{BA}]$ defines the $(n_0 \times n_0)$-dimensional adjacency matrix of the given initial graph $\mathcal{R}_0^{BA}$, the recursive expression (5.113) then delivers for $t = n - n_0$ with

$$
\hat{\mathfrak{a}}[\hat{\mathcal{R}}_{n,k,n_0,k_0}^{BA}] = \hat{\mathfrak{a}}[\hat{\mathcal{R}}_0^{BA}] + \sum_{t=1}^{n-n_0}\sum_{j=1}^{n_0+t-1} \mathfrak{r}^{(\boldsymbol{p}_t)_j}[1]\cdot(\delta_{j,n_0+t}^{n\times n} + \delta_{n_0+t,j}^{n\times n})
\tag{5.114}
$$

the adjacency matrix observable of our canonical model for Barabási–Albert random graphs $\mathcal{R}_{n,k,n_0,k_0}^{BA}$.

Although (5.114) certainly provides a parametrised algebraic expression for the adjacency matrix of Barabási–Albert random graphs, this expression also remains somehwat unsatisfactory due to its inherent dependence on the probability vectors $\boldsymbol{p}_t$. This dependence mirrors that of our generator (5.108), and requires that we evaluate both the total node degree sequence (5.110) and adjacency (5.110) for each $\mathcal{R}_t^{BA}, 0 \leq t < n - n_0$. By utilising $\hat{\mathfrak{a}}[\hat{\mathcal{R}}_{n,k,n_0,k_0}^{BA}]$, however, it is possible to obtain $\boldsymbol{p}_t$ more conveniently without considering concrete realisations of $\mathcal{R}_t^{BA}$ themselves. To that end, we introduce the set

$$
\mathcal{I}_m := \{(i,i) \colon i \in [1,m]\}
\tag{5.115}
$$

of index pairs which for $1 \leq m \leq n$ mark the first m elements on the diagonal of an $n \times n$ matrix, and once more we note that the matrix of adjacency relations of a simple graph equals its adjacency matrix. It can then easily be shown that the total adjacency of $\mathscr{R}_t^{BA}$ is given by

$$A_t := \mathrm{T}[\boldsymbol{A}_t] = \mathrm{T}\left[\hat{\mathbf{a}}[\hat{\mathscr{R}}^{BA}_{n,k,n_0,k_0}] \cdot \Delta^{n \times n}_{\mathcal{I}_{n_0+t}}\right] = A_0 + 2 \sum_{s=1}^{t} \sum_{j=1}^{n_0+s-1} \mathfrak{r}^{(\boldsymbol{p}_s)_j}[1], \quad (5.116)$$

and that

$$\boldsymbol{a}_t^{total} := \boldsymbol{A}_t \cdot \boldsymbol{1}^n = \hat{\mathbf{a}}[\hat{\mathscr{R}}^{BA}_{n,k,n_0,k_0}] \cdot \Delta^{n \times n}_{\mathcal{I}_{n_0+t}} \cdot \boldsymbol{1}^n \quad (5.117)$$

yields the total node degree sequence with elements

$$(\boldsymbol{a}_t^{total})_i = \begin{cases} (\boldsymbol{a}_0^{total})_i + \sum_{s=1}^{t} \mathfrak{r}^{(\boldsymbol{p}_s)_i}[1] & \text{for } i \in [1, n_0], \\ \sum_{j=1}^{i-1} \mathfrak{r}^{(\boldsymbol{p}_{i-n_0})_j}[1] + \sum_{s=i-n_0+1}^{t} \mathfrak{r}^{(\boldsymbol{p}_s)_i}[1] & \text{for } i \in [n_0+1, n_0+t], \\ 0 & \text{for } i \in [n_0+t+1, n] \end{cases}$$

for $1 \leq t \leq n - n_0$, where A_0 and $\boldsymbol{a}_0^{total}$ denote the total adjacency and node degree sequence of the initial graph $\mathscr{R}_0^{BA}$. Together with (5.99), this eventually delivers the elements of the probability vector $\boldsymbol{p}_t$ at any given step t as function of $\boldsymbol{p}_{t'}$ for $t' < t$. In Section 6.5, we will show how the resulting formulation can be further adapted to yield an explicit expression for the probabilities which govern the preferential attachment of edges in the Barabási–Albert random graph model. In so doing, we will demonstrate that our representation, despite its algebraically challenging nature, provides some leverage for assessing various graph observables non-asymptotically.

5.5 Random Graphs with Arbitrary Degree Distribution

Before we revisit Barabási–Albert graphs in Chapter 6, let us conclude our journey through the realms of important random graph models by exploring a conceptually simpler approach which not only alleviates some of the algebraic challenges we encountered earlier in regards to their generation, but also is more general in its scope by targeting the construction of graphs with arbitrary node degree distributions. We begin here by briefly recalling the adjacency matrix observables of the various graph models considered so far. In Gilbert random graphs, for example, both (5.60) and (5.67) define Boolean matrices whose non-zero elements occur uniform randomly with a given probability p. Similarly, realisations of the Watts–Strogatz model effectively amount to constructing Boolean matrices (5.85) or (5.91) with non-zero elements distributed according to two generally distinct probabilities p and p'. Last but not least, in our canonical model of Barabási–Albert random graphs, the interdependent probabilities $\boldsymbol{p}_t$ which govern the occurrence of non-zero elements in its adjacency matrix (5.114) differ for each column and row in order to account for the preferential attachment of edges that describes the incremental growth of the network. What if we could generalise this common feature and associate the probability which guides the random realisation of adjacency relations and, thus, the presence of non-zero elements in a graph's adjacency matrix with specific characteristics of a desired target graph, such as its node degree sequence or node degree distribution?

The historically first and most prominent model which describes the generation of random graphs with a node degree sequence matching that of a given target graph dates back to the work of Bollobás and is called the *configuration model* [21]. Here, a specific "configuration" or arrangement of edges is constructed by assigning to each of n nodes $i \in [1, n]$ a finite number $a_i^{total} \in \mathbb{N}$ of *stubs* or half-edges. One then selects uniformly at random a pair of available stubs and replaces it with an undirected adjacency relation between the nodes to which both stubs belong, thus effectively reducing the number of available stubs by two and increasing the number of edges by one. This process eventually terminates if all stubs are assigned and results in the generation of a graph of order n with exactly $N_e = 1/2 \sum_{i=1}^{n} a_i^{total}$ undirected edges that represents a realisation of a random graph with node degree sequence $\boldsymbol{a}^{total}$.

Despite the conceptual and algorithmic simplicity as well as general mathematical appeal of the configuration model, however, there are also a number of limitations which impair its usefulness as descriptive vessel for real-world phenomena. Firstly, for the generation to work at all, the chosen configuration must ensure that the total number of assigned stubs is even. More importantly, as the realisation of graphs in the configuration model targets an exact number of edges, it mirrors the Erdős–Rényi random graph model in regards to the algebraic challenge of randomly generating a fixed number of edges (see Section 5.1.3). Secondly, the generation does not prevent the random selection of a pair of stubs assigned to the same node and, thus, the construction of self-loops, or the selection of two or more pairs of stubs assigned to the same distinct nodes and, thus, the construction of multiedges. The configuration model, therefore, can no longer be considered as a model of simple graphs, but it does generally represent self-looped undirected multigraphs. Finally, albeit directed configurations of incoming and outgoing stubs are certainly conceivable, a generalisation of the configuration model to directed multigraphs would require imposing further restrictions on the number of assigned stubs in order to cope with the possible generation of directed self-loops.

Addressing the first of these limitations, Chung and Lu proposed an alternative to the original model of Bollobás by replacing the here necessarily exact configuration of edges with an expected configuration such that the generated node degree sequence will be required to only match that of a target graph in the statistical average over many realisations [29, 30]. To explore the rationale behind this arguably more convenient approach, let us take a closer look at the probability p_{ij} that two given nodes i and j are connected. With $A = \sum_{i=1}^{n} a_i^{total}$ stubs available in the network, and two stubs giving rise to a single undirected edge, we have a total of $\binom{A}{2} = A(A-1)/2$ ways to connect two not necessarily distinct nodes with each other. On the other hand, with a_i^{total} stubs assigned to node i, and a_j^{total} stubs assigned to node j, there are only $a_i^{total} a_j^{total}$ ways to draw a link between i and j in the case $i \neq j$, and $\binom{a_i^{total}}{2} = a_i^{total}(a_i^{total} - 1)/2$ ways if $i = j$. As the process of selecting individual pairs of stubs in the configuration model is independent and uniform-random, and a total of $N_e = A/2$ pairs will be selected during the construction of the graph, we then find

$$p_{ij} = N_e \frac{a_i^{total} a_j^{total}}{A(A-1)/2} = \frac{a_i^{total} a_j^{total}}{A-1} \approx \frac{a_i^{total} a_j^{total}}{A} \tag{5.118}$$

for $i \neq j$, and

$$p_{ii} = N_e \frac{a_i^{total}(a_i^{total} - 1)/2}{A(A-1)/2} = \frac{a_i^{total} a_i^{total}}{2(A-1)} - \frac{a_i^{total}}{2(A-1)} \approx \frac{a_i^{total} a_i^{total}}{2A} \tag{5.119}$$

for $i = j$. Instead of constructing a graph by connecting available stubs to form undirected edges, as in the original configuration model, we can now consider all possible ordered pairs (i, j) of not necessarily distinct nodes $i, j \in [1, n]$, and assign each pair with probability p_{ij} to the set of edges which eventually defines an undirected multigraph of order n whose expected node degree sequence $\langle \boldsymbol{a}^{total} \rangle$ and expected total adjacency $\langle A \rangle$ match those of a given target graph in the statistical average.

The element-wise independent and probabilistic nature of assigning adjacency relations to pairs of nodes renders the configuration model of Chung and Lu both conceptually and algebraically similar to the Gilbert random graph model and allows for a variety of algorithmic optimisations which feed into its usefulness as a computational tool [80]. However, this model also has its stringent limitations. For instance, while the original configuration model of Bollobás naturally allows for realisations of graphs in which certain node degrees do not occur, this cannot be ensured in the Chung-Lu model. Indeed, as long as $p_{ij} \neq 0$ for a given node i, the total node degree of i in realisations of a Chung-Lu random graph carries the possibility of being distinct from its expected value $\langle \boldsymbol{a}^{total} \rangle_i = a_i^{total}$, even if no node with the realised node degree exists in the target graph. The consequence of this inherent shortcoming is that some node degree sequences and, thus, node degree distributions, in particular those for which $p[\boldsymbol{a}^{total}; a] = 0$ for one or more $a \in \mathbb{N}$, cannot be realised exactly or even in the statistical average. Furthermore, neither the often-undesirable generation of self-looped nodes and multiedges nor the possibility of constructing directed adjacency relations is addressed in this model.

In order to at least dispose of the latter of these limitations, we will introduce here a slightly modified version of the configuration model of Chung and Lu, the *approximate degree-matched random digraph*, that delivers directed not self-looped relational graphs with a given expected node degree sequence in the statistical average over many realisations. Aiming at an operator graph-theoretical representation of this model, let $\mathscr{G}$ denote a relational digraph of order n with node in-degree and out-degree sequence $\boldsymbol{a}^{in}$ and $\boldsymbol{a}^{out}$, respectively, such that its total adjacency $A = \mathrm{T}[\boldsymbol{a}^{in}] = \mathrm{T}[\boldsymbol{a}^{out}]$. Furthermore, let us impose

$$\max[\boldsymbol{a}^{in}] \cdot \max[\boldsymbol{a}^{out}] \leq A(n-1)/n \tag{5.120}$$

as condition on the node degree sequences of $\mathscr{G}$ to ensure that the probability p_{ij} for randomly assigning an adjacency relation between any two nodes i and j satisfies $0 \leq p_{ij} \leq 1$. We can then define the approximate degree-matched random digraph $\mathscr{R}^{\mathscr{G}}$ associated with $\mathscr{G}$ by marking non-zero elements in its adjacency matrix $\boldsymbol{a}^{\mathscr{G}}$ according to

$$a_{ij}^{\mathscr{G}} := \begin{cases} 1 & \text{for } i \neq j \text{ with probability } p_{ij} := \dfrac{n}{n-1}\dfrac{a_i^{out} a_j^{in}}{A}, \\ 0 & \text{otherwise.} \end{cases} \tag{5.121}$$

The normalising term $n/(n-1)$ accounts here for the absence of self-loops in the construction of $\mathscr{R}^{\mathscr{G}}$ and ensures that, in the case of a complete graph, all non-diagonal elements in $\boldsymbol{a}^{\mathscr{G}}$ are non-zero. Indeed, for a complete relational digraph of order n, we have $a_i^{in} = a_i^{out} = n-1$ for all i and $A = n(n-1)$, and we find $p_{ij} = 1\ \forall i, j \in [1, n] : i \neq j$.

With (5.121) at our disposal, it is now straightforward to construct an operator representation and generator for the approximate degree-matched random graph model. We choose here again the representation (4.74) and (4.75) of the complete relational digraph $\mathscr{K}_n^d$ of order n with nodes $\boldsymbol{n}_i := \boldsymbol{\delta}_i^n \in \mathbb{B}^n$ and edge operators $\mathfrak{E}_{j_1 j_2} := \boldsymbol{\delta}_{j_1 j_2}^{n\times n} \in \mathbb{B}^{n\times n}$ as seed. The generator

$$\hat{\mathfrak{G}}^{\mathscr{G}} = \left(\hat{\mathfrak{G}}_{\mathcal{N}} := \mathrm{id}\,,\, \hat{\mathfrak{G}}_{\mathcal{E}} : \hat{\mathfrak{G}}_{\mathcal{E}}[\mathfrak{E}_{j_1 j_2}] := \mathfrak{r}^{p_{j_1 j_2}}[\mathfrak{E}_j] = \mathfrak{r}^{p_{j_1 j_2}}[\boldsymbol{\delta}_{j_1 j_2}^{n\times n}]\right) \tag{5.122}$$

then yields with $\hat{\mathscr{R}}^{\mathscr{G}} = \hat{\mathfrak{G}}^{\mathscr{G}}[\hat{\mathscr{K}}_n^d]$ an operator representation $\hat{\mathscr{R}}^{\mathscr{G}} = (\hat{\mathcal{N}}^{\mathscr{G}}, \hat{\mathcal{E}}^{\mathscr{G}})$ of $\mathscr{R}^{\mathscr{G}}$, defined by the sets

$$\hat{\mathcal{N}}^{\mathscr{G}} := \left\{\hat{\mathfrak{G}}_{\mathcal{N}}[\boldsymbol{n}] : \boldsymbol{n} \in \hat{\mathcal{N}}^{\mathscr{K}_n^d}\right\} = \hat{\mathcal{N}}^{\mathscr{K}_n^d} \subset \mathbb{B}^n, \tag{5.123}$$

$$\hat{\mathcal{E}}^{\mathscr{G}} := \left\{\hat{\mathfrak{G}}_{\mathcal{E}}[\mathfrak{E}] : \mathfrak{E} \in \hat{\mathcal{E}}^{\mathscr{K}_n^d}\right\} \subset \mathbb{B}^{n\times n} \tag{5.124}$$

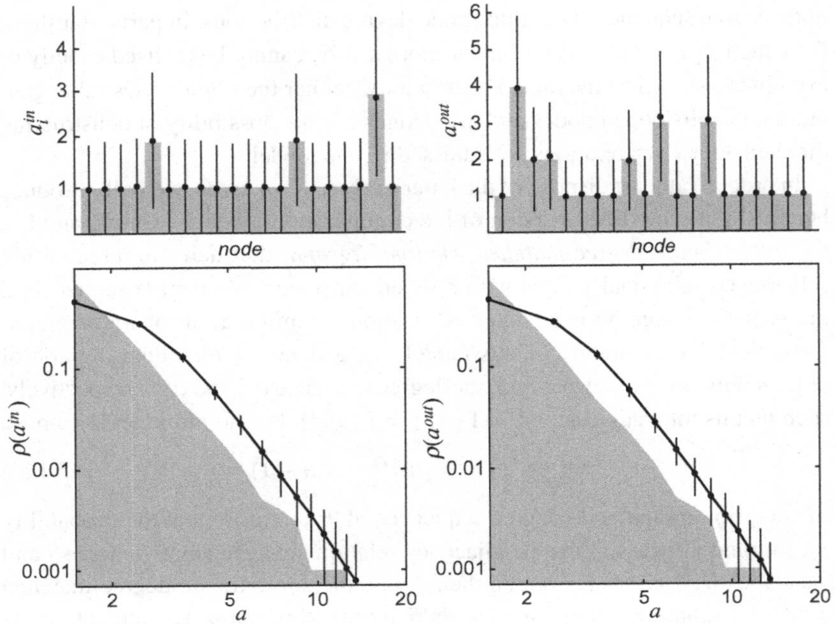

Figure 5.12 Generation of approximate degree-matched random digraphs. Shown are representative node in-degree and out-degree sequences (top; first 20 nodes) and distributions (bottom) resulting from computational realisations of an approximate degree-matched random digraph $\mathscr{R}^{\mathscr{G}}$ using generator (5.122) for a target graph of order n=1,000 with Pareto node degree distribution $\rho_{k,\gamma}(a){\sim}x^{-\gamma-1}$, $a > k$, $k = 1$, $\gamma = 2$. The node degree sequences and distributions of the target graph are shown in grey, the results of the computational model in black (mean ± SD over 100 realisations).

of nodes and edge operators, as well as their classical and auxiliary subsets

$$\begin{aligned} \hat{\mathcal{N}}^{\mathscr{G}}_{cl} &:= \left\{\boldsymbol{n} \in \hat{\mathcal{N}}^{\mathscr{G}} : \mathrm{T}[\boldsymbol{n}] = 1\right\}, \hat{\mathcal{N}}^{\mathscr{G}}_{aux} := \left\{\boldsymbol{n}_0\right\}, \\ \hat{\mathcal{E}}^{\mathscr{G}}_{cl} &:= \left\{\mathfrak{E} \in \hat{\mathcal{E}}^{\mathscr{G}} : \mathrm{T}[\mathfrak{E}] = 1\right\}, \hat{\mathcal{E}}^{\mathscr{G}}_{aux} := \hat{\mathcal{E}}^{\mathscr{G}} \setminus \hat{\mathcal{E}}^{\mathscr{G}}_{cl}. \end{aligned} \tag{5.125}$$

By utilising this representation together with (5.43) and (5.122), the adjacency matrix observable for the approximate degree-matched random digraph can be shown to evaluate to

$$\hat{\boldsymbol{a}}[\hat{\mathscr{R}}^{\mathscr{G}}] := \sum_{\mathfrak{E} \in \hat{\mathcal{E}}^{\mathscr{G}}_{cl}} \mathfrak{E} = \sum_{\substack{j_1, j_2 = 1 \\ j_1 \neq j_2}}^{n} \mathfrak{r}^{p_{j_1 j_2}}[\delta^{n \times n}_{j_1 j_2}], \tag{5.126}$$

and to deliver an $(n \times n)$-dimensional matrix whose non-diagonal elements are determined by independent scalar realisation of the binomial randomisation operator $\mathfrak{r}^{p_{ij}}$, such that

$$\left(\hat{\mathfrak{a}}[\hat{\mathscr{R}}^{\mathscr{G}}]\right)_{ij} = \mathfrak{r}^{p_{ij}}[1] = \begin{cases} 1 & \text{for } i \neq j \text{ with probability } p_{ij}, \\ 0 & \text{otherwise} \end{cases}$$

in accordance with (5.121).

Leaving an exploration of the potential benefits and limitations of our configuration model for approximate degree-matched random digraphs to the interested reader, let us conclude with a brief analysis of the node degree sequences and their associated distributions for a specific computational realisation of this model. As illustrated in Fig. 5.12 – choosing the node degrees of a target graph from a scale-free distribution, for instance – the operator (5.122) defines a generator for the construction of directed Barabási–Albert random graphs which not only circumvents the challenging consideration of interdependent probabilities that govern the process of preferential attachment of edges during the incremental growth of the network, but also presents itself naturally as a generalisation of the Barabási–Albert model that delivers directed scale-free random graphs. More importantly, beyond describing an alternative approach for the generation of a vast variety of relational random graph and digraph models, our configuration model provides the means to obtain randomised realisations of real-world target graphs for which in many cases only one instance is available. This opens the door for thorough statistical investigations and, by adapting (5.121) and (5.122) to reflect properties of the target graph, the algebraic assessment of such graphs within an operator graph-theoretical context. However, as we already cautioned earlier, and will further demonstrate in Chapter 6, the configuration model introduced here does and can only approximate the node degree sequence and total adjacency of a given target graph, while other characteristics might not be reproduced at all.

5.6 Randomised Square Grid Graphs

Up to now, we focused primarily on the algebraic construction of pure random graphs, as such models play a dominant role in the applied graph-theoretical literature across many research fields. However, a vast number of problems associated with real-world phenomena are, or at least can be, described by models that apply random aspects to otherwise finite and exact network constructs subject to stringent boundary conditions. For example, an over century-old yet still unsolved problem at the very heart of condensed matter physics, formulated

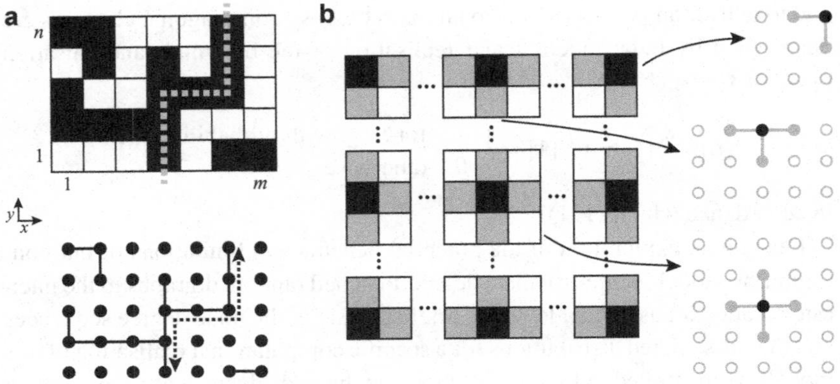

Figure 5.13 Randomised square grid graphs. **a:** Illustration of a model which considers randomly occupied squares arranged in a finite grid of dimension $m \times n$ (top; $m = 7$, $n = 5$, $p = 0.5$; occupied squares marked in black), and its graph-theoretical formulation in which each node represents a square, and each adjacency relation marks a pair of neighbouring occupied squares on the grid (bottom). The goal is to identify all paths which draw a connection between the top and bottom of the grid (dashed). **b:** Possible neighbour relationships in the original model (left) and their graph-theoretical representation (right). Occupied squares are marked in black, possible neighbouring squares and their corresponding graph edges in grey. In all cases, the nodes of the graph are arranged to reflect the spatial characteristics of the original model.

by DeVolson Wood [111] considers the random occupation of squares arranged in a finite square grid and asks about paths comprised of neighbouring occupied which draw a connection between two opposing sides of the given grid (Fig. 5.13a). Due to the importance and prototypical nature of this original problem, we will conclude this chapter by presenting its formalisation within our operator graph-theoretical framework. This will not only lay the groundwork for an exploration of the fundamental challenge conceived by Wood in Section 6.6, but also provide a somewhat different perspective from which to view and eventually tackle the vast number of related problems.

To that end, let us consider a total of mn randomly occupied unit squares arranged in a 2-dimensional rectangular regular grid of dimension $m \times n$ such that each square is uniquely identified by its grid coordinates $(x, y)\colon x, y \in \mathbb{N}$ with $x \in [1, m], y \in [1, n]$ and occupation state

$$O_{xy} = \begin{cases} 1 & \text{with probability } p \text{ (square occupied)}, \\ 0 & \text{otherwise (square not occupied)}, \end{cases} \tag{5.127}$$

as exemplified in Fig. 5.13a. Two squares are said to neighbour each other if and only if they reside next to each other in one of the four cardinal directions (Fig. 5.13b, left). This model naturally calls for a graph-theoretical representation that is furnished by assigning to each given square a unique node, and to each pair of occupied neighbouring squares a unique undirected edge. This direct translation faces two immediate challenges, however. Firstly, in contrast to all other graph models considered so far in this chapter, here the number of edges any node can establish is limited to at most four and, thus, is independent of the graph size. To complicate matters, the finite dimension of the rectangular grid imposes stringent boundary conditions which further restrict the number of possible edges for some nodes (Fig. 5.13b, right). Indeed, any of the $2(m+n)-4$ nodes associated with squares which are not corners but reside at the sides of the grid will allow for at most three edges, while a node associated with any of the four corner squares can have at most two. As we will find later, it is these boundary conditions associated with the finite grid size which render this model and its graph-theoretical formulation both algebraically demanding and leading to interesting results. Secondly, and more importantly, while in all previous models a graph was generated by randomly selecting elements from a pool of possible edges, the assignment of an edge between two nodes associated with a pair of neighbouring squares now depends solely on the uniform randomly chosen occupation state of these squares.

In order to deal with both of these challenges on an algebraic level, we will abstract from the 2-dimensional spatial representation of the original model through introducing mn nodes that are labelled consecutively by integers $i \in \mathbb{N} : i \in [1, mn]$ and adapting (2.126) and (2.127) to yield

$$\begin{aligned} &(x, y) \to i \colon \mathbb{N} \times \mathbb{N} \to \mathbb{N}\,,\ i = m(y-1) + x, \\ &i \to (x, y) \colon \mathbb{N} \to \mathbb{N} \times \mathbb{N}\,,\ (x, y) = \left(i - m\left\lfloor \frac{i-1}{m} \right\rfloor, 1 + \left\lfloor \frac{i-1}{m} \right\rfloor \right) \end{aligned} \tag{5.128}$$

as transformation between grid coordinates and node label (see Fig. 2.8e). All possible adjacency relations between two nodes i and j can then be expressed in terms of the Kronecker delta function as

$$\begin{aligned} j \text{ north/south of } i \quad &\to \quad j = i \pm m \quad \Rightarrow \quad \delta[j - i \mp m], \\ j \text{ east/west of } i \quad &\to \quad j = i \pm 1 \quad \Rightarrow \quad \delta[j - i \mp 1]. \end{aligned} \tag{5.129}$$

These adjacency relations must be further confined to ensure that the boundary conditions imposed by the finite size of the grid are respected. To that end, we recognise that, due to (5.128), two squares associated with subsequent nodes i and $i + 1$ reside on different rows, thus cannot be neighbours, if and only if both squares are situated at either vertical boundary of the grid. Furthermore, due to the chosen labelling of nodes, which starts in the southwest corner and advances eastwards through each row, the horizontal boundaries of the grid are respected by construction. This eventually refines (5.129) to

$$\begin{aligned} j \text{ north/south of } i \quad &\Rightarrow \quad \delta[j-i\mp m], \\ j \text{ east of } i \quad &\Rightarrow \quad \delta[j-i-1]\big(1-\textstyle\sum_{l=1}^{n-1}\delta[i-lm]\big), \\ j \text{ west of } i \quad &\Rightarrow \quad \delta[j-i+1]\big(1-\textstyle\sum_{l=1}^{n-1}\delta[j-lm]\big), \end{aligned} \tag{5.130}$$

and allows us to define a *projection operator*

$$\mathfrak{L}_{m,n}^{(4,4)} : \mathbb{Q}^{mn\times mn} \to \mathbb{Q}^{mn\times mn}, \quad \mathfrak{L}_{m,n}^{(4,4)}[\boldsymbol{A}] := \mathfrak{L}_{m,n}^{(4,4)} \odot \boldsymbol{A} \tag{5.131}$$

for $\boldsymbol{A} \in \mathbb{Q}^{mn\times mn}$ with elements

$$\begin{aligned} (\mathfrak{L}_{m,n}^{(4,4)})_{ij} := {} & \delta[j-i-m] + \delta[j-i+m] + \delta[j-i-1] + \delta[j-i+1] \\ & - \delta[j-i-1]\sum_{l=1}^{n-1}\delta[i-lm] - \delta[j-i+1]\sum_{l=1}^{n-1}\delta[j-lm] \end{aligned} \tag{5.132}$$

such that $\mathfrak{L}_{m,n}^{(4,4)}[\boldsymbol{1}^{mn\times mn}]$ marks all possible adjacency relations in the 2-dimensional square grid graph $\mathcal{L}_{m,n}^{(4,4)}$ of order mn. It should be mentioned here that (5.131) provides an alternative representation of the weight matrix (2.128) of $\mathcal{L}_{m,n}^{(4,4)}$ in terms of an operator which can easily be adapted to also yield the weight matrices of finite triangular or hexagonal grid graphs, as well as exact network models in arbitrary spatial dimensions.

What remains now is to consider the actual occupation state of each square, and to construct a new graph by selecting from the complete set of adjacency relations of $\mathcal{L}_{m,n}^{(4,4)}$ only those which are associated with occupied neighbouring squares. With (5.128), we immediately find

$$o_i = \sum_{x=1}^{m}\sum_{y=1}^{n}\delta[i-x-(y-1)m]O_{xy} \tag{5.133}$$

for $i \in [1, mn]$ as vectorial representation of the occupation state matrix (5.127), which then allows us to formulate

$$\big\{\text{node } i \text{ adjacent to node } j\big\} \Leftrightarrow \big\{o_i = 1 \wedge o_j = 1 \wedge \big(\mathfrak{L}_{m,n}^{(4,4)}[\boldsymbol{1}^{mn\times mn}]\big)_{ij} = 1\big\}$$

as necessary and sufficient condition that governs the occurrence of adjacency relations in our new graph. By noting that

$$\big\{o_i = 1 \wedge o_j = 1\big\} \Leftrightarrow \big\{(\boldsymbol{o}\otimes\boldsymbol{o}^\top)_{ij} = 1\big\}, \tag{5.134}$$

the right-hand side of this expression can be further simplified to yield

$$(\boldsymbol{o}\otimes\boldsymbol{o}^\top)\odot\mathfrak{L}_{m,n}^{(4,4)}[\boldsymbol{1}^{mn\times mn}] = (\boldsymbol{o}\otimes\boldsymbol{o}^\top)\odot\mathfrak{L}_{m,n}^{(4,4)}\odot\boldsymbol{1}^{mn\times mn} = \mathfrak{L}_{m,n}^{(4,4)}\odot(\boldsymbol{o}\otimes\boldsymbol{o}^\top).$$

Here, we made use of (5.131) and the commutative property of the Hadamard product, as well as $(\boldsymbol{o} \otimes \boldsymbol{o}^{\mathsf{T}}) \odot \boldsymbol{1}^{mn\times mn} = \boldsymbol{o} \otimes \boldsymbol{o}^{\mathsf{T}}$. From this, we finally obtain the $(mn \times mn)$-dimensional adjacency matrix

$$\boldsymbol{a} = \mathfrak{L}^{(4,4)}_{m,n}[\boldsymbol{o} \otimes \boldsymbol{o}^{\mathsf{T}}], \tag{5.135}$$

which defines the *randomised square grid graph* $\mathscr{R}^{\mathscr{L}}_{m,n,p}$ that is associated with randomly occupied squares arranged on a finite rectangular grid. An example of this classical graph-theoretical representation is illustrated in Fig. 5.13a.

Employing the algebraic objects introduced above, an operator graph-theoretical representation $\hat{\mathscr{R}}^{\mathscr{L}}_{m,n,p}$ of $\mathscr{R}^{\mathscr{L}}_{m,n,p}$ and its generator can be obtained in a straightforward fashion. The square grid graph $\mathscr{L}^{(4,4)}_{m,n}$ presents itself here as the natural choice for a generator seed, with a suitable operator representation $\hat{\mathscr{L}}^{(4,4)}_{m,n}$ being furnished by the sets

$$\begin{aligned}
\hat{\mathcal{N}}^{\mathscr{L}^{(4,4)}_{m,n}} &= \left\{\boldsymbol{n}_0 := \boldsymbol{0}^{mn}, \boldsymbol{n}_i := \boldsymbol{\delta}^{mn}_i : i \in [1, mn]\right\} \subset \mathbb{B}^{mn}, \\
\hat{\mathcal{E}}^{\mathscr{L}^{(4,4)}_{m,n}} &= \left\{\boldsymbol{\mathfrak{E}}_{00} := \boldsymbol{0}^{mn}, \boldsymbol{\mathfrak{E}}_{j_1 j_2} := \boldsymbol{\delta}^{mn}_{j_1} + \boldsymbol{\delta}^{mn}_{j_2} : (j_1, j_2) \in \mathcal{I}^{\mathscr{L}}_{m,n} \wedge j_2 > j_1\right\} \subset \mathbb{B}^{mn}
\end{aligned} \tag{5.136}$$

of nodes and edge operators along with their classical and auxiliary subsets

$$\begin{aligned}
\hat{\mathcal{N}}^{\mathscr{L}^{(4,4)}_{m,n}}_{cl} &:= \left\{\boldsymbol{n}_i \in \hat{\mathcal{N}}^{\mathscr{L}^{(4,4)}_{m,n}} : i \in [1, mn]\right\}, \ \hat{\mathcal{N}}^{\mathscr{L}^{(4,4)}_{m,n}}_{aux} := \left\{\boldsymbol{n}_0\right\}, \\
\hat{\mathcal{E}}^{\mathscr{L}^{(4,4)}_{m,n}}_{cl} &:= \left\{\boldsymbol{\mathfrak{E}}_{j_1 j_2} \in \hat{\mathcal{E}}^{\mathscr{L}^{(4,4)}_{m,n}} : (j_1, j_2) \in \mathcal{I}^{\mathscr{L}}_{m,n} \wedge j_2 > j_1\right\}, \ \hat{\mathcal{E}}^{\mathscr{L}^{(4,4)}_{m,n}}_{aux} := \left\{\boldsymbol{\mathfrak{E}}_{00}\right\}.
\end{aligned}$$

For notational convenience, we introduced in (5.136) the set

$$\mathcal{I}^{\mathscr{L}}_{m,n} := \left\{(i, j) \colon i, j \in [1, mn], \left(\mathfrak{L}^{(4,4)}_{m,n}[\boldsymbol{1}^{mn\times mn}]\right)_{ij} = 1\right\} \tag{5.137}$$

of ordered index pairs that mark all $2(2mn - m - n)$ adjacency relations between the nodes of $\mathscr{L}^{(4,4)}_{m,n}$.

In order to define a generator which acts on $\hat{\mathscr{L}}^{(4,4)}_{m,n}$ to deliver $\hat{\mathscr{R}}^{\mathscr{L}}_{m,n,p}$, we recall that, according to (5.135), the selection of any edge operator $\boldsymbol{\mathfrak{E}}_{j_1 j_2} \in \hat{\mathcal{E}}^{\mathscr{L}^{(4,4)}_{m,n}}$ is solely informed by the actual occupation states o_{j_1} and o_{j_2} of its associated nodes. As the occupation state O_{xy} of each of the mn squares in the original model is assigned independently in a uniform-random fashion with probability p, the same must hold true for its vectorial representation (5.133) such that

$$\boldsymbol{o} := \mathfrak{r}^p[\boldsymbol{1}^{mn}] \tag{5.138}$$

formalises the occupation vector $\boldsymbol{o}$ in terms of the binomial randomisation operator. It can then easily be shown that

$$(\boldsymbol{o} \otimes \boldsymbol{o}^{\mathsf{T}})_{ij} = \begin{cases} (\mathfrak{r}^p[\boldsymbol{1}^{mn}])_i \cdot (\mathfrak{r}^p[\boldsymbol{1}^{mn}])_j = \mathfrak{r}^p_i[1] \cdot \mathfrak{r}^p_j[1] & \text{for } i \neq j, \\ \left((\mathfrak{r}^p[\boldsymbol{1}^{mn}])_i\right)^2 = \mathfrak{r}^p_i[1] & \text{for } i = j, \end{cases} \tag{5.139}$$

where $\mathfrak{r}_i^p[1]$ denotes independent scalar realisations for which identities (5.58) and (5.59) hold. With this, we can make use of (5.134) to algebraically formulate the selection of edge operators from $\hat{\mathscr{L}}_{m,n}^{(4,4)}$, and we eventually find

$$\hat{\mathfrak{G}}_p^{\mathscr{L}} = \left(\hat{\mathfrak{G}}_{\mathcal{N}} := \mathrm{id}\,,\, \hat{\mathfrak{G}}_{\mathcal{E}}\right) \tag{5.140}$$

with

$$\hat{\mathfrak{G}}_{\mathcal{E}} : \hat{\mathcal{E}}^{\mathscr{L}_{m,n}^{(4,4)}} \to \hat{\mathcal{E}}^{\mathscr{R}_{m,n,p}^{\mathscr{L}}}$$
$$\hat{\mathfrak{G}}_{\mathcal{E}}[\mathfrak{E}_{j_1 j_2}] := (\boldsymbol{o} \otimes \boldsymbol{o}^{\mathsf{T}})_{j_1 j_2} \cdot \mathfrak{E}_{j_1 j_2} = \mathfrak{r}_{j_1}^p[1] \cdot \mathfrak{r}_{j_2}^p[1] \cdot (\delta_{j_1}^{mn} + \delta_{j_2}^{mn})$$

as a suitable generator for an operator representation of the randomised square grid graph such that $\hat{\mathscr{R}}_{m,n,p}^{\mathscr{L}} = \hat{\mathfrak{G}}_p^{\mathscr{L}}[\hat{\mathscr{L}}_{m,n}^{(4,4)}]$. The sets of nodes and edge operators of $\hat{\mathscr{R}}_{m,n,p}^{\mathscr{L}} = (\hat{\mathcal{N}}^{\mathscr{R}_{m,n,p}^{\mathscr{L}}}, \hat{\mathcal{E}}^{\mathscr{R}_{m,n,p}^{\mathscr{L}}})$ are given by

$$\begin{aligned} \hat{\mathcal{N}}^{\mathscr{R}_{m,n,p}^{\mathscr{L}}} &:= \left\{\hat{\mathfrak{G}}_{\mathcal{N}}[\boldsymbol{n}] : \boldsymbol{n} \in \hat{\mathcal{N}}^{\mathscr{L}_{m,n}^{(4,4)}}\right\} = \hat{\mathcal{N}}^{\mathscr{L}_{m,n}^{(4,4)}} \subset \mathbb{B}^n, \\ \hat{\mathcal{E}}^{\mathscr{R}_{m,n,p}^{\mathscr{L}}} &:= \left\{\hat{\mathfrak{G}}_{\mathcal{E}}[\mathfrak{E}] : \mathfrak{E} \in \hat{\mathcal{E}}^{\mathscr{L}_{m,n}^{(4,4)}}\right\} \subset \mathbb{B}^n, \end{aligned} \tag{5.141}$$

with

$$\begin{aligned} \hat{\mathcal{N}}_{cl}^{\mathscr{R}_{m,n,p}^{\mathscr{L}}} &:= \left\{\boldsymbol{n} \in \hat{\mathcal{N}}^{\mathscr{R}_{m,n,p}^{\mathscr{L}}} : \mathrm{T}[\boldsymbol{n}] = 1\right\},\ \hat{\mathcal{N}}_{aux}^{\mathscr{R}_{m,n,p}^{\mathscr{L}}} := \left\{\boldsymbol{n}_0\right\}, \\ \hat{\mathcal{E}}_{cl}^{\mathscr{R}_{m,n,p}^{\mathscr{L}}} &:= \left\{\mathfrak{E} \in \hat{\mathcal{E}}^{\mathscr{R}_{m,n,p}^{\mathscr{L}}} : \mathrm{T}[\mathfrak{E}] = 2\right\},\ \hat{\mathcal{E}}_{aux}^{\mathscr{R}_{m,n,p}^{\mathscr{L}}} := \hat{\mathcal{E}}^{\mathscr{R}_{m,n,p}^{\mathscr{L}}} \setminus \hat{\mathcal{E}}_{cl}^{\mathscr{R}_{m,n,p}^{\mathscr{L}}} \end{aligned} \tag{5.142}$$

as their respective classical and auxiliary subsets.

Let us conclude this section by evaluating the adjacency matrix observable for $\hat{\mathscr{R}}_{m,n,p}^{\mathscr{L}}$. With (4.63), (5.140) and (5.141), we immediately find

$$\begin{aligned} \hat{\mathfrak{a}}[\hat{\mathscr{R}}_{m,n,p}^{\mathscr{L}}] &:= \sum_{\mathfrak{E} \in \hat{\mathcal{E}}_{cl}^{\mathscr{R}_{m,n,p}^{\mathscr{L}}}} \left(\mathfrak{E} \otimes \mathfrak{E}^{\mathsf{T}} - \mathrm{diag}\,[\mathfrak{E}]\right) = \sum_{\substack{(j_1,j_2) \in \mathcal{I}_{m,n}^{\mathscr{L}} \\ j_2 > j_1}} \left(\mathfrak{E}_{j_1 j_2} \otimes \mathfrak{E}_{j_1 j_2}^{\mathsf{T}} - \mathrm{diag}\,[\mathfrak{E}_{j_1 j_2}]\right) \\ &= \sum_{\substack{(j_1,j_2) \in \mathcal{I}_{m,n}^{\mathscr{L}} \\ j_2 > j_1}} \mathfrak{r}_{j_1}^p[1] \cdot \mathfrak{r}_{j_2}^p[1] \cdot (\delta_{j_1 j_2}^{mn \times mn} + \delta_{j_2 j_1}^{mn \times mn}). \end{aligned}$$

The last expression can be further simplified by using (5.137) and the definition (5.131) of our projection operator $\mathfrak{L}_{m,n}^{(4,4)}$. This finally yields

$$\begin{aligned} \hat{\mathfrak{a}}[\hat{\mathscr{R}}_{m,n,p}^{\mathscr{L}}] &= \sum_{\substack{j_1,j_2=1 \\ j_2 > j_1}}^{mn} \left(\mathfrak{L}_{m,n}^{(4,4)}[\boldsymbol{1}^{mn \times mn}]\right)_{j_1 j_2} \cdot \mathfrak{r}_{j_1}^p[1] \cdot \mathfrak{r}_{j_2}^p[1] \cdot (\delta_{j_1 j_2}^{mn \times mn} + \delta_{j_2 j_1}^{mn \times mn}) \\ &= \mathfrak{L}_{m,n}^{(4,4)}\left[\sum_{\substack{j_1,j_2=1 \\ j_2 > j_1}}^{mn} \mathfrak{r}_{j_1}^p[1] \cdot \mathfrak{r}_{j_2}^p[1] \cdot (\delta_{j_1 j_2}^{mn \times mn} + \delta_{j_2 j_1}^{mn \times mn})\right] \end{aligned} \tag{5.143}$$

for the adjacency matrix observable of the randomised square grid graph $\mathscr{R}_{m,n,p}^{\mathscr{L}}$. We note here that this expression is identical to (5.135). Indeed, the argument of $\mathfrak{L}^{(4,4)}_{m,n}$ in (5.143) describes an $mn \times mn$ Boolean matrix in which all diagonal elements are zero, and pairs of symmetric non-zero elements are chosen independently with probability p^2. With the exception of diagonal elements, the same holds true for the Kronecker product $\boldsymbol{o} \otimes \boldsymbol{o}^\top$ due to (5.139). As our projection operator, by construction, only selects non-diagonal elements, both expressions for the adjacency matrix must therefore be algebraically identical.

Last but not least, let us take a brief comparative look at (5.143) and the adjacency matrix observable (5.60) for the undirected Gilbert random graph model $\mathscr{R}^G_{n,p}$. Apart from the presence of the projection operator $\mathfrak{L}^{(4,4)}_{m,n}$, which restricts the number of possible connections each node can establish, the selection of adjacency relations in the randomised square grid graph is governed by a probability p^2, while in the case of the Gilbert model, individual adjacency relations are selected with probability p. This, however, is not surprising, as in the former case the selection is tied to the random occupation state of two nodes, each assigned uniform-randomly with probability p, and suggests that at least some of the characteristics of $\mathscr{R}^{\mathscr{L}}_{m,n,p}$ should be mirrored by a Gilbert random graph $\mathscr{R}^G_{n,p^2}$ with connection probability p^2. We leave an exploration of this intriguing prospect as challenging exercise to the motivated reader.

With the small selection of finite graph models, their algebraic generation and representation, we hope to have illustrated in this chapter a first concrete application of our operator graph-theoretical framework, and to have exemplified some of the potential advantages of this more dynamic perspective over its static classical counterpart. The focus on finite random graph models was here intentional. While such models play an important role in the description of real-world phenomena that cannot be overstated, they also defy in many cases a rigorous algebraic treatment which limits their accessibility to computational realisations and subsequent numerical analysis. Asymptotic considerations certainly provide a viable means to circumnavigate these limitations as well as a frequently used toolset which allows us to assess various characteristics of random graphs on analytic grounds. However, such approaches are approximative at best and all to often discard interesting and defining features of the graphs under investigation by standing in direct opposition to the finite and discrete nature of real-world phenomena, the very makeup of physical reality itself. In the next chapter, we will attempt to overcome some of the principal problems inherent to asymptotic approaches by utilising the generated operator representations of finite random graphs in the algebraically rigorous assessment of various graph observables. In this way, we hope to further motivate the potential usefulness of our operator graph-theoretical framework.

6
Measuring Graphs

On our adventurous journey, we formalised in the previous chapter the generation of various finite random graph models in terms of suitable algebraic objects, and we obtained representations of these models which not only reside beyond their classical or algorithmic descriptions, but also encompass their whole parameter spectra at once without restricting assumptions. This approach naturally paves the way for a more rigorous investigation of the vast plethora of graph-theoretical measures that typically are, or only can be, considered in tedious and demanding numerical studies, or under stringent limitations in asymptotic assessments. In this chapter, we will exemplify how the properties of the algebraic objects governing the generation of graphs can be exploited, and parametrised expressions for a variety of graph measures can be obtained. Also here, unfortunately, we have to restrict our gaze into the sheer limitless realms of possibilities to a few selected directions, namely graph observables which are classically defined as powers of the adjacency matrix, in the hope that these directions will suffice to convey the novelty and prospect of our approach. By highlighting some of the differences to already available results from a conceptual and mathematical vantage point, we will continue to argue for the necessity of a study of networks at finite scales, for which our operator graph-theoretical framework presents itself as one viable approach.

6.1 Total Adjacency of Random Graphs and Digraphs

Let us begin our exploration in the realms of possible graph observables with the total adjacency, a simple graph-theoretic measure for which results are readily available and, thus, easy verifiable (see Table 2.8). With (4.66), we already constructed an observable that is associated with the total adjacency as measure of the cardinality of the classical subset of edge-generating operators in an operator representation of a digraph. In order to arrive at a more general definition which applies to both directed and undirected graphs $\mathscr{G}$, however, we will adapt here the classical definition (2.14) such that

$$\hat{A}: \mathbb{G} \to \mathbb{N}_0\,,\; \hat{A}[\hat{\mathscr{G}}] = A := \mathrm{T}\left[\hat{\mathfrak{a}}[\hat{\mathscr{G}}]\right] \tag{6.1}$$

yields the total adjacency observable for an operator representation $\hat{\mathscr{G}}$ of $\mathscr{G}$ in terms of its adjacency matrix observable $\hat{\mathfrak{a}}[\hat{\mathscr{G}}]$, where $\mathrm{T}[\,.\,]$ denotes the total sum operator introduced in (3.59). By then employing the various algebraic expressions obtained for $\hat{\mathfrak{a}}[\hat{\mathscr{G}}]$ in the previous chapter, it should be straightforward to derive the total adjacency A of the most prominent finite random graph models within the confines of our operator graph-theoretical framework.

6.1.1 Erdős–Rényi Random Graphs and Digraphs

With (5.16) and (5.44), we immediately find

$$\hat{A}[\hat{\mathscr{R}}^{ER}_{n,k}] = \mathrm{T}\left[\hat{\mathfrak{a}}[\hat{\mathscr{R}}^{ER}_{n,k}]\right] = \mathrm{T}\left[\sum_{\substack{j_1,j_2=1\\ j_2>j_1}}^{n} (e^{k_{\max}}_{(k)}{}^{\mathsf{T}})_{j_2-j_1(j_1-2n+1)/2-n} \cdot (\delta^{n\times n}_{j_1j_2}+\delta^{n\times n}_{j_2j_1})\right] = 2k,$$

$$\hat{A}[\hat{\mathscr{R}}^{dER}_{n,k}] = \mathrm{T}\left[\hat{\mathfrak{a}}[\hat{\mathscr{R}}^{dER}_{n,k}]\right] = \mathrm{T}\left[\sum_{\substack{j_1,j_2=1\\ j_1\neq j_2}}^{n} (e^{k_{\max}}_{(k)}{}^{\mathsf{T}})_{nj_1+j_2-\lfloor(nj_1+j_2)/(n+1)\rfloor-n} \cdot \delta^{n\times n}_{j_1j_2}\right] = k$$

for the total adjacency observable of Erdős–Rényi random graphs $\mathscr{R}^{ER}_{n,k}$ and digraphs $\mathscr{R}^{dER}_{n,k}$. Here we made use of (5.26), recalling that, by definition (5.9), the Boolean vector $e^{k_{\max}}_{(k)}$ contains exactly k randomly assigned non-zero elements, and that each term $\delta^{n\times n}_{j_1j_2}$ contributes 1 to the total.

6.1.2 Gilbert Random Graphs and Digraphs

The restriction imposed on the number of non-zero elements in the Boolean matrices (5.16) and (5.44) renders the above results for the total adjacency of directed and undirected Erdős–Rényi graphs exact in the sense that they not only characterise both of these models as a whole but also apply to any of their concrete realisations. Non-zero elements in the adjacency matrix observables (5.60) and (5.67) for the Gilbert random graph model, on the other hand, are assigned in a uniform-random fashion with a given probability and no further constraints. This means that, here, a meaningful algebraic expression for the total adjacency – in fact, for any conceivable graph measure defined as a function of the adjacency matrix – can be obtained only for the expectation value and, thus, can provide an exact result only for the statistical average in the limit of a large number of concrete realisations of the model. In the case of undirected Gilbert random graphs, we eventually find

$$\left\langle \hat{A}[\hat{\mathscr{R}}^{G}_{n,p}] \right\rangle = \left\langle \mathrm{T}\left[\hat{\mathfrak{a}}[\hat{\mathscr{R}}^{G}_{n,p}]\right] \right\rangle = 2 \sum_{\substack{j_1,j_2=1 \\ j_2>j_1}}^{n} \left\langle \mathrm{T}\left[\mathfrak{r}^{p}_{j_1 j_2}[1] \cdot \delta^{n\times n}_{j_1 j_2}\right] \right\rangle \tag{6.2}$$

by making use of the linearity of the total sum operator, and by recalling that $\mathfrak{r}^{p}_{j_1 j_2}[1]$ denotes distinct scalar realisations of the binomial randomisation operator, each of which governs the assignment of a pair of symmetric elements in (5.60). As any $\delta^{n\times n}_{j_1 j_2}$ contributes 1 to the total, and $\mathfrak{r}^{p}$ satisfies (4.43), the right-hand side of (6.2) can be further simplified to finally yield

$$\left\langle \hat{A}[\hat{\mathscr{R}}^{G}_{n,p}] \right\rangle = 2 \sum_{\substack{j_1,j_2=1 \\ j_2>j_1}}^{n} \left\langle \mathrm{T}\left[\mathfrak{r}^{p}_{j_1 j_2}[1]\right] \right\rangle = 2 \sum_{\substack{j_1,j_2=1 \\ j_2>j_1}}^{n} p = pn(n-1) \tag{6.3}$$

for the expectation value of the total adjacency observable in the Gilbert random graph model $\mathscr{R}^{G}_{n,p}$. The expectation value of the total adjacency for the directed model can be obtained in a similar fashion, and doing so delivers

$$\left\langle \hat{A}[\hat{\mathscr{R}}^{dG}_{n,p}] \right\rangle = \left\langle \mathrm{T}\left[\hat{\mathfrak{a}}[\hat{\mathscr{R}}^{dG}_{n,p}]\right] \right\rangle = \left\langle \mathrm{T}\left[\mathfrak{r}^{p}\left[\Delta^{n\times n}_{\mathcal{I}^{dG}_{n}}\right]\right] \right\rangle = \left\langle \mathrm{T}\left[\mathfrak{r}^{p}[\mathcal{I}^{n\times n} - \mathcal{I}^{n}]\right] \right\rangle = pn(n-1).$$

Here, we utilised (4.43) and (5.68) along with the fact that all non-diagonal elements of the Boolean matrix argument of $\mathfrak{r}^{p}$ are non-zero.

6.1.3 Watts–Strogatz Random Graphs and Digraphs

Continuing with the canonical model $\mathscr{R}^{WS}_{n,k,q}$ for undirected Watts–Strogatz random graphs, we first note that its adjacency matrix observable (5.85) is given in terms of two sums over the disjunct index sets $\mathcal{I}^{\mathscr{C}}_{n,k}$ and $\mathcal{I}^{\bar{\mathscr{C}}}_{n,k}$ defined in (5.71) and (5.72) respectively, and that in each of these sums pairs of symmetric non-zero elements are chosen uniform-randomly with the same probability. Both terms can thus be treated independently, and similar to (6.2) and (6.3) for the Gilbert model, to eventually yield

$$\left\langle \hat{A}[\hat{\mathscr{R}}^{WS}_{n,k,q}] \right\rangle = \left\langle \mathrm{T}\left[\hat{\mathfrak{a}}[\hat{\mathscr{R}}^{WS}_{n,k,q}]\right] \right\rangle = 2 \sum_{\substack{(j_1,j_2)\in\mathcal{I}^{\mathscr{C}}_{n,k} \\ j_2>j_1}} \left\langle \mathrm{T}\left[\mathfrak{r}^{p}_{j_1 j_2}[1]\right] \right\rangle + 2 \sum_{\substack{(j_1,j_2)\in\mathcal{I}^{\bar{\mathscr{C}}}_{n,k} \\ j_2>j_1}} \left\langle \mathrm{T}\left[\mathfrak{r}^{p'}_{j_1 j_2}[1]\right] \right\rangle .$$

By further noting that $|\mathcal{I}^{\mathscr{C}}_{n,k}| = 2kn$ and $|\mathcal{I}^{\bar{\mathscr{C}}}_{n,k}| = n(n-1) - 2kn$, and that the sums on the right-hand side in the last expression consider with $j_2 > j_1$ only half of the elements in both index sets, we then find

$$\left\langle \hat{A}[\hat{\mathscr{R}}^{WS}_{n,k,q}] \right\rangle = 2pkn + p'(n(n-1) - 2kn),$$

which, together with p and p' in (5.75) and (5.76), finally evaluates to

$$\left\langle \hat{A}[\hat{\mathscr{R}}^{WS}_{n,k,q}]\right\rangle = 2kn \tag{6.4}$$

for the expectation value of the total adjacency of simple Watts–Strogatz random graphs $\mathscr{R}^{WS}_{n,k,q}$. It certainly comes as little surprise that this result is independent of the rewiring probability q, and that it corresponds to the total adjacency expected for any realisation of the original Watts–Strogatz model (see Section 2.3.6 and Table 2.8). However, while the algorithmic construction in the original model only rewires already-existing edges and, thus, must necessarily preserve the total adjacency of the initial ring graph, our result (6.4) for the canonical model holds true only for the statistical average over many realisations. The same argument applies in the case of the digraph model $\mathscr{R}^{dWS}_{n,k,q}$ which, with (5.91) and (5.97), directly delivers

$$\left\langle \hat{A}[\hat{\mathscr{R}}^{dWS}_{n,k,q}]\right\rangle = \left\langle \mathrm{T}\left[\hat{\mathbf{a}}[\hat{\mathscr{R}}^{dWS}_{n,k,q}]\right]\right\rangle = \left\langle \mathrm{T}\left[\mathbf{r}^{p}[\boldsymbol{\Delta}^{n\times n}_{\mathcal{I}^{<\mathscr{C}}_{n,k}}]\right]\right\rangle + \left\langle \mathrm{T}\left[\mathbf{r}^{p'}[\boldsymbol{\Delta}^{n\times n}_{\mathcal{I}^{\not<\mathscr{C}}_{n,k}}]\right]\right\rangle = 2kn \tag{6.5}$$

for the expectation value of its total adjacency observable.

6.1.4 Barabási–Albert Random Graphs

Despite the arguably challenging algebraic nature of our canonical model for simple Barabási–Albert random graphs (see Section 5.4.2), its total adjacency observable can be evaluated in a straightforward manner. Indeed, with (5.116) we already formalised an expression for the total adjacency as necessary ingredient in the recursive construction of $\mathscr{R}^{BA}_{n,k,n_0,k_0}$. Taking the expectation value of this expression, and noting that

$$A_0 := \hat{A}[\hat{\mathscr{R}}^{BA}_0] = \mathrm{T}\left[\hat{\mathbf{a}}[\hat{\mathscr{R}}^{BA}_0]\right]$$

denotes the total adjacency of the given initial graph $\mathscr{R}^{BA}_0$ of order n_0 and with k_0 undirected edges, we immediately find

$$\left\langle \hat{A}[\hat{\mathscr{R}}^{BA}_{n,k,n_0,k_0}]\right\rangle = \left\langle \mathrm{T}\left[\hat{\mathbf{a}}[\hat{\mathscr{R}}^{BA}_{n,k,n_0,k_0}]\right]\right\rangle = A_0 + 2\sum_{t=1}^{n-n_0}\sum_{j=1}^{n_0+t-1}(\boldsymbol{p}_t)_j = A_0 + 2\sum_{t=1}^{n-n_0}\mathrm{T}\left[\boldsymbol{p}_t\right].$$

By furthermore recalling the definition (5.99) of the probability vector $\boldsymbol{p}_t$ at step t, and recognising that $\mathrm{T}\left[\boldsymbol{a}^{total}_t\right] = A_t$ with $A_0 = 2k_0$, we then finally obtain

$$\left\langle \hat{A}[\hat{\mathscr{R}}^{BA}_{n,k,n_0,k_0}]\right\rangle = 2k_0 + 2k\sum_{t=1}^{n-n_0} 1 = 2k_0 + 2k(n-n_0) \tag{6.6}$$

for the expectation value of the total adjacency in the canonical model of Barabási–Albert random graphs $\mathscr{R}^{BA}_{n,k,n_0,k_0}$.

6.1.5 Random Digraphs with Arbitrary Degree Distribution

Let us conclude this section by evaluating the total adjacency for our model of approximate degree-matched random digraphs. With the adjacency matrix observable $\hat{\mathfrak{a}}[\hat{\mathscr{R}}^{\mathscr{G}}]$ of $\mathscr{R}^{\mathscr{G}}$ given in (5.126), we eventually find

$$\left\langle \hat{A}[\hat{\mathscr{R}}^{\mathscr{G}}]\right\rangle = \left\langle \mathrm{T}\left[\hat{\mathfrak{a}}[\hat{\mathscr{R}}^{\mathscr{G}}]\right]\right\rangle = \sum_{\substack{j_1,j_2=1\\ j_1\neq j_2}}^{n} \left\langle \mathrm{T}\left[\mathfrak{r}^{p_{j_1 j_2}}[\delta^{n\times n}_{j_1 j_2}]\right]\right\rangle = \sum_{\substack{j_1,j_2=1\\ j_1\neq j_2}}^{n} p_{j_1 j_2} \tag{6.7}$$

by again employing the linearity of the total sum operator and identity (4.43), and by recognising that the occurrence of each of the $n(n-1)$ non-diagonal element of $\hat{\mathfrak{a}}[\hat{\mathscr{R}}^{\mathscr{G}}]$ is governed by an independent scalar realisation of the binomial randomisation operator. Due to the very conception of this graph model, the above result solely depends on the probabilities defined in (5.121) as function of the node in-degree and out-degree sequence of a given yet arbitrary target digraph $\mathscr{G}$, and must therefore necessarily remain rather general.

With (6.7) at our disposal, we can now assess the total adjacency of $\mathscr{R}^{\mathscr{G}}$ in relation to the total adjacency

$$A = \hat{A}[\hat{\mathscr{G}}] := \mathrm{T}\left[\hat{\mathfrak{a}}[\hat{\mathscr{G}}]\right] = \mathrm{T}\left[\boldsymbol{a}^{in}\right] = \mathrm{T}\left[\boldsymbol{a}^{out}\right]$$

of its target graph $\mathscr{G}$, where $\boldsymbol{a}^{in} := \hat{\boldsymbol{a}}^{in}[\hat{\mathscr{G}}]$ and $\boldsymbol{a}^{out} := \hat{\boldsymbol{a}}^{out}[\hat{\mathscr{G}}]$ respectively denote the node in-degree and out-degree sequence observables for an operator representation $\hat{\mathscr{G}}$ of $\mathscr{G}$. With $p_{j_1 j_2}$ in (5.121), we then obtain

$$\begin{aligned}
\left\langle \hat{A}[\hat{\mathscr{R}}^{\mathscr{G}}]\right\rangle &= \frac{n}{n-1}\frac{1}{A}\sum_{\substack{j_1,j_2=1\\ j_1\neq j_2}}^{n} a_i^{out} a_j^{in} = \frac{n}{n-1}\frac{1}{A}\left(\sum_{j_1,j_2=1}^{n} a_{j_1}^{out} a_{j_2}^{in} - \sum_{j_1=1}^{n} a_{j_1}^{out} a_{j_1}^{in}\right)\\
&= \frac{n}{n-1}\frac{1}{A}\left(\mathrm{T}\left[\boldsymbol{a}^{in}\right]\mathrm{T}\left[\boldsymbol{a}^{out}\right] - \sum_{i=1}^{n} a_i^{out} a_i^{in}\right)\\
&= \frac{n}{n-1}A - \frac{n}{n-1}\frac{\boldsymbol{a}^{in}\cdot\boldsymbol{a}^{out\mathrm{T}}}{A},
\end{aligned} \tag{6.8}$$

a result which, perhaps unsurprisingly, only approximates the given adjacency A of $\mathscr{G}$ due to the exclusion of self-loops in realisations of $\mathscr{R}^{\mathscr{G}}$. However, in the special case of a complete relational digraph, for which $A = n(n-1)$ and $a_i^{in} = a_i^{out} = n-1$ for all $i \in [1, n]$, or in the more general case of a graph in which the in-degree and out-degree of each node equals the average node degree A/n, the right-hand side of (6.8) recovers the total adjacency of the target graph such that $\left\langle \hat{A}[\hat{\mathscr{R}}^{\mathscr{G}}]\right\rangle = A$. Moreover, if we were to allow self-looped nodes in the generation of $\mathscr{R}^{\mathscr{G}}$, a simple modification of the defining probabilities (5.121) suffices to exactly match the expectation value of $\hat{A}[\hat{\mathscr{R}}^{\mathscr{G}}]$ with the total adjacency of the target graph, even in the case of arbitrary node degree sequences. We leave the inspection of such an adaptation of our approximate degree-matched random digraph model and its link to the configuration model of Chung and Lu (see Section 5.5) as exercise for the interested reader.

6.2 Asymmetry Index of Random Digraphs

In the previous section, we considered with the total adjacency a graph measure which depends linearly on a relational digraph's adjacency matrix. A slightly more involved measure is given by the asymmetry index α of a directed graph, which we defined in (2.21) as the ratio between the number of asymmetrical edges N_{as} and number of symmetrical edges N_{se}. Recalling (2.18) and (2.19), both of these numbers depend, in the most general sense, on the product of the weight or, in the case of relational digraphs, the adjacency matrix with itself and, thus, are of second order. Before evaluating the asymmetry index for some of the random digraph models presented in the last chapter, however, we first need to define a suitable graph observable associated with this classical measure. To that end, recognising that only operator representations $\hat{\mathscr{G}}$ of relational digraphs $\mathscr{G}$ will be considered here, let us simplify (2.18) by discarding self-loops, and define with

$$\hat{N}_{se} : \mathbb{G} \to \mathbb{N}_0 \, , \; \hat{N}_{se}[\hat{\mathscr{G}}] = N_{se} := \frac{1}{2} \mathrm{T}\left[\hat{\mathfrak{a}}[\hat{\mathscr{G}}] \odot \hat{\mathfrak{a}}[\hat{\mathscr{G}}]^{\mathsf{T}}\right] \tag{6.9}$$

a graph observable which delivers the number of symmetrical edges in terms of the Hadamard product (3.52) of the adjacency matrix observable $\hat{\mathfrak{a}}[\hat{\mathscr{G}}]$ with its transpose. Similarly, utilising the general identity (2.20) satisfied by N_{se} and N_{ae}, we easily find with

$$\hat{N}_{ae} : \mathbb{G} \to \mathbb{N}_0 \, , \; \hat{N}_{ae}[\hat{\mathscr{G}}] = N_{ae} := \hat{A}[\hat{\mathscr{G}}] - \mathrm{T}\left[\hat{\mathfrak{a}}[\hat{\mathscr{G}}] \odot \hat{\mathfrak{a}}[\hat{\mathscr{G}}]^{\mathsf{T}}\right] \tag{6.10}$$

an observable that measures the number of asymmetrical edges by involving the graph's total adjacency $\hat{A}[\hat{\mathscr{G}}]$. Targeting an application of these observables which focuses on random graph models, we can then define with

$$\langle\hat{\alpha}\rangle : \mathbb{G} \to \mathbb{Q} \, , \; \left\langle\hat{\alpha}[\hat{\mathscr{G}}]\right\rangle = \langle\alpha\rangle := \frac{\left\langle\hat{N}_{ae}[\hat{\mathscr{G}}]\right\rangle}{\left\langle\hat{A}[\hat{\mathscr{G}}]\right\rangle - \left\langle\hat{N}_{se}[\hat{\mathscr{G}}]\right\rangle} \tag{6.11}$$

a graph observable that yields the expectation value of the asymmetry index for an operator representation $\hat{\mathscr{G}}$ of a directed relational digraph $\mathscr{G}$ as function of the expectation values of its total adjacency (6.1), number of symmetrical edges (6.9) and number of asymmetrical edges (6.10).

6.2.1 Erdős–Rényi Random Digraphs

Let us exemplify the application of (6.11) in the case of Erdős–Rényi random digraphs, and begin by evaluating the Hadamard product of the adjacency matrix observable $\hat{\mathfrak{a}}[\hat{\mathscr{R}}^{dER}_{n,k}]$ with its transpose. Recalling (5.44), we easily find

$$\hat{\mathfrak{a}}[\hat{\mathscr{R}}^{dER}_{n,k}] \odot \hat{\mathfrak{a}}[\hat{\mathscr{R}}^{dER}_{n,k}]^{\mathsf{T}} = \sum_{\substack{j_1,j_2=1 \\ j_1 \neq j_2}}^{n} (\mathbf{e}^{k_{\max}}_{(k)}{}^{\mathsf{T}})_j \cdot (\mathbf{e}^{k_{\max}}_{(k)}{}^{\mathsf{T}})_{j'} \tag{6.12}$$

with $j := nj_1+j_2-\lfloor(nj_1+j_2)/(n+1)\rfloor-n$ and $j' := nj_2+j_1-\lfloor(nj_2+j_1)/(n+1)\rfloor-n$. Here, we made use of the linearity of the Hadamard product, and the fact that each of the $k_{\max} = n(n-1)$ terms in the sum (5.44) contributes one unique element to the adjacency matrix of $\mathscr{R}^{dER}_{n,k}$. In order to simplify this expression further, we recognise that, by definition, the $k_{\max}$-dimensional Boolean vector $\mathbf{e}^{k_{\max}}_{(k)}$ contains exactly k uniform-randomly chosen non-zero elements. As $j \neq j'$ for each j_1, j_2 in the above sum, the scalar product of two distinct elements of $\mathbf{e}^{k_{\max}}_{(k)}$ then returns 1 with a probability of $(k/n(n-1))^2$ such that

$$\left\langle \mathrm{T}\left[\hat{\mathfrak{a}}[\hat{\mathscr{R}}^{dER}_{n,k}] \odot \hat{\mathfrak{a}}[\hat{\mathscr{R}}^{dER}_{n,k}]^{\mathsf{T}}\right]\right\rangle = n(n-1)\left(\frac{k}{n(n-1)}\right)^2 = \frac{k^2}{n(n-1)}.$$

With (6.9) and (6.10) as well as $\langle \hat{A}[\hat{\mathscr{R}}^{dER}_{n,k}]\rangle = k$, we eventually obtain

$$\left\langle \hat{N}_{se}[\hat{\mathscr{R}}^{dER}_{n,k}]\right\rangle = \frac{1}{2}\frac{k^2}{n(n-1)}, \quad \left\langle \hat{N}_{ae}[\hat{\mathscr{R}}^{dER}_{n,k}]\right\rangle = k - \frac{k^2}{n(n-1)} \tag{6.13}$$

for the average number of symmetrical and asymmetrical edges in Erdős–Rényi random digraphs, which with (6.11) finally leads to

$$\left\langle \hat{\alpha}[\hat{\mathscr{R}}^{dER}_{n,k}]\right\rangle = \frac{2n(n-1)-2k}{2n(n-1)-k} = 1 - \frac{k}{2n(n-1)-k} \tag{6.14}$$

for the expectation value of the asymmetry index of $\mathscr{R}^{dER}_{n,k}$. The general functional behaviour of this result for some representative values of n and k is illustrated in Fig. 6.1. It is important to stress here again that, albeit the number of adjacency relations in an Erdős–Rényi random digraph is strictly fixed and remains the same for all realisations of a given model, the evaluation of expressions such as (6.12) or (6.14) must necessarily resort to probabilistic arguments due to the element-wise random assignment of these adjacency relations.

6.2.2 Gilbert Random Digraphs

Arguably simpler on an algebraic level is the treatment of the Gilbert random digraph model as the non-zero elements in its adjacency matrix observable

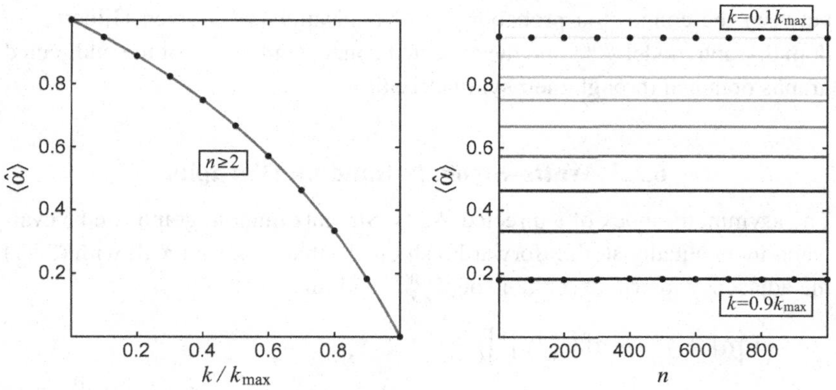

Figure 6.1 Asymmetry index (6.14) of Erdős–Rényi random digraphs as function of $k/k_{\max}$ for any $n \geq 2$ (left), and n for $k = qk_{\max}$, $q \in \{0.1, 0.2, \ldots, 0.9\}$ (right). In both cases, $\langle \hat{\alpha} \rangle$ remains independent of n due to the use of the fraction of connected edges. For some models, the results of a statistical analysis of 100 computational realisations are shown (black dots; mean±SD). Parameters for numerical models: $n = 1000$ (left); $k = 0.1k_{\max}$ and $k = 0.9k_{\max}$ (right).

(5.67) are assigned uniform-randomly with a given probability p and no further constraints. Indeed, with (4.46), (5.69) and (5.70), and by recognising the symmetric nature of the Boolean matrix $\mathbf{\Delta}^{n\times n}_{\mathcal{I}_n^{dG}}$, we easily obtain

$$\begin{aligned}&\left\langle \mathrm{T}\left[\hat{\mathbf{a}}[\hat{\mathcal{R}}^{dG}_{n,p}] \odot \hat{\mathbf{a}}[\hat{\mathcal{R}}^{dG}_{n,p}]^{\mathsf{T}}\right]\right\rangle \\ &\quad = \left\langle \mathrm{T}\left[\mathbf{r}^p[\mathbf{\Delta}^{n\times n}_{\mathcal{I}_n^{dG}}] \odot \mathbf{r}^p[\mathbf{\Delta}^{n\times n}_{\mathcal{I}_n^{dG}}]^{\mathsf{T}}\right]\right\rangle = \left\langle \mathrm{T}\left[\mathbf{r}^p \circ \mathbf{r}^p[\mathbf{\Delta}^{n\times n}_{\mathcal{I}_n^{dG}} \odot \mathbf{\Delta}^{n\times n}_{\mathcal{I}_n^{dG}}]\right]\right\rangle \\ &\quad = \left\langle \mathrm{T}\left[\mathbf{r}^{p^2}[\mathbf{\Delta}^{n\times n}_{\mathcal{I}_n^{dG}}]\right]\right\rangle = p^2 n(n-1),\end{aligned}$$

which together with (6.4) then yields

$$\left\langle \hat{N}_{se}[\hat{\mathcal{R}}^{dG}_{n,p}]\right\rangle = \frac{1}{2} p^2 n(n-1)\,,\ \left\langle \hat{N}_{ae}[\hat{\mathcal{R}}^{dG}_{n,p}]\right\rangle = p(1-p)n(n-1) \qquad (6.15)$$

for the average number of symmetrical and asymmetrical edges, and eventually

$$\left\langle \hat{\alpha}[\hat{\mathcal{R}}^{dG}_{n,p}]\right\rangle = 2\,\frac{p(1-p)n(n-1)}{2pn(n-1) - p^2 n(n-1)} = 2\,\frac{1-p}{2-p} \qquad (6.16)$$

for the expectation value of the asymmetry index in directed Gilbert random graphs $\mathcal{R}^{dG}_{n,p}$. It is important to note here that choosing $p = k/k_{\max} = k/n(n-1)$ will recover our result (6.14) for the Erdős–Rényi random digraph model and lead to a functional behaviour of $\langle \hat{\alpha}[\hat{\mathcal{R}}^{dG}_{n,p}]\rangle$ which is identical to that displayed in Fig. 6.1. Finally, by making use of the asymmetry index (6.16) in (2.22), we find with $\rho^{ud} = p(2-p)$ an interesting relation which draws a link between the connection probability p of realisations of a given Gilbert random digraph model $\mathscr{R}^{dG}_{n,p}$ and the expected connectedness ρ^{ud} of the undirected graphs obtained through their symmetrisation.

6.2.3 Watts–Strogatz Random Digraphs

The asymmetry index of a directed Watts–Strogatz random graph can be evaluated in an equally straightforward fashion. To that end, we recall with (5.91) the adjacency matrix observable of $\mathscr{R}^{dWS}_{n,k,q}$, and find

$$\begin{aligned}
&\left\langle \mathrm{T}\left[\hat{\mathbf{a}}[\hat{\mathscr{R}}^{dWS}_{n,k,q}] \odot \hat{\mathbf{a}}[\hat{\mathscr{R}}^{dWS}_{n,k,q}]^{\mathsf{T}}\right]\right\rangle \\
&= \left\langle \mathrm{T}\left[\left(\mathfrak{r}^{p}[\boldsymbol{\Delta}^{n\times n}_{\mathcal{I}^{\mathscr{C}}_{n,k}}] + \mathfrak{r}^{p'}[\boldsymbol{\Delta}^{n\times n}_{\mathcal{I}^{\not\mathscr{C}}_{n,k}}]\right) \odot \left(\mathfrak{r}^{p}[\boldsymbol{\Delta}^{n\times n}_{\mathcal{I}^{\mathscr{C}}_{n,k}}] + \mathfrak{r}^{p'}[\boldsymbol{\Delta}^{n\times n}_{\mathcal{I}^{\not\mathscr{C}}_{n,k}}]\right)^{\mathsf{T}}\right]\right\rangle \\
&= \left\langle \mathrm{T}\left[\mathfrak{r}^{p}[\boldsymbol{\Delta}^{n\times n}_{\mathcal{I}^{\mathscr{C}}_{n,k}}] \odot \mathfrak{r}^{p}[\boldsymbol{\Delta}^{n\times n}_{\mathcal{I}^{\mathscr{C}}_{n,k}}] + \mathfrak{r}^{p}[\boldsymbol{\Delta}^{n\times n}_{\mathcal{I}^{\mathscr{C}}_{n,k}}] \odot \mathfrak{r}^{p'}[\boldsymbol{\Delta}^{n\times n}_{\mathcal{I}^{\not\mathscr{C}}_{n,k}}]\right.\right. \\
&\qquad \left.\left. + \mathfrak{r}^{p'}[\boldsymbol{\Delta}^{n\times n}_{\mathcal{I}^{\not\mathscr{C}}_{n,k}}] \odot \mathfrak{r}^{p}[\boldsymbol{\Delta}^{n\times n}_{\mathcal{I}^{\mathscr{C}}_{n,k}}] + \mathfrak{r}^{p'}[\boldsymbol{\Delta}^{n\times n}_{\mathcal{I}^{\not\mathscr{C}}_{n,k}}] \odot \mathfrak{r}^{p'}[\boldsymbol{\Delta}^{n\times n}_{\mathcal{I}^{\not\mathscr{C}}_{n,k}}]\right]\right\rangle \\
&= \left\langle \mathrm{T}\left[\mathfrak{r}^{p^2}[\boldsymbol{\Delta}^{n\times n}_{\mathcal{I}^{\mathscr{C}}_{n,k}}] + \mathfrak{r}^{p'^2}[\boldsymbol{\Delta}^{n\times n}_{\mathcal{I}^{\not\mathscr{C}}_{n,k}}]\right]\right\rangle = 2knp^2 + n(n-1-2k)p'^2.
\end{aligned}$$

Here we employed the linearity of the Hadamard product and, recognising the symmetric nature of the Boolean matrix arguments of each binomial randomisation operator, the identities (4.46) and (5.97). With (6.9), this yields

$$\left\langle \hat{N}_{se}[\hat{\mathscr{R}}^{dWS}_{n,k,q}]\right\rangle = \frac{kn((n-1)(1-q) - 2k(1-2q))^2 + 2k^2nq^2(n-1-2k)}{(n-1-2k(1-q))^2} \tag{6.17}$$

for the expectation value of the number of symmetrical edges in $\mathscr{R}^{dWS}_{n,k,q}$. In a similar fashion, (6.10) delivers the expectation value

$$\left\langle \hat{N}_{ae}[\hat{\mathscr{R}}^{dWS}_{n,k,q}]\right\rangle = \frac{2knq(n-1-2k)((n-1)(2-q) - 4k(1-q))}{(n-1-2k(1-q))^2} \tag{6.18}$$

for the number of asymmetrical edges, eventually resulting in the somewhat untidy yet exact algebraic expression

$$\left\langle \hat{\alpha}[\hat{\mathscr{R}}^{dWS}_{n,k,q}]\right\rangle = \frac{2q(n-1-2k)((n-1)(2-q) - 4k(1-q))}{4k^2(1-q^2) - 2k(n-1)(2+q(2-3q)) + (n-1)^2(1+q(2-q))} \tag{6.19}$$

for the expectation value of the asymmetry index for our canonical model of directed Watts–Strogatz random graphs $\mathscr{R}^{dWS}_{n,k,q}$.

Unsurprisingly, (6.19) yields in the special case $q = 0$ the asymmetry index

$$\left\langle \hat{\alpha}[\hat{\mathscr{R}}^{dWS}_{n,k,0}]\right\rangle = \left\langle \hat{\alpha}[\mathscr{C}^{cd}_{n,k}]\right\rangle = 0 \tag{6.20}$$

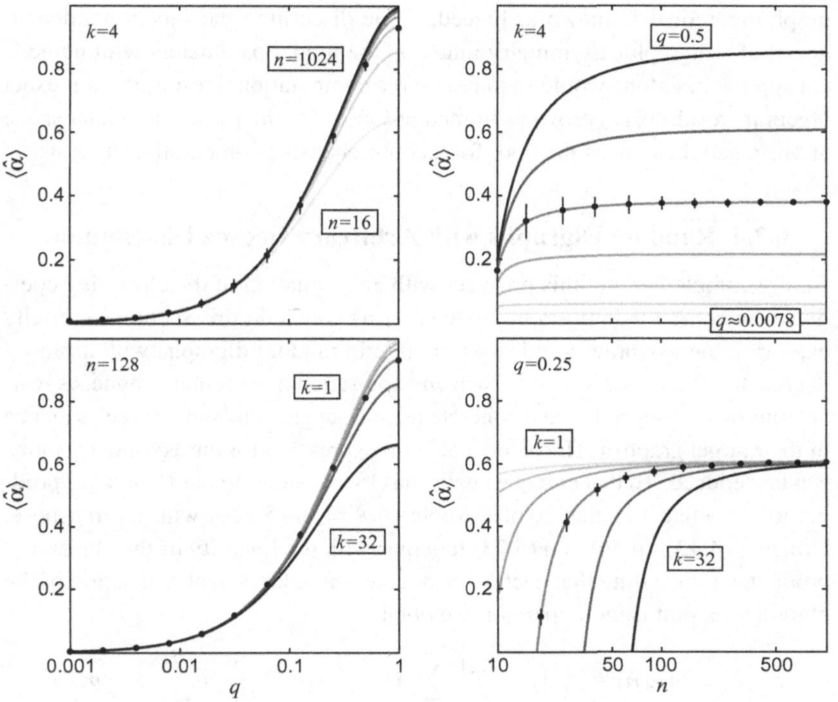

Figure 6.2 Asymmetry index (6.19) of Watts–Strogatz random digraphs as function of the rewiring probability q (left; top: $k = 4$, $n = 2^m$, $m \in [4, 10]$; bottom: $n = 128$, $k = 2^m$, $m \in [0, 5]$) and graph order n (right; top: $k = 4$, $q = 2^m$, $m \in [-7, -1]$; bottom: $k = 2^m$, $m \in [0, 5]$, $q = 0.25$). For some models, the results of a statistical analysis of 100 computational realisations are shown (black dots; mean ± SD). Parameters for numerical models: $n = 64$, $k = 4$ (top left); $n = 128$, $k = 8$ (bottom left); $k = 4$, $q = 0.125$ (top right); $k = 8$, $q = 0.25$ (bottom right).

of a complete relational k-ring digraph $\mathscr{C}^{cd}_{n,k}$. For $q = 1$, we recover with

$$\left\langle \hat{\alpha}[\hat{\mathscr{R}}^{dWS}_{n,k,1}] \right\rangle = \left\langle \hat{\alpha}[\hat{\mathscr{R}}^{dER}_{n,2kn}] \right\rangle = \left\langle \hat{\alpha}[\hat{\mathscr{R}}^{dG}_{n,2k/(n-1)}] \right\rangle = 1 - \frac{k}{n-1-k} \tag{6.21}$$

the expected asymmetry index of a directed Erdős–Rényi random graph $\mathscr{R}^{dER}_{n,k'}$ with $k' := 2kn$ edges and that of a Gilbert random digraph $\mathscr{R}^{dG}_{n,p}$ with connection probability $p = 2k/(n-1)$. In the general case $0 \leq q \leq 1$, the functional behaviour is somewhat more challenging and is illustrated in Fig. 6.2 for various parameter sets along with some numerical results from computational realisations of our canonical model. We hope that these few representative examples suffice to further demonstrate the potential usefulness of our operator graph-theoretical framework. Indeed, while discerning the functional dependence of a digraph's asymmetry index on the model parameters with numerical approaches alone would require notable computational resources, our exact algebraic result (6.19) provides immediate access to the whole parameter space at once, and thus opens the door for a comprehensive comparative analysis.

6.2.4 Random Digraphs with Arbitrary Degree Distribution

Before complementing this prospect with an evaluation of the clustering coefficient in some random graph models, let us conclude this section by briefly exploring the asymmetry index observable in random digraphs with arbitrary degree distributions. Certainly, such an exploration must remain vague, as realisations of $\mathscr{R}^{\mathscr{G}}$ depend on the concrete node in-degree and out-degree sequence of their target graph $\mathscr{G}$. However, a general expression for the asymmetry index can be deduced. To that end, we again start by considering the Hadamard product of the adjacency matrix observable $\hat{\mathfrak{a}}[\hat{\mathscr{R}}^{\mathscr{G}}]$ in (5.126) with its transpose. Utilising (4.43), (4.46) and (5.23) together with the linearity of the Hadamard product, and recalling that each $\mathfrak{r}^{p_{j_1 j_2}}$ denotes an independent realisation of the binomial randomisation operator, we obtain

$$\left\langle \mathrm{T}\left[\hat{\mathfrak{a}}[\hat{\mathscr{R}}^{\mathscr{G}}] \odot \hat{\mathfrak{a}}[\hat{\mathscr{R}}^{\mathscr{G}}]^{\mathsf{T}}\right]\right\rangle = \left\langle \mathrm{T}\left[\sum_{\substack{j_1,j_2=1\\ j_1\neq j_2}}^{n} \mathfrak{r}^{p_{j_1 j_2} p_{j_2 j_1}}\left[\delta^{n\times n}_{j_1 j_2}\right]\right]\right\rangle = \sum_{\substack{j_1,j_2=1\\ j_1\neq j_2}}^{n} p_{j_1 j_2} p_{j_2 j_1},$$

from which with (6.7) for the total adjacency of $\mathscr{R}^{\mathscr{G}}$ immediately yields

$$\left\langle \hat{N}_{se}[\hat{\mathscr{R}}^{\mathscr{G}}]\right\rangle = \frac{1}{2}\sum_{\substack{j_1,j_2=1\\ j_1\neq j_2}}^{n} p_{j_1 j_2} p_{j_2 j_1}\,,\ \left\langle \hat{N}_{ae}[\hat{\mathscr{R}}^{\mathscr{G}}]\right\rangle = \sum_{\substack{j_1,j_2=1\\ j_1\neq j_2}}^{n} (p_{j_1 j_2} - p_{j_1 j_2} p_{j_2 j_1}) \quad (6.22)$$

for the average number of symmetrical and asymmetrical edges follow. This eventually yields

$$\left\langle \hat{\alpha}[\hat{\mathscr{R}}^{\mathscr{G}}]\right\rangle = 2\sum_{\substack{j_1,j_2=1\\ j_1\neq j_2}}^{n} (p_{j_1 j_2} - p_{j_1 j_2} p_{j_2 j_1}) \Bigg/ \sum_{\substack{j_1,j_2=1\\ j_1\neq j_2}}^{n} (2p_{j_1 j_2} - p_{j_1 j_2} p_{j_2 j_1}) \quad (6.23)$$

for the expectation value of the asymmetry index in our model of approximate degree-matched random graphs $\hat{\mathscr{R}}^{\mathscr{G}}$.

This is again a rather general result, and it is important to stress that although a formal link between $\langle \hat{\alpha}[\hat{\mathscr{R}}^{\mathscr{G}}]\rangle$ and the asymmetry index observable $\langle \hat{\alpha}[\mathscr{G}]\rangle$ of its target graph can certainly be drawn by using p_{ij} in (5.121), such a link will remain in most cases meaningless, as a graph's node degree sequences alone do not carry sufficient information about the actual distribution of non-zero elements in its adjacency matrix. Indeed, (6.23) will generally differ from the asymmetry index of its target graph, which is to be expected as our model for approximate degree-matched random graphs, by construction, accounts only for the node in-degree and out-degree sequences of $\mathcal{G}$. Only in special cases do we recover the asymmetry index, such as for $p_{ij} = p\ \forall i, j \in [1, n] : i \neq j$ where (6.23) yields $2(1-p)/(2-p)$, and thus, $\langle \hat{\alpha}[\hat{\mathcal{R}}^{dG}_{n,p}] \rangle$.

6.3 Clustering Coefficient of Random Digraphs

Continuing with our exploration of various graph observables, let us next consider the clustering coefficient as a measure that involves the third power of a graph's adjacency matrix. By focusing here again solely on relational digraphs $\mathcal{G}$ of finite order n, for which the matrix of adjacency relations $\boldsymbol{A}$ equals the adjacency matrix $\boldsymbol{a}$ with $\mathrm{Tr}[\boldsymbol{a}] = 0$, we adapt our definition (2.85) of the total global clustering coefficient C^d to yield

$$C^d := \frac{1}{N^d} \sum_{i,j,k=1}^{n} (a_{ij} + a_{ji})(a_{ik} + a_{ki})(a_{jk} + a_{kj})$$

for $N^d \geq 1$ with

$$N^d := 2 \sum_{i=1}^{n} (a_i^{total})^2 - 2 \sum_{i=1}^{n} a_i^{total} - 4 \sum_{i,j=1}^{n} a_{ij} a_{ji}, \tag{6.24}$$

where $a_i^{total} = a_i^{in} + a_i^{out}$ denotes the total node degree of directed graphs. The last term on the right-hand side of (6.24) counts with $\sum_{i,j=1}^{n} a_{ij} a_{ji} = 2N_{se}$ the number of symmetrical edges in $\mathcal{G}$, and the second term is proportional to the total adjacency A of $\mathcal{G}$ due to (2.28). By further recognising that the total node degree of a digraph can be formulated as $\boldsymbol{a}^{total} = \boldsymbol{a}^{in} + \boldsymbol{a}^{out} = (\boldsymbol{a} + \boldsymbol{a}^{\mathsf{T}}) \cdot \boldsymbol{1}^n$ in terms of its adjacency matrix, we then find the more convenient expression

$$N^d = 2\,\mathrm{T}\left[\left((\boldsymbol{a} + \boldsymbol{a}^{\mathsf{T}}) \cdot \boldsymbol{1}^n\right) \odot \left((\boldsymbol{a} + \boldsymbol{a}^{\mathsf{T}}) \cdot \boldsymbol{1}^n\right)\right] - 4A - 8N_{se} \tag{6.25}$$

for the normalising term entering the definition of C^d.

With (6.24) and (6.25) at our disposal, it is now possible to conceive of a suitable graph observable $\hat{C}^d$ for the total global clustering coefficient of $\mathcal{G}$. To that end, let us denote with $\hat{\boldsymbol{a}}[\hat{\mathcal{G}}]$ the adjacency matrix observable for an operator representation $\hat{\mathcal{G}}$ of $\mathcal{G}$, and with $\hat{A}[\hat{\mathcal{G}}]$ and $\hat{N}_{se}[\hat{\mathcal{G}}]$, the observables measuring the graph's total adjacency and number of symmetrical edges respectively. We certainly have $\mathrm{Tr}\left[\hat{\boldsymbol{a}}[\hat{\mathcal{G}}]\right] = 0$ for any operator representation of a relational digraph, such that no term involving diagonal elements of the adjacency matrix observable will contribute to the sum in (6.24). By furthermore imposing the condition

$$\hat{\mathfrak{a}}[\hat{\mathscr{G}}] = \hat{\mathfrak{a}}[\hat{\mathscr{G}}]^{\mathsf{T}}, \tag{6.26}$$

the numerator eventually simplifies to

$$\begin{aligned}
\sum_{i,j,k=1}^{n} &(a_{ij} + a_{ji})(a_{ik} + a_{ki})(a_{jk} + a_{kj}) \\
&= \sum_{i,j,k=1}^{n} \left(2\, a_{ij}a_{jk}a_{ki} + 6\, a_{ij}a_{jk}a_{ik}\right) \\
&= \sum_{i,j,k=1}^{n} \left(2\, \hat{\mathfrak{a}}[\hat{\mathscr{G}}]_{ij}\, \hat{\mathfrak{a}}[\hat{\mathscr{G}}]_{jk}\, \hat{\mathfrak{a}}[\hat{\mathscr{G}}]_{ki} + 6\, \hat{\mathfrak{a}}[\hat{\mathscr{G}}]_{ij}\, \hat{\mathfrak{a}}[\hat{\mathscr{G}}]_{jk}\, \hat{\mathfrak{a}}[\hat{\mathscr{G}}]_{ik}\right) \\
&= 8 \sum_{i,j,k=1}^{n} \hat{\mathfrak{a}}[\hat{\mathscr{G}}]_{ij}\, \hat{\mathfrak{a}}[\hat{\mathscr{G}}]_{jk}\, \hat{\mathfrak{a}}[\hat{\mathscr{G}}]_{ki} = 8\, \mathrm{Tr}\left[\hat{\mathfrak{a}}[\hat{\mathscr{G}}]^3\right].
\end{aligned} \tag{6.27}$$

It is important to stress here that (6.26) has to be understood as a condition imposed on the algebraic expression returned by the adjacency matrix observable, and thus it is in a conceptually subtle way distinguished from the property of a given adjacency matrix that classically defines an undirected graph. Indeed, recalling (5.44), (5.67) or (5.91), for instance, the adjacency matrix observables associated with our operator representations of directed Erdős–Rényi, Gilbert or Watts–Strogatz random graph models, among others, all formally return matrices in which symmetric elements are randomly assigned with the same probability. These elements are therefore algebraically identical when expressed in terms of a randomisation operator, while the independence of their random assignment ultimately ensures that a concrete realisation will result in a generally directed graph. Restricting ourselves, then, to relational random digraph models $\mathscr{G}$ that satisfy (6.26) such that (6.27) holds, we can proceed with evaluating the expectation value of $\hat{C}^d$, and finally define with

$$\left\langle \hat{C}^d \right\rangle : \mathbb{G} \to \mathbb{Q}\,, \left\langle \hat{C}^d[\hat{\mathscr{G}}] \right\rangle = \langle C^d \rangle := \frac{8}{\left\langle \hat{N}^d[\hat{\mathscr{G}}] \right\rangle} \left\langle \mathrm{Tr}\left[\hat{\mathfrak{a}}[\hat{\mathscr{G}}]^3\right] \right\rangle \tag{6.28}$$

and

$$\left\langle \hat{N}^d[\hat{\mathscr{G}}] \right\rangle = 8 \left\langle \mathrm{T}\left[\left(\hat{\mathfrak{a}}[\hat{\mathscr{G}}] \cdot \mathbf{1}^n\right) \odot \left(\hat{\mathfrak{a}}[\hat{\mathscr{G}}] \cdot \mathbf{1}^n\right)\right] \right\rangle - 4 \left\langle \hat{A}[\hat{\mathscr{G}}] \right\rangle - 8 \left\langle \hat{N}_{se}[\hat{\mathscr{G}}] \right\rangle \tag{6.29}$$

a viable graph observable that yields the expectation value of the total global clustering coefficient for an operator representation $\hat{\mathscr{G}}$ of $\mathscr{G}$ in terms of the expectation values of its adjacency matrix, total adjacency (6.1) and number of symmetrical edges (6.9). In what follows, we will apply (6.28) to the Gilbert random digraph model and our canonical model for Watts–Strogatz random digraphs, both of which deliver a result for the clustering coefficient in directed Erdős–Rényi random graphs as a special case.

6.3.1 Gilbert Random Digraphs

Let us begin with an evaluation of the clustering coefficient for Gilbert random digraphs. Noting that the adjacency matrix observable (5.67) of this model satisfies $\mathrm{Tr}\,[\hat{\mathfrak{a}}[\hat{\mathcal{R}}^{dG}_{n,p}]] = 0$, as well as $\hat{\mathfrak{a}}[\hat{\mathcal{R}}^{dG}_{n,p}] = \hat{\mathfrak{a}}[\hat{\mathcal{R}}^{dG}_{n,p}]^{\mathsf{T}}$ due to the symmetry of the Boolean matrix argument of its binomial randomisation operator, we certainly can apply (6.28) here. In order to eventually arrive at a useful algebraic expression, we first take a closer look at $\langle \hat{N}^d[\hat{\mathcal{R}}^{dG}_{n,p}]\rangle$. With $\langle \hat{A}[\hat{\mathcal{R}}^{dG}_{n,p}]\rangle$ and $\langle \hat{N}_{se}[\hat{\mathcal{R}}^{dG}_{n,p}]\rangle$ already at our disposal, only the first term on the right-hand side of (6.29) remains to be considered. Employing (4.45) and (4.46), we find

$$
\begin{aligned}
&\left(\hat{\mathfrak{a}}[\hat{\mathcal{R}}^{dG}_{n,p}]\cdot \boldsymbol{1}^n\right)\odot\left(\hat{\mathfrak{a}}[\hat{\mathcal{R}}^{dG}_{n,p}]\cdot \boldsymbol{1}^n\right)\\
&\quad= \left(\mathfrak{r}^p\left[\boldsymbol{\Delta}^{n\times n}_{\mathcal{I}^{dG}_n}\right]\cdot \boldsymbol{1}^n\right)\odot\left(\mathfrak{r}^p\left[\boldsymbol{\Delta}^{n\times n}_{\mathcal{I}^{dG}_n}\right]\cdot \boldsymbol{1}^n\right)\\
&\quad= \left(\mathfrak{r}^p\left[\boldsymbol{\Delta}^{n\times n}_{\mathcal{I}^{dG}_n}\right]\cdot \mathfrak{r}^1[\boldsymbol{1}^n]\right)\odot\left(\mathfrak{r}^p\left[\boldsymbol{\Delta}^{n\times n}_{\mathcal{I}^{dG}_n}\right]\cdot \mathfrak{r}^1[\boldsymbol{1}^n]\right)\\
&\quad= \mathfrak{r}^p\left[\boldsymbol{\Delta}^{n\times n}_{\mathcal{I}^{dG}_n}\cdot \boldsymbol{1}^n\right]\odot\mathfrak{r}^p\left[\boldsymbol{\Delta}^{n\times n}_{\mathcal{I}^{dG}_n}\cdot \boldsymbol{1}^n\right] = \mathfrak{r}^{p^2}\left[\left(\boldsymbol{\Delta}^{n\times n}_{\mathcal{I}^{dG}_n}\cdot \boldsymbol{1}^n\right)\odot\left(\boldsymbol{\Delta}^{n\times n}_{\mathcal{I}^{dG}_n}\cdot \boldsymbol{1}^n\right)\right]\\
&\quad= \mathfrak{r}^{p^2}\left[((n-1)\cdot \boldsymbol{1}^n)\odot((n-1)\cdot \boldsymbol{1}^n)\right] = (n-1)^2\cdot \mathfrak{r}^{p^2}[\boldsymbol{1}^n],
\end{aligned}
$$

such that

$$
\left\langle \mathrm{T}\left[\left(\hat{\mathfrak{a}}[\hat{\mathcal{R}}^{dG}_{n,p}]\cdot \boldsymbol{1}^n\right)\odot\left(\hat{\mathfrak{a}}[\hat{\mathcal{R}}^{dG}_{n,p}]\cdot \boldsymbol{1}^n\right)\right]\right\rangle = (n-1)^2\left\langle \mathrm{T}\left[\mathfrak{r}^{p^2}[\boldsymbol{1}^n]\right]\right\rangle = p^2 n(n-1)^2.
$$

This, together with (6.4) and (6.15), then yields

$$
\begin{aligned}
\left\langle \hat{N}^d[\hat{\mathcal{R}}^{dG}_{n,p}]\right\rangle &= 8p^2 n(n-1)^2 - 4pn(n-1) - 4p^2 n(n-1)\\
&= 4pn(n-1)(2pn-3p-1) \qquad (6.30)
\end{aligned}
$$

for the normalising term of $\langle \hat{C}^d[\hat{\mathcal{R}}^{dG}_{n,p}]\rangle$.

The evaluation of the numerator in (6.28), on the other hand, is somewhat more involved as it requires calculating the third matrix power of the adjacency matrix observable $\hat{\mathfrak{a}}[\hat{\mathcal{R}}^{dG}_{n,p}]$. Utilising once more the general identity (4.45) satisfied by the matrix product of binomial randomisation operators, we have

$$
\begin{aligned}
\left\langle \mathrm{Tr}\left[\hat{\mathfrak{a}}[\hat{\mathcal{R}}^{dG}_{n,p}]^3\right]\right\rangle &= \left\langle \mathrm{Tr}\left[\mathfrak{r}^p\left[\boldsymbol{\Delta}^{n\times n}_{\mathcal{I}^{dG}_n}\right]\cdot \mathfrak{r}^p\left[\boldsymbol{\Delta}^{n\times n}_{\mathcal{I}^{dG}_n}\right]\cdot \mathfrak{r}^p\left[\boldsymbol{\Delta}^{n\times n}_{\mathcal{I}^{dG}_n}\right]\right]\right\rangle\\
&= \left\langle \mathrm{Tr}\left[\mathfrak{r}^{p^3}\left[(\boldsymbol{\Delta}^{n\times n}_{\mathcal{I}^{dG}_n})^3\right]\right]\right\rangle, \qquad (6.31)
\end{aligned}
$$

which effectively translates the problem into one of obtaining the third matrix power of $\boldsymbol{\Delta}^{n\times n}_{\mathcal{I}^{dG}_n}$. Fortunately, this can be achieved by recalling with (5.68) the circulant nature of this Boolean matrix, which then allows us to make use of the *circulant diagonalisation theorem* to get algebraic access to its matrix powers (see [33] for a concise introduction). Adapting this theorem to serve our purpose, it states that all circulant matrices $\boldsymbol{C} \in \mathbb{Q}^{n\times n} : \boldsymbol{C} = \mathrm{circ}[\boldsymbol{c}]$ constructed from arbitrary vectors $\boldsymbol{c} \in \mathbb{Q}^n$ according to (3.56) are diagonalised by the same unitary matrix $\boldsymbol{U} \in \mathbb{C}^{n\times n}$, with elements

$$U_{rs} = \frac{1}{\sqrt{n}} \exp\left[-\frac{2\pi i}{n}(r-1)(s-1)\right] \tag{6.32}$$

satisfying

$$\begin{aligned} \boldsymbol{U} \cdot \boldsymbol{U}^\dagger &= \boldsymbol{U}^\dagger \cdot \boldsymbol{U} = \boldsymbol{I}^n, \\ \boldsymbol{U} \cdot \bar{\boldsymbol{U}} &= \bar{\boldsymbol{U}} \cdot \boldsymbol{U} = \boldsymbol{I}^n, \end{aligned} \tag{6.33}$$

where $\boldsymbol{U}^\dagger$ and $\bar{\boldsymbol{U}}$ denote the hermitian transpose and complex conjugate of $\boldsymbol{U}$, respectively. The n eigenvalues $e_r(\boldsymbol{C}) : r \in [1, n]$ of $\boldsymbol{C}$ are explicitly given by

$$e_r(\boldsymbol{C}) := \sum_{l=1}^{n} c_l \exp\left[-\frac{2\pi i}{n}(r-1)(l-1)\right] \tag{6.34}$$

in terms of the n elements of the vector $\boldsymbol{c}$, such that

$$\boldsymbol{C} = \boldsymbol{U} \cdot \mathrm{diag}\left[\boldsymbol{e}(\boldsymbol{C})\right] \cdot \bar{\boldsymbol{U}}, \tag{6.35}$$

and thus with (6.33),

$$\boldsymbol{C}^m = \boldsymbol{U} \cdot \mathrm{diag}\left[\boldsymbol{e}(\boldsymbol{C})\right]^m \cdot \bar{\boldsymbol{U}} \tag{6.36}$$

for arbitrary powers $m \in \mathbb{N}$. Here, $\boldsymbol{e}(\boldsymbol{C})$ denotes the vector of eigenvalues with elements defined in (6.34), and $\mathrm{diag}\left[\boldsymbol{e}(\boldsymbol{C})\right]$ the diagonal matrix with elements

$$\mathrm{diag}\left[\boldsymbol{e}(\boldsymbol{C})\right]_{rs} := \delta[r-s]\, e_r(\boldsymbol{C}) \tag{6.37}$$

such that $(\mathrm{diag}\left[\boldsymbol{e}(\boldsymbol{C})\right]^m)_{rs} = \delta[r-s](e_r(\boldsymbol{C}))^m$.

Using the circulant diagonalisation theorem, we can now proceed with our evaluation of (6.31). To that end, we recognise that the matrix $\boldsymbol{\Delta}^{n\times n}_{\mathcal{I}^{dG}_n} = \mathrm{circ}[\boldsymbol{c}]$ is fully defined by a vector $\boldsymbol{c}$ with components $c_1 = 0$ and $c_l = 1$ for $l \in [2, n]$. Application of (6.34) then delivers the n eigenvalues

$$e_r\left(\boldsymbol{\Delta}^{n\times n}_{\mathcal{I}^{dG}_n}\right) = \sum_{l=2}^{n} \exp\left[-\frac{2\pi i}{n}(r-1)(l-1)\right] = \begin{cases} n-1 & \text{for } r = 1, \\ -1 & \text{for } r \in [2, n] \end{cases}$$

of $\boldsymbol{\Delta}^{n\times n}_{\mathcal{I}^{dG}_n}$, from which with (6.36) and (6.37)

$$\left(\left(\boldsymbol{\Delta}^{n\times n}_{\mathcal{I}^{dG}_n}\right)^m\right)_{rs} = \sum_{l,l'=1}^{n} U_{rl} \left(\mathrm{diag}\left[\boldsymbol{e}\left(\boldsymbol{\Delta}^{n\times n}_{\mathcal{I}^{dG}_n}\right)\right]^m\right)_{ll'} \bar{U}_{l's}$$

$$= \sum_{l,l'=1}^{n} U_{rl}\,\delta[l-l']\big(e_l\big(\mathbf{\Delta}^{n\times n}_{I^{dG}_n}\big)\big)^m\,\bar{U}_{l's}$$

$$= \frac{(n-1)^m}{n} + \frac{(-1)^m}{n}\sum_{l=2}^{n}\exp\left[-\frac{2\pi i}{n}(l-1)(r-s)\right] \qquad (6.38)$$

for the matrix elements of its mth power follows. Noting that the trace operator effectively removes the exponential terms in (6.38), we eventually find

$$\left\langle \mathrm{Tr}\left[\hat{\mathbf{a}}[\hat{\mathscr{R}}^{dG}_{n,p}]^3\right]\right\rangle = \left\langle \sum_{r=1}^{n}\mathbf{r}^{p^3}\left[\frac{(n-1)^3}{n} - \frac{n-1}{n}\right]\right\rangle = p^3(n-1)((n-1)^2-1),$$

which with (6.28) and (6.31) finally delivers

$$\left\langle \hat{C}^d[\hat{\mathscr{R}}^{dG}_{n,p}]\right\rangle = \frac{2p^2((n-1)^2-1)}{n(2pn-3p-1)} \qquad (6.39)$$

for the expectation value of the total global clustering coefficient in directed Gilbert random graphs $\mathscr{R}^{dG}_{n,p}$.

It is important to point out that the necessary condition $N^d \geq 1$ imposed on the normalising term in the classical definition of C^d also applies here, and does restrict the use of (6.39) to Gilbert random graphs with connection probability

$$p \geq p_{\min} := \frac{1}{2\left(\sqrt{n(n^3-4n+3)} - n(n-1)\right)}. \qquad (6.40)$$

However, this restriction does not result from a limitation of our approach, but derives from the very definition of the total global clustering coefficient itself. Indeed, C^d counts the number of graph patterns of order three with two and three edges (see Section 2.2.5) and, thus, is meaningful only if such patterns are possible or expected to be present in the graph under consideration. In extremely sparse graphs, for instance, this is likely to not be the case. Worse still, in such graphs the total degree will certainly be smaller than two for many nodes and will yield a normalising term $N^d < 1$. The lower limit imposed with (6.42) on the connection probability simply ensures that enough edges are present in the graph such that patterns relevant to the clustering coefficient can form.

The functional behaviour of (6.39) for some representative values of n and $p \geq p_{\min}$ is illustrated in Fig. 6.3. With

$$\left\langle \hat{C}^d[\hat{\mathscr{R}}^{dG}_{n,p}]\right\rangle = p + \frac{1-p}{2n} + \mathcal{O}(1/n^2) \overset{n\to\infty}{\to} p$$

in the asymptotic limit of large n, the total global clustering coefficient does remain mostly independent of the graph order and increases linearly with connection probability to eventually reach $\langle \hat{C}^d[\hat{\mathscr{R}}^{dG}_{n,1}]\rangle = 1$ for complete relational

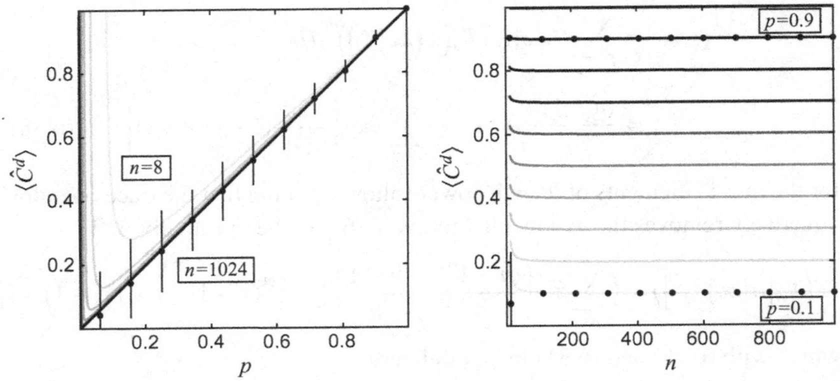

Figure 6.3 Expectation value of the total global clustering coefficient (6.39) for directed Gilbert random graphs as function of the connection probability p for $n = 2^m$, $m \in [3, 10]$ (left), and as function of n for $p \in [0.1, 0.2, \ldots, 0.9]$ (right). For some models, the results of a statistical analysis of 100 computational realisations are shown (black dots; mean ± SD). Parameters for numerical models: $n = 8$ (left); $p = 0.1$ and $p = 0.9$ (right).

digraphs. This behaviour is to be expected because C^d counts the fraction of occurring triangular graph patterns and, therefore, must scale independently of the graph's size. Although this finding and, more importantly, the validity of our result (6.39) are generally confirmed by a computational analysis, a significant discrepancy for small n and p has to be noticed, hinting at a limitation of (6.39) which, as further inspection reveals, can be attributed to the principal challenge of treating conditional statements and discrete case distinctions in algebraic or analytic formalisations. Indeed, despite having with (6.42) a condition at our disposal that corresponds to $N^d \geq 1$ in the classical conception of this measure, our algebraic expression neither considers N^d to be an integer nor requires that $C^d = 0$ for $N^d < 1$ according to (2.85). Due to the probabilistic nature of realising Gilbert random graphs in a computational setting, however, cases in which $N^d < 1$ are likely to occur for small or sparsely connected graphs even if $p > p_{\min}$ and will lead to a conditional modification – and, ultimately, the rejection – of some numerical data points to prevent meaningless infinite or negative clustering coefficients. As our approach only delivers with (6.30) the average value of N^d, this generally results in an underestimation of the normalising term in (6.39) for connection probabilities close to $p_{\min}$, and consequently an expected clustering coefficient larger than that observed in computational models.

Finally, restricting the range of possible connection probabilities in (6.39) to $p = k/n(n-1)$, we obtain with

$$\left\langle \hat{C}^d[\hat{\mathscr{R}}^{dER}_{n,k}] \right\rangle = \frac{2k^2(2-n)}{n(n-1)(k(3-2n)+n(n-1))} \tag{6.41}$$

the expected total global clustering coefficient for directed Erdős–Rényi random digraphs $\mathscr{R}^{dER}_{n,k}$ of order n and

$$k > k_{\min} := \left\lfloor \frac{n(n-1)}{2\left(\sqrt{n(n^3-4n+3)} - n(n-1)\right)} \right\rfloor \tag{6.42}$$

directed edges. This algebraic expression mirrors the functional behaviour depicted in Fig. 6.3, and will be subject to the same limitations in regards to its validity as our result for the Gilbert random digraph model.

6.3.2 Watts–Strogatz Random Digraphs

With the tools presented above, the total global clustering coefficient for our canonical model of Watts–Strogatz random digraphs can be obtained in a similarly straightforward fashion. Let us begin here again by noting that the adjacency matrix observable (5.91) of this model satisfies both $\mathrm{Tr}\,[\hat{\mathbf{a}}[\hat{\mathscr{R}}^{dWS}_{n,k,q}]] = 0$ and $\hat{\mathbf{a}}[\hat{\mathscr{R}}^{dWS}_{n,k,q}] = \hat{\mathbf{a}}[\hat{\mathscr{R}}^{dWS}_{n,k,q}]^{\mathsf{T}}$, such that (6.28) defines a viable graph observable for the clustering coefficient that can be applied to the operator representation $\hat{\mathscr{R}}^{dWS}_{n,k,q}$ of $\mathscr{R}^{dWS}_{n,k,q}$ given in (5.89). By exploiting (4.45) and (4.46), one then finds

$$\begin{aligned}
&\left(\hat{\mathbf{a}}[\hat{\mathscr{R}}^{dWS}_{n,k,q}] \cdot \mathbf{1}^n\right) \odot \left(\hat{\mathbf{a}}[\hat{\mathscr{R}}^{dWS}_{n,k,q}] \cdot \mathbf{1}^n\right) \\
&= \left(\mathfrak{r}^{p}\big[\boldsymbol{\Delta}^{n\times n}_{\mathcal{I}^{\mathscr{C}}_{n,k}}\big] \cdot \mathbf{1}^n + \mathfrak{r}^{p'}\big[\boldsymbol{\Delta}^{n\times n}_{\mathcal{I}^{\bar{\mathscr{C}}}_{n,k}}\big] \cdot \mathbf{1}^n\right) \odot \left(\mathfrak{r}^{p}\big[\boldsymbol{\Delta}^{n\times n}_{\mathcal{I}^{\mathscr{C}}_{n,k}}\big] \cdot \mathbf{1}^n + \mathfrak{r}^{p'}\big[\boldsymbol{\Delta}^{n\times n}_{\mathcal{I}^{\bar{\mathscr{C}}}_{n,k}}\big] \cdot \mathbf{1}^n\right) \\
&= \mathfrak{r}^{p}\big[\boldsymbol{\Delta}^{n\times n}_{\mathcal{I}^{\mathscr{C}}_{n,k}} \cdot \mathbf{1}^n\big] \odot \mathfrak{r}^{p}\big[\boldsymbol{\Delta}^{n\times n}_{\mathcal{I}^{\mathscr{C}}_{n,k}} \cdot \mathbf{1}^n\big] + 2\mathfrak{r}^{p}\big[\boldsymbol{\Delta}^{n\times n}_{\mathcal{I}^{\mathscr{C}}_{n,k}} \cdot \mathbf{1}^n\big] \odot \mathfrak{r}^{p'}\big[\boldsymbol{\Delta}^{n\times n}_{\mathcal{I}^{\bar{\mathscr{C}}}_{n,k}} \cdot \mathbf{1}^n\big] \\
&\quad + \mathfrak{r}^{p'}\big[\boldsymbol{\Delta}^{n\times n}_{\mathcal{I}^{\bar{\mathscr{C}}}_{n,k}} \cdot \mathbf{1}^n\big] \odot \mathfrak{r}^{p'}\big[\boldsymbol{\Delta}^{n\times n}_{\mathcal{I}^{\bar{\mathscr{C}}}_{n,k}} \cdot \mathbf{1}^n\big] \\
&= \mathfrak{r}^{p^2}\Big[\big(\boldsymbol{\Delta}^{n\times n}_{\mathcal{I}^{\mathscr{C}}_{n,k}} \cdot \mathbf{1}^n\big) \odot \big(\boldsymbol{\Delta}^{n\times n}_{\mathcal{I}^{\mathscr{C}}_{n,k}} \cdot \mathbf{1}^n\big)\Big] + 2\mathfrak{r}^{pp'}\Big[\big(\boldsymbol{\Delta}^{n\times n}_{\mathcal{I}^{\mathscr{C}}_{n,k}} \cdot \mathbf{1}^n\big) \odot \big(\boldsymbol{\Delta}^{n\times n}_{\mathcal{I}^{\bar{\mathscr{C}}}_{n,k}} \cdot \mathbf{1}^n\big)\Big] \\
&\quad + \mathfrak{r}^{p'^2}\Big[\big(\boldsymbol{\Delta}^{n\times n}_{\mathcal{I}^{\bar{\mathscr{C}}}_{n,k}} \cdot \mathbf{1}^n\big) \odot \big(\boldsymbol{\Delta}^{n\times n}_{\mathcal{I}^{\bar{\mathscr{C}}}_{n,k}} \cdot \mathbf{1}^n\big)\Big] \\
&= \mathfrak{r}^{p^2}\big[(2k \cdot \mathbf{1}^n) \odot (2k \cdot \mathbf{1}^n)\big] + 2\mathfrak{r}^{pp'}\big[(2k \cdot \mathbf{1}^n) \odot ((n{-}1{-}2k) \cdot \mathbf{1}^n)\big] \\
&\quad + \mathfrak{r}^{p'^2}\big[((n{-}1{-}2k) \cdot \mathbf{1}^n) \odot ((n{-}1{-}2k) \cdot \mathbf{1}^n)\big] \\
&= 4k^2 \cdot \mathfrak{r}^{p^2}[\mathbf{1}^n] + 4k(n{-}1{-}2k) \cdot \mathfrak{r}^{pp'}[\mathbf{1}^n] + (n{-}1{-}2k)^2 \cdot \mathfrak{r}^{p'^2}[\mathbf{1}^n],
\end{aligned}$$

where in the final two steps we applied the definition (5.92) for the Boolean matrices $\boldsymbol{\Delta}^{n\times n}_{\mathcal{I}^{\mathscr{C}}_{n,k}}$ and $\boldsymbol{\Delta}^{n\times n}_{\mathcal{I}^{\bar{\mathscr{C}}}_{n,k}}$, as well as the homogeneity of degree 1 of our binomial randomisation operator (see Table 5.1). This yields

$$\begin{aligned}&\left\langle \mathrm{T}\left[\left(\hat{\mathbf{a}}[\hat{\mathscr{R}}^{dWS}_{n,k,q}]\cdot \boldsymbol{1}^{n}\right)\odot\left(\hat{\mathbf{a}}[\hat{\mathscr{R}}^{dWS}_{n,k,q}]\cdot \boldsymbol{1}^{n}\right)\right]\right\rangle\\ &\qquad = 4p^2k^2n + 4pp'kn(n-1-2k) + p'^2n(n-1-2k)^2 = 4k^2n\end{aligned}$$

with p and p' given in (5.75) and (5.76), from which with $\langle \hat{A}[\hat{\mathscr{R}}^{dWS}_{n,k,q}]\rangle$ in (6.5) and $\langle \hat{N}_{se}[\hat{\mathscr{R}}^{dWS}_{n,k,q}]\rangle$ in (6.17), eventually,

$$\begin{aligned}\left\langle \hat{N}^d[\hat{\mathscr{R}}^{dWS}_{n,k,q}]\right\rangle &= 8kn(4k-1) - 8knp^2 - 4n(n-1-2k)p'^2 \\ &= 8kn\left(4k-1-\frac{((n-1)(1-q)-2k(1-2q))^2 + 2kq^2(n-1-2k)}{(n-1-2k(1-q))^2}\right)\end{aligned} \tag{6.43}$$

for the normalising term (6.29) in $\langle \hat{C}^d[\hat{\mathscr{R}}^{dWS}_{n,k,q}]\rangle$ follows.

In order to evaluate the numerator of (6.28), we follow the path used for the Gilbert random graph model, and with (4.45), we find

$$\begin{aligned}&\left\langle \mathrm{Tr}\left[\hat{\mathbf{a}}[\hat{\mathscr{R}}^{dWS}_{n,k,q}]^3\right]\right\rangle\\ &\quad = \left\langle \mathrm{Tr}\left[\left(\mathfrak{r}^{p}\left[\boldsymbol{\Delta}^{n\times n}_{\mathcal{I}^{\mathscr{C}}_{n,k}}\right] + \mathfrak{r}^{p'}\left[\boldsymbol{\Delta}^{n\times n}_{\mathcal{I}^{\bar{\mathscr{C}}}_{n,k}}\right]\right)^3\right]\right\rangle\\ &\quad = \left\langle \mathrm{Tr}\left[\mathfrak{r}^{p^3}\left[(\boldsymbol{\Delta}^{n\times n}_{\mathcal{I}^{\mathscr{C}}_{n,k}})^3\right]\right]\right\rangle + 3\left\langle \mathrm{Tr}\left[\mathfrak{r}^{p^2p'}\left[(\boldsymbol{\Delta}^{n\times n}_{\mathcal{I}^{\mathscr{C}}_{n,k}})^2\cdot \boldsymbol{\Delta}^{n\times n}_{\mathcal{I}^{\bar{\mathscr{C}}_{n,k}}}\right]\right]\right\rangle\\ &\qquad + 3\left\langle \mathrm{Tr}\left[\mathfrak{r}^{pp'^2}\left[\boldsymbol{\Delta}^{n\times n}_{\mathcal{I}^{\mathscr{C}}_{n,k}}\cdot (\boldsymbol{\Delta}^{n\times n}_{\mathcal{I}^{\bar{\mathscr{C}}_{n,k}}})^2\right]\right]\right\rangle + \left\langle \mathrm{Tr}\left[\mathfrak{r}^{p'^3}\left[(\boldsymbol{\Delta}^{n\times n}_{\mathcal{I}^{\bar{\mathscr{C}}_{n,k}}})^3\right]\right]\right\rangle. \end{aligned} \tag{6.44}$$

This again transforms the problem effectively into one of assessing various matrix power of circulant Boolean matrices. By employing the circulant diagonalisation theorem (6.32)–(6.36), we obtain after a lengthy calculation

$$\begin{aligned}e_r\left(\boldsymbol{\Delta}^{n\times n}_{\mathcal{I}^{\mathscr{C}_{n,k}}}\right) &= \sum_{l=2}^{k+1}\exp\left[-\frac{2\pi i}{n}(r-1)(l-1)\right] + \sum_{l=n-k+1}^{n}\exp\left[-\frac{2\pi i}{n}(r-1)(l-1)\right]\\ &= \begin{cases} 2k & \text{for } r=1,\\ 2\sin\left[\frac{k(r-1)}{n}\pi\right]\cos\left[\frac{(1+k)(r-1)}{n}\pi\right]\Big/\sin\left[\frac{r-1}{n}\pi\right] & \text{for } r\in[2,n],\end{cases}\end{aligned}$$

$$\begin{aligned}e_r\left(\boldsymbol{\Delta}^{n\times n}_{\mathcal{I}^{\bar{\mathscr{C}}_{n,k}}}\right) &= \sum_{l=k+2}^{n-k}\exp\left[-\frac{2\pi i}{n}(r-1)(l-1)\right]\\ &= \begin{cases} n-1-2k & \text{for } r=1,\\ -\sin\left[\frac{(1+2k)(r-1)}{n}\pi\right]\Big/\sin\left[\frac{r-1}{n}\pi\right] & \text{for } r\in[2,n],\end{cases}\end{aligned}$$

for the eigenvalues of $\boldsymbol{\Delta}^{n\times n}_{\mathcal{I}^{\mathscr{C}_{n,k}}}$ and $\boldsymbol{\Delta}^{n\times n}_{\mathcal{I}^{\bar{\mathscr{C}}_{n,k}}}$, and

$$\left(\left(\boldsymbol{\Delta}^{n\times n}_{\mathcal{I}^{\mathscr{C}_{n,k}}}\right)^m\right)_{rs} = \frac{2^m}{n}\sum_{l=1}^{n}\alpha_l^m(n,k)\exp\left[-\frac{2\pi i}{n}(l-1)(r-s)\right], \tag{6.45}$$

$$\left(\left(\mathbf{\Delta}^{n\times n}_{\mathcal{I}^{\mathscr{C}_{n,k}}}\right)^m\right)_{rs} = \frac{(-1)^m}{n}\sum_{l=1}^{n}\beta_l^m(n,k)\exp\left[-\frac{2\pi i}{n}(l-1)(r-s)\right] \quad (6.46)$$

for the elements of their mth matrix powers. Here we introduced for notational convenience the functions

$$\alpha_l(n,k) := \begin{cases} k & \text{for } l=1,\\ \sin\left[\frac{k(l-1)}{n}\pi\right]\cos\left[\frac{(1+k)(l-1)}{n}\pi\right]\Big/\sin\left[\frac{(l-1)}{n}\pi\right] & \text{for } l\in[2,n],\end{cases}$$

$$\beta_l(n,k) := \begin{cases} 2k+1-n & \text{for } l=1,\\ \sin\left[\frac{(1+2k)(l-1)}{n}\pi\right]\Big/\sin\left[\frac{l-1}{n}\pi\right] & \text{for } l\in[2,n],\end{cases} \quad (6.47)$$

which, when viewed as number sequences for $l\in\mathbb{N} : l\in[1,n]$, lend themselves to some interesting number-theoretical applications beyond the scope of this book [96]. In a similar fashion, we find

$$\left(\left(\mathbf{\Delta}^{n\times n}_{\mathcal{I}^{\mathscr{C}_{n,k}}}\right)^m\left(\mathbf{\Delta}^{n\times n}_{\mathcal{I}^{\vec{\mathscr{C}}_{n,k}}}\right)^{m'}\right)_{rs} = \frac{(-1)^{m'}2^m}{n}\sum_{l=1}^{n}\alpha_l^m(n,k)\beta_l^{m'}(n,k)\exp\left[-\frac{2\pi i}{n}(l-1)(r-s)\right] \quad (6.48)$$

for the product of matrix powers of $\mathbf{\Delta}^{n\times n}_{\mathcal{I}^{\mathscr{C}_{n,k}}}$ and $\mathbf{\Delta}^{n\times n}_{\mathcal{I}^{\vec{\mathscr{C}}_{n,k}}}$.

With (6.45), (6.46) and (6.48) at hand, we then obtain

$$\left\langle \mathrm{Tr}\left[\hat{a}[\hat{\mathscr{R}}^{dWS}_{n,k,q}]^3\right]\right\rangle = 8p^3\sum_{l=1}^{n}\alpha_l^3(n,k) - 12p^2p'\sum_{l=1}^{n}\alpha_l^2(n,k)\beta_l(n,k) + 6pp'^2\sum_{l=1}^{n}\alpha_l(n,k)\beta_l^2(n,k) - p'^3\sum_{l=1}^{n}\beta_l^3(n,k)$$

for the numerator (6.44). Together with (6.43), this finally delivers the somewhat challenging algebraic expression

$$\left\langle \hat{C}^d[\hat{\mathscr{R}}^{dWS}_{n,k,q}]\right\rangle = \frac{2}{2kn(4k-1)-2knp^2-n(n-1-2k)p'^2} \times\left(8p^3\sum_{l=1}^{n}\alpha_l^3(n,k) - 12p^2p'\sum_{l=1}^{n}\alpha_l^2(n,k)\beta_l(n,k) + 6pp'^2\sum_{l=1}^{n}\alpha_l(n,k)\beta_l^2(n,k) - p'^3\sum_{l=1}^{n}\beta_l^3(n,k)\right) \quad (6.49)$$

for the expected total global clustering coefficient of directed Watts–Strogatz random graphs. Please note that we present this result for the purpose of notational simplicity in terms of the probabilities p and p' defined in (5.75) and (5.76), as well as the functions $\alpha_l(n,k)$ and $\beta_l(n,k)$ in (6.47). More importantly, we find that, in contrast to the Gilbert model, the troubling condition $N^d \geq 1$ imposed on the normalising term in the classical conception of C^d is here naturally satisfied. Indeed, it can easily be argued that $\langle \hat{N}^d[\hat{\mathcal{R}}^{dWS}_{n,k,q}]\rangle$ for any given n and k can only monotonically increase with q because the number of symmetrical edges is largest in the initial k-ring digraph and, thus, necessarily decreases with the rewiring of existing edges, while the total node degrees remain, on average, unaffected by the rewiring process. Recalling (6.29), the minimum value of our normalising term is therefore taken at $q = 0$, for which $p = 1$ and $p' = 0$, which leaves us with

$$\langle \hat{N}^d[\hat{\mathcal{R}}^{dWS}_{n,k,q}]\rangle \overset{q\to 1}{\to} 16kn(2k-1) \gg 1 \tag{6.50}$$

even for graphs of low order $n \geq 3$ and $1 \leq k \ll \lfloor n/2 \rfloor$.

The functional behaviour of $\langle \hat{C}^d[\hat{\mathcal{R}}^{dWS}_{n,k,q}]\rangle$ for some representative parameter values is illustrated in Fig. 6.4. As expected from (6.49), this behaviour is quite non-trivial and would require non-negligible resources to be discerned in computational studies. By mirroring the results of numerical models, we hope that the obtained algebraic expression for the total global clustering coefficient of Watts–Strogatz random digraphs provides yet another example motivating the potential usefulness of our operator graph-theoretical approach by giving this measure immediate access to the model's full parameter spectrum without restricting assumptions or asymptotic considerations. Before strengthening this prospect further in the next section, however, let us take a brief look at two important special cases. Firstly, for $q = 0$, we obtain with

$$\left\langle \hat{C}^d[\hat{\mathcal{R}}^{dWS}_{n,k,0}]\right\rangle = \frac{4}{kn(2k-1)} \sum_{l=1}^{n} \alpha_l^3(n,k) = \hat{C}^d[\hat{\mathcal{C}}_{n,k}] \tag{6.51}$$

the total global clustering coefficient of the complete relational k-ring digraph $\mathcal{C}_{n,k}$, noting that this observable yields an exact result and not an expectation value, as no random selection of adjacency relations is involved in the construction of $\mathcal{C}_{n,k}$. By careful numerical inspection, it can be shown that

$$\frac{1}{nk(k-1)} \sum_{l=2}^{n} \alpha_l^3(n,k) \overset{n\to\infty}{\to} \frac{3}{8} \tag{6.52}$$

for finite k, which then yields with

$$\lim_{n\to\infty} \left\langle \hat{C}^d[\hat{\mathcal{R}}^{dWS}_{n,k,0}]\right\rangle = \lim_{n\to\infty} \hat{C}^d[\hat{\mathcal{C}}_{n,k}] = \frac{3(k-1)}{2(2k-1)} \tag{6.53}$$

the known result for the clustering coefficient of the k-ring graph in the asymptotic limit of infinite graph size [13].

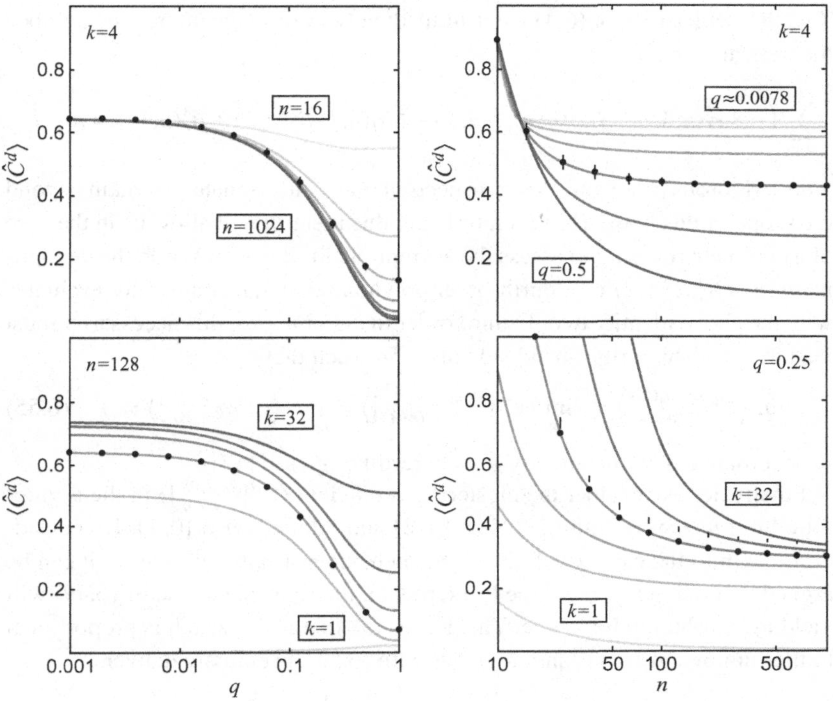

Figure 6.4 Expected total global clustering coefficient (6.49) of Watts–Strogatz random digraphs as a function of the rewiring probability q (left; top: $k = 4$, $n = 2^m, m \in [4, 10]$; bottom: $n = 128$, $k = 2^m$, $m \in [0, 5]$) and graph order n (right; top: $k = 4$, $q = 2^m$, $m \in [-7, -1]$; bottom: $k = 2^m$, $m \in [0, 5]$, $q = 0.25$). For some models, the results of a statistical analysis of 100 computational realisations are shown (black dots; mean±SD). Parameters for numerical models: $n = 64$, $k = 4$ (top left); $n = 128$, $k = 8$ (bottom left); $k = 4$, $q = 0.125$ (top right); $k = 8$, $q = 0.25$ (top right).

In the second special case $q = 1$ which, according to our canonical model, corresponds to Gilbert random digraphs $\mathscr{R}^{dG}_{n,p}$ with a connection probability $p = p' = 2k/(n-1)$ and Erdős–Rényi random digraphs $\mathscr{R}^{dER}_{n,2kn}$ with $2kn$ directed edges, we find an expectation value

$$\begin{aligned}\left\langle \hat{C}^d[\hat{\mathscr{R}}^{dWS}_{n,k,1}]\right\rangle &= \left\langle \hat{C}^d[\hat{\mathscr{R}}^{dG}_{n,2k/(n-1)}]\right\rangle = \left\langle \hat{C}^d[\hat{\mathscr{R}}^{dER}_{n,2kn}]\right\rangle \\ &= \frac{8k^2}{n(n-1)^2(n-1-2k(2n-3))} \sum_{l=1}^{n} \Big(-8\alpha_l^3(n,k) \\ &\quad + 12\alpha_l^2(n,k)\beta_l(n,k) - 6\alpha_l(n,k)\beta_l^2(n,k) + \beta_l^3(n,k)\Big). \qquad (6.54)\end{aligned}$$

Together with (6.39) or (6.41), this immediately leads to the interesting number-theoretical identity

$$\sum_{l=2}^{n}\Big(-8\alpha_l^3(n,k)+12\alpha_l^2(n,k)\beta_l(n,k)-6\alpha_l(n,k)\beta_l^2(n,k)+\beta_l^3(n,k)\Big)=n-1$$

whose rigorous proof and closer inspection must, unfortunately, remain beyond the scope of this book. However, utilising this identity will allow us in the case of a complete rewiring to assess the asymptotic limit $n\to\infty$. While the denominator of $\langle\hat{C}^d[\hat{\mathcal{R}}^{dWS}_{n,k,1}]\rangle$ is a fourth-order polynomial in n, its numerator evaluates with the above identity to only third order in n. For $n\to\infty$, this necessarily must lead to a vanishing right-hand side of (6.54) such that

$$\lim_{n\to\infty}\left\langle\hat{C}^d[\hat{\mathcal{R}}^{dWS}_{n,k,1}]\right\rangle=\lim_{n\to\infty}\left\langle\hat{C}^d[\hat{\mathcal{R}}^{dG}_{n,2k/(n-1)}]\right\rangle=\lim_{n\to\infty}\left\langle\hat{C}^d[\hat{\mathcal{R}}^{dER}_{n,2kn}]\right\rangle=0 \quad (6.55)$$

in accordance with the already-known result (e.g., see [13]).

Finally, let us consider the clustering coefficient $\langle\hat{C}^d[\hat{\mathcal{R}}^{dWS}_{n,k,q}]\rangle$ in the asymptotic limit $n\to\infty$ for finite $1\le k<\lfloor n/2\rfloor$ and arbitrary $q\in[0,1]$. By considering, akin to the case $q=1$ above, the behaviour as a function of n, it can be argued that neither of the three last terms on the right-hand side of (6.49) will yield a contribution for $n\to\infty$. This leaves the first term, which is proportional to the sum over $\alpha_l(n,k)^3$ and, together with (6.52), eventually delivers

$$\lim_{n\to\infty}\left\langle\hat{C}^d[\hat{\mathcal{R}}^{dWS}_{n,k,q}]\right\rangle=\frac{3(k-1)}{2(2k-1)+q(2-q)}(1-q)^3 \quad (6.56)$$

for the clustering coefficient of small-world digraphs $\mathcal{R}^{dWS}_{n,k,q}$ in the asymptotic limit $n\to\infty$ and finite k. Interestingly, this solution differs through the presence of an additional term $q(2-q)$ in the denominator from the asymptotic solution proposed in [13], obtained by interpolating between the clustering values of a k-ring graph and infinite-sized random graph. However, it can easily be shown that for $k>1$ this term becomes negligible, as $q\in[0,1]$ is strictly bound.

6.3.3 Application: Small-Worlds in the Brain

Let us conclude this section by briefly presenting a first concrete application of our algebraic expression (6.49) for the expected total global clustering coefficient in directed Watts–Strogatz random graphs. As already mentioned in Section 2.3.6, Watts and Strogatz demonstrated in their now-seminal work the existence of an intermediate state between regular and random graphs in which connected nodes maintain a small geodesic distance while an abundance of triangular graph patterns results in a high clustering of network connections, and that this intermediate *small-world* state can be reached through the random rewiring of only a small fraction of edges in regular ring graphs [109]. Evidence of a network connectivity which exhibits both a clustering exceeding that of Erdős–Rényi random graphs and an average number of links between nodes on par with that found in Erdős–Rényi random graphs has since been uncovered in a vast array of real-world datasets. However, while in many of these networks the small-world property clearly dominantes the structural makeup, in some cases – and in particular for smaller systems – the difference to a purely random connectivity pattern may not be particularly large and may leave the prospect of identifying the investigated network as small-world in a more questionable light or even untenable.

In order to quantify the "small-worldness" of graphs more rigorously and to provide a viable means for a comparative analysis of this important characteristic in networks of arbitrary order, the *global small-worldness index*

$$S^d \in \mathbb{Q}: S^d := \frac{C^{dWS}}{C^{dER}} \frac{\langle D \rangle^{dER}}{\langle D \rangle^{dWS}} \tag{6.57}$$

was introduced [63]. Here C^{dER}, C^{dWS} and $\langle D \rangle^{dER}$, $\langle D \rangle^{dWS}$ respectively denote the global total clustering coefficient and average geodesic graph distance of Erdős–Rényi and Watts–Strogatz random digraphs of the same order n and with the same number of edges. Immediately upon conception of this classical measure, it became apparent that systems such as the electric power grid of the United States or the co-authorship network of mathematicians could exhibit a global small-worldness index of more than 100, even reaching beyond 10,000 in some instances [63], while other real-world networks appeared to fall into a "borderline" category which was arbitrarily defined for indices $1 < S^d \leq 3$. Interestingly, and somewhat surprisingly, among these borderline cases reside the neural connectivity diagram of the macaque cortex and other *brain networks* [60, 74, 85], including the area-level connectivity diagram of the human cerebral cortex [57]. Although it certainly could be argued that all values $S^d > 1$ indicate the presence of the small-world property, the important question remaining concerns to which extent this property dominantes the structural makeup of the considered graph – that is, whether graphs with the same number of nodes and edges but a larger small-worldness index can be constructed.

A thorough answer to this question would require that we construct computational models of both Erdős–Rényi and Watts–Strogatz random digraphs for given n and k, and to evaluate the global small-worldness index as a function of the rewiring probability q. Only if the maximum value of S^d for $q \ll 1$ remains comparable to the value characterising the corresponding real-world network, the small-world property can be claimed as a dominant feature of the network's structural makeup. However, the computational expenses involved in such an approach are undoubtedly considerable, even for the typically small and only sparsely connected brain networks available in the literature. Fortunately, our algebraic expression (6.49) for the global total clustering coefficient $\langle \hat{C}^d[\hat{\mathcal{R}}^{dWS}_{n,k,q}] \rangle$ of $\mathcal{R}^{dWS}_{n,k,q}$ obtained earlier in this section opens the door for a more efficient alternative to tackle this problem. In order to formalise this alternative, let us define with

$$\langle S^d(n,k,q) \rangle : \mathbb{N}\times\mathbb{N}\times\mathbb{Q} \to \mathbb{Q}\,, \; \langle S^d(n,k,q) \rangle := \frac{\langle \hat{C}^d[\hat{\mathcal{R}}^{dWS}_{n,k,q}] \rangle \, \langle D \rangle^{dER}}{\langle \hat{C}^d[\hat{\mathcal{R}}^{dER}_{n,2kn}] \rangle \, \langle D \rangle^{dWS}} \tag{6.58}$$

the expectation value of the global small-worldness index as a function of the number of nodes $n \geq 3$, $1 \leq k < \lfloor n/2 \rfloor$ and rewiring probability $0 \leq q \leq 1$. It is important to stress here that $\langle S^d(n,k,q) \rangle$ is not a graph observable in the strict sense of Definition 4.6, as its domain is not the set of finite graphs $\mathbb{G}$. Instead, it provides a measure which is defined in terms of the total global clustering coefficient observables (6.54) for Erdős–Rényi and (6.49) for Watts–Strogatz random digraphs, as well as their classical average geodesic graph distances $\langle D \rangle^{dER}$ and $\langle D \rangle^{dWS}$. Although viable observables for the latter are certainly accessible within our operator graph-theoretical framework, the involved challenges are beyond the scope of this introductory exposé and will only briefly be touched upon in Section 6.7. The lack of an observable for the geodesic distance, however, has little bearing on the validity of the overall argument being developed here. Indeed, with

$$\langle D \rangle^{dER} \sim \frac{\ln[n] - \gamma}{\ln[k/(n-1)]} + \frac{1}{2}, \tag{6.59}$$

where γ denotes the Euler–Mascheroni constant, an analytic expression for the geodesic distance in Erdős–Rényi random digraphs that provides an excellent approximation in the parameter range of relevance for our investigation is readily available [47]. Although a similar expression also exists for $\langle D \rangle^{dWS}$ (see [87]), it unfortunately provides a reasonable approximation only in a very narrow parameter regime for $q \ll 1$ and small k, and will therefore not be considered here. Instead, we will estimate $\langle D \rangle^{dWS}$ from computational realisations of the Watts–Strogatz model, a small but acceptable caveat.

Employing the definition in (6.58), we can now formulate our alternative approach for assessing the prevalence of the small-world property in the structural makeup of real-world networks. To that end, we first note that, by conception of the Watts–Strogatz random graph model, $\langle D \rangle^{dWS}$ is a monotonically decreasing function of q which takes with

$$\min_{q\in[0,1]} [\langle D \rangle^{dWS}] = \langle D \rangle^{dER} \; , \; \max_{q\in[0,1]} [\langle D \rangle^{dWS}] = \langle D \rangle^{\mathcal{C}_{n,k}}$$

its minimum at $q = 1$ and maximum at $q = 0$, where $\langle D\rangle^{\mathscr{C}_{n,k}}$ denotes the average geodesic graph distance of the k-ring graph given in (2.117). The average global small-worldness index is thus necessarily bound, leaving us with

$$\left\langle S^d(n,k,q)\right\rangle_{\min} \le \left\langle S^d(n,k,q)\right\rangle \le \left\langle S^d(n,k,q)\right\rangle_{\max}$$

for arbitrary $q \in [0,1]$, where

$$\left\langle S^d(n,k,q)\right\rangle_{\min} := \frac{\langle \hat{C}^d[\hat{\mathfrak{R}}^{dWS}_{n,k,q}]\rangle\,\langle D\rangle^{dER}}{\langle \hat{C}^d[\hat{\mathfrak{R}}^{dER}_{n,2kn}]\rangle\,\langle D\rangle^{\mathscr{C}_{n,k}}},\quad \left\langle S^d(n,k,q)\right\rangle_{\max} := \frac{\langle \hat{C}^d[\hat{\mathfrak{R}}^{dWS}_{n,k,q}]\rangle}{\langle \hat{C}^d[\hat{\mathfrak{R}}^{dER}_{n,2kn}]\rangle}.$$

By studying the behaviour of $\langle S^d(n,k,q)\rangle_{\min}$, $\langle S^d(n,k,q)\rangle_{\max}$ and $\langle S^d(n,k,q)\rangle$ as function of q for given n and k, we then have access not only to the maximum possible value $S^d_{\max}$ of the average global small-worldness index in graphs with a specific number of nodes and edges, but also to the rewiring probability $q_{S^d_{\max}}$ at which this value is reached, such that

$$S^d_{\max} := \max_{q\in[0,1]} \left\langle S^d(n,k,q)\right\rangle = \left\langle S^d(n,k,q_{S^d_{\max}})\right\rangle \tag{6.60}$$

as illustrated in Fig 6.5a. In a similar fashion, given a relational digraph $\mathscr{G}$ of order n with N_e edges and global small-world index $S^d_{\mathscr{G}}$, a numerical evaluation of the functional behaviour of $\langle S^d(n, \lfloor 1/2 + N_e/2n\rfloor, q)\rangle$ will allow us to estimate the rewiring probability $q_{S^d_{\mathscr{G}}}$ which, under the assumption that $\mathscr{G}$ is a Watts–Strogatz random digraph, yields $S^d_{\mathscr{G}}$ such that

$$\left\langle S^d(n, \lfloor 1/2 + N_e/2n\rfloor, q_{S^d_{\mathscr{G}}})\right\rangle = S^d_{\mathscr{G}}. \tag{6.61}$$

Please note that here, the term $\lfloor 1/2 + N_e/2n\rfloor$ approximates the parameter k in the Watts–Strogatz model from the number of edges N_e of $\mathscr{G}$.

With (6.60) and (6.61), we finally have tools at our disposal not only to compare the small-worldness index of any given real-world graph $\mathscr{G}$ with its maximum possible value, but also to quantify the rewiring probability necessary to obtain the measured value. This approach was applied to a number of biological neural networks [85] and revealed that, for all of these networks, $S^d_{\max}$ is significantly larger than the actual value $S^d_{\mathscr{G}}$, suggesting that their assignment to an arbitrarily defined "borderline" category does not equate to a dominance of the small-world property. This finding is corroborated by the observation that $q_{S^d_{\max}}$ is about one order of magnitude lower than $q_{S^d_{\mathscr{G}}}$ (Fig. 6.5b), suggesting that the structural makeup of brain networks exhibits a dominant random component, or at least that a significant rewiring is required to construct these networks with their measured small-worldness indices according to the Watts–Strogatz model. Challenging the still-prevalent view which discusses brain networks almost exclusively in the context of small-worlds, these novel

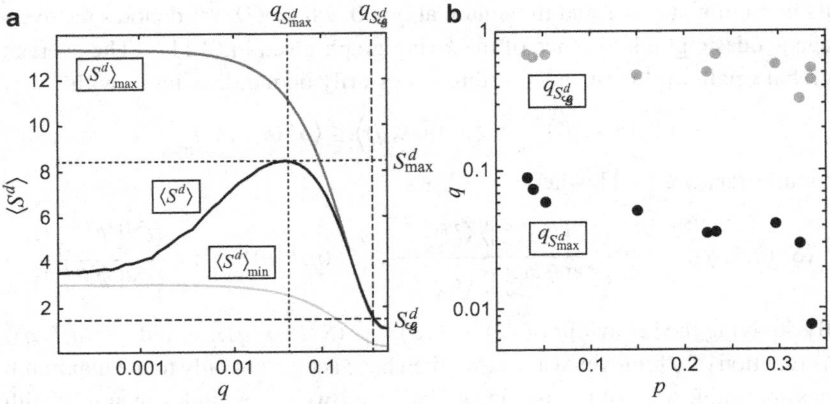

Figure 6.5 Small-worlds in the brain? **a:** Average global small-worldness index $\langle S^d(n,k,q)\rangle$ (black solid) and its bounds (grey solid) as function of the rewiring probability q for a small-world graph with $n = 350$ and $k = 9$. The maximum value $S^d_{\max}$ is here taken at a rewiring probability $q_{S^d_{\max}}$ (dotted), according to (6.60). By comparing these values to the measured small-worldness index $S^d_{\mathcal{G}}$ of a given real-world network $\mathcal{G}$ with the same number of nodes and edges, and the associated rewiring probability $q_{S^d_{\mathcal{G}}}$ (dashed) obtained by applying (6.61), the prevalence of the small-world property can be assessed. The illustrated example (long-distance areal connection network in the macaque brain [82]; data assembled from CoCoMac database [67, 102]; $\mathcal{G}$: $\lambda_d = 1$, $n = 383$, $N_e = 6602$) suggests that $\mathcal{G}$ requires a significant rewiring when constructed according to the Watts–Strogatz random graph model. **b:** Pooled values of $q_{S^d_{\mathcal{G}}}$ and $q_{S^d_{\max}}$ for various brain networks [85]. Interestingly, we find that $q_{S^d_{\mathcal{G}}}$ is about one order of magnitude larger than $q_{S^d_{\max}}$ for all networks considered, suggesting that the structural makeup of brain networks is dominated by a random component and not by the small-world property.

findings might have a significant bearing on the conception of computational models of brain networks, and of our understanding of their functional characteristics in general. The path leading up to these results was made possible by our algebraic expression (6.49) for the global total clustering coefficient of Watts–Strogatz random digraphs, and it certainly can be put on a completely analytic footing once an exact expression for the geodesic graph distance in this model, and thus $\langle S^d(n,k,q)\rangle$, has been made available. The conception of such an expression within our operator graph-theoretical framework does, however, remain as an open challenge, and as invitation to the inspired reader.

6.4 Walks in Gilbert Random Digraphs

So far we considered only observables that are associated with graph measures defined in terms of the adjacency matrix and its second and third powers.

The circulant nature of the adjacency matrix observables for our models of Gilbert and Watts–Strogatz random graphs, however, allows a rigorous access to arbitrary powers and, thus, a much wider spectrum of classical graph measures. In order to exemplify this access and further motivate the potential usefulness of our operator graph-theoretical framework, we will evaluate in this section the number of walks, paths and cycles in Gilbert random digraphs. We will then conclude by demonstrating how the obtained algebraic expressions can be applied to describe the important class of physical phenomena that is governed by a process known as *percolation* in statistical and condensed matter physics.

6.4.1 Number of Walks of Length *m*

Let us first take a look at the number of walks in an arbitrary graph $\mathcal{G} = (\mathcal{N}, \mathcal{E})$ of order n. To that end, we recall from Section 2.2.4 that the mth power of the matrix of adjacency relations $\boldsymbol{A}$ of $\mathcal{G}$ yields an $(n \times n)$-dimensional matrix whose elements $(\boldsymbol{A}^m)_{ij}$ count the number of directed walks of length m between two not necessarily distinct nodes $i, j \in \mathcal{N}$. Denoting with $\mathcal{W}_{ij}^m$ the subset of all possible walks $\mathcal{W}_{ij}$ of length m, we can then define with

$$N_m^{\mathcal{W}} \in \mathbb{N}_0 : N_m^{\mathcal{W}} := \sum_{i,j \in \mathcal{N}} \left|\mathcal{W}_{ij}^m\right| = \sum_{i,j \in \mathcal{N}} (\boldsymbol{A}^m)_{ij}. \tag{6.62}$$

a measure for the total *number of walks* $\mathcal{W}_{ij} \in \mathcal{W}_{ij}^m \subseteq \mathcal{W}_{ij}$ of length $m = |\mathcal{W}_{ij}|$ in $\mathcal{G}$. By distinguishing between diagonal and non-diagonal elements of $\boldsymbol{A}^m$, we further find

$$\begin{aligned} \mathring{N}_m^{\mathcal{W}} \in \mathbb{N}_0 &: \mathring{N}_m^{\mathcal{W}} := \sum_{i \in \mathcal{N}} (\boldsymbol{A}^m)_{ii}, \\ \bar{N}_m^{\mathcal{W}} \in \mathbb{N}_0 &: \bar{N}_m^{\mathcal{W}} := \sum_{\substack{i,j \in \mathcal{N} \\ i \neq j}} (\boldsymbol{A}^m)_{ij} = N_m^{\mathcal{W}} - \mathring{N}_m^{\mathcal{W}} \end{aligned} \tag{6.63}$$

for the number of closed walks of length m, and the number of walks between distinct nodes of $\mathcal{G}$, respectively.

These classical graph measures directly translate into viable observables for suitable operator representations $\hat{\mathcal{G}}$ of $\mathcal{G}$. If we limit ourselves here for the purpose of brevity to relational random graphs, we obtain with

$$\left\langle \hat{N}_m^{\mathcal{W}} \right\rangle : \mathbb{G} \to \mathbb{N}_0 \,,\, \left\langle \hat{N}_m^{\mathcal{W}}[\hat{\mathcal{G}}] \right\rangle = \left\langle N_m^{\mathcal{W}} \right\rangle := \left\langle \mathrm{T}\left[\hat{\mathfrak{a}}[\hat{\mathcal{G}}]^m\right] \right\rangle \tag{6.64}$$

an observable that returns the expected number of walks of length m in terms of the mth power of the adjacency matrix observable $\hat{\mathfrak{a}}[\hat{\mathcal{G}}]$. Similarly,

$$\left\langle \hat{\mathring{N}}_m^{\mathcal{W}} \right\rangle : \mathbb{G} \to \mathbb{N}_0 \,,\, \left\langle \hat{\mathring{N}}_m^{\mathcal{W}}[\hat{\mathcal{G}}] \right\rangle = \left\langle \mathring{N}_m^{\mathcal{W}} \right\rangle := \left\langle \mathrm{Tr}\left[\hat{\mathfrak{a}}[\hat{\mathcal{G}}]^m\right] \right\rangle, \tag{6.65}$$

$$\left\langle \hat{\bar{N}}_m^{\mathcal{W}} \right\rangle : \mathbb{G} \to \mathbb{N}_0, \left\langle \hat{\bar{N}}_m^{\mathcal{W}}[\hat{\mathscr{G}}] \right\rangle = \left\langle \bar{N}_m^{\mathcal{W}} \right\rangle := \left\langle \hat{N}_m^{\mathcal{W}} \right\rangle - \left\langle \hat{\mathring{N}}_m^{\mathcal{W}} \right\rangle \tag{6.66}$$

define two observables which deliver the expectation values of $\mathring{N}_m^{\mathcal{W}}$ and $\bar{N}_m^{\mathcal{W}}$.

In order to demonstrate the application of (6.64)–(6.66), let us evaluate the number of walks in Gilbert random digraphs. To that end, we recall our operator representation $\hat{\mathscr{R}}_{n,p}^{dG}$ of this model from Section 5.2.2, and find

$$\left(\hat{\mathfrak{a}}[\hat{\mathscr{R}}_{n,p}^{dG}]^m\right)_{rs} = \mathfrak{r}^{p^m}\left[\left(\boldsymbol{\Delta}_{\mathcal{I}_n^{dG}}^{n\times n}\right)^m\right] \tag{6.67}$$

for the mth power of its adjacency matrix observable $\hat{\mathfrak{a}}[\hat{\mathscr{R}}_{n,p}^{dG}]$ after employing (4.45). The right-hand side of (6.67) can now be readily treated using the circulant diagonalisation theorem. Indeed, with (6.38) we already obtained an algebraic expression for arbitrary powers of the circulant Boolean matrix $\boldsymbol{\Delta}_{\mathcal{I}_n^{dG}}^{n\times n}$. This expression invites further simplification by recognising that

$$\mathrm{Im}\left[\exp\left[-\frac{2\pi i}{n}(l-1)(r-s)\right]\right] = -\,\mathrm{Im}\left[\exp\left[-\frac{2\pi i}{n}(n-l+1)(r-s)\right]\right]$$

for $l \in [2, \lfloor (n+1)/2 \rfloor]$ and $r \neq s$, and that

$$\mathrm{Im}\left[\exp\left[-\frac{2\pi i}{n}(l-1)(r-s)\right]\right] = 0$$

for $l = 1 + n/2$, $n \in 2\mathbb{N}$ and $r \neq s$, where $\mathrm{Im}[x]$ denotes the imaginary part of $x \in \mathbb{C}$. With this, the elements of $(\boldsymbol{\Delta}_{\mathcal{I}_n^{dG}}^{n\times n})^m$ take the form

$$\left(\left(\boldsymbol{\Delta}_{\mathcal{I}_n^{dG}}^{n\times n}\right)^m\right)_{rs} = \frac{(n-1)^m}{n} + \frac{(-1)^m}{n}\sum_{l=2}^{n}\cos\left[\frac{2\pi}{n}(l-1)(r-s)\right] = \frac{(n-1)^m}{n} - \frac{(-1)^m}{n}$$

for $r \neq s$, and

$$\left(\left(\boldsymbol{\Delta}_{\mathcal{I}_n^{dG}}^{n\times n}\right)^m\right)_{rr} = \frac{(n-1)^m}{n} + (-1)^m\frac{n-1}{n}$$

for diagonal elements. By utilising (4.43), we then obtain

$$\left\langle \mathrm{T}\left[\hat{\mathfrak{a}}[\hat{\mathscr{R}}_{n,p}^{dG}]^m\right]\right\rangle = p^m \sum_{\substack{r,s=1 \\ r\neq s}}^{n}\left(\frac{(n-1)^m}{n} - \frac{(-1)^m}{n}\right) + p^m\sum_{r=1}^{n}\left(\frac{(n-1)^m}{n} + (-1)^m\frac{n-1}{n}\right),$$

which finally delivers

$$\left\langle \hat{N}_m^{\mathcal{W}}[\hat{\mathscr{R}}_{n,p}^{dG}]\right\rangle = p^m n(n-1)^m \tag{6.68}$$

for the expected total number of walks of length m in a Gilbert random digraph of order n and connectedness p. In a similarly straightforward fashion, we find

$$\begin{aligned}\left\langle \hat{\mathring{N}}_m^{\mathcal{W}}[\hat{\mathscr{R}}_{n,p}^{dG}]\right\rangle &= p^m(n-1)^m + (-1)^m p^m (n-1),\\ \left\langle \hat{\bar{N}}_m^{\mathcal{W}}[\hat{\mathscr{R}}_{n,p}^{dG}]\right\rangle &= p^m(n-1)^{m+1} - (-1)^m p^m (n-1)\end{aligned} \tag{6.69}$$

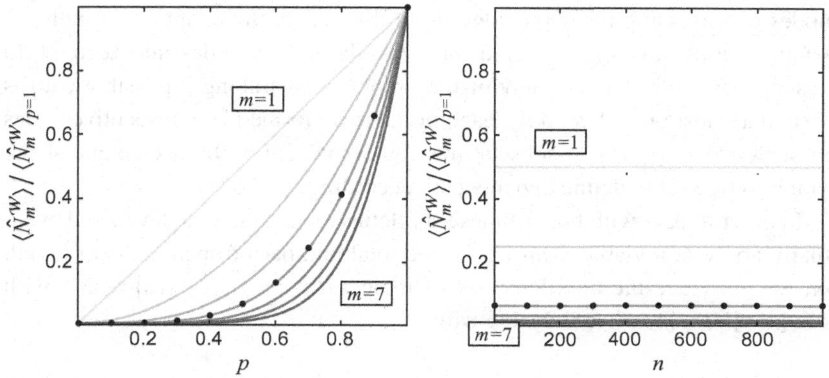

Figure 6.6 Expectation value of the relative number of walks of length $1 \leq m \leq 7$ in Gilbert random digraphs $\mathscr{R}_{n,p}^{dG}$ as function of connectedness p (left) and number of nodes n (right). For some models, results of a statistical analysis of 100 computational realisations are shown (black dots; mean ± SD). Parameters for numerical models: $n = 100$, $m = 4$ (left); $m = 4$, $p = 0.5$ (right).

for the expected number of closed walks of length m and walks connecting distinct nodes in $\mathscr{R}_{n,p}^{dG}$.

The functional behaviour of the relative number of walks, defined here conveniently as $\langle \hat{N}_m^W[\hat{\mathscr{R}}_{n,p}^{dG}]\rangle / \langle \hat{N}_m^W[\hat{\mathscr{R}}_{n,1}^{dG}]\rangle$, for some representative parameter sets is shown in Fig. 6.6. The illustrated results also apply to the relative number of closed walks of length $m \geq 2$. In the special case $m = 1$, we find as expected

$$\left\langle \hat{N}_1^W[\hat{\mathscr{R}}_{n,p}^{dG}] \right\rangle = pn(n-1) = \left\langle \hat{A}[\hat{\mathscr{R}}_{n,p}^{dG}] \right\rangle,$$

as well as

$$\left\langle \hat{\mathring{N}}_1^W[\hat{\mathscr{R}}_{n,p}^{dG}] \right\rangle = 0$$

in accordance with the fact that closed walks in a not self-looped graph must have a length of at least 2. Finally, we note that for $m \geq 2$ and large n, the number of closed walks is dominated by the first term in (6.69) such that $\langle \hat{\mathring{N}}_m^W[\hat{\mathscr{R}}_{n,p}^{dG}]\rangle \sim (pn)^m$.

6.4.2 Number of Paths of Length *m*

Let us next consider the total number of paths of length m that visit $m + 1$ distinct nodes in a graph of order $n \geq m + 1$. Here we face two immediate combinatorial challenges. Firstly, in contrast to walks which, according to the definition in (2.52), are not subject to any constraints in regard to revisiting nodes or traversing the same edge more than once, the counting of paths of length m must take only ordered $(m + 1)$-subsets of n nodes into account, to ensure that each node and any of the graph's edges along a possible path is visited at most once. Secondly, each of the pairs formed by consecutive nodes in such ordered $(m + 1)$-subsets must be associated with an element of the graph's edge set to define a viable path according to (2.53).

In order to deal with both of these subtleties on an algebraic level, and eventually arrive at a viable measure for the total number of open paths of length m, we introduce the unordered set of indices $\mathcal{I}^m := \{i_1, \ldots, i_m\} \in \mathbb{N}^m$ with $i_l \in [1, n]\ \forall l \in [1, m]$, and denote with

$$\mathfrak{C}_2(\mathcal{I}^m) := \left\{\{i_l, i_{l'}\} : i_l, i_{l'} \in \mathcal{I}^m, l \neq l'\right\} \tag{6.70}$$

the set of all 2-combinations over $\mathcal{I}^m$ – that is, the set of all unordered pairs of distinct elements of $\mathcal{I}^m$ such that $|\mathfrak{C}_2(\mathcal{I}^m)| = \binom{m}{2}$. We can then define with

$$\boldsymbol{\delta} : \mathbb{N}^m \to \mathbb{B}\ ,\ \boldsymbol{\delta}[\mathcal{I}^m] := \prod_{(i_l, i_{l'}) \in \mathfrak{C}_2(\mathcal{I}^m)} \delta[i_l - i_{l'}] \tag{6.71}$$

and

$$\bar{\boldsymbol{\delta}} : \mathbb{N}^m \to \mathbb{B}\ ,\ \bar{\boldsymbol{\delta}}[\mathcal{I}^m] := \prod_{(i_l, i_{l'}) \in \mathfrak{C}_2(\mathcal{I}^m)} \left(1 - \delta[i_l - i_{l'}]\right) \tag{6.72}$$

generalisations of the Kronecker delta operator (3.28) and its inverse (3.30) for index sets $\mathcal{I}^m$. The product on the right-hand side of (6.71) is non-zero if and only if both elements in all pairs of indices of $\mathfrak{C}_2(\mathcal{I}^m)$ are equal – that is, iff $i_l = i_{l'}\ \forall l, l' \in [1, m] : l \neq l'$. Similarly, and more importantly, (6.72) returns zero whenever the two elements in at least one pair of indices of $\mathfrak{C}_2(\mathcal{I}^m)$ are equal, and one if and only if all indices in the set $\mathcal{I}^m$ are distinct.

By distinguishing all m-subsets of n nodes from the n^m possible index sets $\mathcal{I}^m$, the operator $\bar{\boldsymbol{\delta}}$ provides the algebraic means to address the first of the combinatorial challenges mentioned above. What remains now is to determine whether any of these subsets itself forms a path through the graph. Instead of considering a combination of edges formed by pairs of consecutive nodes, however, we will here directly utilise the graph's matrix of adjacency relations $\boldsymbol{A}$. For example, the product $A_{i_1 i_2} A_{i_2 i_3}$ of two of its elements does yield one if and only if a walk from node i_1 to node i_3 visiting an intermediate node i_2 exists. The sum over index i_2 then necessarily counts the number of walks of length 2 between node i_1 and i_3. By restricting the summation to nodes $i_1 \neq i_2$, $i_2 \neq i_3$ and $i_1 \neq i_3$ through the utilisation of $\bar{\boldsymbol{\delta}}[\mathcal{I}^3]$ with $\mathcal{I}^3 = \{i_1, i_2, i_3\}$, only walks visiting distinct nodes – that is, paths of length 2 between distinct nodes i_1 and i_3 – will be counted. The restricted summation over all $i_1, i_2, i_3 \in [1, n]$

then delivers the total number of paths of length 2 between distinct nodes in a given graph of order n. Generalising this argument, we eventually find

$$N_m^{\mathcal{P}} \in \mathbb{N}_0 : N_m^{\mathcal{P}} := \sum_{\substack{i,j \in \mathcal{N} \\ i \neq j}} |\mathscr{P}_{ij}^m| = \sum_{i_1,\ldots,i_{m+1}=1}^{n} \bar{\delta}[\mathcal{I}^{m+1}] \prod_{l=1}^{m} (\boldsymbol{A})_{i_l i_{l+1}} \tag{6.73}$$

as the measure for the total *number of paths* $\mathcal{P}_{ij} \in \mathscr{P}_{ij}^m \subseteq \mathscr{P}_{ij} : i \neq j$ in a graph $\mathcal{G} = (\mathcal{N}, \mathcal{E})$. It is important to remember here that (6.73) corresponds for directed graphs to the frequency of occurrence $\bar{F}_{m+1}^d$ of paths defined in (2.79), but that it has to be distinguished from the frequency $\bar{F}_{m+1}^{ud}$ defined in (2.77) for undirected graphs, as for each existing path between distinct nodes, there is an isomorphic reciprocal path which counts towards $N_m^{\mathcal{P}}$ but not $\bar{F}_{m+1}^{ud}$.

Focusing again exclusively on operator representations $\hat{\mathcal{G}}$ of relational random graphs $\mathcal{G}$ of order $n \geq m+1$, the classical measure (6.73) can immediately be translated into a viable graph observable

$$\langle \hat{N}_m^{\mathcal{P}} \rangle : \mathbb{G} \to \mathbb{N}_0 , \langle \hat{N}_m^{\mathcal{P}}[\hat{\mathcal{G}}] \rangle = \langle N_m^{\mathcal{P}} \rangle := \Big\langle \sum_{i_1,\ldots,i_{m+1}=1}^{n} \bar{\delta}[\mathcal{I}^{m+1}] \prod_{l=1}^{m} \big(\hat{a}[\hat{\mathcal{G}}]\big)_{i_l i_{l+1}} \Big\rangle \tag{6.74}$$

for the expected number of paths of length m visiting $m + 1$ distinct nodes. Although a direct evaluation of (6.74) is certainly possible for most random graph models with an available adjacency matrix observable, let us briefly explore an interesting simplification which will, at least in some cases, allow to express $\langle \hat{N}_m^{\mathcal{P}} \rangle$ in terms of the expected number of paths of length $m-1$. To that end, we consider the two index sets $\mathcal{I}^m = \{i_1, \ldots, i_m\}$ and $\mathcal{I}^{m+1} = \{i_1, \ldots, i_{m+1}\}$. By careful inspection, it can be shown that

$$\mathfrak{C}_2(\mathcal{I}^{m+1}) = \left\{ \begin{array}{ccc} \{i_1, i_2\}, \{i_1, i_3\}, \ldots, & \{i_1, i_m\} \;, & \{i_1, i_{m+1}\} \;, \\ \{i_2, i_3\}, \ldots, & \{i_2, i_m\} \;, & \{i_2, i_{m+1}\} \;, \\ & & \vdots \\ & \{i_{m-1}, i_m\}, & \{i_{m-1}, i_{m+1}\}, \\ & & \{i_m, i_{m+1}\} \end{array} \right\}$$

$$= \mathfrak{C}_2(\mathcal{I}^m) \cup \big\{\mathcal{I}^m \times \{i_{m+1}\}\big\} = \mathfrak{C}_2(\mathcal{I}^m) \cup \big\{\{i_l, i_{m+1}\} : l \in [1, m]\big\},$$

which then leads to the useful identity

$$\bar{\delta}[\mathcal{I}^{m+1}] = \bar{\delta}[\mathcal{I}^m] \prod_{l=1}^{m} \big(1 - \delta[i_l - i_{m+1}]\big) \tag{6.75}$$

satisfied by the Kronecker delta operator (6.72). Employing this identity on the right-hand side of the definition (6.74), we find

$$\langle \hat{N}_m^{\mathcal{P}}[\hat{\mathcal{G}}] \rangle = \Big\langle \sum_{i_1,\ldots,i_{m+1}=1}^{n} \bar{\delta}[\mathcal{I}^m] \Big(\prod_{l=1}^{m-1} \big(\hat{a}[\hat{\mathcal{G}}]\big)_{i_l i_{l+1}} \Big) \Big(\prod_{l=1}^{m} \big(1 - \delta[i_l - i_{m+1}]\big) \Big) \big(\hat{a}[\hat{\mathcal{G}}]\big)_{i_m i_{m+1}} \Big\rangle$$

$$
\begin{aligned}
&= \Big\langle \sum_{i_1,\dots,i_{m+1}=1}^{n} \bar{\delta}[\mathcal{I}^m]\Big(\prod_{l=1}^{m-1}\big(\hat{a}[\hat{\mathcal{G}}]\big)_{i_l i_{l+1}}\Big)\Big(1-\sum_{l=1}^{m}\delta[i_l-i_{m+1}]\Big)\big(\hat{a}[\hat{\mathcal{G}}]\big)_{i_m i_{m+1}}\Big\rangle \\
&= \Big\langle \sum_{i_1,\dots,i_m=1}^{n} \bar{\delta}[\mathcal{I}^m]\Big(\prod_{l=1}^{m-1}\big(\hat{a}[\hat{\mathcal{G}}]\big)_{i_l i_{l+1}}\Big)\sum_{i_{m+1}=1}^{n}\big(\hat{a}[\hat{\mathcal{G}}]\big)_{i_m i_{m+1}}\Big\rangle \\
&\quad - \Big\langle \sum_{i_1,\dots,i_m=1}^{n} \bar{\delta}[\mathcal{I}^m]\Big(\prod_{l=1}^{m-1}\big(\hat{a}[\hat{\mathcal{G}}]\big)_{i_l i_{l+1}}\Big)\sum_{l=1}^{m}\big(\hat{a}[\hat{\mathcal{G}}]\big)_{i_m i_l}\Big\rangle. \qquad (6.76)
\end{aligned}
$$

Here we recognised in the second step that all terms with two or more factors $\delta[i_l - i_{m+1}]$ in the argument of the sum necessarily vanish and, in the last step, performed the sum over i_{m+1}. To show the former, it suffices to consider terms of second order. Without loss of generality, let $l' \le l'' \le m$. We then have

$$
\begin{aligned}
&\sum_{i_1,\dots,i_{m+1}=1}^{n} \bar{\delta}[\mathcal{I}^m]\Big(\prod_{l=1}^{m-1}\big(\hat{a}[\hat{\mathcal{G}}]\big)_{i_l i_{l+1}}\Big)\Big(\prod_{l=1}^{m-1}\big(\hat{a}[\hat{\mathcal{G}}]\big)_{i_l i_{l+1}}\Big)\Big(\prod_{\substack{l=1\\ l\neq l',l''}}^{m}\big(1-\delta[i_l-i_{m+1}]\big)\Big) \\
&\qquad \times \delta[i_{l'}-i_{m+1}]\delta[i_{l''}-i_{m+1}]\big(\hat{a}[\hat{\mathcal{G}}]\big)_{i_m i_{m+1}} \\
&= \sum_{i_1,\dots,i_m=1}^{n} \bar{\delta}[\mathcal{I}^m]\Big(\prod_{l=1}^{m-1}\big(\hat{a}[\hat{\mathcal{G}}]\big)_{i_l i_{l+1}}\Big)\Big(\prod_{l=1}^{m-1}\big(\hat{a}[\hat{\mathcal{G}}]\big)_{i_l i_{l+1}}\Big)\Big(\prod_{\substack{l=1\\ l\neq l',l''}}^{m}\big(1-\delta[i_l-i_{m+1}]\big)\Big) \\
&\qquad \times \delta[i_{l'}-i_{l''}]\big(\hat{a}[\hat{\mathcal{G}}]\big)_{i_m i_{l'}}
\end{aligned}
$$

after performing the sum over i_{m+1}. As $l' \le l'' \le m$, the factor $\delta[i_{l'} - i_{l''}]$ forces at least one index pair with identical elements in $\bar{\delta}[\mathcal{I}^m]$ which, by definition (6.72), must yield zero. This argument holds for all terms of second order in $\delta[i_l - i_{m+1}]$ and, as all higher orders contain at least one such term, for all orders larger than two such that $\prod_{l=1}^{m}(1-\delta[i_l-i_{m+1}]) \to (1-\sum_{l=1}^{m}\delta[i_l-i_{m+1}])$.

In the case of the directed Gilbert random graph model and its adjacency matrix observable (5.67), we first recognise that $(\hat{a}[\hat{\mathcal{R}}^{dG}_{n,p}])_{i_m i_{m+1}} = 1$ with probability p for any given i_m and each $i_{m+1} \in [1,n] : i_{m+1} \neq i_m$, and zero otherwise. The sum over i_{m+1} thus yields a total of $(n-1)$ contributions, each with probability p. Moreover, as $\bar{\delta}[\mathcal{I}^m]$ ensures that all indices $i_l, l \in [1,m]$ are distinct, we find that $(\hat{a}[\hat{\mathcal{R}}^{dG}_{n,p}])_{i_m i_l} = 1$ with probability p for each given i_m and $l \neq m$ such that the sum over l yields a total of $(m-1)$ contributions, each again with probability p. With this, the right-hand side of (6.76) then simplifies to

$$
\big\langle \hat{N}^{\mathcal{P}}_m[\hat{\mathcal{R}}^{dG}_{n,p}]\big\rangle = p\big((n-1)-(m-1)\big)\Big\langle \sum_{i_1,\dots,i_m=1}^{n}\bar{\delta}[\mathcal{I}^m]\Big(\prod_{l=1}^{m-1}\big(\hat{a}[\hat{\mathcal{R}}^{dG}_{n,p}]\big)_{i_l i_{l+1}}\Big)\Big\rangle,
$$

and eventually yields the recursive expression

$$
\big\langle \hat{N}^{\mathcal{P}}_m[\hat{\mathcal{R}}^{dG}_{n,p}]\big\rangle = p(n-m)\big\langle \hat{N}^{\mathcal{P}}_{m-1}[\hat{\mathcal{R}}^{dG}_{n,p}]\big\rangle \qquad (6.77)
$$

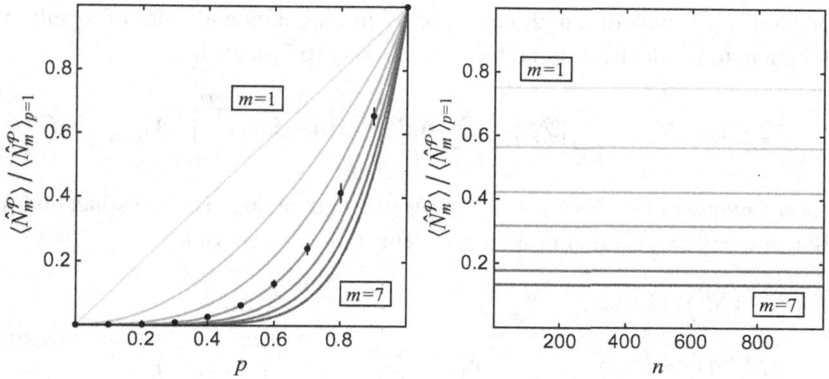

Figure 6.7 Expectation value of the relative number $\langle \hat{N}_m^{\mathcal{P}}[\hat{\mathcal{R}}_{n,p}^{dG}]\rangle / \langle \hat{N}_m^{\mathcal{P}}[\hat{\mathcal{R}}_{n,1}^{dG}]\rangle$ of paths of length $1 \leq m \leq 7$ visiting $m + 1$ nodes in Gilbert random digraphs as function of connectedness p (left) and number of nodes $n \geq m + 1$ (right). For a model with $n = 32$ and $m = 4$, the result of a statistical analysis of 100 computational realisations is shown (black dots; mean ± SD).

for the expected number of paths of length m in $\mathcal{R}_{n,p}^{dG}$. An explicit form of (6.77) can be readily obtained by observing that

$$\left\langle \hat{N}_m^{\mathcal{P}}[\hat{\mathcal{R}}_{n,p}^{dG}]\right\rangle = \left(\prod_{l=2}^{m} p(n-l)\right)\left\langle \hat{N}_1^{\mathcal{P}}[\hat{\mathcal{R}}_{n,p}^{dG}]\right\rangle = p^{m-1}\frac{\Gamma[n-1]}{\Gamma[n-m]}\left\langle \hat{N}_1^{\mathcal{P}}[\hat{\mathcal{R}}_{n,p}^{dG}]\right\rangle,$$

and by noting that $\langle \hat{N}_1^{\mathcal{P}}[\hat{\mathcal{R}}_{n,p}^{dG}]\rangle$ equals the expected total adjacency of the Gilbert model. With (6.4), we finally find

$$\left\langle \hat{N}_m^{\mathcal{P}}[\hat{\mathcal{R}}_{n,p}^{dG}]\right\rangle = p^{m-1}\frac{\Gamma[n-1]}{\Gamma[n-m]}\left\langle \hat{A}[\hat{\mathcal{R}}_{n,p}^{dG}]\right\rangle = p^{m}\frac{\Gamma[n+1]}{\Gamma[n-m]} \qquad (6.78)$$

for the average number of paths of length m that visit $m+1$ nodes in Gilbert random digraphs of order n and connection probability p. The functional behaviour of the relative number of such paths for some representative parameter sets is illustrated in Fig. 6.7.

6.4.3 Number of Cycles of Length *m*

With (6.73), (6.74) and (6.76) for the total number of paths at our disposal, we can now proceed and also conceive of a measure which delivers the number of cycles in a given graph. To that end, we recall from Section 2.2.4 that a cycle of length m is defined as a closed path of length m visiting m distinct nodes. Such a cycle is constructed by either adding one more edge connecting both endnodes to a path of length $m-1$, or by forcing both endnodes of a path of length m to be identical. In both cases, utilising (6.73), we find

$$N_m^{\mathcal{C}} \in \mathbb{N}_0 : N_m^{\mathcal{C}} := \sum_{i \in \mathcal{N}} \left|\mathscr{P}_{ii}^m\right| = \sum_{i_1,\ldots,i_{m+1}=1}^{n} \bar{\delta}[\mathcal{I}^{m+1}]\delta[i_1 - i_{m+1}] \prod_{l=1}^{m} (\boldsymbol{A})_{i_l i_{l+1}} \tag{6.79}$$

for the *number of cycles* $\mathcal{P}_{ii} \in \mathscr{P}_{ii}^m \subseteq \mathscr{P}_{ii}$ of length m that visit m distinct nodes in a graph $\mathcal{G} = (\mathcal{N}, \mathcal{E})$ of order $n \geq m$. This immediately yields

$$\begin{aligned} &\left\langle \hat{N}_m^{\mathcal{C}} \right\rangle : \mathbb{G} \to \mathbb{N}_0 \\ &\left\langle \hat{N}_m^{\mathcal{C}}[\hat{\mathcal{G}}] \right\rangle = \left\langle N_m^{\mathcal{C}} \right\rangle := \left\langle \sum_{i_1,\ldots,i_{m+1}=1}^{n} \bar{\delta}[\mathcal{I}^{m+1}]\delta[i_1 - i_{m+1}] \prod_{l=1}^{m} \left(\hat{\boldsymbol{a}}[\hat{\mathcal{G}}]\right)_{i_l i_{l+1}} \right\rangle \end{aligned} \tag{6.80}$$

as an observable that returns the expectation value of $N_m^{\mathcal{C}}$ when applied to operator representations $\hat{\mathcal{G}}$ of relational random graphs $\mathcal{G}$.

Similar to (6.74), the graph observable (6.80) can be represented in a somewhat more convenient form that will eventually allow us to express $\langle \hat{N}_m^{\mathcal{C}} \rangle$ in terms of the expected number of cycles of length $m-1$. Following the argumentation which, together with identity (6.75), led to (6.76), we find, after a lengthy yet straightforward calculation,

$$\begin{aligned} \left\langle \hat{N}_m^{\mathcal{C}}[\hat{\mathcal{G}}] \right\rangle = &\left\langle \sum_{i_1,\ldots,i_m=1}^{n} \bar{\delta}[\mathcal{I}^m] \left(\prod_{l=1}^{m-1} \left(\hat{\boldsymbol{a}}[\hat{\mathcal{G}}]\right)_{i_l i_{l+1}} \right) \left(\hat{\boldsymbol{a}}[\hat{\mathcal{G}}]\right)_{i_m i_1} \right\rangle \\ &- \left\langle \sum_{i_1,\ldots,i_m=1}^{n} \bar{\delta}[\mathcal{I}^m] \left(\prod_{l=1}^{m-1} \left(\hat{\boldsymbol{a}}[\hat{\mathcal{G}}]\right)_{i_l i_{l+1}} \right) \sum_{l=1}^{m} \delta[i_l - i_1] \left(\hat{\boldsymbol{a}}[\hat{\mathcal{G}}]\right)_{i_m i_1} \right\rangle. \end{aligned}$$

In the case of $\mathscr{R}_{n,p}^{dG}$, we again have $(\hat{\boldsymbol{a}}[\hat{\mathscr{R}}_{n,p}^{dG}])_{i_m i_1} = 1$ with probability p for each $i_1, i_m \in [1, n] : i_1 \neq i_m$ and zero otherwise, such that the first term in the last expression yields a non-zero contribution with probability p. The second term on the right-hand side must necessarily vanish as the presence of $\bar{\delta}[\mathcal{I}^m]$ ensures that $i_l \neq i_1$ for all $l \in [1, m]$, such that $\delta[i_l - i_1] = 0 \, \forall i_1, i_l \in [1, n]$. Recalling with (6.74) our graph observable for the expected number of paths of given length, this then yields

$$\left\langle \hat{N}_m^{\mathcal{C}}[\hat{\mathscr{R}}_{n,p}^{dG}] \right\rangle = p \left\langle \sum_{i_1,\ldots,i_m=1}^{n} \bar{\delta}[\mathcal{I}^m] \left(\prod_{l=1}^{m-1} \left(\hat{\boldsymbol{a}}[\hat{\mathcal{G}}]\right)_{i_l i_{l+1}} \right) \right\rangle = p \left\langle \hat{N}_{m-1}^{\mathcal{P}}[\hat{\mathscr{R}}_{n,p}^{dG}] \right\rangle,$$

and delivers together with (6.77) the recursion

$$\left\langle \hat{N}_m^{\mathcal{C}}[\hat{\mathscr{R}}_{n,p}^{dG}] \right\rangle = p(n - m + 1) \left\langle \hat{N}_{m-1}^{\mathcal{C}}[\hat{\mathscr{R}}_{n,p}^{dG}] \right\rangle \tag{6.81}$$

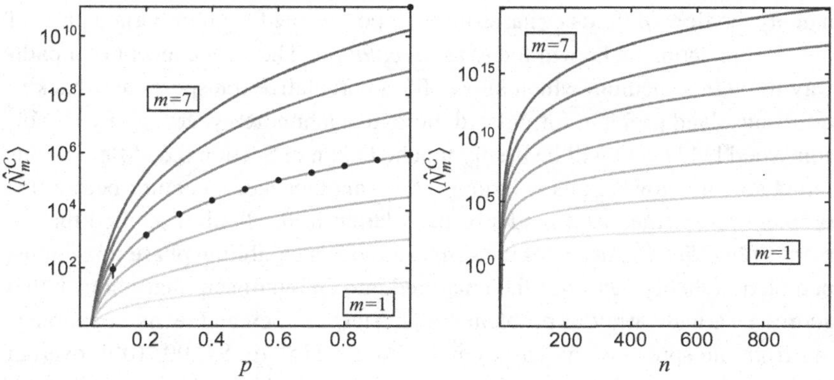

Figure 6.8 Expectation value of the number $\langle \hat{N}^C_m[\hat{\mathcal{R}}^{dG}_{n,p}]\rangle$ of cycles of length m in Gilbert random digraphs as function of connectedness p (left) and number of nodes n (right). For a model with $n = 32$ and $m = 4$, the result of a statistical analysis of 100 computational realisations is shown (black dots; mean ± SD).

for the expectation value of the number of cycles of length m in directed Gilbert random graphs $\mathcal{R}^{dG}_{n,p}$. Similar to the number of paths (6.77), an explicit expression can also be obtained from (6.81) by recognising that

$$\left\langle \hat{N}^C_m[\hat{\mathcal{R}}^{dG}_{n,p}]\right\rangle = \left(\prod_{l=2}^{m-1} p(n-l)\right)\left\langle \hat{N}^C_2[\hat{\mathcal{R}}^{dG}_{n,p}]\right\rangle = p^{m-2}\frac{\Gamma[n-1]}{\Gamma[n-m+1]}\left\langle \hat{N}^C_2[\hat{\mathcal{R}}^{dG}_{n,p}]\right\rangle,$$

and by noting that $\langle \hat{N}^C_2[\hat{\mathcal{R}}^{dG}_{n,p}]\rangle = 2\langle \hat{N}_{se}[\hat{\mathcal{R}}^{dG}_{n,p}]\rangle$. With (6.15), this finally yields

$$\left\langle \hat{N}^C_m[\hat{\mathcal{R}}^{dG}_{n,p}]\right\rangle = p^m \frac{\Gamma[n+1]}{\Gamma[n-m+1]} \qquad (6.82)$$

for the expected number of cycles of length m in $\mathcal{R}^{dG}_{n,p}$. The functional behaviour of (6.82) is illustrated in Fig. 6.8. We note that, as in the case of walks and paths earlier, the order of graphs used in all computational models is deliberately kept small because, firstly, no exact results exist yet in the literature for graphs of low order and, secondly, the computational search for specific walks constitutes a well-known NP-hard problem requiring significant resources even for graphs of modest size. Given these dire circumstances, the observed match between numerical models and our algebraic results then provides further support for the usefulness of our operator graph-theoretical perspective.

6.4.4 Application: Percolation in Porous Media

In order to strengthen this point, let us conclude this section by presenting an interesting application in the field of statistical and condensed matter physics, namely the flow of fluids or gases through porous media, an important class of physical phenomena known today as *percolation*. The very concept of a pathway through a medium which allows for a percolative transport dates back to a still-unsolved problem formulated more than a hundred years ago by DeVolson Wood [111], and will be briefly touched upon in Section 6.6. After various failed attempts towards its solution, it took another half a century before this problem re-emerged as a model of percolation in the field of applied mathematics [24, 25, 58]. As one of the simplest models exhibiting phase transitions, percolation theory has since then matured into an interdisciplinary branch that addresses a wide array of problems in physics, biology and technology, ranging from the spread of epidemics and wildfires [15, 79, 84, 90, 106], over an assessment of the robustness of real-world networks [28], to the study of integrated circuitry [50] (for general reviews, see [37, 86, 98]).

Describing porous media as relational graphs with randomly interconnected nodes, a system was originally conceived of as percolating once a path spanning two spatially defined sides of the system exists [25, 58]. This notion has seen several simplifications in the literature since then, most notably the assumption of infinite system size and the identification of the percolative phase transition with the emergence of a giant connected component spanning the graph, in order to not only deal with a variety of mathematical caveats, but to also circumvent the combinatorially hard problem of finding paths through finite graphs in computational approaches (see [52, 105] for thorough reviews). However, with the exact algebraic expressions (6.78) and (6.78) for the number of paths and cycles in finite Gilbert random digraphs at our disposal, we can now revisit the original conception of the percolation phenomenon and, with two different models, propose its mathematically rigorous formalisation.

In the first model, we consider paths of length $n - 1$ that visit all n nodes in a Gilbert random digraph $\mathscr{R}^{dG}_{n,p}$. Such paths are called Hamiltonian paths (see Section 2.2.4), and with (6.78) we find their expected number to be

$$\left\langle \hat{N}^{\mathcal{P}}_{n-1}[\hat{\mathscr{R}}^{dG}_{n,p}] \right\rangle = p^{n-1}\Gamma[n+1]. \tag{6.83}$$

One can now assert that, for percolation to occur, at least one Hamiltonian path must exist, and thus, ask for which connectedness $p = p_c$ the expected number $\langle \hat{N}^{\mathcal{P}}_{n-1}[\hat{\mathscr{R}}^{dG}_{n,p}] \rangle = 1$. With (6.83), we then obtain

$$p_c = \Gamma[n+1]^{-1/(n-1)} \tag{6.84}$$

for the *critical percolation threshold* of Gilbert random digraphs. In the asymptotic limit of large graphs, p_c furnishes with

$$p_c \overset{n\to\infty}{\to} \mathrm{e}^{(n+1)/(n-1)}(2\pi)^{-1/2(n-1)}(n+1)^{-(2n+1)/2(n-1)} \sim \frac{1}{n} \tag{6.85}$$

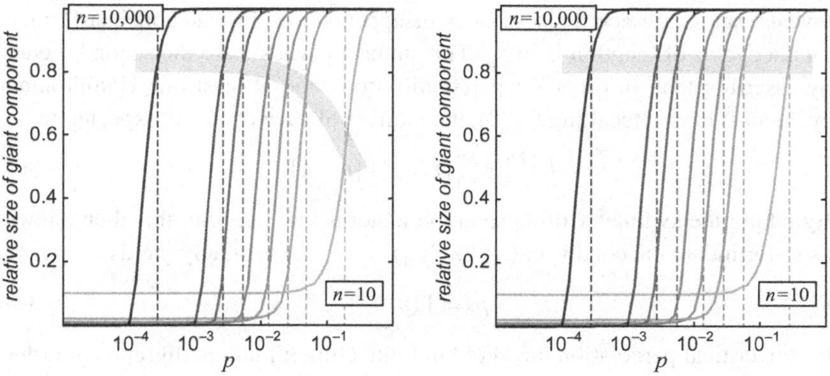

Figure 6.9 Percolation in directed Gilbert random graphs $\mathscr{R}^{dG}_{n,p}$. The relative size of the giant connected component is shown as a function of the connectivity p for $n \in \{10, 50, 100, 200, 500, 1{,}000, 10{,}000\}$ (grey solid). Respective values for the critical percolation threshold p_c (grey dashed) were obtained from (6.84) and (6.87) by considering Hamiltonian paths (left) and Hamiltonian cycles (right). The size of all giant connected components was retrieved from computational models (average over 1,000 realisations; 100 realisations for $n = 10{,}000$) for each parameter set. The grey areas mark the interpolated intersection of p_c with the percolative phase transitions observed in computational models.

a scaling behaviour that is in accordance with the well-known classical result for random graphs in statistical physics [3]. However, in order to compare (6.84) with the connectedness at which a dominating giant connected component emerges, an approach commonly followed to characterise percolation in finite graphs, one must resort to computational models. Such models show that p_c resides well within the sharp sigmoidal-shaped phase transition which marks the emergence of a giant component (Fig. 6.9, left), thus suggesting that the use of Hamiltonian paths constitutes a viable method for identifying and quantifying percolative phase transitions in Gilbert random digraphs. Interestingly, the relative size of the giant component at the critical threshold varies here with graph size, especially in smaller graphs (Fig. 6.9, left, grey band). The reason for this behaviour can be attributed to our conception of the expected number of paths itself. Indeed, (6.74) considers all node pairs as possible endpoints of paths, and therefore must necessarily overcount the Hamiltonian paths which are required for percolation to occur.

It can easily be argued that this overcounting of Hamiltonian paths in our first model will result in an underestimation of the critical percolation threshold p_c when compared to the phase transition marking the emergence of a giant connected component in computational models. However, further investigation reveals that the observed discrepancy disappears if we instead consider Hamiltonian cycles of length n in $\mathscr{R}^{dG}_{n,p}$. This naturally leads us to the second model by asserting that, in order for percolation to occur, at least one Hamiltonian cycle must exist. Recalling (6.82), the number of such cycles is expected to be

$$\left\langle \hat{N}^C_n [\hat{\mathscr{R}}^{dG}_{n,p}] \right\rangle = p^n \Gamma[n+1]. \tag{6.86}$$

By taking the symmetry of these graph patterns into account, this then allows us to formulate the condition $\langle \hat{N}^C_n [\hat{\mathscr{R}}^{dG}_{n,p_c}] \rangle = n$, and eventually yields

$$p_c = \Gamma[n]^{-1/n} \tag{6.87}$$

for the critical percolation threshold in finite Gilbert random digraphs of order n. Also here, we find with

$$p_c \overset{n\to\infty}{\to} \mathrm{e}\,(2\pi)^{-1/2n} n^{-(2n-1)/2n} \sim \frac{1}{n} \tag{6.88}$$

an asymptotic behaviour which is in accordance with already available results (e.g., see [3]). It is important to stress that although (6.87) is functionally similar to the critical threshold (6.84) of our first model, it compensates for the overcounting of endpoint nodes in open paths. Indeed, comparing (6.87) with computational models suggests that p_c coincides with the emergence of a giant component covering about 83% of the graph, independent of the graph's size (Fig. 6.9, right, grey bar). A more rigorous analytical comparison of the critical percolation threshold and size of the giant connected component must, however, remain beyond the scope of this presentation. We nevertheless hope that this second concrete application of our operator graph-theoretical framework to a real-world problem provides a stimulating prospect for future studies. Reminding that the application presented here was made possible by the algebraic expressions (6.78) and (6.82) for the expected number of paths and cycles in Gilbert random digraphs, it certainly is conceivable that a similar approach can be employed in the description and formalisation of the percolation phenomenon in other random graph models for which an algebraic formulation of the adjacency matrix is available.

6.5 Node Degrees of Barabási–Albert Random Graphs

The operator graph-theoretical representation of our canonical model for scale-free Barabási–Albert random graphs in Section 5.4 differs from other random graph models presented in Chapter 5 in that it renders the explicit evaluation of graph observables algebraically somewhat more challenging. However, as we will demonstrate in this section with the evaluation of the total node degree sequence for $\mathscr{R}^{BA}_{n,k,n_0,k_0}$, exact results can also be obtained in this case. Recalling (2.25), the total node degree in simple graphs $\mathscr{G}$ is defined as the sum over the columns, or rows, of the graph's symmetric adjacency matrix. Adapting this classical measure to simple random graphs $\mathscr{G}$ of order n, we then obtain with

$$\left\langle \hat{a}^{total}\right\rangle_i : \mathbb{G} \to \mathbb{N}_0\,, \left\langle \hat{a}^{total}[\hat{\mathscr{G}}]\right\rangle_i = \left\langle a^{total}\right\rangle_i := \left\langle \hat{\boldsymbol{a}}[\hat{\mathscr{G}}]\cdot \boldsymbol{1}^n\right\rangle_i \tag{6.89}$$

a graph observable for the expected total degree of node $i \in [1,n]$. It is important to note here that $\langle a^{total}\rangle_i$ defines the expectation value of the total degree for a given node i and, therefore, has to be distinguished from the average node degree $\langle a_i^{total}\rangle$ which, according to (2.33), measures the first moment of the node degree sequence $\boldsymbol{a}^{total}$. In the case of Barabási–Albert random graphs $\mathscr{R}^{BA}_{n,k,n_0,k_0}$, the observable (6.89) immediately delivers

$$\begin{aligned}
&\left\langle \hat{a}^{total}[\hat{\mathscr{R}}^{BA}_{n,k,n_0,k_0}]\right\rangle_i \\
&= \left\langle \hat{\boldsymbol{a}}^{total}[\hat{\mathscr{R}}^{BA}_0]\cdot \boldsymbol{1}^n\right\rangle_i + \left\langle \sum_{t=1}^{n-n_0}\sum_{j=1}^{n_0+t-1} \mathfrak{r}^{(\boldsymbol{p}_t)_j}[1]\cdot\left(\delta^{n\times n}_{j,n_0+t} + \delta^{n\times n}_{n_0+t,j}\right)\cdot \boldsymbol{1}^n\right\rangle_i \\
&= \begin{cases} (\boldsymbol{a}_0^{total})_i + \sum_{t=1}^{n-n_0} (\boldsymbol{p}_t)_i & \text{for } i\in[1,n_0], \\ \sum_{j=1}^{i-1} (\boldsymbol{p}_{i-n_0})_j + \sum_{t=i-n_0+1}^{n-n_0} (\boldsymbol{p}_t)_i & \text{for } i \in [n_0+1,n], \end{cases}
\end{aligned} \tag{6.90}$$

where we denote with $\boldsymbol{a}_0^{total}$ the exact node degree sequence of the initial simple graph $\mathscr{R}^{BA}_0$ of order n_0 that enters the model as a given parametric component and with $\boldsymbol{p}_t$ the probability vector at step t in the construction of $\mathscr{R}^{BA}_{n,k,n_0,k_0}$.

In order to simplify the right-hand side of (6.90), let us first take a look at the probability vector $\boldsymbol{p}_t$ for each step $t \in [1, n-n_0]$. Recalling the definition from (5.99), the $n_0 + t$ non-zero components $(\boldsymbol{p}_t)_i$, $i \in [1, n_0+t]$ of this vector are given by

$$(\boldsymbol{p}_t)_i = \frac{k}{\left\langle \hat{A}[\hat{\mathscr{R}}^{BA}_{t-1}]\right\rangle}\left\langle \hat{a}^{total}[\hat{\mathscr{R}}^{BA}_{t-1}]\right\rangle_i = \frac{k}{A_0 + 2k(t-1)}\left\langle \hat{a}^{total}[\hat{\mathscr{R}}^{BA}_{t-1}]\right\rangle_i. \tag{6.91}$$

Here $\langle \hat{A}[\hat{\mathscr{R}}^{BA}_t]\rangle$ denotes the expectation value of the total adjacency (5.116) at step t, which evaluates to

$$\begin{aligned}
\left\langle \hat{A}[\hat{\mathscr{R}}^{BA}_t]\right\rangle &= A_0 + 2\sum_{s=1}^{t}\sum_{j=1}^{n_0+s-1} (\boldsymbol{p}_s)_j = A_0 + 2\sum_{s=1}^{t} \mathrm{T}\left[\boldsymbol{p}_s\right] \\
&= A_0 + 2\sum_{s=1}^{t} \frac{k}{\left\langle \hat{A}[\hat{\mathscr{R}}^{BA}_{s-1}]\right\rangle}\mathrm{T}\left[\left\langle \hat{a}^{total}[\hat{\mathscr{R}}^{BA}_{s-1}]\right\rangle_i\right] \\
&= A_0 + 2\sum_{s=1}^{t} \frac{k}{\left\langle \hat{A}[\hat{\mathscr{R}}^{BA}_{s-1}]\right\rangle}\left\langle \mathrm{T}\left[\hat{\boldsymbol{a}}[\hat{\mathscr{R}}^{BA}_{s-1}]\right]\right\rangle = A_0 + 2k\sum_{s=1}^{t} 1 = A_0 + 2kt
\end{aligned}$$

using (6.91) in the second step, and the help of definitions from (6.1) and (6.89) as well as the properties of our total sum operator (3.59) in the last step. With (5.117), we then find

$$
\begin{aligned}
(\boldsymbol{p}_t)_i &= \frac{k}{A_0 + 2k(t-1)}\Big((\boldsymbol{a}_0^{total})_i + \sum_{s=1}^{t-1}(\boldsymbol{p}_s)_i\Big) \\
&= \frac{k}{A_0 + 2k(t-1)}\Big((\boldsymbol{a}_0^{total})_i + \sum_{s=1}^{t-2}(\boldsymbol{p}_s)_i + (\boldsymbol{p}_{t-1})_i\Big) \\
&= \frac{k}{A_0 + 2k(t-1)}\Big(\frac{A_0 + 2k(t-2)}{k}(\boldsymbol{p}_{t-1})_i + (\boldsymbol{p}_{t-1})_i\Big) \\
&= \frac{k}{A_0 + 2k(t-1)}\Big(1 + \frac{A_0 + 2k(t-2)}{k}\Big)(\boldsymbol{p}_{t-1})_i
\end{aligned}
$$

for $i \in [1, n_0]$ and $t > 1$, which eventually yields the explicit expression

$$
\begin{aligned}
(\boldsymbol{p}_t)_i &= (\boldsymbol{p}_1)_i \prod_{s=1}^{t-1} \frac{k}{A_0 + 2k(t-s)}\Big(1 + \frac{A_0 + 2k(t-s-1)}{k}\Big) \\
&= (\boldsymbol{p}_1)_i \frac{(A_0/2k + 1/2)_{t-1}}{(A_0/2k + 1)_{t-1}}
\end{aligned}
\tag{6.92}
$$

for the first n_0 elements of $\boldsymbol{p}_t$. Here $(q)_n := \Gamma[q+n]/\Gamma[q]$ for $q \in \mathbb{Q}$ and $n \in \mathbb{N}$ denotes the Pochhammer symbol, and

$$
(\boldsymbol{p}_1)_i = \frac{k}{A_0}(\boldsymbol{a}_0^{total})_i \tag{6.93}
$$

the probabilities which guide the preferential attachment of edges to the initial graph $\mathscr{R}_0^{BA}$ with node degree sequence $\boldsymbol{a}_0^{total}$ and adjacency A_0 during the first step in the construction of $\mathscr{R}_{n,k,n_0,k_0}^{BA}$. The treatment of the remaining non-zero elements $(\boldsymbol{p}_t)_i$, $i \in [n_0+1, n_0+t]$ follows the same approach and results in

$$
\begin{aligned}
(\boldsymbol{p}_t)_i &= \frac{k}{A_0 + 2k(t-1)}\Big(\sum_{j=1}^{i-1}(\boldsymbol{p}_{i-n_0})_j + \sum_{s=i-n_0+1}^{t-1}(\boldsymbol{p}_s)_i\Big) \\
&= \frac{k}{A_0 + 2k(t-1)}\Big(\sum_{j=1}^{i-1}(\boldsymbol{p}_{i-n_0})_j + \sum_{s=i-n_0+1}^{t-2}(\boldsymbol{p}_s)_i + (\boldsymbol{p}_{t-1})_i\Big) \\
&= \frac{k}{A_0 + 2k(t-1)}\Big(1 + \frac{A_0 + 2k(t-2)}{k}\Big)(\boldsymbol{p}_{t-1})_i \\
&= (\boldsymbol{p}_{i-n_0+1})_i \prod_{s=1}^{n_0+t-i-1} \frac{k}{A_0 + 2k(t-s)}\Big(1 + \frac{A_0 + 2k(t-s-1)}{k}\Big) \\
&= (\boldsymbol{p}_{i-n_0+1})_i \frac{(A_0/2k + 1/2 + i - n_0)_{n_0+t-i-1}}{(A_0/2k + 1 + i - n_0)_{n_0+t-i-1}}
\end{aligned}
\tag{6.94}
$$

for $t > 1$ with

$$\begin{aligned}(\boldsymbol{p}_{i-n_0+1})_i &= \frac{k}{\left\langle \hat{A}[\hat{\mathcal{R}}^{BA}_{i-n_0}]\right\rangle} \left\langle \hat{a}^{total}[\hat{\mathcal{R}}^{BA}_{i-n_0}]\right\rangle_i = \frac{k}{\left\langle \hat{A}[\hat{\mathcal{R}}^{BA}_{i-n_0}]\right\rangle} \sum_{j=1}^{i-1} (\boldsymbol{p}_{i-n_0})_j \\ &= \frac{k}{\left\langle \hat{A}[\hat{\mathcal{R}}^{BA}_{i-n_0}]\right\rangle} \mathrm{T}\left[\boldsymbol{p}_{i-n_0}\right] = \frac{k^2}{\left\langle \hat{A}[\hat{\mathcal{R}}^{BA}_{i-n_0}]\right\rangle} = \frac{k^2}{A_0 + 2k(i-n_0)} \end{aligned} \tag{6.95}$$

as initial probabilities in the recursion defined by (5.99) and (5.117).

With (6.92)–(6.95) at hand, we can now return to (6.90) and proceed with the evaluation of the total node degree sequence . After a lengthy yet straightforward calculation which we leave as an entertaining number-theoretical exercise to the reader, we finally obtain for the expectation value of the total degree of nodes $i \in [1, n]$ in our canonical model of Barabási–Albert random graphs $\mathcal{R}^{BA}_{n,k,n_0,k_0}$ the exact algebraic expression

$$\left\langle \hat{a}^{total}[\hat{\mathcal{R}}^{BA}_{n,k,n_0,k_0}]\right\rangle_i = \begin{cases} \frac{1}{\pi}\left(\frac{A_0}{2k} - \frac{1}{2} + n - n_0\right) B\left[\frac{1}{2}, \frac{A_0}{2k}\right] B\left[\frac{1}{2}, \frac{A_0}{2k} - \frac{1}{2} + n - n_0\right] (\boldsymbol{a}_0^{total})_i \\ \qquad\qquad \text{for } i \in [1, n_0], \\ \frac{A_0 - k + 2k(n-n_0)}{2\pi} B\left[\frac{1}{2}, \frac{A_0}{2k} + i - n_0\right] B\left[\frac{1}{2}, \frac{A_0}{2k} - \frac{1}{2} + n - n_0\right] \\ \qquad\qquad \text{for } i \in [n_0+1, n], \end{cases} \tag{6.96}$$

where $B[p, q] := \Gamma[p]\Gamma[q]/\Gamma[p+q]$ for $p, q \in \mathbb{Q}$ denotes the Euler beta function. This expression can certainly be simplified further, but if should suffice here to illustrate that, not unexpectedly, the characteristics of the given initial graph $\mathcal{R}^{BA}_0$ stringently shape the average node degrees of a Barabási–Albert random graph (see Fig 6.10 for some representative examples), and taint the desired scale-free behaviour of its node degree distribution, especially in the case of small graph size n. Utilising (6.96) might aid a thorough exploration of this interesting dependence and help to confine computational models targeting the construction of finite scale-free random graphs.

Before concluding this section, let us briefly verify the validity of our result (6.96) by evaluating the sum over all total node degrees. After some more entertaining number-theoretical manipulations, we eventually obtain

$$\begin{aligned}&\mathrm{T}\left[\left\langle \hat{a}^{total}[\hat{\mathcal{R}}^{BA}_{n,k,n_0,k_0}]\right\rangle\right] \\ &= \frac{1}{\pi}\left(\frac{A_0}{2k} - \frac{1}{2} + n - n_0\right) B\left[\frac{1}{2}, \frac{A_0}{2k}\right] B\left[\frac{1}{2}, \frac{A_0}{2k} - \frac{1}{2} + n - n_0\right] \sum_{i=1}^{n_0} (\boldsymbol{a}_0^{total})_i \\ &\quad + \frac{A_0 - k + 2k(n-n_0)}{2\pi} B\left[\frac{1}{2}, \frac{A_0}{2k} - \frac{1}{2} + n - n_0\right] \sum_{i=n_0+1}^{n} B\left[\frac{1}{2}, \frac{A_0}{2k} + i - n_0\right]\end{aligned}$$

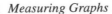

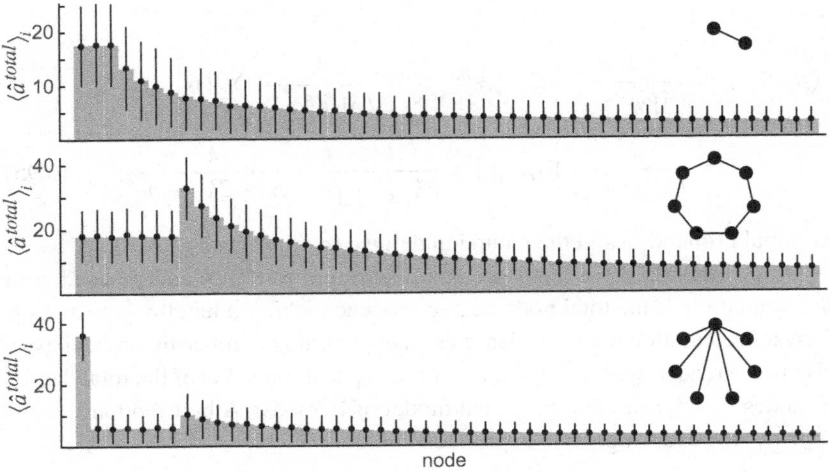

Figure 6.10 Expected total node degrees in Barabási–Albert random graphs for different initial graphs (insets). Compared are the exact solution (grey), Eq. (6.96), with respective numerical results obtained from 100 computational realisations of the corresponding models (black; mean±SD) for the first 50 nodes of the graph. Model parameters: $n = 100$, $k = 2$, $n_0 = 2$, $k_0 = 1$ (top); $n = 100$, $k = 5$, $n_0 = 7$, $k_0 = 7$ (middle); $n = 100$, $k = 2$, $n_0 = 7$, $k_0 = 6$ (bottom). Please note that in all cases, the necessary condition (5.100) imposed on the model parameters is satisfied.

$$\begin{aligned}
&= \frac{A_0}{\pi}\left(\frac{A_0}{2k} - \frac{1}{2} + n - n_0\right) B\left[\tfrac{1}{2}, \tfrac{A_0}{2k}\right] B\left[\tfrac{1}{2}, \tfrac{A_0}{2k} - \tfrac{1}{2} + n - n_0\right] \\
&\quad + \frac{A_0 - k + 2k(n - n_0)}{\pi}\left(\frac{A_0}{2k} + n - n_0\right) B\left[\tfrac{1}{2}, \tfrac{A_0}{2k} - \tfrac{1}{2} + n - n_0\right] B\left[\tfrac{1}{2}, \tfrac{A_0}{2k} + n - n_0\right] \\
&\quad - \frac{A_0 - k + 2k(n - n_0)}{\pi}\frac{A_0}{2k} B\left[\tfrac{1}{2}, \tfrac{A_0}{2k} - \tfrac{1}{2} + n - n_0\right] B\left[\tfrac{1}{2}, \tfrac{A_0}{2k}\right] \\
&= A_0 + 2k(n - n_0) = \left\langle \hat{A}[\hat{\mathfrak{R}}^{BA}_{n,k,n_0,k_0}]\right\rangle
\end{aligned}$$

in accordance with our result (6.6) obtained in Section 6.1.

6.6 Paths in Randomised Square Grid Graphs

The long history of science is filled with countless examples of apparently simple problems, everyday observations or seemingly trivial phenomena whose explanations draw deep roots that span far beyond what can be seen with the naked eye. In the course of solving these problems, new fields of science arose and will continue to arise. The very existence of graph theory with its innocent

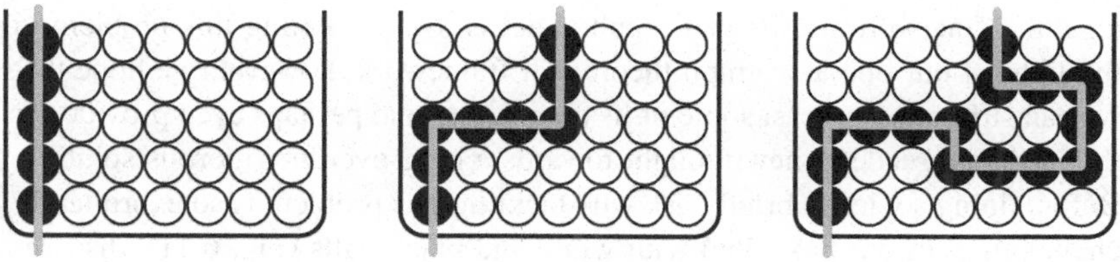

Figure 6.11 Illustration of the problem formulated by DeVolson Wood [111]. In a finite box filled with white and black balls, what is the probability of finding a path comprised of neighbouring balls of one colour that connects top and bottom? At first glance, the counting of possible straight vertical paths appears as a simple exercise in probability (left). Even adding a horizontal path will not add much to the combinatorial complexity (middle). However, both the boundary conditions and the possibility of complex paths winding in all directions (right) render this problem quickly intractable in classical combinatorial approaches. What if white and black balls in the box were to be arranged in a random fashion?

origin in the mystery of Königsberg's seven bridges is an undeniable attest to this ongoing evolution. While Leonard Euler bereaved these bridges of their mystery and planted with his brilliant insights the seed from which a new field of mathematics emerged, in many other cases, solutions to similarly accessible problems and phenomena are still at large. In this section, we will deal with one of these problems, formulated more than 120 years ago [111]. In the first volume of *American Mathematical Monthly* in 1894, DeVolson Wood asked the simple question *"An equal number of white and black balls of equal size are thrown into a rectangular box, what is the probability that there will be contiguous contact of white balls from one end of the box to the opposite end?"* Although Wood's question presents itself on the outside as innocent as the challenge that surrounded the bridges of Königsberg during Euler's time, the answer to that question remains elusive to this day. This is even more surprising as it resides at the heart of a whole family of phenomena which appear, perhaps unnoticed, each day in front of our very eyes – for instance, when brewing the necessary cup of coffee in the morning. At the moment the first drop of the desired dark-coloured excitement enters our cup, the hot water poured in on top found its way through the porous coffee powder, it "percolated" through the coffee. We still use today the old name "percolator" for a specific coffee pot invented by the British physicist Sir Benjamin Thompson in the early years of the nineteenth century, a name which traces its origin to the physical phenomenon that since gave rise to a whole new field in physics and applied mathematics.

An adequate exploration of Wood's original question would certainly warrant its own lenghty textbook, as it requires digging deep into the exciting algebra of network motifs and graph patterns. By presenting this problem in the light of our operator graph-theoretical framework, however, we hope that we can strip away at least some of its complexity and perhaps even provide for the intrigued reader a new thought towards a long-overdue rigorous solution. Before doing so, let us briefly ask why tackling this problem is so exorbitantly challenging. In our box filled with white and black balls (Fig. 6.11), discerning straight vertical paths that are comprised of neighbouring balls of the same colour occurring with probability p is a simple exercise in probability. Indeed, two balls of the same colour will appear as neighbours with a probability of p^2, three with p^3 and so forth. With each ball at the bottom of the box being a potential source of a unique vertical path, their expected number is then given by the product of the number of balls at the bottom and $p^{\text{box height}}$. Not much changes in regard to the combinatorial complexity if we allow for a single horizontal arrangement of balls along each of these vertical paths. Now each ball can be the source of multiple paths, depending on the dimension of the box and the position of the ball within the box, but counting their expected number certainly remains comfortably in reach. Unfortunately, with the possibility of complex paths winding horizontally and vertically in all directions, and the strict boundary conditions defining our finite box, or 'medium', of black and white balls, the problem is quickly rendered intractable within classical combinatorial approaches due to the sheer number of possible path shapes and adjacency relations.

Departing from this doomed combinatorial perspective, the medium of balls in our box and their possible neighbour relationships naturally invites a description in terms of a square grid graph. By distinguishing the balls' colours through the random assignment of an occupation state to each of the nodes in this graph, we eventually arrive at the operator graph-theoretical formulation presented in Section 5.6. Wood's problem can then be addressed by counting the number of paths through a finite randomised square grid graph $\mathcal{R}^{\mathcal{L}}_{m,n,p}$, and by comparing this number to all possible paths in a square grid graph of equal dimension to obtain their probability of occurrence. This approach is complicated by the fact that we still need to distinguish the bottom and top of the box, or any other spatially separated "sides" of our medium, such that only paths $\mathcal{P}_{ij}$ are admissible whose endnodes $i \in \hat{\mathcal{N}}_1$ and $j \in \hat{\mathcal{N}}_2$ reside in disjunct subsets of nodes $\hat{\mathcal{N}}_1, \hat{\mathcal{N}}_2 \subset \hat{\mathcal{N}}_{cl}^{\mathcal{R}^{\mathcal{L}}_{m,n,p}} : \hat{\mathcal{N}}_1 \cap \hat{\mathcal{N}}_2 = \emptyset$. In order to illustrate the principal idea behind our approach, however, we will avoid here the conceptual and algebraic challenges associated with introducing such a spatial component and restrict ourselves to an evaluation of the expected number of lowest-order paths without imposing further limitations on their endnodes.

With (6.74), we are already in possession of a viable observable that delivers the expected number of paths of given length when applied to a suitable operator representation $\hat{\mathscr{G}}$ of a relational random graph $\mathscr{G}$. In the case of our model of randomised square grid graphs with adjacency matrix (5.143), we then easily obtain

$$\begin{aligned}
&\left\langle \hat{N}_1^{\mathcal{P}}[\hat{\mathscr{R}}^{\mathscr{L}}_{m,n,p}]\right\rangle \\
&= \left\langle \sum_{i_1,i_2=1}^{mn} \hat{\delta}[\mathcal{I}^2] \prod_{l=1}^{1} \left(\mathfrak{L}^{(4,4)}_{m,n} \left[\sum_{\substack{j_1,j_2=1\\ j_2>j_1}}^{mn} \mathbf{r}^p_{j_1}[1]\cdot \mathbf{r}^p_{j_2}[1] \cdot (\delta^{mn\times mn}_{j_1 j_2} + \delta^{mn\times mn}_{j_2 j_1}) \right]\right)_{i_l i_{l+1}} \right\rangle \\
&= \left\langle \sum_{\substack{i_1,i_2=1\\ i_l\neq i_2}}^{mn} \left(\mathfrak{L}^{(4,4)}_{m,n} \left[\sum_{\substack{j_1,j_2=1\\ j_2>j_1}}^{mn} \mathbf{r}^p_{j_1}[1]\cdot \mathbf{r}^p_{j_2}[1] \cdot (\delta^{mn\times mn}_{j_1 j_2} + \delta^{mn\times mn}_{j_2 j_1}) \right]\right)_{i_1 i_2} \right\rangle \\
&= p^2 \sum_{\substack{i_1,i_2=1\\ i_l\neq i_2}}^{mn} \left(\mathfrak{L}^{(4,4)}_{m,n} \odot \boldsymbol{I}^{mn\times mn} - \mathfrak{L}^{(4,4)}_{m,n} \odot \boldsymbol{I}^{mn} \right)_{i_1 i_2} \\
&= p^2 \left(\mathrm{T}\left[\mathfrak{L}^{(4,4)}_{m,n} \odot \boldsymbol{I}^{mn\times mn} - \mathfrak{L}^{(4,4)}_{m,n} \odot \boldsymbol{I}^{mn} \right] - \mathrm{Tr}\left[\mathfrak{L}^{(4,4)}_{m,n} \odot \boldsymbol{I}^{mn\times mn} - \mathfrak{L}^{(4,4)}_{m,n} \odot \boldsymbol{I}^{mn} \right] \right)
\end{aligned}$$

for paths of length 1 visiting two distinct nodes. Here we employed the defining property (5.131) of the projection matrix operator $\mathfrak{L}^{(4,4)}_{m,n}$. By noting that

$$\mathrm{T}\left[\mathfrak{L}^{(4,4)}_{m,n} \odot \boldsymbol{I}^{mn\times mn} \right] = \mathrm{T}\left[\mathfrak{L}^{(4,4)}_{m,n} \right] = 2(2mn - m - n) \tag{6.97}$$

yields the number of adjacency relations in a square grid graph $\mathscr{L}^{(4,4)}_{m,n}$, and that

$$\mathrm{Tr}\left[\mathfrak{L}^{(4,4)}_{m,n} \right] = 0, \tag{6.98}$$

we eventually find

$$\left\langle \hat{N}_1^{\mathcal{P}}[\hat{\mathscr{R}}^{\mathscr{L}}_{m,n,p}]\right\rangle = 2p^2(2mn - m - n) = \left\langle \hat{A}[\hat{\mathscr{R}}^{\mathscr{L}}_{m,n,p}]\right\rangle \tag{6.99}$$

for the expected number of paths of length 1 in $\mathscr{R}^{\mathscr{L}}_{m,n,p}$. Interestingly, this result allows us to draw a link between the occupation probability p in the original model and the average connectedness of the associated randomised square grid graph. As grid graphs are both undirected and not self-looped, we define

$$\left\langle \rho[\hat{\mathscr{R}}^{\mathscr{L}}_{m,n,p}]\right\rangle := \frac{1}{mn(mn-1)} \left\langle \hat{A}[\hat{\mathscr{R}}^{\mathscr{L}}_{m,n,p}]\right\rangle \tag{6.100}$$

according to (2.15)–(2.17), and with (6.99) obtain the relation

$$\left\langle \rho[\hat{\mathscr{R}}^{\mathscr{L}}_{m,n,p}]\right\rangle = \frac{2(2mn - m - n)}{mn(mn-1)} p^2, \tag{6.101}$$

which is visualised for various graphs of small size in Fig. 6.12a.

Using (6.99) as initial value, we can now employ the general identity (6.76) and derive a recursive expression for the expected number of paths of arbitrary length, as demonstrated in Section 6.4.2. Unlike in Gilbert random graphs, we

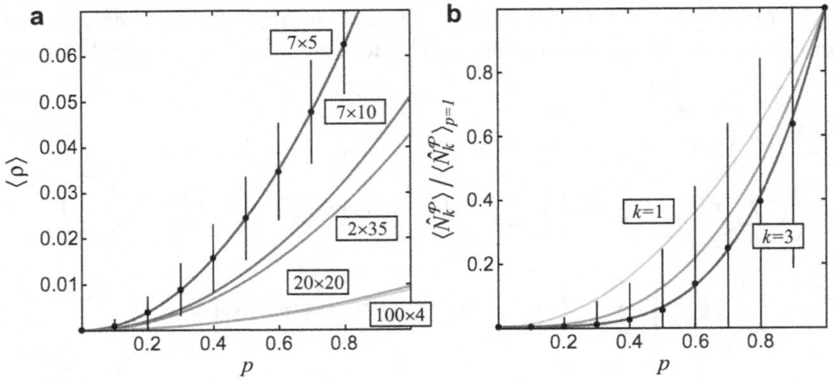

Figure 6.12 Paths in randomised square grid graphs. **a:** Relation between the occupation probability p and average connectedness $\langle\rho\rangle$ in $\mathscr{R}^{\mathscr{L}}_{m,n,p}$ for various graph dimensions $m \times n$. Interestingly, despite describing graphs of the same order mn, the results for 7×10, 2×35 and 20×20, 100×4 differ slightly and suggest that the boundary conditions of the model play a distinctive role. **b:** Relative number of paths of length k (6.103) as function of p for $m = 7$, $n = 5$ and $1 \leq k \leq 3$ (grey). Computational models (black dots; mean ± SD obtained from a statistical analysis of 1,000 realisations): $m = 7$, $n = 5$ and $k = 1$ (**a**), $k = 3$ (**b**).

find here that, depending on their position, individual endnodes will contribute differently when adding a new edge to extend a given path. Indeed, each corner node $i \in \{1, m, m(n-1), mn\}$ allows for at most two adjacency relations, nodes $i \in \{km + l\colon k \in [1, n-2], l \in [2, m-1]\}$ for at most four, and all other nodes for at most three. An application of (6.76) then effectively translates into a representation of the algebra of motifs in a square grid graph that reflects the combinatorial complexity of the original problem. For presentational brevity, we will leave an exploration of this insightful approach as exercise to the interested reader, and instead we will evaluate (6.74) directly. We immediately find

$$\begin{aligned}
&\left\langle \hat{N}^{\mathcal{P}}_2[\hat{\mathscr{R}}^{\mathscr{L}}_{m,n,p}]\right\rangle \\
&= \left\langle \sum_{i_1,i_2,i_3=1}^{mn} \bar{\delta}[\mathcal{I}^3] \prod_{l=1}^{2} \left(\mathfrak{L}^{(4,4)}_{m,n} \left[\sum_{\substack{j_1,j_2=1\\ j_2>j_1}}^{mn} \mathbf{r}^p_{j_1}[1] \cdot \mathbf{r}^p_{j_2}[1] \cdot \left(\delta^{mn\times mn}_{j_1 j_2} + \delta^{mn\times mn}_{j_2 j_1}\right)\right]\right)_{i_l i_{l+1}} \right\rangle \\
&= p^3 \sum_{i_1,\ldots,i_3=1}^{mn} \bar{\delta}[\mathcal{I}^3] \left(\mathfrak{L}^{(4,4)}_{m,n}\right)_{i_1 i_2} \left(\mathfrak{L}^{(4,4)}_{m,n}\right)_{i_2 i_3}
\end{aligned} \tag{6.102}$$

for the expected number of paths of length 2 between distinct nodes in terms of the components (5.132) of the projection operator $\mathfrak{L}^{(4,4)}_{m,n}$. We note that $\mathbf{r}^p_j[1]$ marks for each given j an independent realisation of the binomial randomisation operator and, thus, satisfies (5.58) and (5.59) such that $\langle \hat{N}_2^{\mathcal{P}}[\hat{\mathcal{R}}_{m,n,p}^{\mathcal{L}}]\rangle \sim p^3$. Expression (6.102) can easily be generalised to finally yield

$$\left\langle \hat{N}_k^{\mathcal{P}}[\hat{\mathcal{R}}_{m,n,p}^{\mathcal{L}}]\right\rangle = p^{k+1} \sum_{i_1,\ldots,i_{k+1}=1}^{mn} \bar{\delta}[\mathcal{I}^{k+1}] \prod_{l=1}^{k} \left(\mathfrak{L}_{m,n}^{(4,4)}\right)_{i_l i_{l+1}} \tag{6.103}$$

for the expected number of paths of length k between distinct nodes in $\mathcal{R}_{m,n,p}^{\mathcal{L}}$ in terms of products of the projection operator $\mathfrak{L}_{m,n}^{(4,4)}$. Due to the non-circular nature of this operator, an algebraically exact evaluation of (6.103) is certainly more involved yet not beyond reach (see Fig. 6.12b). By restricting the sum in (6.103) to nodes $i_1 \in [1, m]$ and $i_{k+1} \in [m(n-1), mn]$ that comprise the lower and upper boundary of our grid graph, and by relating the resulting number of paths to the total number of possible paths for $p = 1$, it should then be possible to obtain a definite answer to the question originally posed by DeVolson Wood more than a century ago.

6.7 Challenges and Limitations

Before concluding this chapter, let us take a critical look at some of the challenges and potential limitations faced by measuring graphs within our operator graph-theoretical framework. With a small selection of concrete examples, we hope to have illustrated here an approach that can indeed deliver in a rigorous fashion exact algebraic expressions for a variety of measures which are difficult to access in a classical context without imposing limiting assumptions. These expressions were generally found not only to be in accordance with numerical results obtained in resource-demanding computational realisations, but also to apply to the whole parameter spectrum of a given model at once, thus opening the door for a thorough comparative study of finite graph models for which observables are available. Unfortunately, for certain types of classical measures, the definition of suitable graph observables may be difficult or even impossible to achieve. In other cases, available observables might not reflect all of the conceptual and formal nuances of their classical counterparts.

6.7.1 Validity of Graph Observables

We encountered a first instance of such a limitation with our evaluation of the total global clustering coefficient in Gilbert random digraphs $\mathcal{R}_{n,p}^{dG}$ in Section 6.3.1. There we found that the deduced algebraic expression is not guaranteed to agree in all corners of the model's parameter spectrum with numerical results obtained from computational realisations. In defence of this finding, we argued that the observed discrepancy for smaller and sparsely connected graphs (see Fig. 6.3) is a direct consequence of the rejection of some computational realisations due to a condition imposed on the classical definition of this measure that results in discrete changes of some numerical data points to prevent meaningless infinite or negative clustering coefficients. However, this nuance in the classical conception of the considered measure is not reflected in the definition of our graph observable, which was constructed to deliver the statistical average of the clustering coefficient, meaningful or not, over all conceivable realisations of the model. It is therefore justified to suggest that our algebraic expression for the expected total global clustering coefficient, albeit being close to its classical root, does not provide a valid graph observable for Gilbert random graphs or, for that matter, any other graph model which carries the potential of realising meaningless clustering coefficients.

This example points at a more principal limitation, one that is not specific to our operator graph-theoretical approach alone but that indeed applies generally to any algebraic or analytic formalisation of an algorithm, computational or otherwise, which involves random components, probabilistic arguments or discrete case distinctions. Conditions that lead to the modification or even rejection of some but not all realisations of an algorithm for a given parameter set of a model are inherently difficult to treat in such formalisations unless they retain parts of the original algorithmic representation. Unfortunately, this applies to both the representation of graphs and the formalisation of their measurement in algebraic or analytic terms. As a rule of thumb in addressing this principal limitation in the context of the algebraic approach presented in this book, however, we will assert that each viable evaluation of a graph observable necessitates application of the associated classical measure, without modification or rejection, to all computational realisations of a given model. If this is not the case, the algebraic or analytic expressions obtained for observables within our operator graph-theoretical approach can, and very likely will, deviate from their respective computational results or classical counterparts and must remain limited in regard to their applicability to the model's full parameter spectrum.

6.7.2 Distance-Based Measures

Arguably not a limitation, but certainly a formidable challenge for our operator graph-theoretical approach is furnished by the important class of distance-based measures introduced in Section 2.2.4. While the few examples of classical measures considered in this chapter are well-defined functions of a graph's matrix of adjacency relations, and thus can be directly translated into viable graph observables, distance-based measures are typically defined as functions of the geodesic distance between pairs of nodes whose evaluation, according to (2.54), involves the search for the shortest path of non-zero length between nodes. Viewed from a most general perspective, this search constitutes an optimisation problem, and is therefore inherently difficult to formalise concisely in exact algebraic or analytic terms. Although with (2.57) we conveniently defined this search in terms of the powers of a graph's matrix of adjacency relations, this only translates the optimisation problem into the equally challenging one of dealing with conditional statements in an algebraically rigorous fashion. Due to the importance of distance-based measures in general, and the geodesic distance matrix in particular, let us briefly explore, on the classical level, an alternative definition which might hold the key to a rigorous treatment of such measures within our operator graph-theoretical framework.

To that ambitious end, we recall that in relational graphs and digraphs, the elements $(\boldsymbol{a}^m)_{ij}$ of the mth power of the adjacency matrix $\boldsymbol{a}$ deliver the number of walks of length m between arbitrary nodes i and j such that

$$\delta[(\boldsymbol{a}^m)]_{ij} = \begin{cases} 1 & \text{iff } \exists \text{ walk of length } m \text{ from node } i \text{ to node } j, \\ 0 & \text{otherwise.} \end{cases}$$

Adapting the right-hand side of (2.57), we can then formulate

$$\left.\begin{array}{l} \exists \text{ shortest path of length} \\ m \text{ from node } i \text{ to node } j \end{array}\right\} \Leftrightarrow \left(\delta[\boldsymbol{a}^m]_{ij} = 1\right) \wedge \left(\delta[\boldsymbol{a}^l]_{ij} = 0 \; \forall l \in [1, m-1]\right)$$
$$\Leftrightarrow \delta[\boldsymbol{a}^m]_{ij} \prod_{l=1}^{m-1} \bar{\delta}[\boldsymbol{a}^l]_{ij} = 1$$

as both necessary and sufficient conditions for the existence of a shortest path of length m between nodes i and j, and eventually find

$$d_{ij} = \sum_{m=1}^{n} m\, \delta[\boldsymbol{a}^m]_{ij} \prod_{l=1}^{m-1} \bar{\delta}[\boldsymbol{a}^l]_{ij} = 1 + \sum_{m=1}^{n} \prod_{l=1}^{m} \bar{\delta}[\boldsymbol{a}^l]_{ij} - n \prod_{l=1}^{n} \bar{\delta}[\boldsymbol{a}^l]_{ij} \qquad (6.104)$$

for the elements of the geodesic distance matrix $\boldsymbol{d}$. We note here that this definition not only ensures that $d_{ij} = 0$ if no shortest path exists between nodes i and j, in accordance with our convention in Section 2.2.4, but also naturally applies to diagonal elements of $\boldsymbol{d}$ and, thus, geodesic cycles. More importantly, with (6.104), we effectively replaced the conditional evaluation in (2.57) with a concise algebraic expression in terms of powers of a graph's adjacency matrix which should, at least in some cases, allow us to divorce the construction of the geodesic distance matrix from involving computational resources.

Although the approach proposed above is certainly a cautious first step in the right direction, a naive translation of the so-defined classical measure into a viable graph observable – for instance, by replacing the adjacency matrix with its associated observable – is unfortunately not possible, at least not in the case of random graph models. Indeed, each $\bar{\delta}$-term on the right-hand side of (6.104) evaluates the presence of non-zero elements in powers of the adjacency matrix $\boldsymbol{a}$, and therefore strictly relies on concrete realisations of $\boldsymbol{a}$. From a more probabilistic vantage point, however, we could ask the question of with which probability one is expected to find $(\boldsymbol{a}^k)_{ij} \neq 0$ and, thus, $\bar{\delta}[\boldsymbol{a}^k]_{ij} \neq 0$ for $k \in [1, n]$. An algebraic answer to this question would then allow us to assess the expectation value of each term in (6.104) and eventually lead to the definition of a useful graph observable that measures the geodesic distance matrix in arbitrary random graph models. Although a thorough exploration of this undoubtedly challenging approach, along with its computational validation, lies outside the scope of this brief presentation, we must again impress the need and importance of a rigorous treatment of the geodesic distance within our operator graph-theoretical framework. Such a treatment will not only lift the comparative investigation of the small-world property in real-world networks presented in Section 6.3.3 onto firm algebraic grounds, but it will also provide the necessary algebraic foundation for a rigorous study of distance-based measures in general.

6.7.3 Size of Connected Components

Closely related to both the classical concept and general importance of distance-based measures are measures that delineate and characterise connected components in a graph. An algebraically rigorous formalisation of such measures would undoubtedly render valuable aid to a vast array of concrete real-world applications, such as the study of the percolation phenomenon briefly touched upon in Section 6.4.4, or the investigation of a network's vulnerability and efficiency [97], to mention but two. Unfortunately, also here, computational search algorithms remain the primary tool for an evaluation, at least in the case of random graph models. As we showed above with (6.104), however, a translation of such conditional search algorithms into an algebraically well-defined representation is certainly possible and provides the necessary step towards the formidable challenge of embedding such measures into our operator graph-theoretical framework. Therefore, let us conclude this section by addressing the question of how to formalise in algebraic terms an algorithmic search in graphs – specifically, how to algebraically construct and distinguish a connected component. For reasons of brevity, we must also here remain at the classical level and will only briefly hint at a possible translation into our operator graph-theoretical language.

Let $\mathcal{G} = (\mathcal{N}, \mathcal{E})$ be a simple graph of order n with adjacency matrix $\boldsymbol{a}$. Our goal is to find the subset of nodes of $\mathcal{G}$ which are connected to a given node

$i_0 \in \mathcal{N}$ through at least one walk $\mathcal{W}_{i_0 i} \colon |\mathcal{W}_{i_0 i}| \geq 1$ by constructing in a number of discrete steps the connected component $C_{i_0} := \{i \in \mathcal{N} \colon \exists \mathcal{W}_{i_0 i}\} \subseteq \mathcal{N}$. To that end, we introduce a Boolean node state vector $\boldsymbol{s}_t^n \in \mathbb{B}^n$ at each step $t \in \mathbb{N}_0$ in the construction, and define with $(\boldsymbol{s}_0^n)_{i_0} = 1$ and $(\boldsymbol{s}_0^n)_i = 0 \, \forall i \in [1, n] \colon i \neq i_0$ the initial state vector $\boldsymbol{s}_0^n$. The rationale behind the approach proposed here is to visit the nearest neighbours of all nodes of $\mathcal{G}$ at each step $t \geq 1$, and to then change the state of each nearest neighbour according to the state of its source node. After sufficiently many, but certainly after at most $n - 1$ steps, all node states will necessarily be assigned such that with

$$(\boldsymbol{s}_{n-1}^n)_i = \begin{cases} 1 & \text{iff } i \in C_{i_0}, \\ 0 & \text{iff } i \notin C_{i_0} \end{cases} \tag{6.105}$$

our state vector marks all nodes belonging to C_{i_0}, and

$$N_n^{C_{i_0}} := \mathrm{T}\left[\boldsymbol{s}_{n-1}^n\right] \tag{6.106}$$

delivers the size of the connected component C_{i_0}.

In order to formalise this approach in algebraic terms, we define with

$$\begin{aligned} &(1) \quad a_{ij} = 1 \wedge (\boldsymbol{s}_t^n)_i = 1 && \Rightarrow (\boldsymbol{s}_{t+1}^n)_j = 1, \\ &(2) \quad a_{ij} = 0 \wedge \big((\boldsymbol{s}_t^n)_i = 0 \vee (\boldsymbol{s}_t^n)_i = 1\big) && \Rightarrow (\boldsymbol{s}_{t+1}^n)_j = 0, \\ &(3) \quad a_{ij} = 1 \wedge (\boldsymbol{s}_t^n)_i = 0 && \Rightarrow (\boldsymbol{s}_{t+1}^n)_j = 0, \\ &(4) \quad \big(a_{ij} = 0 \vee a_{ij} = 1\big) \wedge (\boldsymbol{s}_t^n)_i = 1 && \Rightarrow (\boldsymbol{s}_{t+1}^n)_i = 1 \end{aligned} \tag{6.107}$$

for $i, j \in [1, n]$ a set of rules that govern the state change of a node's nearest neighbours. The first rule assigns here all nearest neighbours of $i \in C_{i_0}$ to C_{i_0}. The second rule concerns not adjacent nodes i and j for which, irrespective of the state of node i, the state of node j remains zero. The third rule covers adjacent nodes with a source node i not yet assigned to C_{i_0}, in which case the state of node j will also remain zero. Lastly, rule (4) ensures that the state of all nodes already assigned to C_{i_0} will remain unchanged. It can easily be shown that by using $\tilde{a}_{ii} := a_{ii} + 1 \, \forall i \in \mathcal{N}$ – that is, by replacing the adjacency matrix $\boldsymbol{a}$ in (6.107) with $\tilde{\boldsymbol{a}} := \boldsymbol{a} + \boldsymbol{I}^n$ – this last rule is naturally covered by (1) which then, together with rules (2) and (3), defines a logic AND gate for which the Boolean multiplication (3.1) provides a suitable functional representation. Noting that $a \cdot^{\mathbb{B}} b = ab$ for $a, b \in \mathbb{B}$, we eventually obtain

$$\boldsymbol{s}_{t+1}^n = \bar{\delta}[\boldsymbol{s}_t^n \cdot \tilde{\boldsymbol{a}}] \tag{6.108}$$

for the recursive update of all node states in the construction of C_{i_0}, and with

$$\boldsymbol{s}_{n-1}^n = \bar{\delta}[\boldsymbol{s}_0^n \cdot \tilde{\boldsymbol{a}}^{n-1}] = \boldsymbol{s}_0^n \cdot \bar{\delta}[\tilde{\boldsymbol{a}}^{n-1}] \tag{6.109}$$

an explicit expression for the Boolean node state vector $\boldsymbol{s}^n_{n-1}$ at step $t = n-1$ in terms of the $(n-1)$th power of $\tilde{\boldsymbol{a}} = \boldsymbol{a} + \boldsymbol{I}^n$ and, thus, powers $\boldsymbol{a}^k : k \in [1, n-1]$ of the adjacency matrix defining $\mathscr{G}$.

With (6.109), we have finally arrived at an algebraically rigorous representation of the search for connected components in simple graphs. Indeed, by considering each possible initial node $i_0 \in [1, n]$, we can discern not only all connected components in a given graph, but, with (6.106), also their respective size by evaluating the powers of its adjacency matrix. The approach leading to the above representation can certainly be generalised to encompass relational digraphs. Unfortunately, it faces, not unlike (6.104), a number of challenges when striving for a translation into viable graph observables for random graph models. As in the case of geodesic distances, our approach crucially hinges on the Boolean nature of the adjacency matrix and, thus, is valid only for concrete realisations of a graph model. However, also here, we can ask with which probability non-zero elements in powers of a graph's adjacency matrix will occur. This formidable exercise in the algebra of random Boolean matrices should then, at least in principle, provide the path for defining graph observables for discerning connected components and their properties in random graphs, and eventually expand the scope of our operator graph-theoretical framework into another and undoubtedly important area of real-world applications.

Building on the representation of various graph models introduced in the previous chapter, we hope that this brief excursion into the realms of graph measures further demonstrated the potential usefulness of an operator graph-theoretical perspective. Our focus here was directed towards a rather specific selection of simple measures in order to exemplify how these measures can be embedded into our framework, and how their associated observables can be rigorously evaluated to yield algebraically exact results, even in the case of random graph models for which such results are difficult or even impossible to obtain classically without imposing stringent constraints. Not only does our operator graph-theoretical approach allow us to dispose of such limitations, but the obtained results effectively apply to the full parameter spectrum of a given graph model at once, thus paving the way for a rigorous comparative analysis and characterisation of finite graph models without the involvement of resource-demanding and often prohibitively time-consuming computational studies. Although the examples presented here comprise but a small subset of measures available in the applied graph-theoretical literature – and many challenges still remain before the proposed approach can be elevated to an all-encompassing tool – we nevertheless hope to have provided sufficient motivation and inspiration for a further exploration of graph-theoretical problems and the study of real-world phenomena within an algebraic framework that can be both exact and flexible.

7
Transforming Graphs

Navigating across sometimes treacherous waters, we demonstrated in the previous chapter the construction and utilisation of a small selection of graph observables for measuring various properties of finite random graphs. Together with the generation of operator representations for arbitrary graph models, we should now possess a sufficiently equipped toolset with which to further explore and characterise on rigorous algebraical grounds the plethora of graph models in the applied graph-theoretical literature. However, the adventurous journey we embarked on would not be complete without at least touching upon another crucial aspect exhibited by many real-world networks: their dynamic nature. Indeed, from the directed graphs spanned by neural pathways in our brains to the simple graphs describing the gravitational forces between stars and galaxies, each network that serves as a model of a real-world phenomenon undergoes continual changes, either as part of its development or as realisation of its function. For this reason, let us briefly explore – with one hopefully light-hearted yet certainly playful example, the game of chess – how to formulate such dynamical aspects in our operator graph-theoretical language. As we will witness here, the construction of graphs that describe possible moves of chess pieces at any position during a game, and the transformations that lead to changes of such positional chess graphs, pose a formidable challenge for not only computational algorithms.

7.1 Positional Chess Graphs

With its finite spatio-temporal makeup and set of rules, the game of chess undoubtedly provides a classical example of a discrete dynamical system which lends itself naturally to a representation in terms of finite graphs. Of particular interest here are graph-theoretical representations that encompass all legal moves the pieces on the chess board can potentially perform in any given position. Such descriptions present the conceptual basis on which chess positions are evaluated and advantageous moves are selected, both by human players and computer chess algorithms alike. However, their formalisation also encounters many difficulties due to the peculiar rules that govern this game. As we will show later in this section, our operator graph-theoretical perspective does alleviate some of these difficulties and brings us closer to an algebraic formalisation of the game of chess which not only could allow for the rigorous study of this historic board game within the powerful confines of graph theory, but also could lead to more efficient and sophisticated implementations of computer chess algorithms itself.

7.1.1 Conceptual Preliminaries

The game of chess is played on a fixed board with 64 squares of two alternating colours arranged in a regular (8×8)-dimensional grid. Each square can be occupied by at most one of 32 pieces of 6 types (*king*, *queen*, *rook*, *bishop*, *knight* and *pawn*) and two colours (typically *white* and *black*), one for each of two players. Starting from a defined *initial position*, with a white piece always opening with the first move, a game advances by alternating discrete moves of white and black pieces until the king of the opposing colour is captured (*checkmate*). The legal moves each type of piece can perform are governed by a set of strict rules, now internationally standardised by the Fédération Internationale des Échecs (FIDE; for a review of modern chess rules, see [45]), and will be distinguished here into *regular moves* and *special moves* (*en passant capture* and *castling*) for presentational purposes. By identifying each square on the chess board with a node, and each possible legal move of chess pieces with a directed edge, any position during a game of chess finds a natural representation in terms of a finite digraph which we will call a *positional chess graph*. The defining makeup of these graphs deviates significantly, however, from that of the relational digraphs considered in Chapter 5. Indeed, three major differences must be dealt with before a rigorous classical and, ultimately, operator graph-theoretical representation of the game of chess can be formulated.

Spatial Layout

Firstly, although the squares on the chess board are arranged in a spatial grid, the positional chess graph is not a square grid graph, as all pieces can legally move diagonally and, in most cases, across multiple squares. Moreover, each square has a fixed position, historically labelled by *file* $\boldsymbol{f} \in \{a, b, c, d, e, f, g, h\}$ and *rank* $\boldsymbol{r} \in \{1, 2, 3, 4, 5, 6, 7, 8\}$. The strict spatial layout and boundary conditions of the chess board prohibit the arbitrary relabelling of nodes in a positional chess graph. In order to identify each square, and thus each node, we will introduce a unique node identifier $i \in \mathbb{N}$ ranging from 1 to 64, starting in the lower left-hand corner with the $a1$ square and ending in the upper right-hand corner ($h8$ square). Recalling (2.126) and (2.127), the conversions between file, rank and node identifier are then given by

$$\begin{aligned} (\boldsymbol{f},\boldsymbol{r}) &\longrightarrow i \colon \mathbb{N}\times\mathbb{N}\to\mathbb{N}\,,\; i = 8\boldsymbol{r}+\boldsymbol{f}-8, \\ i &\longrightarrow (\boldsymbol{f},\boldsymbol{r}) \colon \mathbb{N}\to\mathbb{N}\times\mathbb{N}\,,\; (\boldsymbol{f},\boldsymbol{r}) = \left(i-8\left\lfloor\frac{i-1}{8}\right\rfloor, 1+\left\lfloor\frac{i-1}{8}\right\rfloor\right), \end{aligned} \tag{7.1}$$

where for notational convenience we mapped with $(a,\ldots,h) \to (1,\ldots,8)$ the board's files successively into natural numbers.

Graph Nodes

Secondly, each square on the chess board can be occupied by at most one of 12 different pieces (6 types of 2 colours each). Because the type and colour of a piece govern its legal moves and, therefore, the adjacency relations the node associated with an occupied square can establish to other nodes in a positional chess graph, each node must not only distinguish the presence or absence of a piece, but also identify the type and colour of the piece that eventually resides on its associated square. For that purpose, let us introduce with

$$C := \{\mathrm{w},\mathrm{b}\} \tag{7.2}$$

the set of colours (w for *white*, b for *black*) and with

$$\mathcal{T} := \{\mathrm{K},\mathrm{Q},\mathrm{R},\mathrm{B},\mathrm{N},\mathrm{P}\} \tag{7.3}$$

the set of all types (K for *king*, Q for *queen*, R for *rook*, B for *bishop*, N for *knight*, P for *pawn*) of chess pieces, and define with

$$\mathcal{S}^n := \left\{0\,, s^{\mathrm{wK}}, s^{\mathrm{bK}}, s^{\mathrm{wQ}}, s^{\mathrm{bQ}}, s^{\mathrm{wR}}, s^{\mathrm{bR}}, s^{\mathrm{wB}}, s^{\mathrm{bB}}, s^{\mathrm{wN}}, s^{\mathrm{bN}}, s^{\mathrm{wP}}, s^{\mathrm{bP}}\right\} \tag{7.4}$$

a set of 13 possible node states, where $s^{ct} \in \mathbb{Z} : s^{ct} \neq 0$ for $c \in C$ and $t \in \mathcal{T}$ denote distinct integer constants. Any legal chess position is then uniquely described by a node state row vector $\boldsymbol{s}^n$ with 64 elements $s_i^n \in \mathcal{S}^n, i \in [1,64]$. In what follows, we will restrict ourselves to states $s^{\mathrm{w}t} \in \mathbb{N}$ and $s^{\mathrm{b}t} = -s^{\mathrm{w}t}$ for all $t \in \mathcal{T}$, such that $\operatorname{sgn}[s_i^n]$ further distinguishes between squares occupied by white and black pieces, and $\left|\operatorname{sgn}[s_i^n]\right|$ further distinguishes between occupied and not occupied squares.

Graph Edges

Finally, as the game of chess is played by two opposing parties, it is imperative to distinguish between adjacency relations that mark possible moves of white and black pieces. To that end, let us assign to each directed edge between nodes i and j a weight $w_{ij} \in \mathbb{B}_{-1}$ according to the colour of the piece which occupies the square corresponding to the edge's source node, such that

$$w_{ij} = \begin{cases} \operatorname{sgn}[s_i^n] & \text{if node } i \text{ is connected to node } j, \\ 0 & \text{otherwise.} \end{cases} \tag{7.5}$$

The set of target nodes j for which $w_{ij} \neq 0$ depends here on the legal moves the chess piece occupying node i can perform in a given position – that is on its type and colour as well as the placement of all other pieces on the chess board. The complete set of adjacency relations in a positional chess graph is therefore necessarily a function of the node state vector $\boldsymbol{s}^n$, which renders the algebraic rigorous construction of such graphs a formidable challenge.

7.1.2 Classical Representation

Taking these conceptual peculiarities into account, we can now more precisely define a *positional chess graph* as a weighted digraph $\mathscr{C} = (\mathcal{N}, \mathcal{E})$ of order 64 that is comprised of a set of nodes $\mathcal{N}$ whose elements $n_i \in \mathcal{N}, i \in [1, 64]$ are each associated with a node state $s_i^n \in \mathcal{S}^n$ and uniquely describe the placement of pieces on the chess board; and a set of adjacency relations $\mathcal{E}$ whose elements are ordered node pairs $(i, j) \in \mathcal{N} \times \mathcal{N}$, each assigned with a weight $w_{ij} \in \mathbb{B}_{-1}$, and uniquely describe all legal moves the pieces on a chess board can perform. It is important to note here that, albeit formally conforming with Definition 2.1 of a classical graph, the very concept of a positional chess graph requires that we supplement the above definition with a node state vector $\boldsymbol{s}^n$ and weight matrix $\boldsymbol{w}$ in order to arrive at a complete description. So far, both $\boldsymbol{s}^n$ and $\boldsymbol{w}$ remain as mere abstract algebraic objects, and our primary goal will be to formulate a concrete representation of these objects in the remainder of this chapter.

In preparing for the challenge of explicitly constructing the set of weighted directed edges in a positional chess graph $\mathscr{C}$ from a given node state vector, let us premise by taking a brief look at concrete moves of individual chess pieces, and at how these moves will impact and constrain possible node states. For all regular moves, given a source node i in state $s_i^n \neq 0$, a potential target node j can only be in state $s_j^n = 0$ or, in the case of possible capture, a state with $\operatorname{sgn}[s_j^n] = -\operatorname{sgn}[s_i^n]$. The latter does not apply to the *en passant* capture move, for which the target node is required to be in state $s_j^n = 0$. Disregarding for the moment the stringent conditions which govern the realisation of this special move, the source node i for a white pawn *en passant* capture must be in state $s_i^n = s^{\mathrm{wP}}$ and satisfy $33 \leq i \leq 40$, while $s_j^n = 0$ and $s_{j-8}^n = s^{\mathrm{bP}}$ for at least one of the respective potential target nodes $j = i + 8 \pm 1 : 41 \leq j \leq 48$. Similarly, for the *en passant* capture move of a black pawn occupying node i, we require $s_i^n = s^{\mathrm{bP}}$ with $25 \leq i \leq 32$ as well as $s_j^n = 0$ and $s_{j+8}^n = s^{\mathrm{wP}}$ for at least one potential target nodes $j = i - 8 \pm 1 : 17 \leq j \leq 24$. Finally, each of the two possible castling moves of the white king requires two source nodes $i_1 = 5$ and $i_2 \in \{1, 8\}$ with $s_{i_1}^n = s^{\mathrm{wK}}$ and $s_{i_2}^n = s^{\mathrm{wR}}$, and they can be realised if either $s_3^n = s_4^n = 0$ (queenside castling) or $s_6^n = s_7^n = 0$ (kingside castling). In a similar fashion, we require $s_{i_1}^n = s^{\mathrm{bK}}$ and $s_{i_2}^n = s^{\mathrm{bR}}$ with $i_1 = 61$ and $i_2 \in \{57, 64\}$ for the two source nodes, and either $s_{59}^n = s_{60}^n = 0$ for queenside castling or $s_{62}^n = s_{63}^n = 0$ for kingside castling of the black king.

As in the case of the *en passant* capture move of pawns, the potential realisation of castling moves is subject to stringent conditions which make it necessary to keep a reduced record of earlier game positions and, thus, significantly complicate their eventual algebraic formalisation. Another layer of complexity is added by the necessary validation of adjacency relations, as only moves of pieces of a given colour are permissible which do not result in an attack on the king of the same colour. This validation requires us to consider each possible move associated with a given source state $\operatorname{sgn}[s_i^n] \neq 0$, and to disregard the move if the graph resulting from this positional change contains at least one adjacency relation from a source node i' with $\operatorname{sgn}[s_{i'}^n] = -\operatorname{sgn}[s_i^n]$ to a target node j' with $s_{j'}^n \in \{s^{\mathrm{wK}}, s^{\mathrm{bK}}\} : \operatorname{sgn}[s_{j'}^n] = \operatorname{sgn}[s_i^n]$. Last but not least, if a given position permits an adjacency relation from a node i with $s_i^n \neq 0$ to a target node j with a state value $s_j^n \in \{s^{\mathrm{wK}}, s^{\mathrm{bK}}\} : \operatorname{sgn}[s_j^n] = -\operatorname{sgn}[s_i^n]$ (*check* position), the set of possible adjacency relations emanating from nodes i' with $\operatorname{sgn}[s_{i'}^n] = \operatorname{sgn}[s_j^n]$ is restricted to elements which remove node j as potential target in the next position. If this set is empty, the given positional chess graph marks the end of a chess game (*checkmate*). With this, a complete description of a given chess position in the form of a weighted and directed positional chess graph is achieved, and a chess game is fully described by a finite ordered set comprised of graphs $\mathscr{C}$, one for each successive position.

7.1.3 Operator Representation

Before taking on the challenge of algebraically formalising the generation of a positional chess graph $\mathscr{C}$ by constructing its weight matrix $\boldsymbol{w}$, let us explore a viable operator representation $\hat{\mathscr{C}}$ of $\mathscr{C}$. A careful inspection of the moves each type of chess piece can legally perform from any given square on the chess board reveals that a total of $N_e^{\max} = 1{,}792$ edge operators would suffice to encompass all possible positional chess graphs. The complete set of adjacency relations associated with these edge operators is shown in Fig. 7.1 (left; black)

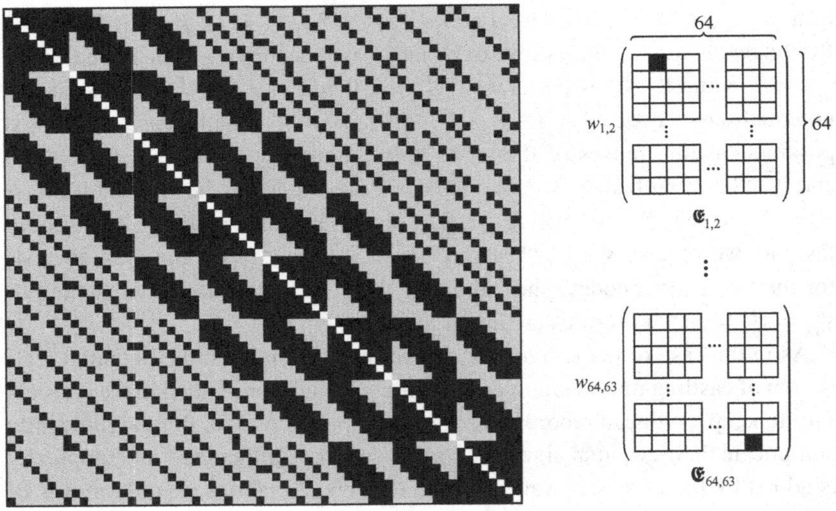

Figure 7.1 Edge operators of positional chess graphs $\mathscr{C}$. A set of 1,792 edge operators, each represented as 64×64 matrix operator and associated with a possible directed edge in $\mathscr{C}$ (left, black), suffices to define a viable operator representation $\hat{\mathscr{C}}$ of $\mathscr{C}$ which encompasses all conceivable positional chess graphs. By instead employing an operator $\mathfrak{w}$ that delivers a matrix $w \in \mathbb{B}_{-1}^{64\times 64}$ and, thus, assigns a weight to each of the 4,032 edge operators associated with non-diagonal elements of a 64×64 Boolean matrix (right), the complete relational digraph $\mathscr{K}_{64}^{d}$ can be used as seed for the generation of $\hat{\mathscr{C}}$.

and comprises less than half of the 4,032 total directed adjacency relations in a complete relational digraph of the same order. Moreover, digraphs associated with positions during a chess game will typically realise only a tiny fraction of these adjacency relations, such that $N_e \ll N_e^{\max}$ for any conceivable positional chess graph. However, for presentational purposes, and for our ultimate goal to algebraically formulate transformations of chess graphs in this chapter, it is most convenient to employ an operator representation of the complete relational digraph $\mathscr{K}_n^d$ of order $n = 64$ as seed in the generation of $\hat{\mathscr{C}}$, and to delegate the selection of edge operators through the assignment of weights to the action of a dedicated operator $\mathfrak{w}$.

This approach is somewhat reminiscent of the generation of random graphs through the use of scalar realisations of a binomial randomisation operator. By adapting the construction of directed Gilbert random graphs in Section 5.2.2, for instance, we then easily find

$$\hat{\mathfrak{G}}^{\mathscr{C}} = \left(\hat{\mathfrak{G}}_{\mathcal{N}}\colon \hat{\mathfrak{G}}_{\mathcal{N}}[\boldsymbol{n}] := s^n \odot \boldsymbol{n}\,,\ \hat{\mathfrak{G}}_{\mathcal{E}}\colon \hat{\mathfrak{G}}_{\mathcal{E}}[\mathfrak{E}] := \boldsymbol{w} \odot \mathfrak{E}\right) \tag{7.6}$$

as a suitable generator for an operator representation $\hat{\mathscr{C}} = \hat{\mathfrak{G}}^{\mathscr{C}}[\hat{\mathscr{K}}^d_{64}]$ of positional chess graphs $\mathscr{C}$. The operator representation $\hat{\mathscr{K}}^d_{64}$ of the complete relational digraph with nodes $\boldsymbol{n}_0 := \boldsymbol{0}^{64}$ and $\boldsymbol{n}_i := \boldsymbol{\delta}^{64}_i, i \in [1, 64]$ as well as edge operators $\mathfrak{E}_{00} := \boldsymbol{0}^{64\times 64}$ and $\mathfrak{E}_{j_1 j_2} := \boldsymbol{\delta}^{64\times 64}_{j_1 j_2}$ with $j_1, j_2 \in [1, 64] : j_1 \neq j_2$ (Fig. 7.1, right) serves here as seed, such that

$$\hat{\mathcal{N}}^{\mathscr{C}} := \left\{\hat{\mathfrak{G}}_{\mathcal{N}}[\boldsymbol{n}] : \boldsymbol{n} \in \hat{\mathcal{N}}^{\mathscr{K}^d_{64}}\right\} \subset \mathbb{Z}^{64},$$
$$\hat{\mathcal{E}}^{\mathscr{C}} := \left\{\hat{\mathfrak{G}}_{\mathcal{E}}[\mathfrak{E}] : \mathfrak{E} \in \hat{\mathcal{E}}^{\mathscr{K}^d_{64}}\right\} \subset \mathbb{B}^{64\times 64}_{-1} \tag{7.7}$$

define the sets of nodes and edge operators of $\hat{\mathscr{C}} := (\hat{\mathcal{N}}^{\mathscr{C}}, \hat{\mathcal{E}}^{\mathscr{C}})$, and

$$\hat{\mathcal{N}}^{\mathscr{C}}_{cl} := \left\{s^n_i \cdot \boldsymbol{n}_i \in \hat{\mathcal{N}}^{\mathscr{C}} : i \in [1, 64]\right\}, \; \hat{\mathcal{N}}^{\mathscr{C}}_{aux} := \left\{\boldsymbol{n}_0\right\},$$
$$\hat{\mathcal{E}}^{\mathscr{C}}_{cl} := \left\{w_{j_1 j_2} \cdot \mathfrak{E}_{j_1 j_2} \in \hat{\mathcal{E}}^{\mathscr{C}} : j_1, j_2 \in [1, 64], j_1 \neq j_2\right\}, \; \hat{\mathcal{E}}^{\mathscr{C}}_{aux} := \left\{\mathfrak{E}_{00}\right\} \tag{7.8}$$

their respective classical and auxiliary subsets. The generator (7.6) here uses the node state vector $\boldsymbol{s}^n \in \mathbb{Z}^{64}$ with elements $s^n_i \in \mathcal{S}^n$ in order to assign a state to each node of our seed graph $\hat{\mathscr{K}}^d_{64}$, and the matrix $\boldsymbol{w} \in \mathbb{B}^{64\times 64}_{-1}$ to assign a weight to each of its edge operators. The classical subsets (7.8) then define a concrete realisation of a positional chess graph $\mathscr{C}$ according to Section 7.1.2. The remainder of this chapter will be dedicated to the task of explicitly constructing $\boldsymbol{w}$ by means of an operator $\mathfrak{w}$ from node state vectors that describe legal positions during a chess game, and to the conception and formalisation of operators that generate successive chess positions by transforming a given node state vector $\boldsymbol{s}^n$ and its associated positional chess graph.

7.2 Generation of Positional Chess Graphs

With the notion of a positional chess graph $\mathscr{C}$ and an operator graph-theoretical representation $\hat{\mathscr{C}}$ of $\mathscr{C}$ finally at our disposal, let us now proceed and explicitly construct an operator $\mathfrak{w}$ that delivers the weights associated with each edge operator of $\hat{\mathscr{C}}$. As all moves a chess piece can legally perform depend primarily on the placement of all other pieces on the board, the operator $\mathfrak{w}$ must necessarily act on the node state vector $\boldsymbol{s}^n_p$ which uniquely describes a given chess position p. Furthermore, recalling the peculiarities of chess moves from Section 7.1.2, the set of arguments of $\mathfrak{w}$ must also include the node state vector $\boldsymbol{s}^n_{p-1}$ of the previous position $p-1$ to account for potential *en passant* capture moves, as well as a suitable algebraic object, which we will denote here by $\boldsymbol{\lambda}_p$, that marks the availability of castling moves at position p based on the history of the game. We then arrive with

$$\mathfrak{w} : \mathbb{Z}^{64} \times \mathbb{Z}^{64} \times \mathbb{B}^4 \to \mathbb{B}^{64\times 64}_{-1}, \; \mathfrak{w}[\boldsymbol{s}^n_p, \boldsymbol{s}^n_{p-1}, \boldsymbol{\lambda}_p] =: \boldsymbol{w}_p \tag{7.9}$$

at a general definition of $\mathfrak{w}$, where $\mathfrak{w}_p$ denotes the weight matrix that describes the chess graph $\mathscr{C}$ at position p during a game. Following the introduction of some necessary algebraic tools, we will formalise the contribution of each regular and special move to $\mathfrak{w}$, and we will eventually obtain a concrete representation of (7.9) after incorporating the algebraic rigorous handling of check positions.

7.2.1 Algebraic Preliminaries

We begin by introducing a set of primary transformation matrices that deliver the adjacency relations associated with moves of chess pieces by one square as well as terminated moves by multiple squares in any of the four cardinal and four intercardinal directions. These matrices form the building blocks for the algebraic formalisation of legal moves for all types of chess pieces later in this section. To prepare for this endeavour, let us define the sets

$$\mathcal{D}_c := \{\mathrm{N}, \mathrm{E}, \mathrm{S}, \mathrm{W}\}, \; \mathcal{D}_{ic} := \{\mathrm{NE}, \mathrm{SE}, \mathrm{SW}, \mathrm{NW}\}, \; \mathcal{D} := \mathcal{D}_c \cup \mathcal{D}_{ic} \qquad (7.10)$$

of all cardinal (N, *north*; E, *east*; S, *south*; W, *west*) and intercardinal directions (NE, *northeast*; SE, *southeast*; SW, *southwest*; NW, *northwest*). Furthermore, let

$$\boldsymbol{S}^n := \mathrm{diag}\,[\boldsymbol{s}^n] \qquad (7.11)$$

denote the diagonal matrix generated from a given node state vector $\boldsymbol{s}^n$, and let

$$\boldsymbol{s}^{nt} := s^{\mathrm{w}t} \cdot \delta[\boldsymbol{s}^n - s^{\mathrm{w}t} \cdot \boldsymbol{1}^{64\mathsf{T}}] + s^{\mathrm{b}t} \cdot \delta[\boldsymbol{s}^n - s^{\mathrm{b}t} \cdot \boldsymbol{1}^{64\mathsf{T}}], \; \boldsymbol{S}^{nt} := \mathrm{diag}\,[\boldsymbol{s}^{nt}] \qquad (7.12)$$

define a vector and its diagonal matrix that will mark all nodes in a state associated with a specific type $t \in \mathcal{T}$ of chess piece in a node state vector $\boldsymbol{s}^n$.

Moves by One Square

As the chess board with its regular (8×8)-dimensional grid has a fixed spatial layout, we can distinguish four primary movements from which every possible move of a chess piece can then be constructed. The first is a northward move by one square which changes the rank of a piece by one while leaving its file unchanged, the second a move eastwards which leaves the rank unchanged and advances the file by one, the third a move southwards reduces the rank by one while leaving the file unchanged and, finally, a westward move by one square which reduces the piece's file by one while preserving its rank. These four cardinal moves can be represented algebraically by $(64{\times}64)$-dimensional Boolean matrices $\boldsymbol{M}^{\mathrm{N}}$, $\boldsymbol{M}^{\mathrm{E}}$, $\boldsymbol{M}^{\mathrm{S}}$ and $\boldsymbol{M}^{\mathrm{W}}$, each with exactly 56 non-zero elements

$$M_{ij}^{\mathrm{N}} := \begin{cases} 1 & \text{for } i \in \mathbb{N} : 1 \le i \le 56, \, j = i + 8, \\ 0 & \text{otherwise,} \end{cases}$$

$$M^{\mathrm{E}}_{ij} := \begin{cases} 1 & \text{for } i \in \mathbb{N} \setminus 8\mathbb{N} : 1 \le i < 64, j = i + 1, \\ 0 & \text{otherwise}, \end{cases} \tag{7.13}$$

$$M^{\mathrm{S}}_{ij} := \begin{cases} 1 & \text{for } i \in \mathbb{N} : 9 \le i \le 64, j = i - 8, \\ 0 & \text{otherwise}, \end{cases}$$

$$M^{\mathrm{W}}_{ij} := \begin{cases} 1 & \text{for } i \in \mathbb{N} \setminus 8\mathbb{N}{+}1 : 1 < i \le 64, j = i - 1, \\ 0 & \text{otherwise} \end{cases}$$

marking directed adjacency relations from a source node i to a target node j in a positional chess graph. Here $\mathbb{N} \setminus 8\mathbb{N}$ denotes the set of all natural numbers that are not divisible by 8, and $\mathbb{N} \setminus 8\mathbb{N}{+}1$ the set of natural numbers which excludes numbers of the form $8i + 1, i \in \mathbb{N}$. It is important to note that the definition (7.13) respects the spatial boundary conditions of the chess board such that, for instance, a piece residing on node 8 (square $h1$) does not establish an adjacency relation associated with a move eastwards ($M^{\mathrm{E}}_{8,9} = 0$) or southwards.

With the matrices (7.13) at our disposal, we can now construct moves by one square in all intercardinal directions. A move in the northeast direction, for example, can be achieved by an unordered combination of a move northwards and eastwards. Considering all possible combinations, we eventually find

$$\begin{aligned} M^{\mathrm{NE}} &:= M^{\mathrm{N}} \cdot M^{\mathrm{E}} = M^{\mathrm{E}} \cdot M^{\mathrm{N}}, \\ M^{\mathrm{SE}} &:= M^{\mathrm{S}} \cdot M^{\mathrm{E}} = M^{\mathrm{E}} \cdot M^{\mathrm{S}}, \\ M^{\mathrm{SW}} &:= M^{\mathrm{S}} \cdot M^{\mathrm{W}} = M^{\mathrm{W}} \cdot M^{\mathrm{S}}, \\ M^{\mathrm{NW}} &:= M^{\mathrm{N}} \cdot M^{\mathrm{W}} = M^{\mathrm{W}} \cdot M^{\mathrm{N}} \end{aligned} \tag{7.14}$$

for the 64×64 Boolean matrices that mark with their non-zero elements every intercardinal move by one square. Given a node state vector s^n, the weighted directed adjacency relations associated with moves by one square that can be performed by all chess pieces on the board in any of the four cardinal or four intercardinal directions are then obtained through application of the operator

$$\mathfrak{w}^d : \mathbb{Z}^{64} \to \mathbb{B}^{64\times 64}_{-1}\,, \ \mathfrak{w}^d[s^n] := \operatorname{sgn}[S^n] \cdot M^d, \tag{7.15}$$

where $d \in \mathcal{D}$. Ignoring for the moment the question for which type of chess pieces the considered moves are legal, we illustrate in Fig. 7.2 (left) representative examples of the application of $\mathfrak{w}^d$.

Moves by Multiple Squares

Akin to the construction of intercardinal moves, multiplication of the matrices defined in (7.13) and (7.14) will yield the adjacency relations associated with moves by multiple squares. For example, the non-zero elements of the product $M^{\mathrm{N}} \cdot M^{\mathrm{N}}$ mark all adjacency relations that describe moves by two squares to

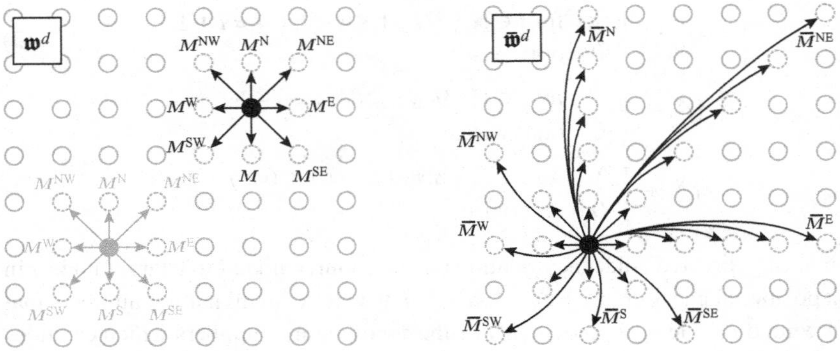

Figure 7.2 Constructing cardinal and intercardinal moves of chess pieces in a positional chess graph. Shown are examples of all weighted directed adjacency relations associated with moves by one square (left) and multiple squares (right) that are generated by the operators $\mathfrak{w}^d$ and $\bar{\mathfrak{w}}^d$ defined in (7.15) and (7.17). Adjacency relations associated with moves of white and black chess pieces are here, and in all forthcoming figures, respectively marked in grey and black, while adjacency relations with zero weight are omitted. Node states: $\text{sgn}\,[s^n_{19}] = 1$, $\text{sgn}\,[s^n_{46}] = -1$ and $s^n_i = 0\ \forall i \in [1, 64]{:}i \notin \{19, 46\}$ (left); $\text{sgn}\,[s^n_{19}] = -1$ and $s^n_i = 0$ $\forall i \in [1, 64]{:}i \neq 19$ (right).

the north for each square on the chess board, $(M^{N})^3$ by three squares and so forth. As there are at most seven squares reachable from any given square on the chess board in both cardinal and intercardinal directions, the sum

$$\bar{M}^d := \sum_{k=1}^{7} (M^d)^k \tag{7.16}$$

over successive matrix powers will thus generate the adjacency relations for all possible moves by multiple squares, and allow us to define the operator

$$\bar{\mathfrak{w}}^d : \mathbb{Z}^{64} \to \mathbb{B}^{64\times 64}_{-1}\,,\ \bar{\mathfrak{w}}^d[s^n] := \text{sgn}\,[S^n] \cdot \bar{M}^d \tag{7.17}$$

for $d \in \mathcal{D}$. However, it is important to stress here that although the adjacency relations obtained by applying $\bar{\mathfrak{w}}^d$ to a node state vector s^n do respect the spatial boundaries of the chess board, such that associated moves will naturally terminate once the border of the board is reached (see Fig. 7.2, right), the generation of a weight matrix according to (7.17) does not yet consider the eventual presence of other occupied nodes.

Termination of Moves

In order to algebraically formalise the termination of moves due to the presence of other pieces along the direction of the move, we need to distinguish two cases. If the first piece encountered along the move is of the same colour as the moving piece, a move to the associated square is not permitted and must terminate on the preceding square along the considered direction. If, on the other hand, the first piece encountered is of the opposing colour, a move up to and including the corresponding occupied square is permissible, thus allowing for the eventual capture of the opponent's piece.

Either of these two cases requires the detection of occupied nodes along the movement direction. If we ignore for a moment the colour state of occupied nodes, it can be shown that $\operatorname{sgn}[\bar{\mathfrak{w}}^d[\boldsymbol{s}^n] \cdot |\bar{\mathfrak{w}}^d[\boldsymbol{s}^n]|]$ generates all weighted adjacency relations that target nodes behind the first occupied node encountered in direction d, irrespective of whether the targeted nodes are occupied or not. Indeed, without loss of generality, let us assume that the state vector $\boldsymbol{s}^n$ contains two non-zero elements s_i^n and $s_{i'}^n$, where i' is the first occupied node in direction d of a move emanating from node i. Denoting with $j_k, k \in [1, m]$ all successive target nodes along d, we then find that $\exists k' \geq 1 : i' = j_{k'}$ and $s_{j_k}^n = 0$ for all $k \in [1, m] : k \neq k'$, such that $\bar{\mathfrak{w}}^d[\boldsymbol{s}^n]$ and $|\bar{\mathfrak{w}}^d[\boldsymbol{s}^n]|$ are represented by

$$\bar{\mathfrak{w}}^d[\boldsymbol{s}^n] = \operatorname{sgn}[s_i^n] \sum_{k=1}^{m} \delta_{i,j_k}^{64\times 64} + \operatorname{sgn}[s_{i'}^n] \sum_{k=k'+1}^{m} \delta_{j_{k'},j_k}^{64\times 64},$$

$$\left|\bar{\mathfrak{w}}^d[\boldsymbol{s}^n]\right| = \sum_{k=1}^{m} \delta_{i,j_k}^{64\times 64} + \sum_{k=k'+1}^{m} \delta_{j_{k'},j_k}^{64\times 64}$$

in terms of sums over Kronecker delta matrices (4.3) for some $m \in [1, 7]$ which depends on the distance of node i from the border of the chess board. Using (5.22), this yields

$$\begin{aligned}
&\bar{\mathfrak{w}}^d[\boldsymbol{s}^n] \cdot \left|\bar{\mathfrak{w}}^d[\boldsymbol{s}^n]\right| \\
&= \left(\operatorname{sgn}[s_i^n] \sum_{k=1}^{m} \delta_{i,j_k}^{64\times 64} + \operatorname{sgn}[s_{i'}^n] \sum_{k=k'+1}^{m} \delta_{j_{k'},j_k}^{64\times 64}\right) \cdot \left(\sum_{l=1}^{m} \delta_{i,j_l}^{64\times 64} + \sum_{l=k'+1}^{m} \delta_{j_{k'},j_l}^{64\times 64}\right) \\
&= \operatorname{sgn}[s_i^n] \sum_{k=1}^{m} \sum_{l=1}^{m} \delta_{i,j_k}^{64\times 64} \cdot \delta_{i,j_l}^{64\times 64} + \operatorname{sgn}[s_i^n] \sum_{k=1}^{m} \sum_{l=k'+1}^{m} \delta_{i,j_k}^{64\times 64} \cdot \delta_{j_{k'},j_l}^{64\times 64} \\
&\quad + \operatorname{sgn}[s_{i'}^n] \sum_{k=k'+1}^{m} \sum_{l=1}^{m} \delta_{j_{k'},j_k}^{64\times 64} \cdot \delta_{i,j_l}^{64\times 64} + \operatorname{sgn}[s_{i'}^n] \sum_{k=k'+1}^{m} \sum_{l=k'+1}^{m} \delta_{j_{k'},j_k}^{64\times 64} \cdot \delta_{j_{k'},j_l}^{64\times 64} \\
&= \operatorname{sgn}[s_i^n] \sum_{k=k'+1}^{m} \delta_{i,j_k}^{64\times 64} \equiv \operatorname{sgn}\left[\bar{\mathfrak{w}}^d[\boldsymbol{s}^n] \cdot \left|\bar{\mathfrak{w}}^d[\boldsymbol{s}^n]\right|\right],
\end{aligned}$$

and delivers all adjacency relations from node i to nodes $j_k : k > k'$ that reside behind i' along the direction d of the considered move.

Cases in which more than one occupied node is present along the direction d of a move originating at node i can be treated in a similar fashion. Adapting the above evaluation by assuming that there exists another occupied node i'' with $s^n_{i''} \neq 0$ behind i', for example, we find that $\exists k'' \geq k' : i'' = j_{k''}$ and $s^n_{j_k} = 0$ for all $k \in [1, m] : k \neq k', k''$ such that

$$\begin{aligned}
&\bar{\mathfrak{w}}^d[s^n] \cdot \left|\bar{\mathfrak{w}}^d[s^n]\right| \\
&\quad = \operatorname{sgn}[s^n_i] \sum_{k=k'+1}^{m} \delta^{64\times 64}_{i,j_k} + \operatorname{sgn}[s^n_i] \sum_{k=k''+1}^{m} \delta^{64\times 64}_{i,j_k} + \operatorname{sgn}[s^n_{i'}] \sum_{k=k''+1}^{m} \delta^{64\times 64}_{j_{k'},j_k} \\
&\quad = \operatorname{sgn}[s^n_i] \sum_{k=k'+1}^{k''} \delta^{64\times 64}_{i,j_k} + 2\operatorname{sgn}[s^n_i] \sum_{k=k''+1}^{m} \delta^{64\times 64}_{i,j_k} + \operatorname{sgn}[s^n_{i'}] \sum_{k=k''+1}^{m} \delta^{64\times 64}_{j_{k'},j_k}.
\end{aligned}$$

Here the counting of multiple edges between the source node i and target nodes $j_k, k \in [k'' + 1, m]$ in the second term is prevented by applying the signum operator, thus leaving us again with $\operatorname{sgn}[\bar{\mathfrak{w}}^d[s^n] \cdot |\bar{\mathfrak{w}}^d[s^n]|]$.

The eventual termination of a considered move due to the presence of occupied nodes along the movement direction can now be algebraically formalised by simply removing all directed edges generated by $\operatorname{sgn}[\bar{\mathfrak{w}}^d[s^n] \cdot |\bar{\mathfrak{w}}^d[s^n]|]$ from those returned by $\bar{\mathfrak{w}}^d[s^n]$. Specifically, the operator

$$\bar{\mathfrak{w}}^{\dagger d} : \mathbb{Z}^{64} \to \mathbb{B}^{64\times 64}_{-1}, \; \bar{\mathfrak{w}}^{\dagger d}[s^n] := \bar{\mathfrak{w}}^d[s^n] - \operatorname{sgn}\left[\bar{\mathfrak{w}}^d[s^n] \cdot \left|\bar{\mathfrak{w}}^d[s^n]\right|\right] \tag{7.18}$$

delivers, for each piece present on the board, the weighted adjacency relations associated with moves by multiple squares in direction d that target nodes up to and including the first occupied node encountered along d. As illustrated in Fig. 7.3 (left), the operator $\bar{\mathfrak{w}}^{\dagger d}$ then correctly constructs not only terminated moves, but also possible legal capture moves in the case that the colour state associated with the moving piece and the first piece encountered are distinct.

Illegal Capture Moves

It remains to exclude from the set of adjacency relations generated by $\bar{\mathfrak{w}}^{\dagger d}$ all those relations which target nodes in a colour state identical to that of the source node. In order to algebraically formalise the removal of such *illegal capture moves*, we recognise that, given a matrix w of weighted adjacency relations describing moves of chess pieces in state s^n, right-hand matrix multiplication of w with $\operatorname{sgn}[S^n] = \operatorname{sgn}[\operatorname{diag}[s^n]]$ yields a matrix which only marks edges to occupied target nodes such that

$$\left(w \cdot \operatorname{sgn}[S^n]\right)_{ij} = \begin{cases} -1 & \text{iff } \operatorname{sgn}[s^n_i] \neq \operatorname{sgn}[s^n_j], \\ 1 & \text{iff } \operatorname{sgn}[s^n_i] = \operatorname{sgn}[s^n_j], \\ 0 & \text{otherwise,} \end{cases}$$

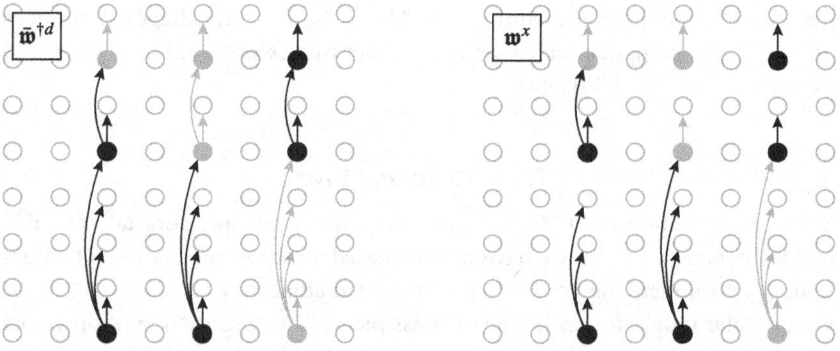

Figure 7.3 Adjacency relations associated with terminated moves of chess pieces. When applied to a node state vector s^n, the operator $\bar{\mathfrak{w}}^{\dagger d}$ in (7.18) returns a weight matrix w that describes terminated moves by multiple squares in any cardinal or intercardinal direction d, and includes illegal capture moves marked by adjacency relations in which source and target nodes have the same colour state (left). The weight matrix generated by $\mathfrak{w}^x[s^n,w]$ in (7.19) excludes all adjacency relations associated with illegal capture moves and, thus, correctly describe both cases of terminated moves (right). Exemplified are moves northwards, with multiple occupied nodes present along the movement direction. Node states: $\operatorname{sgn}[s_i^n] = -1$ for $i \in \{3, 5, 35, 39, 55\}$, $\operatorname{sgn}[s_i^n] = 1$ for $i \in \{7, 37, 51, 53\}$, all other s_i^n=0.

and that right-hand multiplication of $(\operatorname{sgn}[S^n] \cdot w)$ with $|\operatorname{sgn}[S^n]|$ returns the matrix of adjacency relations associated with w such that

$$\left(\operatorname{sgn}[S^n] \cdot w \cdot \left|\operatorname{sgn}[S^n]\right|\right)_{ij} = \left|w \cdot \operatorname{sgn}[S^n]\right|_{ij}$$
$$= \begin{cases} 1 & \text{iff} \left|\operatorname{sgn}[s_i^n]\right| = \left|\operatorname{sgn}[s_j^n]\right| = 1, \\ 0 & \text{otherwise.} \end{cases}$$

Adding both of these constructs will then mark all unweighted edges between occupied source and target nodes of the same colour, from which – through left-hand matrix multiplication with $\operatorname{sgn}[S^n]$ – the corresponding weighted edges can be obtained. This finally leaves us with the operator

$$\mathfrak{w}^x : \mathbb{Z}^{64} \times \mathbb{B}_{-1}^{64\times 64} \to \mathbb{B}_{-1}^{64\times 64}, \tag{7.19}$$
$$\mathfrak{w}^x[s^n, w] := w - \frac{1}{2}\left(\operatorname{sgn}[S^n] \cdot w \cdot \operatorname{sgn}[S^n] + \left|\operatorname{sgn}[S^n]\right| \cdot w \cdot \left|\operatorname{sgn}[S^n]\right|\right),$$

which, when applied to a state vector $s^n \in \mathbb{Z}^{64}$ and weight matrix $w \in \mathbb{B}_{-1}^{64\times 64}$, returns a matrix of weighted adjacency relations which excludes all edges between source and target nodes of the same colour from w, and thus all illegal capture moves. We note here that the presence of the normalising factor 1/2 in the second term ensures edge weights in $\mathbb{B}_{-1}$, and that the definition of $\mathfrak{w}^x$

made use of the general identity $(\mathrm{sgn}[\boldsymbol{A}])^2 = |\mathrm{sgn}[\boldsymbol{A}]|$ for diagonal matrices $\boldsymbol{A} \in \mathbb{Q}^{n \times n}$. The application of $\mathfrak{w}^x$ to a weight matrix obtained through $\bar{\mathfrak{w}}^{\dagger d}$ is exemplified in Fig. 7.3 (right).

7.2.2 Regular Moves

With the definition of $\boldsymbol{M}^d$, $\bar{\boldsymbol{M}}^d$ and construction of operators $\mathfrak{w}^d$, $\bar{\mathfrak{w}}^d$, $\bar{\mathfrak{w}}^{\dagger d}$ and $\mathfrak{w}^x$ in (7.13)–(7.19), we have now gathered all the necessary tools to algebraically formulate the generation of weighted adjacency relations associated with regular moves for each type of chess piece. The construction of operators which deliver the adjacency relations associated with the *en passant* capture of a pawn and castling move of a king will follow in Section 7.2.3. However, it is important to caution here that all these operators will generate weight matrices that could still include illegal capture moves, as well as moves which might leave the king of the same colour as the moving piece in check. Both shortcomings will be dealt with after the complete set of adjacency relations associated with regular and special moves for all types of chess pieces in any conceivable legal position has been made available.

King

Moves by one square in each of the four cardinal and four intercardinal directions constitute the complete set of possible regular moves a king on the chess board can perform. Recalling that (7.15) generates moves by one square in direction $d \in \mathcal{D}$, the sum of $\mathfrak{w}^d$ over all directions then defines an operator

$$\mathfrak{w}^{\mathrm{K}} \colon \mathbb{Z}^{64} \to \mathbb{B}_{-1}^{64 \times 64},\ \mathfrak{w}^{\mathrm{K}}[\boldsymbol{s}^n] := \mathrm{sgn}\,[\boldsymbol{S}^{n\mathrm{K}}] \cdot \sum_{d \in \mathcal{D}} \boldsymbol{M}^d, \qquad (7.20)$$

which returns the weighted and directed adjacency relations associated with all regular moves of the king when applied to a given node state vector $\boldsymbol{s}^n$. We note here that, according to (7.12), the diagonal matrix $\boldsymbol{S}^{n\mathrm{K}}$ on the right-hand side of (7.20) ensures that only nodes in states s^{wK} and s^{bK} – that is, only squares occupied by the white and black king – are considered. A representative example of the action of operator (7.20) is illustrated in Fig. 7.4 (left).

Queen

The queen, as the most mobile type of chess piece, can move multiple squares in each of the four cardinal and four intercardinal directions, ideally until the boundary of the board is reached, or the first occupied square along a movement direction is encountered. By constructing all possible moves through the sum of $\bar{\mathfrak{w}}^d$ over all directions $d \in \mathcal{D}$, and by adapting the argumentation which

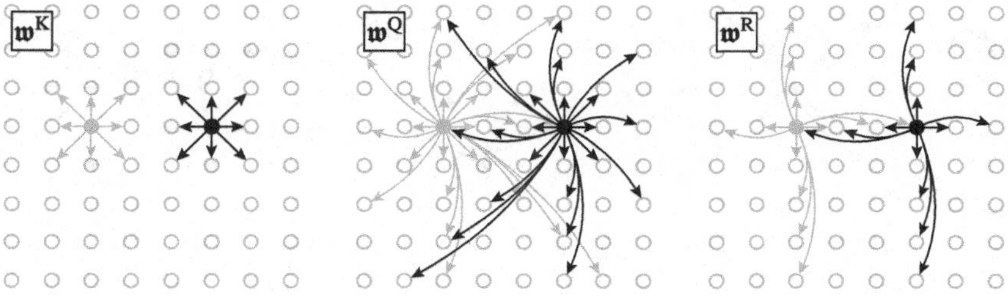

Figure 7.4 Regular moves of king, queen and rook. Representative examples of the application of operators $\mathfrak{w}^{\mathrm{K}}$, $\mathfrak{w}^{\mathrm{Q}}$ and $\mathfrak{w}^{\mathrm{R}}$ defined in (7.20), (7.21) and (7.22). These operators generate all weighted adjacency relations associated with regular moves but do not yet exclude illegal capture moves and moves which could result in a check position for the moving colour. Node states: $s^n_{35} = s^{\mathrm{wK}}$, $s^n_{38} = s^{\mathrm{bK}}$ (left); $s^n_{35} = s^{\mathrm{wQ}}$, $s^n_{38} = s^{\mathrm{bQ}}$ (middle); $s^n_{35} = s^{\mathrm{wR}}$, $s^n_{38} = s^{\mathrm{bR}}$ (right); all other $s^n_i = 0$.

led us to define $\bar{\mathfrak{w}}^{\dagger d}$ in order to algebraically formalise the eventual termination of these moves, we then obtain with

$$\mathfrak{w}^{\mathrm{Q}} : \mathbb{Z}^{64} \to \mathbb{B}^{64\times 64}_{-1}, \tag{7.21}$$
$$\mathfrak{w}^{\mathrm{Q}}[\boldsymbol{s}^n] := \operatorname{sgn}[\boldsymbol{S}^{n\mathrm{Q}}] \cdot \sum_{d\in\mathcal{D}} \bar{\boldsymbol{M}}^d - \operatorname{sgn}\left[\operatorname{sgn}[\boldsymbol{S}^{n\mathrm{Q}}] \cdot \sum_{d\in\mathcal{D}} \bar{\boldsymbol{M}}^d \cdot \left|\operatorname{sgn}[\boldsymbol{S}^n]\right| \cdot \bar{\boldsymbol{M}}^d\right]$$

an operator which, given a node state $\boldsymbol{s}^n$, returns the weighted adjacency relations for all regular moves of a queen (Fig. 7.4, middle).

Rook

By restricting in (7.21) the sum over $d \in \mathcal{D}$ to the subset $\mathcal{D}_c$ of all four cardinal directions, the operator $\mathfrak{w}^{\mathrm{Q}}$ can immediately be adapted to yield with

$$\mathfrak{w}^{\mathrm{R}} : \mathbb{Z}^{64} \to \mathbb{B}^{64\times 64}_{-1}, \tag{7.22}$$
$$\mathfrak{w}^{\mathrm{R}}[\boldsymbol{s}^n] := \operatorname{sgn}[\boldsymbol{S}^{n\mathrm{R}}] \cdot \sum_{d\in\mathcal{D}_c} \bar{\boldsymbol{M}}^d - \operatorname{sgn}\left[\operatorname{sgn}[\boldsymbol{S}^{n\mathrm{R}}] \cdot \sum_{d\in\mathcal{D}_c} \bar{\boldsymbol{M}}^d \cdot \left|\operatorname{sgn}[\boldsymbol{S}^n]\right| \cdot \bar{\boldsymbol{M}}^d\right]$$

an operator that delivers the weighted and directed adjacency relations associated with all regular moves a rook can perform (Fig. 7.4, right).

Bishop

Similar to the construction of (7.22), limiting d to the subset $\mathcal{D}_{ic}$ of all four intercardinal directions defines the operator

$$\mathfrak{w}^{\mathrm{B}} : \mathbb{Z}^{64} \to \mathbb{B}^{64\times 64}_{-1}, \tag{7.23}$$
$$\mathfrak{w}^{\mathrm{B}}[\boldsymbol{s}^n] := \operatorname{sgn}[\boldsymbol{S}^{n\mathrm{B}}] \cdot \sum_{d\in\mathcal{D}_{ic}} \bar{\boldsymbol{M}}^d - \operatorname{sgn}\left[\operatorname{sgn}[\boldsymbol{S}^{n\mathrm{B}}] \cdot \sum_{d\in\mathcal{D}_{ic}} \bar{\boldsymbol{M}}^d \cdot \left|\operatorname{sgn}[\boldsymbol{S}^n]\right| \cdot \bar{\boldsymbol{M}}^d\right]$$

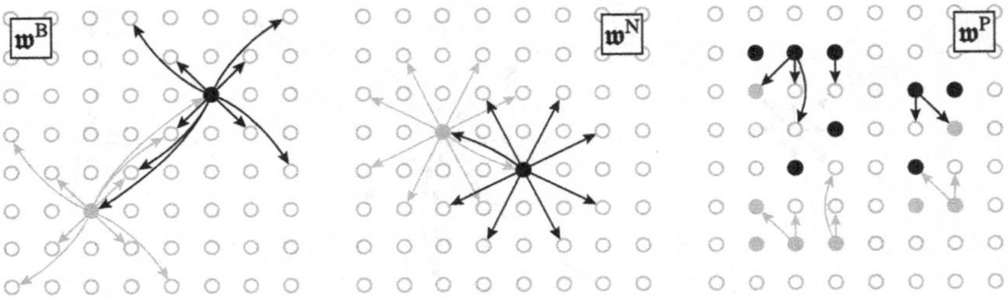

Figure 7.5 Regular moves of bishop, knight and pawn. Examples of the application of operators $\mathfrak{w}^{B}$, $\mathfrak{w}^{N}$ and $\mathfrak{w}^{P}$ defined in (7.23), (7.24) and (7.31). These operators generate all weighted adjacency relations associated with regular moves but do not yet exclude illegal capture moves and moves which could result in a check position for the moving colour. Node states: $s^n_{19} = s^{wB}$, $s^n_{46} = s^{bB}$ (left); $s^n_{35} = s^{wN}$, $s^n_{29} = s^{bN}$ (middle); $s^n_i = s^{wQ}$ for $i \in \{18, 39, 42\}$, $s^n_i = s^{bQ}$ for $i \in \{27, 30, 36\}$, $s^n_i = s^{wP}$ for $i \in \{10, 11, 12, 22, 23\}$, $s^n_i = s^{bP}$ for $i \in \{46, 47, 50, 51, 52\}$ (right); all other $s^n_i = 0$.

for generating the weighted adjacency relations associated with regular moves of bishops from a given node state vector $\boldsymbol{s}^n$. A representative example of the application of (7.23) is illustrated in Fig. 7.5 (left).

Knight

There are moves to at most eight squares a knight can legally perform in any given position. These moves are constructed by combining a move into a cardinal and intercardinal direction, or by combinations of three cardinal moves. Considering all possibilities according to the rules of chess, we then easily find

$$\mathfrak{w}^{N} : \mathbb{Z}^{64} \to \mathbb{B}_{-1}^{64\times 64}\,, \tag{7.24}$$

$$\mathfrak{w}^{N}[\boldsymbol{s}^n] := \operatorname{sgn}[\boldsymbol{S}^{nN}] \cdot \big(\boldsymbol{M}^{N}\cdot\boldsymbol{M}^{NE} + \boldsymbol{M}^{N}\cdot\boldsymbol{M}^{NW} + \boldsymbol{M}^{E}\cdot\boldsymbol{M}^{NE} + \boldsymbol{M}^{E}\cdot\boldsymbol{M}^{SE} + \boldsymbol{M}^{S}\cdot\boldsymbol{M}^{SE} + \boldsymbol{M}^{S}\cdot\boldsymbol{M}^{SW} + \boldsymbol{M}^{W}\cdot\boldsymbol{M}^{SW} + \boldsymbol{M}^{W}\cdot\boldsymbol{M}^{NW}\big)$$

as an operator which, when applied to a given node state vector $\boldsymbol{s}^n$, generates all weighted adjacency relations associated with regular moves of knights present on the chess board (Fig. 7.5, middle).

Pawn

In comparison to all other types of chess pieces, the generation of adjacency relations associated with regular pawn moves is somewhat more involved. Indeed, not only is every possible move of a pawn tied to its colour state, with a white pawn being generally allowed only to advance northwards by one square, and a black pawn being restricted to southward moves by one square, but we also need to distinguish two complementary movements which are subject to stringent conditions. Firstly, in addition to their regular moves by one square, a white pawn residing on rank 2 can also move by two squares to the north, and a black pawn on rank 7 by two squares to the south. As ranks 2 and 7 mark the placement of all 16 pawns in the initial chess position, we will call such a move by two squares *initial pawn move*. Secondly, if a piece of the opposing colour is present on the diagonally neighbouring square in the pawn's general movement direction, the pawn can eventually capture this piece by moving one square in an intercardinal direction (*pawn capture move*).

In order to deal with both of these peculiarities of regular pawn moves on an algebraic level, let us introduce a Boolean row vector $\boldsymbol{h_r} \in \mathbb{B}^{64}$ with elements

$$(\boldsymbol{h_r})_i = \begin{cases} 1 & \text{if } \lfloor (i-1)/8 \rfloor = r-1, \\ 0 & \text{otherwise} \end{cases} \tag{7.25}$$

whose non-zero elements mark all nodes associated with the squares on a given rank r of the chess board. Let

$$\boldsymbol{H_r} := \text{diag}\,[\boldsymbol{h_r}] \in \mathbb{B}^{64\times 64} \tag{7.26}$$

denote the diagonal matrix associated with $\boldsymbol{h_r}$. Considering for a moment only pawns with a state value s^{wP}, we can then define the operator

$$\begin{aligned} \mathfrak{w}^{\text{wP}} &: \mathbb{Z}^{64} \to \mathbb{B}_{-1}^{64\times 64}\,, \\ \mathfrak{w}^{\text{wP}}[\boldsymbol{s}^n] &:= \text{sgn}\,[\boldsymbol{S}^{n\text{wP}}] \cdot \left(\boldsymbol{M}^{\text{N}} + \boldsymbol{H}_2 \cdot (\boldsymbol{M}^{\text{N}})^2\right) \cdot \left(\boldsymbol{I}^{64} - \left|\text{sgn}\,[\boldsymbol{S}^n]\right|\right) \\ &\quad - \text{sgn}\left[\text{sgn}\,[\boldsymbol{S}^{n\text{wP}}] \cdot \boldsymbol{H}_2 \cdot \boldsymbol{M}^{\text{N}} \cdot \left|\text{sgn}\,[\boldsymbol{S}^n]\right| \cdot \boldsymbol{M}^{\text{N}}\right] \cdot \left(\boldsymbol{I}^{64} - \left|\text{sgn}\,[\boldsymbol{S}^n]\right|\right) \\ &\quad + \text{sgn}\,[\boldsymbol{S}^{n\text{wP}}] \cdot \left(\boldsymbol{M}^{\text{NE}} + \boldsymbol{M}^{\text{NW}}\right) \cdot \left|\text{sgn}\,[\boldsymbol{S}^n]\right| \end{aligned} \tag{7.27}$$

for generating all weighted adjacency relations associated with regular moves of white pawns, including initial pawn and pawn capture moves, from a given node state vector $\boldsymbol{s}^n$. Here $\boldsymbol{S}^{n\text{wP}} := \text{diag}\,[\boldsymbol{s}^{n\text{wP}}]$ denotes the diagonal matrix of

$$\boldsymbol{s}^{n\text{wP}} := s^{\text{wP}} \cdot \boldsymbol{\delta}[\boldsymbol{s}^n - s^{\text{wP}} \cdot \boldsymbol{1}^{64\text{T}}], \tag{7.28}$$

which, akin to (7.12), selects all nodes with a state value s^{wP} from $\boldsymbol{s}^n$. The first two terms in (7.27) deliver the adjacency relations for terminated moves by one and, in the case the pawn resides on rank 2, by two squares northwards. In contrast to the termination of moves described by the operator $\bar{\mathfrak{w}}^{\dagger d}$ in (7.18), however, we exclude here also moves to the first occupied node, irrespective of its colour state, as none of these northward moves can be a capture according to the rules of chess. The third term on the right-hand side of (7.27) inspects the given node state vector $\boldsymbol{s}^n$ for the presence of occupied nodes located northeast and northwest of each pawn, and eventually contributes the weighted adjacency relations associated with potential pawn capture moves, including invalid capture moves.

In a similar fashion, the adjacency relations associated with all regular moves of black pawns are generated. By simply replacing the movement direction and the rank requirement for initial pawn moves in (7.27), we find

$$\begin{aligned} \mathfrak{w}^{\mathrm{bP}} &: \mathbb{Z}^{64} \to \mathbb{B}_{-1}^{64\times 64}, \\ \mathfrak{w}^{\mathrm{bP}}[s^n] &:= \operatorname{sgn}[\boldsymbol{S}^{n\mathrm{bP}}] \cdot \left(\boldsymbol{M}^{\mathrm{S}} + \boldsymbol{H}_7 \cdot (\boldsymbol{M}^{\mathrm{S}})^2\right) \cdot \left(\boldsymbol{I}^{64} - \left|\operatorname{sgn}[\boldsymbol{S}^n]\right|\right) \\ &\quad - \operatorname{sgn}\left[\operatorname{sgn}[\boldsymbol{S}^{n\mathrm{bP}}] \cdot \boldsymbol{H}_7 \cdot \boldsymbol{M}^{\mathrm{S}} \cdot \left|\operatorname{sgn}[\boldsymbol{S}^n]\right| \cdot \boldsymbol{M}^{\mathrm{S}}\right] \cdot \left(\boldsymbol{I}^{64} - \left|\operatorname{sgn}[\boldsymbol{S}^n]\right|\right) \\ &\quad + \operatorname{sgn}[\boldsymbol{S}^{n\mathrm{bP}}] \cdot \left(\boldsymbol{M}^{\mathrm{SE}} + \boldsymbol{M}^{\mathrm{SW}}\right) \cdot \left|\operatorname{sgn}[\boldsymbol{S}^n]\right|, \end{aligned} \tag{7.29}$$

where $\boldsymbol{S}^{n\mathrm{bP}} := \operatorname{diag}[\boldsymbol{s}^{n\mathrm{bP}}]$ with

$$\boldsymbol{s}^{n\mathrm{bP}} := s^{\mathrm{bP}} \cdot \delta[\boldsymbol{s}^n - s^{\mathrm{bP}} \cdot \boldsymbol{1}^{64}]. \tag{7.30}$$

With (7.27) and (7.29), we then constructed the complete set of weighted adjacency relations that describe the regular moves of pawns present on the board in any given legal position $\boldsymbol{s}^n$, and we can finally define

$$\mathfrak{w}^{\mathrm{P}} : \mathbb{Z}^{64} \to \mathbb{B}_{-1}^{64\times 64}, \ \mathfrak{w}^{\mathrm{P}}[s^n] := \mathfrak{w}^{\mathrm{wP}}[s^n] + \mathfrak{w}^{\mathrm{bP}}[s^n]. \tag{7.31}$$

An application of this operator to a position that distinguishes every conceivable case is exemplified in Fig. 7.5 (right).

Legal Regular Moves

With operators (7.20)–(7.24) and (7.31) at our disposal, we are now one step closer to generating positional chess graphs according to (7.6)–(7.8). Indeed, by considering the sum

$$\tilde{w}^{reg} = \tilde{\mathfrak{w}}^{reg}[s^n] := \mathfrak{w}^{\mathrm{K}}[s^n] + \mathfrak{w}^{\mathrm{Q}}[s^n] + \mathfrak{w}^{\mathrm{R}}[s^n] + \mathfrak{w}^{\mathrm{B}}[s^n] + \mathfrak{w}^{\mathrm{N}}[s^n] + \mathfrak{w}^{\mathrm{P}}[s^n],$$

we have defined a matrix of weighted adjacency relations that represents the regular moves, and illegal capture moves, which each individual piece in a given position $\boldsymbol{s}^n$ can perform. In order to remove from $\tilde{w}^{reg}$ all those adjacency relations for which both source and target nodes are in the same colour state, we can employ the operator $\mathfrak{w}^x$ introduced in (7.19) and eventually find with

$$\begin{aligned} \mathfrak{w}^{reg} &: \mathbb{Z}^{64} \to \mathbb{B}_{-1}^{64\times 64}, \\ \mathfrak{w}^{reg}[s^n] &:= \tilde{\mathfrak{w}}^{reg}[s^n] - \frac{1}{2}\Big(\operatorname{sgn}[\boldsymbol{S}^n] \cdot \tilde{\mathfrak{w}}^{reg}[s^n] \cdot \operatorname{sgn}[\boldsymbol{S}^n] \\ &\qquad + \left|\operatorname{sgn}[\boldsymbol{S}^n]\right| \cdot \tilde{\mathfrak{w}}^{reg}[s^n] \cdot \left|\operatorname{sgn}[\boldsymbol{S}^n]\right|\Big) \end{aligned} \tag{7.32}$$

an operator that generates, from a given node state vector $\boldsymbol{s}^n$ describing a legal chess position, the weighted adjacency relations associated with every possible regular move and, thus, the overwhelming majority of allowed moves in a typical position during a game of chess. What remains is to take on the arguably more demanding challenges of incorporating with *en passant* capture and castling the two special chess moves, and of detecting, and eventually discarding, from the set of possible moves all those which would result in a check position for the moving colour. By meeting both of these challenges, we will then have accomplished our goal of generating positional chess graphs for any given legal chess position in an algebraically rigorous fashion.

7.2.3 Special Moves

Besides the regular moves described so far, the game of chess also allows for a number of less common moves which demand special attention. These special moves are the *en passant* capture of a pawn, the castling of the king and the promotion of a pawn. While the latter requires a manual change of the node state vector during a game that is solely based on a player's subjective decision and, therefore, will not be considered here, the possible execution of both the *en passant* capture and castling move are subject to stringent yet algebraically formalisable conditions which partially depend on previous positions and, thus, a reduced record of the positional history of a chess game.

En Passant Capture

Let us first take a look at the *en passant* capture move. According to the rules of chess, such a capture is allowed only when a pawn of a given colour advances two squares from its initial position, that is from rank 2 for white or rank 7 for black, and a pawn of the opponent's colour resides next to the square of arrival. If these conditions are satisfied, the opponent's pawn has the right to capture this pawn "in passing" (*en passant*) with and only with the next move by advancing diagonally to the square located directly behind it.

In order to formalise these conditions algebraically, let

$$\boldsymbol{I_r} := \left\{i \in [1,64] : (\boldsymbol{h_r})_i = 1\right\} \tag{7.33}$$

define the index set of nodes residing on rank $\boldsymbol{r}$ of the chess board, and let $\boldsymbol{s}^n_{p-1}$ and $\boldsymbol{s}^n_p$ denote node state vectors defining two successive positions $p-1$ and p during a chess game. The *en passant* capture move of a black pawn is then allowed if and only if

(1) $\exists!\,(i_1 \in \boldsymbol{I}_2, i_2 \in \boldsymbol{I}_4)$ such that
$(\boldsymbol{s}^n_p - \boldsymbol{s}^n_{p-1})_{i_1} = -s^{\mathrm{wP}}, (\boldsymbol{s}^n_p - \boldsymbol{s}^n_{p-1})_{i_2} = s^{\mathrm{wP}}, (\boldsymbol{s}^n_p - \boldsymbol{s}^n_{p-1})_i = 0\;\forall i \notin \{i_1, i_2\},$

(2) $\exists i_3 \in \mathcal{I}_4, i_3 \in \{i_2 - 1, i_2 + 1\}$ such that $(\boldsymbol{s}_p^n)_{i_3} = s^{\text{bP}}$.

These necessary and sufficient conditions directly translate into the operator

$$\mathfrak{w}^{ep\text{bP}} : \mathbb{Z}^{64} \times \mathbb{Z}^{64} \to \mathbb{B}_{-1}^{64\times 64}, \tag{7.34}$$
$$\mathfrak{w}^{ep\text{bP}}[\boldsymbol{s}_p^n, \boldsymbol{s}_{p-1}^n] := \text{sgn}\,[\boldsymbol{S}_p^{n\text{bP}}] \cdot \boldsymbol{H}_4 \cdot \left(\boldsymbol{M}^{\text{SE}} + \boldsymbol{M}^{\text{SW}}\right)$$
$$\times \text{diag}\left[\left(\text{sgn}\,[\boldsymbol{s}_p^n] - \text{sgn}\,[\boldsymbol{s}_{p-1}^n]\right) \cdot \text{sgn}\,[\boldsymbol{S}_p^{n\text{wP}}] \cdot \boldsymbol{H}_4 \cdot \boldsymbol{M}^{\text{S}}\right]$$

for generating the adjacency relations of all possible *en passant* capture moves of black pawns. The first term in this product constructs here for each black pawn residing on rank 4 the edges associated with moves to the southeast and southwest – that is the moves which describe eventual *en passant* captures. The row vector $(\text{sgn}[\boldsymbol{s}_p^n] - \text{sgn}[\boldsymbol{s}_{p-1}^n]) \cdot \text{sgn}\,\boldsymbol{S}_p^{n\text{wP}} \cdot \boldsymbol{H}_4$ in the second term yields the difference of white pawn positions on rank 4 as a result of an initial pawn move according to condition (1), while subsequent right-hand matrix multiplication with $\boldsymbol{M}^{\text{S}}$ describes the temporary placement of the at most one pawn satisfying this condition on the neighbouring square to the south where it can serve as the target for an eventual capture move by a black pawn according to condition (2). After converting this vector into a diagonal matrix, multiplication with the first term selects the at most two adjacency relations which target the temporarily deplaced white pawn and, thus, represent possible *en passant* capture moves.

In a similar fashion, we can formulate

(1) $\exists!\,(i_1 \in \mathcal{I}_7, i_2 \in \mathcal{I}_5)$ such that
$(\boldsymbol{s}_p^n - \boldsymbol{s}_{p-1}^n)_{i_1} = -s^{\text{bP}}, (\boldsymbol{s}_p^n - \boldsymbol{s}_{p-1}^n)_{i_2} = s^{\text{bP}}, (\boldsymbol{s}_p^n - \boldsymbol{s}_{p-1}^n)_i = 0\ \forall i \notin \{i_1, i_2\}$,

(2) $\exists i_3 \in \mathcal{I}_5, i_3 \in \{i_2 - 1, i_2 + 1\}$ such that $(\boldsymbol{s}_p^n)_{i_3} = s^{\text{wP}}$

as both necessary and sufficient conditions for an *en passant* capture move of a white pawn, and obtain with

$$\mathfrak{w}^{ep\text{wP}} : \mathbb{Z}^{64} \times \mathbb{Z}^{64} \to \mathbb{B}_{-1}^{64\times 64}, \tag{7.35}$$
$$\mathfrak{w}^{ep\text{wP}}[\boldsymbol{s}_p^n, \boldsymbol{s}_{p-1}^n] := \text{sgn}\,[\boldsymbol{S}_p^{n\text{wP}}] \cdot \boldsymbol{H}_5 \cdot \left(\boldsymbol{M}^{\text{NE}} + \boldsymbol{M}^{\text{NW}}\right)$$
$$\times \text{diag}\left[\left(\text{sgn}\,[\boldsymbol{s}_p^n] - \text{sgn}\,[\boldsymbol{s}_{p-1}^n]\right) \cdot \text{sgn}\,[\boldsymbol{S}_p^{n\text{bP}}] \cdot \boldsymbol{H}_5 \cdot \boldsymbol{M}^{\text{N}}\right]$$

an operator that returns all weighted adjacency relations associated with such a move. By simply adding (7.34) and (7.35), we then find the operator

$$\mathfrak{w}^{ep} : \mathbb{Z}^{64} \times \mathbb{Z}^{64} \to \mathbb{B}_{-1}^{64\times 64}, \tag{7.36}$$
$$\mathfrak{w}^{ep}[\boldsymbol{s}_p^n, \boldsymbol{s}_{p-1}^n] := \mathfrak{w}^{ep\text{wP}}[\boldsymbol{s}_p^n, \boldsymbol{s}_{p-1}^n] + \mathfrak{w}^{ep\text{bP}}[\boldsymbol{s}_p^n, \boldsymbol{s}_{p-1}^n]$$

for generating the complete set of weighted adjacency relations associated with possible *en passant* capture moves of pawns from two given node state vectors

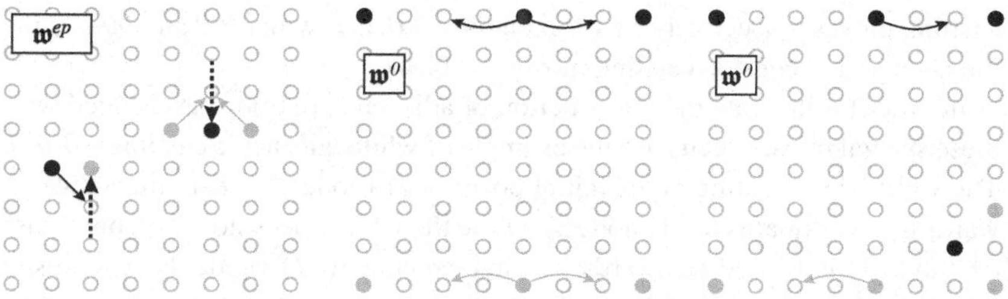

Figure 7.6 Special chess moves. Examples of an application of $\mathfrak{w}^{ep}$ in (7.36) and $\mathfrak{w}^{0}$ in (7.45). In the case of *en passant* capture moves (left), dotted arrows indicate initial pawn moves. For illustrative purposes, both the white pawn on $c2$ (node 11) and black pawn on $f7$ (node 54) were moved from their initial positions. In the case of castling, only adjacency relations associated with moves of the king are generated by $\mathfrak{w}^{0}$ (middle), while all conditions required for castling are considered (right). For both examples, we assumed $\boldsymbol{\lambda} = \{1, 1, 1, 1\}$. Node states: $(\boldsymbol{s}^n_{p-1})_i = s^{\mathrm{wP}}$ for $i \in \{11, 37, 39\}$, $(\boldsymbol{s}^n_{p-1})_i = s^{\mathrm{bP}}$ for $i \in \{26, 54\}$, $(\boldsymbol{s}^n_p)_i = s^{\mathrm{wP}}$ for $i \in \{27, 37, 39\}$, $(\boldsymbol{s}^n_p)_i = s^{\mathrm{bP}}$ for $i \in \{26, 38\}$ (left); $\boldsymbol{s}^n_i = s^{\mathrm{wR}}$ for $i \in \{1, 8\}$, $\boldsymbol{s}^n_i = s^{\mathrm{bR}}$ for $i \in \{57, 64\}$, $\boldsymbol{s}^n_5 = s^{\mathrm{wK}}$, $\boldsymbol{s}^n_{61} = s^{\mathrm{bK}}$ (middle and right); $\boldsymbol{s}^n_{15} = s^{\mathrm{bP}}$, $\boldsymbol{s}^n_{24} = s^{\mathrm{wQ}}$ (right); all other $s^n_i = 0$.

$\boldsymbol{s}^n_{p-1}$ and $\boldsymbol{s}^n_p$ that describe successive positions during a chess game. It is interesting to note here that, in any legal chess position $p > 0$, this set can have a cardinality of at most two, and will contain only elements in a colour state identical to the colour of the capturing pawn. A representative example of the application of $\mathfrak{w}^{ep}$ is illustrated in Fig. 7.6 (left).

Castling

Similar to the *en passant* capture move of a pawn, the castling move of the king also is subject to a number of stringent conditions which render its algebraic rigorous formulation a somewhat challenging endeavour. To complicate matters, the conditions that govern the possible realisation of this second special move not only involve two subsequent positions during a chess game, as in the case of *en passant* capture, but in some capacity require keeping track of the whole history of a game. Indeed, a castling move is permitted only if (1) neither the king nor the eventually castling rook of a given colour have been moved before, (2) no piece is occupying the squares between the castling king and rook and (3) the castling king is not in check, does not pass through squares in which it might result in check, and does not arrive at a square under attack by the opponent. If and only if all three of these conditions are satisfied, one of two possible castling moves for each colour can be executed during a game. For presentational purposes, we will denote the white kingside and queenside castling moves respectively by *w0-0* and *w0-0-0*, and with *b0-0* and *b0-0-0* the kingside and queenside castling moves for black.

In order to illustrate the construction of adjacency relations associated with these special moves, let us use the example of white queenside castling *w0-0-0*. The white king residing on its initial position $e1$ (node 5) is here moved westwards by two squares to $c1$ (node 3), while the white queenside rook on square $a1$ (node 1) is moved eastwards by three squares to $d1$ (node 4). The possibility of this castling move depends on a reduced record of the game's history as condition (1) demands that neither king nor rook must have been moved before. To limit the algebraic challenge of keeping a complete record of a game and extracting from it the necessary information, let us introduce an auxiliary Boolean scalar $\lambda^{w0\text{-}0\text{-}0}$ which takes the value 1 in the case condition (1) is met, and 0 otherwise. If at any position during a chess game either the white king or queenside rook has been moved, $\lambda^{w0\text{-}0\text{-}0}$ is updated from its initial value of 1 to 0, at which it will remain for the rest of the game.

Condition (2) can be inspected by considering the vector $\boldsymbol{h}_{w0\text{-}0\text{-}0}^{\mathsf{T}} \cdot \big|\operatorname{sgn}[\boldsymbol{s}^n]\big|$, where $\boldsymbol{h}_{w0\text{-}0\text{-}0} \in \mathbb{B}^{64}$ denotes a Boolean row vector with elements

$$(\boldsymbol{h}_{w0\text{-}0\text{-}0})_i := \begin{cases} 1 & \text{if } i \in \{2,3,4\}, \\ 0 & \text{otherwise} \end{cases}$$

marking the nodes involved in the white queenside castling move. The product with $\big|\operatorname{sgn}[\boldsymbol{s}^n]\big|$ then yields a non-zero integer scalar if and only if one or more nodes along the castling move of the king are occupied, such that

$$\delta\Big[\big|\operatorname{sgn}[\boldsymbol{s}^n]\big| \cdot \boldsymbol{h}_{w0\text{-}0\text{-}0}^{\mathsf{T}}\Big] = \begin{cases} 1 & \text{iff } s_2^n = s_3^n = s_4^n = 0, \\ 0 & \text{otherwise} \end{cases}$$

eventually provides an algebraic formalisation of condition (2) in terms of the Kronecker delta function (2.13).

Finally, castling condition (3) can be evaluated by considering

$$\delta\Big[\Big(\big(\operatorname{sgn}[\boldsymbol{s}^n] - \big|\operatorname{sgn}[\boldsymbol{s}^n]\big|\big) \cdot \boldsymbol{\mathfrak{w}}^{reg}[\boldsymbol{s}^n] - \operatorname{sgn}[\boldsymbol{s}^{nbP}] \cdot (\boldsymbol{M}^{\mathrm{SE}} + \boldsymbol{M}^{\mathrm{SW}})\Big) \cdot \boldsymbol{h}_{w0\text{-}0\text{-}0}^{\mathrm{K}\,\mathsf{T}}\Big]$$
$$= \begin{cases} 1 & \text{iff nodes 3, 4 and 5 are not in check or under attack}, \\ 0 & \text{otherwise} \end{cases} \tag{7.37}$$

for a given position. Here, $\boldsymbol{h}_{w0\text{-}0\text{-}0}^{\mathrm{K}} \in \mathbb{B}^{64}$ with elements

$$(\boldsymbol{h}_{w0\text{-}0\text{-}0}^{\mathrm{K}})_i := \begin{cases} 1 & \text{if } i \in \{3,4,5\}, \\ 0 & \text{otherwise} \end{cases}$$

defines a Boolean row vector that marks all those nodes which are involved in the westward move of the white king during its castling. The first term in the argument of the Kronecker delta function on the left-hand side of (7.37) extracts from the node state vector s^n all nodes that are occupied by black pieces and evaluates whether any of their regular moves targets node 3, 4 or 5. It is important to recognise here that only regular moves need to be considered, as *en passant* capture moves cannot target any of the nodes involved in castlings. However, the regular moves generated by $\mathfrak{w}^{reg}$ will not include potential capture moves of black pawns unless at least one square associated with a pawn capture move is occupied by an opponent's piece. To adjust for this eventuality in the case of our castling move, the second term in the argument of the Kronecker delta generates pawn capture moves that target the nodes marked by $h^{\mathrm{K}}_{w0\text{-}0\text{-}0}$. By subtracting this term from the first, we ensure that both yield equally signed contributions. If the resulting scalar argument yields a number unequal zero, at least one square along the king's castling line is under attack by the opponent, in which case the Kronecker delta function will then return zero and indicate that condition (3) is not satisfied.

With this, all three conditions required for the queenside castling move of the white king are algebraically accounted for, and we can define the operator

$$\mathfrak{w}^{w0\text{-}0\text{-}0}: \mathbb{Z}^{64} \times \mathbb{B} \to \mathbb{B}^{64\times 64}_{-1}\,, \tag{7.38}$$
$$\mathfrak{w}^{w0\text{-}0\text{-}0}[s^n, \lambda^{w0\text{-}0\text{-}0}] := \mathrm{sgn}\,[S^{n\mathrm{wK}}] \cdot (M^{\mathrm{W}})^2 \cdot \lambda^{w0\text{-}0\text{-}0} \cdot \delta\Big[\big|\,\mathrm{sgn}[s^n]\big| \cdot h^{\mathsf{T}}_{w0\text{-}0\text{-}0}\Big]$$
$$\times\, \delta\Big[\Big(\big(\mathrm{sgn}\,[s^n] - \big|\,\mathrm{sgn}\,[s^n]\big|\big) \cdot \mathfrak{w}^{reg}[s^n] - \mathrm{sgn}\,[s^{n\mathrm{bP}}] \cdot (M^{\mathrm{SE}} + M^{\mathrm{SW}})\Big) \cdot h^{\mathrm{K}\,\mathsf{T}}_{w0\text{-}0\text{-}0}\Big]$$

to generate the associated weighted adjacency relations from a given node state vector s^n and auxiliary scalar $\lambda^{w0\text{-}0\text{-}0}$. Each of the last three terms in the product (7.38) returns a Boolean marking whether the corresponding condition is satisfied or not. Only if all three terms return a non-zero value will the castling move formalised in the first term – here a move of the white king by two squares westwards – contribute an adjacency relation. It is important to note, however, that the generated adjacency relation describes only the move of the white king. The rook's move by three squares eastwards is already accounted for in the set of possible regular moves $\mathfrak{w}^{reg}[s^n]$ as, according to condition (2), no occupied node is allowed between the king and castling rook.

By adapting the above approach, we can construct similar operators for the kingside castling move of the white king as well as the queenside and kingside castling moves of the black king, and eventually we find

$$\mathfrak{w}^{w0\text{-}0}: \mathbb{Z}^{64} \times \mathbb{B} \to \mathbb{B}^{64\times 64}_{-1}\,, \tag{7.39}$$
$$\mathfrak{w}^{w0\text{-}0}[s^n, \lambda^{w0\text{-}0}] := \mathrm{sgn}\,[S^{n\mathrm{wK}}] \cdot (M^{\mathrm{E}})^2 \cdot \lambda^{w0\text{-}0} \cdot \delta\Big[\big|\,\mathrm{sgn}[s^n]\big| \cdot h^{\mathsf{T}}_{w0\text{-}0}\Big]$$
$$\times\, \delta\Big[\Big(\big(\mathrm{sgn}\,[s^n] - \big|\,\mathrm{sgn}\,[s^n]\big|\big) \cdot \mathfrak{w}^{reg}[s^n] - \mathrm{sgn}\,[s^{n\mathrm{bP}}] \cdot (M^{\mathrm{SE}} + M^{\mathrm{SW}})\Big) \cdot h^{\mathrm{K}\,\mathsf{T}}_{w0\text{-}0}\Big],$$

$$\mathfrak{w}^{b0\text{-}0\text{-}0} \colon \mathbb{Z}^{64} \times \mathbb{B} \to \mathbb{B}_{-1}^{64\times 64}, \tag{7.40}$$
$$\mathfrak{w}^{b0\text{-}0\text{-}0}[\boldsymbol{s}^n, \lambda^{b0\text{-}0\text{-}0}] := \operatorname{sgn}[\boldsymbol{S}^{n\mathrm{bK}}] \cdot (\boldsymbol{M}^{\mathrm{W}})^2 \cdot \lambda^{b0\text{-}0\text{-}0} \cdot \delta\Big[\big|\operatorname{sgn}[\boldsymbol{s}^n]\big| \cdot \boldsymbol{h}_{b0\text{-}0\text{-}0}^{\mathsf{T}}\Big]$$
$$\times \delta\Big[\Big(\big(\operatorname{sgn}[\boldsymbol{s}^n] + \big|\operatorname{sgn}[\boldsymbol{s}^n]\big|\big) \cdot \mathfrak{w}^{reg}[\boldsymbol{s}^n] + \operatorname{sgn}[\boldsymbol{s}^{n\mathrm{wP}}] \cdot (\boldsymbol{M}^{\mathrm{NE}} + \boldsymbol{M}^{\mathrm{NW}})\Big) \cdot \boldsymbol{h}_{b0\text{-}0\text{-}0}^{\mathrm{K}\,\mathsf{T}}\Big],$$

$$\mathfrak{w}^{b0\text{-}0} \colon \mathbb{Z}^{64} \times \mathbb{B} \to \mathbb{B}_{-1}^{64\times 64}, \tag{7.41}$$
$$\mathfrak{w}^{b0\text{-}0}[\boldsymbol{s}^n, \lambda^{b0\text{-}0}] := \operatorname{sgn}[\boldsymbol{S}^{n\mathrm{bK}}] \cdot (\boldsymbol{M}^{\mathrm{E}})^2 \cdot \lambda^{b0\text{-}0} \cdot \delta\Big[\big|\operatorname{sgn}[\boldsymbol{s}^n]\big| \cdot \boldsymbol{h}_{b0\text{-}0}^{\mathsf{T}}\Big]$$
$$\times \delta\Big[\Big(\big(\operatorname{sgn}[\boldsymbol{s}^n] + \big|\operatorname{sgn}[\boldsymbol{s}^n]\big|\big) \cdot \mathfrak{w}^{reg}[\boldsymbol{s}^n] + \operatorname{sgn}[\boldsymbol{s}^{n\mathrm{wP}}] \cdot (\boldsymbol{M}^{\mathrm{NE}} + \boldsymbol{M}^{\mathrm{NW}})\Big) \cdot \boldsymbol{h}_{b0\text{-}0}^{\mathrm{K}\,\mathsf{T}}\Big].$$

The auxiliary scalars $\lambda^{w0\text{-}0}$, $\lambda^{b0\text{-}0\text{-}0}$ and $\lambda^{b0\text{-}0}$ are here defined by

$$\lambda^{\{w/b\}\{0\text{-}0\text{-}0\,/\,0\text{-}0\}} := \begin{cases} 1 & \text{iff king and rook involved in} \\ & \text{\{white/black\}\{queenside/kingside\}} \\ & \text{castling have not been moved,} \\ 0 & \text{otherwise,} \end{cases} \tag{7.42}$$

and mark the possibility of castling moves depending on the history of previous positions of the game. Moreover, the Boolean row vectors $\boldsymbol{h}_{\{w/b\}\{0\text{-}0\text{-}0\,/\,0\text{-}0\}} \in \mathbb{B}^{64}$ and $\boldsymbol{h}^{\mathrm{K}}_{\{w/b\}\{0\text{-}0\text{-}0\,/\,0\text{-}0\}} \in \mathbb{B}^{64}$ with elements

$$\big(\boldsymbol{h}_{\{w0\text{-}0\text{-}0\,/\,w0\text{-}0\}}\big)_i := \begin{cases} 1 & \text{for } i\in\{2,3,4\} \,/\, i\in\{6,7\}, \\ 0 & \text{otherwise,} \end{cases}$$
$$\big(\boldsymbol{h}_{\{b0\text{-}0\text{-}0\,/\,b0\text{-}0\}}\big)_i := \begin{cases} 1 & \text{for } i\in\{58,59,60\} \,/\, i\in\{62,63\}, \\ 0 & \text{otherwise,} \end{cases}$$
$$\big(\boldsymbol{h}^{\mathrm{K}}_{\{w0\text{-}0\text{-}0\,/\,w0\text{-}0\}}\big)_i := \begin{cases} 1 & \text{for } i\in\{3,4,5\} \,/\, i\in\{5,6,7\}, \\ 0 & \text{otherwise,} \end{cases}$$
$$\big(\boldsymbol{h}^{\mathrm{K}}_{\{b0\text{-}0\text{-}0\,/\,b0\text{-}0\}}\big)_i := \begin{cases} 1 & \text{for } i\in\{59,60,61\} \,/\, i\in\{61,62,63\}, \\ 0 & \text{otherwise} \end{cases} \tag{7.43}$$

mark all nodes involved in the respective castling moves. Defining with

$$\boldsymbol{\lambda} := (\lambda^{w0\text{-}0\text{-}0}, \lambda^{w0\text{-}0}, \lambda^{b0\text{-}0\text{-}0}, \lambda^{b0\text{-}0}) \in \mathbb{B}^4 \tag{7.44}$$

an auxiliary Boolean vector that marks the availability of castling moves based on the history of the chess game, we finally obtain the operator

$$\mathfrak{w}^{0} \colon \mathbb{Z}^{64} \times \mathbb{B}^4 \to \mathbb{B}_{-1}^{64\times 64}, \tag{7.45}$$
$$\mathfrak{w}^{0}[\boldsymbol{s}^n, \boldsymbol{\lambda}] := \mathfrak{w}^{w0\text{-}0\text{-}0}[\boldsymbol{s}^n, \lambda^{w0\text{-}0\text{-}0}] + \mathfrak{w}^{w0\text{-}0}[\boldsymbol{s}^n, \lambda^{w0\text{-}0}]$$
$$+ \mathfrak{w}^{b0\text{-}0\text{-}0}[\boldsymbol{s}^n, \lambda^{b0\text{-}0\text{-}0}] + \mathfrak{w}^{b0\text{-}0}[\boldsymbol{s}^n, \lambda^{b0\text{-}0}]$$

for generating all weighted adjacency relations associated with castling moves in a given position. Two representative examples of the application of $\mathfrak{w}^0$ are illustrated in Fig. 7.6 (middle and right), reminding that (7.45) returns only adjacency relations describing a potential move of the castling king, while the edges associated with moves of the corresponding rooks are already part of the set of regular moves generated by $\mathfrak{w}^{reg}$.

7.2.4 Generation of Positional Chess Graphs

With the introduction of (7.32), (7.36) and (7.45), we algebraically formalised the generation of all possible regular, *en passant* capture and castling moves for any given legal chess position. Before we can employ this formalisation in the construction of positional chess graphs, however, we still require the detection of all those moves which would leave the king of the moving colour in a check position. According to the rules of chess, such moves and their associated adjacency relations must then be discarded. Certainly, for the adjacency relations generated by $\mathfrak{w}^0$, such a detection is not necessary as, by construction, this operator already discards castling moves which would leave the king in check. For the adjacency relations delivered by $\mathfrak{w}^{reg}$ and $\mathfrak{w}^{ep}$, on the other hand, this is not the case, and we need to assess in each individual case whether the associated move would result in a check position.

To take on this formidable challenge, we will first construct a set of operators which select specific adjacency relations from the weight matrices generated by $\mathfrak{w}^{reg}$, $\mathfrak{w}^{ep}$ and $\mathfrak{w}^0$, and thus provide an algebraic representation of individual moves that advance a given position $p-1$ to position p. We then define an operator which identifies each adjacency relation emanating from source nodes of a given colour, and we assess whether performing the associated move will leave the king of the same colour in check by the opponent. With this, we will finally be in possession of a viable toolset that will allow for the algebraic construction of positional chess graphs for any given legal chess position during a game of chess according to (7.6)–(7.8).

Performing Individual Chess Moves

Each move an individual chess piece performs on the board can be unambiguously identified by the square on which the piece resides and the square on which the piece arrives after the move has been made, thus, by the source and target node of the move's associated adjacency relation. The endnodes of this adjacency relation also mark the elements in the node state vector that undergo discrete changes as a result of a performed move. These changes can be algebraically formulated in terms of a matrix operator that, when applied to a node state vector $\boldsymbol{s}^n_{p-1}$ describing a given chess position $p-1$, generates a new state vector $\boldsymbol{s}^n_p$ for position p by changing the state $(\boldsymbol{s}^n_{p-1})_i$ of the source and state

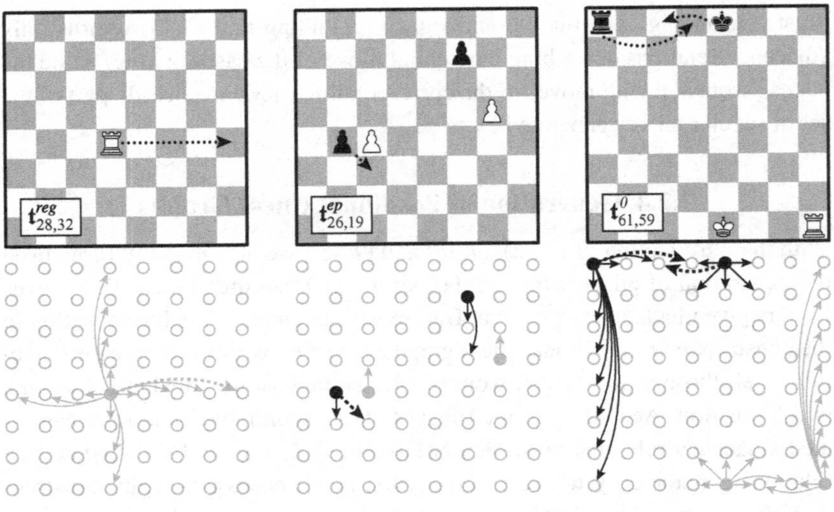

Figure 7.7 Performing individual chess moves. Application of operators $\mathbf{t}^{reg}$, $\mathbf{t}^{ep}$ and $\mathbf{t}^{0}$ defined in (7.46)–(7.48) for generating node state vectors through regular, *en passant* capture and castling moves. In each case, the original chess position $p-1$ (top) and its associated adjacency relations (bottom) are shown, with performed moves indicated by a dotted arrow. For the *en passant* move, the white pawn on $c4$ (node 27) was moved from $c2$ (node 11) in position $p-2$. Node states and moves: $(\boldsymbol{s}^n_{p-1})_{28} = s^{\mathrm{wR}}$, $(\boldsymbol{s}^n_p)_{32} = s^{\mathrm{wR}}$, $\mathbf{t}^{reg}_{28,32}$ (left); $(\boldsymbol{s}^n_{p-1})_i = s^{\mathrm{wP}}$ for $i \in \{11, 39\}$, $(\boldsymbol{s}^n_{p-1})_i = s^{\mathrm{bP}}$ for $i \in \{26, 54\}$, $(\boldsymbol{s}^n_p)_i = s^{\mathrm{wP}}$ for $i \in \{27, 39\}$, $(\boldsymbol{s}^n_p)_i = s^{\mathrm{bP}}$ for $i \in \{26, 54\}$, $\mathbf{t}^{ep}_{26,19}$ (middle); $(\boldsymbol{s}^n_{p-1})_5 = s^{\mathrm{wK}}$, $(\boldsymbol{s}^n_{p-1})_8 = s^{\mathrm{wR}}$, $(\boldsymbol{s}^n_{p-1})_{57} = s^{\mathrm{bR}}$, $(\boldsymbol{s}^n_{p-1})_{61} = s^{\mathrm{bK}}$, $(\boldsymbol{s}^n_p)_5 = s^{\mathrm{wK}}$, $(\boldsymbol{s}^n_p)_8 = s^{\mathrm{wR}}$, $(\boldsymbol{s}^n_p)_{59} = s^{\mathrm{bK}}$, $(\boldsymbol{s}^n_p)_{60} = s^{\mathrm{bR}}$, $\boldsymbol{\lambda} = (0, 1, 1, 0)$, $\mathbf{t}^{0}_{61,59}$ (right); all other $s^n_i = 0$.

$(\boldsymbol{s}^n_{p-1})_j$ of the target node in a fashion which reflects the execution of a move on the board. A regular move from node i to node j, for example, requires us to set the state of i to zero, and to copy the original state of node i to node j such that $(\boldsymbol{s}^n_p)_i = 0$ and $(\boldsymbol{s}^n_p)_j = (\boldsymbol{s}^n_{p-1})_i$. This can be accomplished by the operator

$$\mathbf{t}^{reg}_{ij} : \mathbb{Z}^{64} \to \mathbb{Z}^{64} \, , \, \mathbf{t}^{reg}_{ij}[\boldsymbol{s}^n] := \boldsymbol{s}^n \cdot \left(\boldsymbol{I}^{64} + \boldsymbol{\delta}^{64\times 64}_{ij} - \boldsymbol{\delta}^{64\times 64}_{ii} - \boldsymbol{\delta}^{64\times 64}_{jj} \right), \qquad (7.46)$$

which then formalises the action of performing a specific regular chess move. The first term yields here the diagonal matrix of $\boldsymbol{s}^n$, and thus simply copies its argument node state vector, while the second term copies the state of node i to node j. The last two terms ensure that the original states of nodes i and j are discarded. As a result, $\mathbf{t}^{reg}_{ij}[\boldsymbol{s}^n]$ delivers a new state vector with the state of node i transferred to node j and describes a regular chess move if $(\boldsymbol{s}^n_{p-1})_j = 0$ (Fig. 7.7, left), or a capture move in the case $(\boldsymbol{s}^n_{p-1})_j \neq 0$.

Operators similar to $\mathbf{t}_{ij}^{reg}$ can also be defined for the two special chess moves. For the *en passant* capture move of a pawn, we find

$$\mathbf{t}_{ij}^{ep} : \mathbb{Z}^{64} \to \mathbb{Z}^{64} \ , \ \mathbf{t}_{ij}^{ep}[\boldsymbol{s}^n] := \boldsymbol{s}^n \cdot \left(\boldsymbol{I}^{64} + \boldsymbol{\delta}_{ij}^{64\times 64} - \boldsymbol{\delta}_{ii}^{64\times 64} - \boldsymbol{\delta}_{j'j'}^{64\times 64}\right), \tag{7.47}$$

where i and j respectively mark the source and target nodes of the capturing pawn, and $j' = j + 8\,\mathrm{sgn}[i - j]$ identifies the node of the captured pawn of the opposing colour. In the case of the castling move, we need to account for two pieces, the king and accompanying rook, and eventually obtain

$$\mathbf{t}_{ij}^{0} : \mathbb{Z}^{64} \to \mathbb{Z}^{64} \ , \ \mathbf{t}_{ij}^{0}[\boldsymbol{s}^n] := \boldsymbol{s}^n \cdot \left(\boldsymbol{I}^{64} + \boldsymbol{\delta}_{ij}^{64\times 64} + \boldsymbol{\delta}_{i''j''}^{64\times 64} - \boldsymbol{\delta}_{ii}^{64\times 64} - \boldsymbol{\delta}_{i''i''}^{64\times 64}\right), \tag{7.48}$$

where i and j identify the source and target nodes of the castling king, and the nodes $i'' = i - 7\,\mathrm{sgn}[i - j]/2 - 1/2$ and $j'' = i - \mathrm{sgn}[i - j]$ mark the source and target of the castling rook. Representative examples illustrating the action of operators (7.46)–(7.48) are shown in Fig. 7.7.

Detecting Check Positions

With the operators introduced above, we can now construct a new chess position for each non-zero element in the weight matrices generated by $\mathfrak{w}^{reg}$, $\mathfrak{w}^{ep}$ and $\mathfrak{w}^{0}$. By inspecting all of these newly obtained positions with respect to the possible moves their pieces can perform, in particular the moves which target a specific king, we are then able to distinguish the adjacency relations that are associated with legal chess moves from those which would leave the king of the moving colour in check and, thus, are not legal. After discarding the latter from their respective weight matrices, we will finally have constructed the positional chess graph for a given position.

In order to formalise this approach in algebraic terms, we note that, in some limited capacity, we already delineated squares under attack by pieces of the opponent's colour in our definition of the operator $\mathfrak{w}^{0}$. Indeed, recalling (7.37), the first term in the argument on the Kronecker delta function selects all nodes in a black colour state and evaluates whether the adjacency relations emanating from these nodes target the nodes which need to be traversed by the white king during queenside castling. This construct can easily be adapted to distinguish all those adjacency relations that emanate from nodes of a given colour and target the node on which the king of the opposing colour resides. Given a node state vector $\boldsymbol{s}^n$ and adjacency matrix $\boldsymbol{w}$, we find

$$\delta\Big[\big(\mathrm{sgn}\,[\boldsymbol{s}^n] - |\,\mathrm{sgn}\,[\boldsymbol{s}^n]|\big) \cdot \boldsymbol{w} \cdot \mathrm{sgn}\,[\boldsymbol{s}^{n\mathrm{wK}}]^{\mathrm{T}}\Big] = \begin{cases} 1 & \text{iff white king not in check,} \\ 0 & \text{otherwise,} \end{cases}$$

and a similar expression for the black king under attack by white pieces. Here we introduced the vectors

$$s^{n\mathrm{wK}} := s^{\mathrm{wK}} \cdot \delta[s^n - s^{\mathrm{wK}} \cdot \mathbf{1}^{64\mathsf{T}}]\,,\; s^{n\mathrm{bK}} := s^{\mathrm{bK}} \cdot \delta[s^n - s^{\mathrm{bK}} \cdot \mathbf{1}^{64\mathsf{T}}] \tag{7.49}$$

to mark all nodes with a state value of s^{wP} and s^{bP} in s^n. We can then define the two operators

$$\begin{aligned} \mathfrak{w}^{\mathrm{wK+}}&: \mathbb{Z}^{64} \times \mathbb{B}^{64\times 64} \to \mathbb{B}, \\ \mathfrak{w}^{\mathrm{wK+}}[s^n, w] &:= 1 - \delta\Big[\big(\mathrm{sgn}\,[s^n] - \big|\,\mathrm{sgn}\,[s^n]\big|\big) \cdot w \cdot \mathrm{sgn}\,[s^{n\mathrm{wK}}]^{\mathsf{T}}\Big], \\ \mathfrak{w}^{\mathrm{bK+}}&: \mathbb{Z}^{64} \times \mathbb{B}^{64\times 64} \to \mathbb{B}, \\ \mathfrak{w}^{\mathrm{bK+}}[s^n, w] &:= 1 - \delta\Big[\big(\mathrm{sgn}\,[s^n] + \big|\,\mathrm{sgn}\,[s^n]\big|\big) \cdot w \cdot \mathrm{sgn}\,[s^{n\mathrm{bK}}]^{\mathsf{T}}\Big], \end{aligned} \tag{7.50}$$

which return one if and only if the white or black king is in check by at least one of the opponent's pieces.

By employing (7.50), we are now able to extract from a given weight matrix w all those adjacency relations w_{ij} which will result in a check position for the king in colour state $\mathrm{sgn}\,[w_{ij}]$ if the move associated with w_{ij} is performed. In order to do so, however, it is necessary to distinguish between regular and *en passant* moves, as both differ in their execution according to (7.46) and (7.47). Let us denote with w^{reg} and w^{ep} the weight matrices generated by $\mathfrak{w}^{reg}$ and $\mathfrak{w}^{ep}$, respectively, and introduce the sets

$$\begin{aligned} \mathcal{I}_w(w) &:= \big\{(i,j) : i,j \in [1,64], w_{ij} = \mathrm{sgn}\,[s^n_i] = 1\big\}, \\ \mathcal{I}_b(w) &:= \big\{(i,j) : i,j \in [1,64], w_{ij} = \mathrm{sgn}\,[s^n_i] = -1\big\} \end{aligned} \tag{7.51}$$

of ordered index pairs to mark all weighted adjacency relations whose source nodes are either in a white or in a black colour state. We can then define with

$$\mathfrak{w}^+ : \mathbb{Z}^{64} \times \mathbb{B}_{-1}^{64\times 64} \times \mathbb{B}_{-1}^{64\times 64} \to \mathbb{B}_{-1}^{64\times 64}\,, \tag{7.52}$$

$$\begin{aligned} \mathfrak{w}^+[s^n, w^{reg}, w^{ep}] :=\; & \sum_{(i,j)\in\mathcal{I}_w(w^{reg})} \mathfrak{w}^{\mathrm{wK+}}\Big[\mathbf{t}^{reg}_{ij}[s^n], \mathfrak{w}^{reg}\big[\mathbf{t}^{reg}_{ij}[s^n]\big]\Big] \cdot \delta^{64\times 64}_{ij} \\ &+ \sum_{(i,j)\in\mathcal{I}_w(w^{ep})} \mathfrak{w}^{\mathrm{wK+}}\Big[\mathbf{t}^{ep}_{ij}[s^n], \mathfrak{w}^{reg}\big[\mathbf{t}^{ep}_{ij}[s^n]\big]\Big] \cdot \delta^{64\times 64}_{ij} \\ &- \sum_{(i,j)\in\mathcal{I}_b(w^{reg})} \mathfrak{w}^{\mathrm{bK+}}\Big[\mathbf{t}^{reg}_{ij}[s^n], \mathfrak{w}^{reg}\big[\mathbf{t}^{reg}_{ij}[s^n]\big]\Big] \cdot \delta^{64\times 64}_{ij} \\ &- \sum_{(i,j)\in\mathcal{I}_b(w^{ep})} \mathfrak{w}^{\mathrm{bK+}}\Big[\mathbf{t}^{ep}_{ij}[s^n], \mathfrak{w}^{reg}\big[\mathbf{t}^{ep}_{ij}[s^n]\big]\Big] \cdot \delta^{64\times 64}_{ij} \end{aligned}$$

an operator that returns all those adjacency relations from its argument weight matrices w^{reg} and w^{ep} which, after performing the associated move on the board, will leave the king in check by at least one of the opponent's pieces. In the first term on the right-hand side of (7.52), for example, $\mathbf{t}^{reg}_{ij}[s^n]$ generates a new state vector that describes the position obtained after performing a regular

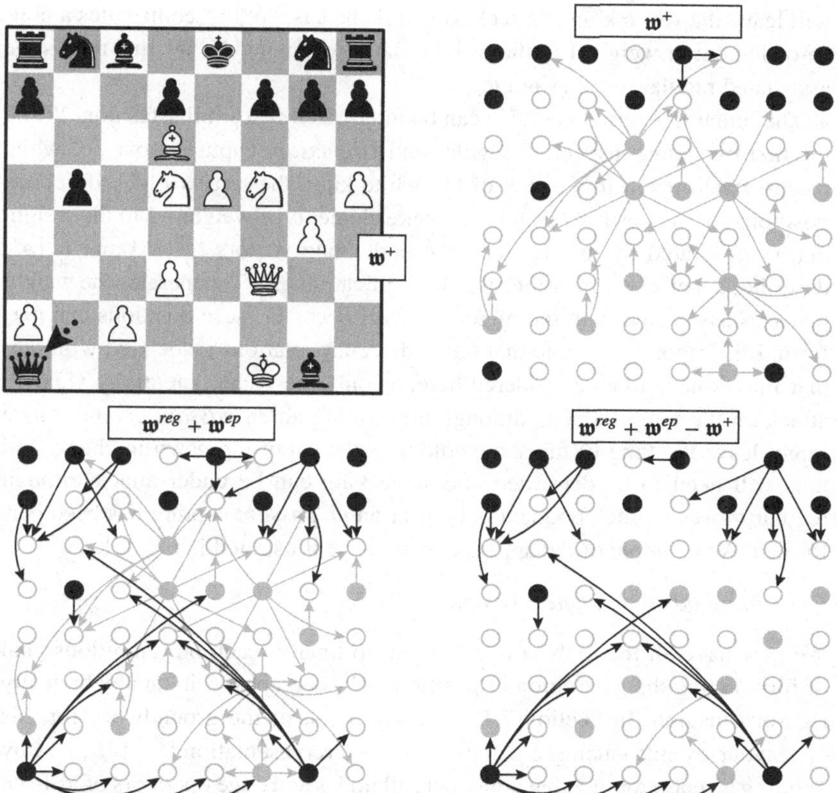

Figure 7.8 Identifying not legal moves. Application of the operator $\mathfrak{w}^+$ defined in (7.52) to a complex chess position (top left; position 39 during the historic game between Anderssen and Kieseritzky in London, 1851). While $\mathfrak{w}^{reg}$ and $\mathfrak{w}^{ep}$ generate an abundance of possible moves for both players (bottom left), most of the moves white pieces can perform are marked not legal by $\mathfrak{w}^+$ (top right) as the capture move of the black queen from square *b*2 in the previous position to *a*1 (dotted arrow) leaves the white king in check. White remains with but three options to resolve the check position (bottom right). Interestingly, after seven more moves, Anderssen (white) brilliantly wins what became known as the "Immortal Game" by sacrificing his queen. Node states: $s_6^n = s^{\mathrm{wK}}$, $s_{22}^n = s^{\mathrm{wQ}}$, $s_{44}^n = s^{\mathrm{wB}}$, $s_i^n = s^{\mathrm{wN}}$ for $i \in \{36, 38\}$, $s_i^n = s^{\mathrm{wP}}$ for $i \in \{9, 11, 20, 31, 37, 40\}$, $s_{61}^n = s^{\mathrm{bK}}$, $s_1^n = s^{\mathrm{bQ}}$, $s_i^n = s^{\mathrm{bR}}$ for $i \in \{57, 64\}$, $s_7^n = s^{\mathrm{bB}}$, $s_i^n = s^{\mathrm{bN}}$ for $i \in \{58, 63\}$, $s_i^n = s^{\mathrm{bP}}$ for $i \in \{59, 34, 49, 52, 54, 55, 56\}$; all other $s_i^n = 0$.

move $(i, j) \in \mathcal{I}_w(w^{reg})$ of the white piece residing on node *i*. The application of $\mathfrak{w}^{reg}$ evaluates this new position in regards to all possible regular moves of its pieces, and the operator $\mathfrak{w}^{\mathrm{wK}+}$ finally inspects whether any of these moves will leave the white king in check. If this is the case, $\delta_{ij}^{64\times 64}$ contributes a non-zero element of weight 1 to the weight matrix generated by $\mathfrak{w}^{+}$ that marks the associated regular move as not legal.

The remaining terms in (7.52) can be interpreted in a similar fashion. While the first two sums inspect all regular and *en passant* capture moves of white pieces which result in a check of the white king, the last two identify check positions for the black king and contribute elements of weight -1 to the weight matrix generated by $\mathfrak{w}^{+}$. Each of the node state vectors $\mathbf{t}_{ij}^{reg}[\boldsymbol{s}^n]$ and $\mathbf{t}_{ij}^{ep}[\boldsymbol{s}^n]$ describes a new chess position, and the application of $\mathfrak{w}^{reg}$ generates the weight matrices associated with the regular moves pieces in these positions can perform. It is important to note that only adjacency relations associated with regular moves have to be considered here, as only these can potentially yield an attack on the king. Indeed, although performing an *en passant* capture move might leave the king of the same colour as the capturing pawn in check, and thus will need to be discarded, the same king can be under attack through regular moves by the opponent only after an *en passant* capture has been performed. An example of the application of $\mathfrak{w}^{+}$ is illustrated in Fig. 7.8.

Generating Positional Chess Graphs

We now have all the tools at our disposal to finally reach our ambitious goal of formulating the generation of positional chess graphs $\mathscr{C}$ in an algebraically rigorous fashion. In Section 7.1.3, we laid most of the groundwork for this endeavour by introducing a suitable operator representation $\hat{\mathscr{C}}$ of $\mathscr{C}$, and by defining a generator $\hat{\mathfrak{G}}^{\mathscr{C}}$ that constructs all nodes and edge operators of $\hat{\mathscr{C}}$ from an operator representation $\hat{\mathscr{K}}_{64}^{d}$ of the complete relational digraph of order 64. What remains is to construct the operator $\mathfrak{w}$ which, according to (7.9), delivers the weight matrix that represents the complete set of legal moves the pieces in a given chess position can perform. To that end, we simply consider all weighted adjacency relations for regular, *en passant* capture and castling moves generated by $\mathfrak{w}^{reg}$, $\mathfrak{w}^{ep}$ and $\mathfrak{w}^{0}$, according to (7.32), (7.36) and (7.45), and then discard from the set of adjacency relations associated with regular and *en passant* moves all those which will leave the king of the corresponding colour in a check position by utilising the operator $\mathfrak{w}^{+}$ defined in (7.52). This eventually leaves us with

$$\begin{aligned} \mathfrak{w} &: \mathbb{Z}^{64}\times\mathbb{Z}^{64}\times\mathbb{B}^{4}\rightarrow\mathbb{B}_{-1}^{64\times 64}, \\ \mathfrak{w}[\boldsymbol{s}_p^n,\boldsymbol{s}_{p-1}^n,\boldsymbol{\lambda}_p] &:= \mathfrak{w}^{reg}[\boldsymbol{s}_p^n]+\mathfrak{w}^{ep}[\boldsymbol{s}_p^n,\boldsymbol{s}_{p-1}^n]+\mathfrak{w}^{0}[\boldsymbol{s}_p^n,\boldsymbol{\lambda}] \\ &\quad -\mathfrak{w}^{+}\Big[\boldsymbol{s}^n,\mathfrak{w}^{reg}[\boldsymbol{s}_p^n],\mathfrak{w}^{ep}[\boldsymbol{s}_p^n,\boldsymbol{s}_{p-1}^n]\Big] \end{aligned} \tag{7.53}$$

and thus concludes our quest for the generation of operator representations of positional chess graphs for any given position p during a game of chess.

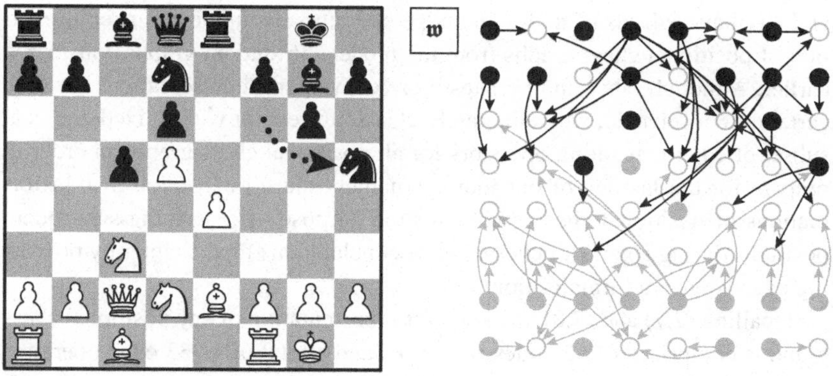

Figure 7.9 Generating positional chess graphs. Application of the operator $\mathfrak{w}$ defined in (7.53) to the iconic position 22 (left) in the game between Spassky (white) and Fischer in Round 3 during the 8th World Championship in 1972. To this day, Fischer's infamous move of the black knight from $f6$ to $h5$ (dotted arrow) remains somewhat of a mystery. With the positional chess graph generated by $\mathfrak{w}$ (right), it will be possible to study this and other chess positions within the powerful confines of graph theory. Node states: $s_7^n = s^{\mathrm{wK}}$, $s_{11}^n = s^{\mathrm{wQ}}$, $s_i^n = s^{\mathrm{wR}}$ for $i \in \{1, 6\}$, $s_i^n = s^{\mathrm{wB}}$ for $i \in \{3, 13\}$, $s_i^n = s^{\mathrm{wN}}$ for $i \in \{12, 19\}$, $s_i^n = s^{\mathrm{wP}}$ for $i \in \{9, 10, 14, 15, 16, 29, 36\}$, $s_{63}^n = s^{\mathrm{bK}}$, $s_{60}^n = s^{\mathrm{bQ}}$, $s_i^n = s^{\mathrm{bR}}$ for $i \in \{57, 61\}$, $s_i^n = s^{\mathrm{bB}}$ for $i \in \{55, 59\}$, $s_i^n = s^{\mathrm{bN}}$ for $i \in \{40, 52\}$, $s_i^n = s^{\mathrm{bP}}$ for $i \in \{35, 44, 47, 49, 50, 54, 56\}$; all other $s_i^n = 0$.

To exemplify the application of $\mathfrak{w}$, we illustrate in Fig. 7.9 the positional chess graph after the infamous move 11 of Robert Fischer (black) in the game against Boris Spassky in Round 3 during the 8th World Championship in Reykjavik in 1972.

7.3 Transformation of Positional Chess Graphs

The algebraic generation of positional chess graphs explored in the previous sections provides us with a rather elaborate application of our operator graph-theoretical framework. At the conceptual level, however, the proposed formalisation mirrors in its simplicity that of the various random graphs introduced in Chapter 5. Indeed, in all considered models, viable operator representations are constructed by selecting edge operators from a given seed graph through the assignment of scalar weights. These weights are either obtained from realisations of a randomisation operator, as in the case of our random graph models, or directly associated with the elements of a matrix operator, such as $\mathfrak{w}$. Only the additional use of node state values to account for the various types and colours of chess pieces and, more importantly, the fixed cardinalities of the classical and auxiliary subsets of nodes and edge operators distinguish our representation of positional chess graphs from the models of random graphs considered earlier. Although other and perhaps more convenient representations are here certainly conceivable, we deliberately choose to remain with a fixed classical subset of edge-generating operators for all positional chess graphs in order to prepare for the last leg of our journey, namely the formalisation of transformations of positional chess graphs for the purpose of describing subsequent positions during a game of chess. Let us conclude this final chapter by proposing exactly such a formalisation.

Recalling (7.7) and (7.8), the operator representation of any positional chess graph is comprised of 65 nodes $\boldsymbol{n}_0$, $s_i^n \cdot \boldsymbol{n}_i$ and a total of 4,033 edge operators $\mathfrak{E}_{00}$, $w_{j_1 j_2} \cdot \mathfrak{E}_{j_1 j_2}$, where $\boldsymbol{n}_0$, $\boldsymbol{n}_i$: $i \in [1, 64]$ and $\mathfrak{E}_{00}$, $\mathfrak{E}_{j_1 j_2}$: $j_1, j_2 \in [1, 64]$, $j_1 \neq j_2$ respectively denote the nodes and edge operators of the seed graph $\hat{\mathscr{K}}_{64}^{d}$. With the exception of the null-node $\boldsymbol{n}_0$, each node of $\hat{\mathscr{C}}$ is assigned an element of a state vector $\boldsymbol{s}^n \in \mathbb{Z}^{64}$. By acting on this node state vector, the operator $\mathfrak{w}$ delivers a weight matrix $\boldsymbol{w} \in \mathbb{B}_{-1}^{64\times 64}$, which also assigns a state value, or weight, to every edge operator of $\hat{\mathscr{C}}$, except $\mathfrak{E}_{00}$. According to Definition 4.3, a transformation $\hat{\mathfrak{M}}[\hat{\mathscr{C}}] = \hat{\mathscr{C}}'$ between operator representations $\hat{\mathscr{C}}$ and $\hat{\mathscr{C}}'$ of two positional chess graphs can then be defined by simply mapping

$$\boldsymbol{n}_0 \to \boldsymbol{n}_0 \ , \ s_i^n \cdot \boldsymbol{n}_i \to s_i^{n\prime} \cdot \boldsymbol{n}_i := \left(\mathbf{t}[\boldsymbol{s}^n]\right)_i \cdot \boldsymbol{n}_i \tag{7.54}$$

through the action of an operator $\mathbf{t}$ on $\boldsymbol{s}^n$, and by utilising $\mathfrak{w}$ to obtain the weight matrix $\boldsymbol{w}'$ for edge operators of $\hat{\mathscr{C}}'$ from $\boldsymbol{s}^{n\prime} := \mathbf{t}[\boldsymbol{s}^n]$ such that

$$\mathfrak{E}_{00} \to \mathfrak{E}_{00} \ , \ w_{j_1 j_2} \cdot \mathfrak{E}_{j_1 j_2} \to w'_{j_1 j_2} \cdot \mathfrak{E}_{j_1 j_2} . \tag{7.55}$$

It therefore suffices to find suitable mappings of the node state vector to fully define operator graph transformations between two positional chess graphs.

In order to give a meaning to any such transformation within the context of a chess game, we certainly should consider here only mappings that describe individual legal moves of chess pieces. Fortunately, with the operators $\mathbf{t}_{ij}^{reg}$, $\mathbf{t}_{ij}^{ep}$ and $\mathbf{t}_{ij}^{0}$ introduced in (7.46)–(7.48), we already possess mappings that meet this requirement. Indeed, by formalising the positional changes associated with regular, *en passant* capture or castling moves, each of these operators acts between node state vectors $\boldsymbol{s}_{p-1}^n$ and $\boldsymbol{s}_p^n$ that describe subsequent positions such that $\exists!\, \mathbf{t}_{p-1} \in \{\mathbf{t}_{ij}^{reg}, \mathbf{t}_{ij}^{ep}, \mathbf{t}_{ij}^{0}\}$ with $\boldsymbol{s}_p^n = \mathbf{t}_{p-1}[\boldsymbol{s}_{p-1}^n]$. Defining with

$$\begin{aligned}\boldsymbol{s}_1^n := \Big\{ & s^{\mathrm{wR}}, s^{\mathrm{wN}}, s^{\mathrm{wB}}, s^{\mathrm{wQ}}, s^{\mathrm{wK}}, s^{\mathrm{wB}}, s^{\mathrm{wN}}, s^{\mathrm{wR}}, \overbrace{s^{\mathrm{wP}}, \ldots, s^{\mathrm{wP}}}^{8 \text{ elements}}, \overbrace{0, \ldots, 0}^{32 \text{ elements}}, \\ & \underbrace{s^{\mathrm{bP}}, \ldots, s^{\mathrm{bP}}}_{8 \text{ elements}}, s^{\mathrm{bR}}, s^{\mathrm{bN}}, s^{\mathrm{bB}}, s^{\mathrm{bQ}}, s^{\mathrm{bK}}, s^{\mathrm{bB}}, s^{\mathrm{bN}}, s^{\mathrm{bR}} \Big\}\end{aligned} \tag{7.56}$$

the node state vector of the initial chess position $p = 1$, repeated application then eventually delivers an ordered sequence

$$\begin{aligned} &\boldsymbol{s}_1^n, \\ &\boldsymbol{s}_2^n = \mathbf{t}_1[\boldsymbol{s}_1^n], \\ &\boldsymbol{s}_3^n = \mathbf{t}_2[\boldsymbol{s}_2^n] = \mathbf{t}_2\big[\mathbf{t}_1[\boldsymbol{s}_1^n]\big] = \mathbf{t}_2 \circ \mathbf{t}_1[\boldsymbol{s}_1^n], \\ &\quad\vdots \\ &\boldsymbol{s}_p^n = \mathbf{t}_{p-1} \circ \mathbf{t}_{p-2} \circ \cdots \circ \mathbf{t}_1[\boldsymbol{s}_1^n] =: \bigcirc_{t=1}^{p-1} \mathbf{t}_t[\boldsymbol{s}_1^n] \end{aligned} \tag{7.57}$$

of node state vectors that represents successive positions in a complete game of chess. This sequence will naturally terminate once a checkmate or draw position is reached – that is once, for example, the condition

$$\mathit{checkmate} \Leftrightarrow \begin{cases} \Big(\mathrm{T}\big[\boldsymbol{w}_p - \boldsymbol{1}^{64\times64}\big] = 0 \wedge \mathfrak{w}^{\mathrm{wK+}}[\boldsymbol{s}_p^n, \boldsymbol{w}_p] = 1\Big) \\ \vee\Big(\mathrm{T}\big[\boldsymbol{w}_p + \boldsymbol{1}^{64\times64}\big] = 0 \wedge \mathfrak{w}^{\mathrm{bK+}}[\boldsymbol{s}_p^n, \boldsymbol{w}_p] = 1\Big) \end{cases} \tag{7.58}$$

for $\boldsymbol{w}_p := \mathfrak{w}[\boldsymbol{s}_p^n, \boldsymbol{s}_{p-1}^n, \boldsymbol{\lambda}_p]$ is satisfied. Termination conditions for other game endings, such as the stalemate, draws by threefold repetition or the fifty-move rule, and the "in dead position" [45] can be algebraically formulated in a similar fashion. We leave this task as entertaining exercise for the interested reader.

Instead, let us conclude with formalising the transformation which maps an operator representation $\hat{\mathscr{C}}_{p-1}$ of a positional chess graph at position $p-1$ into $\hat{\mathscr{C}}_p$. With an eye on (7.54) and (7.55), such an operator graph transformation is defined by the tuple

$$\hat{\mathfrak{M}}^{\mathscr{C}} = \big(\hat{\mathfrak{M}}_{\mathcal{N}}, \hat{\mathfrak{M}}_{\mathcal{E}}\big) \tag{7.59}$$

with

$$\hat{\mathfrak{M}}_{\mathcal{N}} : \hat{\mathcal{N}}^{\mathscr{C}_{p-1}} \to \hat{\mathcal{N}}^{\mathscr{C}_p}, \begin{cases} \hat{\mathfrak{M}}_{\mathcal{N}}[\boldsymbol{n}_0] := \boldsymbol{n}_0, \\ \hat{\mathfrak{M}}_{\mathcal{N}}[\boldsymbol{n}_i] := \big(\mathbf{t}_{p-1}[\boldsymbol{s}_{p-1}^n]\big)_i \cdot \boldsymbol{n}_i \end{cases}$$

for $i \in [1, 64]$ and $\mathbf{t}_{p-1} \in \{\mathbf{t}_{ij}^{reg}, \mathbf{t}_{ij}^{ep}, \mathbf{t}_{ij}^{0}\}$, and

$$\hat{\mathfrak{M}}_{\mathcal{E}} : \hat{\mathcal{E}}^{\mathscr{C}_{p-1}} \to \hat{\mathcal{E}}^{\mathscr{C}_p}, \begin{cases} \hat{\mathfrak{M}}_{\mathcal{E}}[\mathfrak{E}_{00}] := \mathfrak{E}_{00}, \\ \hat{\mathfrak{M}}_{\mathcal{E}}[\mathfrak{E}_{j_1 j_2}] := \Big(\mathfrak{w}\big[\mathbf{t}_{p-1}[\boldsymbol{s}_{p-1}^n], \boldsymbol{s}_{p-1}^n, \boldsymbol{\lambda}_p\big]\Big)_{j_1 j_2} \cdot \mathfrak{E}_{j_1 j_2} \end{cases}$$

for $j_1, j_2 \in [1, 64]$, $j_1 \neq j_2$ such that $\hat{\mathscr{C}}_p := \hat{\mathfrak{M}}^{\mathscr{C}}[\hat{\mathscr{C}}_{p-1}]$ for positions $p > 1$. The operator representation $\hat{\mathscr{C}}_1$ of the positional chess graph for the initial position $p = 1$ is here defined by the node state vector $\boldsymbol{s}_1^n$ introduced in (7.56) and the weight matrix $\boldsymbol{w}_1 := \mathfrak{w}[\boldsymbol{s}_1^n, \boldsymbol{s}_1^n, \boldsymbol{\lambda}_1]$ with $\boldsymbol{\lambda}_1 := (1, 1, 1, 1)$. More importantly, the auxiliary vector $\boldsymbol{\lambda}_p$ has to be updated if and only if $\mathbf{t}_{p-1} = \mathbf{t}^0$, depending on the actual castling move performed. The operator graph transformation $\hat{\mathfrak{M}}^{\mathscr{C}}$

then provides an algebraically rigorous means not only to represent positional changes during a game of chess, but also to explore the dynamic changes that are associated with the complete set of possible legal moves each player can perform over the course of a game. By defining graph observables for classical measures such as the average node reach, mobility, dominance, offensiveness or defensiveness, for example, the utilisation of (7.59) should allow us to go beyond the resource-demanding numerical analysis of chess games. Indeed, the algebraic representation proposed here opens the door for a rigorous graph-theoretical analysis of the game of chess, and perhaps it will prove a useful tool in the algebraic implementation of chess strategies for the purpose of optimising existing algorithms, or even conceiving a new generation of computer chess players.

In this final chapter of our introduction to the mathematics of finite networks, we took on the arguably challenging yet hopefully also entertaining task of conceiving an algebraic means to describe the game of chess. With its discrete spatio-temporal makeup and strict set of rules governing the dynamical changes between a sheer unlimited, or at least inconceivably large, set of distinct positional configurations, this historic board game presents itself naturally as an example of a classical finite graph that defied for far too long a mathematically rigorous description. We hope that our approach for tackling the inherent difficulties associated with an algebraic formalisation of this game not only provides enough incentive for its consideration as a viable research subject within the powerful confines of graph theory, but also inspires new analysis methods which will help to understand and improve the decision process and strategical considerations of human and computer players alike. Choosing chess as the final example for demonstrating the application and potential usefulness of our operator graph-theoretical framework had another, more nefarious reason, however. By taking on a well-known real-world phenomenon, by carefully dissecting its defining makeup and by abstracting from colourful yet less relevant details, our presentation was intended also to serve as an educational exercise to convey at least some of the unique thought process that allowed Leonard Euler to approach the mystery of Königsberg's seven bridges. In this sense, we hope to have, one final time, intrigued the interested reader with sufficient motivation and stimulation to go further and beyond in the never-ending quest to unravel the secrets of our universe.

Afterthought

We have finally reached the end of our brief, yet adventurous journey. Having embarked from the rich shores of classical graph and operator theory whose beautiful vistas appear to stretch endlessly far beyond the perceivable horizon and paint, each with its own conceptual premises and toolsets, detailed descriptions of an evergrowing number of real-world phenomena and mysteries that reside at the very heart of our physical world, we travelled across a widely unexplored ocean which encompasses both of these cherished shores of applied mathematics. In this ocean's ghastly depths, we searched for a connecting ridge, a fusion of the static perspective provided by classical graph theory and the inherently dynamic vantage point that forms the conceptual basis of operator theory. What we discovered and tried to explore, perhaps too naively so, from different angles is a picture of a unified framework, ambitiously called *operator graph theory*, which not only generalises the very notion of a graph but, under the justifiable architectural premise that each real-world system is comprised of discrete finite constituents interacting with each other in an intoxicating dynamic dance, touches upon the very fabric of physical reality itself.

Where do we go from here? In short, only the sky is the limit. A less euphoric and more honest answer to this question, however, must prelude that our journey merely served as a careful initial exploration of a possibility, with the primary goal of providing sufficient motivation for taking one small step outside the well-set boundaries of classical graph theory on a more dynamic path. Although the conceptual basis of this challenging endeavour is certainly sound, its devilish details are at this point arguably nothing more than an often improvised collection of loosely intertwined thoughts and their attempted formalisations which have yet to satisfy the unforgiving demands of mathematical rigour. With the arguments presented in these pages, we nevertheless hope to have provided the interested reader with a meaningful source of inspiration to partake in the furthering of the yet-to-be-fleshed-out theoretical foundations of an operator graph-theoretical framework, and with sufficient motivation and excitement to consider such a framework as basis and potentially powerful ally in the graph-theoretical description and analysis of real-world phenomena in the never-ending conquest of understanding nature.

Some of you will undoubtedly be relieved that our at-times-unwieldy journey has finally come to an end. Some of you might be eager to continue and snatch other inspiring pictures from the depths of the ocean we travelled across, perhaps more in focus than those presented in the book about to end in front of you. Irrespective of on which side of the aisle you find yourself after our little adventure, I, the author, owe a deep gratitude to all of you who took part in this journey, with the bliss of optimism that you share with me perhaps the most important insight at the end – namely, that no single journey into the mysteries of nature is ever finished, and that it is ultimately up to each and every one of us how we proceed to the next journey. The picture presented in this book is but a mere preliminary shot, a first humble attempt to explore a formalisation which satisfies the author's deeply held and still somewhat heretical view that our physical reality, the universe itself, is inherently finite and discrete, and that the intriguing beauty of its observed complexity and dynamical richness which we experience all around us must and only can be explained on the basis of this uncompromising philosophical stance. I, for one, will continue the journey because nothing is more exhilarating, more intoxicating, than to dive on an unexplored path into the Unknown, and to eventually return with a tiny fragment of Truth in the finite time before we ourselves become unconscious participants in the eternal cosmic dance.

Bibliography

[1] *Common Crawl Foundation*. http://commoncrawl.org. 2020.

[2] Albert, R., and Barabási, A.-L. 2000. Topology of evolving networks: local events and universality. *Phys. Rev. Lett.*, **85**, 5234.

[3] Albert, R., and Barabási, A.-L. 2002. Statistical mechanics of complex networks. *Rev. Mod. Phys.*, **74**, 47–97.

[4] Albert, R., Hawoong, J., and Barabási, A. 1999. The diameter of the world wide web. *Nature*, **401**, 130–131.

[5] Amaral, L.A.N., Scala, A., Barthélémy, M., and Stanley, H.E. 2000. The diameter of the world wide web. *Proc. Natl. Acad. Sci. USA*, **97**, 11149–11152.

[6] An, Y., Janssen, J., and Milios, E. 2004. Characterizing and mining the citation graph of the computer science literature. *Knowl. Inf. Syst.*, **6**, 664–678.

[7] Appel, K., Haken, W., and Koch, J. 1977. Every planar map is four colorable. II: Reducibility. *Illinois J. Math.*, **21**, 491–567.

[8] Appel, K., and Haken, W. 1977. The solution of the four-color map problem. *Sci. Am.*, **237**, 108–121.

[9] Appel, K., Haken, W., and Koch, J. 1977. Every planar map is four colorable. I: Discharging. *Illinois J. Math.*, **21**, 429–490.

[10] Asratian, A.S., Denley, T.M.J., and Häggkvist, R. 1998. *Bipartite Graphs and Their Applications*. Cambridge University Press.

[11] Azevedo, F.A.C., Carvalho, L.R.B., Grinberg, L.T., Farfel, J.M., Ferretti, R.E.L., Leite, R.E.P., Filho, W.J., Lent, R., and Herculano-Houzel, S. 2009. Equal numbers of neuronal and nonneuronal cells make the human brain an isometrically scaled-up primate brain. *J. Comp. Neurol.*, **513**, 532–541.

[12] Barabási, A.-L., and Albert, R. 1999. Emergence of scaling in random networks. *Science*, **286**, 509–512.

[13] Barrat, A., and Weigt, M. 2000. On the properties of small-world network models. *Eur. Phys. J. B*, **13**, 547560.

[14] Barrat, A., Barthélemy, M., Pastor-Satorras, R., and Vespignani, A. 2004. The architecture of complex weighted networks. *Proc. Natl. Acad. Sci. USA*, **101**, 3747–3752.

[15] Beer, T., and Enting, I.G. 1990. Fire spread and percolation modelling. *Math. Comp. Mod.*, **13**, 77–96.

[16] Bianconi, G., and Barabási, A.-L. 2001a. Bose-Einstein condensation in complex networks. *Phys. Rev. Lett.*, **86**, 5632.

[17] Bianconi, G., and Barabási, A.-L. 2001b. Competition and multiscaling in evolving networks. *Europhys. Lett.*, **54**, 436–442.

[18] Biggs, N. 1993. *Algebraic Graph Theory*. Cambridge University Press.

[19] Bilke, S., and Peterson, C. 2001. Topological properties of citation and metabolic networks. *Phys. Rev. E*, **64**, 036106.

[20] Boccaletti, S., Latora, V., Moreno, Y., Chavez, M., and Hwang, D.-U. 2006. Complex networks: structure and dynamics. *Phys. Rep.*, **424**, 175–308.

[21] Bollobás, B. 1980. A probabilistic proof of an asymptotic formula for the number of labelled regular graphs. *Eur. J. Combin.*, **1**, 311–316.

[22] Bollobás, B. 2001. *Random Graphs*. 2nd ed. Cambridge University Press.

[23] Braitenberg, V., and Schüz, A. 1998. *Cortex: Statistics and Geometry of Neuronal Connectivity*. 2nd ed. Springer.

[24] Broadbent, S.R. 1964. In discussion of symposium on Monte Carlo methods. *J. Roy. Stat. Soc. B*, **16**, 68.

[25] Broadbent, S.R., and Hammersley, J.M. 1957. Percolation processes. I. Crystals and mazes. *Proc. Camb. Philos. Soc.*, **53**, 629–641.

[26] Broder, A., Kumar, R., Maghoul, F., Raghavan, P., Rajagopalan, S., Stata, R., Tomkins, A., and Wiener, J. 2000. Graph structure in the Web: experiments and models. *Comput. Netw.*, **33**, 309–320.

[27] Burt, R.S. 1976. Positions in networks. *Soc. Forces*, **55**, 93–122.

[28] Callaway, D.S., Newman, M.E.J., Strogatz, S.H., and Watts, D.J. 2000. Network robustness and fragility: percolation on random graphs. *Phys. Rev. Lett.*, **85**, 5468.

[29] Chung, F., and Lu, L. 2002a. The average distances in random graphs with given expected degrees. *Proc. Natl. Acad. Sci. USA*, **99**, 15879–15882.

[30] Chung, F., and Lu, L. 2002b. Connected components in random graphs with given expected degree sequences. *Combinatorics*, **6**, 125–145.

[31] Cohn, P.M. 1981. *Universal Algebra*. Springer.

[32] Conyon, M.J., and Muldoon, M.R. 2006. The small world of corporate boards. *J. Bus. Finan. Account.*, **33**, 1321–1343.

[33] Davis, P.J. 1970. *Circulant Matrices*. Wiley.

[34] Donato, D., Leonardi, S., Laura, L., Millozzi, S., Meyer, U., and Sibeyn, J.F. 2006. Algorithms and experiments for the webgraph. *J. Graph Algorithms and Applications*, **10**, 219–236.

[35] Dorogovtsev, S.N., and Mendes, J.F.F. 2000. Scaling behaviour of developing and decaying networks. *Europhys. Lett.*, **52**, 33.

[36] Dorogovtsev, S.N., Mendes, J.F.F., and Samukhin, A.N. 2000. Structure of growing networks with preferential linking. *Phys. Rev. Lett.*, **85**, 4633.

[37] Durrett, R. 2006. *Random Graph Dynamics*. Cambridge University Press.

[38] Erdős, P., and Rényi, A. 1959. On random graphs. I. *Publicationes Mathematicae*, **6**, 290–297.

[39] Erdős, P., and Rényi, A. 1960. On the evolution of random graphs. *Magyar Tudományos Akadémia Matematikai Kutató Intézetének Közleményei (Publ. Math. Inst. Hung. Acad. Sci., Ser. A)*, **5**, 17–61.

[40] Erdős, P., and Rényi, A. 1961. On the evolution of random graphs. II. *Bull. Inst. Int. Stat.*, **38**, 343–347.

[41] Euclid. 1956. Book XIII. In: *The Thirteen Books of the Elements, Vol. 3: Books X-XIII*, 2nd, unabridged ed. Dover.

[42] Euler, L. 1736. Solutio problematis ad geometriam situs pertinentis. *Comment. Acad. Sci. U. Petrop*, **8**, 128–140.

[43] Fagiolo, G. 2007. Clustering in complex directed networks. *Phys. Rev. E*, **76**, 026107.

[44] Farkas, I., Derényi, I., Barabási, A.-L., and Vicsek, T. 2001. Spectra of "real-world" graphs: Beyond the semicircle law. *Phys. Rev. E*, **64**, 26704.

[45] FIDE. 2021. *World Chess Federation Handbook*. http://www.fide.com/fide/handbook.html.

[46] Fine, T.L. 1999. *Feedforward Neural Network Methodology*. Springer.

[47] Fronczak, A., Fronczak, P., and Hoł yst, J.A. 2004. Average path length in random networks. *Phys. Rev. E*, **70**, 056110.

[48] Garlaschelli, D., and Loffredo, M.I. 2004. Patterns of link reciprocity in directed networks. *Phys. Rev. Lett.*, **93**, 268701.

[49] Gilbert, E.N. 1959. Random graphs. *Ann. Math. Statist.*, **30**, 1141–1144.

[50] Gingl, A., Pennetta, C., Kiss, L.B., and Reggiani, L. 1996. Biased percolation and abrupt failure of electronic devices. *Semicond. Sci. Technol.*, **11**, 1770–1775.

[51] Goh, K.-I., Kahng, B., and Kim, D. 2001. Spectra and eigenvectors of scale-free networks. *Phys. Rev. E*, **64**, 051903.

[52] Grimmett, G.R. 1999. *Percolation*. Springer.

[53] Gross, J.T., and Yellen, J. 2006. *Graph Theory and Its Applications*. 2nd ed. CRC Press.

[54] Guillaume, J.-L., and Latapy, M. 2002. *The web graph: an overview*. Actes d'ALGOTEL'02 (Quatrièmes Rencontres Francophones sur les aspects Algorithmiques des Télécommunications), Mèze, France.

[55] Guimera, R., Mossa, S., Turtschi, A., and Amaral, L.A.N. 2005. The world-wide air transportation network: anomalous centrality, community structure, and cities' global roles. *Proc. Natl. Acad. Sci. USA*, **102**, 7794–7799.

[56] Hagar, A. 2014. *Discrete or Continuous?: The Quest for Fundamental Length in Modern Physics*. Cambridge University Press.

[57] Hagmann, P., Cammoun, L., Gigandet, X., Meuli, R., Honey, C.J., V.J., Wedeen, and Sporns, O. 2008. Mapping the structural core of human cerebral cortex. *PLoS Biology*, **6**, e159.

[58] Hammersley, J.M., and Morton, K.W. 1954. Poor man's Monte Carlo. *J. Roy. Stat. Soc. B*, **16**, 23–38.

[59] Harary, F. 1969. *Graph Theory*. Addison-Wesley.

[60] He, Y., Chen, Z.J., and Evans, A.C. 2007. Small-world anatomical networks in the human brain revealed by cortical thickness from MRI. *Cereb. Cortex*, **17**, 2407.

[61] Holland, P.W., and Leinhardt, S. 1971. Transitivity in structural models of small groups. *Small Gr. Res.*, **2**, 107–124.

[62] Holme, P., and Kim, B.J. 2002. Growing scale-free networks with tunable clustering. *Phys. Rev. E*, **65**, 026107.

[63] Humphries, M.D., and Gurney, K. 2008. Network 'small-world-ness': a quantitative method for determining canonical network equivalence. *PLoS ONE*, **3**, e0002051.

[64] Kennedy, J.W., Quintas, L.V., and Sysło, M.M. 1985. The theorem on planar graphs. *Hist. Math.*, **12**, 350–368.

[65] Kőnig, D. 1936. *Theorie der endlichen und unendlichen Graphen*. Akademische Verlagsgesellschaft, Leipzig. Translated from German by Richard McCoart, Theory of finite and infinite graphs, Birkhäuser, 1990.

[66] Kirman, A. 1997. The economy as an evolving network. *J. Evol. Econ.*, **7**, 339353.

[67] Kötter, R. 2004. Online retrieval, processing, and visualization of primate connectivity data from the CoCoMac database. *Neuroinformatics*, **2**, 127–144.

[68] Kraitchik, M. 1953. *Mathematical Recreations*. 2nd revised ed. Dover Publications.

[69] Krapivsky, P.L., and Redner, S. 2001. Organization of growing random networks. *Phys. Rev. E*, **63**, 66123.

[70] Krapivsky, P.L., Redner, S., and Leyvraz, F. 2000. Connectivity of growing random networks. *Phys. Rev. Lett.*, **85**, 4629.

[71] Krapivsky, P.L., Rodgers, G.J., and Redner, S. 2001. Degree distributions of growing networks. *Phys. Rev. Lett.*, **86**, 5401.

[72] Kuratowski, K. 1930. Sur le problème des courbes gauches en topology. *Fund. Math.*, **15**, 271–283.

[73] Lehmann, S., Lautrup, B., and Jackson, A.D. 2003. Citation networks in high energy physics. *Phys. Rev. E*, **68**, 026113.

[74] Li, M., Chen, H., Wang, J., Liu, F., Long, Z., Wang, Y., Iturria-Medina, Y., Zhang, J., Chunshui, Y., and Chen, H. 2014. Handedness- and hemisphere-related differences in small-world brain networks: a diffusion tensor imaging tractography study. *Brain Connectivity*, **4**, 145.

[75] Maynard, M. 2020. *Neural Networks*. Independently published.

[76] Menger, K. 1952. *You Will Like Geometry: Guidebook of the Illinois Institute of Technology Geometry Exhibit*. Museum of Science and Industry, Chicago.

[77] Meusel, R., Vigna, S., Lehmberg, O., and Bizer, C. 2015. The graph structure in the web - analyzed on different aggregation levels. *The Journal of Web Science*, **1**, 33–47.

[78] Milgram, S. 1967. The small world problem. *Psychol. Today*, **1**, 61–67.

[79] Miller, J.C. 2009. Percolation and epidemics in random clustered networks. *Phys. Rev. E*, **80**, 020901.

[80] Miller, J.C., and Hagberg, A. 2011. Efficient generation of networks with given expected degrees. Pages 115–126 of: Frieze, A., Horn, P., and Pralat, P. (eds), *Algorithms and Models for the Web-Graph (WAW 2011)*.

[81] Minkowski, H. 1967. *Gesammelte Abhandlungen*. Chelsea Publishing Co..

[82] Modhaa, D.A., and Singh, R. 2010. Network architecture of the long-distance pathways in the macaque brain. *Proc. Natl. Acad. Sci. USA*, **107**, 13485–13490.

[83] Montoya, J.M., and Solé, R.V. 2002. Small world patterns in food webs. *J. Theor. Biol.*, **214**, 405–412.

[84] Moore, C.M., and Newman, M.E.J. 2000. Epidemics and percolation in small-world networks. *Phys. Rev. E*, **61**, 5678–5682.

[85] Muller, L.E., Destexhe, A., and Rudolph-Lilith, M. 2014. Brain networks: small-worlds, after all? *New J. Phys.*, **16**, 105004.

[86] Newman, M. 2010. *Networks*. 2nd ed. Oxford University Press.

[87] Newman, M.E.J., Moore, C., and Watts, D.J. 2000. Mean-field solution of the small-world network model. *Phys. Rev. Lett.*, **84**, 3201.

[88] Newman, M.E.J., Forrest, S., and Balthrop, J. 2002. Email networks and the spread of computer viruses. *Phys. Rev. E*, **66**, 035101.

[89] Nishizeki, T., and Chiba, N. 1988. *Planar Graphs: Theory and Algorithms*. Elsevier.

[90] Pastor-Satorras, R., and Vespignani, A. 2001. Epidemic spreading in scale-free networks. *Phys. Rev. Lett.*, **86**, 3200–3203.

[91] Price, D.J. de Solla. 1965. Networks of scientific papers. *Science*, **149**, 510515.

[92] Ravasz, E., and Barabási, A.-L. 2003. Hierarchical organization in complex networks. *Phys. Rev. E*, **67**, 026112.

[93] Reed, R., and Marks, R., II. 1999. *Neural Smithing*. MIT Press.

[94] Rozenblat, C., Melançon, G., Bourqui, R., and Auber, D. 2013. Comparing Multilevel Clustering Methods on Weighted Graphs: The Case of World-wide Air Passenger Traffic 2000–2004. Pages 141–154 of: Rozenblat, C., and Melançon, G. (eds.), *Methods for Multilevel Analysis and Visualisation of Geographical Networks*. Springer.

[95] Rudolph-Lilith, M., and Muller, L.E. 2014. Aspects of randomness in neural graph structures. *Biol. Cybern.*, **108**, 381–396.

[96] Rudolph-Lilith, M., and Muller, L.E. 2015. On a link between Dirichlet kernels and central multinomial coefficients. *Discrete Math.*, **338**, 1567–1572.

[97] Rudolph-Lilith, M., Destexhe, A., and Muller, L.E. 2012. *Structual vulnerability of the nematode worm neural graph*. arXiv:1208.3383v1 [cond-mat.dis-nn].

[98] Sahimi, M. 1994. *Applications of Percolation Theory*. Taylor & Francis.

[99] Scott, J.P. 2000. *Social Network Analysis: A Handbook*. SAGE Publications.

[100] Seary, A.J., and Richards, W.D. 2003. *Spectral Methods for Analyzing and Visualizing Networks: An Introduction* (209–228). National Academy Press.

[101] Serrano, M.A., and Boguñá, M. 2003. Topology of the world trade web. *Phys. Rev. E*, **68**, 015101.

[102] Stephan, K.E., Kamper, L., Bozkurt, A., Burns, G.A., Young, M.P., and Kötter, R. 2001. Advanced database methodology for the Collation of Connectivity data on the Macaque brain (CoCoMac). *Philos. Trans. R. Soc. Lond. B Biol. Sci.*, **356**, 1159–1186.

[103] Tadić, B. 2001. Dynamics of directed graphs: the world-wide web. *Physica A*, **293**, 273–284.

[104] Thomassen, C. 1981. Kuratowski's theorem. *J. Graph Theor.*, **5**, 225–241.

[105] van der Hofstad, R. 2010. *New Perspectives on Stochastic Geometry*. Oxford University Press.

[106] von Niessen, W., and Blumen, A. 1986. Dynamics of forest fires as a directed percolation model. *J. Phys. A*, **19**, L289–L293.

[107] Wasserman, S., and Faust, K. 1994. *Social Network Analysis: Methods and Applications*. Cambridge University Press.

[108] Watts, D.J. 1999. *Small Worlds*. Princeton University Press.

[109] Watts, D.J., and Strogatz, S.H. 1998. Collective dynamics of 'small-world' networks. *Nature*, **393**, 440–442.

[110] West, D.B. 1995. *Introduction to Graph Theory*. Prentice-Hall.

[111] Wood, D. 1894. Problem 5. *Amer. Math. Monthly*, **1**, 211–212.

[112] Yook, S.H., Jeong, H., Barabási, A.-L., and Tu, Y. 2001. Weighted evolving networks. *Phys. Rev. Lett.*, **86**, 5835.

Index of Notations

Subject Index